Race, Ethnicity, and Social Change

Readings
in the Sociology of Race
and Ethnic Relations

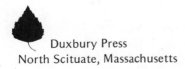

JOHN STONE
St. Antony's College, Oxford

NEW YORK INSTITUTE
OF TECHNOLOGY LIBRARY

Duxbury Press
North Scituate, Massachusetts

Duxbury Press
A Division of Wadsworth Publishing Company, Inc.

Race, Ethnicity, and Social Change: Readings in the Sociology of Race and Ethnic Relations, was edited and prepared for composition by Katharine Gregg. Interior design was provided by Jane Lovinger and the cover was designed by Oliver Kline.

L. C. Cat. Card No.: 76-17713
ISBN 0-87872-122-3
Printed in the United States of America
1 2 3 4 5 6 7 8 9 10-81 80 79 78 77

For My Parents

CONTENTS

PREFACE

While teaching courses in the sociology of race and ethnic relations to undergraduate and graduate students at Columbia University, I felt a need for a collection of articles that would both satisfy the intellectual demands of the social scientist and sustain the interest and enthusiasm of the student. It is my firm belief that students will not be content for long with essentially journalistic accounts of topical "racial" problems without a deeper understanding of the theoretical issues involved and an appreciation of a broader comparative context. I intend no disparagement of journalism as such, for, as Max Weber pointed out long ago, it is intrinsically more difficult to be a brilliant journalist than to be a distinguished scholar. However, there is no greater betrayal of the sociological imagination than to obscure the intimate relationship between practical problems and theoretical understanding: a position that can be shared by writers of radically different ideological convictions.

With this basic principle in mind I have selected articles that have a relevance far beyond the specific problems of race and ethnicity so that the student can begin to consider the fundamental issues involved. A number of core problems recur significantly, and they can be found, contrary to general belief, in the writings of the classical sociological tradition. They include: the problems of defining "race" sociologically, the relationship of race and ethnicity to social stratification, the significance of racism, the importance of racial and ethnic factors in the process of social change, and the diverse responses to racial and ethnic domination. While I have included a large number of selections on the American experience, I wish to stress greatly the comparative importance of these issues. I also wish to emphasize the dynamic quality of racial relationships and to recognize their central contribution to social change in the modern world.

I would like to thank my students at Columbia who have taught me, during the last few years, much more than they probably realize about race and ethnicity. A special word of appreciation goes to Robert K. Merton who gave me invaluable encouragement and perceptive advice during the early stages of the project. Of the many colleagues and friends who have helped me, either directly or indirectly, in the development of the book I would particularly like to thank Norman Fainstein, Herb Gans, Kenneth Kirkwood, Henry Lever, Allan Silver, William Wilson and Neil Van Zeyl. Finally, to Roleen and Dulcie I owe a debt that only those who live with an author can appreciate.

INTRODUCTION

RACE, ETHNICITY, AND SOCIOLOGY

It is surprising that such an influential writer and social critic as C. Wright Mills
should have placed so little stress on race relations in his discussion of the sociological imagination.[1] The case of Mills is symptomatic of the rather uneven attention
that modern social scientists have paid to questions of race and ethnicity. Many
sociologists have also assumed that the founding fathers of their discipline largely
ignored the topic, even though such an assessment of their work is inaccurate. A
close reading of the first section of this book will show the essential continuity between the classical sociologists' understanding of race and ethnic relations and many
of the key problems that concern contemporary students of the subject. Clearly,
major writers in the sociological tradition, like Marx, Tocqueville, Weber, and
Simmel, did consider that race relations were a significant force in social life and an
integral part of the subject matter of sociology.

Two further qualities of great importance typify the classical sociologists' analysis, not merely of these specific issues but of society generally. First is a desire to
place particular case studies or examples into a comparative frame of reference, as
seen in the writings of Weber or Pareto. Second is a strong emphasis on social conflict and change, which characterizes the approach of Marx or Simmel. Both these
attributes are of great value for the study of race relations and have been used as
criteria in the selection of articles for this anthology.

Several central problems are present in both the classical and contemporary discussion of race and ethnicity. The first major problem is the definition of "race"
from a sociological point of view—by no means a simple task as John Rex illustrates in his paper on the concept of race in sociological theory. Few of the classical
theorists accepted Gobineau's argument about the fundamental racial determination
of social institutions and the racial dynamic behind social change. Karl Marx, whose
position was not always consistent, tended to assume that racial and ethnic groups
were really classes lurking behind a particular façade of race, color, or culture.
Alexis de Tocqueville specifically attacked Gobineau's thesis concerning the innate
inequality of the human races on the grounds that it neither fitted the historical
facts nor was supported by scientific evidence. Emile Durkheim explicitly dismissed
racial theorizing as an illegitimate exercise in biological reductionism. Thus, the
classical sociologists understood the fundamental point: the study of race and ethnic
relations has little or nothing to do with biological "race" and a lot to do with patterns of social relationships and structures of power and domination.

A second basic issue for the student of race relations is the determination of the connection between race and ethnicity on the one hand, and class and social stratification on the other. Can race relations be analyzed in terms of class relations, as certain Marxists claim, or should they be seen as part of a broader framework of stratification, as suggested by Max Weber? Are there elements of a race relations situation that are unique and irreducible to other social categories? Rex argues that there are certain distinct properties of such situations that are not strictly analyzable in terms of even a flexible stratification theory. The question is a controversial one, and many of the papers in the anthology, particularly those of Bastide, Kuper, and Pitt-Rivers, contribute to the debate.

Another core issue stems from a further difference in emphasis between Marxian and Weberian sociology.[2] It concerns the role of ideas, in our case racist or non-racist ideas, in the process of historical change. Does racism have an independent causal effect on inter-group relations, or are such beliefs and values mere reflections of the underlying economic and political balance of power? Myrdal in his formulation of the "American Dilemma" puts a considerable stress on such values; he sees the American universalistic creed against discriminatory practices and regards this conflict as an important force in the evolution of race relations in the United States. Despite the oversimplification of his thesis, which Merton elegantly exposes, Myrdal does suggest the need for a more careful exploration of this theme. The articles of Bastide and Goldhagen consider aspects of that issue in relation to Christianity and communism.

Such problems are linked further to questions about the manner in which race relations are affected by and, in turn, influence social change. Can we discern any distinct patterns that connect the major forces of industrialization and urbanism to particular types of racial and ethnic structures? Do certain forms of racial and ethnic contact invariably result in the same structures of subordination and inequality? How can we explain the diversity of responses to racial and ethnic domination?

It is my contention that the classical sociologists considered many of these fundamental questions in terms of the main forms of race and ethnic relations that existed in their day, particularly slavery, colonialism, nationalism, and anti-Semitism. Furthermore, most of them were acutely aware of race and ethnicity as important areas of sociological concern, while avoiding, and often consciously refuting, theories that attributed unique and socially significant characteristics to certain racial or ethnic groups. However, the judicious caution of the classical sociologists was not maintained by their immediate academic successors. As the center of sociological theory and research began to shift from Europe towards America, so the cultural milieu in which sociology developed changed. While nationalism and colonialism pervaded the intellectual climate of the Old World, most of the major sociologists retained a skepticism towards the prevailing ethnocentrism and racism. In the New World the legacy of slavery combined with Anglo-Saxon dominance blended easily with the theories of social Darwinism. Herbert Spencer's views, as propagated by Sumner, were selectively interpreted: the "survival of the fittest" resonated with theories of racial superiority. Indeed, many of the early American sociologists adopted these assumptions in a totally uncritical manner.[3]

The situation gradually changed during the course of the early twentieth century. The classical tradition began to reassert itself as the core problems and issues of race and ethnic relations received renewed attention by academic sociologists. The Chicago School, and particularly Thomas, Znaniecki, and Park, focused on the amazing diversity of the urban ethnic environments that had so fascinated Max Weber when he visited America in 1904.[4] Here were examples of ethnic survival, marginality, racial conflict, and cooperation taking place within a setting of industrialization, urbanization, and increasing social mobility. While a major source of this ethnic diversity—the transatlantic migration—dried up after the restrictive immigration legislation of 1924, no legal barriers stood in the way of the internal migration of Southern blacks, who became an increasingly important element of the urban mosaic. During this period the foundations of future race riots and urban class conflict in the black ghettoes of the Northern cities were reinforced, thereby fulfilling Tocqueville and Weber's gloomy predictions about American race relations.

The Second World War marked a major turning point for race relations. Several fundamental forces have influenced both the popular conception and the academic study of race and ethnicity. The full revelation of the Nazi genocide in Europe, the leap of Afro-Asian societies out of the frying pan of colonial racial domination into the fire of national integration, and the continuing flow of migrants across national and regional frontiers in all parts of the world have heightened a sense of racial and ethnic awareness and raised it to an issue of crucial national and international concern. At the same time, contemporary sociologists have become increasingly aware of the possible contribution of the study of race and ethnic relations to the more general and theoretical field of sociology. Despite the interesting case of C. Wright Mills, cited earlier, there can be little doubt that social and political changes have influenced the critical reevaluation of modern social theory.

Social scientists attempting to analyze social change have constantly encountered racial, cultural, and linguistic barriers as complicating factors in the societies they have been studying.[5] They have been forced to reexamine the basic tools and concepts of sociology when applying them to cultures and situations significantly different from those in which they were first developed. The outcome of that process has been to emphasize alternative strands of thought within the mainstream of contemporary sociology. For example, Gluckman's analysis of the "bonds within the colour bar" lends added weight to Coser's restatement of the functions of social conflict; van den Berghe's explicit critique of the value consensus of Parsonian theory in the context of South African society reemphasizes the prior inadequacies noted by Lockwood and Dahrendorf, who were focusing primarily on the class relations of Europe and North America.[6]

Since the middle of the 1950s, the trend in social theory has been to place a greater stress on the role of conflict in social change. Such a development is particularly crucial for the sociological study of race and ethnic relations because so many cases are fluid and exhibit a constant straining towards change. That change may take on a continuous or discontinuous form, though it is not easy to determine whether one mode of change is more fundamental than another. The less spectacular, yet often more pervasive influence of migration, mobility, and industrialization

deserves at least as much attention as such dramatically discontinuous social phenomena as riots, revolutions, and struggles for national independence.

No meaningful discussion of the contemporary dynamics of race relations can
ignore the changes that have occurred in the "Third World" during the postwar
period. At a more theoretical level such changes are concerned with the process of decolonization, the thesis of neocolonialism, and the concept of the plural society.
Once again, these issues can be related to the classical sociologists' interest in imperialism. Furnivall's analysis is strongly rooted in economic variables and borrows
extensively from Marx. However, the notion of the plural society and the developments that are taking place in many postcolonial societies pose interesting theoretical questions for both the Marxist and the functionalist sociological perspectives.[7]

Another perspective on social change, considered in several of the articles, concerns the degree of resistance produced by different types of racial and ethnic barriers. The formation and maintenance of group boundaries are fundamental
processes in the analysis of racial conflict and consensus. The variety of possible
social structures and the range and fluidity of barriers set up by racial and ethnic
groups have important practical and theoretical implications. The classical sociologists did not ignore those issues, though they did consider them alongside a diverse
range of sociological questions. Marx, Weber, and Durkheim found aspects of the
Indian caste system—that supreme example of boundary maintenance—intriguing in
relation to their conceptions of social change and social stability. For Marx caste
exemplified the "Asiatic mode of production" soon to be destroyed by the inroads
of capitalist-inspired colonialism. For Weber the powerful and pervasive influence of
Brahmanic ethics was an important aspect of the sociology of world religions. For
Durkheim the custom whereby the Hindu widow died on her husband's funeral
pyre supplied a graphic illustration of altruistic suicide. Contemporary sociologists
have a vast number of cases, ranging from the fluidity of racial definition in much
of Latin America to the rigid exclusiveness of separatist sects like the Black Muslims,
on which to test their hypotheses about race relations.

The immense range of possible racial and ethnic definitions and the manner in
which they are linked to the social structure pose the inevitable final question about
future trends and currents in intergroup relations. Prediction is always dangerous,
but the sociologist can take courage from Tocqueville's dictum that "history is like
a picture gallery in which there are few originals and many copies."[8] One new, but
possibly simplifying, factor is that the great diversity of situations is becoming increasingly interconnected to an extent that has never been true before. Interracial
conflict and persecution now have implications on a worldwide scale and rapidly become associated with the international power struggle. It is a fact of life that in the
second half of the twentieth century race and ethnic issues are firmly established in
the competing ideological stances of capitalist, communist, and Third World countries.

Three dominant strands of thought, which can be loosely described as liberal,
Marxist, and separatist, underlie most of the major sociological predictions concerning future patterns of race and ethnic relations. The liberal philosophy tends to be

ameliorative, seeing a gradual dissolution of discriminatory barriers and prejudiced attitudes as a result of expanding education, the "logic" of industrialism, and the increasing interdependence of the world community. The Marxist approach calls for revolution in which ethnic and racial identity is submerged in the overwhelming conflict between a wealthy bourgeoisie and an impoverished proletariat that are defined with little regard for race, religion, or national origin.[9] The separatist theory contains two major approaches: the race war thesis in which cataclysmic racial and ethnic polarization, superimposed on rich and poor nations, leads to a holocaust;[10] and the Black Power thesis that usually entails a tactical separatism before a more just balance of racial and ethnic power can be established.[11]

The real world is much more complex than any of the three models, but one way to evaluate their rival claims is to focus on certain critical societies. The Republic of South Africa, including the future of apartheid, is one such case where theories of race and ethnic relations can be subjected to rigorous scrutiny. Elsewhere I have argued that the white power structure in South Africa has the means to contain the forces for radical social change at least for the next two decades.[12] However, the papers by Lever and Wagner and by Heribert Adam reveal some of the basic internal changes in South African society that may well determine the long-run outcome of race and ethnic relations. Those forces may be more significant than the political and military changes in Angola, Mozambique, and Rhodesia. Whether the situation in Southern Africa will escalate into full-scale racial conflict and violence or whether some other and perhaps unique resolution will emerge from the world's most explicit form of legalized racial domination remains the enduring fascination and relevance of the country for the student of race relations.

Whatever the outcome in South Africa, it will probably be less influential on a world scale than events in the United States. The rise of the Black Power movement during the 1960s marked a growing disillusionment with the strategy of conventional civil rights and also highlighted the needs of "other" minorities.[13] Spurred by a sense of relative deprivation, the militant quest for a new black identity also stimulated a resurgence of ethnicity amongst many other groups in American society. Those trends set off a dialectic between integration and separatism: the theory of apartheid echoing strangely in the ghettoes of Northern cities. For most Americans the concept of pluralism raised as a pragmatic compromise between the two extremes, seemed to be the most satisfactory resolution of a painful dilemma.

While the ideal of pluralism—the achievement of equality of opportunity without losing group identity—seems simple enough, its practice is highly complex. How can one distinguish between legitimate exclusiveness and unjust discrimination? Will pluralism simply evolve into a rationalization for the status quo, or will it lead to a positive strengthening of disadvantaged minority groups, placing them in a better position to utilize full citizenship in a real rather than a token manner?[14] Those are some of the crucial questions facing American society, and much will depend, both for the United States and the rest of the world, on how they are answered. Sociologists are as divided as others in their assessment of the probable outcome, but they can at least point to the critical relationships of social structure and culture and to the underlying forces creating the social and political change on which the balance rests. It is the aim of this book to draw attention to just such forces and to leave the reader to weigh the evidence. While we have argued that many of the questions have a firm rooting in the classical sociological tradition, it is their present-day significance that is most striking. Indeed, few contemporary issues stretch the sociological imagination more fully than the problems associated with race and ethnicity.

NOTES

1. C. W. Mills, *The Sociological Imagination* (New York: Oxford University Press, 1959).
2. This difference should not be exaggerated. Cf. Anthony Giddens, *Capitalism and Modern Social Theory* (London: Cambridge University Press, 1971).
3. E. F. Frazier, "Sociological Theory and Race Relations," *American Sociological Review* 12, no. 3 (1947): 265–71.
4. John Stone, "Race Relations and the Sociological Tradition" appears as article 7 of this volume.
5. David Lockwood, "Race, Conflict, and Plural Society," in *Race and Racialism,* ed. Sami Zubaida (London: Tavistock, 1970).
6. Max Gluckman, *Custom and Conflict in Africa* (Oxford: Blackwell, 1955); L. A. Coser, *The Functions of Social Conflict* (New York: The Free Press, 1956); P. L. van den Berghe, *South Africa: A Study in Conflict* (Middletown, Conn.: Wesleyan University Press, 1965); David Lockwood, "Some Remarks on 'The Social System,'" *British Journal of Sociology* 7, no. 2 (1956): 134–46; and Ralf Dahrendorf, *Class and Class Conflict in Industrial Society* (London: Routledge, 1959).
7. Lockwood, "Race, Conflict, and Plural Society."
8. Alexis de Tocqueville, *The Ancien Regime and the French Revolution* (New York: Doubleday, 1955).
9. Of course, there are many neo-Marxist perspectives that do not fit this model. Cf. Herbert Marcuse, *Counter-Revolution and Revolt* (Boston: Beacon, 1972).
10. Ronald Segal, *The Race War* (New York: Viking Press, 1967).
11. Stokely Carmichael and C. V. Hamilton, *Black Power: The Politics of Liberation in America* (Harmondsworth: Penguin, 1969).
12. John Stone, *Colonist or Uitlander?* (Oxford: Clarendon Press, 1973).
13. Edward Sagarin, ed, *The Other Minorities* (Waltham, Mass.: Xerox College Publishing, 1971).
14. Talcott Parsons, "Full Citizenship for the Negro American," in *The Negro American,* ed. T. Parsons and K. B. Clark (Boston: Beacon, 1967).

PART ONE

Theories
and
Typologies

RACE RELATIONS

AND CLASSICAL SOCIAL THEORY

The essays in the first section of the book support the argument made in the introduction that the study of race and ethnic relations was a much more significant part of the classical theorists' sociological imagination than has often been implied. No man has had a greater influence on the development of both modern society and contemporary social theory than Karl Marx. Indeed, his importance is such that the history of recent social thought has often been characterized as a "debate with the ghost of Marx." Marx's analysis of the effects of British colonialism in India, written for the *New York Daily Tribune,* illustrates his belief that the relations between racial and ethnic groups can only be understood within the context of modern capitalism. Colonial expansion is the inevitable outcome of the dialectical laws governing European capitalism, and it results in the savage plundering of imperial possessions. That exploitation, which superimposes race and ethnic difference on class divisions, is even more crude than the exploitation in the metropolitan country. In Marx's words "bourgeois civilization goes naked in the colonies." Marx assumed too readily that the caste system would simply dissolve in the path of expanding communications and industrialization. Such a position is analogous to that attacked by Blumer in his article in the second section of the book.[1] However, Marx is less certain of the exact mechanism of political change: whether colonial rule will be overthrown as a result of a proletarian revolution in the metropolitan country, or as a result of a struggle for national liberation in the colonies themselves. The logic of Marx's system seemed to suggest the former, while historical circumstance actually promoted the latter.

Gobineau's *The Inequality of Human Races* was published in the same year as Marx's article, and it is on this work that his reputation as the "Father of European Racism" rests.[2] Unlike Marx, who saw race and ethnicity as largely irrelevant for the development of society, Gobineau argued that innate racial qualities were of paramount importance in the origin, growth, and decline of civilizations. His theories (now totally discredited) enjoyed an enormous popularity during the second half of the nineteenth century and the early part of the twentieth, when European imperial expansion had reached its height, because they provided a convenient rationalization for racial inequality and exploitation. However, the issues involved in this debate are by no means irrelevant today since certain social scientists have attempted to link intelligence to heredity. The basic question concerns the impor-

3

tance of institutions and environmental factors and the debate over whether one can safely attribute all socially meaningful differences between racial and ethnic groups (always assuming that they can be identified as distinct units in the first place) to variations in cultural and social structural conditions.

The extract from Simmel's sociological writings is an acute portrayal of the social forms that determine the position of the marginal man—the stranger—so often found in situations of racial and ethnic heterogeneity. Simmel was well qualified to describe that social type being himself the "stranger in the academy." Anti-Semitism was one reason for his retarded academic career at Berlin University. Simmel's discussion of the stranger explores many of the features associated with the marginal man and antedates the analysis of merchant minorities or marginal trading groups like the Indians in East Africa, the Chinese in South East Asia, and the Jews in many European countries.[3] Racially or ethnically distinct groups are forced into certain roles, frequently defined as pariah roles by members of the dominant group, because they are not full citizens of a particular society. The vulnerability of such groups to scapegoating and persecution, which Simmel mentions, has often been seen during periods of rapid social change or social unrest.

Max Weber's paper considers, with characteristic breadth of vision, several aspects of nationalism and ethnic solidarity. He reveals the complexity of defining a nation, for sometimes nationalism is fostered by language, sometimes by religion, and sometimes simply by a sense of common history or identity. He stresses the power of ethnic identity, which frequently overrides any semblance of class solidarity—a critical issue in relation to the Marxist analysis of race relations—but he firmly discounts the mystical theorizing of the racial fanaticists. While rejecting a simple economic interpretation, Weber is quick to recognize the material basis of many aspects of linguistic and nationalist movements.

NOTES

1. H. Blumer, "Industrialization and Race Relations" appears as article 16 of this volume.
2. Cf. M. D. Biddiss, *Father of Racist Ideology: The Social and Political Thought of Count Gobineau* (London: Weidenfeld and Nicolson, 1970).
3. H. Blalock, *Toward a Theory of Minority Group Relations* (New York: Wiley, 1967), pp. 79–84. Edna Bonacich, "A Theory of Middleman Minorities," *American Sociological Review* 38 (1973): 583–94.

1 The Future Results
of British Rule in India

Karl Marx

How came it that English supremacy was established in India? The pàramount power of the Great Mogul was broken by the Mogul Viceroys. The power of the Viceroys was broken by the Mahrattas. The power of the Mahrattas was broken by the Afghans, and while all were struggling against all, the Briton rushed in and was enabled to subdue them all. A country not only divided between Mohammedan and Hindoo, but between tribe and tribe, between caste and caste; a society whose framework was based on a sort of equilibrium, resulting from a general repulsion and constitutional exclusiveness between all its members. Such a country and such a society, were they not the predestined prey of conquest? If we knew nothing of the past history of Hindostan, would there not be the one great and incontestable fact, that even at this moment India is held in English thralldom by an Indian army maintained at the cost of India? India, then, could not escape the fate of being conquered, and the whole of her past history, if it be anything, is the history of the successive conquests she has undergone. Indian society has no history at all, at least no known history. What we call its history, is but the history of the successive intruders who founded their empires on the passive basis of that unresisting and unchanging society. The question, therefore, is not whether the English had a right to conquer India, but whether we are to prefer India conquered by the Turk, by the Persian, by the Russian, to India conquered by the Briton.

England has to fulfill a double mission in India: one destructive, the other regenerating—the annihilation of old Asiatic society, and the laying of the material foundations of Western society in Asia.

Arabs, Turks, Tartars, Moguls, who had successively overrun India, soon became Hindooized, the barbarian conquerors being, by an eternal law of history, conquered themselves by the superior civilization of their subjects. The British were the first conquerors superior, and therefore, inaccessible to Hindoo civilization. They destroyed it by breaking up the native communities, by uprooting the native industry, and by levelling all that was great and elevated in the native society. The historic pages of their rule in India report hardly anything beyond that destruction. The work of regeneration hardly transpires through a heap of ruins. Nevertheless it has begun.

The political unity of India, more consolidated, and extending farther than it ever did under the Great Moguls, was the first condition of its regeneration. That unity, imposed by the British sword, will now be strengthened and perpetuated by

From *The New York Daily Tribune,* 8 August 1853.

the electric telegraph. The native army, organized and trained by the British drill-sergeant, was the *sine qua non* of Indian self-emancipation, and of India ceasing to be the prey of the first foreign intruder. The free press, introduced for the first time into Asiatic society, and managed principally by the common offspring of Hindoos and Europeans, is a new and powerful agent of reconstruction. The Zemindaree and Ryotwar themselves, abominable as they are, involve two distinct forms of private property in land—the great desideratum of Asiatic society. From the Indian natives, reluctantly and sparingly educated at Calcutta, under English superintendence, a fresh class is springing up, endowed with the requirements for government and imbued with European science. Steam has brought India into regular and rapid communication with Europe, has connected its chief ports with those of the whole south-eastern ocean, and has revindicated it from the isolated position which was the prime law of its stagnation. The day is not far distant when, by a combination of railways and steam vessels, the distance between England and India, measured by time, will be shortened to eight days, and when that once fabulous country will thus be actually annexed to the Western World.

The ruling classes of Great Britain have had, till now, but an accidental, transitory and exceptional interest in the progress of India. The aristocracy wanted to conquer it, the moneyocracy to plunder it, and the millocracy to undersell it. But now the tables are turned. The millocracy have discovered that the transformation of India into a reproductive country has become of vital importance to them, and that, to that end, it is necessary, above all, to gift her with means of irrigation and of internal communication. They intend now drawing a net of railroads over India. And they will do it. The results must be inappreciable.

It is notorious that the productive powers of India are paralyzed by the utter want of means for conveying and exchanging its various produce. Nowhere, more than in India, do we meet with social destitution in the midst of natural plenty, for want of the means of exchange. It was proved before a Committee of the British House of Commons, which sat in 1848, that

> when grain was selling from 6s. to 8s. a quarter at Khandesh, it was sold for 64s. to 70s. at Poonah, where the people were dying in the streets of famine, without the possibility of gaining supplies from Khandesh, because the clay roads were impracticable.

The introduction of railroads may be easily made to subserve agricultural purposes by the formation of tanks, where ground is required for embankment, and by the conveyance of water along the different lines. Thus irrigation, the *sine qua non* of farming in the East, might be greatly extended, and the frequently recurring local famines, arising from the want of water, would be averted. The general importance of railways, viewed under this head, must become evident, when we remember that irrigated lands, even in the districts near Ghats, pay three times as much in taxes, afford ten or twelve times as much employment, and yield twelve or fifteen times as much profit, as the same area without irrigation.

Railways will afford the means of diminishing the amount and the cost of the military establishments. Col. Warren, Town Major of the Fort St. William, stated before a Select Committee of the House of Commons:

> The practicability of receiving intelligence from distant parts of the country in as many hours as at present it requires days and even weeks, and of sending instructions with troops and stores, in the more brief period, are considerations which cannot be too highly estimated. Troops could be kept at more distant and healthier stations than at present, and much loss of life from sickness would by this means be spared. Stores could not to the same extent be required at the various depots, and the loss by decay, and the destruction incidental to the climate, would also be avoided. The number of troops might be diminished in direct proportion to their effectiveness.

We know that the municipal organization and the economical basis of the village communities have been broken up, but their worst feature, the dissolution of society into stereotype and disconnected atoms, has survived their vitality. The village isolation produced the absence of roads in India, and the absence of roads perpetuated the village isolation. On this plan a community existed with a given scale of low conveniences, almost without intercourse with other villages, without the desires and efforts indispensable to social advance. The British having broken up this self-sufficient *inertia* of the villages, railways will provide the new want of communication and intercourse. Besides,

> one of the effects of the railway system will be to bring into every village affected by it such knowledge of the contrivances and appliances of other countries, and such means of obtaining them, as will first put the hereditary and stipendiary village artisanship of India to full proof of its capabilities, and then supply its defects.[1]

I know that the English millocracy intend to endow India with railways with the exclusive view of extracting at diminished expenses, the cotton and other raw materials for their manufactures. But when you have once introduced machinery into the locomotion of a country, which possesses iron and coals, you are unable to withhold it from its fabrication. You cannot maintain a net of railways over an immense country without introducing all those industrial processes necessary to meet the immediate and current wants of railway locomotion, and out of which there must grow the application of machinery to those branches of industry not immediately connected with railways. The railway system will therefore become, in India, truly the forerunner of modern industry. This is the more certain as the Hindoos are allowed by British authorities themselves to possess particular aptitude for accommodating themselves to entirely new labour, and acquiring the requisite knowledge of machinery. Ample proof of this fact is afforded by the capacities and expertness of the native engineers in the Calcutta mint, where they have been for years employed in working the steam machinery, by the natives attached to the several steam-engines in the Hurdwar coal districts, and by other instances. Mr.

Campbell himself, greatly influenced as he is by the prejudices of the East India Company, is obliged to avow

> that the great mass of the Indian people possesses a great *industrial energy,* is well fitted to accumulate capital, and remarkable for a mathematical clearness of head, and talent for figures and exact sciences. "Their intellects," he says, "are excellent."[2]

Modern industry, resulting from the railway system, will dissolve the hereditary divisions of labour, upon which rest the Indian castes, those decisive impediments to Indian progress and Indian power.

All the English bourgeoisie may be forced to do will neither emancipate nor materially mend the social condition of the mass of the people, depending not only on the development of the productive powers, but of their appropriation by the people. But what they will not fail to do is to lay down the material premises for both. Has the bourgeoisie ever done more? Has it ever effected a progress without dragging individuals and peoples through blood and dirt, through misery and degradation?

The Indians will not reap the fruits of the new elements of society scattered among them by the British bourgeoisie, till in Great Britain itself the now ruling classes shall have been supplanted by the industrial proletariat, or till the Hindoos themselves shall have grown strong enough to throw off the English yoke altogether. At all events, we may safely expect to see, at a more or less remote period, the regeneration of that great and interesting country, whose gentle natives are, to use the expression of Prince Saltykov, even in the most inferior classes, "plus fins et plus adroits que les Italiens," whose submission even is counterbalanced by a certain calm nobility, who, notwithstanding their natural languor, have astonished the British officers by their bravery, whose country has been the source of our languages, our religions, and who represent the type of the ancient German in the Jat and the type of the ancient Greek in the Brahmin.

I cannot part with the subject of India without some concluding remarks.

The profound hypocrisy and inherent barbarism of bourgeois civilization lies unveiled before our eyes, turning from its home, where it assumes respectable forms, to the colonies, where it goes naked. They are the defenders of property, but did any revolutionary party ever originate agrarian revolutions like those in Bengal, in Madras, and in Bombay? Did they not, in India, to borrow an expression of that great robber, Lord Clive himself, resort to atrocious extortion, when simple corruption could not keep pace with their rapacity? While they prated in Europe about the inviolable sanctity of the national debt, did they not confiscate in India the dividends of the rajahs, who had invested their private savings in the Company's own funds? While they combatted the French revolution under the pretext of defending "our holy religion," did they not forbid, at the same time, Christianity to be propagated in India, and did they not, in order to make money out of the pilgrims streaming to the temples of Orissa and Bengal, take up the trade in the murder and prostitution perpetrated in the temple of Juggernaut? These are the men of "Property, Order, Family, and Religion."

The devastating effects of English industry, when contemplated with regard to India, a country as vast as Europe, and containing 150 millions of acres, are palpable and confounding. But we must not forget that they are only the organic results of the whole system of production as it is now constituted. That production rests on the supreme rule of capital. The centralization of capital is essential to the existence of capital as an independent power. The destructive influence of that centralization upon the markets of the world does not reveal, in the most gigantic dimensions, the inherent organic laws of political economy now at work in every civilized town. The bourgeois period of history has to create the material basis of the new world—on the one hand the universal intercourse founded upon the mutual dependency of mankind, and the means of that intercourse; on the other hand the development of the productive powers of man and the transformation of material production into a scientific domination of natural agencies. Bourgeois industry and commerce create these material conditions of a new world in the same way as geological revolutions have created the surface of the earth. When a great social revolution shall have mastered the results of the bourgeois epoch, the market of the world and the modern powers of production, and subjected them to the common control of the most advanced peoples, then only will human progress cease to resemble that hideous pagan idol, who would not drink the nectar but from the skulls of the slain.

NOTES

1. John Chapman, *The Cotton and Commerce of India, Considered in Relation to the Interests of Great Britain: with Remarks on Railway Communication in the Bombay Presidency* (London, 1851), p. 91.
2. George Campbell, *Modern India: A Sketch of the System of Civil Government* (London, 1852), pp. 59–60.

2   Racial Inequality is not the Result of Institutions

Arthur de Gobineau

The idea of an original, clear-cut, and permanent inequality among the different races is one of the oldest and most widely held opinions in the world. We need not be surprised at this, when we consider the isolation of primitive tribes and communities, and how in the early ages they all used to "retire into their shell"; a great number have never left this stage. Except in quite modern times, this idea has been the basis of nearly all theories of government. Every people, great or small, has begun by making inequality its chief political motto. This is the origin of all systems of caste, of nobility, and of aristocracy, in so far as the last is founded on the right of birth. The law of primogeniture, which assumes the pre-eminence of the first born and his descendants, is merely a corollary of the same principle. With it go the repulsion felt for the foreigner and the superiority which every nation claims for itself with regard to its neighbours. As soon as the isolated groups have begun to intermingle and to become one people, they grow great and civilized, and look at each other in a more favourable light, as one finds the other useful. Then, and only then, do we see the absolute principle of the inequality, and hence the mutual hostility, of races questioned and undermined. Finally, when the majority of the citizens have mixed blood flowing in their veins, they erect into a universal and absolute truth what is only true for themselves, and feel it to be their duty to assert that all men are equal. They are also moved by praiseworthy dislike of oppression, a legitimate hatred towards the abuse of power; to all thinking men these cast an ugly shadow on the memory of races which have once been dominant, and which have never failed (for such is the way of the world) to justify to some extent many of the charges that have been brought against them. From mere declamation against tyranny, men go on to deny the natural causes of superiority against which they are declaiming. The tyrant's power is, to them, not only misused, but usurped. They refuse, quite wrongly, to admit that certain qualities are by a fatal necessity the exclusive inheritance of such and such a stock. In fact, the more heterogeneous the elements of which a people is composed, the more complacently does it assert that the most different powers are, or can be, possessed in the same measure by every fraction of the human race, without exception. This theory is barely applicable to these hybrid philosophers themselves; but they extend it to cover all the generations which were, are, and ever shall be on the earth. They end one day by summing up their views in the words which, like the bag of Æolus, contain so many storms—"All men are brothers."[1]

This is the political axiom. Would you like to hear it in its scientific form? "All

From *The Inequality of Human Races,* trans. Adrian Collins (London: Heineman, 1915).

men," say the defenders of human equality, "are furnished with similar intellectual powers, of the same nature, of the same value, of the same compass." These are not perhaps their exact words, but they certainly give the right meaning. So the brain of the Huron Indian contains in an undeveloped form an intellect which is absolutely the same as that of the Englishman or the Frenchman! Why then, in the course of the ages, has he not invented printing or steam power? I should be quite justified in asking our Huron why, if he is equal to our European peoples, his tribe has never produced a Caesar or a Charlemagne among its warriors, and why his bards and sorcerers have, in some inexplicable way, neglected to become Homers and Galens. The difficulty is usually met by the blessed phrase, "the predominating influence of environment." According to this doctrine, an island will not see the same miracles of civilization as a continent, the same people will be different in the north from what it is in the south, forests will not allow of developments which are favoured by open country. What else? the humidity of a marsh, I suppose, will produce a civilization which would inevitably have been stifled by the dryness of the Sahara! However ingenious these little hypotheses may be, the testimony of fact is against them. In spite of wind and rain, cold and heat, sterility and fruitfulness, the world has seen barbarism and civilization flourishing everywhere, one after the other, on the same soil. The brutish fellah is tanned by the same sun as scorched the powerful priest of Memphis; the learned professor of Berlin lectures under the same inclement sky that once beheld the wretched existence of the Finnish savage.

The curious point is that the theory of equality, which is held by the majority of men and so has permeated our customs and institutions, has not been powerful enough to overthrow the evidence against it; and those who are most convinced of its truth pay homage every day to its opposite. No one at any time refuses to admit that there are great differences between nations, and the ordinary speech of men, with a naïve inconsistency, confesses the fact. In this it is merely imitating the practice of other ages which were not less convinced than we are—and for the same reason—of the absolute equality of races.

While clinging to the liberal dogma of human brotherhood, every nation has always managed to add to the names of others certain qualifications and epithets that suggest their unlikeness from itself. The Roman of Italy called the Græco-Roman a *Græculus,* or "little Greek," and gave him the monopoly of cowardice and empty chatter. He ridiculed the Carthaginian settler, and pretended to be able to pick him out among a thousand for his litigious character and his want of faith. The Alexandrians were held to be witty, insolent, and seditious. In the Middle Ages, the Anglo-Norman kings accused their French subjects of lightness and inconstancy. To-day, every one talks of the "national characteristics" of the German, the Spaniard, the Englishman, and the Russian. I am not asking whether the judgments are true or not. My sole point is that they exist, and are adopted in ordinary speech. Thus, if on the one hand human societies are called equal, and on the other we find some of them frivolous, others serious; some avaricious, others thriftless; some passionately fond of fighting, others careful of their lives and energies;—it stands to reason that these differing nations must have destinies which are also absolutely different, and,

in a word, unequal. The stronger will play the parts of kings and rulers in the tragedy of the world. The weaker will be content with a more humble position.

I do not think that the usual idea of a national character for each people has yet
been reconciled with the belief, which is just as widely held, that all peoples are
equal. Yet the contradiction is striking and flagrant, and all the more serious because
the most ardent democrats are the first to claim superiority for the Anglo-Saxons of
North America over all the nations of the same continent. It is true that they
ascribe the high position of their favourites merely to their political constitution.
But, so far as I know, they do not deny that the countrymen of Penn and Washington, are, as a nation, peculiarly prone to set up liberal institutions in all their places
of settlement, and, what is more, to keep them going. Is not this very tenacity a
wonderful characteristic of this branch of the human race, and the more precious
because most of the societies which have existed, or still exist, in the world seem to
be without it?

I do not flatter myself that I shall be able to enjoy this inconsistency without
opposition. The friends of equality will no doubt talk very loudly, at this point,
about "the power of customs and institutions." They will tell me once more how
powerfully the health and growth of a nation are influenced by "the essential quality of a government, taken by itself," or "the fact of despotism or liberty." But it is
just at this point that I too shall oppose their arguments.

Political institutions have only two possible sources. They either come directly
from the nation which has to live under them, or they are invented by a powerful
people and imposed on all the States that fall within its sphere of influence.

There is no difficulty in the first hypothesis. A people obviously adapts its institutions to its wants and instincts; and will beware of laying down any rule which
may thwart the one or the other. If, by some lack of skill or care, such a rule is laid
down, the consequent feeling of discomfort leads the people to amend its laws, and
put them into more perfect harmony with their express objects. In every autonomous State, the laws, we may say, always emanate from the people; not generally
because it has a direct power of making them, but because, in order to be good laws,
they must be based upon the people's point of view, and be such as it might have
thought out for itself, if it had been better informed. If some wise lawgiver seems,
at first sight, the sole source of some piece of legislation, a nearer view will show
that his very wisdom has led him merely to give out the oracles that have been dictated by his nation. If he is a judicious man, like Lycurgus, he will prescribe nothing
that the Dorian of Sparta could not accept. If he is a mere doctrinaire, like Draco,
he will draw up a code that will soon be amended or repealed by the Ionian of
Athens, who, like all the children of Adam, is incapable of living for long under laws
that are foreign to the natural tendencies of his real self. The entrance of a man of
genius into this great business of law-making is merely a special manifestation of the
enlightened will of the people; if the laws simply fulfilled the fantastic dreams of
one individual, they could not rule any people for long. We cannot admit that the
institutions thus invented and moulded by a race of men make that race what it is.
They are effects, not causes. Their influence is, of course, very great; they preserve

the special genius of the nation, they mark out the road on which it is to travel, the end at which it must aim. To a certain extent, they are the hothouse where its instincts develop, the armoury that furnishes its best weapons for action. But they do not create their creator; and though they may be a powerful element in his success by helping on the growth of his innate qualities, they will fail miserably whenever they attempt to alter these, or to extend them beyond their natural limits. In a word, they cannot achieve the impossible.

NOTES

The man
1. Of virtuous soul commands not, nor obeys;
   Power, like a desolating pestilence,
   Pollutes whate'er it touches; and obedience,
   Bane of all genius, virtue, freedom, truth,
   Makes slaves of men, and of the human frame
   A mechanized automaton.
                                          Shelley, "Queen Mab."

3   The Stranger

Georg Simmel

If wandering is the liberation from every given point in space, and thus the conceptional opposite to fixation at such a point, the sociological form of the "stranger" presents the unity, as it were, of these two characteristics. This phenomenon too, however, reveals that spatial relations are only the condition, on the one hand, and the symbol, on the other, of human relations. The stranger is thus being discussed here, not in the sense often touched upon in the past, as the wanderer who comes today and goes tomorrow, but rather as the person who comes today and stays tomorrow. He is, so to speak, the *potential* wanderer: although he has not moved on, he has not quite overcome the freedom of coming and going. He is fixed within a particular spatial group, or within a group whose boundaries are similar to spatial boundaries. But his position in this group is determined, essentially, by the fact that he has not belonged to it from the beginning, that he imports qualities into it, which do not and cannot stem from the group itself.

Reprinted with permission of Macmillan Publishing Co., Inc. from *The Sociology of Georg Simmel* by K. H. Wolff, trans. & ed. Copyright © 1950 by The Free Press, a division of Macmillan Publishing Co., Inc.

The unity of nearness and remoteness involved in every human relation is organized, in the phenomenon of the stranger, in a way which may be most briefly formulated by saying that in the relationship to him, distance means that he, who is close by, is far, and strangeness means that he, who also is far, is actually near. For, to be a stranger is naturally a very positive relation; it is a specific form of interaction. The inhabitants of Sirius are not really strangers to us, at least not in any sociologically relevant sense: they do not exist for us at all; they are beyond far and near. The stranger, like the poor and like sundry "inner enemies," is an element of the group itself. His position as a full-fledged member involves both being outside it and confronting it. The following statements, which are by no means intended as exhaustive, indicate how elements which increase distance and repel, in the relations of and with the stranger produce a pattern of coordination and consistent interaction.

Throughout the history of economics the stranger everywhere appears as the trader, or the trader as stranger. As long as economy is essentially self-sufficient, or products are exchanged within a spatially narrow group, it needs no middleman: a trader is only required for products that originate outside the group. Insofar as members do not leave the circle in order to buy these necessities—in which case *they* are the "strange" merchants in that outside territory—the trader *must* be a stranger, since nobody else has a chance to make a living.

This position of the stranger stands out more sharply if he settles down in the place of his activity, instead of leaving it again: in innumerable cases even this is possible only if he can live by intermediate trade. Once an economy is somehow closed, the land is divided up, and handicrafts are established that satisfy the demand for them, the trader, too, can find his existence. For in trade, which alone makes possible unlimited combinations, intelligence always finds expansions and new territories, an achievement which is very difficult to attain for the original producer with his lesser mobility and his dependence upon a circle of customers that can be increased only slowly. Trade can always absorb more people than primary production; it is, therefore, the sphere indicated for the stranger, who intrudes as a supernumerary, so to speak, into a group in which the economic positions are actually occupied—the classical example is the history of European Jews. The stranger is by nature no "owner of soil"—soil not only in the physical, but also in the figurative sense of a life-substance which is fixed, if not in a point in space, at least in an ideal point of the social environment. Although in more intimate relations, he may develop all kinds of charm and significance, as long as he is considered a stranger in the eyes of the other, he is not an "owner of soil." Restriction to intermediary trade, and often (as though sublimated from it) to pure finance, gives him the specific character of *mobility*. If mobility takes place within a closed group, it embodies that synthesis of nearness and distance which constitutes the formal position of the stranger. For, the fundamentally mobile person comes in contact, at one time or another, with every individual, but is not organically connected, through established ties of kinship, locality, and occupation, with any single one.

Another expression of this constellation lies in the objectivity of the stranger.

He is not radically committed to the unique ingredients and peculiar tendencies of the group, and therefore approaches them with the specific attitude of "objectivity." But objectivity does not simply involve passivity and detachment; it is a particular structure composed of distance and nearness, indifference and involvement. I refer to the discussion of the dominating positions of the person who is a stranger in the group; its most typical instance was the practice of those Italian cities to call their judges from the outside, because no native was free from entanglement in family and party interests.

With the objectivity of the stranger is connected, also, the phenomenon touched upon above, although it is chiefly (but not exclusively) true of the stranger who moves on. This is the fact that he often receives the most surprising openness—confidences which sometimes have the character of a confessional and which would be carefully withheld from a more closely related person. Objectivity is by no means non-participation (which is altogether outside both subjective and objective interaction), but a positive and specific kind of participation—just as the objectivity of a theoretical observation does not refer to the mind as a passive *tabula rasa* on which things inscribe their qualities, but on the contrary, to its full activity that operates according to its own laws, and to the elimination, thereby, of accidental dislocations and emphases, whose individual and subjective differences would produce different pictures of the same object.

Objectivity may also be defined as freedom: the objective individual is bound by no commitments which could prejudice his perception, understanding, and evaluation of the given. The freedom, however, which allows the stranger to experience and treat even his close relationships as though from a bird's-eye view, contains many dangerous possibilities. In uprisings of all sorts, the party attacked has claimed, from the beginning of things, that provocation has come from the outside, through emissaries and instigators. Insofar as this is true, it is an exaggeration of the specific role of the stranger: he is freer, practically and theoretically; he surveys conditions with less prejudice; his criteria for them are more general and more objective ideals; he is not tied down in his action by habit, piety, and precedent.[1]

Finally, the proportion of nearness and remoteness which gives the stranger the character of objectivity, also finds practical expression in the more *abstract nature* of the relation to him. That is, with the stranger one has only certain *more general* qualities in common, whereas the relation to more organically connected persons is based on the commonness of specific differences from merely general features. In fact, all somehow personal relations follow this scheme in various patterns. They are determined not only by the circumstance that certain common features exist among the individuals, along with individual differences, which either influence the relationship or remain outside of it. For, the common features themselves are basically determined in their effect upon the relation by the question whether they exist only between the participants in this particular relationship, and thus are quite general in regard to this relation, but are specific and incomparable in regard to everything outside of it—or whether the participants feel that these features are common to them because they are common to a group, a type, or mankind in general. In the case of the second alternative, the effectiveness of the common features becomes diluted in proportion to the size of the group composed of members who are similar in this sense. Although the commonness functions as their unifying basis, it does not make *these* particular persons interdependent on one another, because it could as easily connect everyone of them with all kinds of individuals other than the members of his group. This too, evidently, is a way in which a relationship includes both nearness and distance at the same time: to the extent to which the common features are general, they add, to the warmth of the relation founded on them, an element of coolness, a feeling of the contingency of precisely *this* relation—the connecting forces have lost their specific and centripetal character.

In the relation to the stranger, it seems to me, this constellation has an extraordinary and basic preponderance over the individual elements that are exclusive with the particular relationship. The stranger is close to us, insofar as we feel between him and ourselves common features of a national, social, occupational, or generally human, nature. He is far from us, insofar as these common features extend beyond him or us, and connect us only because they connect a great many people.

A trace of strangeness in this sense easily enters even the most intimate relationships. In the stage of first passion, erotic relations strongly reject any thought of generalization: the lovers think that there has never been a love like theirs; that nothing can be compared either to the person loved or to the feelings for that person. An estrangement—whether as cause or as consequence it is difficult to decide—usually comes at the moment when this feeling of uniqueness vanishes from the relationship. A certain skepticism in regard to its value, in itself and for them, attaches to the very thought that in their relation, after all, they carry out only a generally human destiny; that they experience an experience that has occurred a thousand times before; that, had they not accidentally met their particular partner, they would have found the same significance in another person.

Something of this feeling is probably not absent in any relation, however close, because what is common to two is never common to them alone, but is subsumed under a general idea which includes much else besides, many *possibilities* of commonness. No matter how little these possibilities become real and how often we forget them, here and there, nevertheless, they thrust themselves between us like shadows, like a mist which escapes every word noted, but which must coagulate into a solid bodily form before it can be called jealousy. In some cases, perhaps the more general, at least the more unsurmountable, strangeness is not due to different and unundderstandable matters. It is rather caused by the fact that similarity, harmony, and nearness are accompanied by the feeling that they are not really the unique property of this particular relationship: they are something more general, something which potentially prevails between the partners and an indeterminate number of others, and therefore gives the relation, which alone was realized, no inner and exclusive necessity.

On the other hand, there is a kind of "strangeness" that rejects the very commonness based on something more general which embraces the parties. The relation of the Greeks to the Barbarians is perhaps typical here, as are all cases in which it is precisely general attributes, felt to be specifically and purely human, that are disallowed to the other. But "stranger," here, has no positive meaning; the relation to him is a non-relation; he is not what is relevant here, a member of the group itself.

As a group member, rather, he is near and far *at the same time,* as is characteristic of relations founded only on generally human commonness. But between nearness and distance, there arises a specific tension when the consciousness that only the quite general is common stresses that which is not common. In the case of the person who is a stranger to the country, the city, the race, etc., however, this noncommon element is once more nothing individual, but merely the strangeness of origin, which is or could be common to many strangers. For this reason, strangers are not really conceived as individuals, but as strangers of a particular type: the element of distance is no less general in regard to them than the element of nearness.

This form is the basis of such a special case, for instance, as the tax levied in Frankfort and elsewhere upon medieval Jews. Whereas the *Beede* [tax] paid by the Christian citizen changed with the changes of his fortune, it was fixed once for every single Jew. This fixity rested on the fact that the Jew had his social position as a *Jew,* not as the individual bearer of certain objective contents. Every other citizen was the owner of a particular amount of property, and his tax followed its fluctuations. But the Jew as a taxpayer was, in the first place, a Jew, and thus his tax situation had an invariable element. This same position appears most strongly, of course, once even these individual characterizations (limited though they were by rigid invariance) are omitted, and all strangers pay an altogether equal head-tax.

In spite of being inorganically appended to it, the stranger is yet an organic member of the group. Its uniform life includes the specific conditions of this element. Only we do not know how to designate the peculiar unity of this position other than by saying that it is composed of certain measures of nearness and distance. Although some quantities of them characterize all relationships, a *special* proportion and reciprocal tension produce the particular, formal relation to the "stranger."

NOTES

1. But where the attacked make the assertion falsely, they do so from the tendency of those in higher position to exculpate inferiors, who, up to the rebellion, have been in a consistently close relation with them. For, by creating the fiction that the rebels were not really guilty, but only instigated, and that the rebellion did not really start with *them,* they exonerate themselves, inasmuch as they altogether deny all real grounds for the uprising.

4   On Nationalism, Ethnicity and Race

Max Weber

The fervor of this emotional influence [i.e. nationalism] does not, in the main, have
an economic origin. It is based upon sentiments of prestige, which often extend
deep down to the petty bourgeois masses of political structures rich in the historical
attainment of power-positions. The attachment to all this political prestige may fuse
with a specific belief in responsibility towards succeeding generations. The great
power structures *per se* are then held to have a responsibility of their own for the
way in which power and prestige are distributed between their own and foreign
polities. It goes without saying that all those groups who hold the power to steer
common conduct within a polity will most strongly instill themselves with this ideal
fervor of power prestige. They remain the specific and most reliable bearers of the
idea of the state as an imperialist power structure demanding unqualified devotion.

In addition to the direct and material imperialist interests, discussed above,
there are partly indirect and material and partly ideological interests of strata that
are in various ways intellectually privileged within a polity and, indeed, privileged
by its very existence. They comprise especially all those who think of themselves
as being the specific 'partners' of a specific 'culture' diffused among the members of
the polity. Under the influence of these circles, the naked prestige of 'power' is un-
avoidably transformed into other special forms of prestige and especially into the
idea of the 'nation.'

If the concept of 'nation' can in any way be defined unambiguously, it certainly
cannot be stated in terms of empirical qualities common to those who count as
members of the nation. In the sense of those using the term at a given time, the concept undoubtedly means, above all, that one may exact from certain groups of men
a specific sentiment of solidarity in the face of other groups. Thus, the concept belongs in the sphere of values. Yet, there is no agreement on how these groups should
be delimited or about what concerted action should result from such solidarity.

In ordinary language, 'nation' is, first of all, not identical with the 'people of a
state,' that is, with the membership of a given polity. Numerous polities comprise
groups among whom the independence of their 'nation' is emphatically asserted in
the face of the other groups; or, on the other hand, they comprise parts of a group
whose members declare this group to be one homogeneous 'nation' (Austria before
1918, for example). Furthermore, a 'nation' is not identical with a community
speaking the same language; that this by no means always suffices is indicated by
the Serbs and Croats, the North Americans, the Irish, and the English. On the con-

From *Max Weber: Essays in Sociology,* trans. & ed. by H. H. Gerth & C. W. Mills. Copyright 1946 by Oxford University Press, Inc. Renewed 1973 by Dr. Hans H. Gerth. Reprinted by
permission of the publisher.

trary, a common language does not seem to be absolutely necessary to a 'nation.' In official documents, besides 'Swiss People' one also finds the phrase 'Swiss Nation.' And some language groups do not think of themselves as a separate 'nation,' for example, at least until recently, the white Russians. The pretension, however, to be considered a special 'nation' is regularly associated with a common language as a culture value of the masses; this is predominantly the case in the classic country of language conflicts, Austria, and equally so in Russia and in eastern Prussia. But this linkage of the common language and 'nation' is of varying intensity; for instance, it is very low in the United States as well as in Canada.[1]

'National' solidarity among men speaking the same language may be just as well rejected as accepted. Solidarity, instead, may be linked with differences in the other great 'culture value of the masses,' namely, a religious creed, as is the case with the Serbs and Croats. National solidarity may be connected with differing social structure and mores and hence with 'ethnic' elements, as is the case with the German Swiss and the Alsatians in the face of the Germans of the Reich, or with the Irish facing the British. Yet above all, national solidarity may be linked to memories of a common political destiny with other nations, among the Alsatians with the French since the revolutionary war which represents their common heroic age, just as among the Baltic Barons with the Russians whose political destiny they helped to steer.

It goes without saying that 'national' affiliation need not be based upon common blood. Indeed, everywhere the especially radical 'nationalists' are often of foreign descent. Furthermore, although a specific common anthropological type is not irrelevant to nationality, it is neither sufficient nor a prerequisite to found a nation. Nevertheless, the idea of the 'nation' is apt to include the notions of common descent and of an essential, though frequently indefinite, homogeneity. The nation has these notions in common with the sentiment of solidarity of ethnic communities, which is also nourished from various sources. But the sentiment of ethnic solidarity does not by itself make a 'nation.' Undoubtedly, even the white Russians in the face of the Great Russians have always had a sentiment of ethnic solidarity, yet even at the present time they would hardly claim to qualify as a separate 'nation.' The Poles of Upper Silesia, until recently, had hardly any feeling of solidarity with the 'Polish Nation.' They felt themselves to be a separate ethnic group in the face of the Germans, but for the rest they were Prussian subjects and nothing else.

Whether the Jews may be called a 'nation' is an old problem. The mass of the Russian Jews, the assimilating West-European-American Jews, the Zionists—these would in the main give a negative answer. In any case, their answers would vary in nature and extent. In particular, the question would be answered very differently by the peoples of their environment, for example, by the Russians on the one side and by the Americans on the other—or at least by those Americans who at the present time still maintain American and Jewish nature to be essentially similar, as an American President has asserted in an official document.

Those German-speaking Alsatians who refuse to belong to the German 'nation' and who cultivate the memory of political union with France do not thereby consider themselves simply as members of the French 'nation.' The Negroes of the United States, at least at present, consider themselves members of the American 'nation,' but they will hardly ever be so considered by the Southern Whites.

Only fifteen years ago, men knowing the Far East, still denied that the Chinese qualified as a 'nation'; they held them to be only a 'race.' Yet today, not only the Chinese political leaders but also the very same observers would judge differently. Thus it seems that a group of people under certain conditions may attain the quality of a nation through specific behavior, or they may claim this quality as an 'attainment'—and within short spans of time at that.

There are, on the other hand, social groups that profess indifference to, and even directly relinquish, any evaluational adherence to a single nation. At the present time, certain leading strata of the class movement of the modern proletariat consider such indifference and relinquishment to be an accomplishment. Their argument meets with varying success, depending upon political and linguistic affiliations and also upon different strata of the proletariat; on the whole, their success is rather diminishing at the present time.

An unbroken scale of quite varied and highly changeable attitudes toward the idea of the 'nation' is to be found among social strata and also within single groups to whom language usage ascribes the quality of 'nations.' The scale extends from emphatic affirmation to emphatic negation and finally complete indifference, as may be characteristic of the citizens of Luxembourg and of nationally 'unawakened' peoples. Feudal strata, strata of officials, entrepreneurial bourgeois strata of various categories, strata of 'intellectuals' do not have homogeneous or historically constant attitudes towards the idea.

The reasons for the belief that one represents a nation vary greatly, just as does the empirical conduct that actually results from affiliation or lack of it with a nation. The 'national sentiments' of the German, the Englishman, the North American, the Spaniard, the Frenchman, or the Russian do not function in an identical manner. Thus, to take only the simplest illustration, national sentiment is variously related to political associations, and the 'idea' of the nation may become antagonistic to the empirical scope of given political associations. This antagonism may lead to quite different results.

Certainly the Italians in the Austrian state-association would fight Italian troops only if coerced into doing so. Large portions of the German Austrians would today fight against Germany only with the greatest reluctance; they could not be relied upon. The German Americans, however, even those valuing their 'nationality' most highly, would fight against Germany, not gladly, yet, given the occasion, unconditionally. The Poles in the German State would fight readily against a Russian Polish army but hardly against an autonomous Polish army. The Austrian Serbs would fight against Serbia with very mixed feelings and only in the hope of attaining common autonomy. The Russian Poles would fight more reliably against a German than against an Austrian army.

It is a well-known historical fact that within the same nation the intensity of solidarity felt toward the outside is changeable and varies greatly in strength. On the whole, this sentiment has grown even where internal conflicts of interest have not diminished. Only sixty years ago the *Kreuzzeitung*[2] still appealed to the intervention of the emperor of Russia in internal German affairs; today, in spite of increased class antagonism, this would be difficult to imagine.

In any case, the differences in national sentiment are both significant and fluid and, as is the case in all other fields, fundamentally different answers are given to the question: What conclusions are a group of people willing to draw from the 'national sentiment' found among them? No matter how emphatic and subjectively sincere a pathos may be formed among them, what sort of specific joint action are they ready to develop? The extent to which in the diaspora a convention is adhered to as a 'national' trait varies just as much as does the importance of common conventions for the belief in the existence of a separate 'nation.' In the face of these value concepts of the 'idea of the nation,' which empirically are entirely ambiguous, a sociological typology would have to analyze all sorts of community sentiments of solidarity in their genetic conditions and in their consequences for the concerted action of the participants. This cannot here be attempted.

Instead, we shall have to look a little closer into the fact that the idea of the nation for its advocates stands in very intimate relation to 'prestige' interests. The earliest and most energetic manifestations of the idea, in some form, even though it may have been veiled, have contained the legend of a providential 'mission.' Those to whom the representatives of the idea zealously turned were expected to shoulder this mission. Another element of the early idea was the notion that this mission was facilitated solely through the very cultivation of the peculiarity of the group set off as a nation. Therewith, in so far as its self-justification is sought in the value of its content, this mission can consistently be thought of only as a specific 'culture' mission. The significance of the 'nation' is usually anchored in the superiority, or at least the irreplaceability, of the culture values that are to be preserved and developed only through the cultivation of the peculiarity of the group. It therefore goes without saying that the intellectuals, as we have in a preliminary fashion called them, are to a specific degree predestined to propagate the 'national idea,' just as those who wield power in the polity provoke the idea of the state.

By 'intellectuals' we understand a group of men who by virtue of their peculiarity have special access to certain achievements considered to be 'culture values,' and who therefore usurp the leadership of a 'culture community.'[3]

* * * * *

In so far as there is at all a common object lying behind the obviously ambiguous term 'nation,' it is apparently located in the field of politics. One might well define the concept of nation in the following way: a nation is a community of sentiment which would adequately manifest itself in a state of its own; hence, a nation is a community which normally tends to produce a state of its own.

The causal components that lead to the emergence of a national sentiment in this sense may vary greatly. If we for once disregard religious belief—which has not yet played its last role in this matter, especially among Serbs and Croats—then common purely political destinies have first to be considered. Under certain conditions, otherwise heterogeneous peoples can be melted together through common destinies. The reason for the Alsatians not feeling themselves as belonging to the German nation has to be sought in their memories. Their political destiny has taken its course outside the German sphere for too long; their heroes are the heroes of French history. If the custodian of the Kolmar museum wants to show you which among his treasures he cherishes most, he takes you away from Grünewald's altar to a room filled with tricolors, *pompier,* and other helmets and souvenirs of a seemingly most insignificant nature; they are from a time that to him is a heroic age.

An existing state organization whose heroic age is not felt as such by the masses can nevertheless be decisive for a powerful sentiment of solidarity, in spite of the greatest internal antagonisms. The state is valued as the agency that guarantees security, and this is above all the case in times of external danger, when sentiments of national solidarity flare up, at least intermittently. Thus we have seen how the elements of the Austrian state, which apparently strove to separate without regard for consequences, united during the so-called Nibelung danger.[4] It was not only the officials and officers, who were interested in the state as such, who could be relied upon, but also the masses of the army.

The conditions of a further component, namely, the influence of race, is especially complex. Here we had better disregard entirely the mystic effects of a community of blood, in the sense in which the racial fanaticists use the phrase. The differences among anthropological types are but one factor of closure, social attraction, and repulsion. They stand with equal right beside differences acquired through tradition. There are characteristic differences in these matters. Every Yankee accepts the civilized quarter-breed or octoroon Indian as a member of the nation; he may himself claim to have Indian blood. But he behaves quite differently toward the Negro, and he does so especially when the Negro adopts the same way of life as he and therewith develops the same social aspirations. How can we explain this fact?

Aesthetic aversions may come into play. The 'odor of Negroes,' however, of which so many fables are told, is, according to my experience, not to be discovered. Black wet-nurses, black coachmen riding shoulder to shoulder with the lady steering the cabriolet, and above all, several million mixed bloods are all too clear proof against the allegedly natural repulsion between these races. This aversion is social in nature, and I have heard but one plausible explanation for it: the Negroes have been slaves; the Indians have not.

Of those cultural elements that represent the most important positive basis for the formation of national sentiment everywhere, a common language takes first place. But even a common language is not entirely indispensable nor sufficient by itself. One may state that there was a specific Swiss national sentiment in spite of the lack of common language; and, in spite of a common language, the Irish have no common national sentiment with the British. The importance of language is necessarily increasing along with the democratization of state, society, and culture. For the masses a common language plays a more decisive economic part than it does for the propertied strata of feudal or bourgeois stamp. For these latter, at least in the language areas of an identical culture, usually speak the foreign language, whereas the petty bourgeois and the proletarian in a foreign language area are much more dependent upon cohesion with those speaking the same language. Above all, the language, and that means the literature based upon it, is the first and for the time being the only cultural value at all accessible to the masses who ascend toward participation in culture. The enjoyment of art requires a far greater degree of education, and art has a far more aristocratic nature than has literature. This is precisely the case in literature's greatest achievements. It is for this reason that the notion held in Austria that democratization must soften the language conflicts was so utopian. The facts have, in the meanwhile, thoroughly disproved such notions. Common cultural values can provide a unifying national bond. But for this the objective quality of the cultural values does not matter at all, and therefore one must not conceive of the 'nation' as a 'culture community.'

Newspapers, which certainly do not assemble what is most sublime in literary culture, cement the masses most strongly. Concerning the actual social conditions that make for the rise of a unified literary language and for a literature in the vernacular, which is something else, all research is now only in its beginnings. For the case of France, one may refer to the essays of my esteemed friend Vossler.

I should like to point to only one typical supporter of this development, because it is one seldom recognized as such, namely, women. They contributed specifically to the formation of national sentiment linked to language. An erotic lyric addressed to a woman can hardly be written in a foreign language, because then it would be unintelligible to the addressee. The courtly and chivalrous lyric was neither singular, nor always the first literature to displace Latin by the national language, as happened in France, Italy, Germany, or to displace Chinese, as happened in Japan. Nevertheless, the courtly lyric has frequently and permanently done so, and has sublimated national languages into literary languages. I cannot here describe how after this initial displacement the importance of the vernacular steadily progressed under the influence of the broadening administrative tasks of state and church, hence as the language of administration and of the sermon. I may, however, add one more word about the economic determination of modern language conflicts.

Today quite considerable pecuniary and capitalist interests are anchored in the maintenance and cultivation of the popular language: the interests of the publishers, editors, authors, and the contributors to books and periodicals and, above all, to newspapers. Once Polish and Latvian newspapers existed, the language fight conducted by governments or ruling strata of another language community had become as good as hopeless, for reasons of state are powerless against these forces. And to the interests in profits of the capitalist another material interest of great weight has to be added: the bilingual candidates in competing for office throw their bilingualism into the balance and seek to lay claim upon as large an area of patronage as possible. This occurred among the Czechs in Austria with their surplus of intellectual proletariat bred *en masse.* The tendency as such is old.

The conciliar, and at the same time nationalist, reaction against the universalism of the papacy in the waning Middle Ages had its origin, to a great extent, in the interests of the intellectuals who wished to see the prebends of their own country reserved for themselves and not occupied by strangers *via* Rome. After all, the name *natio* as a legal concept for an organized community is found first at the universities and at the reform councils of the church. At that time, however, the linkage to the national language *per se* was lacking; this linkage, for the reasons stated, is specifically modern.

If one believes that it is at all expedient to distinguish national sentiment as something homogeneous and specifically set apart, one can do so only by referring to a tendency toward an autonomous state. And one must be clearly aware of the fact that sentiments of solidarity, very heterogeneous in both their nature and their origin, are comprised within national sentiments.

NOTES

1. Weber was writing at the turn of the century. J. S.
2. Organ of Prussian Junkers.
3. The text breaks off here. Notes on the manuscript indicate that Weber intended to deal with the idea and development of the national state throughout history. The supplementary passage that follows is from Max Weber's comment on a paper by Karl Barth; *Gesammelte Aufsaetze zur Soziologie und Sozialpolitik* (Tübingen, 1924), pp. 484–6.
4. A war scare during the early nineteen hundreds.

CONTEMPORARY

THEORETICAL PERSPECTIVES

Contemporary social science views race and ethnic relations from several different perspectives. Robert Merton's classic paper considers a number of critical aspects of prejudice and discrimination. These aspects have a bearing not simply on the theoretical analysis of race relations, but by clearing up areas of theoretical ambiguity and confusion they point the way towards more precise and realistic policy proposals. Starting from a critique of Gunnar Myrdal's *An American Dilemma,* Merton shows that American race relations are not just a problem of moral ideas clashing with discriminatory behavior. Rather, the situation should be seen as arising out of the complex interplay of three variables: a cultural creed only partially enacted in law, a set of beliefs and attitudes towards that creed, and actual individual behavior. Merton's typology derived from those variables—the "unprejudiced non-discriminator," the "unprejudiced discriminator," the "prejudiced non-discriminator," and the "prejudiced discriminator"—illustrates the important point that prejudiced attitudes and discriminatory behavior are not necessarily related. In practice, social-structural and psychological variables are elaborately intertwined, but an understanding of this phenomenon is an essential prerequisite for those seeking to promote a greater degree of racial justice.

In his paper John Rex also insists that correct theoretical analysis is a vital first step in the implementation of political goals. The most fundamental problem for him is to seek a precise sociological definition of race relations. Rex considers a number of possibilities from the perspectives of social stratification to the phenomenological stress on the individual's subjective definition of the situation. While each approach is valuable none provides an adequate explanation on its own of major problems in race relations. Rex synthesizes aspects of those various approaches into a composite definition that not only emphasizes the structural basis of race relations in economic, political, and military inequalities but also attempts to account for the fact that such inequalities should be defined in racial or ethnic terms. Such a synthesis involves a critical assessment of the nature and role of racist belief systems. Rex then considers the practical implications of his analysis for the sociology of race relations with particular reference to the United Kingdom.

Finally, my paper draws partly on the preceding extracts but also on the more extensive literature of classical sociology. I examine in greater detail the thesis mentioned in the introduction, that the major writers of the classical sociological tradition—Montesquieu, Tocqueville, Marx, Spencer, Pareto, Durkheim, and Weber—paid significant attention to the problem area of race relations in formulating their general theories of society. I relate their concern with race and ethnicity to the three major issues of slavery, imperialism, and nationalism. In each case, these writers developed concepts and theories similar to those used in the modern analysis of racial conflict, stratification, and interaction, and their work contrasts with the racist assumptions and arguments of most of their contemporaries. In conclusion I relate the relative neglect of this classical legacy to a number of factors in the development of Anglo-American sociology.

5   Discrimination and the
           American Creed

Robert K. Merton

The primary function of the sociologist is to search out the determinants and consequences of diverse forms of social behavior. To the extent that he succeeds in fulfilling this role, he clarifies the alternatives of organized social action in a given situation and of the probable outcome of each. To this extent, there is no sharp distinction between pure research and applied research. Rather, the difference is one between research with direct implications for particular problems of social action and research which is remote from these problems. Not infrequently, basic research which has succeeded only in clearing up previously confused concepts may have an immediate bearing upon the problems of men in society to a degree not approximated by applied research oriented exclusively to these problems. At least, this is the assumption underlying the present paper: clarification of apparently unclear and confused concepts in the sphere of race and ethnic relations is a step necessarily prior to the devising of effective programs for reducing intergroup conflict and for promoting equitable access to economic and social opportunities.

In an effort toward such clarification, I shall consider first the place of the creed of equitable access to opportunity in American culture; second, the relations of this creed to the beliefs and practices of Americans; third, the diverse types of orientation toward discrimination *and* prejudice; fourth, the implications for organized action of the recognition of these diverse types; and fifth, the expectable consequences of alternative lines of action in diverse social contexts.

THE AMERICAN CREED: AS CULTURAL IDEAL, PERSONAL
BELIEF AND PRACTICE

The American creed as set forth in the Declaration of Independence, the preamble
of the Constitution and the Bill of Rights has often been misstated. This part of
the cultural heritage does *not* include the patently false assertion that all men are
created equal in capacity or endowment. It does *not* imply that an Einstein and a
moron are equal in intellectual capacity or that Joe Louis and a small, frail Columbia professor (or a Mississippian Congressman) are equally endowed with brawny
arms harboring muscles as strong as iron bands. It does *not* proclaim universal
equality of innate intellectual or physical endowment.

Instead, the creed asserts the indefeasible principle of the human right to full
equity—the right of equitable access to justice, freedom and opportunity, irrespective of race or religion or ethnic origin. It proclaims further the universalist doctrine
of the dignity of the individual, irrespective of the groups of which he is a part. It
is a creed announcing full moral equities for all, not an absurd myth affirming the
equality of intellectual and physical capacity of all men everywhere. And it goes
on to say that though men differ in innate endowment, they do so as individuals,
not by virtue of their group memberships.

Viewed sociologically, the creed is a set of values and precepts embedded in
American culture, to which Americans are expected to conform. It is a complex of
affirmations, rooted in the historical past and ceremonially celebrated in the present, partly enacted in the laws of the land and partly not. Like all creeds, it is a
profession of faith, a part of cultural tradition sanctified by the larger traditions
of which it is a part.

It would be a mistaken sociological assertion, however, to suggest that the
creed is a fixed and static cultural constant, unmodified in the course of time, just
as it would be an error to imply that as an integral part of the culture, it evenly
blankets all subcultures of the national society. It is indeed dynamic, subject to
change and in turn promoting change in other spheres of culture and society. It is,
moreover, unevenly distributed throughout the society, being institutionalized as
an integral part of local culture in some regions of the society and rejected in
others.

Nor does the creed exert the same measure of control over behavior in diverse
times and places. In so far as it is a "sacred" part of American culture, hallowed by
tradition, it is largely immune to direct attack. But it may be honored simply in
the breach. It is often evaded, and the evasions themselves become institutionalized, giving rise to what I may call the "institutionalized evasion of institutional
norms." Where the creed is at odds with local beliefs and practices, it may persist
as an empty cultural form partly because it is so flexible. It need not prove overly
obstructive to the social, psychological and economic gains of individuals, because
there are still so many avenues for conscientiously ignoring the creed in practice. When necessary for peace of mind and psychological equilibrium, individuals

indoctrinated with the creed who find themselves deviating from its precepts may readily explain how their behavior accords with the spirit of the creed rather than with its sterile letter. Or the creed itself is re-interpreted. Only those of equal endowment should have equal access to opportunity, it is said, and a given race or ethnic group manifestly does not have the requisite capacity to be deserving of opportunity. To provide such opportunities for the inferior of mind would be only wasteful of national resources. The rationalizations are too numerous and too familiar to bear repetition. The essential point is that the creed, though invulnerable to direct attack in some regions of the society, is not binding on practice. Many individuals and groups in many areas of the society systematically deny through daily conduct what they affirm on periodic ceremonial or public occasions.

This gap between creed and conduct has received wide notice. Learned men and men in high public positions have repeatedly observed and deplored the disparity between ethos and behavior in the sphere of race and ethnic relations. In his magisterial volumes on the American Negro, for example, Gunnar Myrdal called this gulf between creed and conduct "an American dilemma," and centered his attention on the prospect of narrowing or closing the gap. The President's Committee on Civil Rights, in their report to the nation, and . . . President [Truman] himself, in a message to Congress, have called public attention to this "serious gap between our ideals and some of our practices."

But valid as these observations may be, they tend so to simplify the relations between creed and conduct as to be seriously misleading both for social policy and for social science. All these high authorities notwithstanding, the problems of racial and ethnic inequities are not expressible as a discrepancy between high cultural principles and low social conduct. It is a relation not between two variables, official creed and private practice, but between three: first, the cultural creed honored in cultural tradition and partly enacted into law; second, the beliefs and attitudes of individuals regarding the principles of the creed; and third, the actual practices of individuals with reference to it.

Once we substitute these three variables of cultural ideal, belief and actual practice for the customary distinction between the two variables of cultural ideals and actual practices, the entire formulation of the problem becomes changed. We escape from the virtuous but ineffectual impasse of deploring the alleged hypocrisy of many Americans into the more difficult but potentially effectual realm of analyzing the problem in hand.

To describe the problem and to proceed to its analysis, it is necessary to consider the official creed, individuals' beliefs and attitudes concerning the creed, and their actual behavior. Once stated, the distinctions are readily applicable. Individuals may *recognize* the creed as part of a cultural tradition, *without having any private conviction of its moral validity or its binding quality.* Thus, so far as the beliefs of individuals are concerned, we can identify two types: those who genuinely believe in the creed and those who do not (although some of these may, on public or ceremonial occasions, profess adherence to its principles). Similarly, with respect to actual practices: conduct may or may not conform to the creed. But, and this is the salient consideration: *conduct may or may not conform with individuals' own beliefs concerning the moral claims of all men to equal opportunity.*

Stated in formal sociological terms, this asserts that attitudes and overt behavior vary independently. *Prejudicial attitudes need not coincide with discriminatory behavior.* The implications of this statement can be drawn out in terms of a logical syntax whereby the variables are diversely combined, as can be seen in the following typology.

By exploring the interrelations between prejudice and discrimination, we can identify four major types in terms of their attitudes toward the creed and their behavior with respect to it. Each type is found in every region and social class, though in varying numbers. By examining each type, we shall be better prepared to understand their interdependence and the appropriate types of action for curbing ethnic discrimination. The folklabels for each type are intended to aid in their prompt recognition.

Type I: The Unprejudiced Non-Discriminator or All-Weather Liberal

These are the racial and ethnic liberals who adhere to the creed in both belief and practice. They are neither prejudiced nor given to discrimination. Their orientation toward the creed is fixed and stable. Whatever the environing situation, they are likely to abide by their beliefs: hence, the *all-weather* liberal.

This is, of course, the strategic group which *can* act as the spearhead for the progressive extension of the creed into effective practice. They represent the solid foundation both for the measure of ethnic equities which now exist and for the future enlargement of these equities. Integrated with the creed in both belief and practice, they would seem most motivated to influence others toward the same democratic outlook. They represent a reservoir of culturally legitimatized goodwill which can be channeled into an active program for extending belief in the creed and conformity with it in practice.

Most important, as we shall see presently, the all-weather liberals comprise the group which can so reward others for conforming with the creed, as to transform deviants into conformists. They alone can provide the positive social environment

TABLE 1
A Typology of Ethnic Prejudice and Discrimination

	Attitude Dimension:* Prejudice and Non-prejudice	Behavior Dimension:* Discrimination and Non-discrimination
Type I: Unprejudiced non-discriminator	+	+
Type II: Unprejudiced discriminator	+	−
Type III: Prejudiced non-discriminator	−	.+
Type IV: Prejudiced discriminator	−	−

*Where (+) = conformity to the creed and (−) = deviation from the creed.

for the other types who will no longer find it expedient or rewarding to retain their prejudices or discriminatory practices.

But though the ethnic liberal is a *potential* force for the successive extension of the American creed, he does not fully realize this potentiality in actual fact, for a variety of reasons. Among the limitations on effective action are several fallacies to which the ethnic liberal seems peculiarly subject. First among these is the *fallacy of group soliloquies*. Ethnic liberals are busily engaged in talking to themselves. Repeatedly, the same groups of like-minded liberals seek each other out, hold periodic meetings in which they engage in mutual exhortation and thus lend social and psychological support to one another. But however much these unwittingly self-selected audiences may reinforce the creed among themselves, they do not thus appreciably diffuse the creed in belief or practice to groups which depart from it in one respect or the other.

More, these group soliloquies in which there is typically wholehearted agreement among fellow-liberals tend to promote another fallacy limiting effective action. This is the *fallacy of unanimity*. Continued association with like-minded individuals tends to produce the illusion that a large measure of consensus has been achieved in the community at large. The unanimity regarding essential cultural axioms which obtains in these small groups provokes an overestimation of the strength of the movement and of its effective inroads upon the larger population which does not necessarily share these creedal axioms. Many also mistake participation in the groups of like-minded individuals for effective action. Discussion accordingly takes the place of action. The reinforcement of the creed for oneself is mistaken for the extension of the creed among those outside the limited circle of ethnic liberals.

Arising from adherence to the creed is a third limitation upon effective action, the *fallacy of privatized solutions* to the problem. The ethnic liberal, precisely because he is at one with the American creed, may rest content with his own individual behavior and thus see no need to do anything about the problem at large. Since his own spiritual house is in order, he is not motivated by guilt or shame to work on a collective problem. The very freedom of the liberal from guilt thus prompts him to secede from any *collective* effort to set the national house in order. He essays a *private* solution to a *social* problem. He assumes that numerous individual adjustments will serve in place of a collective adjustment. His outlook, compounded of good moral philosophy but poor sociology, holds that each individual must put his own house in order and fails to recognize that privatized solutions cannot be effected for problems which are essentially social in nature. For clearly, if each person *were* motivated to abide by the American creed, the problem would not be likely to exist in the first place. It is only when a social environment is established by conformists to the creed that deviants can in due course be brought to modify their behavior in the direction of conformity. But this "environment" can be constituted only through collective effort and not through private adherence to a public creed. Thus we have the paradox that the clear conscience of many ethnic liberals may promote the very social situation which permits deviations from the creed to continue unchecked. Privatized liberalism invites social inaction. Accordingly, there appears the phenomenon of the inactive or passive liberal, himself at spiritual ease, neither prejudiced nor discriminatory, but in a measure tending to contribute to the persistence of prejudice and discrimination through his very inaction.

The fallacies of group soliloquy, unanimity and privatized solutions thus operate to make the potential strength of the ethnic liberals unrealized in practice.

It is only by first recognizing these limitations that the liberal can hope to overcome them. With some hesitancy, one may suggest initial policies for curbing the scope of the three fallacies. The fallacy of group soliloquies can be removed only by having ethnic liberals enter into organized groups not comprised merely by fellow-liberals. This exacts a heavy price of the liberal. It means that he faces initial opposition and resistance rather than prompt consensus. It entails giving up the gratifications of consistent group support.

The fallacy of unanimity can in turn be reduced by coming to see that American society often provides large rewards for those who express their ethnic prejudice in discrimination. Only if the balance of rewards, material and psychological, is modified will behavior be modified. Sheer exhortation and propaganda are not enough. Exhortation verges on a belief in magic if it is not supported by appropriate changes in the social environment to make conformity with the exhortation rewarding.

Finally, the fallacy of privatized solutions requires the militant liberal to motivate the passive liberal to collective effort, possibly by inducing in him a sense of guilt for his unwitting contribution to the problems of ethnic inequities through his own systematic inaction.

One may suggest a unifying theme for the ethnic liberal: goodwill is not enough to modify social reality. It is only when this goodwill is harnessed to social-psychological realism that it can be used to reach cultural objectives.

Type II: The Unprejudiced Discriminator or Fair-Weather Liberal

The fair-weather liberal is the man of expediency who, despite his own freedom from prejudice, supports discriminatory practices when it is the easier or more profitable course. His expediency may take the form of holding his silence and thus implicitly acquiescing in expressions of ethnic prejudice by others or in the practice of discrimination by others. This is the expediency of the timid: the liberal who hesitates to speak up against discrimination for fear he might lose status or be otherwise penalized by his prejudiced associates. Or his expediency may take the form of grasping at advantages in social and economic competition deriving solely from the ethnic status of competitors. This is the expediency of the self-assertive: the employer, himself not an anti-Semite or Negrophobe, who refuses to hire Jewish or Negro workers because "it might hurt business"; the trade union leader who expediently advocates racial discrimination in order not to lose the support of powerful Negrophobes in his union.

In varying degrees, the fair-weather liberal suffers from guilt and shame for departing from his own effective beliefs in the American creed. Each deviation through which he derives a limited reward from passively acquiescing in or actively supporting discrimination contributes cumulatively to this fund of guilt. He is, therefore, peculiarly vulnerable to the efforts of the all-weather liberal who would help him bring his conduct into accord with his beliefs, thus removing this source of guilt. He is the most amenable to cure, because basically he wants to be cured. His is a split conscience which motivates him to cooperate actively with those who will help remove the source of internal conflict. He thus represents the strategic group promising the largest returns for the least effort. Persistent re-affirmation of the creed will only intensify his conflict; but a long regimen in a favorable social climate can be expected to transform the fair-weather liberal into an all-weather liberal.

Type III: The Prejudiced Non-Discriminator or Fair-Weather Illiberal

The fair-weather illiberal is the reluctant conformist to the creed, the man of prejudice who does not believe in the creed but conforms to it in practice through fear of sanctions which might otherwise be visited upon him. You know him well: the prejudiced employer who discriminates against racial or ethnic groups until a Fair Employment Practice Commission, able and willing to enforce the law, puts the fear of punishment into him; the trade union leader, himself deeply prejudiced, who does away with Jim Crow in his union because the rank-and-file demands that it be done away with; the businessman who foregoes his own prejudices when he finds a profitable market among the very people he hates, fears or despises; the timid bigot who will not express his prejudices when he is in the presence of powerful men who vigorously and effectively affirm their belief in the American creed.

It should be clear that the fair-weather illiberal is the precise counterpart of the fair-weather liberal. Both are men of expediency, to be sure, but expediency dictates different courses of behavior in the two cases. The timid bigot conforms to the creed only when there is danger or loss in deviations, just as the timid liberal deviates from the creed only when there is danger or loss in conforming. *Superficial similarity in behavior of the two in the same situation should not be permitted to cloak a basic difference in the meaning of this outwardly similar behavior,* a difference which is as important for social policy as it is for social science. Whereas the timid bigot is under strain when he conforms to the creed, the timid liberal is under strain when he deviates. For ethnic prejudice has deep roots in the character structure of the fair-weather bigot, and this will find overt expression unless there are powerful countervailing forces, institutional, legal and interpersonal. He does not accept the moral legitimacy of the creed; he conforms because he must, and will cease to conform when the pressure is removed. The fair-weather liberal, on the other hand, is effectively committed to the creed and does not require strong institutional pressure to conform; continuing interpersonal relations with all-weather liberals may be sufficient.

This is the one critical point at which the traditional formulation of the problem of ethnic discrimination as a departure from the creed can lead to serious errors of theory and practice. Overt behavioral deviation (or conformity) may signify importantly different situations, depending upon the underlying motivations. Knowing simply that ethnic discrimination is rife in a community does not, therefore, point to appropriate lines of social policy. It is necessary to know also the distribution of ethnic prejudices and basic motivations for these prejudices as well. Communities with the same amount of overt discrimination may represent vastly different types of problems, dependent on whether the population is comprised by a large nucleus of fair-weather liberals ready to abandon their discriminatory practices under slight interpersonal pressure or a large nucleus of fair-weather illiberals who will abandon discrimination only if major changes in the local institutional setting can be effected. Any statement of the problem as a gulf between creedal ideals and prevailing practice is thus seen to be overly-simplified in the precise sense of masking this decisive difference between the type of discrimination exhibited by the fair-weather liberal and by the fair-weather illiberal. That the gulf-between-ideal-and-practice does not adequately describe the nature of the ethnic problem will become more apparent as we turn to the fourth type in our inventory of prejudice and discrimination.

Type IV: The Prejudiced Discriminator or the All-Weather Illiberal

This type, too, is not unknown to you. He is the confirmed illiberal, the bigot pure and unashamed, the man of prejudice consistent in his departures from the American creed. In some measure, he is found everywhere in the land, though in varying numbers. He derives large social and psychological gains from his conviction that "any white man (including the village idiot) is 'better' than any nigger (including George Washington Carver)." He considers differential treatment of Negro and white not as "discrimination," in the sense of unfair treatment, but as "discriminating," in the sense of showing acute discernment. For him, it is as clear that one "ought" to accord a Negro and a white different treatment in a wide diversity of situations, as it is clear to the population at large that one "ought" to accord a child and an adult different treatment in many situations.

This illustrates anew my reason for questioning the applicability of the usual formula of the American dilemma as a gap between lofty creed and low conduct. For the confirmed illiberal, ethnic discrimination does *not* represent a discrepancy between *his* ideals and *his* behavior. His ideals proclaim the right, even the duty, of discrimination. Accordingly, his behavior does not entail a sense of social deviation, with the resultant strains which this would involve. The ethnic illiberal is as much a conformist as the ethnic liberal. He is merely conforming to a different cultural and institutional pattern which is centered, not about the creed, but about a doctrine of essential inequality of status ascribed to those of diverse ethnic and racial origins. To overlook this is to overlook the well-known *fact* that our national culture is divided into a number of local subcultures which are not consistent among themselves in all respects. And again, to fail to take this fact of different subcultures into account is to open the door for all manner of errors of social policy in attempting to control the problems of racial and ethnic discrimination.

This view of the all-weather illiberal has one immediate implication with wide bearing upon social policies and sociological theory oriented toward the problem of discrimination. The extreme importance of the social surroundings of the confirmed illiberal at once becomes apparent. For as these surroundings vary, so, in some measure, does the problem of the consistent illiberal. The illiberal, living in those cultural regions where the American creed is widely repudiated and is no effective part of the subculture, has his private ethnic attitudes and practices supported by the local mores, the local institutions and the local power-structure. The illiberal in cultural areas dominated by a large measure of adherence to the American creed is in a social environment where he is isolated and receives small social support for his beliefs and practices. In both instances, the *individual* is an illiberal, to be sure, but he represents two significantly different *sociological types.* In the first instance, he is a *social conformist,* with strong moral and institutional reinforcement, whereas in the second, he is a *social deviant,* lacking strong social corroboration. In the one case, his discrimination involves him in further integration with his network of social relations; in the other, it threatens to cut him off from sustaining interpersonal ties. In the first cultural context, personal change in his ethnic behavior involves alienating himself from people significant to him; in the second context, this change of personal outlook may mean fuller incorporation in groups meaningful to him In the first situation, modification of his ethnic views requires him to take the path of greatest resistance whereas in the second, it may mean the path of least resistance. From all this, we may surmise that any social policy aimed at changing the behavior and perhaps the attitudes of the all-weather illiberal will have to take into account the cultural and social structure of the area in which he lives.

SOME ASSUMPTIONS UNDERLYING SOCIAL POLICIES FOR THE REDUCTION OF RACIAL AND ETHNIC DISCRIMINATION

To diagnose the problem, it appears essential to recognize these several types of men, and not to obscure their differences by general allusions to the "gulf-between-ideals and practice." Some of these men discriminate precisely because their local cultural ideals proclaim the duty of discrimination. Others discriminate only when they find it expedient to do so, just as still others fail to translate their prejudices into active discrimination when *this* proves expedient. It is the existence of these three types of men, in a society traditionally given over to the American creed, who constitute "the racial problem" or "the ethnic problem." Those who practice discrimination are *not* men of one kind. *And because they are not all of a piece, there must be diverse social therapies, each directed at a given type in a given social situation.*

Were it not for widespread social policies to the contrary, it would be unnecessary to emphasize that there is no single social policy which will be adequate for all these types in all social situations. So far as I know, sociological science has not yet evolved knowledge for application to this problem sufficient to merit great confidence in the results. But it has reached the point where it can suggest, with some assurance, that different social types in different social contexts require different social therapies if their behavior is to be changed. To diagnose these several types, therefore, may not be an "academic" exercise, in the too-frequent and dolorous sense of the word "academic." However scanty our knowledge, if action is to be taken, such diagnoses represent the first step toward pragmatic social therapy. The unprejudiced discriminator will respond differently from the prejudiced non-discriminator and he, in turn, differently from the prejudiced discriminator or all-weather illiberal. And each of these will respond according to the social composition of the groups and community in which he is involved.

In setting forth my opinions on the strategy of dealing with ethnic and racial discrimination, I hope it is plain that I move far beyond the adequately accredited knowledge provided by sociology to this point. In 1948, neither the rigorous theory nor many needed data are at hand to "apply" sociological science to this massive problem of American society. But moving from the slight accumulation of sociological knowledge at my disposal, it may be possible to suggest some considerations which it presently seems wise to take into account. For at scattered points, our knowledge may be sufficient to detect probably erroneous assumptions, though it is not always adequate to set out probably sound assumptions.

It is sometimes assumed that discrimination and its frequent though not invariable adjunct, prejudice, are entirely the product of ignorance. To be sure, ignorance *may* support discrimination. The employer unfamiliar with the findings of current anthropology and psychology, for example, may discriminate against Negroes on the ground of the honest and ignorant conviction that they are inherently less intelligent than whites. But, in general, there is no indication that ignorance is the major source of discrimination. The evidence at hand does not show that ethnic and racial discrimination is consistently less common among those boasting a college education than among the less well educated.

To question the close connection between ignorance and discrimination is to raise large implications for social policy. For if one assumes that ignorance and error are alone involved, obviously all that need be done by way of curbing prevalent discriminatory practices is to introduce a program of education concerning racial and ethnic matters, on a scale yet unimagined. Mass education and mass propaganda would at once become the sole indicated tools for action. But there are few who will accept the implications of this assumption that simple ignorance is a major or exclusive source of discrimination and urge that formal education alone can turn the trick. If some seem to be saying this, it is, I suspect, because they are begging the question; they are using the phrase "education on racial and ethnic matters" in an equivocal sense to mean "eradication of racial and ethnic prejudices." But, of course, that is precisely the question at issue: what *are* the procedures most likely to eradicate prejudice and discrimination?

If the assumption of ignorance as the root-source of discrimination is put to one side, then we must be prepared to find that discrimination is in part sustained by a socialized reward-system. When a population is divided into sub-groups, some of which are set apart as inferior, even the lowliest member of the ostensibly superior group derives psychic gains from this institutionalized superiority of status. This system of discrimination also supplies preferential access to opportunity for the more favored groups. The taboos erect high tariff walls restricting the importation of talent from the ethnic outgroups. But we need not assume that such psychic, social and economic gains are *sufficient* to account for the persistence of ethnic discrimination in a society which has an ideal pattern proclaiming free and equal access to opportunity. To be sure, these rewards supply motivation for discrimination. But men favor practices which give them differential advantages only so long as there is a moral code which defines these advantages as "fair." In the absence of this code, special advantage is not typically exploited. Were this not the case, the doctrine of Hobbes would stand unimpaired: everyone would cheat—in personal, economic and other institutional relations. Yet even the most cynical observer would not suggest that chicanery and cheating are the typical order of the day in all spheres, even where fear of discovery is at a minimum. This suggests that discrimination is sustained not only by the direct gains to those who discriminate, but also by cultural norms which *legitimize* discrimination.

To the extent that the foregoing assumptions are valid, efforts to minimize discrimination must take into account at least three sets of factors sustaining discriminatory practices. And each of these points toward distinct, though interrelated, lines of attack on the forces promoting discrimination. First, mass education and propaganda would be directed toward the reduction of sheer ignorance concerning the objective attributes of ethnic groups and of the processes of intergroup relations and attitudes. Second, institutional and interpersonal programs would seek to reduce the social, psychic and economic gains presently accruing to those who discriminate. And third, long-range efforts would be required to reinforce the legitimacy of the American creed as a set of cultural norms applicable to all groups in the society.

One gains the impression that certain secular trends in the society are slowly affecting each of these three fronts. On the educational front, we find an increasing proportion of the American population receiving higher schooling. And in the course of schooling, many are exposed for the first time to salient *facts* regarding ethnic and racial groups. Preconceptions notwithstanding, higher educational institutions even in the Deep South do not teach discredited myths of race superiority; if race is treated at all, it is in substantially factual terms countering the cognitive errors now sustaining race discrimination. Without assuming that such education plays a basic role, I suggest that in so far as it is at all effective, it undermines erroneous conceptions of racial and ethnic qualities.

On the economic front, secular change moves with geological speed but consistently in the same positive direction. This secular trend is represented in slow shifts in the occupational composition of Negroes and other ethnic groups toward a perceptibly higher average level. Again, the importance of these slight shifts should not be exaggerated. As everyone knows, prejudice and its frequent corollary in action, discrimination, are resistant, if not entirely immune, to the coercion of sheer facts. Yet the white agricultural laborer does recognize, at some level of his self, the improbability of his "superiority" to the Negro physician or university president. The discrepancy between achieved occupational status and ascribed caste status introduces severe strains upon the persistence of rationalized patterns of social superiority. As occupational and educational opportunity expand for Negroes, the number of Negroes with class status higher than that of many whites will grow and with it the grounds for *genuinely believing,* no matter what one's protestations, that "any white man is better than any nigger" will be progressively eroded. This secular change is, of course, a two-edged sword: every economic advance of the Negro invites increased hositility and resentment. But no major change in social structure occurs without the danger of temporarily increased conflict (though it is a characteristic of the liberal to want the rose without the thorn, to seek major change without conflict). In any event, it seems plausible that the secular trend of occupational change presently militates against the unimpeded persistence of discrimination.

On the third front of the reinforcement of the American creed, the impressionistic picture is not so clear. But even here, there is one massive fact of contemporary history which points to a firmer foundation for this cultural doctrine. In a world riven with international fears, the pressure for national consensus grows stronger. Ethnic and racial fissures in the national polity cannot so lightly be endured. (Consider the concessions commonly given these groups in times of war.) This tendency is enhanced as men become sensitized to the balance of world population and recognize that firm alliances must be built with non-white peoples, ultimately, it is hoped, in a world alliance. From these pressures external to the nation, there develops an increasing movement toward translating the American creed from a less than fully effective ideology into a working code governing the behavior of men. Slight, yet not unimpressive, signs of this change are evident. In the realm of institutional organizations, there is growing pressure upon government, universities, trade unions and churches to govern themselves by the words they profess. In the realm of interpersonal relations, one has a marked impression of increasing relations between members of diverse racial and ethnic groups. (This change in the pattern of private relations must remain conjectural, until social research searches out the needed *facts.* Periodic researches into the frequency of interracial and interethnic friendships would provide a barometer of interpersonal relations [necessarily invis-

ible to the individual observer] which could be used to supplement current information on institutional changes and public decisions.)

These assumptions of the strategic significance of the three major fronts of
social policy on race and ethnic relations and these impressions of secular trends
now in progress on each front provide the basis for a consideration of social strategies for the reduction of discrimination.

IMPLICATIONS OF THE TYPOLOGY FOR SOCIAL POLICY

This necessary detour into the assumptions underlying social policy leads us back
to the main path laid down in the account of the four main types appearing in our
typology of prejudice and discrimination. And again, however disconcerting the
admission may be, it is essential to note that we must be wholly tentative in drawing out the implications of this typology for social policy, for the needed sociological theory and data are plainly inadequate to the practical demands of the
situation. Yet if we cannot confidently establish the procedures which should be
followed, we can perhaps exclude the procedures which are likely to be unproductive. The successive elimination of alternative procedures is some small gain.

In approaching problems of policy, two things are plain. First, these should be
considered from the standpoint of the militant ethnic liberal, for he alone is sufficiently motivated to engage in positive action for the reduction of ethnic discrimination. And second, the fair-weather liberal, the fair-weather illiberal and the
all-weather illiberal represent types differing sufficiently to require diverse kinds
of treatment.

Treatment of the Fair-Weather Liberal

The fair-weather liberal, it will be remembered, discriminates only when it appears
expedient to do so, and experiences some measure of guilt for deviating from his
own belief in the American creed. He suffers from this conflict between conscience
and conduct. Accordingly, he is a relatively easy target for the all-weather liberal.
He represents the strategic group promising the largest immediate returns for the
least effort. Recognition of this type defines the first task for the militant liberal
who would enter into a collective effort to make the creed a viable and effective
set of social norms rather than a ceremonial myth. And though the tactics which
this definition of the problem suggests are numerous, I can here only allude to one
of these, while emphasizing anew that much of the research data required for fuller
confidence in this suggestion are not yet at hand. But passing by the discomforts
of our ignorance for the moment, the following would seem to be roughly the case.

Since the fair-weather liberal discriminates only when it seems rewarding to do
so, the crucial need is so to change social situations that there are few occasions in

which discrimination proves rewarding and many in which it does not. This would suggest that ethnic liberals self-consciously and deliberately seek to draw into the social groups where they constitute a comfortable majority a number of the "expedient discriminators." This would serve to counteract the dangers of self-selection through which liberals come to associate primarily with like-minded individuals. It would, further, provide an interpersonal and social environment for the fair-weather liberal in which he would find substantial social and psychological gains from abiding by his own beliefs, gains which would more than offset the rewards attendant upon occasional discrimination. It appears that men do not long persist in behavior which lacks social corroboration.

We have much to learn about the role of numbers and proportions in determining the behavior of members of a group. But it seems that individuals generally act differently when they are numbered among a minority rather than the majority. This is not to say that minorities abdicate their practices in the face of a contrary-acting majority, but only that the same people are subjected to different strains and pressures according to whether they are included in the majority or the minority. And the fair-weather liberal who finds himself associated with militant ethnic liberals may be expected to forego his occasional deviations into discrimination; he may move from category II into category I; this at least is suggested by the Columbia-Lavanburg researches on ethnic relations in the planned community.

This suggestion calls attention to the possible significance for policy of the composition of a local population with respect to the four types found in our typology, a consideration to which I shall presently return in some detail. But first it is necessary to consider briefly the problems attending policies for dealing with the illiberal.

Treatment of the Fair-Weather Illiberal

Because his *beliefs* correspond to those of the full-fledged liberal, the fair-weather liberal can rather readily be drawn into an interpersonal environment constituted by those of a comparable turn of mind. This would be more difficult for the fair-weather illiberal, whose beliefs are so fully at odds with those of ethnic liberals that he may, at first, only be alienated by association with them. If the initial tactic for the fair-weather liberal, therefore, is a change in interpersonal environment, the seemingly most appropriate tactic for the fair-weather illiberal is a change in the institutional and legal environment. It is, indeed, probably this type which liberals implicitly have in mind when they expect significant changes in behavior to result from the introduction of controls on ethnic discrimination into the legal machinery of our society.

For this type—and it is a major limitation for planning policies of control that we do not know his numbers or his distribution in the country—it would seem that the most effective tactic is the institution of legal controls administered with strict efficiency. This would presumably reduce the amount of *discrimination* practiced by the fair-weather illiberal, though it might *initially* enhance rather than reduce his *prejudices.*

Despite large libraries on the subject, we have little by way of rigorous knowledge indicating how this group of prejudiced but coercible conformists can be brought to abandon their prejudices. But something is known on a research basis of two methods which are *not* effective, information important for social policy since groups of ethnic liberals do commonly utilize these two apparently ineffectual methods. I refer, first, to mass propaganda for "tolerance" and second, the formation of interracial groups seeking to promote tolerance among their members.

Available evidence suggests rather uniformly that propaganda for ethnic equity disseminated through the channels of mass communication does not appreciably modify prejudice. Where prejudice is deep-seated, it serves too many psychological functions for the illiberal to be relinquished in response to propaganda, emanating from howsoever prestigeful a source. The propaganda is either evaded through misinterpretation or selectively assimilated into his prejudice-system in such a fashion as to produce a "boomerang" effect of intensified prejudice. Seemingly, propaganda for ethnic tolerance has a more important effect upon the propagand*ist,* who comes to feel that he "is doing something" about diffusing the American creed, than upon the prejudiced people who are the ostensible objects of the propaganda. It is at least plausible that *the great dependence of ethnic liberals upon propaganda for tolerance persists because of the morale function the propaganda serves for the liberals who feel that something positive is being accomplished.*

A second prevalent tactic for modifying the prejudice of the fair-weather illiberal is that of seeking to draw him into interethnic groups explicitly formed for the promotion of tolerance. This, too, seems largely ineffectual, since the deeply prejudiced individual will not enter into such groups of his own volition. As a consequence of this process of self-selection, these tolerance groups soon come to be comprised by the very ethnic liberals who initiated the enterprise.

This barrier of self-selection can be partially hurdled only if the ethnic illiberals are brought into continued association with militant liberals in groups devoted to significant common values, quite remote from objectives of ethnic equity as such. Thus, as our Columbia-Lavanburg researches have found, many fair-weather illiberals *will* live in interracial housing projects in order to enjoy the rewards of superior housing at a given rental. And some of the illiberals thus brought into personal contact with various ethnic groups under the auspices of prestigeful militant liberals come to modify their prejudices. It is, apparently, only through interethnic collaboration, initially enforced by pressures of the situation, for immediate and significant objectives (other than tolerance) that the self-insulation of the fair-weather illiberal from rewarding interethnic contacts can be removed.

But however difficult it may presently be to affect the *prejudicial sentiments* of the fair-weather illiberal, his *discriminatory practices* can be lessened by the uniform, prompt and prestigeful use of legal and institutional sanctions. The critical problem is to ascertain the proportions of fair-weather and all-weather illiberals in a given local population in order to have some clue to the probable effectiveness or ineffectiveness of anti-discrimination legislation.

Treatment of the All-Weather Illiberal

It is, of course, the hitherto confirmed illiberal, persistently translating his prejudices into active discrimination, who represents the most difficult problem. But though he requires longer and more careful treatment, it is possible that he is not beyond change. In every instance, his social surroundings must be assiduously taken into account. It makes a peculiarly large difference whether he is in a cultural region of bigotry or in a predominantly "liberal" area, given over to verbal adherence to the American creed, at the very least. As this cultural climate varies, so must the prescription for his cure and the prognosis for a relatively quick or long delayed recovery.

In an unfavorable cultural climate—and this does not necessarily exclude the benign regions of the Far South—the immediate resort will probably have to be that of working through legal and administrative federal controls over extreme discrimination, with full recognition that, in all probability, these regulations will be systematically evaded for some time to come. In such cultural regions, we may expect nullification of the law as the common practice, perhaps as common as was the case in the nation at large with respect to the Eighteenth Amendment, often with the connivance of local officers of the law. The large gap between the new law and local mores will not *at once* produce significant change of prevailing practices; token punishments of violations will probably be more common than effective control. At best, one may assume that significant change will be fitful, and excruciatingly slow. But secular changes in the economy may in due course lend support to the new legal framework of control over discrimination. As the economic shoe pinches because the illiberals do not fully mobilize the resources of industrial manpower nor extend their local markets through equitable wage-payments, they may slowly abandon some discriminatory practices as they come to find that these do not always pay—even the discriminator. So far as discrimination is concerned, organized counteraction is possible and some small results may be expected. But it would seem that wishes father thoughts, when one expects basic changes in the immediate future in these regions of institutionalized discrimination.

The situation is somewhat different with regard to the scattered, rather than aggregated, ethnic illiberals found here and there throughout the country. Here the mores and a social organization oriented toward the American creed still have some measure of prestige and the resources of a majority of liberals can be mobilized to isolate the illiberal. In these surroundings, it is possible to move the all-weather illiberal toward Type III—he can be brought to conform with institutional regulations, even though he does not surrender his prejudices. And once he has entered upon this role of the dissident but conforming individual, the remedial program designed for the fair-weather illberal would be in order.

ECOLOGICAL BASES OF SOCIAL POLICY

Where authenticated data are few and scattered and one must make *some* decision, whether it be the decision to act in a given fashion or not to take action at all, then one must resort to reasonable conjecture as the basis for policy. This is what I have done in assuming throughout that policies designed to curb ethnic discrimination must be oriented toward differences in the composition of a population with respect to the four types here under discussion. It is safe to assume that communities and larger areas vary in the proportion of these several types. Some communities may have an overwhelming majority of militant liberals, in positions of authority and among the rank-and-file. Others may be short on ethnic liberals but long on fair-weather illiberals who respond promptly though reluctantly to the pressure of institutional controls. It would seem reasonable to suppose that different social policies of control over discrimination would be required as these ecological distributions of prejudice-discrimination types vary.

This assumption is concretized in the conjectural distributions of these types set forth in the following four figures. Consider the same legislation aimed at curbing job discrimination against the Negro as this might operate in a community in the Far South and in New England. Since it runs counter to the strongly entrenched attitudes of the large majority in the one community and not in the other, we may suppose that the same law will produce different results in the two cases. This must be put in a reasonable time perspective. Conceivably, the short-term and the long-term effects may differ widely. But with respect to both the long and the short term, it matters greatly whether there is a sufficient local nucleus of ethnic liberals in positions of prestige and authority. The ecological and social distribution of the prejudice-discrimination types is of central importance in assessing the probable outcome. Whether a law providing for equitable access to jobs will in fact produce this result depends not only on the law itself but also on the rest of the social structure. The law is a small, though important, part of the whole. Unless a strong economic and social base for its support exists in a community, the law will be nullified in practice.

Figures 3 and 4 set forth, again conjecturally, the distribution of the prejudice-discrimination types with respect to the Jew among middle-class "strainers" and industrial workers. Should research find that the industrial worker stratum indeed has a larger proportion of militant ethnic liberals than the middle classes, then initial support of an active anti-discrimination policy might most effectively be sought there. But whatever the actual facts might show, the policy-maker attuned to the realities as well as the objectives of the problem would do well to take these into account in the design of his program.

If makers of policy are to escape utopianism on the one hand and pessimistic inaction on the other, they must utilize diverse procedures for modifying attitudes and behavior according to the distribution of these prejudice-discrimination types.

Finally, though action cannot, perhaps, wait upon continued research, it is

A Deep South Community
(Distribution of Attitudes and Practices with Respect to the Negro)

TYPES   LOCAL CULTURAL CLICHES
                                         IDENTIFYING TYPE

I   – "Nigger lover"
II   – (Clandestine liberal conformist)
III   – (This type virtually non-existent here)
IV   – "Any white man's better than any nigger."

A New England Community
(Distribution of Attitudes and Practices with Respect to the Negro)

I   – "All men are created equal . . ."
II   – "Some of my good friends are Negroes . . ."
III   – "A Negro's dollar's as good as a white's."
IV   – "They're all right in their place."

Middle Class "Strainers" for "Success"
(Distribution of Attitudes and Practices with Respect to the Jew)

I   – "All men should be judged as individuals."
II   – "But he was just too pushy, too aggressive."
III   – (The well-bred anti-Semite)
IV   – "Like to out-Jew a Jew"

Industrial Workers
(Distribution of Attitudes and Practices with Respect to the Jew)

I   – "We'll unite to fight our *real* enemies."
II   – "Maybe you're right, but some Jews are O.K."
III   – "You can't afford to step on a Jew . . ."
IV   – "The Jews have got all the money."

suggested that the following kinds of information are needed as a basis for effective anti-discrimination policy:

1) An inventory to determine the relative proportions in various areas of these four prejudice-discrimination types;

2) Within each area, an inventory of these proportions among the several social classes, major associations, and nationality groups;

3) Periodic audits of these proportions, thus providing a barometric map of ethnic attitudes and practices repeatedly brought up to date and marking the short-run and secular trends in diverse areas and groups;

4) Continuing studies of the consequences of various programs designed to promote ethnic equities, thus reducing the wastage presently entailed by well-intentioned, expensive and ineffecual programs.

This is a large research order. But the American creed, as set down in the basic moral documents of this nation, seems deserving of the systematic exercise of our social intelligence fully as much as it is deserving of our moral resolution.

6   The Concept of Race in Sociological Theory

John Rex

THE POLITICAL IMPORTANCE OF A THEORETICAL PROBLEM

The problem of race relations challenges the consciences of sociologists in a way that probably no other problem does. Just as physicists have been reminded of their social and political responsibilities as the full meaning of nuclear warfare became apparent, so sociologists, who are expected to understand the relationships that exist between groups, have been confronted in our own time with problems of racial conflict and racial persecution of a quite unprecedented kind. Before and during the Second World War millions of Jews were exterminated, allegedly because of their race, and with the support of a phoney kind of biological and sociological theory. In our own day discrimination against, or exploitation of, men distinguished by their skin colour prevents millions of human beings from enjoying basic human rights. And in the pattern of international history that is being woven for our future, the one overriding theme seems to be that of race war.

In the world of 1945, still reeling from the experience of Nazism, it was the

From *Race and Racialism,* (ed.) S. Zubaida, London, Tavistock, 1970. Reprinted by permission of Tavistock Publications Ltd.

biologists who were asked by the United Nations to analyse the phenomenon of racism, and their work led to the formulation of expert statements in 1941, 1951, and 1964. But, while the biologists were able to answer the question, 'In what sense does biological science distinguish races and other genetically based groups?'—a question that itself requires a highly technical answer—they were not able to answer the separate question, 'Why are groups of men between whom political differences exist sometimes called races?' All they could say was that such groups bore no relation to 'races' in the biological sense. The problem therefore was handed over to the sociologists (UNESCO 1969).

The problem with which we are faced is not, however, simply an empirical one. It is not a question, for example, of discovering what correlations there are between prejudice towards coloured persons, on the one hand, and a variety of other sociological indices, on the other. There have probably been more than enough studies of this kind already. The real problem is to distinguish among the various studies made by sociologists those which are distinguishable as race-relations studies. This is a complex *theoretical* question. It is one that must be answered, however, before any really systematic approach to the full range of situations leading to the growth of racism can be analysed. The fact that so little attention has been directed towards it can only be regarded as something of a professional scandal.

CURRENT DEFINITIONS OF THE FIELD OF RACE RELATIONS STUDIES

Before I proceed to make some preliminary suggestions as to how this field of study should be mapped, I should like to look at four separate approaches that seem to me, when taken individually, to be inadequate. When I have done this, however, I shall show that, taken together, they do help us to define the key variables of the race-relations field considered systematically.

The first of these approaches claims that there are no race-relations problems as such. All the problems with which race-relations experts deal, it argues, are really problems of stratification and, once these problems are fully understood, their racial aspect disappears.

There is a great deal to be said for this view, particularly if the term stratification is used in an inclusive rather than a narrow sense (referring not to classes in the Marxist sense or to hierarchically rated occupational groups but to all the kinds of differentiation and conflict that arise out of the military, political, and economic relations between men). It is certainly not sufficient to dismiss the whole group of theories involved here as 'Marxist'. But, none the less, there do seem to be aspects of what are called race-relations encounters which are not fully explained even by fairly flexible use of stratification theory, and the factor of role ascription and stereotyping according to observable characteristics does seem to add something new to these situations, as does their explanation and justification in terms of racist theory.

If, however, we turn to the second and third of the approaches made to the definition of their field by sociologists of race relations, we find that these too are inadequate if taken by themselves. If we say that race-relations problems arise when groups distinguish themselves in terms of perceived physical differences, we find that there are cases in which the perception of physical differences does not lead to race-relations problems and that, in any case, those who are classified as belonging to one group actually have a range for any characteristic that overlaps with the range for the same characteristic exhibited by another group (e.g. the darkest Sicilian might be darker than the lightest Negro). Moreover, such a definition excludes from the field the phenomenon of anti-Semitism, usually recognized as the outstanding expression of racism in our time.

Yet, if we simply try to confine out study as sociologists to the study of groups distinguished by cultural characteristics, nearly every phenomenon of culture contact comes within our field. The problem of the nationalisms that are to be found within and across national boundaries would certainly have to be included. So also would the study of religious minorities and the subculture of classes. Obviously, there must be some other feature of the situation in terms of which a subclass of racially defined situations can be distinguished.

Finally, we should note the existence of another approach that might loosely be called phenomenological. This approach recognizes that social phenomena and mental phenomena are meaningful and that the approach to discriminating any kind of structural situation must depend upon a consideration of 'definitions of the situation' used by participant actors. Hence it would seem that the problem disappears. If men typify a situation as racial, racial it must be, and all that the sociologist can do is to concentrate on the careful analysis of the structure of belief systems from which the concept derives. He cannot be expected to distinguish between false and true consciousness or between actually held and valid meanings.

The problem with this approach is not merely that it appears to sell the pass to the racists and to leave them to define the sociologist's field for him. It is that the complexity of meaning systems and their inextricable relations with structure are insufficiently explored. It is not surprising then that the real value of this approach only becomes evident when it is employed in conjunction with the other approaches mentioned above.

Similar problems arise in the use of the definitions suggested by Margaret Nicolson and referred to by Michael Banton.[1] According to Nicolson, 'racism is more often applied to the doctrine, racialism to the practice of the doctrine.' Such a terminology could either lead to a one-sided view of the cause of racialism, tracing it simply to false beliefs, or to a disjunction between the theory and the practice. The latter alternative is preferred by Banton, who suggests that we keep the term racism for the doctrine and that 'We can use racialism more widely to denote, for example, political policies which do not rely on biological ideas.'

If Banton's alternative is pursued, two consequences follow. In the first place no defining criterion of racialism, which distinguishes it from other political policies, remains. In the second place the definition of racism, since it refers only to theory, ceases to depend in any way on structural factors. Hence the only clearly demarcated field that remains is that of the study of ideas, and the problem of racism disappears as soon as politicians and others change their style of theorizing.

The approach taken here is as much against the study of theories in isolation as it is against the reduction of theoretical definitions of the situation to mere epiphenomena arising from structural sources. We envisage a two-way interplay between theoretical and structural factors. Or, putting this in another way, what we envisage is a combination of all four of the approaches mentioned above so that their genuine insights may not be outweighed by their one-sidedness. We therefore tentatively suggest the following definition:

> We shall speak of a race-relations structure or problem, in so far as the inequalities and differentiation inherent in a social structure are related to physical and cultural criteria of an ascriptive kind and are rationalized in terms of deterministic belief systems, of which the most usual in recent years has made reference to biological science.

I believe that such a composite definition is the most useful one we could employ and that it has the merit of recognizing both the similarities and the differences between race-relations and other types of problems. What follows is a detailed explication and illustration of this definition.

Lest there should be any misunderstanding of our purpose here, it must be emphasized that we are by no means attempting to make an exact empirical report on the actual pattern of race relations in, say, the United States, Britain, or Latin America. In so far as we make reference to empirical and historical material in what follows we do so simply in order to clarify our typology by suggesting the questions to which it leads. We aim to draw up an agenda of possible studies, so that, with the questions better understood, we may be more aware of where the answers are likely to be found.

STRATIFICATION AND OTHER STRUCTURAL ASPECTS OF RACE-RELATIONS SITUATIONS

We said above that the notion that race-relations situations were explicable in terms of the theory of stratification had some validity, if the term stratification was used in an inclusive sense. I now wish to suggest that there are at least six kinds of situations that would have to be included. They are:

1 Frontier situations, in which a politically organized group, with an advanced technology and education, encounters another such group whose levels of technology are lower.

2 The particular form of the social relations of production, which is to be found on slave plantations, and in the societies that come into existence immediately after the abolition of slavery.

3 Situations of class conflict in the Marxist, and in the rather wider Weberian, sense, where there is a confrontation of groups possessing differing degrees of market power.

4 Estate and caste systems, in which groups enjoying differing degrees of prestige and of legal rights take on a corporate character and may become occupationally specialized.

5 Situations in which esteem and prestige are not accorded to corporate groups, as such, but are thought of as providing a basis for a continuum, so that any one individual may be thought of as having more or less prestige.

6 Situations of cultural pluralism, such that a number of distinguishable groups interact for limited (e.g. economic) purposes but continue to lead separate communal lives.

Arising from these appear to be a number of particular problems of metropolitan societies that are recurrently regarded as racial problems:

(a) Urban situations in which a complex system of 'stratification' based upon several of the factors mentioned above exists.

(b) Situations in which a particular group of outsiders is called upon to perform a role, which, although essential to the social and economic life of a society, is in conflict with its value system, or is thought to be beneath the dignity of the society's own members.

(c) Situations in which, in times of crisis, a group that is culturally or physically distinguishable is blamed for the existence of a threat to the society's wellbeing, i.e. scapegoat situations. This process is often connected with the structural situation under *(b)* above.

The first kind of situation listed is that which Toynbee refers to as characterized by the presence of an external proletariat. It existed when the 'barbarians' were at the gates of Rome, and it has existed on nearly every frontier during the expansion of European nations overseas. It may lead to the extermination of the external proletariat, to their slow subordination and incorporation into the more advanced society, or to a more complex process in which the external proletariat is, militarily speaking, victorious but, culturally speaking, absorbed. Whatever the outcome, however, the encounter between the groups is marked by tension and by the emergence of stereotypes and belief systems that govern the interaction of members of one group with those of another. These may range from those based upon simple moral derogation, as in the case of Jan Van Riebeck's description of the Hottentots as 'dull, stupid, stinking people', through Aristotle's claim that the barbarian is less than a man, to modern theories that different moral characteristics derive from differing genetic inheritance.

Such frontier situations are one of the basic starting-points from which colonial societies emerge. Another alternative, however, is that in which the colonialist, as a part of his economic enterprise, introduces an alien labour force of varying degrees of freedom or unfreedom. Here the central institution is the slave plantation. Slave plantations are characterized by labour-intensive agricultural work and by the fact that the workers are owned by their employer. That is to say they are essentially productive enterprises. Racist belief systems are not necessary to their existence. Slave plantations existed in antiquity without being justified in racist terms, and it is clear that they have existed without masters and slaves being physically distinguishable. None the less, the capacity to regard other human beings as slaves does impose strains on the belief system of any society and bridging beliefs of some kind will nearly always be found. Racist beliefs are to be found in modern plantation situations as well as in the aftermath of abolition, and would seem to be meaningfully related to the legal and economic institution of slavery.

Turning from these colonial situations to what are more commonly thought of as problems of class and stratification, we find that the dominant theory, based upon experience of the race problem in the United States, was for a long time that of Lloyd Warner (1936), that the race-relations situation was best understood as caste in its incipient phase.

The distinguished Negro Marxist sociologist, Oliver Cromwell Cox (1959), has performed a useful service in reminding us, in opposition to this view, that a great many of the situations classified as racial in modern industrial societies are nothing more or less than class situations in the classic Marxist sense. Thus, for example, the black proletariat of South Africa is clearly distinguishable, both from the white owning class and from white organized labour, by the fact that is has a distinct relationship to the means of production. Equally, the almost permanently unemployed Negro youth of America's urban ghettos look more and more like a class in revolt.

One feature of this class-conflict aspect of race relations that is of the very first importance is the development of a militant or revolutionary Black Power movement on an international scale. The situation here appears to be analogous to that which Marx was suggesting when he wrote of the transition from a local trade-union consciousness to a world-wide revolutionary consciousness. In that case, as in this, we are not necessarily dealing with an actual organized revolutionary class, but the sort of quasi-group that arises from a belief in the existence of a common political destiny. In any case the study of this black-power revolution is central to the study of race relations.

Cox is perhaps wrong, however, in suggesting that class conflict has always been the determining factor in black–white relations. Underdeveloped societies and those undergoing one-sided development through agriculture and mining might well produce some of the main features of the social and political systems to which he attaches the terms caste and estate. The existence of legal inequality and inequality of esteem, together with the maintenance of the authority of a land-owning ruling class, has been a feature of some Latin American societies and it is this which leads some students to the view that a caste-like situation often underlies a problem that comes to be thought of as racial.

It is not sufficient to characterize such societies as paternalist (see, for example, Van den Berghe 1967). Indeed it is gravely misleading, for the actual relations between upper and lower 'classes' are often brutally exploitative. If they are distinguishable from what some sociologists call competitive situations, it is not because the lower orders regard their masters as fathers but because, as in medieval Europe, their social situation, and sometimes their legal status, makes any challenge to the authority of their superiors impossible. It is this which leads us to the view that some race-relations situations are in fact based on caste and estate systems.

An objection might be made here by either Warner or Cox that in the case of true caste systems an exploitative element such as we have described is not present. We concede that this may be so in the Indian case. But no other society has attained a fully developed caste system, even by Warner's reckoning. The main point in our using the term is that estate systems mentioned above could develop in the direction of considerable occupational specialization. Where this occurs we may say that an estate system is developing in a caste-like direction.

Another feature of the Caribbean and Latin American situations, however, is the sheer fact of cultural pluralism brought about through the coming together of Negro, Asiatic, and European labour. It is not surprising, therefore, that the concept of the plural society first pioneered by J. S. Furnivall in Indonesia[2] has been applied there. According to Furnivall's ideal type, a situation might be expected in which ethnically distinct groups meet only in the market-place. And while relations there are based upon exploitation of the harshest sort, each group can and does withdraw to its own independent quarter, where it is not subject to the authority of the others.

In fact, most sociologists found that in applying this concept a measure of inequality of power and status extending beyond the market-place had to be accounted for, but this is not to say that the simple differentiated and pluralist society described by Furnivall is not useful, at least as an extreme ideal type against which degrees of inequality can be measured.

Again, while it is useful in order to grasp the flux and variety of historical experience, to see some Latin American and African situations as approximating to a feudal estate system, it is none the less clear that such a system nowhere exists in a pure form. What does seem to be the case, however, is that as a system of this kind or, for that matter, a plantation system becomes less and less perfect, it breaks down into a status system. Everyone is therefore allocated a certain standing in the society along a quantitatively varying status scale. Thus the position accorded to a man may be high or low according to the lightness or darkness of his skin.

Nearly all of the problems so far discussed are problems that have been encountered at one time or another by British people in their colonial dealings. What is new, however, is the fact of the emergence of a 'racial problem' in the cities of the metropolitan country itself. The more complex subcategories I have listed are intended to provide a framework for the analysis of this problem.

The first fact to notice about colonial immigrants in British society is that not only are they distinguishable on the basis of their skin colour, language, religion, and domestic culture but also they are known through these indicators to have come from fulfilling colonial roles to adopting the role of worker in the metropolitan society. Thus there is at the moment of encounter with the native metropolitan population a double-banked criterion for role ascription. With this said, however, it has still to be noted that relations between such a differentiated group and their hosts are further shaped by the nature and structure of the metropolitan society itself.

One feature of that metropolitan society that increasingly comes to notice, and has been even more clearly brought to notice by the arrival of immigrants, is the existence of a number of unwanted and low-status industrial roles. The more technological advance and educational levels make other kinds of work less arduous or more satisfying, the greater the relative deprivation of those who fulfil these roles. They are therefore shunned by native workers and an alien group can easily be assimilated into them.

Thus far in the British post-war experience, however, it has not been on the industrial front that the immigrant has faced the most acute conflict. Rather it has been with his neighbours in the city. Elsewhere it has been argued that the city can at least in part be analysed as a system of housing class conflict, modified by the emergence of a status-stratified neighbourhood system.[3] I suggest that it is within a system of this kind that immigrants already identified as colonials, and already marked by their past colonial roles, have to take up positions and to encounter their fellow citizens and workers. Of course, the problem comes to be defined as primarily a racial problem, but it should also be clear from what has been said that the pattern of interaction and conflict with which we are dealing here derives partly from the structure of colonialism and partly from the urban class system; neither of which is simply and solely a racial situation.

Taking together the two facts of the emergence of relatively deprived industrial roles and of deprived neighbourhoods, one can see that the immigrant worker is likely to be categorized as belonging to a pariah group, and, in times of crisis, made a scapegoat. Immigrants form pariah groups both in doing unwanted jobs and in providing a kind of housing and neighbourhood that the city needs but that its value system cannot allow it to tolerate. Along with other clearly visible minority groups (e.g. students), they can easily act as scapegoat to be blamed for any hardship suffered by majority groups.

Scapegoating is too often discussed as though it were a purely psychological phenomenon. True, the punishment of the scapegoat is a means of restoring mental equilibrium to those whose personality systems are disturbed. But scapegoating is also a means of restoring *social* equilibrium. Thus certain groups or individuals are threatened because of the hostility their actions or incompetence have engendered. The indication of a scapegoat is a social mechanism whereby resentment may be expressed and the existing power structure maintained. It is the social process *par excellence* that literally fulfils Parsons's description of one of his functional sub-systems as pattern maintenance and tension management.

Pariah groups may exist without becoming scapegoat groups. Pariah status simply refers to the fact that the group's social function, though necessary, is held to be undesirable. The group may be hated and may even be punished. It does not, however, become a scapegoat unless or until it is blamed for acts it has not committed.

In most cases, of course, a pariah role does go with scapegoating. Jewish moneylenders in European history, the Asian trader in Colonial Africa, the immigrant landlord in European cities, have all performed this double function. One part of it, the pariah part, lies in actually carrying out or even being forced to carry out certain duties and being punished for so doing. The other, or scapegoat part, consists in being held generally to blame for failures of the system.

THE ASCRIPTIVE BASIS OF ROLE ALLOCATION

What we have been trying to do thus far is to distinguish structures of social interaction of a major socio-political kind that may be associated with the notion of racial differentiation. In no case does the interaction take its character from the fact that men with perceptibly different physical characteristics (let alone of different biological races) are parties to the social encounter. What we are dealing with as a rule is the deployment of power by one group against another, whether that power be military, political, or economic. This is the point that those who argue that the study of race relations is simply a part of the more general study of stratification are seeking to emphasize.

Overemphasis on this point, however, might lead to the view that whether or not such structural situations become defined in terms of race is purely a matter of accident. This would be a mistake, for, while it is true that the rationalization and justification of power must depend in part on the belief systems available, and that some of these lend themselves more readily than others to providing justifications of a racist kind, it is also the case that *there are certain kinds* of 'stratification' situations that, belief systems apart, are more likely to develop into racially defined situations than others. That is to say, whether or not a 'stratification situation' leads to 'racial problems' depends in part on the particular nature of that situation itself and in part on ideological factors.

The functionalist view that all social structures must have some mechanism for the allocation of personnel to roles and that there is a broad divide between mechanisms based upon ascription and those based upon achievement seems to beg the question here. For it is rarely the case that we are simply dealing with an ongoing social system in which the choice between one mechanism and another is available. Mostly we are dealing with situations that have emerged out of colonial conquest and the absorption of one society by another or with situations of immigration by relatively powerless groups into established social systems. Hence the social systems involved have a hybrid character. The settlers and the natives in the one case, and the immigrants and their native-born hosts in the other, are easily distinguishable by physical or cultural characteristics, so that it is not surprising that in structures arising from their interaction sociologists claim that role allocation is ascriptive. It is, of course, ascriptive and this distinguishes these structures from others with 'open-class' systems. But the crux of the matter is the living together of groups with differing degrees of power in a plural society.

The important issues involved here are those raised by Franz Oppenheimer (1914) in his critique of the Marxian theory of the origin of the state. We need not go so far as to extend Oppenheimer's theory to argue that stratification is always and everywhere the result of conquest, but we can see that in many cases, directly or indirectly, a stratification system might be skewed from the pattern it might have been expected to follow had only 'internal' factors (i.e. relations to the domestic means of production) been involved. One of the indicators of such a situation is the existence of a situation in which role allocation appears to occur on an ascriptive basis.

It would be difficult to maintain a theory that some actual factor of conquest was always involved in ascriptive stratification situations, for the actual connection is sometimes tenuous, especially where we are dealing not with situations in colonial countries but with problems of immigration into the metropolitan societies themselves. None the less, we should insist that it is always the case that the groups who are parties to such a situation are differentiated in terms of their access to legitimate political power. This would apply as much to Jews in a country in which anti-Semitism flourishes as to immigrants from a colonial dependency.

We seem, in fact, to be concerned in race-relations studies with two broad classes of situations. One is that which arises directly from the business of colonial conquest and which involves the assignment of the conquered to the most menial roles. The other is the case in which, either in a metropolitan or in a colonial society, an alien group of immigrants, culturally or physically distinguishable from the rest of the population, are allowed or required to perform what in the society's own terms are morally questionable roles. The unifying social theme is that groups of differing ethnic or national origins live together in a single socio-economic system in circumstances where some of the groups involved have less access than others to legitimate political power.

THE NATURE AND ROLE OF RACIST BELIEF SYSTEMS

The presence of these two factors (i.e. in the broadest sense of the term, a 'stratification' factor and the possibility of ready classification of those who perform different social roles in terms of some simple ascriptive criterion) is, according to the view adopted here, a necessary condition for the emergence of a race-relations problem. That is to say, we are arguing that any attempt to explain the structure and dynamics of race-relations situations in terms of the strangeness of the newcomer, of culture shock, or in terms of immigrant and host, is inadequate if taken by itself. We would insist that without the power or stratification element there would be no race-relations problem.

On the other hand, it must be pointed out that neither 'stratification' taken by itself, nor even stratification coupled with role allocation in terms of ascriptive criteria, is by itself sufficient reason for describing a problem as a race-relations problem. The other necessary condition is that the belief systems in terms of which roles are explained, described, and justified should have a particular character. In other words, it is not possible to give an adequate and complete account of a race-relations situation without reference to the fact of racism. Even if it could not be argued that racist beliefs played an independent causal role within the total structure, it would still be the case that a complete description and analysis of that structure required a consideration of racism and its relation to structural factors. As we see it, however, racism has a double importance as a part of the total situation and as having an independent causal role in the dynamics of stratification and race-relations structures.

All social situations depend for their character upon the definitions we give to them in our culture. We cannot see society or social institutions or social relations. We simply learn to accept that the occurrence of certain sorts of behaviour may be read as indicating the operations of a social institution or that the presence of a person with certain characteristics implies the existence of a certain pattern of rights. We do not, however, rest content with labelling the various sorts of social interaction in which we engage any more than we rest content with a world of discreet physical things. We grope after anchoring and validating principles that explain why things are as they are and why they should be so. Myth and theology, philosophy and science, all provide us with systematic ways of meeting this need.

There are, however, two quite distinct kinds of belief system that, for lack of a better word, we may call deterministic and undeterministic. When the former is applied to the justification of a social structure the social structure comes to be seen as inevitable and unalterable, and transition from one kind of role to another may be held to be impossible.

The clearest example of such a deterministic theory is the one to which the term racist is most often confined. What happens in this case is that the fact that a particular group suffers discrimination is attributed to an incapacity to perform a role or a special capacity to behave in particular ways that is determined by genetic inheritance. This is the most completely deterministic theory in that it is argued that nothing any individual can do can alter the situation and the pattern of rights in the society.

The specific problem of racism as it was posed to the United Nations in 1945 was concerned with a consideration of a belief system of this kind. It therefore seemed sufficient to gather together expert opinion to show that role performance in modern social systems did not depend upon man's genetic inheritance. This, however, left open a number of other possibilities and the disrepute into which racist theories in the narrow sense have fallen has simply meant that those who profited from them have sought other means of ideological support.

Long before justifications for inequality and exploitation were drawn from biological science they were drawn from theology. Indeed, it could be argued that it was only because the ideological extremism of nineteenth-century positivism demanded the justification of everything in terms of natural science, that biological theories assumed the predominance they did and that the decline of scientism would inevitably lead to the recurrence of other forms of theory. Theology, it is true, might play only a small part but *sociological* doctrines about the superiority of particular cultures and social systems might come to play their part. Thus we should not take the disappearance of the specifically biologically oriented theories of race that were so important in the thirties to mean that the class of sociological problems to which they referred has disappeared. Other deterministic theories would still be used and the essential distinguishing feature of this class of situations, namely inequality between men being justified in a deterministic way, would still be present.

Thus we seem to have arrived at a clearer understanding of the specific field of study with which the sociology of race relations should be concerned. It is concerned with a broad range of stratification situations (using this term in a wide sense to include any situation in which power and privilege are unequally distributed between groups or individual role-players in a social structure), but only in so far as roles or group-memberships are ascribed in terms of observable physical or cultural characteristics such as those which distinguish groups of colonial conquerors and conquered and only if the system as a whole is justified by deterministic beliefs.

It should perhaps be pointed out here that the distinction between deterministic and undeterministic belief systems is not absolute and that deterministic assumptions might well be found hidden in a theory of an undeterministic kind. Thus it may be said that a group of people are not yet ready in terms of education or economic advancement to assume equal rights, but if it is also held that the group concerned cannot be expected to advance economically or educationally during 25, 50, or 100 years, the belief operates deterministically. Furthermore, it might well be that, while the implicit belief of a governing group might be that the governed are inferior from a biological or theological point of view, their explicit statements might all refer to non-ascriptive criteria of role allocation. In this case the sociologists' task would not merely lie in describing the structure and the explicit belief system in terms of which it was justified (a process that itself has the character of unmasking or demystification); it would first involve the discovery or unmasking of the implicit theory that itself had to be unmasked by reference to the actual social structure.

THE INDEPENDENT CAUSAL ROLE OF BELIEF SYSTEMS

A further group of problems is suggested, however, by the definition at which we have now arrived. This may be described in the language of Marxism as assessing the relative causal role in race-relations situations of basis and superstructure, or of the stratificational and power element on the one hand and the ideological element on the other. We suggest that, although the existence of some kind of stratificational problem is a necessary precondition of the emergence of a race-relations problem, it is not by itself a sufficient condition. A further precondition is the existence of certain kinds of belief system. Moreover, it must further be recognized that once a deterministic belief system is used to justify a particular stratification situation, that situation is itself changed thereby and the belief system may set in motion wholly new social processes.

Of some importance with regard to the development of stratification situations in a racist direction is the sort of religious or political ideology that is available. Thus it does seem to be the case that race looms less large as a problem in Catholic countries because Catholic social teaching is inhospitable to the notion of deterministic differences between men, and in this may be contrasted with Calvinism, which contains within itself the deterministic distinction between the elect and the damned. Equally, it could be that Marxism as a political philosophy may not be made readily compatible with racialism. A great many comparative and case studies would have to be made, however, before a conclusion on this problem could be reached, and it would be of particular importance to look at deviant cases, i.e. those in which, say, Catholicism or Marxism was redefined in practice to allow for racial discrimination.

But ideological factors may not serve merely to arrest or facilitate the development of racial discrimination. They may, in Marxist terms, 'take on a life of their own'. As we have already seen, they may lead to the social process of punishing a scapegoat group and this will in turn lead, as Myrdal has pointed out, to increased hostility and discrimination and hence to increased demands for punishment.

Even this hypothesis, however, is compatible with an ebb or flow in the intensity of scapegoating according to the intensity of a social, political, or economic threat. What is often overlooked, however, is that although the tide of racism continues to flow after it has started and may flow more or less slowly according to the structural situation, it may not ebb at all, unless action is taken on the ideological level. Thus to point the issue in terms of Britain's predicament in 1969, the racism that has been evident in the community since the speeches of Mr. Enoch Powell and others might have arisen from the failure of the social and economic programmes of successive governments and the need for a scapegoat, but, once started, racism has threatened to become a regular election issue and a regular political theme.

If it is recognized that the ideological factor does make a difference in its own right, however, there is cause for optimism as well as pessimism among liberals on race-relations matters. True, what we have called Powellism may outrun even the functional need of the social system for a scapegoating mechanism. But equally it is possible that alternative beliefs authoritatively stated by political leaders will have a braking effect. This is not, of course, a purely ideological battle and the core of an anti-racist programme must lie on the structural level. None the less, words, speeches, and political actions also matter, either for the intensification or for the abatement of racial discrimination, exploitation, and conflict.

What we are saying in effect is that, even after we have given a comprehensive structural account (including under the heading 'structural' not merely patterns of social relations, but also the belief systems and ideologies that are intimately inter-woven with them) of possible race-relations situations, we should still have to study racism, both in the way in which it varies in relation to changes in the structural base and as an independent factor with a possible cumulative effect on social struc-tures. Indeed, in circumstances like that in contemporary Britain, it might be that this type of study should have priority over all others.

CONCLUSION: THE CENTRAL ROLE OF THEORY AND COMPARATIVE STUDIES IN RACE-RELATIONS RESEARCH

The programme and definition of the field that we have suggested for race-relations research is in no way remarkable. Indeed, it would appear to conform to the socio-logical procedure outlined by Durkheim when he suggests that in the study of any social phenomenon we should,

> indicate first of all by what characteristic one might recognize the thing so designated, then classify its varieties, investigate by methodical in-ductions what the causes of its variation are, and, finally, compare these results in order to abstract a general formula (Durkheim 1950: 25).

The really surprising thing is that so little of the sociology of race relations in Britain has conformed to this plan of attack.

The principal obstacle to the development of this programme has probably been quite simply and quite discreditably a disinclination on the part of some sociologists to look at race-relations problems in ways that might be disturbing to the liberal political establishment. Clearly, though, if the assumptions outlined here are correct, the study of race relations is, among other things a part of political sociology. This must mean that when we consider race-relations problems in Britain, the behaviour of governments and the policies advocated by all political parties must be up for description and analysis along with other phenomena. We cannot simply assume that there is a basic situation of good will in Westminster or Whitehall and that what we have to do is merely to test particular hypotheses as part of a programme of piecemeal social engineering. All too often this is precisely what sociologists have been asked or encouraged or have undertaken to do.

This response has necessarily led to trivialization of sociological concepts in the race-relations field. But sometimes trivialization seems to have been chosen for its own sake. Thus, although I believe that there is a great deal of scope within an overall framework such as I have outlined for micro-sociological studies, too often the cart has been put before the horse and potentially useful concepts referring to immigrant—host relations, to the stranger and colour—class hypotheses, to role theory and to status-crystallization, have been used as though they by themselves provide a sufficient theoretical foundation for the study of race relations. I find it difficult, myself, to regard work such as this as professionally serious.

I believe that in the field of race relations what we are faced with today is a test of our professional integrity, of our capacity to pursue an objective and systematic programme of sociological study. The area of race-relations research is and will continue to be politically sensitive and those who work in it will be under continual pressure to confine themselves to undertaking only those studies or producing only those conclusions which are least disturbing to government. Work of an alternative kind has only just begun. The object of this paper is to urge that we agree on our theoretical programme and then set out to produce the research workers and to create the necessary institutions to carry it out.

NOTES

1. See Michael Banton's paper on 'Racism' in *New Society,* April 1969.
2. J. S. Furnivall (1948). For a further discussion of the concept of the plural society, see M. G. Smith (1965).
3. J. Rex and R. Moore (1967). For detailed statistical evidence on the distribution of coloured immigrants in Britain, see C. Peach (1968).

REFERENCES

Banton, Michael 1969. What do we mean by Racism. *New Society,* 9 April.
Cox, Oliver Cromwell 1959. *Caste, Class, and Race.* New York: Monthly Review Press.
Durkheim, E. 1950. *Rules of Sociological Method.* Glencoe, Ill.: The Free Press.
Furnivall, J. S. 1948. *Colonial Policy and Practice.* London: Cambridge University Press.
Oppenheimer, F. 1914. *The State.* Indianapolis.
Peach, C. 1968. *West Indian Migration to Britain.* London: Oxford University Press.
Rex, J., & Moore, R. 1967. *Race, Community, and Conflict.* London: Oxford University Press.
Smith, M. G. 1965. *The Plural Society in the British West Indies.* Berkeley: University of California Press.
UNESCO 1969. *Four Statements on the Race Question.* Paris.
van den Berghe, P. L. 1967. *Race and Racism.* New York: Wiley.
Warner, W. Lloyd 1936. American Class and Caste. *American Journal of Sociology* 42: 234–7, Sept.

7   Race Relations and
the Sociological Tradition

John Stone

It has often been remarked that sociologists have an undue veneration for the founding fathers of their discipline. Some see it as a tribute to the insight and genius of the precursors of modern sociology; others consider it an indictment against those who would elevate the subject to the status of a "science."[1] A quotation from Marx, Weber, or Durkheim lends intellectual respectability to the most abstruse jargon of the grand theorist or to the most trivial correlation of the abstract empiricist. However, there is one interesting exception to this rule and that is the field of race and ethnic relations. In this case most sociologists have written as if the sociological tradition had little relevant to say on the matter.

The extent and manner in which this generalization holds is illustrated by the writing of three social scientists who are well versed in the main currents of sociological theory. In his influential textbook *Race Relations* Michael Banton outlines in some detail the racial doctrines of nineteenth- and early twentieth-century writers like Robert Knox, Gobineau, Karl Pearson, and Sir Arthur Keith, while hardly mentioning the fact that the masters of sociological theory also had some relevant observations to make about those issues. Banton's position is clear: "None of the major sociological theorists, Comte, Marx, Spencer, Simmel, Durkheim or Weber, paid much attention to questions of race relations."[2] While such a statement accurately describes Comte,[3] it is an exaggeration with respect to the others and creates the impression that their contribution is of little contemporary interest.

A somewhat different emphasis appears in John Rex's discussion of *Race Relations in Sociological Theory*. Rex in no way ignores the insights of Marx, Weber, Durkheim, or Pareto for the study of race relations, but he argues that "a sociological approach to race relations was *first* adopted in the United States."[4] He does not refer to European sociologists like Tocqueville or Weber, who visited America and wrote about the race situation there, or even to those who simply wrote about American race relations, like Marx. While Rex appreciates the value of the classical social theorists' contribution to the resolution of key problems in sociological theory, it is the application of these general theories to race relations by later sociologists, rather than the classical theorists' direct analysis of race and ethnicity, that he considers important.

A third and most striking example of this tendency to underplay the relationship between the classical sociological tradition and the study of race and ethnic relations is seen in the work of C. Wright Mills. It is surprising that Mills, the symbol of American radical sociology during the late nineteen fifties and early sixties, placed such a minor stress on race relations in his discussion of the sociological imagination.[5] Clearly Mills was aware of the importance of race and ethnic divisions both in the United States and as an aspect of the international scene, but, with the exception of his participation in a study of the early migration of Puerto Ricans to New York City,[6] very little of his extensive research and writing mentioned those issues.

There are a number of possible explanations for Mills's curious omission. One, with only a limited degree of plausibility, is that the level of overt conflict between racial and ethnic groups in the United States, and in the rest of the world, has risen sharply in the decade following Mills's death. But such an explanation is hardly sufficient. Another and more critical reason can be found in the widespread assumption that the classical social theorists largely ignored the problem area of race relations. Mills's respect for the intellectual giants of classical sociology is well known, and it is that view of their work that may have led him to neglect the sociological analysis of race and ethnic divisions.

Despite their differences, Banton, Rex, and Mills share the common assumption that the classical tradition has little direct relevance for the analysis of race and ethnicity. The purpose of this paper is to explore three related questions concerning the sociology of race relations. Is it true that the classical social theorists, and in particular Montesquieu, Tocqueville, Marx, Spencer, Durkheim, Pareto, and Weber, substantially ignored the problem area of race relations in formulating their general theories of society? If, in fact, they did pay considerable attention to questions of race relations, what was the nature of their contribution? And, finally, if the importance of their contribution is established, why was that particular legacy of the founding fathers disregarded?

Throughout the nineteenth century, and during the early years of the present century, race and ethnic relations were usually discussed as aspects of certain broad social problems rather than as topics to be isolated and analyzed alone. That practice may also have contributed to the belief that race and ethnic factors were regarded as relatively unimportant. These social problems can be grouped into three major, but overlapping, issues: the problem of slavery, dealing particularly with the sociological significance of racial slavery; the problem of imperialism, focusing on the sociology of colonial domination; and the problem of nationalism, exploring the social consequences of ethnic, linguistic, and cultural separatism.[7] I will argue that the classical sociologists wrote about these issues in considerable detail, attempted to relate their findings to a general interpretation of society, and often, though not always, adopted an essentially "modern" perspective, in as much as it would not seem anachronistic in contemporary academic discussions of the subject.

THE PROBLEM OF SLAVERY

The institution of slavery held a peculiar fascination for the founding fathers of sociology as it posed some of the most basic problems of the nature of social order, social conflict, and social change. As far as race relations were concerned, the primary focus of interest was on the slavery of the New World and the European colonies of Africa and Asia. However, an awareness of the existence of slavery in classical antiquity formed a useful comparative point of reference, since most of the pioneers of sociology were steeped in an education that emphasized the language and civilization of ancient Greece and Rome. Great differences certainly existed between the institutions of slavery at different times and in different places, but the refusal to separate racial slavery from slavery per se mitigated the tendency toward racial theorizing.

Some controversy surrounds Montesquieu's importance for the sociology of slavery, but to dismiss him as a "negrophobe and anti-Semite" is a cavalier treatment of the author of the *Persian Letters*.[8] While some critics have taken certain passages of the *Spirit of the Laws* at their face value, such a practice seems to be a basic misinterpretation of one of the fathers of the Enlightenment. It was not the view of several American colonists in the late eighteenth century, who cited Montesquieu as an authority to back their increasingly active agitation against slavery. Charles Crawford, writing in 1784, declared: "That all black persons should be slaves, says Montesquieu, is as ridiculous as that law of a certain country, that all red-haired persons should be hanged."[9] Montesquieu was not seen by his contemporaries as a negrophobe, and his account of the cynical and unjust persecution of mediaeval Jewry hardly supports the charge of anti-Semitism.[10]

Montesquieu not only derided the logic of racial ascription but pointed to key elements in the social dynamics of the slave system. He perceptively discussed relative deprivation as a factor that influenced the incidence of slave revolts and that explained the paradoxical discrepancy in this respect between despotic states and moderate governments.[11] His observations concerning the impact of slavery on sections of the dominant as well as the suppressed groups were penetrating,[12] and he commented acutely on the social functions of religion as a means of rationalizing enslavement.[13] To recognize his contribution involves much the same interpretative problem as that surrounding the meaning of his "climatic determinism." Are we to understand certain passages literally, or are we to view them within the wider context of his argument and analysis? If the latter course is chosen, following the judgement of Raymond Aron,[14] then Montesquieu ranks as a significant pioneer of the sociology of slavery.

Whatever the merits of Montesquieu's case, there can be little doubt about the contribution of his fellow countryman, Alexis de Tocqueville. Robert Merton has described Tocqueville's analysis of race relations in the United States as the work of a brilliant "outsider," but one not entirely immune from the "insider" myth of racial superiority.[15] Judged on the basis of *Democracy in America*, Merton's appraisal is typically fair, though it is interesting to note that in his later writings and speeches Tocqueville displayed even less acceptance of conventional stereotypes and prejudice. This is indicated by the attack levelled at Tocqueville himself in the Chamber of Deputies, during 1845, by the abolitionist Lavasseur. He quoted Tocqueville's "sinister prediction" concerning race relations found in his masterpiece on America:

> Heretofore, whenever the whites have been the more powerful, they have
> held the blacks in debasement or slavery, whenever the negroes have been
> the stronger they have destroyed the whites; it is the only relationship that
> has ever been opened between the two races.[16]

Lavasseur sought to expose critical inconsistencies between that statement and
Tocqueville's current position on slavery in the French colonies. Tocqueville's reply was simple: he did not need to repudiate what he had written earlier, for the
principle of racial antagonism was valid as long as there was no outside authority
capable of imposing an alternative relationship on the two groups. However, "if
the State was in a position to dominate both races then the situation was different."[17] In that way, he attempted to differentiate the structure of slavery under
varying power situations and to show how external political influence could alter
the racial power balance in such a manner as to modify the consequences of unimpeded local control. The conception is similar to that advanced by Tannenbaum
and Elkins in their comparison between slavery in the antebellum South and the
slavery in Latin America, or, more generally, to Banton's distinction between a
dominative as opposed to a paternalist order of race relations.[18] In both cases, the
crucial variable is the extent to which racial subordination is dictated by local
conditions or tempered by external political controls.

Tocqueville's enduring interest in race relations is seen both at the practical and
the theoretical levels. He was the major figure behind the *Report of the Commission on Slavery in the Colonies,* which paved the way towards the abolition of
bondage in the French Empire. But it was in his correspondence with his lifelong
friend Gobineau that he most clearly demolished the logical and intellectual foundations of racial theorizing. In a letter, dated 17 November 1853, Tocqueville
drew a comparison, a particularly fascinating one for sociologists, between Calvinist
predestination and Gobineau's racial theories.

> The consequence of both theories is that of a vast limitation, if not a com-
> plete abolition, of human liberty. Thus I confess that after having read your
> book I remain, as before, opposed in the extreme to your doctrines. I be-
> lieve that they are probably quite false; I know that they are certainly
> very pernicious.
>
> Surely among the different families which compose the human race there
> exist certain tendencies, certain proper aptitudes resulting from thousands of
> different causes. But that these tendencies, that these capacities should be
> insuperable has not only never been proven but no one will ever be able to
> prove it since to do so one would need to know not only the past but also
> the future. I am sure that Julius Caesar, had he had the time, would have
> willingly written a book to prove that the savages he had met in Britain did
> not belong to the same race as the Romans, and that the latter were destined
> thus by nature to rule the world while the former were destined to vegetate
> in one of its corners![19]

Tocqueville stated his position clearly: the existence of innate and immutable racial characteristics is to be regarded with skepticism and theories founded on such doctrines are mere rationalizations for slavery and other forms of racial oppression. That Tocqueville's writings are largely free from the taint of racist thinking does not imply that he was uninterested in the social implications of racism. He was fully aware of the function of racism as an instrument of group domination, and it was on this basis that he described Gobineau's treatise as "immoral and pernicious."[20] The fact that one of the first American titles claiming to spring from the discipline, Fitzhugh's *Sociology of the South,* was an ideological defense of slavery amply justified his fears.[21]

His observations concerning the present and probable future condition of the "three races" in America, as well as the reports, newspaper articles, and correspondence generated during his struggle for the abolition of slavery in the French colonies, are full of insight into the processes of racial interaction. He noted the phenomenon that later social scientists term minority group self-hatred,[22] he outlined the cluster of characteristics that comprise the "competitive" ideal-type of race relations and contrasted it with the "paternalistic" pattern,[23] elegantly explaining the "paradoxical" results of emancipation on interracial attitudes and actions; he anticipated the rise of informal barriers against racial equality as the legal basis of inequality is struck down;[24] he revealed the circular force of the self-fulfilling prophecy;[25] he demonstrated the principle of relative deprivation that applies both to the incidence of racial protest and to the generation of minority group leadership; [26] he observed the defense mechanism of deliberate ignorance among the threatened white elite;[27] and he dismissed the "humanitarian" theory of emancipation by unveiling the material basis of both slavery and its abolition.[28]

Tocqueville's analysis of race relations fits within his overall conception of social change. The inexorable levelling of social ranks, as aristocratic power decays in the path of democracy, has its counterpart in the field of racial privilege. However, just as he was alive to the dangers that democracy posed for liberty, so he was apprehensive about the consequences of the final collapse of slavery.[29] In view of his direct and perceptive contribution to our understanding of race relations, it is strange indeed that an authority so much respected in other spheres of sociology should have been so little regarded in this one.

THE PROBLEM OF IMPERIALISM

Tocqueville's interest in race relations was not confined to slavery, for he was also concerned with the related issue of imperialism. He visited Algeria on two occasions and predicted that the future of French rule there would depend very much on the treatment of the Arab population. If colonial policy was selfish and unenlightened, then the society would degenerate into "a fortified area in which the two races would fight without mercy, and where one of the two would die."[30] Tocqueville combined a recognition of the power of racism with an almost Marxian appreciation of the force of economic exploitation.

One hundred years later, this Algerian conflict spawned another theorist of colonialism, Frantz Fanon, who was more consciously influenced by the French Marxist tradition than by French liberal thought. However, Fanon argued that Marxism needed to be "slightly stretched" in the colonial context to account adequately for the relationship between colonizer and colonized: an argument that brought him remarkably close to Tocqueville's position.[31] On the other hand, a considerable degree of flexibility did exist within Marx's writings on imperialism, if not within the more rigid framework developed by later Marxists or, indeed, within Marx's own more simplified, polemical formulations of materialism. Despite its ethnocentric bias, Marx did provide one of the most systematic interpretations of colonialism developed by the classical sociologists.

The significance of colonialism for Marx was its contribution to the development of capitalist societies. Colonialism was an extension, or to use Lenin's later terminology, a "higher stage" of capitalism, and it could be analyzed in terms of the proletariat and the bourgeoisie but translated onto a world stage. The detailed mechanics of the model might indeed have to be slightly stretched, but such stretching could be useful, as Lenin was to argue, in accounting for the split in the socialist movement.[32] Surplus value generated by imperial exploitation could be used to bribe a section of the metropolitan proletariat from fulfilling its revolutionary destiny, not that this need take place at a conscious, conspirational level.

Of course, Marx viewed such a situation as a temporary state of static disequilibrium, analogous to the Bonapartist stalemate that he had described in the *Eighteenth Brumaire*, but once such a possibility was recognized it raised genuine problems for his general model of social change. As in the case of false consciousness and the distinction between a class in itself and a class for itself, qualifications that make the theory a more penetrating representation of social reality open the door to basic structural modifications of the theory itself. Thus there is no doubt that Marx totally underestimated the power and the resilience of the caste system or that he underplayed the degree to which racial prejudice combined with imperialism might serve as persistent forces subverting a world proletarian revolution. He luridly described human progress as continuing indefinitely in the form of "the hideous pagan idol who would not drink the nectar but from the skulls of the slain."[33]

That many aspects of Marx's sociology of imperialism contain a glaring ethnocentric bias is well illustrated in his concept of the Asiatic mode of production—a realm of reality outside the pale of dialectical laws, if for no more compelling reason than geographical location.[34] However, to ignore Marx's conception of colonialism on those grounds, or because it has proved to be empirically incorrect on many counts, is indefensible. It is equivalent to dismissing his writings on class conflict and revolutionary change because the working classes of capitalist societies have not become increasingly impoverished or because no socialist revolution has ever succeeded in an advanced capitalist state. In fact, Marx's formulation of imperialism was extended and developed by influential writers both in the Marxist tradition, by Lenin and Fanon, and outside it, by Hobson and Furnivall, but not, significantly enough, by the mainstream of contemporary academic sociologists.

While concern and interest in imperialism were strongly entrenched in the Marxist sociological tradition, it was by no means confined to it. Social theorists as much opposed to the basic tenets of Marxism as Spencer, Sumner, and Pareto developed devastating critiques of imperialist expansion that contain much in common with the work of their socialist counterparts. Thus, it was Herbert Spencer, and not Marx or Veblen, who objected to "our Christian creed and our pagan doings, our professed philanthropy and our actual savagery" and expressed his hatred of colonialism in a letter of 1898:

> Now that the white savages of Europe are over-running the dark savages everywhere—now that the European nations are vying with one another in political burglaries—now that we have entered upon an era of social cannibalism in which strong nations are devouring the weaker—now that national interests, national prestige, pluck and so forth are alone thought of, and equity has dropped utterly out of thought, while rectitude is scorned as "unctuous," it is useless to resist the wave of barbarism. There is a bad time coming, and civilized mankind will morally be uncivilized before civilization can again advance.[35]

Quite apart from his moral objections to it, imperialism posed analogous, and perhaps even more fundamental, problems for Spencer's model of social evolution than it did for Marx's account of the dynamics of revolution. Spencer conceived of social development in terms of increasing differentiation and integration—"coherent heterogeneity"—taking place within the overall transition from the militant to the industrial type of society. His idealization of industrial society as a peaceful association of voluntarily cooperating individuals was based on his distorted view of mid-nineteenth-century Britain. As the century wore on, Spencer had to account for the simultaneous increase in militancy and industrialism that he could only describe as a regression into an earlier phase of social evolution, resulting from collectivism and the enlargement of the role of the state. While Spencer failed to give a convincing explanation of that regression in terms of his wider developmental hypothesis, his analysis was never racist in the social Darwinist sense.[36] In contrast to Bagehot, Kidd, or Pearson, Spencer subscribed to a power analysis of race relations and imperialism that was not tied to assumptions about racial or national superiority or inferiority.

Pareto's analysis of imperialism shared Spencer's general perspective. However, it differed from both Spencer's or Marx's approach in as much as it fitted without difficulty into his cyclical model of sociohistorical change. As with Spencer, but with even less justification, Pareto has often been regarded as a racist sociologist, but that view derives more from attempts to overplay his fleeting connection with Mussolini's Fascists at the very end of his life than from a careful evaluation of his sociology. His conception of residues, however innate and biologically reductionist, was related to a distribution on the basis of color blindness and knew no boundaries of language, nation, or culture. The prevalence of racialist derivations—rationalizations in contemporary language—were, in Pareto's view, the inevitable accompaniment to "the unceasing succession of crimes, cruelties, barbarities, massacres and infamies recorded by history, and in which individuals, races and nations in course of time became *by turns* the tormentors and the victims."[37] Pareto was a sociologist of racism without being a racist sociologist.

In his writings can be found clear statements of a power analysis of both racial discrimination and imperial domination not unrelated to later formulations of Blalock and Lieberson.[38] He was also sharply critical of the crude Marxist interpretation of social conflict and stressed the noneconomic bases of societal cleavage. On imperialism he declared:

> There is not perhaps on this globe a single foot of ground which has not been conquered by the sword at some time or other, and where the people occupying it have not maintained themselves on it by force. If the Negroes were stronger than the Europeans, Europe would be partitioned by the Negroes and not Africa by the Europeans. The "right" claimed by people who bestow on themselves the title of "civilized" to conquer other peoples whom it pleases them to call "uncivilized," is altogether ridiculous, or rather, this right is nothing other than force. For as long as the Europeans are stronger than the Chinese, they will impose their will on them; but if the Chinese should become stronger than Europeans, then the roles would be reversed, and it is highly probable that humanitarian sentiments could never be opposed with any effectiveness to an army.[39]

With respect to the Marxian view of race relations, Pareto recognized the reality of the class struggle, the tokens of which were to be found on "every page of history," but it was not the only form of conflict and frequently not the most important. Nationality, religion, race, language, and sex could serve as the basis for contending power groups that often cut across the economic division between proletarian and capitalist.[40]

THE PROBLEM OF NATIONALISM

Pareto's criticism of Marx's analysis is particularly telling in the area of nationalism and ethnicity. However, in his papers on Ireland Marx moved toward a greater recognition of the independent significance of language, culture, and national sentiment as factors affecting social change. His interpretation of the Irish situation varied during his lifetime. He first claimed that a proletarian revolution in Britain would be the gateway to national liberation in Ireland; later he saw the struggle in Ireland as the path to class war in England.[41] The reality of nineteenth-century nationalism, no matter how much it was ultimately related to material conditions, could no more be ignored by Marx than by Spencer.

Durkheim and Max Weber, writing some twenty years after Marx's death, also found the issues of nationalism both intellectually interesting and closely linked to their daily lives. Of all the great social theorists of the nineteenth and early twentieth centuries, Durkheim was perhaps the least concerned with the immediate aspects of race and ethnicity. Nevertheless, several of his works contain interesting discussions of the problem of defining race and its irrelevance for the explanation of social facts. In his most famous study, *Suicide,* he insisted that the Germans commit suicide more than other peoples not because of their blood but because of the civilization in which they are reared."[42] He rejected racial—innate rather than cultural—explanations of variations in suicide rates and was entirely skeptical of the claim that races could be seen as "concrete, living factors of historical development."[43] A similar interpretation can be found in both *The Division of Labor in Society* and the *Rules of Sociological Method*. In the former work Durkeim minimized the importance of hereditary factors as an explanation of individual variety in modern societies.[44] He joined the attack on Galton whose "veritable dynasties of scholars, poets and muscians" were a product of "family, fortune and education" and not biologically transmitted aptitude.[45] He anticipated major themes of the "Jensen" controversy by exposing the impossibility of "isolating the action of heredity from that of environment,"[46] for with the advance of the division of labor "civilization . . . becomes less and less an organic thing, more and more a social thing."[47] In this respect, Durkheim stuck to his methodological guns. He maintained that biological reductionism was a totally inadequate means of explaining differences between racial, ethnic, or national groups, just as it was inadequate for explaining the existence of any other set of social facts.[48]

Max Weber, much more than his great French contemporary, was extremely sensitive to the theoretical implications of recognizing nationalism, ethnicity, and race as elements in the stratification systems of diverse societies. Several sections of his incomplete masterwork, *Economy and Society,* are devoted to those issues.[49] His earlier writings, comparing German and Polish ethnic groups in Prussia, attributed national differences to race and culture in a rather indiscriminate fashion. In the later studies, however, he began to analyze race in a more precise and rigorous manner. The encounter with American race relations, after his visit of 1904, made him more aware of the significance of these factors and their relationship to his general theories of social stratification. Visiting the United States some seventy years after Tocqueville, he was impressed by the clearly visible ethnic heterogeneity of the great urban centers like New York and Chicago.

> The Greek shining the Yankee's shoes for five cents, the German acting as his waiter, the Irishman managing his politics, and the Italian digging his dirty ditches . . . the whole gigantic city . . . is like a man whose skin has been peeled off and whose entrails one sees at work.[50]

He shared Tocqueville's opinion about America's most visible minority group, finding the problem of the American Negro particularly intractable as it hovered over the society like a "big black cloud."[51] Like Tocqueville he contrasted the position of the Negroes to that of the American Indian and saw in the differential reaction of whites to those two subordinate groups a consequence of slavery.[52]

As far as his general theories are concerned the discussion of nationality, as well as race and ethnicity, is immensely interesting and, like Pareto's studies, forms another aspect of the idealistic modification of Marxist materialism. Weber was sensitive to the ambiguity of the concept of nation, just as he was aware of the complexity of the term race. He noted that nationalism varied among different strata of society, that it was based largely on sentiments of prestige, and that it lay partly in the sphere of values and did not have an exclusively economic origin.[53] A nation was not synonymous with the people of a given political state, nor with a given language group, and it was not true that a common language was a necessary condition of national identity. The same variability applied to religious and other cultural attributes, and Weber illustrates that complex interpretation by referring to a great diversity of examples drawn from Europe, North America, and China. At no stage in his mature work did he subscribe to the thesis that nationalism was a product of "a common blood," and he perceptively pointed out that the most radical nationalists were often of foreign descent.[54]

Weber's approach to nationalism and race fits in with his conception of sociology as the science that aims at the interpretative understanding of social action. His stress on subjective definitions explains why it is that once qualities are defined as "racial," whether they are innate or culturally created, in fact, becomes irrelevant as far as social behavior is concerned. That Weber, in his own opinion, accepted the environmental viewpoint is further illustrated in his explanation of the cultural roots of Chinese stereotypes,[55] in his dismissal of the alleged "natural repulsion of the races,"[56] and in his demolition of racial-historical theories purporting to account for the decline of the Roman Empire.[57] While he shared Marx's stress on the economic foundations of imperialism and the economic determination of many language conflicts, he differed from him when it came to interpreting how class conflict might be affected by racial and national divisions, as seen, for example, in the case of the "poor white trash" of the southern United States.[58] That analysis parallels the criticisms of the Marxian class struggle found in Pareto's writings, particularly *Les Systemes Socialistes, Mind and Society* and *Fatti e Teorie,* where the importance of nationality, religion, race, and language is explicitly recognized and elevated alongside class as a fundamental basis of social cleavage. Thus the sociological analysis of race and ethnic relations joins social stratification as a legitimate and crucial area of social investigation.

CONCLUSION

In this paper I have tried to demonstrate that the range and wealth of the sociological tradition applies as much to the sphere of race and ethnic relations as it does to most other areas of sociological inquiry. While it is true that no one text of the classical social theorists was devoted exclusively to race relations, we cannot assume that they lacked interest in the subject.[59] My brief survey of some of the key works in literature of classical sociology suggests that Montesquieu,

Tocqueville, Marx, Spencer, Durkheim, Weber, and Pareto were all acutely aware of race and ethnicity as important areas of sociological concern, though they carefully avoided theories based on a racial or ethnic dynamic. That awareness is evident even if we confine our attention to their major publications, most of which have been available in translation for many years. The classical sociologists differed radically from their contemporaries like Gobineau, Gumplowicz, and Bagehot in the emphasis they attached to "race" as a factor in social life.[60] It is not that they doubted the empirical significance of race relations; their skepticism turned on the relevance of "race" as an explanation for them.

There are several reasons why such a significant body of knowledge has been generally ignored. One possible explanation is based on an extension of the criticism of influential American theorists like Talcott Parsons for selectively interpreting the classical sociologists. I am not arguing, to use Gouldner's terminology, that the "infrastructure" and "domain assumptions" of recent Western sociology militated against a "conflict orientation" appropriate for the analysis of race relations.[61] To do so one would have to demonstrate the all pervasive influence of Parsons (or those factors determining his outlook) on sociologists who have studied race relations since the late 1930s. That is not the case, for such sociologists have rarely ignored the role of conflict and scarcely ever made explicit reference to Parsons's work in their analyses.[62] The influence of Parsons has been more subtle, coloring the interpretation of the scope of the sociological tradition for sociologists as far removed from Parsons's theoretical orientation as C. Wright Mills, and leading them to the assumption that the classical theorists could not shed much light on the issues of race and ethnicity. It is not so much that Parsons has defined the approach taken by social scientists in their studies of race and ethnic relations as deflected attention away from the fact that this problem area has been an important part of the sociological tradition.

However important this bias may have been for the development of contemporary social theory, it accounts for only some of the neglect of the classical analysis of race relations. Other factors must also have been responsible for this curious omission, and they can be traced to certain disciplinary trends in Anglo-American social science, research, and teaching. There has been a tendency among many American sociologists to view the "peculiar institution" of American slavery as uniquely their own, a perspective not shared by the classical sociologists with their incessant comparative bent.[63] In as much as many of the early American sociologists did accept racist assumptions and theories,[64] it is not surprising that later researchers should have overlooked the contribution of European sociologists towards an understanding of what was defined as an essentially American problem. A comparable ethnocentrism on the part of many British sociologists has led them to focus on class relations at home while relegating colonial affairs to their anthropological colleagues. When confronted with race relations in Britain, sociologists have tended to draw on American research rather than to look for inspiration in the writings of the classical tradition. Such American research has been further influenced by the great impact of Freudian psychology, which has channeled so much attention into psychodynamic theories of prejudice at the expense of studies of the structures of discrimination.[65] This last perspective is at variance with the classical viewpoint, which tended, on the whole but with the notable exception of Pareto, to see social life in terms of rational domination, rather than as the consequence of irrational urges.

Two other factors may also be significant. Some of the classical theorists wrote about race relations in their less well-known works, and much information can be found in letters, reports, newspaper articles, and in unfamiliar sections of their major studies.[66] In addition, it may be that the occasional lapses into stereotyped language, however much contrary to the great bulk of the classical sociologists' theories and known beliefs—Marx's so-called anti-Semitism, Pareto's fascism, or even the erroneously ascribed imperialism that links the passivist Spencer to the more bellicose social Darwinists—offended the liberal consciences or ideological sensibilities of many later social scientists. Rather than seeing these slips as genuine intellectual mistakes, or simply as moments of incautious writing, some sociologists have refused to look further, lest their intellectual idols turn out to have feet of clay. If they have done so, it is most unfortunate, for otherwise they would have discovered that the insight and penetration of the sociological tradition did not stop short of the field of race relations.

NOTES

I am grateful to Robert K. Merton, Kenneth Kirkwood and Michael Banton for critical comments on an earlier draft of this paper. The writing of the paper was assisted by a grant from the Social Science Research Council of Columbia University.

1. See John Goldthorpe's introduction to *The Founding Fathers of Social Science* (Harmondsworth: Penguin, 1969), pp. 9–16.
2. Michael Banton, *Race Relations* (London: Tavistock, 1967), p. 62.
3. Comte's references to race relations are brief and not very enlightening. Perhaps it is not surprising that the apostle of positivism could jump to the conclusion that "the white race . . . in all its branches is superior to the other two races." Auguste Comte, *System of Positive Polity*, trans. H. Martineau, 4 vols. (New York: B. Franklin, 1968), 1: 314. Nevertheless, Comte opposed the "iniquitous yoke of slavery" (Ibid., 1: 315–16), and his former mentor and intellectual twin, Saint-Simon, "used to justify racial cross-breeding in the interests of humanity." Felix Markham, ed., *Henri de Saint-Simon: Social Organization, the Science of Man and Other Writings* (New York: Harper & Row, 1964), p. xv.
4. John Rex, *Race Relations in Sociological Theory* (London: Weidenfeld & Nicolson, 1970), p. 13. Emphasis added.
5. Rex comments: "One wonders whether the insensitivity to the race relations problem, which he shared with so many of his New Left friends, would have been overcome had he still been alive in the summer of 1967." "Wright Mills," *New Society* 5 (October 1967): 467.
6. Even this participation is not a significant exception since Mills did not initiate the study. Personal communication from Robert K. Merton to the author, 25 December 1973.
7. A fourth problem area that has fallen within the traditional scope of race relations deals with the concept of marginality and is exemplified in the case of anti-Semitism. Once again the sociological tradition contains many references to both the concept and the example. Of course, marginality is by no means confined to Jewish experience, and

Tocqueville, Bryce, and Weber wrote with great perception about the dilemmas and contradictions—the status inconsistency—of rich blacks and poor whites in racially stratified societies. However, the position of the Jews has a special interest partly because many of the founding fathers were of Jewish parentage, most notably Marx, Durkheim, and Simmel, and partly because Veblen, whose own marginality was notorious, argued that is was an anomalous social situation, rather than any notion of genetic purity, that accounted for the "intellectual preeminence" of the Jews. Simmel presents the most abstract analysis of marginality in his discussion of the formal relationships that characterize the social situation of the stranger. Cf. John Stone, "James Bryce and the Comparative Sociology of Race Relations," *Race* 13, no. 3 (1972): 319–21; R. Misrahi, *Marx et la question juive* (Paris, 1972); Thorstein Veblen, "The Intellectual Preeminence of Jews in Modern Europe," *Political Science Quarterly*, 34 (1919): 33–39. K. H. Wolff, ed., *The Sociology of Georg Simmel* (New York: Free Press, 1950) pp. 402–8.

8. C. Dover, "The Racial Philosophy of Johann Herder," *British Journal of Sociology* 3, no.2 (1952): 125. For a different assessment: R. Shackleton, *Montesquieu: A Critical Biography* (London: Oxford University Press, 1961), pp. 354–55.

9. Charles Crawford, *Observations on Negro Slavery* (Philadelphia: 1784) quoted in W. D. Jordan, *White over Black: American Attitudes toward the Negro, 1550–1812* (Baltimore: Penguin, 1969), pp. 278–79.

10. T. Nugent, trans., *Montesquieu: The Spirit of the Laws* (New York: Hafner, 1949), 1: 364–65.

11. Ibid., p. 243.

12. Ibid., P. 235

13. Ibid., p. 238; Montesquieu, *The Persian Letters* (New York: Meridian, 1961), No. 75, pp. 167–69.

14. Raymond Aron, *Main Currents in Sociological Thought* (London: Weidenfeld & Nicolson, 1965), 1: 35–38.

15. R. K. Merton, "Insiders and Outsiders: A Chapter in the Sociology of Knowledge," *American Journal of Sociology* 1, no. 78 (July 1972): 33–34.

16. Alexis de Tocqueville, *Oeuvres complètes*, 2 vols., ed. J. P. Mayer (Paris: Gallimard, 1951), I, i, p. 359.

17. Alexis de Tocqueville, *Le Moniteur universal*, 31 mai 1845.

18. Frank Tannenbaum, *Slave and Citizens: The Negro in the Americas* (New York: Knopf, 1946); S. M. Elkins, *Slavery: A Problem in American Institutional and Intellectual Life* (Chicago: University of Chicago Press, 1959); Banton, *Race Relations*, pp. 71–72.

19. Alexis de Tocqueville, *The European Revolution and Correspondence with Gobineau*, ed. J. Lukacs (Gloucester, Mass.: Peter Smith, 1968), pp. 227–28. See also: M. Lawlor, *Alexis de Tocqueville in the Chamber of Deputies: His View on Foreign and Colonial Policy* (Washington, D. C.: The Catholic University of American Press, 1959). The exact title of Tocqueville's report was: *Rapport fait au nom de la commission chargée d'examiner la proposition de M. de Tracy relative aux esclaves des colonies* (Paris: A. Henry, 1839). The correspondence with Gobineau has been discussed by Michael Biddiss in his article, "Prophecy and Pragmatism: Gobineau's Confrontation with Tocqueville," *The Historical Journal* 13, no. 4, (1970): 624–33.

20. Tocqueville to Gobineau, 30 July 1856. Here we find Tocqueville making a distinction similar to that drawn by Weber between an ethic of responsibility and an ethic of ultimate ends: "Even though this act in itself may not be immoral; its consequences assuredly are." Tocqueville, *European Revolution and Correspondence*, p. 291.

21. Tocqueville had written to Gobineau: "For those Americans whom you mention and who translated your book are known to me as perfervid leaders of the anti-abolitionist party. They translated the part of your book which suits their prejudices, the part which tends to prove that the Negroes belong to another, to a different and inferior race; but they suppressed the part which tends to argue that, like every other, the Anglo-Saxon race is also decaying." Ibid., p. 294.

22. Alexis de Tocqueville, *Democracy in America* (New York: Vintage Books, n.d.), 1: 346; cf. K. Lewin, *Resolving Social Conflicts* (New York: Harper, 1948).

23. Tocqueville *Democracy in America*, 1: 374, 390; P. L. van den Berghe, *Race and Ethnicity* (New York: Basic Books, 1970), pp. 21–41.

24. Tocqueville *Democracy in America*, 1: 372, n. 32.

25. R. K. Merton, "Insiders and Outsiders," pp. 33–34; R. K. Merton, *Social Theory and Social Structure* (New York: Free Press, 1957), pp. 421–36.

26. Tocqueville, *Democracy in America*, 1: 387–88, 395.

27. Ibid., 1: 392; Gunnar Myrdal, *An American Dilemma* (New York: Harper, 1944), 1: 42.

28. Tocqueville *Democracy in America*, 1: 375; cf. E. Williams, *Capitalism and Slavery* (London: Deutsch, 1964). In this final respect Tocqueville's irony contrasts with the bitter sarcasm of Pareto. The style is different but the message remains the same. "So the Europeans are performing a sacrosanct duty in exterminating Africans in an effort to teach them to be civilized. . . .The cat catches the mouse and eats it; but it does not pretend to be doing so for the good of the mouse. It does not proclaim any dogma that all animals are equal, nor lift its eyes hypocritically to heaven in worship of the Father of us all." Vilfredo Pareto, *The Mind and Society: A Treatise on General Sociology* (New York: Dover, 1963), 1: 626–27 (S1050).

29. Tocqueville, *Democracy in America*, 1: 345, 397.

30. Lawlor, *Tocqueville in the Chamber of Deputies*, p. 158.

31. Frantz Fanon, *The Wretched of the Earth* (New York: Grove Press, 1968), p. 40, i.e. nearer to a race war than a class war thesis. Many parallels can be found in the two writers who, apart from their common French culture, are in other respects so different. Take for example their observations on the pressure for conformity among settlers with regard to race relations. Ibid., p. 92; Tocqueville to J. S. Mill, 14 November 1839 quoted in Lawlor, *Tocqueville in the Chamber of Deputies*, p. 104.

32. V. I. Lenin, *Collected Works*, vol. 19, 1916–17 (Moscow: Foreign Publishing House, 1942), pp. 337–51.

33. Karl Marx, "The Future Results of British Rule in India," *New York Daily Tribune*, 8 August 1853. See also: S. Avineri, *Karl Marx on Colonialism and Modernization* (New York: Doubleday, 1968); R. Blauner, "Marxist Theory, Nationality, and Colonialism" mimeographed, 1973.

34. See K. A. Wittfogel, *Oriental Despotism* (New Haven: Yale University Press, 1957); G. Lichtheim, *The Concept of Ideology* (New York: Random House, 1967), pp. 62–93.

35. Spencer to M. D. Conway, 17 July 1898, quoted in J. D. Y. Peel, *Herbert Spencer: The Evolution of a Sociologist* (London: Heinemann, 1971), p. 233.

36. On this point Spencer insisted that he had been misinterpreted even by his old friends. In reply to Huxley's *Romanes Lecture* of 1893, Spencer claimed: "No one has so often insisted that 'the ethical process' is hindered by the cowardly conquests of bullet and shell over arrow and assegai, which demoralizes the one side while slaughtering the other." "Evolutionary Ethics," *Popular Science Monthly* Vol. 99, no. 37, (1898): 499.

37. Vilfredo Pareto, *Fatti e teorie*, (Florence: Vallecchi editore, 1920). Emphasis added. See also S. E. Finer, ed., *Vilfredo Pareto: Sociological Writings* (London: Pall Mall Press, 1966), p. 294. All his major works point to this conclusion: Finer, p. 17 and Pareto, *The Mind and Society*, 2: 962 (S1508), 2: 1519 (S2180).

38. H. M. Blalock, "A Power Analysis of Racial Discrimination," *Social Forces* 39 (1960): 53–59; Stanley Lieberson, "A Societal Theory of Race and Ethnic Relations," *American Sociological Review* 26, no. 6 (1961): 902–910.

39. Vilfredo Pareto, *Les Systemes socialistes*, 1902, in Finer, *Pareto: Sociological Writings*, pp. 135–36.

40. "In our own day the struggle of the Czechs and the Germans in Bohemia is more intense than that of the proletariat and capitalists in England." Ibid., 1; Chap. 2; p. 140.

41. Karl Marx and Friederich Engels, *Ireland and the Irish Question*, ed. R. Dixon (New York:

International Publishers, 1972), p. 29. Tocqueville visited Ireland in 1835, and his notes on the class and religious conflicts are typically perceptive. On 9 July 1835 he wrote: "If you want to know what can be done by the spirit of conquest and religious hatred combined with the abuses of aristocracy, go to Ireland." J. P. Mayer, ed., *Alexis de Tocqueville: Journeys to England and Ireland* (New Haven: Yale University Press, 1958), p. 122.

42. Emile Durkheim, *Suicide,* ed. G. Simpson (New York: Free Press, 1951), p. 89.

43. Ibid., pp. 82–85.

44. Emile Durkheim, *The Division of Labor in Society,* trans. G. Simpson (New York: Free Press, 1964), pp. 308–9.

45. Ibid., pp. 312–13.

46. Ibid., pp. 316–17; See also: A. R. Jensen, "How Much Can We Boost I.Q. and Scholastic Achievement?" *Harvard Educational Review* 39 (1969): 1–123; A. L. Stinchcombe, "Environment: The Cumulation of Effects Is Yet To Be Understood," *Harvard Educational Review* 39 (1969): 511–22.

47. Durkheim, *Division of Labor,* p. 321.

48. Durkheim wrote: "No social phenomenon is known which can be placed in indisputable dependence on race. No doubt we cannot attribute to this proposition the value of a principle; we can merely affirm it as invariably true in practical experience." Emile Durkheim, *The Rules of Sociological Method* (New York: Free Press, 1964), p. 108.

49. Max Weber, *Wirtschaft und Gesellschaft* (Tübingen: Mohr, 1922), p. 216; H. Gerth & C. W. Mills, eds., *From Max Weber: Essays in Sociology* (London: Routledge & Kegan Paul, 1948), pp. 171–75. See also E. M. Manasse, "Max Weber on Race," *Social Research* 14 (1947): 191–221; G. Roth and C. Wittich, eds., *Max Weber: Economy and Society* (New York: Bedminster, 1968), 1: 385–95; 2: 492–99, 913–26, 933–35.

50. Gerth and Mills, eds., *From Max Weber: Essays,* p. 15.

51. Ibid., pp. 15–16.

52. Ibid., p. 177; Tocqueville, *Democracy in America,* 1: 344–48.

53. Gerth and Mills, eds., *From Max Weber: Essays,* p. 172.

54. Ibid., p. 173.

55. Manasse, "Max Weber on Race," pp. 211–14; cf. Max Weber, *Gesammelte Aufsätze zur Sozial und Wirtschaftsgeschichte* (Tübingen: Mohr, 1924), pp. 289–90.

56. Manasse pp. 211–14. Cf. Max Weber, *Gesammelte Aufsätze zur Soziologie und Sozialpolitik* (Tübingen: Mohr, 1926), p. 489.

57. Manasse pp. 211–14. Cf. Max Weber, *Gesammelte Aufsätze zur Religionssoziologie* (Tübingen: Mohr, 1920–21), 1: 518–20.

58. Max Weber, *The Theory of Social and Economic Organization,* ed. Talcott Parsons (New York: Free Press, 1964), p. 426.

59. There is evidence from W. E. B. Du Bois that Weber may have planned such a work. Manasse, "Max Weber on Race," p. 199, n. 20.

60. Cf. D. H. Wrong's comment: "Modern sociology, after all, originated as a protest against the partial views of man contained in such doctrines as utilitarianism, classical economics, social Darwinism, and vulgar Marxism." "The Oversocialized Conception of Man in Modern Sociology," *American Sociological Review* 26 (1961): 191–92.

61. See A. W. Gouldner, *The Coming Crisis of Western Sociology* (New York: Basic Books), 1970.

62. Parsons gave little emphasis to race and ethnicity before the early 1960s; cf. Talcott Parsons, *The Social System* (London: Routledge & Kegan Paul, 1951), pp. 172–73. The two most specific essays on the subject are: Talcott Parsons, "Full Citizenship for the Negro American?" in Talcott Parsons & K. B. Clark, *The Negro American* (Boston: Beacon Press, 1967), pp. 709–54; Talcott Parsons, "The Problem of Polarization on the Axis of Color" in J. H. Franklin, ed., *Color and Race* (Boston: Beacon Press, 1969), pp. 349–67.

63. For the lack of a comparative dimension to research and teaching in American race relations see P. I. Rose, *The Subject is Race: Traditional Ideologies and the Teaching of Race Relations* (New York: Oxford University Press, 1968), p. 95. See also the highly relevant

comments in two recent papers by Michael Banton, "1960, a Turning Point in the Study of Race Relations," *Daedalus* 103, no. 2 (Spring 1974): 31–44; "Race in the American Sociological Tradition: From Park to Parsons," *Jewish Journal of Sociology* 16; no. 1 (June 1974): 85–93.

64. See. E. F. Frazier, "Sociological Theory and Race Relations," *American Sociological Review* 12 (1947): 265–71; Stanford M. Lyman, *The Black American in Sociological Thought* (New York: Putnam, 1972); and R. Hofstadter, *Social Darwinism in American Thought* (Boston: Beacon Press, 1955).

65. See B. Bettelheim and M. Janowitz, *Social Change and Prejudice* (New York: Harper & Row, 1964), p. 52; Rose, *The Subject is Race,* pp. 132–37.

66. Avineri makes the same point in relation to Marx: *Karl Marx on Colonialism and Modernization,* p. 1.

MODELS

AND TYPOLOGIES

A science of society requires systematic measurement, comparison, and synthesis. Although the initial attempts at such studies may be crude and inaccurate, they are, nonetheless, indispensable. The articles in this section of the book try to provide a greater degree of coherence to the vast array of empirical findings and theoretical propositions outlined earlier.

Lieberson's societal theory of race and ethnic relations draws a basic distinction between those contact situations where an indigenous group is the stronger and can impose its will on other groups and those where a migrant group has greater power. He then explores the effects of this difference on various aspects of race relations such as political and economic control, multiple ethnic contacts, and conflict and assimilation. Lieberson argues that in situations where the migrant group has more power at the time of contact there will be a greater degree of conflict often resulting in open warfare, the decimation of the indigenous peoples, and, at a later stage, outbursts of militant nationalism. On the other hand, where there is indigenous superordination the likelihood of intense racial and ethnic conflict is much less.

Pierre van den Berghe's quest for order lies in a somewhat different distinction between two ideal types of race relations, which he labels "paternalistic" and "competitive." The paternalistic pattern of race relations is usually approximated in nonindustrial societies such as the slave plantations of the antebellum South or the European colonial regimes that existed in many parts of Africa. A competitive system is typically found in urbanized, industrial economies based on capitalist manufacturing industry where there is a breakdown of a rigid racial or ethnic division of labor. Thus, members of different racial and ethnic groups are placed in situations where they are more openly in competitive conflict with one another, and a whole series of social and psychological consequences results from that contact. Van den Berghe relates his ideal types to other theoretical models of social change and points to their relevance for a wide range of situations of prejudice and discrimination.

A third possible classification of types of racial contact and patterns of race relations is suggested by Michael Banton. Banton's "six orders" of race relations start from the simplest kinds of contact and then explore a number of possible developments resulting from interaction between more complex societies. It is important to recognize that Banton and van den Berghe use the same term *paternalism* to describe different social and political relationships. For Banton, the term indicates a degree of control exercised by a metropolitan society over the internal race relations of a colonized territory; for van den Berghe, it represents the cluster of characteristics found in his first ideal type.

These three typologies abstract from and thereby oversimplify complex relationships. They have also been criticized on the grounds that, in certain cases, they do not seem to fit the facts.[1] However, Lieberson, van den Berghe, and Banton have quite deliberately overgeneralized in order to reveal parallel structures of domination and similar patterns of interethnic behavior that might have been overlooked without a comparative frame of reference.

NOTES

1. P. Mason, *Patterns of Dominance* (London: Oxford University Press, 1970), pp. 57–65.

8   A Societal Theory of Race and Ethnic Relations

Stanley Lieberson

"In the relations of races there is a cycle of events which tends everywhere to repeat itself."[1] Park's assertion served as a prologue to the now classical cycle of competition, conflict, accommodation, and assimilation. A number of other attemps have been made to formulate phases or stages ensuing from the initial contacts between racial and ethnic groups.[2] However, the sharp contrasts between relatively harmonious race relations in Brazil and Hawaii and the current racial turmoil in South Africa and Indonesia serve to illustrate the difficulty in stating—to say nothing of interpreting—an inevitable "natural history" of race and ethnic relations.

Many earlier race and ethnic cycles were, in fact, narrowly confined to a rather specific set of groups or contact situations. Bogardus, for example, explicitly limited his synthesis to Mexican and Oriental immigrant groups on the west coast of the United States and suggested that this is but one of many different cycles of relations between immigrants and native Americans.[3] Similarly, the Australian

From Stanley Lieberson, "A Societal Theory of Race and Ethnic Relations," in *American Sociological Review*, 26 (1961), pp. 902–910. Reprinted by permission of the author and the American Sociological Association.

anthropologist Price developed three phases that appear to account for the relationships between white English-speaking migrants and the aborigines of Australia,
Maoris in New Zealand, and Indians of the United States and Canada.[4]

This paper seeks to present a rudimentary theory of the development of race
and ethnic relations that systematically accounts for differences between societies
in such divergent consequences of contact as racial nationalism and warfare, assimilation and fusion, and extinction. It postulates that the critical problem on a
societal level in racial or ethnic contact is initially each population's maintenance
and development of a social order compatible with its ways of life prior to contact.
The crux of any cycle must, therefore, deal with political, social, and economic
institutions. The emphasis given in earlier cycles to one group's dominance of another in these areas is therefore hardly surprising.[5]

Although we accept this institutional approach, the thesis presented here is that
knowledge of the nature of one group's domination over another in the political,
social, and economic spheres is a necessary but insufficient prerequisite for predicting or interpreting the final and intermediate stages of racial and ethnic contact.
Rather, institutional factors are considered in terms of a distinction between two
major types of contact situations: contacts involving subordination of an indigenous population by a migrant group, for example, black-white relations in South
Africa; and contacts involving subordination of a migrant population by an indigenous racial or ethnic group, for example, Japanese migrants to the United States.

After considering the societal issues inherent in racial and ethnic contact, the
distinction developed between migrant and indigenous superordination will be
utilized in examining each of the following dimensions of race relations: political
and economic control, multiple ethnic contacts, conflict and assimilation. The
terms "race" and "ethnic" are used interchangeably.

DIFFERENCES INHERENT IN CONTACT

Most situations of ethnic contact involve at least one indigenous group and at
least one group migrating to the area. The only exception at the initial point in
contact would be the settlement of an uninhabited area by two or more groups. By
"indigenous" is meant not necessarily the aborigines, but rather a population sufficiently established in an area so as to possess the institutions and demographic
capacity for maintaining some minimal form of social order through generations.
Thus a given spatial area may have different indigenous groups through time. For
example, the indigenous population of Australia is presently largely white and
primarily of British origin, although the Tasmanoids and Australoids were once in
possession of the area.[6] A similar racial shift may be observed in the populations
indigenous to the United States.

Restricting discussion to the simplest of contact situations, i.e., involving one
migrant and one established population, we can generally observe sharp differences
in their social organization at the time of contact. The indigenous population has

an established and presumably stable organization prior to the arrival of migrants, i.e., government, economic activities adapted to the environment and the existing techniques of resource utilization, kinship, stratification, and religious systems.[7] On the basis of a long series of migration studies, we may be reasonably certain that the social order of a migrant population's homeland is not wholly transferred to their new settlement.[8] Migrants are required to make at least some institutional adaptations and innovations in view of the presence of an indigenous population, the demographic selectivity of migration, and differences in habitat.

For example, recent post-war migrations from Italy and the Netherlands indicate considerable selectivity in age and sex from the total populations of these countries. Nearly half of 30,000 males leaving the Netherlands in 1955 were between 20 and 39 years of age whereas only one quarter of the male population was of these ages.[9] Similarly, over 40,000 males in this age range accounted for somewhat more than half of Italy's male emigrants in 1951, although they comprise roughly 30 per cent of the male population of Italy.[10] In both countries, male emigrants exceed females in absolute numbers as well as in comparison with the sex ratios of their nation. That these cases are far from extreme can be illustrated with Oriental migration data. In 1920, for example, there were 38,000 foreign-born Chinese adult males in the United States, but only 2,000 females of the same group.[11]

In addition to these demographic shifts, the new physical and biological conditions of existence require the revision and creation of social institutions if the social order known in the old country is to be approximated and if the migrants are to survive. The migration of eastern and southern European peasants around the turn of the century to urban industrial centers of the United States provides a well-documented case of radical changes in occupational pursuit as well as the creation of a number of institutions in response to the new conditions of urban life, e.g., mutual-aid societies, national churches, and financial institutions.

In short, when two populations begin to occupy the same habitat but do not share a single order, each group endeavors to maintain the political and economic conditions that are at least compatible with the institutions existing before contact. These conditions for the maintenance of institutions can not only differ for the two groups in contact, but are often conflicting. European contacts with the American Indian, for example, led to the decimation of the latter's sources of sustenance and disrupted religious and tribal forms of organization. With respect to a population's efforts to maintain its social institutions, we may therefore assume that the presence of another ethnic group is an important part of the environment. Further, if groups in contact differ in their capacity to impose changes on the other group then we may expect to find one group "superordinate" and the other population "subordinate" in maintaining or developing a suitable environment.

It is here that efforts at a single cycle of race and ethnic relations must fail. For it is necessary to introduce a distinction in the nature or form of subordination before attempting to predict whether conflict or relatively harmonious assimilation will develop. As we shall shortly show, the race relations cycle in areas where the migrant group is superordinate and indigenous group subordinate differs sharply from the stages in societies composed of a superordinate indigenous group and subordinate migrants.[12]

POLITICAL AND ECONOMIC CONTROL

Emphasis is placed herein on economic and political dominance since it is assumed that control of these institutions will be instrumental in establishing a suitable milieu for at least the population's own social institutions, e.g., educational, religious, and kinship, as well as control of such major cultural artifacts as language.

Migrant Superordination

When the population migrating to a new contact situation is superior in technology (particularly weapons) and more tightly organized than the indigenous group, the necessary conditions for maintaining the migrants' political and economic institutions are usually imposed on the indigenous population. Warfare, under such circumstances, often occurs early in the contacts between the two groups as the migrants begin to interfere with the natives' established order. There is frequently conflict even if the initial contact was friendly. Price, for example, has observed the following consequences of white invasion and subordination of the indigenous populations of Australia, Canada, New Zealand, and the United States:

> During an opening period of pioneer invasion on moving frontiers the whites decimated the natives with their diseases; occupied their lands by seizure or by pseudo-purchase; slaughtered those who resisted; intensified tribal warfare by supplying white weapons; ridiculed and disrupted native religions, society and culture, and generally reduced the unhappy peoples to a state of despondency under which they neither desired to live, nor to have children to undergo similar conditions.[13]

The numerical decline of indigenous populations after their initial subordination to a migrant group, whether caused by warfare, introduction of venereal and other diseases, or disruption of sustenance activities, has been documented for a number of contact situations in addition to those discussed by Price.[14]

In addition to bringing about these demographic and economic upheavals, the superordinate migrants frequently create political entities that are not at all coterminous with the boundaries existing during the indigenous populations' supremacy prior to contact. For example, the British and Boers in southern Africa carved out political states that included areas previously under the control of separate and often warring groups.[15] Indeed, European alliances with feuding tribes were often used as a fulcrum for the territorial expansion of whites into southern Africa.[16]

The bifurcation of tribes into two nations and the migrations of groups across newly created national boundaries are both consequences of the somewhat arbitrary nature of the political entities created in regions of migrant superordination.[17] This incorporation of diverse indigenous populations into a single territorial unit under the dominance of a migrant group has considerable importance for later developments in this type of racial and ethnic contact.

Indigenous Superordination

When a population migrates to a subordinate position considerably less conflict occurs in the early stages. The movements of many European and Oriental populations to political, economic, and social subordination in the United States were not converted into warfare, nationalism, or long-term conflict. Clearly, the occasional labor and racial strife marking the history of immigration of the United States is not on the same level as the efforts to expel or revolutionize the social order. American Negroes, one of the most persistently subordinated migrant groups in the country, never responded in significant numbers to the encouragement of migration to Liberia. The single important large-scale nationalistic effort, Marcus Garvey's Universal Negro Improvement Association, never actually led to mass emigration of Negroes.[18] By contrast, the indigenous American Indians fought long and hard to preserve control over their habitat.

In interpreting differences in the effects of migrant and indigenous subordination, the migrants must be considered in the context of the options available to the group. Irish migrants to the United States in the 1840s, for example, although clearly subordinate to native whites of other origins, fared better economically than if they had remained in their mother country.[19] Further, the option of returning to the homeland often exists for populations migrating to subordinate situations. Jerome reports that net migration to the United States between the midyears of 1907 and 1923 equaled roughly 65 per cent of gross immigration.[20] This indicates that immigrant dissatisfaction with subordination or other conditions of contact can often be resolved by withdrawal from the area. Recently subordinated indigenous groups, by contrast, are perhaps less apt to leave their habitat so readily.

Finally, when contacts between racial and ethnic groups are under the control of the indigenous population, threats of demographic and institutional imbalance are reduced since the superordinate populations can limit the numbers and groups entering. For example, when Oriental migration to the United States threatened whites, sharp cuts were executed in the quotas.[21] Similar events may be noted with respect to the decline of immigration from the so-called "new" sources of eastern and southern Europe. Whether a group exercises its control over immigration far before it is actually under threat is, of course, not germane to the point that immigrant restriction provides a mechanism whereby potential conflict is prevented.

In summary, groups differ in the conditions necessary for maintaining their respective social orders. In areas where the migrant group is dominant, frequently the indigenous population suffers sharp numerical declines and their economic and political institutions are seriously undermined. Conflict often accompanies the establishment of migrant superordination. Subordinate indigenous populations generally have no alternative location and do not control the numbers of new ethnic populations admitted into their area. By contrast, when the indigenous population dominates the political and economic conditions, the migrant group is introduced into the economy of the indigenous population. Although subordinate in their new habitat, the migrants may fare better than if they remained in their homeland. Hence their subordination occurs without great conflict. In addition, the migrants usually have the option of returning to their homeland and the indigenous population controls the number of new immigrants in the area.

MULTIPLE ETHNIC CONTACTS

Although the introduction of a third major ethnic or racial group frequently occurs in both types of societies distinguished here, there are signifant differences between conditions in habitats under indigenous domination and areas where a migrant population is superordinate. Chinese and Indian migrants, for example, were often welcomed by whites in areas where large indigenous populations were suppressed, but these migrants were restricted in the white mother country. Consideration of the causes and consequences of multi-ethnic contacts is therefore made in terms of the two types of racial and ethnic contact.

Migrant Superordination

In societies where the migrant population is superordinate, it is often necessary to introduce new immigrant groups to fill the niches created in the revised economy of the area. The subordinate indigenous population frequently fails, at first, to participate in the new economic and political order introduced by migrants. For example, because of the numerical decline of Fijians after contact with whites and their unsatisfactory work habits, approximately 60,000 persons migrated from India to the sugar plantations of Fiji under the indenture system between 1879 and 1916.[22] For similar seasons, as well as the demise of slavery, large numbers of Indians were also introduced to such areas of indigenous subordination as Mauritius, British Guiana, Trinidad, and Natal.[23] The descendents of these migrants comprise the largest single ethnic group in several of these areas.

McKenzie, after observing the negligible participation of the subordinate indigenous populations of Alaska, Hawaii, and Malaya in contrast to the large numbers of Chinese, Indian, and other Oriental immigrants, offers the following interpretation:

The indigenous peoples of many of the frontier zones of modern industrial-

ism are surrounded by their own web of culture and their own economic
structure. Consequently they are slow to take part in the new economy
especially as unskilled laborers. It is the individual who is widely removed
from his native habitat that is most adaptable to the conditions imposed
by capitalism in frontier regions. Imported labor cannot so easily escape to
its home village when conditions are distasteful as can the local population.[24]

Similarly, the Indians of the United States played a minor role in the new economic activities introduced by white settlers and, further, were not used successfully
as slaves.[25] Frazier reports that Negro slaves were utilized in the West Indies and
Brazil after unsuccessful efforts to enslave the indigenous Indian populations.[26]
Large numbers of Asiatic Indians were brought to South Africa as indentured
laborers to work in the railways, mines, and plantations introduced by whites.[27]

This migration of workers into areas where the indigenous population was
either unable or insufficient to work in the newly created economic activities was
also marked by a considerable flow back to the home country. For example,
nearly 3.5 million Indians left the Madras Presidency for overseas between 1903
and 1912, but close to 3 million returned during this same period.[28] However, as
we observed earlier, large numbers remained overseas and formed major ethnic
populations in a number of countries. Current difficulties of the ten million
Chinese in Southeast Asia are in large part due to their settlement in societies
where the indigenous populations were subordinate.

Indigenous Superordination

We have observed that in situations of indigenous superordination the call for new
immigrants from other ethnic and racial populations is limited in a manner that
prevents the indigenous group's loss of political and economic control. Under such
conditions, no single different ethnic or racial population is sufficiently large in
number or strength to challenge the supremacy of the indigenous population.

After whites attained dominance in Hawaii, that land provided a classic case
of the substitution of one ethnic group after another during a period when large
numbers of immigrants were needed for the newly created and expanding plantation economy. According to Lind, the shifts from Chinese to Japanese and Portuguese immigrants and the later shifts to Puerto Rican, Korean, Spanish, Russian,
and Philippine sources for the plantation laborers were due to conscious efforts to
prevent any single group from obtaining too much power.[29] Similarly, the exclusion of Chinese from the United States mainland stimulated the migration of the
Japanese and, in turn, the later exclusion of Japanese led to increased migration
from Mexico.[30]

In brief, groups migrating to situations of multiple ethnic contact are thus
subordinate in both types of contact situations. However, in societies where whites
are superordinate but do not settle as an indigenous population, other racial and
ethnic groups are admitted in large numbers and largely in accordance with economic needs of the revised economy of the habitat. By contrast, when a dominant

migrant group later becomes indigenous, in the sense that the area becomes one of permanent settlement through generations for the group, migrant populations from new racial and ethnic stocks are restricted in number and source.

CONFLICT AND ASSIMILATION

From a comparison of the surge of racial nationalism and open warfare in parts of Africa and Asia or the retreat of superordinate migrants from the former Dutch East Indies and French Indo-China, on the one hand, with the fusion of populations in many nations of western Europe or the "cultural pluralism" of the United States and Switzerland, on the other, one must conclude that neither conflict nor assimilation is an inevitable outcome of racial and ethnic contact. Our distinction, however, between two classes of race and ethnic relations is directly relevant to consideration of which of these alternatives different populations in contact will take. In societies where the indigenous population at the initial contact is subordinate, warfare and nationalism often—although not always—develop later in the cycle of relations. By contrast, relations between migrants and indigenous populations that are subordinate and superordinate, respectively, are generally without long-term conflict.

Migrant Superordination

Through time, the subordinated indigenous population begins to participate in the economy introduced by the migrant group and, frequently, a concomitant disruption of previous forms of social and economic organization takes place. This, in turn, has significant implications for the development of both nationalism and a greater sense of racial unity. In many African states, where Negroes were subdivided into ethnic groups prior to contact with whites, the racial unity of the African was created by the occupation of their habitat by white invaders.[31] The categorical subordination of Africans by whites as well as the dissolution and decay of previous tribal and ethnic forms of organization are responsible for the creation of racial consciousness among the indigenous populations.[32] As the indigenous group becomes increasingly incorporated within the larger system, both the saliency of their subordinate position and its significance increase. No alternative exists for the bulk of the native population other than the destruction or revision of the institutions of political, economic, and social subordination.

Further, it appears that considerable conflict occurs in those areas where the migrants are not simply superordinate, but where they themselves have also become, in a sense, indigenous by maintaining an established population through generations. In Table 1, for example, one can observe how sharply the white populations of Algeria and the Union of South Africa differ from those in nine other African countries with respect to the percent born in the country of settlement. Thus, two among the eleven African countries for which such data were

TABLE 1

Nativity of the White Populations of Selected African Countries, Circa 1950

Country	Per Cent of Whites Born in Country
Algeria	79.8
Basutoland	37.4
Bechuanaland	39.5
Morocco[a]	37.1[c]
Northern Rhodesia	17.7
Southern Rhodesia	31.5
South West Africa[b]	45.1
Swaziland	41.2
Tanganyika	47.6
Uganda	43.8
Union of South Africa	89.7

Source: United Nations, *Demographic Yearbook,* 1956, Table 5.
Note: Other non-indigenous groups included when necessary breakdown by race is not given.
[a]Former French zone.
[b]Excluding Walvis Bay.
[c]Persons born in former Spanish zone or in Tangier are included as native.

available[33] are outstanding with respect to both racial turmoil and the high proportion of whites born in the country. To be sure, other factors operate to influence the nature of racial and ethnic relations. However, these data strongly support our suggestions with respect to the significance of differences between indigenous and migrant forms of contact. Thus, where the migrant population becomes established in the new area, it is all the more difficult for the indigenous subordinate group to change the social order.

Additionally, where the formerly subordinate indigenous population has become dominant through the expulsion of the superordinate group, the situation faced by nationalities introduced to the area under earlier conditions of migrant superordination changes radically. For example, as we noted earlier, Chinese were welcomed in many parts of Southeast Asia where the newly subordinated indigenous populations were unable or unwilling to fill the economic niches created by the white invaders. However, after whites were expelled and the indigenous population obtained political mastery, the gates to further Chinese immigration were fairly well closed and there has been increasing interference with the Chinese already present. In Indonesia, where Chinese immigration had been encouraged under Dutch domain, the newly created indigenous government allows only token immigration and has formulated a series of laws and measures designed to interfere with and reduce Chinese commercial activities.[34] Thompson and Adloff observe that

> since the war, the Chinese have been subjected to increasingly restrictive
> measures throughout Southeast Asia, but the severity and effectiveness of

these has varied with the degree to which the native nationalists are in control of their countries and feel their national existence threatened by the Chinese.[35]

Indigenous Superordination

By contrast, difficulties between subordinate migrants and an already dominant indigenous population occur within the context of a consenual form of government, economy, and social institutions. However confused and uncertain may be the concept of assimilation and its application in operational terms,[36] it is important to note that assimilation is essentially a very different phenomenon in the two types of societies distinguished here.

Where populations migrate to situations of subordination, the issue has generally been with respect to the migrants' capacity and willingness to become an integral part of the on-going social order. For example, this has largely been the case in the United States where the issue of "new" vs. "old" immigrant groups hinged on the alleged inferiorities of the former.[37] The occasional flurries of violence under this form of contact have been generally initiated by the dominant indigenous group and with respect to such threats against the social order as the cheap labor competition of Orientals in the west coast,[38] the nativist fears of Irish Catholic political domination of Boston in the nineteenth century,[39] or the desecration of sacred principles by Mexican "zoot-suiters" in Los Angeles.[40]

The conditions faced by subordinate migrants in Australia and Canada after the creation of indigenous white societies in these areas are similar to that of the United States; that is, limited and sporadic conflict, and great emphasis on the assimilation of migrants. Striking and significant contrasts to the general pattern of subordinate immigrant assimilation in these societies, however, are provided by the differences between the assimilation of Italian and German immigrants in Australia as well as the position of French Canadians in eastern Canada.

French Canadians have maintained their language and other major cultural and social attributes whereas nineteenth and twentieth century immigrants are in the process of merging into the predominantly English-speaking Canadian society. Although broader problems of territorial segregation are involved,[41] the critical difference between French Canadians and later groups is that the former had an established society in the new habitat prior to the British conquest of Canada and were thus largely able to maintain their social and cultural unity without significant additional migration from France.[42]

Similarly, in finding twentieth-century Italian immigrants in Australia more prone to cultural assimilation than were German migrants to that nation in the 1800's, Borrie emphasized the fact that Italian migration occurred after Australia had become an independent nation-state. By contrast, Germans settled in what was a pioneer colony without an established general social order and institutions. Thus, for example, Italian children were required to attend Australian schools and learn English, whereas the German immigrants were forced to establish their own educational program.[43]

Thus the consequences of racial and ethnic contact may also be examined in terms of the two types of superordinate-subordinate contact situations considered. For the most part, subordinate migrants appear to be more rapidly assimilated than are subordinate indigenous populations. Further, the subordinate migrant group is generally under greater pressure to assimilate, at least in the gross sense of "assimilation" such as language, than are subordinate indigenous populations. In addition, warfare or racial nationalism—when it does occur—tends to be in societies where the indigenous population is subordinate. If the indigenous movement succeeds, the economic and political position of racial and ethnic populations introduced to the area under migrant dominance may become tenuous.

A FINAL NOTE

It is suggested that interest be revived in the conditions accounting for societal variations in the process of relations between racial and ethnic groups. A societal theory of race relations, based on the migrant-indigenous and superordinate-subordinate distinctions developed above, has been found to offer an orderly interpretation of differences in the nature of race and ethnic relations in the contact situations considered. Since, however, systematic empirical investigation provides a far more rigorous test of the theory's merits and limitations, comparative cross-societal studies are needed.

NOTES

1. Robert E. Park, *Race and Culture* (Glencoe, Ill.: The Free Press), 1950, p.150.
2. For example, Emory S. Bogardus, "A Race-Relations Cycle," *American Journal of Sociology*, 35 (January, 1930), pp. 612–617; W. O. Brown, "Culture Contact and Race Conflict" in E. B. Reuter, editor, *Race and Culture Contacts* (New York: McGraw-Hill, 1934), pp. 34–47; E. Franklin Frazier, *Race and Culture Contacts in the Modern World* (New York: Alfred A. Knopf, 1957), pp. 32 ff.; Clarence E. Glick, "Social Roles and Types in Race Relations" in Andrew W. Lind, editor, *Race Relations in World Perspective* (Honolulu: University of Hawaii Press), 1955, pp. 243–262; Edward Nelson Palmer, "Culture Contacts and Population Growth" in Joseph J. Spengler and Otis Dudley Duncan, editors, *Population Theory and Policy* (Glencoe, Ill.: The Free Press), 1956, pp. 410–415; A. Grenfell Price, *White Settlers and Native Peoples*, Melbourne: Georgian House, 1950. For summaries of several of these cycles, see Brewton Berry, *Race and Ethnic Relations* (Boston: Houghton Mifflin, 1958), Chapter 6.
3. Bogardus, *op. cit.*, p. 612.
4. Price, *op. cit.*
5. Intra-urban stages of contact are not considered here.
6. Price, *op. cit.*, chaps. 6 and 7.
7. Glick, *op. cit.*, p. 244.
8. See, for example, Brinley Thomas, "International Migration" in Philip M. Hauser and Otis Dudley Duncan, editors, *The Study of Population* (Chicago: University of Chicago Press, 1959), pp. 523–526.

9. United Nations, *Demographic Yearbook* (1957), pp. 147, 645.
10. United Nations, *Demographic Yearbook* (1954), pp. 131, 669.
11. R. D. McKenzie, *Oriental Exclusion* (Chicago: University of Chicago Press, 1928), p. 83.
12. See, for example, Reuter's distinction between two types of direct contact in E. B. Reuter, editor, *op. cit.*, pp. 4–7.
13. Price, *op. cit.*, p. 1.
14. Stephen Roberts, *Population Problems of the Pacific* (London: George Routledge & Sons, 1927).
15. John A. Barnes, "Race Relations in the Development of Southern Africa" in Lind, editor, *op. cit.*
16. *Ibid.*
17. Witness the current controversies between tribes in the newly created Congo Republic. Also, for a list of tribes living on both sides of the border of the Republic of Sudan, see Karol Józef Krótki, "Demographic Survey of Sudan" in *The Population of Sudan*, report on the sixth annual conference (Khartoum: Philosophical Society of Sudan, 1958), p. 35.
18. John Hope Franklin, *From Slavery to Freedom*, second edition (New York: Alfred Knopf, 1956), pp. 234–238, 481–483.
19. Oscar Handlin, *Boston's Immigrants*, revised edition (Cambridge, Mass.: The Belknap Press of Harvard University Press, 1959), Chap. 2.
20. Harry Jerome, *Migration and Business Cycles* (New York: National Bureau of Economic Research, 1926), pp. 43–44.
21. See, George Eaton Simpson and J. Milton Yinger, *Racial and Cultural Minorities*, revised edition (New York: Harper & Brothers, 1958), pp. 126–132.
22. K. L. Gillion, "The Sources of Indian Emigration to Fiji," *Population Studies*, 10 (November 1956), p. 139; I. M. Cumpston, "A Survey of Indian Immigration to British Tropical Colonies to 1910," *ibid.*, pp. 158–159.
23. Cumpston, *op. cit.*, pp. 158–165.
24. R. D. McKenzie, "Cultural and Racial Differences as Bases of Human Symbiosis" in Kimball Young, editor, *Social Attitudes* (New York: Henry Holt, 1931), p. 157.
25. Franklin, *op. cit.*, p. 47.
26. Frazier, *op. cit.*, pp. 107–108.
27. Leo Kuper, Hilstan Watts, and Ronald Davies, *Durban: A Study in Racial Ecology* (London: Jonathan Cape, 1958), p. 25.
28. Gillion, *op. cit.*, p. 149.
29. Andrew W. Lind, *An Island Community* (Chicago: University of Chicago Press, 1938), pp. 218–229.
30. McKenzie, *Oriental Exclusion, op. cit.*, p. 181.
31. For a discussion of territorial and tribal movements, see James S. Coleman, "Current Political Movements in Africa," *The Annals of the American Academy of Political and Social Science*, 298 (March 1955), pp. 95–108.
32. For a broader discussion of emergent nationalism, see, Thomas Hodgkin, *Nationalism in Colonial Africa* (New York: New York University Press, 1957); Everett C. Hughes, "New Peoples" in Lind, editor, *op. cit.*, pp. 95–115.
33. United Nations, *Demographic Yearbook*, 1956, Table 5.
34. B. H. M. Vlekke, *Indonesia in 1956* (The Hague: Netherlands Institute of International Affairs, 1957), p. 88.
35. Virginia Thompson and Richard Adloff, *Minority Problems in Southeast Asia* (Stanford, Calif.: Stanford University Press, 1955), p. 3.
36. See, for example, International Union for the Scientific Study of Population, "Cultural Assimilation of Immigrants," *Population Studies*, supplement, March 1950.
37. Oscar Handlin, *Race and Nationality in American Life* (Garden City, N. Y.: Doubleday Anchor Books, 1957), Chap. 5.

38. Simpson and Yinger, *op. cit.*

39. Oscar Handlin, *Boston's Immigrants, op. cit.,* Chap. 7.

40. Ralph Turner and Samuel J. Surace, "Zoot-Suiters and Mexicans: Symbols in Crowd Behavior," *American Journal of Sociology,* 62 (July 1956), pp. 14–20.

41. It is, however, suggestive to consider whether the isolated settlement of an area by a racial, religious, or ethnic group would be permitted in other than frontier conditions. Consider, for example, the difficulties faced by Mormons until they reached Utah.

42. See Everett C. Hughes, *French Canada in Transition* (Chicago: University of Chicago Press, 1943).

43. W. D. Borrie assisted by D. R. G. Packer, *Italians and Germans in Australia* (Melbourne: F. W. Cheshire, 1954), *passim.*

9   Paternalistic versus Competitive Race Relations: An Ideal-Type Approach

Pierre van den Berghe

Our general contention is that manifestations of racial prejudice have historically polarized around two ideal-types which we shall call *paternalistic* and *competitive.* The choice of labels is always a difficult one. Rather than use arbitrary symbols and thereby hinder readability, we adopted two words which are in some way descriptive of our two types. Obviously the common-sense meanings of the labels do not exhaust the content of the two types.[1]

THE PATERNALISTIC TYPE: ITS CHARACTERISTICS

The paternalistic type is incompatible with a complex manufacturing economy and with large-scale industrial capitalism. The most congenial form of economy is agricultural, pastoral, or handicraft. Mercantile capitalism and a large-scale plantation agriculture geared to the export of staple products (cotton, coffee, rubber, sugar, and the like) are also compatible with the paternalistic type. This type of economy coincides with an "intermediate" level of differentiation in the division of labor. By "intermediate" is meant here a degree of specialization which has gone considerably beyond a "primitive" division of labor based primarily on sex and age criteria, and yet which is not as complex as in the case of large-scale manufacturing industry.

Typically, in this intermediate stage of the division of labor, the mass of the

From Chapter 1, "Paternalistic versus Competitive Race Relations: An Ideal-Type Approach," in *Race and Ethnicity: Essays in Comparative Sociology,* by Pierre L. van den Berghe, © 1970 by Basic Books, Inc.

labor force still consists of a fairly unspecialized, servile, or quasi-servile peasantry. But there is already considerable differentiation. Handicraft production is in the hands of full-time specialized artisans. Trading is concentrated in the hands of a merchant class, though the latter is often not very powerful. A rudimentary professional specialization is present. Warriors, priests, judges, and officials constitute the ruling group. This intermediate stage corresponds to what Weber called the "traditional" type of authority and is exemplified by most large-scale premodern societies. This stage implies both urbanization and fairly advanced social stratification. In paternalistic interracial situations with which we are concerned, the division of labor is along racial lines. A servile or quasi-servile racial caste (serfs, slaves, indentured laborers, "recruited" labor, *peones,* and so on) performs the heavy manual labor, in particular the agricultural tasks.[2]

The dominant upper caste confines itself to such occupations as war, the priesthood, the professions, government, supervision of labor, and commerce. The upper caste is, in fact, a ruling aristocracy, usually a small minority of the total population. This ruling caste is fairly homogeneous in social status. Class distinctions within the ruling caste are secondary to the paramount caste distinctions between the racial groups.[3]

A wide and unbreachable gap exists between the castes, as indicated by living standards, income, occupations, education, death rates, for example. There is a horizontal color bar with no intercaste mobility. Intracaste mobility is possible but limited, as there is little status differentiation within the castes. A slave can be manumitted, or gain a privileged position as house servant, skilled craftsman, foreman, but he remains in a subordinate position. Spatial mobility is also limited: serfs are attached to the land, slaves and servants to their masters. Such a non-mobile labor is clearly incompatible with large-scale industry, which requires a flexible allocation of resources.

The form of government found in paternalistic society is aristocratic or oligarchic. Autocratic authority of Weber's traditional type prevails, either in a centralized form as in colonial governments or in a decentralized feudal form. The legal system is on the side of the racial status quo. The lower caste has a clearly defined legal status which entails both rights and obligations, though the latter are often more numerous than the former. Nevertheless, the lower caste is protected under law and punished within the framework of the law.

Paternalistic attitudes and stereotypes are well integrated in the value system of the society. Elaborate sets of rationalizations come to the defense of the racial status quo and are subjectively, if not logically, consistent with the basic religious and ethical premises of the society. Examples of such rationalizations are the "white man's burden" theory, the "civilizing mission of the West," the "Christianizing of the heathen," among others. In short, there is no ideological conflict between the existing norms of prejudice and the basic value system of the society.

Racial rules and statuses are sharply defined. An elaborate and rigid etiquette of race relations stabilizes the master-servant relationship. Indeed, etiquette seems to be the primary mechanism of social control to maintain intimacy of contact coupled with status inequality.[4] To borrow Talcott Parsons' pattern variables, roles are based on ascription, particularism, diffuseness, collectivity orientation, and affectivity.

Spatial segregation is minimal because the wide status gap allows close but unequal contact. In other words, spatial distance can be thought of as an alternative mechanism of social control to status distance. Slaves and servants live in close intimacy with their masters, particularly household servants. Although caste endogamy (prohibition of intermarriage) is rigidly adhered to, miscegenation between upper-caste males and lower-caste females is condoned and frequent. It takes the form of institutionalized concubinage and is accepted at all class levels in the upper caste. Wealthy masters interbreed freely with their female slaves without any opprobrium or fear of censure. This miscegenation leads to the rise of a group of half-breeds who generally remain in the lower caste but with privileged status. The half-breeds may, by intermarriage among themselves, constitute an intermediate caste of their own. Some half-breeds do, of course, become assimilated to the upper caste through "passing," and when interbreeding has been extensive for several generations, the racial caste system may eventually break down. Such complete interbreeding has only rarely taken place wherever physical characteristics of the groups in presence were widely different. The closest approximation to it is the "color continuum" situation which prevails in Haiti, Mexico, or, to a somewhat lesser extent, Brazil.

Generally speaking, race relations in the paternalistic type are stable. The lower caste is "accommodated" to its inferior status, which it may even internalize. What Dollard has called "white folks' manner," and Kardiner and Ovesey, the "mark of oppression" are illustrations of such internalized subservient status.[5] To use the southern United States phraseology, the "old time darky knows his place." The converse of accommodation on the part of the lower caste is paternalism on the part of the upper caste. The upper caste adopts an attitude of benevolent despotism toward members of the lower caste, whom it treats as perpetual children. Stereotypes of members of the lower caste describe them as immature, exuberant, impulsive, uninhibited, lazy, fun-loving, good-humored, happy-go-lucky. In short, they are inferior by lovable. They ought to be treated sternly and kindly at the same time. Corporal punishment is to be used as one uses it to keep one's own children in line.

This paternalistic prejudice might also be described as pseudo-tolerance. The slave, or servant, is acceptable "in his place," even "loved" in a condescending way. It should be fairly apparent that this paternalistic syndrome bears little relation to "authoritarianism" of "high F." The psychological characteristics of the bigot which have come out of research in the United States are, we think, more typical of a competitive situation when the ethos of the culture is opposed to prejudice. This is not to say that no high F's will be found in a paternalistic situation, but rather that in a paternalistic society the authoritarian syndrome will not be a good predictor of racial attitudes, opinions, and behavior. It would also be a misunderstanding of our position to interpret us as saying that psychological variables are not operative in the paternalistic type of prejudice. In fact, we suspect that there might be a corresponding psychological syndrome in the paternalistic type. Roger Bastide, a psychoanalytically oriented social scientist, has suggested that paternalistic master-servant relationships are an extension of the nuclear family situation.[6] He suggests an ambivalent oedipal relationship between master and slave in the plantation situation and an incest taboo between white mistress and male slaves. We are not equipped to pass judgment on such interpretations. But although our own primary theoretical focus is sociological, we do not deny the operation of psychological factors or the existence of individual differences in the paternalistic situation.

An important note of caution should be added here. The romantic myth of the kindly master who led an existence of genteel leisure on his plantation amid the happy singing of his slaves should, of course, be dismissed. Violence and aggression do occur in the paternalistic type. But they take different forms than in the competitive case. They generally originate from the lower caste and are not directly and specifically racial in character. Slave rebellions and nationalistic, revivalistic, or messianistic movements are typical of the paternalistic type and indicate a lack of complete integration of the society. Such movements are usually repressed with utmost vigor by the upper caste, because if they are allowed to develop, they tend to lead to a violent and cataclysmic overthrow of the "old regime," as exemplified by the Haitian revolution.

Generally speaking, however, the paternalistic type of prejudice can be said to be "adjustive," "functional," or "integrative" for the social system. This statement implies, of course, no value judgment. We simply mean that, barring external influences and other disruptive factors such as industrialization, the more the racial ideology is believed in and practiced in a paternalistic society, the more integrated and stable the social system is. In other words, the more the hierarchal norms have been internalized in the personalities of both upper- and lower-caste members, the greater the stability of the social system, everthing else remaining constant. But this inherent stability of the paternalistic type is accompanied by inherent inflexibility and inadaptability; that is, when the system is attacked from the outside, as is colonialism today, or when internal developments such as industrialization are incompatible with paternalism, the whole social system collapses altogether or evolves into a competitive situation.

Examples of the paternalistic type of racial prejudice are the slave plantation regimes of the ante-bellum United States South, of the West Indies, of Brazil; the encomienda or hacienda system in various parts of Spanish America; the colonial regimes of the various European powers in Africa, some of which, such as the former Belgian Congo, have survived in fairly pure form to the recent past. All the preceding examples were taken from Western societies because the cases are more familiar. But paternalism is not limited to Western societies. In Ruanda-Urundi (Central Africa), for example, the Watuzi, a group of pastoralists famous for their tall stature, have imposed their domination over an overwhelming majority of shorter and physically quite distinguishable Bahutu. The latter, who were already tillers of land before the Watuzi conquest, have become the serfs of the Watuzi; the situation is typically paternalistic.

Likewise, paternalism as a type of relationship is not limited to interracial situations, as we shall see later.

THE COMPETITIVE TYPE: ITS CHARACTERISTICS

In our ideal-type dichotomy, the competitive type is the polar opposite of the paternalistic type. Generally, the competitive type is found in the large-scale manufacturing economy based on industrial capitalism. However, competitive prejudice has existed in preindustrial societies. The case of the Jews in medieval Europe, though not racial according to our definition of the word, was competitive. The problem whether the competitive type is linked with capitalism, as a Marxist might contend, is not easy to settle empirically. Ethnic relations in the Soviet Union and Soviet policies toward the "nationalities" are not easy to investigate. However, the USSR has known waves of anti-Semitism indicative of competive prejudice. At any rate, urbanization seems a prerequisite for a competitive situation, and, empirically, the latter is very much associated with an industrial and capitalistic society.

The division of labor is complex and based on rational and universalistic criteria as required by a differentiated manufacturing economy. The bulk of the labor force is no longer unskilled, and technical competence and efficiency become paramount criteria of selection. Hence any rigid racial division of labor based on ascription and particularism cannot be maintained without entailing serious economic dysfunctions. Racial criteria of selection are not altogether absent, however. Indeed, they can be operative, due to prejudice, but they can be maintained only at a cost to the efficiency of the system of production, and the tendency is toward a breakdown of the industrial color bar. As a corollary of the factors above, there is much mobility, both social and spatial. Any complex industrial economy based on "organic solidarity" requires a spatially and socially mobile labor force; one that is responsive to the demand for labor and skills. Again, social mobility is hampered by racial prejudice, but only at a cost to the production system, and the tendency is toward *"la carrière ouverte aux talents."*

In typical form, the competitive situation is accompanied by a caste system, but the distance between the castes in education, occupation, income, living standards, death rates, and so on, tends to diminish; that is, the color bar tends to tilt from a horizontal to a vertical position, though the vertical position has never been fully achieved. Within each color caste, there is more and more class differentiation. In other words, the status gap *between* castes tends to diminish and the status range *within* the castes tends to increase. With the tilting of the color bar, an upper-class lower-caste person may have a higher education, occupation, living standard, and the like, than a lower-class upper-caste person. Hence, there often comes about a status panic of lower-class persons from the upper caste, who feel threatened by rising lower-caste members as soon as class status and caste status cease to have a one-to-one correspondence. Though threat to status is probably not the whole story, it goes a long way to account for the higher virulence of competitive prejudice among poor whites in the United States, for example.

The dominant caste, in the competitive situation, is usually a majority which has within itself great status and class differences. The upper caste is not a homogeneous ruling group, as in the paternalistic case. On the contrary, a large segment of the upper caste engages in manual labor and hence is in direct competition with members of the lower caste. The sheer numerical ratio between the castes makes this situation inevitable. A certain percentage of the population must engage in manual occupations, and only a minority can be "on top."

In some interracial situations where miscegenation has been so extensive as to blur physical distinctions, and where the criteria of group membership are at least partly cultural rather than purely racial, the rigid color-caste system has broken down in part. This has been the case to some extent in most of Latin America. In Mexico, for example, a mestizo or Ladino can be a full-blooded Indian, provided he speaks fluent Spanish and is acculturated to Hispanic ways. But that still does not make him a "Spaniard." Prejudice is still present, though it is a mixture of ethnic and racial prejudice, and a quasi-caste system exists, though in much less rigid form than in the United States.

The competitive type is usually accompanied by ideological conflict, at least in a Western, "Christian," "democratic," and "liberal" sort of society. This conflict was the central core of Myrdal's analysis of the United States' situation.[7] Whether the ideological conflict is simply a superstructural reflection of the more basic incompatibility between the production system and prejudice, as the Marxist line of argument would run, is an open question, and one which cannot easily be settled empirically.

The form of government found in a competitive situation is generally a restricted or partial democracy from which the lower caste is excluded by various means and to a greater or lesser degree. The lower caste has generally no definite legal status. Discriminatory legislation can be passed, but usually without explicitly mentioning race as the basis of exclusion. Devious devices such as poll taxes, rezoning, and the like are used. Extralegal sanctions against the minority are resorted to, such as lynching in the southern United States. The law generally is on the side of the general value system of the society and hence opposed to the prejudice norms. In terms of Max Weber's typology, the form of authority found in the competitive type is "rational-legal."

Racial roles and statutes are ill defined and in a constant state of flux. In terms of Parsons' pattern variables, they are based on achievement, universalism, specificity, self-orientation, and affective neutrality. There is no elaborate etiquette. Rather, members of the lower caste are in constant doubt as to the behavior expected from them. Conversely, members of the upper caste are in constant difficulty as to how to address educated lower-caste members, for example. The old etiquette is no longer applicable, and no new one has been evolved.

Unequal caste status is constantly assailed by the leveling forces discussed above. Since etiquette has broken down as a mechanism to maintain intimate unequal contacts, spatial segregation is resorted to in order to minimize interracial contacts which threaten to become equal and which are replete with uneasiness, ambiguity, and tension because of mutual prejudices.[8] Suspicion, hatred, antagonism prevail between the racial groups. Competition, real or imaginary, for status, for jobs, for women, or the threat of competition, poisons race relations. Miscegenation is severely condemned and infrequent. If it takes place at all, it will assume the form of transitory or commercialized contacts between the finge members of both castes (as between poor whites and Negro prostitutes in the United States). Lasting concubinage is not institutionalized. A few cases of intermarriage will occur, at the cost of much disapproval, and usually among fringe groups (such as artists, bohemians, political radicals, low-class white immigrants).

Forms of aggression are numerous and originate both from the upper and from the lower caste. The basis of such aggression involves specifically racial issues. Besides the more violent manifestations of prejudice, such as sabotage, bombing, lynchings, race riots, and pogroms, other forms of resistance and antagonism are organized mass protests, strikes, passive resistance, and the like. The lower caste often seems to turn also to in-group aggression as a response to frustration. Typical of the competitive situation is a recurrent pattern of increase and decrease in prejudice which is in contrast with the relatively stable level of prejudice in the paternalistic case. In the competitive case, prejudice against groups seems to build up to a point of dangerous tension in response to such conditions as rapid influx of lower-caste migrants or rising unemployment. The slightest incident will then trigger off interracial violence. Such a gradual building up of tension seems to precede most race riots, pogroms, waves of terrorism, and the like.

Naturally, competitive prejudice, irrespective of these cyclical trends, can operate at an average level which is lower in one society than in another (anti-Semitism is stronger in Germany than in France, but still there has been a Dreyfus affair in France. Anti-Negro prejudice is stronger in the United States than in Brazil, but is far from absent in the latter country).

Stereotypes held about the lower caste are colored by fear. Lower-caste members are held to be aggressive, "uppity," insolent, oversexed, dirty. In short, they are despicable and dangerous as well as inferior. Clearly, stereotypes and prejudice are reciprocal. Lower-caste members describe upper-caste members as overbearing, bullying, brutal.

It appears that competitive prejudice is linked with authoritarian personality variables in members of the upper caste. This relationship is probably even closer when the values of total society are opposed to prejudice. In the United States, this aspect of prejudice has been widely studied, and the link between competitive prejudice and sexuality, sadism, anality, and so on, has been established. Scapegoating and frustration-aggression are clearly not complete explanations of prejudice even at the psychological level, but the relevance of these psychological mechanisms is beyond question. One may speak of a personality "need," or, as Allport puts it, of the "functional significance" of prejudice for the high F's.[9] It is still an open question how this relationship between authoritarianism and competitive prejudice holds when the values of the society are not openly against prejudice. Fragmentary evidence from the southern United States suggests, however, that the relationship becomes lesser. In other words, conformity to prejudicial norms in the southern United States accounts for a good deal of anti-Negro prejudice.[10]

One point stands out clearly from our description of competitive prejudice; it is a highly maladjusting or dysfunctional phenomenon in an industrial society. Again, no value judgment is implied. Not for a moment would we assert that the paternalistic type is any "better." By "maladjusting" we mean that the higher the level of competitive prejudice is, the less smoothly the social system will operate. Competitive prejudice, then, is a luxury which can be bought only at a price.

The reason for this built-in maladjustive factor in competitive prejudice lies primarily, we think, in the functional prerequisites of an industrial society which conflict with prejudicial norms. Mobility of labor and rationality of recruitment based on achievement and universalism are all in conflict with racial prejudice which is ascriptive and particularistic. Competitive prejudice finds itself in the inherently paradoxical position of operating both within a rational-legal system and against it.

Some empirical examples of competitive types of prejudice are the anti-Negro prejudice in the United States since the Civil War, the anti-Asiatic prejudice in California, anti-Semitism in Europe and the United States, anti-non-European prejudice in South Africa in recent years, and anti-Negro prejudice in Brazil, at least in the large industrial centers such as São Paulo, Santos, and Rio de Janeiro.

THE TWO TYPES OF PREJUDICE:
A SUMMARY AND ANALYTICAL SCHEMA

Such a broad description of the two types of prejudice as we have presented is rather unmanageable for analytical purposes. We shall now attempt to isolate the main variables, classify them for purposes of analysis, and present a schema contrasting the two types side by side to ensure that they do indeed constitute polar opposites and differ on the same dimensions.

We propose to classify the main variables of analysis into dependent, independent, and social control variables. Since these terms call to mind the experimental model, we should immediately emphasize that we are using them, for lack of better words, only in an analogical manner, not in a strict experimental sense. As variables interact, the words dependent and independent are interchangeable. In the present context, they are only meant to clarify the starting point of our analysis and to disentangle somewhat the relationship between variables.

TABLE 1

	Paternalistic	*Competitive*
	A. Independent Variables	
1. Economy	Nonmanufacturing, agricultural, pastoral, handicraft; mercantile capitalism; plantation economy.	Typically manufacturing, but not necessarily so. Large-scale industrial capitalism.
2. Division of labor	Simple (primitive) or intermediate (as in preindustrial large-scale societies). Division of labor along racial lines. Wide income gap between racial groups.	Complex (manufacturing) according to rational universalistic criteria. Narrow gap in wages. No longer strictly racial.
3. Mobility	Little mobility either vertical or horizontal (slaves, servants, or serfs "attached" in space).	Much mobility both vertical and horizontal (required by industrial economy).
4. Social stratification	Caste system with horizontal color bar. Aristocracy vs. servile caste with wide gap in living standards (as indexed by income, education, death and birth rates). Homogeneous upper caste.	Caste system but with tendency for color bar to tilt to vertical position. Complex stratification into classes within castes. Narrower gaps *between* castes and greater range *within* castes.
5. Numerical ratio	Dominant group a small minority.	Dominant group a majority.
6. Value conflict	Integrated value system. No ideological conflict.	Conflict at least in Western, Christian, democratic, liberal type of society.
	B. Dependent Variables	
1. Race relations	Accommodation. Everyone in his place and "knows it." Paternalism. Benevolent despotism.	Antagonism. Suspicion, hatred. Competitiveness (real or imaginary).
2. Roles and statuses	Sharply defined roles and statuses based on ascription, particularism, diffuseness, collectivity orientation, affectivity. Unequal status unthreatened.	Ill defined and based on achievement, universalism, specificity, self-orientation, affective neutrality. Unequal status threatened.
3. Etiquette	Elaborate and definite.	Simple and indefinite.
4. Forms of aggression	Generally from lower caste: slave rebellions, nationalistic, revivalistic, or messianistic movements. Not directly racial. "Righteous" punishment from the master.	Both from upper and lower caste. More frequent and directly racial: riots, lynchings, pogroms. Passive resistance, sabotage, organized mass protests.
5. Miscegenation	Condoned and frequent between upper-caste males and lower-caste females. Institutionalized concubinage.	Severely condemned and infrequent.

(continued)

TABLE 1 continued

	Paternalistic	*Competitive*
6. Segregation	Little of it. Status gap allows close but unequal contact.	Much of it. Narrowing of status gap makes for increase of spatial gap.
7. Psychological syndrome	Internalized subservient status. No personality "need" for prejudice. No high F. Pseudo-tolerance.	"Need" for prejudice. High F. Linked with sexuality, sadism, frustration. Scapegoating.
8. Stereotypes of lower caste	Childish, immature, exuberant, uninhibited, lazy, impulsive, fun-loving, good-humored. Inferior but lovable.	Aggressive, uppity, insolent, oversexed, dirty. Inferior, despicable, and dangerous.
9. Intensity of prejudice.	Fairly constant.	Variable, and sensitive to provocative situations.
C. Social Control Variables		
1. Form of government	Aristocratic, oligarchic, autocratic. Either centralized or feudal. Colonial.	Restricted or partial democracy.
2. Legal system	Lower cast has separate legal status. Law on side of racial status quo. Weber's traditional type of authority.	Lower caste has no separate legal status. Resort to extralegal sanctions. Weber's rational-legal type of authority.

We shall call "dependent variables" those that are directly concerned with race relations and prejudice, such as stereotypes, patterns of segregation, psychological syndromes, for instance. They are the variables which we shall attempt to "predict" ex post facto from the independent variables. The latter are broader social structure variables—the social framework in which prejudice expresses itself. They are the type of economy, the division of labor, the social stratification, and so on. Lest we be accused of economic, sociological, or some other form of determinism, we must again emphasize that the primacy we give to these independent variables is strictly heuristic and in no way precludes reciprocal causation.

A third set of variables we shall call "social control" variables, though we depart again from the strict experimental model. By "social control" we mean here deliberate attempts to modify, restore, or preserve an existent set of social conditions. This set of variables includes primarily governmental action in its executive, legislative, and judicial forms.

Table 1 presents the schema.

THE TWO TYPES OF PREJUDICE IN RELATION TO OTHER THEORETICAL SCHEMES

We have already indicated explicitly our borrowings from Parsons and from Weber. Weber's traditional type of authority tends to coincide with our paternalistic type of prejudice, whereas his rational-legal type of authority both coincides and conflicts with competitive prejudice. Weber's third type of authority, the charismatic one, is unstable and rarely found in a pure state. Insofar as charisma is revolutionary and unstable, it is incompatible with our paternalistic type. An example of competitive prejudice under a system which had strong charismatic elements is anti-Semitism under National Socialism in Germany. But anti-Semitism was already present in the rational-legal Germany of pre-Hitler days. Hence, charisma and the competitive type are not incompatible, but the relationship is not a necessary one.

In our use of Parsons' pattern variables, we have seen that they polarized along our two types. The pattern variables are conceived of by Parsons as being *independently* variable, however. That such is the case in many of the possible applications of the scheme, we shall not dispute. But in application to racial roles, there does not seem to be independent variation.

Our dichotomy is obviously related to some of the classical distinctions in sociology. Our competitive type coincides largely with the type of social solidarity which Durkheim called "organic." However, the reverse relationship between paternalism and mechanical solidarity does not hold. Most cases of paternalistic prejudice are found in a functionally differentiated, though preindustrial, society with a division of labor which we have termed "intermediate." Such a level of differentiation in the division of labor already contains strong "organic" elements and no longer represents a primitive "mechanical" level of solidarity, at least not in anywhere near a pure state.

Redfield's "folk" versus "urban" distinction likewise bears only a partial relationship to our own typology. Although the competitive type is associated with urbanism, and although paternalism is compatible with a folk society, the paternalistic situation is also found in urban societies. As regards Toennies' *Gemeinschaft-Gesellschaft* dichotomy, the correspondence to our two types is perhaps closer. The paternalistic type has many *Gemeinschaft* characteristics, and a *Gesellschaft* society is most compatible with the competitive type.

Subject to the reservations mentioned above, Table 2 schematizes the relationship between our dichotomy and the distinctions reviewed above.

APPLICABILITY OF THE PATERNALISTIC-COMPETITIVE DISTINCTION AND THE PROBLEM OF "MIXED TYPES"

We must first answer the question: Is our scheme synchronic or diachronic? The answer is that it is both. Historically, at least in Western societies since the first period of overseas expansion in the fifteenth century, the general tendency has been away from the paternalistic type and toward competitive prejudice. In that sense, then, our scheme is diachronic and evolutionary. But each of the two types can also be viewed as an existing situation in a given society. There is no *necessary* evolution from one type to the other. A competitive situation can prevail without having been preceded by a paternalistic one, as with Jews in medieval Europe; conversely, a paternalistic system can endure, barring disruptive factors, without

TABLE 2

	Paternalistic Type	*Competitive Type*
Max Weber's types of authority	Traditional	Rational-legal (occasionally: charismatic)
Parsons' pattern variables	Ascription, particularism, affectivity, collective orientation, diffuseness	Achievement, universalism, affective neutrality, self orientation, specificity
Durkheim's forms of solidarity	Mechanical-organic mixture	Organic
Toennies	*Gemeinschaft*	*Gesellschaft*
Redfield	Folk or urban	Urban

leading to the competitive type, as between Watuzi and Bahutu in Ruanda-Urundi until the eve of independence.

There is another sense in which our scheme is to be regarded as synchronic. The two types of prejudice can coexist in different segments of the same society and toward different groups. One example comes to mind to illustrate this point, though it is not a case of racial prejudice. In medieval Europe, the prejudice against Jews in the cities was competitive, while the feudal lord-serf relationship in the rural areas was paternalistic.

We have already hinted that our scheme was applicable cross-culturally to non-Western societies. The argument that racial prejudice is a recent development limited to Western societies, and intended to rationalize the economic exploitation of subject peoples, is only a half-truth. True, the pseudo-scientific theories of racial differences have attained their most thorough elaboration in the Western world with the writings of Gobineau and the popularization of Social Darwinism. That such theories provided convenient justifications for the exploitation of "native" labor and slaves in the European colonies is likewise incontrovertible. But the exploitation preceded the development of the theories, and a simplistic view that the theories were devised with the Machiavellian purpose of justifying the colonial system is untenable. The main point, however, is that racial prejudice is much older than Gobineau and not limited to the Western world. Whenever phenotypical differences have existed between groups of people, racial prejudice seems to have arisen. The Bantu groups of Central Africa regard the pygmies who live among them as intermediate between chimpanzees and men. The Japanese express contempt for the bearded Ainu of Hokkaido. The Chinese expressed bewilderment at the sight of the first Europeans who landed in their country and compared the Europeans to monkeys because of their hairiness. In India, there is considerable evidence that the caste system originated in racial differences between Aryan conquerors and Dravidians, though, of course, race alone does not account for the florescence of caste. In short, physically distinguishing characteristics are generally

seized upon to perpetuate group differences and establish the superiority of one
group over the other.

Not only does our scheme apply to non-Western societies. It also applies
mutatis mutandis to forms of prejudice other than racial. The competitive ethnic
and religious prejudice against Jews in Europe and the United States is an example
of nonracial prejudice. Similarly, the paternalistic syndrome can be found in a
wide variety of contexts: between the factory owner and his workers; between the
company or ship commander and his men. In this study, however, we shall limit
ourselves to specifically racial prejudice.[11]

The problem of "mixed types" is crucial to any ideal-type scheme. As ideal
types are logical constructs, it is important not to reify them. The fact that no
empirical situation coincides exactly with one of the types does not invalidate a
typology. But, as in any scientific theory, heuristic usefulness is a paramount consideration. A distinction should be made here between schemes that are constructed
in terms of a continuum between two or more poles and schemes based on what
we may call a "true typology." The first sort of scheme admits of all intermediate
positions on the continuum; even a normal distribution where most cases are found
in the middle of the continuum, and none at the extremes, is compatible with this
sort of scheme.

A true typology, in the restricted sense in which we use that term, implies an
empirical polarization of cases around the extremes and qualitative rather than
quantitative differences. "Mixed cases" must be inherently unstable and tend to
move toward one of the ideal types. We believe that our dichotomy satisfies this
condition. Societies have moved from the paternalistic to the competitive type of
prejudice and hence must have gone through a "mixed" stage. But the social system
as a whole tends to continue to evolve until the competitive situation is rather
closely approximated. It cannot remain in a stable intermediate position between
the polar opposites. Mixed types at the total society level of analysis can only be
transitory. But there is another sense in which mixed types can occur. Subsystems
in the society can belong in different types, as in the case of medieval Europe
mentioned earlier. Different groups in the same society can be the object of different types of prejudice. Also, in the case of a society in transition, different segments of the total society (as rural versus urban) can be in different stages in the
process of evolution. The isolated rural areas will tend to remain paternalistic
longer than the industrial centers, for example. All these possibilities can make the
over-all characterization of a total society a complex matter. But again, this does
not invalidate the criterion of polarization. It is only a question of defining the
boundaries of the social system or subsystem under analysis.

NOTES

1. The labels *paternalistic* and *competitive* will be used in conjunction with the term "prejudice" when the psychological reference is emphasized and with the term "race relations"
   when sociological or social system factors are stressed.

2. In agreement with Dollard, Warner, Myrdal, and others, we shall call "caste" a group which satisfies all three of the following criteria: (1) endogamy, (2) membership therein by birth and for life, and (3) a position of superiority or inferiority vis-à-vis other such groups.

3. Professor Parsons suggested to us an important distinction between social stratification as a product of internal differentiation in the social system and social stratification imposed from the outside. In the latter case, the hierarchy is likely to be rigid. In fact, most caste or quasi-caste systems, such as estates, have their origin in conquest. The greater the disparity in physical characteristics, level of organization, technology, and so forth between conqueror and conquered, the greater is the likelihood of a caste system arising. Of course, a caste system may perpetuate itself long after these differences have been blurred, as exemplified by India.

4. Cf. Robert E. Park, *Race and Culture* (Glencoe: The Free Press, 1950), p. 183; Bertrand W. Doyle, *The Etiquette of Race Relations in the South* (Chicago: University of Chicago Press, 1937); and Pierre L. van den Berghe, "Distance Mechanisms of Stratification," *Sociology and Social Research* 44 (1960): 155–164.

5. John Dollard, *Caste and Class in a Southern Town* (New Haven: Yale University Press, 1937); Abraham Kardiner and Lionel Ovesey, *The Mark of Oppression* (New York: Norton, 1951).

6. Roger Bastide, *Sociologie et Psychanalyse* (Paris: Presses Universitaires de France, 1950), pp. 241–245.

7. Gunnar Myrdal, *An American Dilemma* (New York: Harper, 1944), pp. 21, 39, 84–89, 460, 614, 899.

8. If one conceives of spatial distance and social distance as alternative mechanisms of social control in a racial caste situation, certain theoretical considerations follow. Both mechanisms are based on the ascriptive criterion of race and hence involve a "cost" in efficiency, at least in the sense of economic rationality. To quote Linton, "The ascription of status sacrifices the possibility of having certain roles performed superlatively well to the certainty of having them performed passably well." (Cf. Ralph Linton, *The Study of Man* [New York: Appleton-Century, 1936], p. 129.) But social distance involves a great measure of functional differentiation insofar as the members of the various castes perform tasks that are largely complementary. Spatial distance, on the contrary, involves a large degree of segmentation without differentiation, insofar as tasks, facilities, and functions are duplicatory rather than complementary. If the considerations above are correct, they may in part account for the greater degree of in-built maladjustment in the competitive type of race relations. An industrial competitive type of society which "needs all the differentiation it can get" can afford the luxury of segmentation even less than a preindustrial paternalistic society. Yet the tendency is toward spatial segregation as a substitute for social distance. This is one of the inherent paradoxes of the competitive type.

9. Gordon W. Allport, *The Nature of Prejudice* (Cambridge: Addison-Wesley, 1954), pp. 285–286.

10. Thomas F. Pettigrew, "Regional Differences in Anti-Negro Prejudice," (Thesis, Harvard University, 1956).

11. This limitation of our subject matter is heuristic rather than substantive. We do not believe that racial prejudice is fundamentally different from the other forms of prejudice. We conceive rather of racial prejudice as a special case of a more general phenomenon. But the relative permanency of physical characteristics makes for a more rigid definition of groups and for more clear-cut and enduring situations than in other forms of prejudice.

10   Six Orders of Race Relations

Michael Banton

When members of two different societies first have dealings with one another their transactions may be peripheral to their societies, having no influence upon relations within them nor bringing about any change of outlook. The type case of such forms of contact is probably the kind of exchange known as 'silent trade', in which peoples exchange goods without actually meeting. Herodotus describes the practice of this form of trade by the Carthaginians, and it has been reported from all over the world, from Sierra Leone, Guatemala, England, China, Timor, Eskimo regions, etc.[1] There is always some pricing mechanism. The Pygmies of the Ituri forest of the Congo have been described as exchanging game and forest products for manufactures and fruit produced by neighbouring Negro settlements of agriculturalists. One group places piles of goods at the trading place and retires. The other group places opposite these piles the goods it offers in exchange. The first group returns and, where the terms are acceptable, picks up the proffered exchange items. Such cases of peripheral contact either are short-lived or arise in restricted ecological circumstances. It may be helpful to think of them diagrammatically, as in *Figure 1*.

Figure 1   Peripheral contact

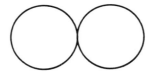

When contact between members of two groups is continuous it may develop along either of two principal courses, institutionalized contact or acculturation. When one of the two groups has a centralized political structure so that a few leaders control the action of other members, these leaders are likely to use their power to try to dominate the other group. When two such societies enter into contact through some of the outlying members and there is no strong competition for resources, a situation arises in which members of each society look inwards towards their own institutions; the people who live on the social boundaries are those most affected by contact and they may make exchanges with the strangers. Such people may come to occupy positions in two social systems, their own society and the new system of interrelations between the societies. They play different roles in the two systems. Frequently, the roles they play in the system of interrelations seem

Figure 2   Institutionalized contact

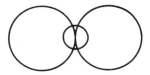

rather crude because the agents of the strangers may not speak the same language or participate in the same cultural universe of shared meanings, but, however undeveloped this system may initially be, it is a system of interrelations in a way that peripheral contact is not. When it is necessary to distinguish these two forms of contact, the adjectives peripheral and institutional will be used. In general, however, the term contact will signify institutional contact, because it is only this variety that constitutes an interracial social order.

In situations of contact, there is no common political order or integral social system. Racial differences serve to signalize roles only in the area of overlap, for in the two major societies pre-contact institutions and customs are maintained with little modification, and the roles related to them have their own signs. If relations between members of the two societies start on a basis of trade and not violence, the first patterns of interrelation are formed by the personal acquaintance of individuals with individuals. Then the expectations a man has of one individual in the other society are extended to a category of people in it or to all members of that society. In so far as these expectations are reinforced by conforming behaviour, roles are created. The people, on both sides, who are involved in the interrelational system develop that system, but, being themselves members of their own societies, they are subject to other pressures. Very frequently, this interrelational system is unable to develop freely because of the power wielded by external interests. When one of the societies is an expanding industrial nation, the balance of power in the contact situation rapidly tips in its favour; to explain the course of events as they affect the participants it is then constantly necessary to refer back to features of the industrial nation's affairs.

When the societies in contact are small in scale and have no centralized power structure, especially when there is little competition and contact is gradual, then change takes the form of acculturation. The people who are in contact can themselves adjust to the strangers, being under little pressure from more distant members of their own society. The two societies and cultures tend to merge, with the weaker making more changes than the stronger. Examples of such change can be represented diagrammatically as in *Figure 3*. Processes of acculturation are also present when one society subordinates the other, but then it is the political balance that most determines the interracial order.

The contact and growth of ties between racially distinguished groups or nations have, in several important instances, resulted in the domination of one by the other and in the constitution of a single society. The pattern of such an order, both sociologically and historically, can be better appreciated if a distinction is drawn between local and national systems of relations. The local system has been the farm or plan-

Figure 3   Acculturation

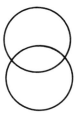

Figure 4   Domination

tation, for example, in which the master exercises a personal domination over members of the subjugated group, many or all of whom he knows as individuals. His power over them is frequently more limited than may appear at first sight, for even slaves have their methods of obtaining retribution when they feel they have been treated with particular injustice. The harshness of subjugation in the local system is therefore often tempered by appreciation of a man's or woman's qualities as an individual and by the need to provide effective incentives if the social arrangements are to work. When the pattern of relations prevailing locally is extended to the national system so that all members of the one category are universally subordinated, then in many of the situations in which members of the two categories meet they are not acquainted with one another; they therefore respond to each other not as individuals, but as representatives of a category. This kind of subordination is far harsher, and it provides the most clear-cut illustration of race as a role sign. Whatever their personal qualities, individuals are ascribed to one or the other category, and those in the lower are prevented from claiming the privileges of those in the upper category. As racial distinctions are drawn in a wide variety of situations (indeed, there is often scarcely a single kind of situation in which they are irrelevant), race is a sign of a basic role like sex or age.[2] Where race relations show a pattern of domination, the two categories are differentiated by other attributes than those of race: income, education, religion, norms of family relations, etc. Differentiation by these means complicates the picture, but, as will be shown later, is often essential to it, for it makes the gap between the categories greater and more difficult to bridge.

When members of a more powerful nation enter the territory of another and contact is established, a major variable is the political independence of the newcomers. If they are free to determine and enforce their own policy towards the local society, a dominative order is likely to be created (e.g. the 'white settler' society in Africa). If they are subject to control by a home government which formulates its own policy, there is a greater probability of a paternalist order being established.

This is a special form of institutionalized contact depending, unlike domination,

Figure 5   Paternalism

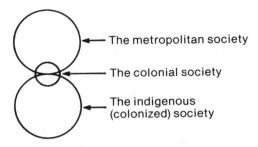

The metropolitan society

The colonial society

The indigenous
(colonized) society

upon maintaining the distinctiveness of the interacting societies. It is exemplified in some forms of colonial rule, such as those that sanctioned and often reinforced the control tribal chiefs exercised over their peoples. In the pure form of paternalism, the only representatives of the metropolitan society who have dealings with the indigenous society are approved agents responsible for their actions to authorities in their homeland. In this case, race serves as a sign of a basic role, relevant whenever members of the two groups meet, but the liberty of the agents to intrude into various spheres of indigenous life is restricted; the development of roles within the colonial society (i.e. the sphere of overlap) is influenced by metropolitan policies, in particular by the regulation of the career structure of the agents. If the agents spend long periods in the territory in question they may identify themselves with groups that do not altogether approve metropolitan policy, and they may acquire interests of their own in the territory. This sort of tendency is stronger when—in a departure from the pure form of paternalism—persons from the metropolitan country other than official agents are allowed to establish relations (as traders or settlers) with the indigenous people. The immigrant section of the colonial society will acquire greater strength from the diversification of its personnel; the tension between its interests and those of the metropolitan society may then become as important as the tension between the colonialists and the colonized. Paternalistic orders of race relations in practice frequently show divergencies in this direction. The essential point is, however, that whereas the relevance and character of roles in a dominative order are determined by the desire of the upper group to maintain control over all significant spheres of activity, in a paternalistic order the relevance and character of the upper group's roles are decided chiefly, or to a considerable extent, by metropolitan policies.

In other circumstances it is possible that much less attention will be paid to racial distinctions, though it seems that they are never ignored completely. The characteristics of a few individuals may be forgotten, but, if such characteristics distinguish a category of people systematically, they are almost certain to acquire social significance (differences, for example, of hair colour, would not be sufficiently systematic because they arise between one brother and another, between parent and child). When minimal attention is paid to racial differences, an integrated order of race relations is constituted. The nearest approach to integration is achieved by

Figure 6   Integration

countries in which there are several different racial groups and many people of mixed descent. Race is then still used as a social sign, though as a sign indicating an individual's background and probable claims to deference. It is one sign among many others, being irrelevant in some sectors (e.g. political rights) but of some account in status-sensitive situations of social acceptance or rejection. For nearly all purposes, race has much less significance than the individual's occupation and his other status-conferring roles. Thus, in a racially integrated social order, race is a sign of an independent role, signalizing rights and obligations in only a few restricted sets of circumstances.[3]

Equality in political and civic rights may be achieved without dissolution of the boundaries of minority group membership. Some minorities may have to preserve a high solidarity if they are to achieve such equality, and the significance of membership may be enhanced. When minorities compete with one another for jobs and status, they may become identified with particular sectors of the economy and this strengthens their distinctiveness. On the other hand, separation in marriage and leisure-time relations may be entailed by religious differences. Where equal political rights are maintained by minority representation, internal distinctions are reinforced; this kind of social order is better referred to as pluralistic. The balance of power which it presupposes is more likely to develop when there are more than two distinctive groups. In a pluralist order there are no separate racial roles with different political rights and claims to deference: race is not relevant to behaviour in many important situations, so it is not a sign of a basic role. But racial differences do signalize variations in expected behaviour in far more situations than under an

Figure 7   Pluralism

integrated order, so neither is it a sign of an independent role. Elsewhere, roles of an intermediate range of relevance have been identified as general roles,[4] and in a pluralistic order race will serve as a sign of such a general role.

It will be apparent that there are resemblances and points of difference between certain of these six orders that make it more likely that one order will be transformed into another than into a third. Acculturation leads fairly easily to integration. Initial situations of contact have often been succeeded by either domination or paternalism. In modern circumstances a rapid transition to an integrated or pluralist order is perhaps possible, although, considering the technologically backward position of the relatively isolated peoples, it is not probable. Whether contact gives way to domination or paternalism depends upon the extent to which those who build up relations with the indigenous people can operate as an independent political power. In a paternalist order it is probable that the power of the metropolitan country will be weakened after a time, and that this will be reflected in changes in the skills of the personnel that country sends out and in the definition of their roles. In such ways the transition to an integrated order is facilitated; it may entail the withdrawal of all representatives of the former metropolitan country and the creation of a society without racial minorities. A dominative order is so structured that the pattern of domination is continually reinforced, and fundamental change becomes increasingly difficult. The purest form of domination is one in which there are only two racial categories and the superior one normally resists the entry (by immigration) or creation (by miscegenation) of any additional categories. However, because of economic and political tendencies, the whole society may be absorbed into some larger society; the subordinated racial category may then be accorded political privileges previously denied its members; thus they and their former superiors will become minorities within the larger order, though this does not mean that the inequalities between them will necessarily be reduced rapidly or substantially. It can be argued that a dominative order can be maintained over long periods

Figure 8   Sequence of racial orders

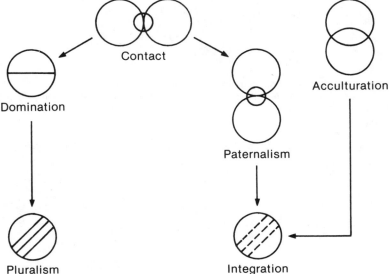

only if the economic basis of the society is unchanging. Economic development affects a dominative order in such a way that it must either modify some of its fundamentals or explode. If it is to shift from absolute domination, it is more likely to change in the direction of an unequal pluralism than in any other.

This suggestion of typical sequences in changing patterns of race relations is reminiscent of the cyclical theories of race relations elaborated by several authors. R. E. Park maintained that contact is followed by competition, then by accommodation, and finally by assimilation and amalgamation. E. S. Bogardus, who had in mind immigrants to California rather than to the American north-east, outlined a different kind of cycle: curiosity, economic welcome, industrial and social antagonism, legislative antagonism, fair-play tendencies, quiescence, second-generation difficulties. Other American sociologists have proposed variants upon these ideas.[5] These cyclical theories concern themselves with race relations in a country of immigration and make little allowance for the characteristics of the interacting groups or for the institutional context within which contact occurs. In so far as they posit assimilation as an inevitable conclusion, events of recent years have cast further doubt upon their validity. The sequences outlined here are not cycles of race relations. They are used to draw attention to what seem to be the chief factors relating the use of racial distinctions to economic and political features of the wider social order. They are first approximations, not polished classifications, and will invite further elaboration if they are of use. No assumptions are made about ultimate assimilation or continuing friction, because the future is problematic. It is probable that technological change will continue at an ever-increasing pace and that the substitution of machines for human activity will have important implications for intergroup relations. It is difficult to know whether an age of fully automated production would generate pressures favouring an integrated or a pluralistic order, or whether it might not give rise to some new pattern.

NOTES

1. P. J. Hamilton Grierson, *The Silent Trade* (Edinburgh: Green, 1903).
2. Michael Banton, *Roles: An Introduction to the Study of Social Relations* (London: Tavistock, 1965). pp. 33–35.
3. Ibid., pp. 33–35.
4. Ibid., pp. 33–35.
5. Brewton Berry, *Race & Ethnic Relations,* 3rd. ed. (Boston: Houghton Mifflin, 1965). pp. 129–135.

PART TWO

Perspectives
on
Social Change

CONTINUOUS SOCIAL CHANGE:

MIGRATION AND MARGINALITY

The studies in the second part of this book consider the effects of various types of social change on race and ethnic relations. Thomas and Znaniecki's famous account of the Polish peasant in Europe and America is not only a sociological investigation of the causes and consequences of a particular migration but also one of the earliest formulations of the thesis that the persistence of ethnicity is a crucial feature of American society. The fate of the Polish migrant in the large American cities like Chicago and New York should not be seen in terms of individual assimilation into an American way of life, but rather in relation to his integration into a Polish-American subgroup. This subgroup, far from dissolving into an ethnic melting pot, turned out to be, as Glazer and Moynihan were to argue, a new social form of enduring vitality and resilience.

Robert Ezra Park was a colleague of Thomas and Znaniecki and another founding member of the Chicago School of Sociology. Although he only turned to sociology in his later life, starting out as a journalist, he was a most influential scholar and teacher. "Human Migration and the Marginal Man" combines theoretical insights derived from Simmel with Park's extensive knowledge of the literature and experience of interracial and interethnic encounters. It provides a penetrating and far-ranging definition of the marginal man in terms of the conflicting cultures associated with human migrations. The concept of the marginal man has been employed in many subsequent studies from Stonequist's *The Marginal Man,*[1] published in the 1930s, to Dickie-Clark's *The Marginal Situation,*[2] written in the 1960s.

One of the classic examples of marginality that Park cites is the case of the emancipated Jew in Europe during the late nineteenth and early twentieth centuries. Andreski continues with this focus on Jewish life by considering the role of economic competition in the social derivation of anti-Semitism. He attempts to synthesize some of the insights of Marx with those of Gumplowicz, and his conclusions fit other theories that link intensified intergroup conflict with competitive patterns of race and ethnic relations. Andreski's main concern is with the anti-Semitism of Eastern Europe prior to the rise of the Nazis, and at no stage does he assert that economic factors are the only explanation of such prejudice and discrimination. However, the understandable emphasis on explaining the persecution of Jews in the

Third Reich has led to a preoccupation with irrational psychopathic forces which may not be the major element in other cases of anit-Semitism.

NOTES

1. E. V. Stonequist, *The Marginal Man: A Study in Personality and Culture Conflict* (New York: Scribners, 1937).
2. H. F. Dickie-Clark, *The Marginal Situation: A Sociological Study of a Coloured Group* (London: Routledge & Kegan Paul, 1966).

11   Migration and Ethnic Survival

W. I. Thomas & Florian Znaniecki

The preceding parts of this work, though far from exhaustive, give a general outline of the psychology and organization of the peasant communities in Poland and of the evolution by which these communities, formerly almost isolated, became integral parts of the Polish national body. We have found that, except for the higher forms of cultural productivity (literature, art, science, large-scale industry and commerce) in which the peasant class did not appreciably participate and for the maintenance and development of a state system, of which Poland was deprived, our study has involved nearly all the sociological problems which can be raised with reference to a concrete, ethnically homogeneous society which has occupied a certain territory for many generations and come into the possession of a set of social values either originally produced or completely assimilated during its historical existence.

But during the last three-quarters of a century, numerous isolated components of the peasant (and lower city) class—individuals, marriage groups, sometimes fragments of large families and primary communities—have been leaving their original milieu and settling in America, intentionally or accidentally grouping themselves into colonies of various sizes scattered over the territory of an ethnically and culturally different society. The evolution of these fragments separated from their social whole presents a series of new problems, interesting not only from the practical standpoint of the relation of the immigrants to American society but also in view of their general sociological significance.

The situation is really much more complicated than most of the popular Ameri-

From *The Polish Peasant in Europe and America*, Boston, Richard G. Badger—The Gorham Press, Vol. 5., (1918–1920) pp. vii–ix.

can literature concerning immigration and Americanization sees it. It would seem *a priori* and it is generally assumed that the main problems concerning the immigrants can be stated in terms of individual assimilation or non-assimilation. Since the immigrant is no longer a member of the society from which he came, since he lives in the midst of American society, is connected with it by economic bonds and dependent on its institutions, the only line of evolution left to him seems to be the one leading to a gradual substitution in his consciousness of American cultural values for Polish cultural values and of attitudes adapted to his American environment for the attitudes brought over from the old country. This substitution may be slower or faster and various factors—among others living in racial groups—may influence its pace; but the immigrant (or the immigrant's descendant) is considered as still a Pole in traditions and attitudes, or already an American, or somewhere on the way from Polonism to Americanism, and it is supposed that the essential thing to be studied in relation to him is, how he makes this passage.

But in fact, if we look at the Poles in America not from the standpoint of Polish or American national interests but from that of an objective sociological inquiry, we find that the problem of individual assimilation is at present an entirely secondary and unimportant issue. Of course there have been many Poles—a few of the first, many more of the second generation—who have become individually absorbed in American society and are now more or less completely assimilated: but the number of such cases in proportion to the total population of Polish origin in this country has been rapidly decreasing in the last fifty years. The fundamental process which has been going on during this period is *the formation of a new Polish-American society* out of those fragments separated from Polish society and embedded in American society. This Polish-American society as a whole is, indeed, slowly evolving from Polonism to Americanism, as is shown by the fact that its members, particularly those of the second generation, are continually acquiring more American attitudes and being more influenced by American civilization. But this "assimilation" is not an individual but a group phenomenon, to be compared with such processes as the progressive Germanization of Czech society up to a hundred years ago or the adoption of French culture by the Polish, Russian and German aristocracies in the course of the 18th century. Here the individual does not stand isolated in the midst of a culturally different group. He is part of a homogeneous group in contact with a civilization which influences in various degrees all of the members. And the striking phenomenon, the central object of our investigation, is the formation of this coherent group out of originally incoherent elements, the creation of a society which in structure and prevalent attitudes is neither Polish nor American but constitutes a specific new product whose raw materials have been partly drawn from Polish traditions, partly from the new conditions in which the immigrants live and from American social values as the immigrant sees and interprets them. It is this Polish-American society, not American society, that constitutes the social milieu into which the immigrant who comes from Poland becomes incorporated and to whose standards and institutions he must adapt himself.

12   Human Migration and the Marginal Man

Robert Park

Students of the great society, looking at mankind in the long perspective of history, have frequently been disposed to seek an explanation of existing cultural differences among races and peoples in some single dominating cause or condition. One school of thought, represented most conspicuously by Montesquieu, has found that explanation in climate and in the physical environment. Another school, identified with the name of Arthur de Gobineau, author of *The Inequality of Human Races,* has sought an explanation of divergent cultures in the innate qualities of races biologically inherited. These two theories have this in common, namely, that they both conceive civilization and society to be the result of evolutionary processes— processes by which man has acquired new inheritable traits—rather than processes by which new relations have been established between men.

In contrast to both of these, Frederick Teggart has recently restated and amplified what may be called the catastrophic theory of civilization, a theory that goes back to Hume in England, and to Turgot in France. From this point of view, climate and innate racial traits, important as they may have been in the evolution of races, have been of only minor influence in creating existing cultural differences. In fact, races and cultures, so far from being in any sense identical—or even the product of similar conditions and forces—are perhaps to be set over against one another as contrast effects, the results of antagonistic tendencies, so that civilization may be said to flourish at the expense of racial differences rather than to be conserved by them. At any rate, if it is true that races are the products of isolation and inbreeding, it is just as certain that civilization, on the other hand, is a consequence of contact and communication. The forces which have been decisive in the history of mankind are those which have brought men together in fruitful competition, conflict, and co-operation.

Among the most important of these influences have been—according to what I called the catastrophic theory of progress—migration and the incidental collisions, conflicts, and fusions of people and cultures which they have occasioned.

"Every advance in culture," says Bücher, in his *Industrial Evolution,* "commences, so to speak, with a new period of wandering," and in support of this thesis he points out that the earlier forms of trade were migratory, that the first industries to free themselves from the household husbandry and become independent occupations were carried on itinerantly. "The great founders of religion, the earliest poets and philosophers, the musicians and actors of past epochs, are all great wanderers. Even today, do not the inventor, the preacher of a new doctrine, and the virtuoso

From *The American Journal of Sociology,* Vol. XXXIII, May 1928, No.6, pp. 881–893. Reprinted by permission of The University of Chicago Press.

travel from place to place in search of adherents and admirers—notwithstanding the immense recent development in the means of communicating information?"[1]

The influences of migrations have not been limited, of course, by the changes which they have effected in existing cultures. In the long run, they have determined the racial characteristics of historical peoples. "The whole teaching of ethnology," as Griffith Taylor remarks, "shows that peoples of mixed race are the rule and not the exception."[2] Every nation, upon examination, turns out to have been a more or less successful melting-pot. To this constant sifting of races and peoples, human geographers have given the title "the historical movement," because, as Miss Semple says in her volume *Influences of Geographic Environment,* "it underlies most written history and constitutes the major part of unwritten history, especially that of savage and nomadic tribes."[3]

Changes in race, it is true, do inevitably follow, at some distance, changes in culture. The movements and mingling of peoples which bring rapid, sudden, and often catastrophic, changes in customs and habits are followed, in the course of time, as a result of interbreeding, by corresponding modifications in temperament and physique. There has probably never been an instance where races have lived together in the intimate contacts which a common economy enforces in which racial contiguity has not produced racial hybrids. However, changes in racial characteristics and in cultural traits proceed at very different rates, and it is notorious that cultural changes are not consolidated and transmitted biologically, or at least to only a very slight extent, if at all. Acquired characteristics are not biologically inherited.

Writers who emphasize the importance of migration as an agency of progress are invariably led to ascribe a similar rôle to war. Thus Waitz, commenting upon the rôle of migration as an agency of civilization, points out that migrations are "rarely of a peaceful nature at first." Of war he says: "The first consequence of war is that fixed relations are established between peoples, which render friendly intercourse possible, an intercourse which becomes more important from the interchange of knowledge and experience than from the mere interchange of commodities."[4] And then he adds:

> Whenever we see a people, of whatever degree of civilization, not living in contact and reciprocal action with others, we shall generally find a certain stagnation, a mental inertness, and a want of activity, which render any change of social and political condition next to impossible. These are, in times of peace, transmitted like an everlasting disease, and war appears then, in spite of what the apostles of peace may say, as a saving angel, who rouses the national spirit, and renders all forces more elastic.[5]

Among the writers who conceive the historical process in terms of intrusions, either peaceful or hostile, of one people into the domain of another, must be reckoned such sociologists as Gumplowicz and Oppenheim. The former, in an effort to define the social process abstractly, has described it as the interaction of heterogeneous ethnic groups, the resulting subordination and superordination of races constituting the social order—society, in fact.

In much the same way, Oppenheim, in his study of the sociological origin of the state, believes he has shown that in every instance the state has had its historical beginnings in the imposition, by conquest and force, of the authority of a nomadic upon a sedentary and agricultural people. The facts which Oppenheim has gathered to sustain his thesis show, at any rate, that social institutions have actually, in many instances at least, come into existence abruptly by a mutation, rather than by a process of evolutionary selection and the gradual accumulation of relatively slight variations.[6]

It is not at once apparent why a theory which insists upon the importance of catastrophic change in the evolution of civilization should not at the same time take some account of revolution as a factor in progress. If peace and stagnation, as Waitz suggests, tend to assume the form of a social disease; if, as Sumner says, "society needs to have some ferment in it" to break up this stagnation and emancipate the energies of individuals imprisoned within an existing social order; it seems that some "adventurous folly" like the crusades of the middle ages, or some romantic enthusiasm like that which found expression in the French Revolution, or in the more recent Bolshevist adventure in Russia, might serve quite as effectively as either migration or war to interrupt the routine of existing habit and break the cake of custom. Revolutionary doctrines are naturally based upon a conception of catastrophic rather than of evolutionary change. Revolutionary strategy, as it has been worked out and rationalized in Sorel's *Reflections on Violence,* makes the great catastrophe, the general strike, an article of faith. As such it becomes a means of maintaining morale and enforcing discipline in the revolutionary masses.[7]

The first and most obvious difference between revolution and migration is that in migration the breakdown of social order is initiated by the impact of an invading population, and completed by the contact and fusion of native with alien peoples. In the case of the former, revolutionary ferment and the forces which have disrupted society have ordinarily had, or seem to have had, their sources and origins mainly if not wholly within, rather than without, the society affected. It is doubtful whether it can be successfully maintained that every revolution, every *Aufklärung,* every intellectual awakening and renaissance has been and will be provoked by some invading population movement or by the intrusion of some alien cultural agency. At least it seems as if some modification of this view is necessary, since with the growth of commerce and communication there is progressively and relatively more movement and less migration. Commerce, in bringing the ends of the earth together, has made travel relatively secure. Moreover, with the development of machine industry and the growth of cities, it is the commodities rather than men which circulate. The peddler, who carries his stock on his back, gives way to the traveling salesman, and the catalogue of the mail order house now reaches remote regions which even the Yankee peddler rarely if every penetrated. With the development of a world-economy and the interpenetration of peoples, migrations, as Bücher has pointed out, have changed their character:

The migrations occurring at the opening of the history of European peoples are migrations of whole tribes, a pushing and pressing of collective units from east to west which lasted for centuries. The migrations of the Middle Ages never affect individual classes alone; the knights in the crusades, the merchants, the wage craftsmen, the journeymen hand-workers, the jugglers and minstrels, the villeins seeking protection within the walls of a town. Modern migrations, on the contrary, are generally a matter of private concern, the individuals being led by the most varied motives. They are almost invariably without organization. The process repeating itself daily a thousand times is united only through the one characteristic, that it is everywhere a question of change of locality by persons seeking more favourable conditions of life.[8]

Migration, which was formerly an invasion, followed by the forcible displacement or subjugation of one people by another, has assumed the character of a peaceful penetration. Migration of peoples has, in other words, been transmuted into mobility of individuals, and the wars which these movements so frequently occasioned have assumed the character of internecine struggles, of which strikes and revolutions are to be regarded as types.

Furthermore, if one were to attempt to reckon with all the forms in which catastrophic changes take place, it would be necessary to include the changes that are effected by the sudden rise of some new religious movement like Mohammedanism or Christianity, both of which began as schismatic and sectarian movements, and which by extension and internal evolution have become independent religions. Looked at from this point of view, migration assumes a character less unique and exceptional than has hitherto been conceived by the writers whom the problem has most intrigued. It appears as one, merely, of a series of forms in which historic changes may take place. Nevertheless, regarded abstractly as a type of collective action, human migration exhibits everywhere characteristics that are sufficiently typical to make it a subject of independent investigation and study, both in respect to its form and in respect to the effects which it produces.

Migration is not, however, to be identified with mere movement. It involves, at the very least, change of residence and the breaking of home ties. The movements of gypsies and other pariah peoples, because they bring about no important changes in cultural life, are to be regarded rather as a geographical fact than a social phenomenon. Nomadic life is stabilized on the basis of movement, and even though gypsies now travel by automobile, they still maintain, comparatively unchanged, their ancient tribal organization and customs. The result is that their relation to the communities in which they may at any time be found is to be described as symbiotic rather than social. This tends to be true of any section or class of the population—the hobos, for example, and the hotel dwellers—which is unsettled and mobile.

Migration as a social phenomenon must be studied not merely in its grosser effects, as manifested in changes in custom and in the mores, but it may be envisaged in its subjective aspects as manifested in the changed type of personality which it produces. When the traditional organization of society breaks down, as a result of contact and collision with a new invading culture, the effect is, so to speak, to emancipate the individual man. Energies that were formerly controlled by custom

and tradition are released. The individual is free for new adventures, but he is more
or less without direction and control. Teggart's statement of the matter is as follows:

> As a result of the breakdown of customary modes of action and of thought,
> the individual experiences a "release" from the restraints and constraints to
> which he has been subject, and gives evidence of this "release" in aggressive
> self-assertion. The overexpression of individuality is one of the marked fea-
> tures of all epochs of change. On the other hand, the study of the psychologi-
> cal effects of collision and contact between different groups reveals the fact
> that the most important aspect of "release" lies not in freeing the soldier, war-
> rior, or berserker from the restraint of conventional modes of action, but in
> freeing the individual judgment from the inhibitions of conventional modes of
> thought. It will thus be seen (he adds) that the study of the *modus operandi*
> of change in time gives a common focus to the efforts of political historians,
> of the historians of literature and of ideas, of psychologists, and of students
> of ethics and the theory of education.[9]

Social changes, according to Teggart, have their inception in events which "release" the individuals out of which society is composed. Inevitably, however, this
release is followed in the course of time by the reintegration of the individuals so
released into a new social order. In the meantime, however, certain changes take
place—at any rate they are likely to take place—in the character of the individuals
themselves. They become, in the process, not merely emancipated, but enlightened.

The emancipated individual invariably becomes in a certain sense and to a certain degree a cosmopolitan. He learns to look upon the world in which he was born
and bred with something of the detachment of a stranger. He acquires, in short, an
intellectual bias. Simmel has described the position of the stranger in the community, and his personality, in terms of movement and migration.

"If wandering," he says, "considered as the liberation from every given point in
space, is the conceptual opposite of fixation at any point, then surely the sociological form of the stranger presents the union of both of these specifications." The
stranger stays, but he is not settled. He is a potential wanderer. That means that he
is not bound as others are by the local proprieties and conventions. "He is the freer
man, practically and theoretically. He views his relations to others with less prejudice; he submits them to more general, more objective standards, and he is not confined in his action by custom, piety or precedents."

The effect of mobility and migration is to secularize relations which were formerly sacred. One may describe the process, in its dual aspect, perhaps, as the
secularization of society and the individuation of the person. For a brief, vivid, and
authentic picture of the way in which migration of the earlier sort, the migration of
a people, has, in fact, brought about the destruction of an earlier civilization and
liberated the peoples involved for the creation of a later, more secular, and freer
society, I suggest Gilbert Murray's introduction to *The Rise of the Greek Epic,* in
which he seeks to reproduce the events of the Nordic invasion of the Aegean area.

What ensued, he says, was a period of chaos:

A chaos in which an old civilization is shattered into fragments, its laws set at naught, and that intricate web of normal expectation which forms the very essence of human society torn so often and so utterly by continued disappointment that at last there ceases to be any normal expectation at all. For the fugitive settlers on the shores that were afterwards Ionia, and for parts too of Doris and Aeolis, there were no tribal gods or tribal obligations left, because there were no tribes. There were no old laws, because there was no one to administer or even to remember them; only such compulsions as the strongest power of the moment chose to enforce. Household and family life had disappeared, and all its innumerable ties with it. A man was now not living with a wife of his own race, but with a dangerous strange woman, of alien language and alien gods, a woman whose husband or father he had perhaps murdered—or, at best, whom he had bought as a slave from the murderer. The old Aryan husbandman, as we shall see hereafter, had lived with his herds in a sort of familiar connexion. He slew "his brother the ox" only under special stress or for definite religious reasons, and he expected his women to weep when the slaying was performed. But now he had left his own herds far away. They had been devoured by enemies. And he lived on the beasts of strangers whom he robbed or held in servitude. He had left the graves of his fathers, the kindly ghosts of his own blood, who took food from his hand and loved him. He was surrounded by the graves of alien dead, strange ghosts whose names he knew not, and who were beyond his power to control, whom he tried his best to placate with fear and aversion. One only concrete thing existed for him to make henceforth the centre of his allegiance, to supply the place of his old family hearth, his gods, his tribal customs and sanctities. It was a circuit wall of stones, a *Polis;* the wall which he and his fellows, men of diverse tongues and worships united by a tremendous need, had built up to be the one barrier between themselves and a world of enemies.[10]

It was within the walls of the *polis* and in this mixed company that Greek civilization was born. The whole secret of ancient Greek life, its relative freedom from the grosser superstitions and from fear of the gods, is bound up, we are told, with this period of transition and chaos, in which the older primitive world perished and from which the freer, more enlightened social order sprang into existence. Thought is emancipated, philosophy is born, public opinion sets itself up as an authority as over against tradition and custom. As Guyot puts it, "The Greek with his festivals, his songs, his poetry, seems to celebrate, in a perpetual hymn, the liberation of man from the mighty fetters of nature."[11]

What took place in Greece first has since taken place in the rest of Europe and is now going on in America. The movement and migration of peoples, the expansion of trade and commerce, and particularly the growth, in modern times, of these vast melting-pots of races and cultures, the metropolitan cities, has loosened local bonds, destroyed the cultures of tribe and folk, and substituted for the local loyalties the freedom of the cities; for the sacred order of tribal custom, the rational organization which we call civilization.

In these great cities, where all the passions, all the energies of mankind are released, we are in position to investigate the processes of civilization, as it were, under a microscope.

It is in the cities that the old clan and kinship groups are broken up and replaced by social organization based on rational interests and temperamental predilections. It is in the cities, more particularly, that the grand division of labor is effected which permits and more or less compels the individual man to concentrate his energies and his talents on the particular task he is best fitted to perform, and in this way emancipates him and his fellows from the control of nature and circumstance which so thoroughly dominates primitive man.

It happens, however, that the process of acculturation and assimilation and the accompanying amalgamation of racial stocks does not proceed with the same ease and the same speed in all cases. Particularly where peoples who come together are of divergent cultures and widely different racial stocks, assimilation and amalgamation do not take place so rapidly as they do in other cases. All our so-called racial problems grow out of situations in which assimilation and amalgamation do not take place at all, or take place very slowly. As I have said elsewhere, the chief obstacle to the cultural assimilation of races is not their different mental, but rather their divergent physical traits. It is not because of the mentality of the Japanese that they do not so easily assimilate as do the Europeans. It is because

> the Japanese bears in his features a distinctive racial hallmark, that he wears, so to speak, a racial uniform which classifies him. He cannot become a mere individual, indistinguishable in the cosmopolitan mass of the population, as is true, for example, of the Irish, and, to a lesser extent, of some of the other immigrant races. The Japanese, like the Negro, is condemned to remain among us an abstraction, a symbol—and a symbol not merely of his own race but of the Orient and of that vague, ill-defined menace we sometimes refer to as the "yellow peril."[12]

Under such circumstances peoples of different racial stocks may live side by side in a relation of symbiosis, each playing a rôle in a common economy, but not interbreeding to any great extent; each maintaining, like the gypsy or the pariah peoples of India, a more or less complete tribal organization or society of their own. Such was the situation of the Jew in Europe up to modern times, and a somewhat similar relation exists today between the native white and the Hindu populations in Southeast Africa and in the West Indies.

In the long run, however, peoples and races who live together, sharing in the same economy, inevitably interbreed, and in this way if in no other, the relations which were merely co-operative and economic become social and cultural. When migration leads to conquest, either economic or political, assimilation is inevitable. The conquering peoples impose their culture and their standards upon the conquered, and there follows a period of cultural endosmosis.

Sometimes relations between the conquering and the conquered peoples take the form of slavery; sometimes they assume the form, as in India, of a system of caste. But in either case the dominant and the subject peoples become, in time, integral parts of one society. Slavery and caste are merely forms of accommodation, in which the race problem finds a temporary solution. The case of the Jews was different. Jews never were a subject people, at least not in Europe. They were never reduced to the position of an inferior caste. In their ghettos in which they first elected, and then were forced, to live, they preserved their own tribal traditions and their cultural, if not their political, independence. The Jew who left the ghetto did not escape; he deserted and became that execrable object, an apostate. The relation of the ghetto Jew to the larger community in which he lived was, and to some extent still is, symbiotic rather than social.

When, however, the walls of the medieval ghetto were torn down and the Jew was permitted to participate in the cultural life of the peoples among whom he lived, there appeared a new type of personality, namely, a cultural hybrid, a man living and sharing intimately in the cultural life and traditions of two distinct peoples; never quite willing to break, even if he were permitted to do so, with his past and his traditions, and not quite accepted, because of racial prejudice, in the new society in which he now sought to find a place. He was a man on the margin of two cultures and two societies, which never completely interpenetrated and fused. The emancipated Jew was, and is, historically and typically the marginal man, the first cosmopolite and citizen of the world. He is, par excellence, the "stranger," whom Simmel, himself a Jew, has described with such profound insight and understanding in his *Sociologie.* Most if not all the characteristics of the Jew, certainly his preeminence as a trader and his keen intellectual interest, his sophistication, his idealism and lack of historic sense, are the characteristics of the city man, the man who ranges widely, lives preferably in a hotel—in short, the cosmopolite. The autobiographies of Jewish immigrants, of which a great number have been published in America in recent years, are all different versions of the same story—the story of the marginal man; the man who, emerging from the ghetto in which he lived in Europe, is seeking to find a place in the freer, more complex and cosmopolitan life of an American city. One may learn from these autobiographies how the process of assimilation actually takes place in the individual immigrant. In the more sensitive minds its effects are as profound and as disturbing as some of the religious conversions of which William James has given us so classical an account in his *Varieties of Religious Experience.* In these immigrant autobiographies the conflict of cultures, as it takes place in the mind of the immigrant, is just the conflict of "the divided self," the old self and the new. And frequently there is no satisfying issue of this conflict, which often terminates in a profound disillusionment, as described, for example, in Lewisohn's autobiography *Up Stream.* But Lewisohn's restless wavering between the warm security of the ghetto, which he has abandoned, and the cold freedom of the outer world, in which he is not yet quite at home, is typical. A century earlier, Heinrich Heine, torn with the same conflicting loyalties, struggling to be at the same time a German and a Jew, enacted a similar rôle. It was, according to his latest biographer, the secret and the tragedy of Heine's life that circumstance condemned him to live in two worlds, in neither of which he ever quite belonged. It was this that embittered his intellectual life and gave to his writings that character of spiritual conflict and instability which, as Browne says, is evidence of "spiritual distress."

His mind lacked the integrity which is based on conviction: "His arms were weak"—to continue the quotation—"because his mind was divided; his hands were nerveless because his soul was in turmoil."

Something of the same sense of moral dichotomy and conflict is probably characteristic of every immigrant during the period of transition, when old habits are being discarded and new ones are not yet formed. It is inevitably a period of inner turmoil and intense self-consciousness.

There are no doubt periods of transition and crisis in the lives of most of us that are comparable with those which the immigrant experiences when he leaves home to seek his fortunes in a strange country. But in the case of the marginal man the period of crisis is relatively permanent. The result is that he tends to become a personality type. Ordinarily the marginal man is a mixed blood, like the Mulatto in the United States or the Eurasian in Asia, but that is apparently because the man of mixed blood is one who lives in two worlds, in both of which he is more or less of a stranger. The Christian convert in Asia or in Africa exhibits many if not most of the characteristics of the marginal man—the same spiritual instability, intensified self-consciousness, restlessness, and *malaise.*

It is in the mind of the marginal man that the moral turmoil which new cultural contacts occasion manifests itself in the most obvious forms. It is in the mind of the marginal man—where the changes and fusions of culture are going on—that we can best study the processes of civilization and of progress.

NOTES

1. Carl Bücher, *Industrial Evolution*, p. 347.
2. Griffith Taylor, *Environment and Race: A Study of the Evolution, Migration, Settlement, and Status of the Races of Men*, p. 336.
3. Ellen Churchill Semple, *Influences of Geographic Environment* (London & New York, 1911), p. 75.
4. Theodor Waitz, *Introduction to Anthropology*, p. 347.
5. *Ibid.*, p. 348
6. Franz Oppenheim, *The State: Its History and Development Viewed Sociologically* (1914).
7. Georges Sorel, *Reflections on Violence* (New York, 1914).
8. Carl Bücher, *Industrial Evolution*, p. 349.
9. Frederick J. Teggart, *Theory of History* (New Haven, 1925), p. 196.
10. Gilbert Murray, *The Rise of the Greek Epic* (Oxford: Clarendon Press, 1907), pp. 78–79.
11. A. H. Guyot, *Earth and Man* (Boston, 1857), cited by Franklin Thomas, *The Environmental Basis of Society* (New York, 1921), p. 205.
12. "Racial Assimilation in Secondary Groups," *Publication of the American Sociological Society*, Vol. VIII (1914).

13   An Economic Interpretation of Antisemitism

Stanislav Andreski

One of the chief contributions of Karl Marx to our understanding of society was his insistence on the necessity of explaining political struggles and ideologies in terms of conflicts of economic interest. In the more moderate form suggested by Engels, which admits the possibility of a reflexive influence of an ideology upon the conditions which nurtured it, this idea is very helpful. It does not explain everything, but it does explain a great deal. There is no reason, however, to assume that struggles for economic prizes must always be fought between classes—that is to say, collectivities differentiated principally in virtue of their economic positions.

In a way, the interpretation presented here might be described as a synthesis of Marx's thesis on the economic nature of all conflicts, with Gumplowicz's antithesis, which emphasized the paramount importance of struggles between races. Gumplowicz, who lived in the Habsburg empire, which abounded in ethnic, racial and religious divisions, had ample opportunities for making observations which supported his theory.

On the basis of the following analysis of antisemitism, with some references to analogous phenomena, I propose the following thesis.

The strength of popular movements and currents of animosity directed against a non-dominant minority is stimulated by the following factors:

1 The conspicuousness and indelibility of the distinguishing marks.

2 The coincidence of cultural and religious and racial dividing lines.

3 General poverty and, particularly, processes of impoverishment.

4 The ratio of the minority to the majority, and, particularly, the process of increase of this ratio.

5 The minority's share of the total wealth, and, particularly the process of growth of this share.

6 The extent to which economic complementarity is absent.

7 Absence of common foes.

Among the movements and currents of animosity directed against various racial, religious and ethnic minorities, antisemitism has been without any doubt most thoroughly studied. In the writings on it two kinds of approach predominate: one is psychological, the other is through genealogy of ideas. The latter is wholly inade-

This article was first published in *The Jewish Journal of Sociology*, Vol. 5, No. 2, Dec. 1963, pp. 201–213, and is reprinted by permission of the editor of the *J.J.S.* Also reprinted by permission of the author and The Regents of the University of California Press.

quate. As shown elsewhere,[1] we can throw light on the causes of historical processes by investigating the genealogy of ideas when we deal with ideas which are difficult to conceive, such as in the field of science, technology or the art of organizing, whereas anything so primitive as ideological justifications for the dislike of strangers can occur spontaneously to any untutored mind. Ideas of this kind are always being proclaimed by somebody, and the important question, from the point of view of social causation, is to discover which social circumstances enhance their appeal. It is of little help in understanding the rise of Hitler to be told that he got his notions from Nietzsche or Stewart Houston Chamberlain, because if he did not get them from their writings he could have got them from many others, including the Old Testament. It is ethnocentrism with its ingredients of pride and hatred that has been common throughout history—not its opposites. The real problem is to explain why among the Germans in the thirties of the 20th century these commonplace sentiments turned into an insane passion.

The psychological approach is more fruitful. Unquestionably, sadism and the scapegoat mechanism operate among human beings and play a large part in the persecutions of minorities. These psychological factors must be taken into account but any interpretation solely in terms of them is bound to be inadequate because it cannot explain the variations. There are grounds to believe that sadistic propensities—as distinct from indulgence—are an irradicable feature of the human species. There is probably a little sadism in all men (though perhaps not in all women), and in any population there is a sizeable number of downright sadists who will use every opportunity for venting their lusts. The existence of a non-dominant minority may provide them with such an opportunity, for the obvious reason that its members are handicapped in defending themselves. Naturally, sadism breeds sadism, but there is an apparently irreducible core of it, which it is very difficult to relate to general social conditions even with the aid of the frustration-aggression theory, for it appears even among populations whose material needs are fully satisfied, and where there is no institutionalized brutality. This does not prove that the theory which explains sadism as a form of aggression generated by frustration is wrong: there are many forms of frustration possible even when the material needs are provided for, the most obvious being sexual. It may not have been accidental that the burning of witches began soon after celibacy had been enjoined upon the clergy, and that the most ardent inquisitors were recruited from among the monks, but on the other hand, the wealthy spectators at Roman circuses savoured gruesome sights in spite of indulging in sexual pleasures to the limits of physical capacity. We might still rescue the theory by pointing out that these people had to endure frightful humiliations and insecurity, which might have accounted for their unbridled and perverse sybaritism. There are, however, many cases described by psychiatrists which do not reveal any forms of frustration beyond what is the inescapable lot of all human beings. We must, then, draw the conclusion that in trying to discover the social circumstances which stimulate hostility against minorities, we must consider sadism as a factor which is always present, at least potentially, and which is partially independent of social conditions.

The frustration-aggression theory purports to explain displaced aggression, that is to say aggression directed at objects other than those which cause the frustration. Such aggression obviously is very important in social life and particularly in the persecutions of minorities, but equally important is simple aggression—rational in a way—which assumes the form of attempts to wrest from the minority goods which some or all members of the majority covet, or to prevent the minority from obtaining these goods in the first place.

The scapegoat theory is very enlightening. It can be interpreted as a special application of the frustration-aggression theory, and can be likewise related in some measure to economic fluctuations. It enables us to understand some spectacular events like the massacres of Jews after the epidemics in the Middle Ages, as well as the customs of human sacrifice, but it fails to account for one important feature of animosity directed towards minorities: namely, its connection with the numerical proportions between minorities and majorities.

The stress on the irrational psychopathic elements in antisemitism is due to the concentration on the phenomenon of Nazism, which was essentially a mass psychosis in spite of its economic and military conditioning. For this reason Hitlerism differed profoundly from the more prosaic and less cruel antisemitic currents which prevailed in eastern Europe. Furthermore, Hitlerite antisemitism was ordained by the charismatic leader. Before the rise of Hitler there was antisemitism in Germany, but it was weaker than in Poland and Hungary: its relative strength corresponded more or less to the relation of the proportion of the Jews in the total population of Germany to the equivalent proportions in other countries. The cruelty of the persecution of the Jews in the Third Reich was probably due to the particularly strong streak of sadism, infused into the Germans by disciplinarian social relations, the tradition of unquestioning and dutiful obedience, Hitler's insane hatred and his scheme to bind the German nation inescapably to himself by involving it in complicity in an enormous crime. In the milder antisemitic movements in eastern Europe these features were not present; in Hungary Horthy did try to divert popular discontent into this channel, but in Poland the government tried to contain it within the limits of the law of equality for all citizens.

Persecutions ordered by governments must be clearly distinguished from those which surge spontaneously from the masses. We must remember, however, that all concrete cases present inextricable mixtures of both of these ideal types, though in very varying measures. This distinction is very important for attributions of causal efficacity because a course of action which is decided upon by a small number of persons is less determined by social conditions than an action which is the result of a large number of independent decisions. For this reason acts like the expulsions of the Jews from Spain and quasi-expulsions from Russia are not easily explicable in economic terms: less bigoted monarchs might have left them alone. Ferdinand and Isabella as well as Alexander III ascended their thrones by inheritance, which had nothing to do with their views on this matter, whereas Hitler rose to power in virtue of the appeal of his propaganda, in which antisemitism figured in the first place. So it cannot be said that given the social situation, Hitler's personal inclinations were the cause of the persecutions—they determined only their severity.

Even if we consider only the behaviour of the masses we must take into account a factor which we can hardly call economic: namely, the desire for invidious self-esteem, practically universal among humanity. We assign importance to various criteria of excellence in accordance with what we excel in. One of the most accessible ways of satisfying this desire is to disdain strangers. This tendency, however, though very important in preserving any existing discriminatory institutions and attitudes, and in facilitating their establishment, cannot be regarded as a factor which initiates variations affecting whole societies. There are no reasons to think that this tendency varies greatly from one society to another, although individuals differ greatly in this respect. Among individuals whose desire for invidious self-esteem is of more or less equal strength, and whose economic interests are similar, the ones most prone to espouse the cause of racial or ethnic discrimination are those who have least other grounds for feelings of superiority, given the scale of values prevalent in their environment.

We have thus delimited the field: what is to be explained are the variations in the intensity of spontaneous mass currents of animosity towards ethnic and/or racial and/or religious non-dominant minorities. Antisemitism will be treated as a case which throws light on this general issue.

A comparative survey suggests that (like other minorities) the Jews can live unmolested only where they are few—which does not mean that where they are few they must be unmolested.

The only exception to this rule is New York, but there they are too powerful to be persecuted. Moreover, the enormous wealth of the United States makes economic competition less lethal than it is in the poor countries. For this reason psychological factors (other than the simple desire to satisfy elementary needs) play a more important role in the causation of racial and ethnic frictions in the United States than is the case in indigent societies, whilst the opposite is true of the strictly economic factor of the struggle for the division of wealth. Nevertheless, notwithstanding the great wealth available to Americans, there seems to be more hostility and discrimination against the Jews there than in England or France where they are proportionately fewer.

If we take Europe in the 20th century we see that the differences in the intensity of antisemitism roughly correspond to the ratios of the Jews to the total populations. It was most intense in Poland (where more than 10 per cent of the population was Jewish), Hungary and Rumania. It was less intense in Czechoslovakia, where they were fewer and which was more prosperous, and in Germany until Hitler whipped it up. Although the Tzarist government deliberately used the Jews as a scapegoat for the wrath of the populace, antisemitism was less deeply rooted in Russia proper than in Poland, Rumania and Hungary because the Jewish population was proportionately much smaller, and the country offered greater economic opportunities. The Tzarist government pushed most of the Jews into Poland and the Ukraine, thus intensifying antisemitism there. Antisemitism had least effect upon the prosperous countries of western Europe where Jews amounted to less than 1 per cent of the population.

As an approximate rule, there is a critical ratio which is most conducive to popular persecutions, and which seems to lie around 10 per cent. With this ratio the non-dominant minority is very conspicuous, has many points of friction with the majority, but is still small enough to be persecuted with ease. Harassing a minority of 30 or 40 per cent often entails great danger, whereas a minority of 1 or 2 per cent (provided that it is not particularly conspicuous for other reasons) can more easily escape the attention of the majority unless it is put into the limelight by organized hostile propaganda. Naturally even a majority of 99 per cent can be cruelly oppressed but this can be done only with the aid of the entire apparatus of the state—not by unorganized crowds.

The ratio is important. Nevertheless the numerical factor explains neither Hitlerism nor why antisemitism was stronger in eastern Europe in the 20th century than a century earlier, which shows that it is not a simple matter of numbers. One reason why there was less incentive a century ago to violent attacks upon the Jews was that the laws kept them in inferior positions. An exactly analogous consideration explains why there are no lynchings in South Africa as there are in the southern states of the USA.

The story of pogroms and discriminations in eastern Europe is too well known to be repeated here. What might be worth mentioning is the role which antisemitism has played in Stalin's success. When Lenin died there was a mere sprinkling of non-Jews in the highest organ of the party. By the time Stalin died there was only one Jew in the Politburo—Kaganovitch (since removed by Khrushchev). In all Stalin's purges Jews figured more prominently than chance would warrant.

Everywhere there are more aspirants than good places. The struggle for the good things of life goes on all the time. Its intensity depends primarily on how much there is to share out. This struggle is waged with all kinds of weapons, and one can view racial or religious or ethnic discrimination simply as a tool for eliminating some of the rivals. The larger the ratio of the minority to the total population, the more numerous are the points of contact and, therefore, opportunities for friction. It is clear, however, that the intensity of the hostility cannot depend on the frequency of contacts alone. As far as the conflict of economic interests is concerned, the number factor is supremely important because it determines the total amount of wealth held by the minority—for any given level of opulence of its members. A mass movement aiming at spoliation needs a prospect of a booty of some size. Although usually this size is grossly magnified in the imagination of the covetous or necessitous multitudes, there is normally some relation between the reality and the image.

Eastern Europe between the wars was, as it still is today, a poor and over-populated area. The Jews had succeeded in monopolizing certain lucrative trades, and in entering certain attractive professions in very large numbers. For example, about 60 per cent of the doctors and lawyers in Cracow (and more in some smaller towns) were Jews. Something like 95 per cent of the trade in hides and furs in Poland was in the hands of the Jews. This, of course, does not mean that all the Jews were rich (actually most of them were desperately poor) but they did own a sufficient slice of the total wealth to excite the envy of others. Disregarding clearly exaggerated estimates, it seems that it amounted to about 20 per cent. Under these circumstances, it would be surprising if some of the non-Jews did not strike on the idea that they could make a better living if the Jews were eliminated or despoiled, or at least fettered. The rioting students, for instance, demanded that the Jews should not be admitted into universities in numbers larger than corresponding to their proportion in the total population. In a way, eastern European antisemitism was an attempt to counteract the economic superiority of the Jews by the fists of the greater number.

The superior economic prowess of the Jews in eastern Europe was due to a number of causes, of which the first was the increase in importance of the activities traditionally allotted to them: in consequence of urbanization and industrialization commerce was continually gaining in weight as a source of income in comparison with agriculture; and in this field the Jews possessed not only the advantage of acquired positions but also the tradition of necessary skills. Being a closely-knit community, they often combined to try to keep the Gentiles out of their ground, thus defending, in fact, the *status quo* sanctified by tradition. Apart from the very rich families who acquired the habits of the nobility, the Jews were not impeded from attaining business success by the proclivity to conspicuous and ruinous consumption instilled into the Poles and the Hungarians by the example of their nobility, who regarded spendthriftiness as one of the chief virtues.

In intellectual occupations the success of the Jews was connected in the first place with their tradition of reverence for knowledge and the book, and secondly, with the stimulus to excel produced by their inner conviction of superiority combined with their exposure to outward humiliations. Furthermore, the tradition of parental solicitude and family solidarity seem to be particularly strong among the Jews, and, together with the readiness of mutual help within the Jewish community, they provided a counterweight to the hindrances of antisemitic discrimination. As far as intellectuals in the strict sense are concerned, the prominence of the Jews in their ranks was also due to the marginal social position of unorthodox Jews: being suspended at cross-roads of loyalties, beliefs and customs always stimulates curiosity and independence of thought.

In the old Polish kingdom there was an ethnic division of labour: commerce was a Jewish occupation. In the regions which now form part of Poland both the peasants and the nobles were of Polish ethnic stock. In the eastern territories there was a proper ethnic stratification; the nobility was Polish, the commercial class Jewish and the peasants Ukrainian. As Gumplowicz pointed out eighty years ago, the situation in Java was very similar, the homologous elements being the Dutch, the Chinese and the Javanese. The same can be said about the English, the Indians and the Africans in south-eastern Africa. In the two latter cases, however, the ruling race retained the largest businesses, which just did not exist in old Poland, and where consequently the nobility remained purely rural. The attitude of the Polish or Ukrainian peasant to the Jew was similar to that of the African peasant to the Indian: a mixture of disdain with admiration for the cleverness of the trading race, of resentment at their pretensions to superiority and their economic exploitation. Sometimes this resentment turned into burning hatred, and led to outbreaks of violence.

The pogroms of the Jews in eastern Europe, the recent slaughter of the Chinese in Indonesia, and the anti-Indian riots in Africa, were truly popular movements. Even in such cases as the Durban riots in 1949, or the post-1905 pogroms in Russia, the police provided only a few *agents-provocateurs,* and turned a blind eye on what was going on—they did not hire or command the assailants. The explosive material was there—the *agents-provocateurs* acted as a spark. As mentioned earlier, there is in all such phenomena a constant element: in any human mass, particularly if it consists of uncouth lads, there are many who will jump at the opportunity of beating up somebody with impunity. Being constant, however, this factor explains neither the timing nor the dimensions of the outbreaks. These can be understood only if we take into account the economic processes.

Money flows into the hands of those who manipulate it, and in all cases where peasants coexist with traders and moneylenders, the peasants fall into debt, and the others increase their share of wealth. This is a well-known process already described in the Bible as well as in modern economic studies of India and other countries. On very large estates the conflict between the Jew and the peasant was aggravated by the practice of rent-farming: big landowners, who could not supervise their estates, sometimes gave their Jewish 'factors' the right to collect the rents in exchange for a lump sum. Like the Roman tax-farming, or the sale of offices, this practice produced some of the worst forms of exploitation. In the Ukraine, where the largest estates were to be found and where the big peasant wars were fought, the slogan of the rebels was: 'Kill the lords and the Jews'. The smaller pogroms, however, which did not form part of peasant uprisings, did not aim at the elimination of the Jews. In so far as they had an aim, it was the cancellation of debts.

The nobles were in a peculiar position: on the one side they had superior force, on the other, many of them were in debt to Jewish moneylenders. This ambiguity led to erratic behaviour in which patronizing friendship and even humble entreaties alternated with insults and assaults. Anyway, the nobles and the Jews lived in a symbiosis: the nobles relied on the commercial services of the Jews, and protected them. Indeed, the decisive fact in the history of Poland was that the nobles succeeded in suppressing the Christian commercial class, and replacing it by the Jews who, being isolated from the rest of the population, were more docile. This explains the downfall of the royal authority: the kings were unable to resist the encroachments of the nobility because—unlike their counterparts in western Europe—they could not use the *bourgeoisie* as the counterweight. The erratic symbiosis between the nobles and the Jews was somewhat undermined after the partitions by the policy of 'divide and rule' pursued by the Tzarist government, but in the main it continued until the appearance of the non-Jewish professional and commercial classes. Antisemitism as a mass movement appeared when economic competition replaced economic complementarity.

If we follow the history of the expulsions of the Jews from various places in western Europe, which took place towards the end of the Middle Ages, we find that whether we take England or the Rhineland these expulsions were preceded by the growth of a non-Jewish commercial class. The princes of eastern Europe welcomed

the Jews—and the population did not oppose them—because, owing to the paucity
of native traders, they were economically complementary. There was one medieval
case which did not fit this rule: the Jews were expelled from Spain in spite of being
economically complementary. This expulsion, however, was prompted not so much
by mass antipathy as by the kings' bigotry. Moreover, it occurred as aftermath of
the victory in a war against the infidel which lasted several centuries. In so far as
there was popular hostility to the Jews, it was due to what the psychologists call
nowadays 'stimulus generalization', and what they used to call association of ideas:
the war against the Moslems made all infidels odious. For nowhere in medieval
Europe were the Jews less racially distinguishable, or more assimilated culturally.
Whereas eastern European Jews spoke Yiddish (derived from German), some of the
Sephardic Jews, whose ancestors lived in the Orient after the expulsion from Spain,
spoke Spanish at home until their arrival in the new state of Israel. This example
proves that persecutions can occur in spite of economic complementarity, but it
does not disprove the thesis that economic complementarity is a necessary condition of the lack of persecutions. This proposition was first advanced by Leon
Petrajitski (Petrazycki) forty years ago in a memorable essay which, unfortunately,
is available only in Polish. It can be formulated as follows: in any society composed
of cohesive, ethnically heterogeneous sections, a relative absence of conflict is possible only if these sections are economically complementary.

The foregoing considerations allow us to view the growth of antisemitism in
eastern Europe as a consequence of the erosion of economic complementarity. The
abolition of serfdom and the increase in the density of the rural population led to
an influx of young peasants to towns. Most of them became servants or journeymen
or industrial workers; some took up petty trade (which some of their descendants
succeeded in developing) where they came up against the Jewish monopoly. On the
other side, the Jews, when liberated from their legal disabilities, began to flock into
liberal professions where they entered into competition with impoverished nobles
and the 'mobiles' from below. Apart from the argument from co-variance in time,
an examination of the class composition of the antisemitic organizations in Poland
between the wars also supports this view. This interpretation can be applied to
equivalent movements in other countries of eastern Europe.

The Polish Socialist Party, supported in the main by the industrial workers, was
not antisemitic. In Russian Poland before the First World War about one third of its
members were Jewish; and many remained in it even after the specifically Jewish
parties came into existence. Although the peasants rioted against the Jews sporadically, their organizations were certainly not to the fore in demanding that the Jews
should be deported to Palestine or locked up in ghettoes. As the peasants sold their
produce mostly to the Jews they blamed them for low prices. As far as the industrial
workers are concerned, the explanation is not, of course, that their occupation gen-
erates superior virtue: there are many examples from all over the world of how
xenophobic industrial workers can be when it comes to admitting foreigners into
their kind of job. The reason for the relative weakness of antisemitism among the
Polish industrial workers was that, although there were Jews in this occupation, they

were relatively few, and did not present a serious threat to employment. The political circles connected with the landowning nobility did not propagate antisemitism either: they maintained the tradition of patronizing tolerance. There were two parties devoted to the cause of antisemitism. One was the Radical National Party—a small body of violent men, whose admiration for Hitler's methods and outlook verged on anticlericalism. (Its ex-leader, incidentally, is now a *persona grata* of the Communist régime, and heads the National Catholics who defy Rome.) It attracted all kinds of desperadoes and delinquents. In so far as its recruitment tended towards any class, it seems to have been what the Germans call *'Lumpenintelligenz'*; failed students with neither jobs nor private means. This party was born at the nadir of the economic crisis. The traditionalist and clerical National Party was far older and bigger.

Owing to the existence of multi-national states, citizenship in central and eastern Europe is clearly distinguished from nationality, in the sense of belonging to an ethnic collectivity. So, by calling itself 'national', the party proclaimed that it was against the co-citizens who were not co-nationals. The word 'national', incidentally, has the same connotation in the name of the ruling party of South Africa. It must be added that the overwhelming majority of Jews in eastern Europe were not merely distinguished by religion and physical traits, but had a special kind of customary dress, spoke Yiddish and were neither considered, nor considered themselves, as belonging to the Russian, Polish, Hungarian or the Ukrainian nations. With the exception of the Ukrainians, each of these nations had its 'assimilated' Jews. In Poland people whom the antisemites classified as Jews comprised the following categories: (1) Jews resident in Poland who did not know Polish and lived in complete segregation; (2) Polish Jews who spoke Polish (though not always well) and had strong links with the Polish nation without identifying themselves with it; (3) Poles of Jewish faith who did not speak Yiddish, and regarded themselves as belonging to the Polish nation in spite of humiliations; (4) persons of Jewish origin who cut themselves off from the Jewish community and identified themselves wholly with the Gentile Polish nation—they were either converts to Catholicism or free thinkers; (5) persons of partly Jewish origins who had no links with the Jewish community although they would be branded as Jews by the antisemites if their antecedents were known.

Assimilation occurred as a rule only among the educated or the rich. For this reason it was more extensive in Great Russia, where poor Jews were fewer, than in the western provinces of the Russian Empire. In the old kingdom of Poland converts to Christianity came exclusively from among the rich Jews who desired to enter the ranks of the nobility. Notwithstanding the temptation of ennoblement as the usual reward for conversion, very few Jews abandoned their faith. In later times, when the spread of religious scepticism made more of them willing to do so, they were pushed back by the rising tide of antisemitism. The fact that antisemitism assumed extreme forms precisely at the time when increasing numbers of Jews were abandoning their ghettoes and the special dress, and even ceasing to speak Yiddish, proves that its chief roots lay in the growing acerbity of economic competition rather than in sheer heterophobia.

The National Party in Poland drew its strength mainly from the artisans and traders, with a large ingredient of members of the class which used to be, and still is, called the 'intelligentsia', and which has no equivalent in western Europe. The 'intelligentsia' was the section of society which consisted of families who derived their subsistence from employment as civil servants, teachers and army officers, or the liberal professions. In order to qualify as a member of the intelligentsia, a person had to have academic or at least secondary education, do non-commercial work for which such education was at least formally necessary, and have requisite manners. The antisemitism of this group was also economically conditioned: it became acute after the establishment of universities in a number of towns, and the consequent increase in the number of graduates beyond what could be absorbed by the market. It became frantic during the economic crisis of the thirties when redundancy hit even the well-established members of this class. Before independence there were only two Polish universities, both located in Austrian Poland. Even in Warsaw higher education was only intermittently available before the First World War. In German Poland the people who corresponded occupationally to the 'intelligentsia' were mostly Germans, and did not form a class segregated from the business sectors: they belonged to the fairly unified middle class of the western European type, which had no equivalent farther east. In any case, there were very few Jews there, because after the incorporation of these regions into Prussia the Jews who lived there in mass migrated to economically more advanced parts of Germany. In western Poland antisemitism passed from latency to virulence when the Jews from the eastern parts began to arrive after the reunification. To come back to the 'intelligentsia': in Russian Poland there was relatively little antisemitism amongst this class; primarily because of the weakness of economic competition, and secondly because of the existence of a common enemy in the shape of the Tzarist government which oppressed the Poles and the Jews alike. Two factors explain the weakness of the competition on the pasturages of the intelligentsia in Russian Poland: the first was the smallness of the supply, itself the consequence of the virtual non-existence of institutions of higher learning. Secondly, in spite of being oppressed at home, the Poles with professional qualifications of any kind had ample openings in Russia itself, where often they were even given preference over the Russians, owing to their reputation for being more reliable and less addicted to dissipation.

Unlike the persecution of the Jews in Hitler's Germany, the antisemitic outbreaks in independent Poland were entirely unofficial, and the government tried to repress them—with fair success, for they never turned into massacres, and were normally confined to shouting and breaking windows. The police beat the demonstrators as much as these beat the Jews. Pilsudski (the dictator from 1926 to 1935) represented the old traditions of the nobility which regarded the Jews as a natural part of the body of citizens. The chief and the most effective slogan against him was that he sold the country to the Jews. After his death his heirs began reluctantly to make concessions to the mood of the masses: though still maintaining the prohibition of violence, they allowed organized boycott. To understand the situation, one must take into consideration the odd circumstance that in spite of being a dictatorship with a developing taste for totalitarian paraphernalia, the government could not control the masses very well: in fact, in some places it was dangerous to admit that one was pro-government. In the university of Poznan, for instance, the few students who belonged to the pro-government organization were exposed to intimidation and chicanery from their fellows, as well as to victimization from some of the professors. Some professors from various universities, who did not conceal their anticlericalism or disapproval of antisemitism, had to endure whistles and shouts in lecture rooms, and on some occasions were pelted with rotten eggs. Sometimes the students started riots which assumed the proportions of battles against the police.

The curious feature of the National Party was the anti-capitalist streak in its ideology. In this it resembled the National Party of South Africa, and for the same reason: the big industrialists were not of their stock. In Poland they were mostly Germans or Jews, and some of the biggest establishments were owned by foreign companies. Similar circumstances gave an anti-capitalist tinge to nationalist ideologies in a number of Latin American and ex-colonial countries. The Polish National Party fought battles on many fronts, one of them being of the small and middle size business against big business. It remains to be noted that even the wing whose programmes and values could without exaggeration be described as Fascist, and whose members admired Mussolini and Hitler, was violently anti-German. Obviously the creed of sacred egoism of the nation provides no basis for an international.

To understand the whole situation one must bear in mind the extremely hard economic conditions, which did not yet last long enough to induce despondency: aggressive resentment, not fatalistic lethargy, was the prevailing mood of the people. This was combined with the tradition of disobedience and wilfulness, bred by centuries of disorder and foreign rule, and the inclination to violence in everyday life, which was unparalleled in western Europe. These pent-up animosities would probably have discharged themselves in a civil war, were it not for the German invasion.

There is nothing surprising in the connection between antisemitism and economic distress. A similar relationship has been observed in many other cases, and there is no reason to believe that antisemitism is exempt from social causation, or that the sufferings of the Jews are something absolutely unique. Unfortunately, the annals of cruelty are inexhaustible and other minorities have experienced at some time or other all the iniquities inflicted upon the Jews. The extermination of the Christians in Japan was just as thorough as Hitler's genocide. If fewer were killed it was because they were fewer. When massacring the Armenians, the Turks perpetrated all the deeds of which the SS men are guilty. If the history of antisemitism is particularly long it is because the Jews have clung to their separateness with unique tenacity. Most minorities could not be persecuted for so long because they dissolved themselves in the surrounding population.

In so far as there could be no antisemitism without Jews, the economic interpretation is incomplete because it fails to account for the unique continuity of the Jewish cultural tradition and ethnic identity. Nor could the tenacity of the Jews in preserving their identity be the consequence of oppression, because other oppressed minorities did not acquire it.

The most general conclusion which emerges from this analysis of the economic roots of antisemitism, as well as from the preceding examination of other forms of racial discrimination, is that preaching alone will not extirpate them, and that they cannot be attenuated if the economic conflicts do not abate. The lesson for social engineering is plain.

Economic conflict is not a necessary condition of ethnic and racial animosity but it is a sufficient condition thereof. As the position of Negroes in the USA shows, animosity may exist without serious economic conflict, but it is inevitable where such conflict is bitter.

When goods are growing scarce men will fight for the shares, but whether they will divide themselves on class lines, or according to religious or ethnic or racial distinctions, depends on the relative strength of the various kinds of social bonds: a fissure occurs along the line of least cohesion. The difficulty of harmonizing conflicting interests will be greatest if more than one distinguishing mark coincides: if, for instance, class positions correspond to differences in religion, language, culture and physical traits. Obversely, where such differences cut across the stratification they tend to prevent the crystallization of conflict along the class lines.

The part played by the struggle for a share in wealth in exacerbating antagonisms between collectivities in no way ensures that the movements thus generated offer a real solution to economic ills. Normally the contrary is the case: strife aggravates instead of alleviating poverty, and a vicious circle comes into existence.

NOTES

1. See S. Andreski, *Elements of Comparative Sociology* (London: Weidenfeld & Nicolson, 1964), chap. 12.

CONTINUOUS SOCIAL CHANGE:

SOCIAL MOBILITY, URBANIZATION, AND

INDUSTRIALIZATION

It would not seem surprising if three such major processes as social mobility, urbanization, and industrialization had a profound impact on the relations between racial and ethnic groups. The papers in this section of the book arrive at rather similar conclusions. They reject oversimple theories based on a single-factor determinism and argue that no clear-cut result can be seen as the invariable consequence of such patterns of social change. Much greater knowledge of the particular context of race contact must be secured before reliable predictions about the outcome of these forces can be made.

Bettelheim and Janowitz focus on the issue of social mobility in American society by considering the results of studies bearing on their theoretical formulation of prejudice (derived in part from the insights of Durkheim) in terms of personal and social controls. In general they confirm the hypothesis associating downward mobility with ethnic intolerance. The suggestive finding that sharp upward mobility—as opposed to a more moderate rise in status—is also linked to ethnic hostility gives added support to their theories uniting social and psychological variables.

Lever and Wagner are concerned with an even more narrowly defined variation on the same basic theme: disputing the claim that there will be an automatic increase in tolerance among urbanized Afrikaners in South Africa simply as a result of living in towns and cities. By undermining this crude ecological determinism they expose the dangers of the common tendency to oversimplify the complex interaction of race and ethnicity with highly generalized social trends.

Blumer continues the argument by examining the impact of industrialization. In several respects his approach parallels the debates over two related theories: the *embourgeoisement* thesis,[1] which claims that advanced industrialism erodes class consciousness and breaks down class barriers; and the *convergence* thesis,[2] which maintains that capitalist and communist societies are becoming increasingly alike in a "post-industrial" world. Blumer's conclusion that industrialization "will continue to be an incitant to change, without providing the definition of how the change is to be met" is applicable to each aspect of the debate. It is a convincing refutation of those theories that proclaim a logic of industrialism that will inevitably determine

135

the shape of society in the future. The truth seems to be that a wide variety of social, racial, and ethnic relations can coexist with similar types of economic and technological substructures.

NOTES

1. J. H. Goldthorpe, D. Lockwood, F. Bechofer, and J. Platt, *The Affluent Worker in the Class Structure* (Cambridge: Cambridge University Press, 1969).
2. J. H. Goldthorpe, "Social Stratification in Industrial Society," *Sociological Review Monograph* no. 8 (1964): 97–122.

14   The Consequences
of Social Mobility

Bruno Bettelheim & Morris Janowitz

In studying the effects of social mobility, we called our approach that of personal and social control, because we were interested in how inner and interpersonal processes interact with patterns of social control. Our underlying assumption was that the effects of social mobility on beliefs and attitudes, including prejudice, derive not only from differing group norms but also from how the person responds to group norms. We were interested not only in explaining how group norms evolve, but in understanding the range of attitudes held by persons within a relatively homogeneous group as well.

By personal controls, we mean the internalized patterns that regulate and influence human predispositions and emotions and thereby condition overt behavior. By social control, we mean the institutionalized patterns regulating and influencing groups as they pursue social values and social goals. The approach of personal and social control was used to compare and contrast the correlates of prejudice against Jews and Negroes.[1] We hardly sought to contribute to a unified theory of behavior that would be applicable to prejudice. But neither did we give priority to either social or psychological variables. Our frame of reference was interdisciplinary and our objectives were limited. We believed that the concept of control—personal and social—supplied a useful coordinating device. By using a sociological approach to prejudice and its correlates, we felt that psychological mechanisms could be studied as mediating variables. For example, one of our central hypotheses was that downward social mobility would increase ethnic intolerance. Downward social mobility is seen as a sociological process which has effects on psychological processes connected with personal control. We are aware, of course, that psychological processes contribute to mobility, particularly to mobility different from dominant societal trends. But the underlying rationale was that downward mobility as a social process would increase feelings of subjective deprivation and insecurity, which in turn would contribute to hostility and prejudice. Likewise, from a psychological orientation, the sociological variables would lend understanding of the context. We believe the same approach would be relevant for a range of social behavior broader than ethnic intolerance.

This approach of personal and social control stems from the work of Émile Durkheim, who focused attention on the disruptive consequences of social mobility in his classic study of suicide.[2] Durkheim sought to explain in social terms what was looked on as a psychological act. For him, the higher incidence of certain types of suicide indicated a weakening of the social bond or of "collective representations." He recognized that a special type of suicide could also be linked to overintegration and overrigidity of social norms.

Durkheim saw a weakening of social bonds as a result of the growth of the industrial division of labor, which alters the basic institutions of society. For him, social mobility was a specially important manifestation of the industrial division of labor. He felt it would weaken the collective representations on which social stability rests. Therefore, he expected—and found—higher rates of suicide among groups with greater social mobility.

In retrospect, we would note three limitations of Durkheim's analysis. First, he overlooked the positive contribution that social mobility with its widening horizons can make to personal well-being and social stability. This takes the forms of releasing personal and group creativity, a process that we still understand only dimly. Second, he underestimated the potential of social institutions and of new social inventions to contain, and even overcome, the disruptive effects of social mobility. Third, he did not concern himself with the interpersonal mechanisms by which a person may give up old values and incorporate new ones. He overlooked the variation in the capacity of human beings with similar social backgrounds to develop requisite new personal controls and incorporate new norms.

In our analysis, a person with stronger personal controls—as opposed to rigid inner controls—would be a person who was able to adjust to varying conditions connected with social mobility; that is, he would have a stronger ego and more effective psychological resources for coping with the personal consequences of social change. He would be able to withstand the pressure and disruption of social mobility more than would a person with weaker personal controls. Moreover, since Durkheim's time, the "world view" toward mobility has changed. Social mobility has emerged as a desirable social goal in the United States, an end to be sought after by "good" people. Thus, in our efforts to study the consequences of social mobility on ethnic prejudice, we sought to go beyond the frame of reference supplied by Durkheim; we sought to incorporate—directly or indirectly—a person's reactions to mobility, that is, his definition of the situation.

Our hypotheses about social mobility and ethnic prejudice were limited by the following considerations. First, we were concerned with the effects of personal mobility; that is, the movement of persons and families from one social stratum to another. Social shifts in the position of a whole group, as they affect prejudice, provide a closely related but distinct issue, although we did not focus on this problem in *Dynamics of Prejudice.* In the writings of Robert E. Park,[3] one finds a discussion of prejudice and group mobility. For him, prejudice was a social response—a resistant response—to change in the social order. When Negroes as a group moved up the social scale, there would necessarily be an increase in social competition and therefore in social prejudice, as a defensive reaction for maintaining the older social order. But our materials on social change and prejudice, over the last 20 years, do not support the view that a rise in social position for the Negro directly increases prejudice. The process seems to be more complex, more varied, and more interactive. Higher social position, including social benefits won by direct action, as by the "sit-ins," also brings greater respect for the particular minority group. Thus, group mobility is an important influence on ethnic prejudice. Nevertheless, our empirical data dealt with a narrower problem: namely, that as a society moves into advanced industrialism, personal mobility is fundamental to the process of social change. In investigating trends that might slow or even operate against the growth of tolerance, personal mobility is of special importance.

Second, in the original study and in evaluating the various new studies, we speak of a particular time and place. Our focus was on the United States as an advanced industrial society. We were concerned with social mobility in the metropolitan community, where the bulk of the American population resides. The changes that take place in urbanization, in moving from the agricultural sector to the urban sector, are not directly covered by our hypotheses. We do not believe our hypotheses are directly applicable to rural areas. They might not apply directly to the South with its special historical traditions.

Third, the period during which we were studying social mobility was one of economic expansion and without prolonged economic depression. On historical and theoretical grounds, we rejected the assumption that the effects of upward and downward mobility would be the same. There was every reason to believe that downward mobility would be the more disruptive. It not only would weaken social bonds, but would forcibly confront the person with the fact that his social experience was at variance with the cultural ideal and with major societal trends. Both pressures would weaken or strain his personal control and increase his feelings of deprivation and insecurity. These psychological mechanisms would increase his level of prejudice, even above what existed in the group he was entering.

Upward social mobility during this recent period would not have had the same effect. A moderate amount of upward mobility is widespread and in a sense typical or "normal." With this pattern so widespread, there was no reason to suppose that moderate upward mobility would create high levels of social and personal disruption. Only among persons who had experienced extreme upward mobility could we expect to find the consequences described by Durkheim. What is required is a measure of normal or "expected" upward mobility so that mobility beyond that is extreme or "abnormal."

We were, of course, fully aware that certain social institutions, such as voluntary associations and religious groups, operate to contain the disruptive consequences of social mobility. Yet, on balance we expected both downward mobility and extreme upward mobility to have the over-all effect of increasing the incidence of high ethnic hostility. We rejected, as not being overriding, the reverse proposition that ethnic prejudice would influence these patterns of mobility because there was no theoretical rationale to support it; neither did it seem plausible. This might operate for some cases but not as a systematic factor, especially not for extreme upward mobility.

Fourth, social mobility variables cannot explain the historical genesis of ethnic prejudice in any particular social group. They are relevant only in explaining the mobile person's deviation from or conformity to group norms.[4] In the original study and in all of the subsequent studies, the research approach was to focus on the correlates of high versus low ethnic prejudice. This was done by cross-sectional analysis at a particular time period. It meant that the norms of ethnic prejudice had to be identified for each group—that is, the group's central tendency and its range from high to low. Thus, the more we know about the "norms" of intolerance in a particular group, the more precisely can we identify the effects of mobility. To study these effects in national samples is highly complex, because the norms of the many social groupings become much harder to identify. That is why relatively homogeneous samples were necessary to test our hypotheses.

In summary, no simple assumption can be made about the effects of mobility on prejudice, or for that matter on other types of social behavior. In the search for generalizations, we must keep in mind the direction and extent of movement, the norms of the groups to and from which the person is moving, and the economic context of the mobility process.

DOWNWARD SOCIAL MOBILITY

Efforts to study the hypothesis that downward social mobility increases ethnic hostility have been rewarding. They also demonstrate that sociological investigations can be cumulative. The seven relevant efforts to restudy the problem have produced evidence to support the hypothesis, at least for the period of the last 15 years of economic expansion. (See Table 1.) At the same time they help to reformulate the original proposition by more clearly identifying which social groups are most vulnerable to the disruptive effects of mobility.

It was assumed in the *Dynamics of Prejudice* that a single variable can explain only limited aspects of ethnic prejudice. This makes a multivariate analysis appropriate. Since the original study was completed, however, such techniques have been greatly improved. We sought a partial solution by using a relatively homogeneous sample. Our sampling procedures de-emphasize the difference in levels of prejudice at the extremes of the social structure. We sought to reduce or eliminate the special

TABLE 1

Replication Studies Proposition: Downward Social Mobility Increases Ethnic Prejudice

Investigator	Sample	Instrument	Target Group	Prejudice Measure	Type of Mobility	Comparison Group	Replication
Bettelheim and Janowitz[1]	150 World War II veterans of Chicago, under 35 years, interviewed 1945	Intensive structured interviews	Jews; Negroes	Typology based on 12 response categories	Intra-generation	a. No mobility b. Upward mobility	a. Confirmed b. Confirmed
Curtis[2]	Probability sample of Detroit Area Study, interviewed 1954	Standard survey research interview	Negroes	Coding of spontaneous references	Inter-generation	a. No mobility b. Upward mobility	a. Confirmed b. Confirmed
Greenblum and Pearlin[3]	Representative sample of 664 adults from Elmira, N.Y., interviewed 1948	Standard survey research interview	Jews; Negroes	Responses to individual questions	Inter-generation	a. No mobility b. Upward mobility	a. Confirmed on 6 items; tied on 1 item b. Not confirmed
Silberstein and Seeman[4]	Sample of 665 persons of Morgantown, West Virginia, published 1960	Standard survey research interview	Jews; Negroes	Anti-Semitic and anti-Negro scale of authoritarian personality	Inter-generation	a. No mobility b. Upward mobility	a. Partially confirmed b. Confirmed
Lenski[5]	Probability sample of 640 adults, interviewed 1959 in Detroit Area	Standard survey research interview	Negroes	Responses to individual questions	Inter-generation	a. No mobility b. Upward mobility	a. Confirmed b. Confirmed
Pettigrew[6]	180 New England adults and 186 Southern adults from Carolina and Georgia, interviewed 1955	Standard survey research interview	Jews; Negroes	8-item scale of anti-Semitic; 12-item measure of anti-Negro	Inter-generation	a. No mobility	a. Confirmed for Northern sample; reversal for Southern sample
Tumin[7]	Sample of 287, Guilford County, North Carolina, published 1958	Standard survey research interview	Negroes	6 Guttman type scales	Inter-generation	a. No mobility b. Upward mobility	a. Partially confirmed b. Confirmed
Leggett[8]	375 blue collar male heads of households in Detroit, interviewed 1960	Intensive structured interview	Negroes	Coding of spontaneous references	Intra-generation	a. No mobility	a. Confirmed

[1] Bruno Bettelheim and Morris Janowitz, *Dynamics of Prejudice*, New York, Harper and Bros., 1950, pp. 59, 150.

[2] Richard F. Curtis, *Consequences of Occupational Mobility in a Metropolitan Community*, Unpublished Ph.D. dissertation, University of Michigan, 1958, p. 196.

[3] Joseph Greenblum, and Leonard I. Pearlin, "Vertical Mobility and Prejudice: A Socio-Psychological Analysis," in Reinhard Bendix and S. M. Lipset (eds.), *Class, Status and Power*, New York, The Free Press of Glencoe, 1953, pp. 486–91.

[4] Fred B. Silberstein and Melvin Seeman, "Social Mobility and Prejudice," *American Journal of Sociology*, LX, November, 1959, pp. 258–64.

[5] Gerhard E. Lenski, Special tabulations prepared on data presented in *The Religious Factor: A Sociological Study of Religions Impact on Politics, Economics and Family Life*, Garden City, N.Y., Doubleday and Co., 1961.

[6] Thomas F. Pettigrew, "Regional Differences in Anti-Negro Prejudice," *Journal of Abnormal and Social Psychology*, LIX, July, 1959, p. 33.

[7] Melvin M. Tumin, *Desegregation: Resistance and Readiness*, Princeton University Press, 1958, p. 130.

[8] John Carl Leggett, *Working Class Consciousness in an Industrial Community*, Unpublished Ph.D. thesis, University of Michigan, 1962.

problems of studying prejudice at the very top of the social structure. And by excluding Negroes, we reduced representation from the very bottom. Nevertheless, it needs to be emphasized that to the extent that prejudice varies between social status groups, we sought to correct these differences in testing our mobility hypotheses.

The first test of our downward mobility hypothesis was to compare levels of prejudice between those who were stationary in the middle classes, and those who were downwardly mobile from the middle class. But, the downward mobility hypothesis could be put to a more severe test. We could examine whether persons who move downward are not only more prejudiced than the group they left but also more prejudiced than the lower status group they enter. It is a more severe test because prejudice in the stationary, lower status groups is usually greater than in the middle status groups. The downwardly mobile were also compared with those moving upward.

Using the more stringent test, these seven studies produced a general pattern of confirmation (Table 1). Four studies produced clear-cut confirmation; two yielded partial confirmation. Uniform measures of statistical significance were not possible because of how the data were collected and published; however, two samples were significant at the .01 level or better. (Partial confirmation implies either that results were in the predicted direction but did not achieve statistical significance, or that the relationship could be observed for the more limited test of the middle class stables versus the downwardly mobiles.) The seventh study confirmed the proposition at the statistical level for its Northern sample, while the finding was reversed for its Southern sample. Of the six Northern samples, there was not a single reversal, only one partial confirmation, and all the remaining were confirmed. When comparing the downwardly mobile with the upwardly mobile as another test of the proposition, roughly similar results were obtained.

The samples covered a variety of populations and methodologies. Three samples represent the Northern urban metropolis; two of them were drawn from the Detroit Area Study by the Department of Sociology of the University of Michigan, which used probability sampling and standardized interview procedures (Richard F. Curtis and Gerhard Lenski). A third made use of an urban working class population (John Leggett). Another sample studied by similar research procedures was the one used by Joseph Greenblum and Leonard I. Pearlin in their reanalysis of the Elmira voting study data. The special relevance of this latter study is that it reflects attitudes among the minority of the population who live in small industrial communities. Silberstein and Seeman interviewed a group of residents of Morgantown, West Virginia, for the specific purpose of probing the relationship between social mobility and prejudice. Two studies involved Southern samples: one included a North-South comparison, undertaken by Thomas F. Pettigrew; the other, by Melvin M. Tumin, made possible a very careful study of attitudes toward desegregation in North Carolina.[5]

Both John Leggett and Richard Curtis used spontaneous expressions of hostility as their operational measures of ethnic prejudice. Leggett's work in particular is an interesting example of the field approach required for studying ethnic and moral values, especially among working class persons. His study was designed to probe class consciousness—not in a rigid Marxian sense, but in the concrete realities: style of life, job opportunities, and political power in the daily life of a worker in a metropolitan community. His particular insight was that class consciousness in the working class—the person's awareness of the class-based limitations on his style of life (or of limitations imposed by the social order)—depends on the ethnic factor. He found, holding income and skill constant, that Poles were more class conscious than Germans, and Negroes more class conscious than Poles. In general terms, the lower the ethnic status the higher was the level of class consciousness. The order was Negroes, Poles, Germans.

While probing social class consciousness, Leggett had an ideal opportunity to elicit expressions of anti-Negro hostility among white members of his working-class sample. Because his sample was sociologically homogeneous, and because the interview probed effectively for levels of hostility, the results were noteworthy in that the downwardly mobile workers were most prejudiced. Among the workers with stable mobility backgrounds, 26.9 per cent gave spontaneous responses that were anti-Negro as against 43.3 per cent among the downwardly mobile.

Curtis' findings had further relevance. He was able to measure the extent of downward mobility—moderate, high, and extreme—on the basis of a more refined occupational stratification code than was used in most of the other studies (but similar to that employed in *Dynamics of Prejudice*). This enabled him to confirm the proposition that more extensive downward social mobility was linked to higher levels of ethnic intolerance. His findings indicate that the downward mobility proposition operates both within and between the white collar and blue collar stratification system.

Greenblum and Pearlin's re-examination of the downward mobility hypothesis took the supplementary step of studying subgroups. The proposition was validated for the entire sample: men and women, for the subsample of the gainfully employed; for males only; and for gainfully employed males under thirty-five. They also broke down their data by social class of origin into manual stationary, downwardly mobile, and nonmanual stationary. Again the findings were that the downwardly mobile are more prejudiced than the stationary, manual or nonmanual.

Silberstein and Seeman introduce a related distinction between two different outlooks on status—those stressing mobility and those stressing achievement. They report that the distinction "lies in the fact that the latter tend to give status and prestige a lower value—i.e., they choose to emphasize the relative importance of, for example, friendship, political freedom, community life, or intrinsic interest in the job as compared with the value of social rank."[6] For our purpose, this distinction is relevant for locating those persons most vulnerable to the disruptive effects of downward mobility. They offer the hypothesis that among the downwardly mobile, those persons who stress mobility would be more prejudiced than those stressing achievement. Empirical results support this proposition when objective measures of mobility are used.[7]

UPWARD SOCIAL MOBILITY

By contrast to the extensive restudy of the downward mobility hypothesis, new data on upward social mobility are limited and incomplete. In retrospect, we attribute this in part to our not being more explicit about the link between rational inner controls and the effects of upward mobility. Added to this, full replication requires both direction and extent of mobility, and only one of the seven studies examined both.

Our central hypothesis did not state that upward social mobility would increase prejudice. Upward social mobility is widespread in the United States, and there is no reason to expect a moderate amount to be particularly stressful or disruptive. The linkage of upward mobility and ethnic intolerance was based on extent of mobility; i.e., if a person had experienced extreme (not just moderate) upward mobility, one would expect higher levels of prejudice on the basis of an approach seeking to link personal and social controls to levels of prejudice.

What prediction could be made about moderate or average upward mobility? In the original research, it was found that for our sample of young veterans, the total group of upwardly mobile persons (characterized mainly by moderate upward mobility) were more tolerant than those who had experienced no change in social position. Among the rapidly upward subgroup, a higher level of ethnic intolerance was found. We have no theoretical grounds for stating, as a general proposition, that moderate upward mobility would reduce prejudice for the period studied. We can merely suggest that moderate upward mobility would be associated with levels of tolerance equal to *or* higher than those of the nonmobile group. The approach of personal and social control implies that moderate upward mobility would not create inner pressures that would show up in greater prejudice; either no change would take place or else prejudice would decrease. One can argue that, given American values which legitimate gradual social mobility, both economic and status, the moderately upwardly mobile person is likely to have relatively effective personal controls. Likewise, the process of moderate social mobility is likely to strengthen the personal controls under which the individual functions.

Of the seven studies, one did not investigate upward mobility (Leggett). Of the remaining six, five included Northern samples. In three of these five cases, results demonstrated that the upwardly mobile group as a whole was more tolerant than the nonmobile. (For both the Curtis and Lenski samples, the findings are clear-cut; the Silberstein and Seeman study is a partial confirmation in that some subsamples were equal to that of the nonmobile group, but there were no significant reversals.) Only one Northern sample presents a clear-cut case in which the upward mobility group is more intolerant than the stable group (Greenblum and Pearlin). This alternative pattern appears partially due to the reported structure of prejudice in Elmira. There, in contrast to general expectation, a very low level of ethnic intolerance was found in the lower class, particularly as to residential location of Negroes.

Of the two Southern samples, the larger and more comprehensive study by Tumin indicates that upward mobility was linked to lower levels of prejudice than in the stable lower class groups. The Pettigrew sample, which is more limited in scope, did not confirm the hypothesis.

Thus, the evidence gathered from these new studies goes a long way to support the minimum observation that moderate upward mobility does not increase ethnic prejudice and often brings some decline in hostility.

For the more important theoretical proposition that rapid and extreme upward mobility would increase prejudice, only the study by Curtis can be cited. In his Detroit sample, he found that persons who had experienced extreme upward mobility had markedly higher levels of ethnic hostility. Since it was the only study to collect comparable findings, no case can be built to confirm this hypothesis. But the lack of adequate data does not cancel its relevance.

In summary, our investigation of sociological variables was designed to determine which trends in an advanced industrialized society operate for and against greater ethnic tolerance. New studies strongly support the view that under advanced industrialism downward personal mobility operates against the general social trend toward ethnic tolerance. Estimates of the impact of automation on the occupational structure indicate new sources of downward social mobility for displaced workers, along with higher levels of skill being required of other population segments. We cannot estimate the magnitude of these trends from available data. But one can speculate that their effects on attitudes toward ethnic minorities are likely to be felt, despite the generally higher levels of education in the society.

NOTES

1. See Bruno Bettelheim and Morris Janowitz, *Dynamics of Prejudice*, New York, Harper and Bros., 1950; Chapter VII, *Tolerance: A Function of Control*, and Chapter VIII *Condoning Intolerance: Anti-Negro Attitudes*, pp. 94–161.
2. Emile Durkheim, *Le Suicide: étude de sociologie*, Paris, F. Alcan, 1897, (In English: *Suicide: A Study in Sociology*, New York, The Free Press of Glencoe, 1951.)
3. Robert E. Park, *Race and Culture*, New York, The Free Press of Glencoe, 1950.
4. We focused on social mobility because we were concerned with social change and not because we considered it to be the "key" sociological variable in understanding prejudice.
5. While these studies used a variety of operational measures of prejudice, all the findings point in the same direction. However, the findings were most revealing and most significant when relatively homogeneous samples were used, and when the measure of prejudice was not a response pattern to a standardized direct probe, but spontaneous expressions of ethnic hostility on neutral or indirect questions designed to elicit expressions of hostility. This device isolated the very intolerant on a more meaningful basis than by arbitrary statistical measures of limited and highly structured responses. Both devices were used in the *Dynamics of Prejudice*.

6. Fred B. Silberstein and Melvin Seeman, "Social Mobility and Prejudice," *American Journal of Sociology*, LX, November, 1959, p. 259.

7. The authors' attempts to show that mobility orientations are more important than actual mobility patterns are subject to two reservations. The data on ethnic intolerance collected by the scales of *The Authoritarian Personality* do not permit the analysis of variance as performed. More fundamentally, the issue is a theoretical one. The authors seek to develop a theory of prejudice based on status striving. We feel that such a concept is relevant, but it is much too narrow a theoretical base for explaining ethnic hostility and prejudice.

15 Urbanization and the Afrikaner

H. Lever & O. J. M. Wagner

INTRODUCTION

In a recent publication, Reverend Beyers Naudé sought to analyse the racial attitudes of the Afrikaner.[1] His analysis is unsatisfactory in a number of respects. Concepts are used incorrectly (more particularly the concepts of nation and attitude); effect is mistaken for cause; there is a lack of familiarity with the relevant literature; religious factors are over-emphasized; and there are a number of propositions which, to say the least, are of doubtful validity. However, in spite of this, Reverend Naudé does present at least one hypothesis which is of interest to the social scientist. He maintains, *inter alia*, that the continued urbanization of the Afrikaner is leading to 'changes which must in the long run influence the whole outlook of the Afrikaner people towards his fellow-men of other cultures and colours'.[2] He envisages a more benign attitude to the non-Whites of South Africa and a disenchantment with the policy of apartheid. As far as the writers are aware, the relationship between the attitudes of the Afrikaner and the extent of his urbanization has not been tested.[3]

It is reasonable to expect the urban environment to influence the development of tolerant attitudes. The heterogeneity of the larger South African cities encourages contact with persons of diverse backgrounds, nationalities, and cultures. Some aspect of the culture of other groups is apt to be assimilated. On the other hand, a case could be, and has been, made out for the opposite effect of the city on intergroup attitudes. Arnold Rose, for example, points out that there are many frustrations in city life. Since the city is essential to modern life, it is not possible for most individuals to express their hatred of the city openly. Their hatred is repressed into

From *Race*, Vol. XI, 2, 1969, pp. 183–188. Reprinted by permission of the Institute of Race Relations.

the unconscious. Hatred of the city may be expressed by directing animosity towards a substitute object, a minority group.[4]

PROCEDURE

Data obtained from a social survey of the 'Flatland' (Hillbrow) area of Johannesburg will be used to test Reverend Naudé's hypothesis. The survey was conducted in 1962 and 1963 by the Social Research Unit of the Department of Sociology of the University of the Witwatersrand. 'Flatland' was chosen for particular study because it approximated to an ideal model of a contemporary South African urban community. Its extremely high population density (one of the highest in the world), the preponderance of residential flats (from whence the name 'Flatland' is derived), an advanced development of commercial facilities, and its 'cosmopolitan atmosphere' and 'bright light' parts make it an area of special interest to the urban sociologist. Although 'Flatland' is not an exact counterpart of all South African urban communities, it reveals the features characteristic of a high degree of urbanization.

A sample of 482 residents of 'Flatland' were interviewed, of whom fifty-two were Afrikaans-speaking South Africans. Respondents were selected by means of a multi-stage sample. In the initial stage, an enumeration of all buildings in the area was made. These buildings were then assigned to one of three strata according to their age. A simple random sample of buildings within each stratum was then made. Within each of the selected buildings, a list of all dwelling units was then made. Dwelling units were assigned to strata according to their size. With the assistance of the Department of Census and Statistics, the average number of persons for each size of dwelling unit was determined. These numbers were used as the basis for a weighted selection of dwelling units (flats, rooms, or apartments). Dwelling units were selected at random within each stratum according to the proportion required from that stratum. The final stage of the sample involved selecting a respondent within each of the selected dwelling units according to the table constructed by Kish.[5]

In the course of the interview, a detailed residential history of each respondent was obtained. This information was used to form an index of urbanization. The index of urbanization provided a measure of the extent, or duration, of exposure to an urban environment. Values of 0, 1, 2, or 3 were assigned for residence in a farming or rural area, small town, large town, or city, respectively. The relevant values were multiplied by the number of years spent in each of the areas concerned. The products were then summed and divided by the total number of years of residential history recorded. The result was multiplied by 100 to obtain the index. The range of scores of urbanization was from a little less than fifty (low urbanization) to a maximum of 300 (high urbanization).

After completion of the interview, respondents were handed an attitude inventory which they were required to complete without the assistance of the interviewer (except for explanatory comments). The inventory contained twenty-three attitude scales. Each scale was composed of a number of short opinion statements to which the respondent was required to indicate the extent of his agreement or disagreement. Each opinion statement contained five categories: strongly agree, agree, undecided, disagree, strongly disagree. Nondiscriminatory statements were eliminated by use of the method of 'internal consistency' devised by Likert.[6]

The attitude inventory contained a scale of 'anti-African prejudice' and a scale of 'pro-apartheid ideology'. The anti-African prejudice scale consisted of the following statements:

> One cannot deny that most Bantu tend to be lazy, aggressive, and overly-emotional.
> In spite of their many good qualities, the Bantu generally just do not have the intelligence and ability of the White man.
> No self-respecting European could ever willingly allow himself to be treated as an equal by or take instructions from a Bantu.

The following statements comprised the scale of pro-apartheid ideology:

> If we are to prevent trouble and maintain our way of life, it is essential that European and Bantu have separate areas in which to live and work.
> Any attempt to provide for the separate development of the Bantu in his own areas is not worth the economic and other sacrifices involved.
> Seeing that the Bantu, with his labour, has helped to develop South Africa, he should be allowed to share certain political and social privileges with the White man.

As the latter two statements represent opposition to apartheid, they were scored in such a way that agreement with the policy of apartheid received a high score.

A test of Reverend Naudé's hypothesis can be made by relating the scale of urbanization to the two attitude scales described above. However, as an extension of the hypothesis, it was decided to ascertain the relationship between extent of urbanization and a number of other attitudes relevant to anti-African prejudice. The additional scales were those of authoritarianism, anomie, humanitarianism, and democratic political ideology. The authoritarianism scale used in the 'Flatland' survey was an abridged fifteen item version[7] of the well-known Berkeley Scale.[8] The scale of anomie consisted of five statements[9] used by Srole.[10] The scales of humanitarianism and democratic political ideology (designed to measure tolerance for the beliefs of others) each comprised five opinion statements.

RESULTS

On average, the Afrikaans respondents were less urbanized than the other residents of 'Flatland'. The distribution of Afrikaans respondents on the urbanization scale was roughly similar to a normal curve with the modal group being approximately in the middle of the distribution. The relationship between the extent of urbanization of the Afrikaans respondents and their scores on the six attitude scales are presented in Table 1. Product-moment correlation coefficients are presented.

Table 1 shows that there is no relationship between extent of urbanization and (1) unfavourable attitude towards the African and (2) belief in the policy of apartheid. The hypothesis relating urbanization to prejudice is accordingly not substantiated. There is also no relationship between extent of urbanization and anomie, authoritarianism, or democratic political ideology. There appears to be a slight relationship between urbanization and humanitarianism. However, the relationship is in the opposite direction to that which Reverend Naudé would predict. That is, there is a slight tendency for increasing urbanization to be associated with decreasing humanitarianism. However, the size of the correlation coefficient is not very large and could be accounted for by chance.

It is of some interest to consider the relationship between anti-African prejudice and belief in the policy of apartheid. The advocates of apartheid maintain that that policy is not motivated by a dislike of, or animosity towards, the African. Some of their critics argue that apartheid is a rationalization for an underlying dislike of the African. In the 'Flatland' sample as a whole (482 respondents), a correlation coefficient of +.529 was found between the scales of anti-African prejudice and pro-apartheid ideology. This coefficient was clearly significant ($p < .001$). This finding is *consistent* with the view that apartheid is motivated by dislike of the African. The coefficient is not as high as the critics of apartheid might have supposed, but is statistically significant.

The correlation coefficient, of course, does not demonstrate a causal relationship. However, it is a prerequisite for a causal relationship. It seems less likely that a belief in apartheid would give rise to unfavourable attitudes to the African. (The advocates of apartheid would probably not wish to claim such an effect in any case.) It is more likely that an anti-African attitude has prompted the policy of apartheid. In the Afrikaans group, the relationship between anti-African prejudice and belief in the policy of apartheid was slightly lower ($r = +.449$) than for the 'Flatland' sample as a whole. Nevertheless, the correlation coefficient was statistically significant ($p < .01 > .001$).

TABLE 1
Correlation Coefficients of Degree of Urbanization with Six Attitude Scales

Attitude Scale	*r*
Anti-African Prejudice	.025
Pro-Apartheid Ideology	.040
Authoritarianism	−.052
Humanitarianism	−.239
Democratic Ideology	−.044
Anomie	.097

DISCUSSION

Perhaps the most conspicuous feature of Afrikaans-speaking South Africans is the very considerable homogeneity in their racial attitudes.[11] Associated with this homogeneity is a strong disapproval and condemnation of those who transgress the norm (Reverend Naudé is, no doubt, able to attest to this).[12] 'A phenomenon that has puzzled observant visitors to South Africa', says Marquard, 'is that the bitterest enmity exists, not between Afrikaner and English, but between Afrikaner and Afrikaner. Afrikaner politicians and editors reserve their sharpest darts for their fellow-Afrikaners.[13] One of the consequences of maintaining group solidarity at a high pitch is that membership of the group is able to act as a buffer against external influences. It is suggested that the group belongingness of the Afrikaner has offset any effects of urbanization on racial attitudes.

The present study does not show that the attitudes of Afrikaners are not susceptible to change. It is merely asserted that urbanization, in itself, will not lead to a more tolerant attitude to Africans or to disenchantment with apartheid, at least in the near future. Attempts to modify the attitudes of the Afrikaner may have to be linked to group membership or seek to dissipate the effects of group membership.

NOTES

The survey of the 'Flatland' area of Johannesburg which is reported here was supported by a grant from the Department of Education, Arts and Science of the Republic of South Africa (National Council for Social Research) which is gratefully acknowledged. Opinions expressed, or conclusions reached, are those of the writers and are not to be regarded as representative of those of the Department of Education, Arts and Science (National Council for Social Research).

The writers also wish to acknowledge the work done by Professor L. T. Badenhorst in the initial planning and execution of the 'Flatland' survey while he was Honorary Director of the Social Research Unit of the Department of Sociology, University of the Witwatersrand.

1. Beyers Naudé, *The Afrikaner and Race Relations* (Johannesburg, South African Institute of Race Relations, 1968).
2. Ibid., p. 9.
3. Of course, the assertion of a general relationship between urbanization and a declining prejudice has been suggested by many other writers, for example, see B. Bettelheim and M. Janowitz, *Social Change and Prejudice* (New York, Free Press of Glencoe, 1950), p. 82, and E. J. B. Rose and associates, *Colour and Citizenship: A Report on British Race Relations* (London, Oxford University Press, for Institute of Race Relations, 1969), Chapter 28.
4. A. M. Rose, 'The Causes of Prejudice', in M. L. Barron (ed.), *American Minorities* (New York, Knopf, 1957), p. 85.
5. L. Kish, 'A Procedure for Objective Respondent Selection within the Household', *Journal of the American Statistical Association* (Vol. 44, 1949), pp. 380–7.
6. R. Likert, 'A Technique for the Measurement of Attitudes', *Archives of Psychology* (No. 140, 1932).
7. H. Lever, L. Schlemmer and O. J. M. Wagner, 'A Factor Analysis of Authoritarianism', *Journal for Social Research* (South African) (Vol. XVI, 1968), pp. 41–8.

8. T. W. Adorno et al., *The Authoritarian Personality* (New York, Harper, 1950).
9. H. Lever and O. J. M. Wagner, 'A Factor Analysis of Anomie', *Journal for Social Research* (South African) (Vol. XVI, 1967), pp. 1–6.
10. L. Srole, 'Social Integration and Certain Corollaries: An Exploratory Study', *American Sociological Review* (Vol. XXI, 1956), pp. 709–16.
11. I. D. MacCrone, *Race Attitudes in South Africa* (London, Oxford University Press, 1937), p. 212, and 'The Functional Analysis of a Group Attitude towards the Native', *South African Journal of Science* (Vol. XXX, 1933), pp. 687–9; and H. Lever, *Ethnic Attitudes of Johannesburg Youth* (Johannesburg, Witwatersrand University Press, 1968), p. 179.
12. Reverend Naudé, a minister of the Nederduitsch Hervormde Kerk, has been subjected to a great deal of criticism and pressure because of his leadership of the Christian Institute and his objection to apartheid.
13. L. Marquard, *The Peoples and Policies of South Africa* (London, Oxford University Press, 1960), p. 70.

16 Industrialisation and Race Relations

Herbert Blumer

INTRODUCTION

The relation of industrialisation to changing race relations poses a problem of special significance in the present stage of world development. The problem brings together in single focus two of the most outstanding forms of transformation at work in our contemporary world. Each in its own right is compelling peoples and countries to work out new lines of destiny. Before considering the relation between them it is desirable to point out the extraordinarily important place of each in our current world scene.

Industrialisation is usually assigned the central role in the shaping of modern life. This is reflected in the common designation of our modern civilisation as 'industrial'. Advanced nations and peoples today are thought to derive their eminence from an industrial base. Likewise, it is commonly assumed that the elevation of so-called underdeveloped countries is to be achieved by bringing them as viable units into an industrial world. Such beliefs, which enjoy almost axiomatic status, signify that the process of industrialisation is the master force at work in modern civilisation, fabricating its life and institutions and setting its peculiar mould. Its operation constitutes, so to speak, a watershed between 'traditional' society and 'modern' so-

From Guy Hunter (ed.), *Industrialisation and Race Relations*, London, Oxford University Press for The Institute of Race Relations, 1965, pp. 220–40. Reprinted by permission of the Institute of Race Relations.

ciety—between agrarian, village, feudal and tribal societies on one hand, and on the other hand a new complex of life centring upon the machine, the factory, and resulting urban aggregations. The process of industrialisation is thus accorded in general thought a dual role of paramount significance. It operates in the first instance as a powerful solvent of pre-established orders of life, undermining traditional institutions, social relations, and values of life. In the second instance, it functions to forge a new framework of relations between people, new institutional forms, and new values and goals of living. In both respects industrialisation is assigned profound transforming influence.

In its turn, the changing character of race relations in different parts of the world must be seen as constituting one of the most significant developments of our times. To appreciate this one merely needs to note the troubled racial situation in such diverse countries as the United States of America, the Republic of South Africa, the emerging nations of Central Africa, and countries in South-east Asia. It is appropriate to say that today races are on the move. This is not a mere metaphor. One of the significant happenings of recent decades has been the disruption of the colonial order—a disruption which has freed many diverse and large racial groups from fixed positions and forced them to work out new relations. We should note, also, the increased restlessness of subservient racial groups in other parts of the world—an animation which is leading them to press vigorously for changes in their social position, or to threaten shortly to do so. Further, we should recognise that on the international scene, apart from domestic situations, the major races are being thrust into a new changing arena—an operational arena which challenges old postures, sets new problems, and requires the forging of new accommodations. Amid these widespread changes which are taking place, domestically and internationally, racial groups are breaking away from old alignments and moving into new, uncharted and generally shaky relations.

If we grant that industrialisation is a master agent of social transformation and if race relations in our contemporary world are in the throes of profound change, it is both timely and highly important to ask what effect the process of industrialisation exercises on the relations between racial groups. Oddly, despite the obvious importance of this question, there has been little effort to study the problem systematically. The literature shows a marked paucity of empirical studies of this matter; and, indeed, the large body of scattered first-hand observations which deal with the associations of races touches only sporadically and casually on the play of industrial factors. This relative absence of empirical evidence does not mean that there is a void of thought on how industrialisation affects race relations. On the contrary, one can piece together from the literature a rather imposing body of theoretical conception of what industrialisation is said to do to race relations. As we shall come to see, this body of conception is chiefly a projection to the racial field of a variety of social consequences which are alleged to stem from the intrinsic or logical character of industrialisation. It is highly desirable that we stake out this body of deductive views since an understanding of them will serve as a very convenient point of departure for an analytic treatment of the relation of industrialisation to race relations. In the next section of this paper, accordingly, we will sketch the distinguishing character of industrialism and designate what are usually regarded as its logical imperatives.

CENTRAL CHARACTERISTICS OF INDUSTRIALISM

Industrialisation is conceived to be the process which brings into being a distinctive type of economy, usually identified as 'industrialism'. The distinguishing mark of this economy is the use of power-driven machinery for the production of goods. A vastly differentiated system may develop from this distinguishing kernel. The compositional features which we wish to note are: (1) the production of manufactured products, usually in large quantity, at low unit cost; (2) the assembling of workers and other industrial personnel around the producing enterprises; (3) the formation of structures of diversified jobs and positions within the enterprises; (4) the development of an auxiliary apparatus providing for the procurement of materials and the disposition of products; and (5) the domination of the productive system by motifs of efficiency and profitability (in the accounting sense).

The operation of this kind of productive system depends on adherence to a number of fundamental conditions or principles—conditions which can be spoken of as the structural requirements or the logical imperatives of industrialism. Since these structural requirements are of crucial importance for an understanding of industrialism and of its alleged lines of influence, it is desirable to spell them out briefly.

The first of these structural requirements is a *commitment to a rational and secular outlook*. It is contended that the needs of productive efficiency and profitable operation force and fashion a rational perspective on the participants in industry. Under this perspective matters are judged not in terms of traditional, sentimental, or sacred concerns, but in terms of their contributory role to the successful operation of the productive enterprise. This rational and secular orientation has the effect of reducing the world of industrial operations to a series of mechanical or instrumental components.

Second, industrialism is regarded as demanding and forging *contractual relations in place of status relations*. The employees of the industrial enterprise, whether in the labour force or in management, are judged in terms of productive need and productive efficiency; they are hired, assigned, or dismissed on the basis of these considerations. The industrial enterprise, to be viable, cannot entertain or honour claims from employees stemming from non-industrial conditions such as community position, institutional affiliation, class memberships, or outside prestige or authority. The dominance exercised by the needs of the enterprise, in place of claims of social status, shifts relations in industry to an impersonal contractual basis. Such pre-eminence of contractual arrangements extends over all other important areas of industrialism—procurement of materials, sale of products, marketing transactions, and banking and credit arrangements.

Third, as a result of the two foregoing features, industrialism brings into being a number of *impersonal markets*. Of these, the labour market has special significance. Having freedom to hire, assign, and dismiss employees on the basis solely of industrial needs and being guided in doing so by the criterion of productive efficiency, employers fall into a rational, detached and non-obligatory relation to the labour force. In their turn, employees, having no personal or social claim to employment, are put in the position of competing with one another on the basis of the possible productivity which they may bring to available jobs and positions. Employees become interchangeable units. Employees are not tied to jobs nor are jobs vested in employees. Both shift impersonally with regard to the other.

A fourth significant characteristic of industrialism, following from those which have been mentioned, is the *physical mobility* of its components. Markets shift, capital flows from one area to another, industrial plants spring up in new areas and decline in others, entrepreneural effort shifts from one field to another, and above all the industrial personnel move about. Employees must seek jobs and positions and are free to respond to the attraction of better ones. This makes for movement, shifting from job to job and frequently from one residential location to another.

Similarly, as a fifth characteristic, industrialism allows and promotes *social mobility*. Since jobs and positions in industry are arranged hierarchically in terms of differential compensation and reward and since they are filled impersonally by employees possessing the requisite skills and experience, the doors are opened to upward movement by those who have or develop the essential skills or experience. Correspondingly, the loss of skill or the unavailability of jobs calling for skills and experience which one possesses may result in movement downward to jobs of lesser value. It is this upward and downward mobility which sociologists are particularly prone to stress in their declaration that industrialisation displaces 'status by ascription' by 'status by achievement'. Social mobility, in a similar manner, attends the fate of industrial owners and employers. Successful entrepreneurship, favourable market advantages, efficient operation of the industrial enterprise, or the gainings of needed capital for investment may allow for significant upward advance in social position. And, of course, converse conditions may lead to a downward movement.

Finally, we need to note a sixth characteristic of industrialism in the form of an *in-built dynamic condition* which presses to keep the five foregoing characteristics in play. This in-built dynamic condition is set by the stimulations that arise from such varied sources as changes in technology, shifting consumer demands, expansion or decline of markets, development of new products, new entrepreneurship, changes in the business cycle, shifts in monetary policy, shifts in capital, and changes in conditions of efficient operation. Such forms of change, which in shifting degree are part and parcel of industrialism, introduce strains and set a need for more or less continuous accommodation. They function, accordingly, to call anew into play the five characteristic features previously discussed.

In sketching the abstract character of industrialisation as a system of production we should add to the above set of six structural requirements a brief note on three concomitant conditions to which scholars are prone to give appreciable importance.

One of these is the introduction of cash or monetary relations at all points in the in-dustrial undertaking—compensation of employees, market activities, returns of the enterprise, and the use of a monetary yardstick in assessing the efficacy of all parts of the industrial operation. It is held that monetary relations promote impersonal-ity, increase freedom in individual decision and action, and promote individual con-trol of careers. A second concomitant condition is an improvement of the standard of living which it is asserted follows naturally from industrialism; this is due to the greater quantity of cheaper goods yielded by industrial production and to cash in-come which allows choice in their acquisition. The third concomitant is the provi-sion of educational and training arrangements enabling the acquisition of the skills required by the jobs and positions in the industrial structure.

It is evident from the foregoing sketch that industrialism is seen conventionally as a compendent system of production, centring upon a number of distinctive struc-tural requirements and carrying with it several important concomitant conditions. This composition distinguishes industrialism from other systems of production and gives it a superior survival value. Industrialism, it is held, acts imperiously towards other systems of production when brought into contact with them, supplanting them and thus undercutting the social order of life built around them.

Let me now delineate the major social changes which it is commonly supposed are produced by industrialisation, and note how these social changes are projected in conventional thought to the area of race relations.

CONVENTIONAL VIEWS OF THE SOCIAL EFFECTS OF INDUSTRIALISATION ON RACE RELATIONS

There are three grand ways by which industrialisation wields its influence as an agent of social change. These are (1) to undermine the traditional social order into which industrialism is introduced; (2) to throw people into new situations and set the need for establishing new relations; and (3) to fashion a new social order around the intrinsic features of industrialism. These represent three stages in a process of development—an initial stage of uprooting the old order, a transitional stage of re-shuffling people and of stimulating new modes of living, and a terminal stage of shaping and consolidating a new order of life. The effects exercised by industrialisa-tion on race relations depends on which of these three stages is under consideration. Let us spell out what is supposed to happen in each stage.

(1) Undermining of the Established Social Order. The ways in which industriali-sation is thought to undermine a pre-established social order are legion. To begin with, we note that each of the first five structural requirements of industrialism which we have previously identified would disarrange the pre-industrial or tradition-al order of life; and that the sixth would assure the continuation of persistency of the process. Rational and secular perspectives challenge and undercut sentimental and sacred pillars of the traditional society; contractual relations displace status relations

around which traditional life is organised; the development of impersonal markets, particularly of an impersonal labour market, force aside traditional and personal claims; physical mobility disrupts the ecological foundations of the old order; and social mobility upsets the established structure of status positions. More concretely, industrialisation is said to undermine subsistence economy, displace handicraft production, shift production from home and village to factory and city, abolish old occupations, inaugurate migratory movements from rural regions to industrial centres, remove workers from their native communities and weaken their kinship ties, throw them into association with strangers, shift concern with survival from a collective to an individual basis, provide new purchasing power through cash income, change old consumption patterns, replace old wants and expectations, destroy old career lines, and weaken traditional status positions. These lines of change have the effect of destroying the old economy, undermining rural and village life, disrupting the traditional family, undercutting the traditional class or caste structure, disarranging the old occupational structure, destroying the old status and role structure, dislocating existing institutions, undermining paternalistic relations, transforming traditional tastes, eroding established values, weakening established systems of authority, and breaking down established schemes of social control.

This conventional conception of industrialisation as a pervasive solvent of pre-industrial orders of life has obvious application to the topic of race relations. With few exceptions, present-day instances of race relations have emerged from a background of ordered association of racial groups within some form of pre-industrial society. This is to be noted clearly in the case of colonial societies, agricultural societies operating under slavery, and plantation economies employing imported contract labour. The picture is very familiar. In essentially all of the colonial societies formed during the past three centuries an outside racial group—European whites—established a position of domination and control over a native population of different ancestry. Where the institution of slavery flourished as in the United States, Brazil, and other parts of the Western Hemisphere, vast numbers of an alien racial people were imported and assigned to a fixed subservient position. A similar kind of racial arrangement came into being in many scattered areas where alien racial peoples were imported as contract labour to work on plantations. In the case of each of these three major forms of association an order grew up with fixed positions and relations between the racial groups. The arrangement consisted of a dominant racial group and one or more subordinate racial groups, with the drawing of lines between them, and with a differential allocation to each of authority, prestige, privileges and opportunities. Subordinate races were confined to inferior occupations, restricted in residential location, barred from most areas of intimate association with the dominant race, limited in their access to the institution of the dominant race, restricted in legal rights, tied to dependency roles, and walled in from opportunities to advance upward in the social scale.

Now, it would seem reasonable that the introduction of an industrial system would undermine such a racial order. The demands which such a system makes and the forces which it releases would combine to attack the racial order at many points.

The typical innovations of industrialisation—the liquidation of old occupations, the opening of new occupations, the dislodgment of people from established residence in villages and rural regions, and their shift to cities, the severing of old dependency relations, particularly paternalistic relations, the change in consumption habits, the acquisition of cash income with the greater freedom which this yields, the openings to upward movement in the industrial structure by virtue of developing higher levels of industrial skill, and opportunities for entrepreneurship—suggest some of the major lines along which the structure of fixed relations in a racial order breaks down. The general tenor of conventional scholarly views is that industrialisation functions as such a solvent when brought into a pre-industrial racial order. Its initial line of effect is to sap many of the pillars of the established racial arrangement, to dislodge racial groups from their respective positions, and to sever or weaken the bonds prevailing between them.

(2) Setting New Relations for People. A second major kind of social change conventionally attributed to industrialisation is that of bringing people together in unfamiliar forms of association, thus requiring them to forge new relations. Obviously, the many lines of movement initiated by the industrialising process should result in many new forms of intermingling. Physical mobility, especially in the form of migration to industrial centres, brings people together in new residential communities. Employment of workers in industrial establishments throws such employees together in new work situations. Shifts in occupation in such establishments continue to lead to new aggregations of workers. The operation of an impersonal labour market throws workers indirectly into new kinds of competitive relations. Similarly, new directions of entrepreneural effort lead to new networks of indirect relations, such as new areas of competition, new lines of dependency, and new arrangements of interest groups. Social mobility leads upward and downward movement of individuals, as in the case of the successful entrepreneur, the 'nouveau riche', new managerial and professional people, workers with newly acquired occupational skills, displaced craftsmen, owners and managers of outmoded enterprises, and individuals forced out of a variety of traditional posts which dwindle or vanish in the new industrial setting. These various lines of movement initiated in industrialisation reshuffle people, removing them from old networks of relations, bringing them into new varieties of direct and indirect contact and setting for them the need to develop new forms of association.

The application of this conventional view to the field of race relations has been made only sparsely in the literature. The scattered accounts that deal somewhat directly with the reshuffling of racial peoples in the process of industrialisation are prone to emphasise strain and conflict. In minor measure, racial tension is thought to arise from the mere fact that members of different racial or ethnic groups are forced to associate with each other under unfamiliar circumstances, particularly to live with each other in new residential communities and to work side by side in industrial plants. But of far more importance is the thought that under new conditions of association, members of racial groups are thrown into competition with each other and thus become threats to one another. The threat may be posed merely by the fact that each views the other as a rival claimant to scarce opportunities. More frequently and more seriously the threat arises as a challenge to traditional status and thus to the special privileges and social standing attached to such status. Thus, it is believed that where members of a traditional subordinate racial group begin to compete with members of the superordinate racial group in arenas where the latter feel they have prior and superior claims, racial tension and conflict are prone to occur. Such arenas are likely to be those of skilled and prestigeful occupations and professions, higher levels of entrepreneurship, areas of business competition, and 'middle-class' positions in the industrial structure. The entrance of members of a subordinate racial group as competitors in such arenas constitutes a challenge not merely to economic position but to social standing; hence such lines of competitive contact become focal points of racial discord.

The net import of this conventional view—even though it is not well developed— is that industrialisation introduces a transitional stage into race relations—a stage marked by unfamiliar association, competitive contact, and a challenge to previous social standing. Race relations become uncertain and unstable. The shifts in them awaken suspicion, arouse resentment, occasion strain and provoke discord.

(3) Consolidation of an Industrial Order. Scholars of industrialisation usually endow it with intrinsic tendencies which are declared to move persistently to mould a given type of social order. These tendencies are those spoken of previously as the structural requirements of industrialism: the primacy of rational perspectives; the inevitability of contractual relations; the need of an impersonal market; the certainty of physical mobility; the allocation of personnel, capital and resources on the basis of productive returns; and built-in pressures which repeatedly activate the requirements. In the long run these imperious tendencies are held to triumph; thus there emerges a social order with a distinctive character. The social order is one which places a premium on a rational perspective, a social order in which people gain social positions on the basis of industrial aptitude and merit, an order which promotes individuation at the expense of traditional group affiliation, and an order which favours shifting alignments on the basis of secular interests. It is a social order marked by movement, by change, by the reshuffling of individuals, and by shifting accommodations—an order which fundamentally and ultimately is guided in its formation by a rational imperative of instrumental efficiency.

To apply the image of such a social order to the area of race relations yields a clear-cut depiction of the ultimate effects of industrialisation. In the long run, race vanishes as a factor which structures social relations. Workers will compete with one another on the basis of industrial aptitude and not on the basis of racial make-up. Correspondingly, members of the managerial force will be chosen and placed on the basis of managerial competence and not of racial affiliation. Imagination, ingenuity, and energy and not racial membership will determine success in industrial entrepreneurship. Ascent on the social ladder will depend on the possession of necessary skills and ability, wealth or capital; racial make-up becomes extraneous. The premium placed on rational decisions will relegate racial prejudice and discrimination to the periphery. The dominance of contractual relations and the resulting impersonal markets will undermine identification with racial groups. Physical movement from job to job and from one to another entrepreneural opportunity, social mobility upward and downward in the occupational structure, differential accumulations of wealth and capital, and different directions of specialisation in the expanding array of career lines in industry—all these will have the effect of parcelling out and intershuffling racial members among one another in the industrial and social structure.

This picture of the order of life formed by the consolidation of industrialism is likely to be judged by the reader as an ideal or utopian vista. Yet it must be taken seriously in the light of the type of thought which one finds in the literature. It is very common to presume that industrialisation presses continuously to achieve a state of complete realisation—a state in which its intrinsic imperatives would operate without restraint and thus shape industrial life to their demands. That this mode of thought is deeply implanted is shown by the disposition to construct an 'ideal-type' of industrialism as it would be if it could operate freely according to its logical imperatives, and then to use this construct to throw light on current happenings. We note this disposition among students of race relations. For example, it is fairly common to presume that industrial managers, who ideally are concerned only with economical productivity, actually hire, assign or dismiss workers solely on this factor, and thus ignore or downgrade the factor of race. Or, since relations in industry are believed to be logically contractual and impersonal, race ceases to be significant in industrial transactions. Or, since the extension of credit to entrepreneurs is made, logically, solely on the basis of the prospects of profitable repayment, the racial make-up of the entrepreneur loses significance. Or, to cite the well-worn proposition of sociologists, since industrialism logically establishes 'status by achievement' to replace 'status by ascription', the racial factor loses relevancy in determining social position. Running through these instances of reasoning is the theme that the logical imperatives of industrialism forge an order of life to their form. This point of view must be recognized as being held seriously by scholars.

In the foregoing discussion in this section we have outlined the conventional views of how industrialisation affects race relations. Let us turn now to a consideration of what is shown by empirical evidence. The intention in the following section of the paper is to see how the three major lines of influence attributed to industrialisation stand up in the face of factual information and in the face of critical analysis.

TEST OF CONVENTIONAL VIEWS

Our critical consideration of the conventional views of how industrialisation affects race relations must be prefaced by two observations. First, as mentioned earlier, the literature is conspicuously lacking in the desired round of factual or descriptive accounts of what has happened to race relations when industrialism is introduced and expanded. We are limited, by and large, to a sparse and uneven array of such accounts. Second, attention must be called to the marked lack of clarity and consistency in conceptions of 'industrialisation' and of 'race relations'. It is only rarely that the term 'industrialism' is defined and held to a specific meaning. All too frequently it is used in a broad and vague way without specification of reference. As a result, it is easily confused with other kinds of happening such as commercialisation, urbanisation, mechanisation, economic development, and modernisation. Such looseness and inconsistency in usage sets frustrating barriers to careful analysis. Somewhat similarly, the meaning of the term 'race relations' is usually not drawn tightly. It may be applied to relations (1) between biologically distinctive groups which pay little or no attention to their biological distinctiveness; (2) between biologically diffuse or mixed groups which, however, treat each other as racially different; (3) between groups with little biological difference but with deeply established religious differences; (4) between groups with different nationality backgrounds; and (5) between different caste groups in an overbridging society. This variation in reference is a formidable impediment to effective comparative treatment.

Despite the limitations outlined in the preceding paragraph enough reliable empirical evidence exists to allow us to assess in broad outline the conventional views of how industrialisation affects race relations. We shall consider the three major lines of alleged influence discussed in the previous section of this paper.

(1) Industrialisation as a Factor Which Undermines the Traditional or Established Racial Order. As our previous discussion has indicated, industrialisation is thought to undermine an established racial system by disrupting the social order in which it is embedded and by direct attack on crucial points of the system itself.

It is evident that as a new system of production, industrialism brings multiple attack to bear on a pre-existing social order which is organised around a different system of production. Yet it is a grievous mistake to assume that this attack necessarily results in a general displacement or transformation of the traditional order. The movement is not merely in one direction. Instead, the traditional order may act back, so to speak, on the process of industrialisation blocking it at many points, forcing it sometimes to develop alongside yet outside of the traditional order, and frequently assimilating it inside of the traditional structure of life. Thus, while industrialisation may have disruptive effects at certain points it may be held in check at other points, and above all may be made to accommodate to and fit inside of the traditional order at many other points. These general observations have a great deal of relevance to the more specific question of how industrialisation affects an established racial system—the question which I now wish to consider.

Our discussion will centre around what we have spoken of earlier as the structural or logical requirements of industrialism. The empirical evidence indicates that no one of these need operate to change or disrupt an established racial system. In early industrialisation the rational or secular perspective, which industrialism admittedly fosters and stresses, may compel an adherence to the racial system rather than a departure from it. The manager of an industrial plant who may be willing to hire workers of a subordinate racial group for high-level jobs or promote them to ad-

vanced positions suited to their aptitudes or skills may definitely refrain from doing
so in order not to provoke difficulties with other workers. This is a *rational* decision
which has occurred innumerable times in industrial establishments introduced into
a society with a strongly established racial system. Openings in managerial positions
may be barred to qualified members of a subordinate race not because of prejudice
but because of a rational realisation that their employment would affront others
and disrupt efficient operation. Credit may be refused to entrepreneurs emerging
out of the subordinate racial group solely because their racial make-up implies possible credit risks. Contracts for construction work may not be awarded to qualified
bidders from the subordinate racial groups solely because it is realised that their
presence on the job may cause resentment and provoke trouble. Employment may
be refused to subordinate racial members as salesmen, outside representatives, professionals, receptionists, and similar types of employees dealing with the public
solely because of the resentment which it is believed their presence might awaken.
These are typical kinds of rational decision—decisions which are guided just as much
by the aim of efficient operation and economic return as if they took into account
only the productive capacity of the individual racial member. They show clearly
that *rational* operation of industrial enterprises which are introduced into a racially
ordered society may call for a deferential respect for the canons and sensitivities of
that racial order. This observation is not a mere *a priori* speculation. It is supported
by countless instances of such decisions in the case of industrial enterprises in the
Southern region of the United States, in South Africa and in certain colonial areas.
One notes the frequent declaration of the industrial manager or financier in such
places that he has no prejudice against the subordinate race, that he would like to
help members of that race but that he cannot afford to be a 'missionary' or a 'crusa-
der' at the expense of interfering with the successful operation of his enterprise. It
is a mistake, accordingly, to assume that the rational motif of industrialism signifies
an automatic undermining of a racial order into which industrialism enters. To the
contrary, the rational imperative in industrial operations may function to maintain
and reinforce the established racial order.

Empirical evidence requires us to make a similar observation in the case of the
other structural requirements of industrialism. The substitution of contractual relations for status relations in early industrialisation need not mean at all that the respective positions of the races are changed. The whole texture of the new contract
relations may reproduce and continue the social position of the races. Workers from
the subordinate race may be restricted to the menial and lower-paid industrial occupations, contractors from the racial group may be narrowly confined in the jobs on
which they can bid, and entrepreneurs from the racial group may find that the areas
into which they may enter are severely curtailed. While their contractual status gives
them freedom to enter into new relations—gaining new employment, bidding on
new jobs, seeking new business, entering new lines of industrial endeavour—their
choices may be markedly confined to areas set by their subordinate racial status.
This same condition may mark the impersonal labour market introduced by industrialism. The employing agent is likely to guide his hiring of workers by his calcula-

tion of where they can fit; their racial make-up rather than their potential productive capacity may be decisive in this determination. The physical mobility stimulated by industrialism—the migration of workers, the shifting around of managerial personnel, the movement of investment capital, and the re-location of industrial plants—need not challenge the principles of the established social order. Those who move—workers, managerial personnel, industrial owners and entrepreneurs—may continue to have residence in areas set by their racial make-up and to enter a framework of social relations carrying the stamp of the pre-existing racial order. Finally, while industrialisation opens up a large array of new lines of social mobility in the form of new occupations, new areas of investment, and new opportunities for industrial enterprise, these new lines of social mobility may quickly come under the sway of the established racial scheme. Low ceilings may be placed on how far subordinate racial members may ascend in the occupational structure; their opportunities for capital investment may be limited and they may have great difficulty in getting credit; and their opportunities for business entrepreneurship may be confined to servicing their own racial group.

The central import of the above observations is to attach a large question mark to the conventional view that industrialisation operates naturally to undermine a pre-existing racial system. The intrinsic structural requirements of industrialism need not, contrary to much *a priori* theorising, force a rearrangement of the relations set by the racial system. We have here, indeed, somewhat of a paradoxical situation in that while industrialisation may alter greatly the social order, it may leave the racial system that is embedded in that order essentially intact. No one can gainsay that the entrance of industrialism may undercut and transform much in traditional life and social structure. One need only think of such changes as the undermining of a subsistence economy, the displacement of handicraft production, the abolition of old occupations, the shift from a rural agricultural economy to an urban manufacturing economy, the initiation of migratory movements, the removal of workers from village, tribal, and kinship ties, the organisation of family or personal economy around cash income, the change in consumption patterns, the replacement of old wants and desires, and the formation of new career lines. Changes of these sorts involve, obviously, significant transformations of social relations and forms of group life. Yet, as the foregoing observations indicate, amidst such transformation of the traditional social order the framework of the established racial system may be retained, even though the content of the framework may change.

This is precisely what has happened during the early stages of industrialisation in the Southern region of the United States, in South Africa, and in many areas under colonial domination. In such regions, where a superordinate-subordinate racial arrangement was deeply entrenched, industrialisation meant essentially a transfer of the framework of the established racial scheme to the new industrial setting. Members of the subordinate race were assigned to and essentially confined to the lower levels of the industrial occupational structure; no positions were opened to them inside of the managerial ranks of the industrial enterprises operated by members of the dominant race; doors were shut to their entrepreneurship in the operating world of the dominant racial group; and the traditional colour line was firmly held. We are forced by empirical evidence to recognise, accordingly, that early industrialisation in these regions did not undermine the established racial system but merely came to fit inside it.

(2) Industrialisation as a Factor Producing Racial Tension. In our earlier discussion we have outlined the conventional view that in the transitional stage of its development industrialisation promotes racial tension and conflict. The thought is that in being moved around by industrialisation members of different racial groups are thrown into new relations, particularly competitive relations. Thus, they come to live together in new residential areas, compete with each other in the labour market, enter one another's occupations as they move up and down the industrial hierarchy, and compete with one another in entrepreneural fields. The strangeness of these new forms of association and particularly the condition of striving against one another are regarded as provocative of racial discord.

The empirical evidence pertaining to this matter presents a very varied picture. It is clear that the alleged happenings are not typical at all of what takes place in the industrialisation of a society which has had a strongly ordered racial system. In such a society, as we have been explaining, even though racial groups may be subject to much movement the traditional pattern of their positions usually continues. Thus, the movement of members of the subordinate racial group from rural regions to industrial centres and their entrance into industrial occupations are likely to bring them into assigned positions which are separate from those occupied by members of the dominant racial group. There is minimal likelihood that inside the industrial structure the dominant and subordinate racial groups will enter into competitive relations with each other. The assumption of open access in such a society to one another's occupations, lines of industrial endeavour, areas of entrepreneural opportunities, and residential areas is not true. Understandings quickly arise, frequently buttressed by legal sanctions, as to the occupations, industrial positions, business and residential locations which subordinate racial members may enter and those which they may not enter. In the event that at given points of contact their relations are not initially clear, they come to be defined quickly—defined under the overbridging sway of traditional views of the appropriate position of the races. The net effect is that members of the dominant and subordinate racial groups are not thrown into the competitive relationship that is presupposed by *a priori* theorising.

The only place in which racial competition and friction is likely to occur in the industrialisation of a strongly organised racial society is at the points of contact between different subordinate racial groups, if there be such. In the reshuffling which industrialisation induces, such subordinate racial groups may be brought into competition at scattered points in the industrial structure with resulting strain and discord. This may be noted, for example, in sporadic outbreaks of friction between Negroes and Mexicans in the United States, or in the case of Africans, Coloured and Indians in South Africa, or between different tribal groups in colonial Africa. Such competition and discord occurs at the lower levels of the industrial structure and does not touch the basic racial framework as constituted by the relations between the dominant and the subordinate racial groups. That framework shapes the re-shuffling process under industrialisation rather than being shaped by it.

The conventional view that industrialisation fosters competition and strain be-tween racial groups in the emerging industrial structure is much more likely to be true in other kinds of settings. It may apply to (a) societies which do not have a firmly established racial order or (b) societies in which a firmly established racial order is definitely undergoing disintegration. In the first of these two settings indus-trialisation may bring together racial groups which previously have not had relations with each other or only tenuously defined positions with regard to each other. Com-petition may arise between them in this kind of setting and lead to tension and dis-cord. This kind of happening may be noted in the case of various ethnic groups entering industry in the North in the United States, or in the case of French Cana-dians and 'Anglo-Saxons' in Eastern Canada, or in the case of racial groups in South-east Asia. However, such mingling of diverse racial groups in the industrial structure may also take place without a sense of racial competition and so without producing racial tension. The second of the two settings—where a firmly established racial or-der is undergoing disintegration—poses its own special problem, a problem with which we shall be concerned in later discussion. Here, to foreshadow the subsequent discussion of this matter, we wish merely to say that the disintegration of a firmly established racial system is apparently not initiated or brought about by the pres-sure of industrial forces but results instead from the play of non-industrial influ-ences. The question which we will have to address is how is the pattern of the reshuffling of racial members in the industrial structure changed so that they are led to enter each other's domain. This is a most vital question which has to be treated when one considers the play of industrialisation in a racially ordered society.

The above remarks give some idea of the variety of settings in which different racial groups may come to face each other during industrialisation. Only in a few of these settings does one find support for the conventional view that industrialisation produces through the play of its own inner forces an intermediate stage in which racial groups are thrown into competitive relations with resulting strain and discord. Despite its plausibility on *a priori* grounds this conventional view has only limited application.

(3) Industrialisation as a Factor Which Dissolves the Significance of Race. Earlier we sketched the widely held view that the logical imperatives of industrialism move to the elimination of race as a factor of importance in the industrial order. The view is basically simple. Since industrialism necessarily places its supreme premium on economical productivity and efficient operation all usable elements are ultimately chosen in terms of such standards. Thus, workers come to be hired and assigned solely on the basis of industrial aptitude, management personnel selected solely on the basis of managerial efficiency, contracts awarded only to lowest qualified bid-ders, industrial opportunities exploited solely on the basis of entrepreneural ability, and credit extended solely on the basis of prospects of reliable repayment. In the

impersonality of these transactions non-industrial factors such as class membership, family connection, religious affiliation and racial make-up become irrelevant. As we have noted in our earlier remarks students are strongly disposed to use this image of the 'pure' or logical character of industrialism to interpret present-day happenings, as for example in the declaration that workers of different racial make-up become interchangeable units.

As applied to the actual racial situations in our recent and present world the view that industrialisation moves ahead naturally to dissolve the racial factor is not borne out by the facts, certainly not in the case of racially ordered societies. Attention has already been called to the racial situation in Southern United States, South Africa, and some of the colonial areas. In these places the hiring and assignment of industrial workers from subordinate racial groups did not follow the postulates of industrialism; members of such groups have not found entrance into managerial ranks; and entrepreneurs from such groups were confronted by high walls barring them from exploiting opportunities lying in the province of the dominant group. Instead, we note a transfer of the lines of racial patterning to the industrial enterprise. Seemingly, many scholars would believe that this general condition represents merely a temporary stage in which the forces of industrialisation have not had opportunity to come to natural expression; with time, or in the long run, the industrial imperatives would gain ascendency, stripping the racial factor of any importance. We do not know how much time is needed to constitute the 'long run'; certainly half a century of industrial experience in both South Africa and the South in the United States brought no appreciable change in the position of the races in the industrial structure. The picture presented by industrialisation in a racially ordered society is that industrial imperatives accommodate themselves to the racial mould and continue to operate effectively within it. We must look to outside factors rather than to a maturation of these imperatives for an explanation of the disintegration of the racial mould.

Our discussion of three major ways in which industrialisation is conventionally regarded as affecting race relations shows the weakness and danger of treating this topic by deductive reasoning from the logical premises of industrialism. The topic needs to be addressed from a different perspective—from a perspective which is empirically oriented and which takes into account the array of forces which may come into play where industrialisation and racial alignment meet. We now undertake this broad and difficult task.

ANALYSIS OF INDUSTRIALISATION AND RACE RELATIONS

A realistic treatment of industrialisation and race relations must be based, in my judgment, on an acceptance of the following points: (1) industrialisation and racial alignment act on each other; (2) their interaction is profoundly influenced by the character of the setting in which it occurs; and (3) the setting, in turn, changes under the play of social and political happenings. These seem to be simple and self-evident propositions. Yet, an approach grounded on them is different from that which is implied by conventional scholarly views. The latter presupposes, by and large, that industrialisation is a unitary constant, acting as an independent variable to affect and shape race relations along relatively fixed lines. In contrast, the approach which I believe to be demanded by empirical happenings presupposes that racial alignment is shaped in major measure by non-industrial influences, that resulting patterns of racial alignment permeate the industrial structure, and that changes in such patterns are traceable mainly to movements in social and political happenings.

We should clearly understand, in beginning our discussion, that neither industrialisation nor the body of race relations is uniform or constant. Each may have many different forms and each may change over time. Scholars tend to treat industrialisation as a homogeneous item subject only to quantitative variation. However, the industrialising process may differ significantly along such qualitative dimensions as type of ownership, managerial policies, kinds of occupation, levels of skill, concentration or dispersal of plants, diversity of products, and relation to markets. Such differences in make-up result in differing points of contact with the social order, differing kinds of situations which are set at these points of contact, and differing ways in which these situations are met and handled. Stated otherwise, industrialisation varies significantly in how it meets and enters a social order and in what it presents, so to speak, to that order. Further, in the course of its career in any given region industrialisation may undergo significant transformation, giving rise to new sets of interactions. It should be evident that industrialisation is not a homogeneous variable operating along fixed lines. Its organisation and its thrusts are dependent in large measure on the influences which play upon it.

Patterns of race relations in different parts of the world, likewise, show great differences. Relations may be between a small administrative and commercial racial group on the one hand and on the other a number of diverse tribes, as was true in Ghana. The relations may involve a sizeable group of alien settlers amidst a number of tribes, as in Kenya. Relations may be between a large dominant racial group and a variety of native tribes who have been forced into reservations, as in the case of whites and American Indians in the United States. They may be between a large dominant racial group and a smaller sized dominant group as in South Africa. The relations in a given country may involve a number of sizeable subordinate racial groups, as in the case of Africans, Coloureds, and Indians in South Africa. In some countries a hybrid racial group may occupy a distinctive social position, as in the case of the Coloureds in South Africa, of the Anglo-Indians in India prior to India's independence. It would be boring to continue this recital by referring to other kinds of racial alignment to be found in such countries as Brazil, Mexico, Peru, Malaya, Indonesia, Nigeria, the Belgian Congo, Hawaii, and regions of Soviet Russia. In addition to differences in racial alignment around the world there are conspicuous differences in the points at which racial exclusion is drawn, the extent of the exclusion, and the rigidity of the exclusion. A reasonably full portrayal of the variations in racial patterning to be found in different parts of the world would fill a good-sized book.

The position of industrialisation in the reshaping of race relations will be no different, in my judgment, from that which it has had in the past. Industrialisation will continue to be an incitant to change, without providing the definition of how the change is to be met. It will contribute to the reshuffling of people without determining the racial alignments into which people will fall. Its own racial ordering, to the extent that it has any, will be set by that in its milieu or that forced on it by the authority of a superior control. In general, it will move along with, respond to, and reflect the current of racial transformation in which it happens to be caught.

DISCONTINUOUS SOCIAL CHANGE:

RIOTS, REVOLUTIONS, AND REBELLIONS

Present-day race and ethnic relations are frequently characterized by outbursts of collective violence and protest that can be seen as a legacy of past conquests, slavery, and other types of subordination. Race riots are some of the most spectacular forms of interracial strife, but their exact significance is a subject of much debate. Allan Silver places the American race riot within the context of a broad history of collective violence: riots earlier in the century were usually white attacks on blacks during periods of postwar dislocation and severe social strain; more recent riots resemble the protests of those European workers who took to the streets as a means of securing remedial action for specific hardships and grievances. The dominant response to these riots is partly influenced by the reports and recommendations of successive riot commissions who have frequently incorporated the assumptions of "liberal" social science—what Silver calls the perspective of "diagnostic sociology"— in their analyses. One of the major political problems arising out of this situation is the attempt to justify concessions to rioters to a majority public whose empathy for the black ghetto dweller is limited.

Leo Kuper considers the broad phenomenon of the revolution in which a subordinated group attempts or succeeds in overthrowing the structure of racial or ethnic domination. He addresses the basic issue of the importance of race and class as factors in revolutionary change, against the background of several African societies like Zanzibar, Rwanda, and the Republic of South Africa. Kuper points to the many complications in a class analysis of racial movements such as the lack of uniformity in class position found among members of specific racial groups and the "encompassing principles" whereby members of an ethnic group are slaughtered regardless of their individual wealth or position in the economic structure. Kuper concludes that racial revolutions cannot be reduced to a purely class basis, as some Marxists have implied, and that it is necessary to pay as much attention to the dynamics of racial revolutions as has been given to revolutions based on social class.

While Kuper rejects an exclusive class analysis of racial revolutions, Herbert Gans points to the complex interplay of race and class factors in recent American urban riots, or what he prefers to call "spontaneous rebellions." Like Silver he emphasizes the desperate logic behind such collective outbursts: the sense of community evoked by taking revenge against the most visible agents of ghetto exploitation, the sense of power temporarily given to the powerless. But much of the violence associated with riots is a result of the overreaction of law enforcement officers and national guardsmen, drawn, significantly enough, from members of the white working class. This group is nearest to the Negroes in terms of residential location and occupational positions and often defines blacks as a competitive threat. The conflict between the white working class and the Negro population has a long history and represents the struggle between two relatively deprived groups. Gans discusses the factors that account for the lack of rebelliousness among white, European immigrants and underlines the fallacy that equates the immigrant and the black experience in the United States. Despite some similarities, important differences remain between these two disadvantaged groups that helps to explain their distinctive destinies.

17   Official Interpretations of Racial Riots

Allan A. Silver

America has had an affinity for collective violence—the violence of vigilante groups, lynch mobs, strikes, strike breakers, and private police. Unlike the violence of daily life, unorganized crime or juvenile delinquents, collective violence expresses the values and interests of groups which must be taken into account by reason of their power, size, or strategic location. To describe America as prone to collective violence is to say that significant conflicts among groups contending for political, economic, and social goals have often been expressed in joint acts of attack on life and property.

   Nevertheless, there is a special sense in which America can be said not to have developed a *tradition*—as distinct from a *history*—of collective violence. As Daniel Bell has observed about labor violence, the great bulk of it took place far removed from political centers—indeed, it might be added, often remote from relatively cosmopolitan cities. Minefields in Pennsylvania and Colorado, steel towns along the Monongahela River, lumbering centers in the Far West, mill towns in New England, factory districts in Detroit—these, rather than New York, Chicago, Washington, Philadelphia, and Boston, were the characteristic sites of large-scale labor violence, especially after the tense decade of the 1870s triggered the building of armories in urban locales. There were few American counterparts to Paris, Berlin, St. Petersburg, and Moscow—cities where large numbers of political, social, and intellectual elites resided, and also where class violence recurred. Regional traditions of popular

Reprinted with permission from the Proceedings of the Academy of Political Science, Volume 29, Number 1 (July 1968), 146–68.

violence—such as Southern lynching and Western vigilantism—were also typically found in smaller cities and rural settings. Large-scale racial violence in American cities characteristically took the predominant form of white attacks on Negroes in circumstances aggravated by dislocations stemming from war—New York in 1863, East St. Louis in 1917, Chicago and Washington in 1919, and Los Angeles and Detroit in 1943. Morris Janowitz has suggested the term "communal riots" for these outbursts. They featured white invasion of Negro areas, centered on the struggle to dominate areas whose social character was put in question by rapid demographic and social change, and involved extensive struggles between the races.

In part for such reasons, America has never developed a tradition of collective violence in urban settings by an "underclass" expressing discontent and demanding change, the forms and content of which are jointly understood by rioters and their targets alike. A group of social historians—George Rudé, Eric Hobsbawm, Charles Tilly, Joseph Hamburger—have documented the requirements for a tradition of riot: a variety of formats for disorder, demonstration, or violence occasioned by recurrent difficulties such as the price of bread, grain, or labor. As Hobsbawm in *Primitive Rebels* has summed up the character of these riots: "There was the claim to be considered. The classical mob did not merely riot as a protest, but because it expected to achieve something by its riot. It assumed that the authorities would be sensitive to its movements, and probably also that they would make some immediate concession; for the 'mob' was not simply a casual collection of people united for some ad hoc purpose, but . . . a permanent entity, even though rarely permanently organized as such." (p. 111)

Both for pre-industrial and early industrial societies, many of these writers document that these rioting crowds were composed not of drifting, unattached, semi-criminal rabble—the "dangerous classes," or the "lumpenproletariat," as they were variously called in the nineteenth century—but of residentially stable artisans, shopkeepers, and workers solidly integrated into their societies. Indeed, they expressed that integration in terms of the tradition of riot itself. Local and national elites, the targets and audiences of these riots, faced them at different points and in different circumstances, with dread and fear, or with confidence and calm, but usually in no doubt about the causes of the riotous behavior and the policies, typically lying well within the repertoire of the times, which would placate popular unruliness. It was a feature of "traditional" political society that it often provided the unorganized poor "with a language by which, in the absence of representative institutions or the ability to participate in them, they might articulately address the propertied classes through riot or disorder. . . . However richly endowed with representative and responsive institutions, [America] has not provided such a language for those in its cities who have long been outside their compass—a language whose grammar is shared by speaker and listener, rioter and pillaged, violent and frightened."[1]

The point is beautifully caught in a comment by a Boston notable in 1837. Reacting to local riots, and aware of contemporary riots in Europe, he declared: "Whatever may be the case in other countries, it is manifestly impossible that any sufficient or justifying cause for popular violence exists in this, where republican institutions secure to every individual his just share of the government of the whole."[2] The early and pervasive development of representative institutions in America thus helped to do away with the classical popular riot as a mode of relationship between governors and the governed.

Collective disorder among urban Negroes appears to be shaping itself into modern equivalents of the traditional forms of riotous protest: a self-conscious drama that substitutes shops, consumer goods, police, and white passers-by for granaries and grain carts, tax officials, local notables, and town houses. The burst of rioting that followed Martin Luther King's assassination was the first time that Negro collective disorder was set off in response to a single, politically significant national event. Potentials for disorder heretofore activated by local incidents of a routine character may increasingly be catalyzed by the course of distinctively political affairs.

Of immediate concern, however, is the character of white responses to urban riot. The focus is not on the responses of groups unremittingly or overtly hostile to Negro aspirations, but rather on those responses that have taken concerned, remedial, and egalitarian forms. Thus, less will be said about the substance of policy proposals than about the ideologies and methods of the people who formulate these latter "liberal" responses to the events they seek to interpret.

Obvious places to start are the reports of commissions occasioned by one or another riot, the latest and most comprehensive of which—the *Report of the National Advisory Commission on Civil Disorders* (Kerner Commission)—has recently been published. Such reports date back to 1921, when the Chicago Commission on Race Relations made its report on the 1919 riot in that city. The 1935 Harlem riot led to a commission appointed by Mayor LaGuardia. State-sponsored reports on the riots in Watts in 1965 and Newark in 1967 have also appeared. In all these reports, with the exception of the McCone Commission's on Watts, the "liberal" mentality dominated among commission members, and free use was made not only of legal expertise but of social scientists. Indeed, the Chicago report is dominated by the tone and approach of the University of Chicago's Robert Park, a founder of American urban sociology; its most influential research director was a graduate student of Park, as were many of the research staff. The research director of the Harlem report in 1936 was E. Franklin Frazier, at the time professor of sociology at Howard University. This style of officially interpreting collective violence in America did not begin in 1921, nor was it restricted to the theme of race. In 1915, a Presidential Commission on Industrial Relations included John R. Commons, and the reports of its staff, many of whom were his students, widely reflected the perspectives of institutional economics. It is of special interest, as we shall see, that the social-science view of things did not prevail in the case of the commission on labor violence. With the Kerner Commission, the utilization of social science as an interpretive tool proceeded on a very large scale, and could no longer be identified with a dominant personality. All of these commissions, whether dealing with labor or racial violence, attempted in some part to analyze outbursts of collective violence in terms of causal doctrines prevailing in American social science at the time.

This is surely not surprising, and that social science has much to contribute in these matters one has no doubt. But the perspective of "diagnostic sociology," to speak in a broad, not a specialized and professional sense, is not without its ideological assumptions, functions, and consequences. It is, to begin with, a way of coping with a dilemma. The American notables who made up these commissions—like those middle- and upper-class liberals and professionals who form a sympathetic audience for their reports—have tended broadly to support some or many key aspirations of Negroes. At the same time, they are perhaps among those most likely to accord high priority to the vision of a pervasively pacific society. Certainly their commitment to what Sorel called the "doctrine of social peace" is greater by far than is the case for the unruly poor, for radical ideologues, or those committed to the continued subordination or segregation of Negroes. To adopt the methods of diagnostic sociology is to objectify the causes of violence, to show their roots in environment and social structure, to depersonalize the connection between particular violent groups and the specific content of violent acts.

Apart from the Kerner report's national scope, more urgent tone, and explicit indictment of "white racism," there is hardly an interpretive diagnosis, as the report conspicuously admits, that has not been fully anticipated in the earlier statements. Migration patterns, police brutality and disrespect, unemployment, exclusion from key labor unions, poor and segregated housing, inferior education, inadequate garbage collections—all made their appearance in the reports as causal factors long before Kerner. Indeed, even in 1936, the Harlem riot of the previous year was ascribed, in part, to "smoldering resentments . . . against poverty in the midst of plenty." That report also described looting in ways that adumbrate current interpretations of looting in terms of exclusion from the "consumer society":

> People seized property when there was no possible use it could serve. They acted as if there were a chance to seize what rightfully belonged to them but had long been withheld. . . . Some of the destruction was carried on in a playful spirit. Even the looting, which has furnished many an amusing tale, was sometimes done in the spirit of children taking preserves from a closet to which they have accidentally found the key.

Just as the group of social historians of riot mentioned earlier is concerned to document the meaningful and patterned character of earlier riotous protest in Europe, so the American commission reports from the beginning stress the socially caused, uncollusive character of collective violence in twentieth-century America. As early as 1915, the majority report of the Commission on Industrial Relations described "the origin of industrial violence" in these terms:

> Violence is seldom, if ever, spontaneous, but arises from a conviction that fundamental rights are being denied and that peaceful methods of adjustment cannot be used. . . . The arbitrary suppression of violence by force produces only resentment which will rekindle into greater violence when opportunity

affords. Violence can be prevented only by removing the causes of violence; industrial peace can rest only on industrial justice.

The Chicago report, after a lengthy analysis of the 1919 riot, begins its summary of its extensive investigation into "the conditions that made possible so serious and sudden an outbreak" with a more perfunctory statement of the diagnostic perspective: "The riot was merely a symptom of serious and profound disorders lying beneath the surface of race relations in Chicago." The language of the 1936 report on Harlem is similar.

> The explosion on March 19 would never have been set off by [a] trifling incident . . . had not existing economic and social forces created a state of emotional tension which sought release on the slightest provocation. As long as the economic and social forces which were responsible for that condition operate, a state of tension will exist in Harlem and recurrent outbursts may occur.

The Kerner report is but an elaborated version of the same imagery.

It is the lack of an indigenous tradition of collective violence by the urban poor—a tradition which would have involved the kind of people that have dominated the commissions—that gives special point to the use of social-science techniques and imagery. They supply at once a basis for understanding and an acceptable definition of the situation. What social-science perspectives do for liberals is to make it possible for them to maintain broad political sympathy for the urban Negro "underclass" and simultaneously come to terms with popular unruliness, riot, and violence even though these things are especially disturbing to them. This function of social-science perspectives also testifies to the remoteness of the relationship between the rioting classes and those officially designated to interpret this behavior.

In the classical tradition of riot, the targets and audience were not insulated by social position, professional police, residential separation, or anonymity from the riots themselves. Their very homes, clubs, and persons were the primary objects of attack by a population that dwelt in close proximity, and could discriminate shrewdly among potential targets. Analogously, in the classical tradition of riot, rioters and their audiences shared a set of understandings about the role, content, and purposes of popular violence in terms of which conflicts of interest were expressed. But over the last two centuries there has been a profound rise in standards of public order in civil society, and no group has been more unconditionally committed to this development, its maintenance, and its enhancement than the professional, upper, and middle classes concerned with liberal democracy and social meliorism. Diagnostic sociology, in a sense, supplements general notions of social justice in aiding liberals to come to terms with riotous and violent behavior about which they especially are likely to feel squeamish.

But the stance of diagnostic sociology is subject to erosion as a means of ideologically coping with riot and collective violence that may increase in frequency, scale, and spatial dispersion in the cities—that is, make its appearance on a more organized basis in residential and business areas heretofore largely immune. The demand for law and order as part of the constitutional fabric may well strain the ideological resilience of diagnostic sociology. This is likely to happen before it strains egalitarian commitments, because the perspectives of social science are, after all, commitments of a secular rather than a sacred kind. In any case, using sociology as a diagnostic tool may explain and depersonalize collective violence but does not serve—as the Kerner report makes utterly clear at its outset—to legitimate it: "Those few who would destroy civil order and the rule of law strike at the freedom of every citizen. They must know that the community cannot and will not tolerate coercion and mob action." It is instructive to contrast this statement with the majority report of the Commission on Industrial Relations in 1915, which was largely carried by labor union representatives: "Through history where a people or group have been arbitrarily denied rights which they conceived to be theirs, reaction has been inevitable. Violence is a natural form of protest against injustice." In such a formulation, diagnostic sociology has scant function: it is a matter of natural law, of elemental and self-evident justice. Diagnostic sociology is not required because collective violence as a response to injustice is rooted in the innate order of things.

Interestingly enough, this formulation was rejected not only by the representatives of industrial capitalism on the commission but also, in a separate report, by John R. Commons and the upper-class reformer, Mrs. Florence J. Harriman. Their recommendations stressed the costs of the "civil war" over industrial questions since 1877 and of military solutions, warned of extremist potentials if the causes of industrial violence were unremedied, and endorsed a program of research, applied expertise, and class reconciliation through remedial legislation and nonpartisan industrial commissions. Commons was acting in the spirit of the "Wisconsin Idea," that early and seminal instance of the institutionalized relationship between social-science expertise and public policy in the service of social reform, then in flower at the University of Wisconsin. Frank Walsh, the commission's chairman—a Progressive radical and leader of the labor union majority—successfully prevented this style from dominating the commission's works.[3] But the affinity of diagnostic sociology and liberal reformism was thus palpable before the emergence of racial violence as an officially acknowledged problem. That affinity is all the stronger, one might suggest, for being tied not to the theme of race as such but to the whole question of popular disorder and collective violence.

This sort of ideological response to riot and disorder is potentially fragile not only because of possible strains between a diagnostic stance and a profound commitment to civil order. Its case for responding positively to riot in terms of remedy and justice rests, implicitly but crucially, upon a view of collective violence as remorselessly caused rather than as an active choice by oppressed people. Obviously one cannot here enter into the bearing of doctrines of social causation on the possibilities of initiative and choice. It is sufficient to suggest that in the world of riot commission reports, it is legitimate for political authority and the general society to respond positively and remedially to acts of collective violence that, in terms of democratic doctrines, cannot enjoy intrinsic legitimacy, to the extent that violence is causally inevitable. The medical metaphor is worn but unavoidable, since the reports themselves constantly invoke it. The sick body cannot but produce symptoms like fever and pain that it finds distressing; a society afflicted by gross injustice cannot but produce violence—in ways, however, amenable to diagnosis, intervention, and cure.

But Negro urban violence has already produced spokesmen—not only visible ideologues but anonymous rioters briefly quoted in the Kerner report itself—whose definitions of Negro rioting affirm it as a positive and voluntary act. It is not only that such affirmations are likely to outrage the great white public that shares the commission's perspectives partially if at all and, in the end, also to offend the commission's sympathetic audience. Also, much would be lost—humanly, politically, and from the viewpoint of social science—if official interpretive ideology functions to elide or ignore Negro definitions of riot as purposeful, affirmative, and actively chosen. Men who engage in dangerous and desperate behavior—indeed, any behavior—have a certain claim to have taken seriously the meanings which they see in their own acts, and wish others to see in them.

But even if such voluntaristic definitions of riot do not become current, we are likely to face, in the seeable future, a period in which some sort of remedial action, at an unknown level of scope and investment, is likely to coexist with continuing and perhaps mounting levels of collective violence among Negroes.[4] The Kerner Commission itself predicts that not only the continuation of present national policy, but also the "enrichment" option and even that program which represents the most radical restructuring of American society in its repertoire, the "integration" option, are likely to result in roughly equal levels of urban riot and violence in the short run. It does so, wisely, on the grounds that even strong integration policies are unable to deflect the massive momentum of the present situation quickly and thoroughly, and that the enhanced contrast between current reality and elevated expectations—already a cause of collective violence under present conditions—would almost certainly not result in a rapid diminution of the disposition to riot and might even increase it.

This exercise in the social causation of riot may satisfy the commission and part, at least, of its sympathetic audience, but it implies political and ideological strains of a considerable order. One could not do better than take one's text from Sorel's discussion in *Reflections on Violence* of a comparable state of affairs six decades ago, as social reformism and the parliamentary state sought to incorporate the industrial working classes:

> To repay with *black ingratitude* the benevolence of those who would protect the workers, to meet with insults the homilies of the defenders of human fraternity, and to reply by blows to the advances of the propagators of social peace . . . is a very practical way of indicating to the middle class that they must mind their own business and only that. . . . It may be useful to thrash the orators of democracy and the representatives of the Government, for in this way you insure that none shall retain any illusions about the character of acts of violence. But these acts can have historical value only if they are the *clear and brutal expression of the class war*. . . . The middle classes must not

be allowed to imagine that, aided by cleverness, social science or high-flown sentiments, they might find a better welcome at the hands of the proletariat. (Italics in the original.)

Fittingly enough among the objects of Sorel's scorn was "Professor Durkheim," who in his classic analysis of modern society's potential for social integration had analyzed the "class war" as an "abnormal form" of social organization.

Certainly, diagnostic sociology will do its best to interpret, and thus to soften, the ideological strains of continued civic disorder in the face of massive "enrichment" or "integrationist" policies. But one may wonder whether explanations of, say, the role of frustrated rising expectations in promoting riots will suffice to alter the Sorelian scenario. Even the optimal American short run will thus be a most perilous time.

The great white public remains, on the whole, unconvinced of the premises and conclusions of such reports as that of the Kerner Commission. More will be learned about the perspectives on these matters of the general public, white and Negro, when an opinion survey of residents in fifteen cities sponsored by the commission is published. Meanwhile, one must make do with data from less satisfactory, scattered surveys based on less sharply focused samples—not of key cities but of the national population. These preliminary indications are not encouraging. Louis Harris reports that at most a third of whites, usually less, agree with the Kerner Commission that "white racism" brought on the riots, that riot arrestees should get better legal counsel and fairer trials, that the rioting is not organized, and that the level of welfare payments should be raised. Only slightly more agree that lack of progress in extending equality to Negroes and too few jobs are major causes of riots. Forty-five per cent see lack of decent housing as a cause of riot, but only 23 per cent are willing to pay higher taxes to remedy this. Only one in ten think police brutality has conduced to riot. On the positive side, however, relatively few whites see urban Negroes as actively preferring riot—a quarter or less agree that among the causes are Negroes' desires for violence and wish to loot stores.

The picture afforded by surveys taken before Kerner is generally also dreary. Just under half of whites in national samples, a heavy plurality, think that high among the major causes of riots is "outside agitation" (45 per cent) and that Communist involvement is major (48 per cent). Asked to perform an extraordinary act of empathy, to imagine how they would react to discrimination if they were Negroes, only a quarter produce such responses as being "mad, resentful, and fighting back." Two-thirds endorse the shooting of looters and firebombers. To prevent riots, 41 per cent of whites suggest stronger repressive measures, the punishment of outside agitators, and increasing police forces; a comparable number propose a variety of remedial actions, including some that echo the spirit of the Kerner report, but no one of these attracts the proportions that prefer repression. Between June 1963 and October 1966, the percentage of whites believing that "demonstrations by Negroes have helped . . . the advancement of Negro rights" fell from 36 to 15; the percentage believing that they have "hurt" rose from 45 to 85. In proportions that range in recent years from 45 to 59, whites report that they have increased fears for their personal safety in daily life. Echoing the belief that most Negroes are peaceful, however, more than eight in ten believe that "only a minority of Negroes" support riots, as do three-quarters of Negroes interviewed. Relatively few whites see Negroes as actively preferring riots and a quarter or less agree that major causes of riots are that Negroes desire violence and wish to loot stores. Whites in lower-income groups, however, are much less likely than those with higher incomes to agree that most Negroes believe in nonviolence.[5]

These responses must be placed in the broad setting that verbal standards of racial tolerance and egalitarianism, as measured by opinion polls over the last few decades, show an uninterrupted rise.[6] It is too soon to tell whether Paul Sheatsley, who has helped document this trend, is correct in predicting that sustained rioting "will [not] halt the massive attitudinal changes we have demonstrated over the last generation."[7] If the American dilemma was severe before a new and unprecedentedly large population of urban Negroes began to question basic assumptions about public order, it is surely premature to expect its favorable resolution under these transformed conditions. The most one can say is that the dilemma's terms have both shifted and sharpened.

Perspectives on race alone do not exhaust these matters. Pluralities or majorities of whites surely do not share the perspective toward disorder and violence that characterizes the social and professional groupings from which the commissions are drawn, and which attend sympathetically to their analyses. The long-range rise in standards of public order, and in the extent to which legitimate violence has tended increasingly to become in America a monopoly of government, has been accompanied by—indeed, has required—a kind of "psychic disarming" of a large number of Americans. The "softening of manners" which is a theme of the older social historians, the rise in standards of peacefulness in family life, and occupational experience that Sorel saw as critical to the bourgeois doctrine of "social peace"—perhaps all have operated psychologically to disarm the middle and professional classes, especially liberals, more than any comparable group. Indeed, the loss of the capacity or will for voluntary self-defense among the new commercial and urban middle classes would appear to be among the conditions that promoted the creation of professional policing. But one's impression of Southern life, of the volume of gun sales in many cities, and of the few—so far controlled—instances of incipient "communal riot" of the older type (Chicago, Milwaukee, and East New York) all suggest strongly that the "psychic disarming" of very many white Americans is far from complete or advanced. Combined with the widely shared demand for historically unprecedented levels of civil order, and with continuing racial hostility, these are ominous convergences. So far, the ecology of segregation, police tactics, and the dispositions dominant among rioting populations have forestalled the fulfillment of these potentials.

The American dilemma persists, and the reports of the commissions on racial disorders are essentially elitist in assumption, tone, and values—more so than was the case of the majority report of the Commission on Industrial Relations with respect to labor violence more than fifty years ago. But the elite that has produced them is significantly different in social composition in one critical respect: formerly dominated by interest-group representatives and civic and philanthropic notables, the Kerner Commission was dominated by the most significant of modern elites, professional politicians. The relationship among professional politicians, popular democracy, egalitarianism, and elitist functions is one of the most charged themes in American society. Historically, elites in America—in Karl Mannheim's classic definition as special groups responsible for the maintenance of standards—have not easily been drawn from professional politicians.

Under present conditions, however, the critical burden of response can fall on no other group. To sponsor hard decisions in the political economy, to mobilize sufficient assent for these decisions, and to win elective office while doing these things—all present a trial without precedent for American professional politicians. Above all, the attempt to define as legitimate remedial responses to illegitimate violence creates extraordinary strains on the ideological resources of egalitarianism, diagnostic sociology, and the capacities of professional politicians to respond, manage, and lead. Never have professional politicians in this greatest of popular democracies been summoned to a role at once more profoundly democratic and more distinctively elitist.

NOTES

1. Allan Silver, "The Demand for Order in Civil Society," in David Bordua (ed.), *The Police* (New York, 1967), 23–24.
2. Samuel A. Eliot, quoted in Roger Lane, *Policing the City* (Cambridge, Massachusetts, 1967), 30–31.
3. Graham Adams, Jr., *Age of Industrial Violence* (New York, 1966), 204–214.
4. This and other matters connected with what I have called the "diagnostic sociology" of collective violence are acutely considered in Aaron Wildavsky's "Black Rebellion and White Reaction," *The Public Interest* (Spring 1968), 3–16.
5. All these results are drawn from Hazel Erskine's compilation, "The Polls: Demonstrations and Race Riots," *Public Opinion Quarterly* (Winter 1967–1968), 655–677.
6. See Herbert H. Hyman and Paul Sheatsley, "Attitudes towards Desegregation," *Scientific American*, CCXI (July 1964), 16–23; Paul Sheatsley, "White Attitudes towards the Negro," *Daedalus*, XCV (Winter 1966), 217–238; and Mildred A. Schwartz, *Trends in White Attitudes toward Negroes*, National Opinion Research Center, University of Chicago, Report No. 119 (1967).
7. Sheatsley, 236.

18   Theories of Revolution
and Race Relations

Leo Kuper

I

Most contemporary theories of revolution are derived from the analysis of conflict between social classes in racially homogeneous societies, and they may not be very illuminating when applied to situations of revolutionary struggle between racial groups. This is the problem I discuss in the present paper, and my purpose, in general, is to raise some questions concerning the applicability of theories of class revolution to racial revolution.

The main source of many of these theories is the Marxist theory of revolution as a product of a dialectical process of polarization between classes, defined in their relationship to the means of production, and I shall deal with it in the more general terms of the role of economic stratification in racial revolutions.

I shall define revolution as a form of "internal war"[1] in which there is a violent assumption of power and substantial change in the structure and values of the society.[2] I shall exclude from the concept of revolution used in this paper internal wars between sections which occupy roughly the same level in the hierarchy (as for example Ibo and Hausa), and struggles for liberation from colonial rule, save where the structure of the colonial society comprised also a settled racially distinct dominant section (as for example, a stratum of white settlers or of pastoral ruling aristocracies). Thus, the cases of racial revolution (or attempted revolution) I have in mind include the revolution of Hutu against Tutsi in Rwanda (where the Belgian tutelary power supported the domination of the pastoral Tutsi over the agricultural Hutu until almost the final stage of independence), the revolution of Africans against Arabs in Zanzibar (where the British supported the Sultan and the Arab oligarchy), and the revolutionary movement of Africans and Indians against white domination in South Africa in the period 1948–64. The Algerian revolution, though not a revolution involving racially different groups, is also relevant, since it has provided a model for racial revolutionary struggle.

II

If a major theme in revolutionary theory is the Marxist dialectic in the economic process, resulting in the polarization of classes, the variations on this theme appear

From *Comparative Studies in Society and History*, Vol. 13, January, 1971. Reprinted by permission of the author and Cambridge University Press.

to exhaust almost every logical possibility.[3] There are theories of a predisposing condition in immiserization of the masses, or in economic advance,[4] or in economic growth followed by recession, or in the disjunction between desire (or aspiration) and reality, or in the tension between the processes and relations of production (such as has characterized South African society for over a generation). What these situations have in common is that they involve disequilibrium, between classes as in the immiserization of the masses, or within a class, as in the disequilibrium resulting from economic progress followed by recession. The theories may then be reduced to the more basic theory that economic disequilibrium is a precondition, or precipitant, of revolutions between classes. Since classes are defined in economic terms, or largely in economic terms, the basic theory may be somewhat tautologous.

In regard to the relevance of these theories for racial revolutions, two extreme positions may be taken. The first position attaches overwhelming significance to economic relations, arguing that racial discrimination is only found in association with economic exploitation, and that racial conflict is simply a particular expression of class conflict. The causes of racial revolution are therefore the same as those of class revolution, for example, polarization of the races in their relationship to the means of production. The second extreme position emphasizes the absolute primacy of the racial structure. Racial revolutions are viewed as inherent or endemic in structures of racial domination, opportunity being the precondition or precipitant. From this perspective, economic change is somewhat marginally relevant to the preconditions or precipitants of revolution.

Theories of Revolution and Race Relations

There is a long-standing and continuing controversy between advocates of these different perspectives. In the U.S.A., shortly after the Second World War, Cox (1948) sought to establish the origins of racial discrimination in the growth of capitalism, and to demonstrate that black and white workers shared common class interests. In the U.S.A. today, the failure of black and white proletariat to combine, and the clashes of interest between them, lend support to the contrary view of many black revolutionaries that the conflict is essentially racial.[5] There is a similar controversy in the interpretation of African revolutions, which take the manifest form of racial conflict. Marxists find in these a class basis. Thus, with reference to Zanzibar, Bochkaryov (1964: 13-15), writing in *New Times,* charged that the British colonial administration and the imperialist press sought to interpret as racialist, a revolution which arose out of class differences and was directed against the big landowners and the Sultan. Rey, in the *New Left Review* (1964:31), viewed the revolution in Zanzibar as a social, not an ethnic, revolution, carried out by groups representing, first and foremost, the Zanzibar City proletariat, but supported after the revolution by a general rallying of all the exploited against the Arab ruling class. In South Africa, these different perspectives of the society in terms of class or race were influential in the political division of Africans into two parties, the African National Congress being more Marxist in its ideological orientation, while the Pan-Africanist Congress emphasized the primacy of racial discrimination against Africans (Kuper, 1965:

Chapter 23). Fanon (1966: 32–3, first publication in 1961), examined this problem of class and race, no doubt largely in the context of the Algerian revolution, and emphasized the racial aspect, but with a complex lyricism, which gives an elusive quality to his meaning. Standing Marxism somewhat on its head (the phrase used in the translation is that Marxist analysis must be "slightly stretched"), he argued that:

"In the colonies the economic substructure is also a superstructure. The cause is the consequence; you are rich because you are white, you are white because you are rich . . . It is neither the act of owning factories, nor estates, nor a bank balance which distinguishes the governing classes. The governing race is first and foremost those who come from elsewhere, those who are unlike the original inhabitants, 'the others.' "

III

Both aspects of Fanon's paradox, "you are rich because you are white" and "you are white because you are rich," are in fact inaccurate. But they do bring out a basic problem in the controversy, namely the difficulty of clearly distinguishing racial divisions from class divisions, and hence the difficulty of assessing the relative significance of class and race in racial revolutions. In the abstract the terms are quite distinct: race refers to physical differences, whether measured by 'objective' criteria or by social definitions, and class refers to socio-economic differentiation, whether defined by "objective" measures such as the relationship to the means of production, or by social perception. In the concrete situation, however, it may be difficult to differentiate the two structures. Race and class divisions generally overlap. Race and class may be closely related genetically, since a system of stratification which is socially defined as a class system, may have originated in a system of racial stratification, the contemporary class differences coinciding appreciably with racial differences, as in many Latin-American and West Indian societies. And separation of the phenomena may be further complicated by the presence of socio-economic differentiation within each of the racial divisions. The problems raised by this merging of the phenomena can only be resolved partly. They are the empirical basis for the ideological controversy, whether racial stratification is epiphenomenal and simply a particular manifestation of class stratification, or whether racial differences provide an independent basis in the genesis and persistence of social stratification.

If racial divisions and class divisions coincided, so that, for example, the whites in a particular society were all members of the bourgeoisie, and the blacks were all members of the proletariat or peasants, some insight into the relative significance of race or class could no doubt be derived from a comparison of revolutions in such societies with revolutionary struggles between social classes in racially homogeneous societies. Where economic differentiation and racial stratification are in some measure divergent, as in the contemporary revolutions involving racial groups, interpretation becomes exceedingly complex.

The two recent revolutions, in Zanzibar and in Rwanda, may serve as an illustration of some of the complexities of the relationship between race and class, or race, class and caste.[6]

In the Protectorate of Zanzibar, comprising Zanzibar and Pemba Island, the main racial and ethnic sections were the Shirazis, Mainland Africans, Arabs and Asians; there were also small numbers of Comorians, Goans and Europeans. The total population, according to the 1958 Census, was some 299,000, comprising over 165,000 on Zanzibar Island, and almost 134,000 on Pemba Island. The Shirazis were the largest section, constituting in 1948 over half the population on both islands (see Table 1). The Shirazis, who claimed that they had intermingled with Persians who migrated to Zanzibar in about the tenth century, most nearly correspond to indigenous African groups. The second largest section was Mainland African, comprising in 1948, almost one-fifth of the total population, that is 25.1 percent of the population on Zanzibar Island, and 12.1 percent on Pemba.[7] Figures are not available for 1958, but in that census, 10.9 percent of the population on Zanzibar Island and 6.7 percent on Pemba were shown as born on the East African mainland: most of these would be Mainland African. The foreign born population in general was an older population, 81.4 percent being over twenty years of age as compared with 51.1 percent of the local born, and had a higher sex ratio, 215.9 males per 100 females as compared with 101.7 (Zanzibar, 1960: 32, 35). The indications therefore are of an appreciable adult male African migrant population. The Arab population which included a variety of Arab groups, was the third largest section: in 1948, Arabs comprised 16.9 percent of the total population, i.e. 9.3 percent on Zanzibar and 26.7 percent on Pemba (Zanzibar, 1953: 2, 4). Mainland Africans, that is to say, were almost three times as numerous as Arabs on Zanzibar Island, whereas on Pemba Island they were less than one-half the number of Arabs. Finally, Asians, mostly Indians and some Goans, comprised 6.1 percent of

TABLE 1

Distribution of Population, Zanzibar Protectorate, 1948*

Section	Zanzibar Island		Pemba Island		Total Zanzibar Protectorate	
	NO.	*%*	*NO.*	*%*	*NO.*	*%*
Arab	13,977	9.3	30,583	26.7	44,560	16.9
Indian and Goan	13,705	9.2	2,187	1.8	15,892	6.1
Mainland African	37,502	25.1	13,878	12.1	51,380	19.5
Shirazi	81,150	54.2	67,330	58.8	148,480	56.2
Other	3,241	2.2	609	0.6	3,850	1.3
Total	149,575	100.0	114,587	100.0	264,162	100.0

*Source: Notes on the Census of the Zanzibar Protectorate, 1948, Tables I and XV. A small number of persons who did not state their tribal origins, I have classified with Mainland Africans.

the total population in 1958, the great majority residing on Zanzibar Island, and indeed in Zanzibar City (Zanzibar, 1960: 18, 21).

Zanzibar economy rested largely on the marketing of cloves, and on subsistence agriculture and fishing. There was some employment by Government, some development of commerce, but little in industry, and that mainly in the processing of foods.[8] Cloves, the main export, were uncertain both as a crop and as a commodity. There was an appreciable seasonal immigration from the mainland for the picking of cloves, most of the plantations being located on Pemba Island. The dependence of the economy on cloves was such that decline in the world market for cloves created a serious economic crisis for the government, and resulted in a reduction of social services in the period immediately preceding the revolution.

It is difficult to give a clear picture of the distribution of resources and occupations among the different sections. The image of Arabs as senior bureaucrats and large plantation owners, of Indians as merchants, and of Africans, both Shirazi and Mainland, as fishermen, cultivators and laborers is of course, quite false. Most Arabs, Shirazis and Africans were poor, and there were many poor Indians. What can be said is that senior bureaucrats and many of the large plantation owners were Arab, that merchants tended to be Indian, that most of the cultivators and fishermen were Shirazi, and that most Mainland Africans were either employed as laborers in Zanzibar City, where many of them lived, or they were occupied as squatters or seasonally in clove-picking. There was, however, considerable overlapping of the occupations followed by members of different sections. Middleton and Campbell (1965: 39) comment on an intermingling of Arab and Shirazi plantation owners on Pemba Island, but not on Zanzibar Island. Lofchie (1969: 293–309) examines landownership (measured by number of clove trees), occupational distribution and access to education in the year 1948, when a survey was conducted; the tables he presents show appreciable overlapping. Lofchie concludes "that Zanzibar's major communal groups were differentiated by economic and social status" and that "Zanzibaris of different races did not share sufficient common occupational or economic interests to create politically meaningful bonds of solidarity across racial lines" (306). But it is here that difficulties begin to arise, since the figures show similarities between the different sections, and there is need for a valid measure of similarities and differences in socio-economic situation (occupation, landownership and education) and for a valid methodology for drawing conclusions as to their political significance. (Tables 2, 3, and 4 are from Lofchie, 1969: 303–305).

The population of Rwanda at the time of the revolution was some 2.5 million, predominantly Hutu (about 85 percent), ruled by an aristocracy drawn from the Tutsi (totalling about 14 percent) and including small numbers of Twa. The sections varied somewhat in physical characteristics, perceiving their differences in terms of racial stereotypes.[9]

The country was, and continues to be, exceedingly poor and densely populated.[10] Its economy rested essentially on subsistence farming and herding. Productivity was greatly limited by geographic environmental factors, by ignorance, by poor health consequent upon malaria, intestinal parasites, tuberculosis, dysentery and malnutrition, by the rudimentary techniques of hoe cultivation and by the so-

TABLE 2

Landownership in Zanzibar by Racial Community, 1948

Number of Trees	Percentage of Parcels				Total Number of Owners
	Arab	*Asian*	*Shirazi*	*Mainland African*	
3,000 or more	68.8	31.2	–	–	240
1,000–2,999	56.1	6.1	20.2	17.7[a]	570
250–999	51.9	5.2	33.8	9.1	3,635
50–249	14.5	0.3	74.2	11.0	13,680
Less than 50	16.0	0.1	66.6	17.3	10,250

[a]This figure, which represents 100 Mainland African landowners, was recorded entirely in Pemba.

TABLE 3

Occupational Distribution in Zanzibar by Racial Community, 1948

Occupational Level	Percentage of Workers				Total Number of Workers
	Arab	*Asian*	*Indigenous African*	*Mainland African*	
Upper	4.2	95.8	–	–	120
Upper middle	26.0	59.2	6.3	8.5	710
Middle (non-manual)	26.1	33.3	27.3	13.3	5,400
Middle (manual)	6.0	34.9	12.1	47.0	1,735
Lower middle	17.1	4.7	54.1	24.1	35,160
Lower	13.5	0.9	36.9	48.7	14,635

TABLE 4

Access to Higher Education in Zanzibar by Racial Community, 1948

Educational Level	Percentage of Students				Total Number of Students
	Arab	*Asian*	*Indigenous African*	*Mainland African*	
Standards I–VI	30.4	7.8	40.2	21.6	12,205
Standards VII–IX	29.9	41.3	12.8	16.0	1,440
Standards X–XII	31.4	46.8	3.2	18.6	620

The figures are for 1948, and though they are the best available, they relate to a period some fifteen to sixteen years before the revolution.

cial and political order (Leurquin, 1960: Part I). With a narrow margin over bare subsistence, famine constantly threatened. Coffee was the main cash crop and export. There was little urbanization, the most important agglomeration having a population of about 20,000, and little industrialization, that being mainly in mining. Foreigners largely controlled both industry and commerce. The different sectors of industry, commerce and agriculture provided some employment for, on the one hand, the "proletarized worker, torn from his tribal roots, living only from his work . . . and, on the other hand, the peasant laborer, the occasional plantation worker, the roadman's or foreman's often undependable day worker" (*Ruanda-Urundi, Economy I,* 1960: 16). About 54,000 were so employed in 1958. In addition, there was a small professional stratum.

The nature of the distribution of resources between the sections is conveyed by the description usually applied to Rwanda, namely caste or feudal society. Maquet compares the relationship between Tutsi and Hutu to that between nobles and peasants in the Ancien Regime, or, in certain respects, to the relation between industrial capitalists and proletarian workers in Europe in the nineteenth century (1964: 552). The two sections were distinguished by their hereditary occupations of agriculture for the Hutu and pastoralism for the Tutsi. In fact, many Hutu looked after cattle and many Tutsi were not engaged in pastoral activities, but, nevertheless, a Hutu was always a man of the hoe, and a Tutsi a man of the cow (Maquet, 1964: 553). Economic and political relations were organized in such a way that rights over cattle provided some exemption from manual labor for the Tutsi.

Maquet, drawing on an analogy to the concept of surplus profit in Marxist class analysis, argues that the system was possible by reason of an agricultural surplus: he was obliged to add, however, that agricultural production was very little above the subsistence level, and that both surplus and malnutrition often co-existed (1964: 554). The Tutsi appropriated the agricultural "surplus" by the effective monopoly of government, the imposition of the corvee and of heavier taxes on the Hutu, and the system of clientage through which the client, in exchange for protection and the use of cattle, undertook to render services and produce to his patron.[11]

Given the low level of economic productivity, there could not have been a great difference in standard of living between many Tutsi and Hutu. The Tutsi however constituted the privileged section. They provided the ruling class, the aristocracy of wealth, the warriors; they appropriated the control over cattle, and they enjoyed a more favored position than the Hutu in the system of clientage, though Tutsi were also involved as clients in a hierarchical system which extended throughout the society. But the near monopoly by the Tutsi of power, privilege and wealth was an attribute of the Tutsi viewed as a collectivity. Seen as individuals or as family units, in their daily routine, there was considerable similarity between Tutsi and Hutu in material conditions of living.

Leurquin, in a careful study of the standard of living of the rural populations of Ruanda-Urundi during the period from September 1955 to August 1956, provides some measure of similarity between Tutsi and Hutu in terms of subsistence production, daily consumption of food, distribution of cattle, monetary revenue, and expenditure. His sample of six regions included four regions in Rwanda. Traditional authorities, from whom a measure of collaboration was necessary, traders with large establishments at the beginning of the inquiry, and persons living in indigenous towns and non-traditional centers ("centres extra-coutumiers"), were excluded from the study (132–3). Thus the sample excludes chiefs and subchiefs, almost entirely Tutsi, and the functionaries and bureaucrats living in the urbanized zones, also predominantly Tutsi (203, 250, 277–8). These were the categories of rich Tutsi (278).

The most important economic sector for the sample population was production for subsistence which contributed two-thirds in money value, while revenue from the money economy contributed one-third (179, 274). Table 5 provides a comparison between Hutu and Tutsi in the sample population, in Ruanda-Urundi: where Leurquin gives separate comparative figures for Rwanda and Urundi, these are shown.

The figures given in the table are averages, but it is clear from the relatively small differences between Tutsi and Hutu in the annual value of subsistence production (4,439 francs as compared with 4,249 francs per family) and in the annual value of monetary revenue (2,795 francs as against 2,189 francs per family) that there must have been considerable continuity and overlapping of standards of living in the two sections. The main difference is in the annual production of milk (181 litres per family compared with 66 litres) and in the distribution of cattle (2.6, 1.2, 2.4 and 1.6 as compared with 1.7, 0.7, 1.2 and 0.5 in the Rwanda regions).

Leurquin (1960: 203–4), in summarizing the position, comments that the material superiority of Tutsi over Hutu is always established by reference to the holders of positions of authority, that is chiefs and subchiefs, and civil servants, categories virtually excluded from the sample. He points out that the cleavage (Tutsi = pastoralism = riches, Hutu = agriculture = poverty) has ceased to be always true. In regions where an artisan category had developed, or where coffee plantations had multiplied, there were to be found rich Hutu, while Tutsi small-owners of cattle, deprived of their prerogatives and obliged to tend the soil, often proved to be mediocre cultivators: in a group of forty families studied at Karama, eighteen Tutsi of thirty-four possessed no cattle and in Rukoma a Tutsi died of hunger, because he had no servants and had never learnt to cultivate. Leurquin comments that the modest advantage enjoyed by Tutsi in the subsistence economy seemed to be concentrated in certain sectors, the most marked being in the production of milk. "Pour le reste, les differences de caste ne suffisent plus aujourd'hui a expliquer les differences de revenue en milieu rural."

IV

Among the many difficulties of interpretation which flow from the lack of correspondence between racial and economic differentiation, there is first of all the prob-

TABLE 5

Comparison of the Value of Subsistence Production and of Monetary Revenue, Quantity of Milk Consumed, and Distribution of Cattle per Family—for Tutsi and Hutu in Rwanda and Urundi in the Period September 1955–August 1956

Category	Value of Subsistence Production (Francs)[1]	Value of Monetary Revenue (Francs)[2]	Production of Milk (Litres)[3]	Distribution of Cattle by Region[4]					
				Rwanda				Urundi	
				Vallee de l'Akanyaru	Bwana-Mukare	Nduga	Kinyaga	Buyenzi	Mugamba
Tutsi	4,439	2,795	181	2.6	1.2	2.4	1.6	1.9	0.5
Hutu	4,249	2,189	66	1.7	0.7	1.2	0.5	0.3	0.2

Sources: All figures are from Philippe Leurquin, *Le Niveau de Vie des Populations Rurales du Ruanda-Urundi* (Louvain: Editions Nauwelaerts, 1960).
[1] Table 26, p. 203.
[2] Table 50, p. 278.
[3] pp. 229–30.
[4] Table 45, p. 263.

lem of the differential impact of economic change on different strata within each of the racial sections. Then, in view of this diversity within each racial section, there is the problem whether it is meaningful to define the racial sections as entities. What is the relationship between collective attributes and individual situation? In what sense were the Tutsi the dominant caste in Rwanda, or Arabs the ruling stratum in Zanzibar? Finally, there is the problem of the disjunction between the objective situation and the perception of it, facilitated precisely by the lack of coincidence between racial and economic differentiation.

First, in regard to economic change, it cannot be assumed that the consequences are the same for all members of a social class, and such general measures as economic growth and *per capita* income may be quite misleading in the analysis of class structures.[12] The assumption of a uniform impact of economic change on members of a racial category may be even more misleading in the analysis of racial structures. The economic position of professionals and businessmen of the subject race may continue to improve, while that of the workers remains constant or deteriorates: or the position of the urban proletariat may improve, and that of the peasantry deteriorate. Similarly, the economic changes may have quite varied consequences for different strata in the dominant group. It is possible that the crucial stimulus which serves as a catalyst of revolution is some particular combination of these consequences for different strata within the dominant and subordinate racial sections.

The second difficulty arises from the equating of collective attributes with individual attributes. Thus, it is a very common practice among scholars, as well as laymen, to describe Indians in East Africa or South Africa as a trading class. The position varies in the different countries from situations in which most trade is (or was) in Indian hands, as in Zanzibar, to situations in which Indian trading is a negligible portion of the total trade, as in South Africa. In the case of Zanzibar, there is no published information regarding the distribution of occupations among Indians at about the time of the revolution, though there is earlier evidence, in a proposal for a survey conducted by Batson in 1946, that "among the Indians there are a great many petty traders who are as poverty-stricken as the natives or even more so, and undernourishment exists, particularly among the Hindus" (1948: 26). Most Indians at the time were engaged as uncertified professional workers, clerical personnel, skilled and semiskilled workers, vendors, itinerant peddlers and unskilled laborers (Lofchie, 1965: 88–9). Clearly the fact that the main traders and financiers in Zanzibar were Indian by no means constitutes Indians as a trading class. In South Africa, the great majority of Indians are working class and poor. In what sense then can they be described as a trading class? If Indians, as a category, are legally entitled to acquire the means of production in some areas of South Africa, and if in fact a few Indians have started industrial enterprises and a larger number have entered into commerce, does this constitute a class of Indian bourgeoisie? If the criterion is the theoretical possibility of mobility into the ruling stratum, or the legal right to acquire productive property, then the Marxist distinction between bourgeoisie and proletariat would be quite meaningless outside of such countries as South Africa, where the laws largely deny Africans the right to acquire productive property.

Similar problems arise with reference to the Tutsi caste in Rwanda and the Arab oligarchy in Zanzibar. The fact that the rulers were Tutsi or Arab, and monopolized positions of power traditionally and under colonial administration, by no means implies that these qualities of power of the dominant caste or oligarchy inhered in the rank and file of impoverished Tutsi or Arabs. Nor do the attributes of Tutsi or Arabs viewed as a collectivity necessarily affect the class situation of commoners. And yet in certain circumstances, as for example in the type of society van den Berghe characterizes as "Herrenvolk Democracy" such as South Africa and U.S.A. (1969: 73), the attributes of the racial section clearly affect the situation of the individual members of that race. Thus the monopoly of political power by whites in South Africa so sharply differentiates the economic position or life chances of white and black workers that they can hardly be regarded as sharing a common class situation. The relationship between collective and individual attributes is clearly an empirical question, requiring systematic analysis and more refined categories than such descriptions as Tutsi dominant caste.

The perceptions of the structure of the society may be at least as significant in the revolutionary process as the "objective reality" and they may be quite varied in their relationship to that reality.[13] Indeed, part of the revolutionary struggle consists essentially in a conflict of ideologies, and the attempt to mobilize sections of the population behind particular perceptions of the structure of the society. The very complexity of the relations of race, class and caste in a society, and the diversity of positions within the structure of that society, would encourage these varied perceptions. If Mainland Africans in Zanzibar perceived Arabs collectively as racial oppressors, or if Hutu peasants perceived Tutsi collectively as a dominant caste, what significance is to be attached to the fact that the great majority of Arabs and Tutsi did not share in the enjoyment or in the exercise of wealth and power, and had no prospects of access to wealth and power?

V

Given the complex interrelations between racial and economic differentiation, and the consequent problems of interpretation, is it possible to test the relative significance of racial factors and of economic factors? Perhaps, the distinction used by Dumont (1966: 17–32) between the encompassing principle and that which is encompassed may be helpful. Thus, when Lofchie (1965: 10) writes that the Afro-Shirazi Party, which had attempted to unite Mainland Africans and Shirazi in Zanzibar, was motivated by a resentment of the Arab oligarchy, a resentment "which expressed itself in virulently anti-Arab propaganda and in the publicly expressed desire of ASP leadership to transform Zanzibar into an African-ruled nation," he would seem to be describing a situation in which the encompassing principle is that of race. It can only be by virtue of this encompassing principle that an antagonism against a section of the Arabs is expressed in antagonism against all Arabs. So too, when Africans and Whites in South Africa see Indians as wealthy traders, when most Indians are working class and poor, it can only be by reason of a transformation of perception in terms of a general encompassing principle of racial stratification: in an objective situation, where some Indians are traders, the subjective perception is that all Indians are traders. Similarly in Zanzibar, where most trade was in Indian hands, the categorization of Indians as traders involves the transformation of the attributes of individual Indians into the attributes of Indians as a collectivity. Again, the encompassing principle is race, and the description of Indians in Zanzibar, or East Africa generally, as traders, though seemingly a description in terms of class, is in fact a racial categorization.

There are obviously very great difficulties in attempting to determine which is the encompassing principle and which the encompassed. In the context of revolutionary change, two measures may be suggested. The first measure relates to the target group, the persons actually killed by the revolutionaries, whether persons of a particular class, or persons of a particular race and class, or members of a particular race, regardless of class. Presumably where revolutionary violence expresses itself in the indiscriminate slaughter of members of a racial group, then the encompassing principle is race. The second measure is that of the precipitating events, in terms of differences between impulses affecting racial differentiation and activating racial conflict on the one hand, and impulses affecting economic differentiation and activating class conflicts on the other. This is a more dubious measure, since subjective factors enter into the interpretation of the precipitating events by the analyst, and into the perception by the participants themselves of exacerbating events in the prelude to revolution. The measure is certainly more ambiguous than a counting and racial identification of corpses.[14]

In the Zanzibar revolution, the encompassing principle appears to have been racial. The initial revolutionary assumption of power was effected by a force made up largely of Mainland Africans on Zanzibar Island. Thereafter, Mainland Africans on Zanzibar Island came out in violent support of the revolution, with the participation of Shirazi, more particularly the Hadimu Shirazi who had been most affected by Arab occupation. Arabs were slaughtered, regardless of class.

Economic change appears to have been of little significance. Prior to the revolution, there was extreme economic stagnation as a result of a decline in Zanzibar's market for cloves, and schools had been closed and welfare programs cut back (Lofchie, 1965: 273). But the market for cloves was always variable, and previous crises had not led to revolution. Moreover, about 85 percent of the cloves were produced on Pemba Island (Middleton and Campbell, 1965: 35), and the revolutionary activity was on Zanzibar Island. Middleton and Campbell (1965: 40–2) refer to changing economic relationships among farmers on Zanzibar Island, expressed in competition between Africans, Shirazis and Arabs in the marketing of food crops; but this competition was between Africans and Shirazis as well as with Arabs. There was, however, a common class situation for Shirazi and African squatters in their relations with Arab landlords.

In Rwanda, the complex interweaving of race, ethnic group, caste and economic differentiation served, like a Rorschach test, to stimulate the most varied interpretations as to the dominant or encompassing principle. There was, for example, the declaration by Hutu leaders in their manifesto of March 1957, that the question whether the conflict was a social or racial conflict was a literary question, and that it was in fact both one and the other (Nkundabagenzi, 1961: 22). Here the implication is that racial or economic differentiation could not be separated out as an encompassing principle. Tutsi students at Lovanium University, on the other hand, argued that the problem must be social because if it were racial, this would mean that all the Hutu were oppressed, and all the Tutsi oppressors, whereas, in fact, the great majority of Tutsi (99.9 percent) were entirely without political, social, cultural or other privilege (Nkundabagenzi, 1961: 107). The argument perhaps carries the implication that the encompassing structural principle is a division between a small Tutsi oligarchy and a mass of oppressed Tutsi and Hutu. But the fact that many Tutsi were as underprivileged as Hutu by no means necessarily implies that racial division was not perceived as the encompassing principle or that it could not become the encompassing principle in the unfolding of the revolution. Luc de Heusch (1964), in his analysis of the revolution, in fact asserts that it did become racial, in the sense of emphasizing physical differences, during the course of the struggle. It is possible to derive from this the suggestion that the racial hierarchy was the encompassing principle, because it is otherwise difficult to understand why the struggle should ultimately have taken a racial form.

There was certainly a process of economic change in Rwanda as a result of action by the Belgian administration for the suppression of the clientage system, the development of cash crops and wage employment. Lemarchand (1966: 602) argues that the entire political structure collapsed with the abolition of clientship, ushering in a bitter struggle for supremacy between Tutsi and Hutu. Economic change was clearly relevant for the role of the rural proletariat and intellectuals. But the conflict was not between economically differentiated groups, but between the two collectivities of Tutsi and Hutu. The actual empirical socio-economic differentiation which cut across the division between Tutsi and Hutu was encompassed within a more general principle, opposing Tutsi and Hutu as collectivities, whether by racial, ethnic and/or caste criteria. The targets of the revolutionary uprising were Tutsi, again apparently without discrimination in terms of economic position, and the precipitating events were such as to activate Hutu and Tutsi in a struggle for power, and not economically differentiated strata in Rwanda society.

In neither Zanzibar nor Rwanda, did the revolutions arise out of an economic polarization of classes, or increasing immiserization of the masses, or in economic growth followed by recession, nor are the revolutions to be explained by economic advance. The economy in Zanzibar was stagnating. In Rwanda, there was some economic growth, the development of new economically differentiated strata, and some modification of traditional patterns of economic relationship. But the struggle was not between sections defined by economic criteria; it was a struggle between racial or ethnic sections stimulated by democratization and the movement toward independence.

VI

However fundamental racial differences may be in particular societies, it is clearly impossible to develop a general theory of society and history based on racial differentiation, as was possible with class differentiation. Nothing could be more absurd than the proposition that the history of all living societies is the history of racial struggle. Racial difference has no intrinsic significance. Even when it is present in a society, as an objective fact, it may not be relevant in social relationships; and where it is recognized as relevant, its significance is highly variable, depending entirely on the way in which it is socially elaborated.

Under certain circumstances however, race may come to have a primary significance in the social structure. Demands for civic rights by a racial section are accompanied by labor disturbances, school and trade boycotts. An accident involving people of different race sets off racial rioting. Race is so woven into the fabric of the society that conflict between races in one situation or structure immediately ramifies to a wide range of situations and structures, whether related or unrelated; and conversely, a conflict on non-racial issues is readily transformed into a racial conflict. Racial consciousness becomes acute, and racial identity becomes the basis for political organization.

These are societies, characterized by a high degree of racial pluralism,[15] in which there has been an elaboration of racial differentiation into an encompassing principle. The structural basis of this elaboration and pluralism would seem to be 'differential incorporation', a system of racial stratification in which the racial sections are incorporated into the society on a basis of inequality (Kuper and Smith, 1969: Chapters 4 and 13). This may be *de jure,* as in South Africa where the constitution denies Africans the franchise, or largely *de facto* as in the U.S.A. It is associated with segregation, with unequal access to power, status and material resources, and often with cultural differences, resulting in sharp discontinuities between the racial sections. Issues of conflict are superimposed on each other, lines of cleavage tend to coincide, providing the social basis for the escalation of conflict from minor incidents.

For analysis of revolutions in this type of society, it may be useful to develop hypotheses on the assumption that change in racial status is the crucial variable, in much the same way as hypotheses have been developed regarding the crucial role of economic change in revolutions between social classes. Thus the propositions in Section II of this paper, dealing with theories of economic change as predisposing factors in revolution, would yield a range of propositions, one or other of which might be used to explain particular racial revolutions with some plausibility. The predisposing conditions might be found in increasing racial subordination and discrimination (corresponding to immiserization of the masses) or in the advancing status of the subordinates, or in the disjunction between aspiration and reality, or in the tension between *de facto* racial interaction and mobility, on the one hand, and *de jure* separation and rigidity on the other. No doubt, in some cases, several of these propositions might be applied with equal plausibility to the interpretation of a particular racial revolution.

But the emphasis on either race or class invites an ideological commitment. If class is seen as the major determinant, then racial differences are subordinated to the role of a dependent variable, as in the theory that they provide the bourgeoisie with the means for a more thoroughgoing exploitation of workers of the subordinate race, by a process of dehumanization. If the emphasis is on race, then Marxism may be declared irrelevant to the black experience, or the significance of class differences may be minimized.

The more promising perspective would be to assume that these racially plural societies are in certain respects somewhat *sui generis* and that theories of revolution derived from the analysis of revolutions in racially homogeneous societies cannot readily be applied to societies in which there is differential incorporation of racial sections. Rather, an approach should be developed which analyzes the revolutionary process in terms of the interrelations between class and race, between economic and racial differentiation.

This is an approach which is becoming well established in the analysis of ethnic conflicts in Africa. Thus Balandier (1965: 140) sees the crises in African states since 1960 as determined by two sets of facts, namely the resurgence of old antagonisms, notably tribal and religious, and the struggle for power between members of the directing class *(des dirigeants et des bureaucrates)*. Le Tourneau (1962) systematically analyzes the role of different classes (Muslim bourgeoisie, both traditional and modern, proletariat, peasants) in the conflict between the indigenous peoples of Algeria and the French. Sklar (1967:1–11) examines class factors in the ethnic conflict in Nigeria, arguing that the activating force was an intra-class conflict between sections of the bourgeoisie, who set the ethnic groups against each other in the interests of their own struggle for power. While Sklar is concerned to show the significance of the class factor, his argument may also be interpreted from the point of view that the social force which provided the raw power for the conflict and made it possible was the force of ethnic antagonism. The position would be similar to class conflict in Marxist theory, in which the raw power is the antithetical relationship of sections to the means of production, but in which leadership may be governed by a different principle.

If a general theory of racial revolutions is to be developed, it is not sufficient simply to demonstrate that a conflict of classes, or a process of class formation, was interwoven with the racial conflict. There is need to develop a set of propositions concerning the interrelations of economic and racial stratification in revolutionary change, as Fanon (1966) attempted in his controversial theory of the revolutionary role of peasants in the colonial situation. The two main variables would relate to economic development and stratification on the one hand, and to racial structure on the other. Presumably revolutionary potential and process will be affected by the nature of the economy, whether highly industrialized as in the U.S.A. or rapidly industrializing as in South Africa, or largely subsistence pastoralism and agriculture as in Rwanda, or combining dependence on a major marketable crop with subsis-

tence agriculture and a stagnating economy, as in Zanzibar. Similarly, racial structure will affect revolutionary change, with extreme racial division being represented
by the systematic development of differential racial incorporation, as in South
Africa. If, in addition to consummated revolutions, revolutionary movements are
included, such as those in South Africa and the U.S.A., then there is a sufficient
range of cases available to cover wide variations in economic and racial structure.

VII

My initial assumption was that theories of revolution derived from the analysis of
conflict between social classes in racially homogeneous societies might not be very
illuminating when applied to situations of revolutionary struggle between racial
groups. Indeed, I would argue more positively that the theories may be quite misleading in the context of racially structured societies. In the rapidly industrializing
society of South Africa, working class movements across the racial boundaries between whites and Africans have been negligible, and white workers have strongly
supported the government in its racially oppressive apartheid policies. In the U.S.A.,
under conditions of the most advanced industrialization, there are tensions between
the races as white workers resist movements by black workers for equality of participation; white workers constitute a conservative stratum in race relations, and black
and white workers have not come together in a significant working class movement.
As for the Zanzibar and Rwanda revolutions, I have presented a discussion in this
paper to suggest that the encompassing principle was racial rather than economic,
and that economic change was not the catalyst of revolution.

Of course, I do not question the very great significance of economic factors in
racially structured societies. I would suppose that wherever there is racial stratifica-
ion there is also economic stratification. The relations between them may be conceived as a continuum. At one extreme, racial and economic divisions tend to
coincide, as in the initial stages of colonial domination. At the other extreme, perhaps purely hypothetical, there has ceased to be stratification by race, and racial
differences though present, are no longer salient in a system of stratification based
on differences in economic status. Between the two extremes fall those societies in
which both racial and economic stratification are present, but do not fully coincide.
This is the more general case in the contemporary world, and the one with which I
' in the present paper.

s a result of the intermingling of race and class, and of incongruities in racial
economic status, the situation is ambiguous and encourages different perspec-
nd ideologies. The consequences of this ambiguity may be seen in the vacillat-
cies of communist parties committed to a theory of revolution which is
ist and obliged to come to terms with racially based nationalist move-
e ambiguity is often expressed in divergent political tendencies among
rdinate groups, a dualism in political parties, committed either to ac-
n and reform, or to radical opposition and revolution. At the level of

the dominant racial group, the ambiguity may be expressed in conflicting theories of economic change, as for example, the theory that the creation of a bourgeoisie among the subordinate race would be counter-revolutionary, or conversely, that it would be the catalyst of revolution. In social theory, the ambiguity may be resolved by distillation into two extreme theories, either that the causes of racial revolution are the same as those of class revolution, namely polarization of the races in their relationship to the means of production, or alternatively that the racial structure is primary and economic change somewhat marginally relevant. And it is precisely because of the ambiguity in the intermingling of class and race, that ideologies assume an added significance as directions to perceive the society, and to act, in terms of racial or class perspectives.

If the problem of the relevance of theories of revolution between social classes for the interpretation of racial revolutions is not to be left at the level of ideological preference, or in the form of a projective test into which the analyst pours his own inclinations, there is a need for comparative studies. The main variables would be different forms of economic structure and stratification, and of racial structure and stratification. This paper stresses in various contexts the salience of subjective perceptions, and it is necessary to analyze these perceptions and the ideologies in which they are conveyed. The historical dimension is also an essential aspect for analysis of the changing salience of class and race in periods preceding the revolution and during the course of the revolution itself.

In this way, it may be possible, by the comparative study of revolutionary struggles between racial groups, to test the argument in this paper, that under certain conditions of racial pluralism, such as characterized Zanzibar and Rwanda, the racial divisions are the propelling force in the revolutions, the predisposing factors are those that affect racial status in any of its many social dimensions, and the dialectic of conflict is essentially racial.

NOTES

The research on which this paper is based was supported by a grant from the National Science Foundation. I would like to acknowledge gratefully this support, help from my research assistant Sondra Hale, and criticism of an earlier draft by Sam Surace.
1. Following Harry Eckstein's use of internal war, namely 'any resort to violence within a political order to change its constitution, rulers, or policies' (1965: 133).
2. See Bienen (1968: Section 3) for critical comments concerning the emphasis on change i conceptions of revolution.
3. See Harry Eckstein (1965: 136–40) for a discussion of the somewhat chaotic abundan hypotheses about the etiology of revolutions, and his listing of different emphases on tellectual' factors, economic factors, social structure and social mobility, political f and such social processes as rapid or uneven social changes. See also the comment (1965: 250 ff.) on the different emphases in Marx and Tocqueville, both explain conflicts in terms of social conflicts, but Tocqueville maintaining 'the specificit the relative autonomy, of the political order'.
4. Olson (1963: 543) makes the interesting point that there is nothing inconsist

both rapid economic growth and rapid economic decline would tend toward political in-stability, and that it is economic stability that should be regarded as conducive to social and political tranquility.

5. See Timothy Ricks (1969: 21–6) and Cruse (1968: Chapter 10) for a discussion of some aspects of this controversy in the U.S.A.

6. See Rene Lemarchand, 'Revolutionary Phenomena in Stratified Societies: Rwanda and Zanzibar' (1968), for an analysis of the problem of revolutionary change in racially or ethnically stratified societies.

7. *Notes on the Census of the Zanzibar Protectorate 1948* (Zanzibar Protectorate, 1953: 11–12). There are difficulties in specifying the numbers of different sections in the 1958 Census, since the "racial grouping" is Afro-Arab, Asian other than Arab, European, Somali and other. Political agitation had preceded the Census, and some persons, at the instance of political parties, returned themselves as Zanzibaris (*Report on the Census of the Population of Zanzibar Protectorate, 1958.* Zanzibar Protectorate, 1960: 17). Composition of the population had probably not changed greatly since 1948.

8. For figures of employment in Government, Commerce and Industry, see Zanzibar Protectorate, *Labour Report for the Years 1960 and 1961* (Zanzibar: Government Printer, 1963), 11–12.

9. I am following Maquet here, but I do not know how adequate his evidence is. Maquet (1964: 553) writes of the differences between Hutu and Tutsi that they were distinct, 'enfin par leur apparence physique: les Tutsi etaient grands, minces, au teint clair; les Hutu, de taille moyenne, trapus, de peau foncee. Tels etaient au moins les stereotypes acceptes par tous les Rwandais memes s'ils ne se verifiaent que chez certains individus'. The Twa are pygmoid.

10. In *Rwanda Carrefour d'Afrique* (May-June 1967: 21), the caption to a photograph of a child beside a banana tree quotes the dictum: 'sous chaque feuille de bananier se cache un Rwandais'.

11. *Rwanda Carrefour d'Afrique* in a discussion of the animal resources of Rwanda quotes the Tutsi proverb, 'Toi, vache qui m'epargne la honte et la fatigue de la houe' (April 1965: 8).

12. See Anthony Oberschall, 'Group Violence: Some Hypotheses and Empirical Uniformities'. Paper presented at the meeting of the American Sociological Association, San Francisco, 1969, and Mancur Olson, 'Rapid Growth as a Destabilizing Force', *Journal of Economic History*, 23 (1963: 529–52).

13. See my paper, "Race Structure in the Social Consciousness," *Civilizations* (1970: 88–102).

14. However, counts of corpses in revolutionary contexts are exceedingly unreliable. Le Tourneau (1962: 350) comments in relation to the Algerian rising in 1945, that 'les discussions statistics autour des cadavres sont aussi vaines que derisoires'.

15. See Kuper and Smith, 1969, Chapter 14.

BIBLIOGRAPHY

Aron, Raymond
    1965 *Main Currents in Sociological Thought*. New York and London: Basic Books.
Balandier, Georges
    1965 "Problematique des Classes Sociales en Afrique Noire." *Cahiers Internationaux de Sociologie*, XXXVIII, 131–42.
Batson, Edward
    1948 *Report on Proposals for a Social Survey of Zanzibar, 1946*. Zanzibar: Government Printer.
Belgian Congo and Ruanda-Urundi Information and Public Relations Office
    1960 *Ruanda-Urundi, Economy I*. Brussels.

Bienen, Henry
    1968 *Violence and Social Change: A Review of Current Literature.* Chicago and London: The University of Chicago Press.
Bochkaryov, Yuri
    1964 'Background to Zanzibar.' *New Times.* 5 (February 5), 13–15.
Cox, Oliver Cromwell
    1948 *Caste, Class, and Race.* New York: Doubleday & Company.
Cruse, Harold
    1968 *Rebellion or Revolution?* New York: William Morrow & Company.
de Heusch, Luc
    1964 'Massacres Collectifs au Rwanda?' *Syntheses,* 221 (October), 416–26.
Dumont, Louis
    1966 'A Fundamental Problem in the Sociology of Caste.' *Contributions to Indian Sociology,* IX (December), 17–32.
Eckstein, Harry
    1965 'On the Etiology of Internal Wars.' *History and Theory,* IV, 2, 133–63.
Fanon, Frantz
    1966 *The Wretched of the Earth.* (First publication 1961.) New York: Grove Press.
Kuper, Leo
    1965 *An African Bourgeoisie: Race, Class and Politics in South Africa.* New Haven: Yale University Press.
    1969a "Ethnic and Racial Pluralism: Some Aspects of Polarization and Depluralization," in Leo Kuper and M. G. Smith, eds., *Pluralism in Africa.* Berkeley and Los Angeles: University of California Press.
    1970 'Race Structure in the Social Consciousness.' *Civilisations,* XX, 1, 88–102.
Kuper, Leo and Smith, M. G., eds.
    1969 *Pluralism in Africa.* Berkeley and Los Angeles: University of California Press.
Le Tourneau, Roger
    1962 *Afrique Nord Musulmane.* Paris: Librairie Armand Colin.
Lemarchand, Rene
    1966 "Power and Stratification in Rwanda: A reconsideration." *Cahiers d'Etudes Africaines,* VI, 4, 592–610.
    1968 "Revolutionary Phenomena in Stratified Societies. Rwanda and Zanzibar." *Civilisations,* XVIII, 1, 16–51.
Leurquin, Philippe
    1960 *Le Niveau de Vie des Populations Rurales du Ruanda-Urundi.* Louvain: Editions Nauwelaerts.
Lofchie, Michael F.
    1965 *Zanzibar: Background to Revolution.* Princeton: Princeton University Press.
    1969 "The Plural Society in Zanzibar" in Leo Kuper and M. G. Smith, eds., *Pluralism in Africa.* Berkeley and Los Angeles: University of California Press.
Maquet, Jacques-J.
    1964 "La Participation de la Classe Paysanne au Mouvement d'Independance du Rwanda," *Cahiers d'Etudes Africaines,* IV, 4, 552–68.
Middleton, John and Jane Campbell
    1965 *Zanzibar—Its Society and Politics.* London and New York: Oxford University Press.
Nkundabagenzi, F., ed.
    1961 *Rwanda Politique.* Brussels: Centre de Recherches et d'Information Socio-Politiques.
Oberschall, Anthony
    1969 "Group Violence: Some Hypotheses and Empirical Uniformities," paper presented at the meeting of the American Sociological Association, San Francisco.
Olson, Mancur
    1963 "Rapid Growth as a Destabilizing Force." *Journal of Economic History,* 23 (December), 529–52.

Rey, Lucien
    1964 "The Revolution in Zanzibar," *New Left Review*, 25 (May-June), 29–32.
Ricks, Timothy
    1969 Black Revolution: A Matter of Definition." *American Behavioral Scientist*, XII, 4
    (March-April), 21–6.
Rwanda Carrefour d'Afrique
    1965 April.
    1967 "L'Economic Rwandaise." 66–7 (May-June), 1–27.
Sklar, Richard
    1967 "Political Science and National Integration—A Radical Approach." *The Journal of
    Modern African Studies*, V, 1, 1–11.
van den Berghe, Pierre L.
    1967 *Race and Racism*. New York: John Wiley.
    1969 "Pluralism and the Polity: A Theoretical Exploration," in Leo Kuper and M. G.
    Smith, eds., *Pluralism in Africa*. Berkeley and Los Angeles: University of California Press.
Zanzibar Protectorate
    1953 *Notes on the Census of the Zanzibar Protectorate 1948*. Zanzibar: Government
    Printer.
    1960 *Report on the Census of the Population of Zanzibar Protectorate, 1958*. Zanzibar:
    Government Printer.
    1963 *Labour Report for the Years 1960 and 1961*. Zanzibar: Government Printer.

19   The Ghetto Rebellion
and Urban Class Conflict

Herbert J. Gans

Events commonly described as riots or civil disorders are in reality *spontaneous rebellions,* carried out impulsively by Negroes disenchanted with the way they have been treated by white American society. These rebellions are the natural outcome of years of anger that have been building up in the ghettos of the nation's cities and towns.

THE REBELLION AS SOCIAL PROCESS

The rebellions must also be understood as a social process. This process begins with mounting community anger that is expressed at an inciting incident, expands into a communitywide uprising, and often ends with revengeful repression by the forces of law and order.

Grievances obviously lead to anger, but anger must be widely shared, and it

Reprinted with permission from the *Proceedings of the Academy of Political Science,*
Volume 29, Number 1 (July 1968), 42–51.

must be expressed against a target that is hated by people with different grievances. So far, the target has usually been an incident, either a fight between Negroes and whites in which the latter use unfair tactics, or, more often, an incident in which policemen deal roughly with a ghetto resident who has broken a minor law before witnesses. The incident may itself be no different from many others in the past, but this time a bystander reacts. Other bystanders agree with him, initiating further incidents that may spiral into a full-fledged rebellion. No one knows exactly what sets off the spiraling process, for incidents involving interracial conflict or police harassment occur frequently in the ghetto without resulting in a rebellion. The kind of incident, the location near an easily assembled crowd, and hot weather may play roles in the process; but most likely the spiral is the outcome of a series of incidents during prior weeks that raised the community's level of anger to the boiling point. If enough people are sufficiently angry, the spiraling process spreads so rapidly that it is virtually beyond stopping. Even if it can be stopped momentarily, a new incitement is almost certain to take place when ghetto and police tempers are frayed, and the temporarily halted rebellion then resumes.

The rebellion is an act of collective behavior. However, it is not the behavior of a mob acting impulsively; in most cases, people destroy or loot only the property of those who have exploited them, and they take as few risks as they can. In some cities, they may be joined by more desperate ghetto residents who resort to arson or sniping, and although such people may be few, they can create the kind of chaos that makes the rebellion seem more violent and destructive than it actually is and leads to unrestrained shooting by the police and the troops.

But most of the rebellious activity is property destruction and looting, and often it takes on the mood of a carnival. This is not because the participants are callous, but because they are happy at the sudden chance to exact revenge against those who have long exploited and harassed them. The rebellion becomes a community event; for once, the ghetto is united, and people feel they are acting together in a way that they rarely can. But, most important, the destruction and looting allows ghetto residents to exert power. The evidence from many cities shows that looting is difficult to stop. Ghetto residents realize that they can do something to overcome their fate, that for once they have some control over their environment, if only for a little while.

As in all rebellions throughout history, eventually agitators and professional revolutionaries come into the picture, but only after the ordinary and usually law-abiding ghetto residents have begun the rebellion, and they succeed only because these residents are willing to follow and listen, because they see truth in the desperate message of the revolutionary. Even so, the rebellions of the past few years are not yet the beginning of a revolution—they are too impulsive, too chaotic and too homemade. They do not seek to overthrow the city government, and they are not based on a considered strategy which would achieve that, or any other, revolutionary aim. This is why they must be considered spontaneous rebellions.

A rebellion in one city does not, however, automatically cause rebellions elsewhere. The mass media diffuse information about rebellions to other cities, but this is not sufficient to encourage additional ghettos to rebel. Rather, the knowledge that a rebellion is going on elsewhere, particularly in a nearby city, raises tension levels in the ghetto, outside it, and among the police, increasing the likelihood of an inciting incident. Ghetto residents in one city may become angrier when they hear rumors that Negroes in another city are dying, and police officials may be tougher with law violators because they know that fellow professionals are under attack in another city. Given the nature of this process, it is unlikely that changes in mass media coverage would do much to prevent additional rebellions. The information that a rebellion is taking place in another city can easily be transmitted by telephone. Only a complete news blackout and the shutting down of telephone lines would prevent the diffusion of the needed information, and such solutions are inconceivable in a democratic society.

The mass media can improve their coverage by including more than just the most extreme actions by the rebels and the police, for such highlighting gives newspaper readers and television viewers the impression that the rebellion is more violent and more widespread than it really is. This impression builds on stereotypes among ghetto residents, whites, and the police about mutual readiness to resort to violence; and these stereotypes help heighten the anger of ghetto residents and increase the feeling of threat among the police and in the white community.

Although the mass media have described the rebellions as extremely violent—and although people would probably think of them as violent even without the mass media emphasis on the most extreme incidents—the rebellions so far have been violent mainly against property, particularly the property of hated white exploiters. Amazingly little violence has been exerted against human beings, even against white policemen. The evidence suggests few snipers, and in many cases they have only shot into the air to create confusion and chaos. They may escalate the violence, particularly by panicking the police and the National Guard, but they have apparently not used their many opportunities to kill those whom they consider their enemies.

In fact, as the chronological and other reports from a variety of cities indicate, most of the violence against persons resulted from police and National Guard actions. This does not justify the ghetto's resort to violence, but it indicates that there was violence on both sides. There are three important reasons for this exchange of violence: First, a spontaneous mass rebellion and a communitywide looting rampage is threatening to even the best-trained policemen, and it should not have surprised anyone that some of the policemen and many of the National Guard troops panicked and shot looters, curfew violators, and even innocent bystanders. Second, and perhaps more important, the police and the troops had expected the ghetto to be much more violent than it was, and they acted on their stereotyped conceptions rather than on reality. This was best illustrated in Cambridge, Maryland, where police believed that the burning of a hated ghetto institution was a ruse to draw the firemen away from the central business district, after which, they imagined, the Negroes would rush downtown. As a result, the firemen were told not to enter the ghetto, and fire destroyed many other buildings.

Third, and perhaps most important, the people and institutions to whom American society assigns the unpleasant task of maintaining order tend to be drawn from the working-class, less affluent population, just one step above the Negro in status, sometimes competing with him for jobs, and who are often the most militantly anti-Negro. Moreover, policemen sometimes have to take considerable abuse from ghetto residents whom they arrest. As a result, they are angry and feel threatened by ghetto residents even when there is no rebellion. When they are forced to restore order in the ghetto, this anger turns into revenge, and this results in the wild shooting and property destruction by police and troops at the end of some rebellions.

The overreaction of white working-class protectors of law and order is also stimulated by the political power of that class. In many cities the dominant urban political machine, old-style or new-style, is caught between the conflicting demands of the white working-class population and the ghetto. Usually the former is more powerful, partly because the ghetto is often racially gerrymandered so that city governments usually draw most of their support from the white working class and therefore tend to be more responsive to its demands. Nor will this change until the Negro population increases, the courts extend the one-man, one-vote principle to the cities, and more federal funds become available to subsidize the bankrupt cities. Even in communities with liberal-reform mayors, such as Detroit and New Haven, many of the lower-echelon officials are more responsive to the demands of white voters than of nonwhite voters. As a result, cities with "model" governments and antipoverty programs are for ghetto residents—who only meet the underlings— often illiberal and even repressive.

THE GHETTO AND THE WHITE WORKING CLASS

One can take this analysis a step further and argue that the rebellions represent, at one level, a continuation of an old American tradition—the conflict between the white working class and the Negro population. This conflict began in nineteenth-century America with, for example, the New York draft riots, and continued with white-initiated race riots in several American cities during the twentieth century. One should remember that, relatively speaking, the white working class is also a deprived group in American society, particularly now when participation in the affluent society requires a college diploma. Thus, the current rebellions are a conflict between two deprived groups, one only slightly better off than the other but with some measure of power at city hall. The white working class is fighting the rising number and potentially rising power of a group just below it in the socioeconomic hierarchy.

If this analysis is correct, more and more violent Negro rebellions and white reactions can be expected in those cities that have an increasing Negro population and a large white working-class population, either of European or Southern poor-white origin. Los Angeles, Newark, Detroit, New Haven, Cambridge, Maryland, and other cities that have experienced rebellions fall in this category—although a few

Southern cities of this type have not yet experienced them, for example, Dallas and St. Louis. Of the cities with such a population mix, the ones most prone to rebellion would probably be those whose major municipal services—particularly the services with which the ghetto comes into contact—are provided by city officials who are, for political and other reasons, primarily responsive to the white working-class voters.

Urban white working-class antagonism toward the ghetto is based partly on fear, for when the ghetto expands, it is often into white working-class neighborhoods. In addition, Negro workers frequently compete with members of the white working class for jobs, and in an era when blue-collar jobs are disappearing, the Negro demand for integration of the unions is seen as competition for scarce jobs. The feelings of fear are reinforced, however, by other grievances, which have nothing to do with Negroes, but for which Negroes become scapegoats. One of the major white grievances is that the government does more for the ghetto than for the not-so-affluent whites, and although government expenditures in behalf of the ghetto are small, governmental programs for whites tend more often to benefit the middle class. Indeed, an analysis of all federal programs which subsidize local communities and institutions would probably show that the largest proportion goes to the middle class.

Consequently, the white working class feels that its demands are ignored by the federal government. In addition, this population is anxious to send children to college due to the declining number of blue-collar jobs, and this not only causes financial problems but also makes parents fearful of losing their children to the sophisticated culture of the campus. Also, the white working class tends to own older homes, and rising maintenance costs and property taxes present them with further financial problems, as well as the fear that their neighborhoods are going downhill. The young people who have gone to college—as yet a small proportion among working-class people—may be moving into the mainstream of the affluent society, but their parents and the young people who do not go to college undoubtedly experience both financial and status strains. Thus they feel, with some justification, that their social position in American society is weaker than it once was, and that they are losing prestige and political power. Although this prestige and power loss must be attributed to the changes in the American economy that have made the college-going, white-collar, and professional middle class the dominant political and cultural force in the society, the working class tends to hold the Negro population responsible for its decline. To be sure, declining groups always blame the groups below them in the socio-economic hierarchy for their troubles.

Related grievances are held by the rural and small-town populations of America, for their affluence and power are also declining in a rapidly urbanizing and suburbanizing society. And even the suburbanites have their grievances. The less affluent young families who have moved to the suburbs in the last decade find themselves beset with rising taxes and other costs of homeownership, so that they, too, need to find scapegoats for their problems. Lower, middle-class homeowners in the city are in a roughly similar position, and although they are usually not as directly threatened by the ghetto as working-class homeowners, they are at best ambivalent about antipoverty and integration programs. Indeed only the upper middle and upper classes are untouched by the events in the ghetto, and among them can be found the largest proportion with favorable opinions toward anti-poverty programs and integration (partly because they know few Negroes can afford to move into their neighborhoods), although these two classes tend to be politically conservative, and therefore opposed to increases in governmental spending *sui generis.*

A COMPARISON OF IMMIGRANT AND
NEGRO REACTIONS TO GHETTO POVERTY

If many groups in our society have major problems and grievances, it becomes relevant to ask why so far only Negro groups have rebelled, and also why the slum dwellers of earlier generations, the European immigrants who came in the nineteenth and twentieth centuries, never resorted to spontaneous uprisings. Of course, not all rebellions have taken place in the ghetto; some have occurred in Puerto Rican neighborhoods, but not as often, and Mexican-Americans have not rebelled at all. Why the European immigrants never rebelled, except occasionally against Negroes, is worth discussing, for the reasons shed light on why the ghetto is in rebellion today.

The primary reason is that when the immigrants came to America, unskilled work was in relatively large supply. They arrived at a time when the urban industrial economy was beginning to grow rapidly, and by the sweat of their labor, they built the cities and factories of the modern era. Moreover, they emigrated from much poorer societies with a low standard of living, and they came at a time when job aspirations were minimal. When most jobs in the American economy were unskilled, they did not feel so deprived in being forced to take the dirty and poorly paid jobs. Their families were large, and many breadwinners, including children, contributed to the total family income. As a result, family units could live off even the lowest paid jobs and still put some money away for savings or investment to purchase a house, a tenement, a store, or a factory.

Since the immigrants lived in their own ethnic cultures and could not speak English, they needed stores which supplied them with ethnic foods and services. It took little capital to start stores and even factories at that time, and the rapid growth of the cities made it possible for them to succeed in these commercial ventures. Also, the immigrant family structures were patriarchal, so that the men could find satisfactions in family life which compensated somewhat for the bad jobs, the hard work, and the poverty they had to endure.

The immigrants, moreover, were white and they came into a society in which the Negro was already discriminated against. In fact, had it not been for discrimination, the North might well have recruited Southern Negroes after the Civil War. Instead, Northern employers recruited workers in Europe, and once the immigrants came they were able to take jobs away from Negroes, even pushing them out of the few urban occupations they had dominated, for example, catering and barbering.

For all these reasons, the immigrants were able to obtain an economic and political foothold in American society, making it possible for their children to obtain better jobs, better housing, and most of the rights and privileges open to other white Americans. This is important, because it is probably always the second generation that rebels, and the second generation, the children of the immigrants, did not have to rebel—at least not against American society, but only against the ethnic culture of their own parents.

The Negro came to the city under quite different circumstances. The urban-industrial economy had been built, and the number of unskilled jobs had begun to decline. Negroes were relegated to the jobs which no one else would take, and which paid so little that they could not put away money for savings, houses, or stores. They spoke English and did not need their own stores, and besides, the areas they occupied were by then already well supplied with stores. In addition, Negroes lacked the extended family and employed children so that each household usually had only one or two breadwinners. Moreover, a Negro man had fewer cultural incentives to work in a dirty job for the sake of the family, for the matriarchal Negro family provided him few of the cultural and psychological rewards of home life available to the immigrant. Instead, many Negroes took to the male street-corner group, which often gave them more dignity and respect than the female-dominated society of home and family.

Even so, most Negro men worked as hard as the immigrants to support their families but the payoff was not the same. Nor could they look to the political machines for help. By the time the Negroes arrived in the city, the power of these machines had been blunted by business reform groups, and the completion of the task of building the city had deprived them of many patronage jobs. As a result, they took over the area settled by Negroes but did not share either the political jobs or the power. Discrimination played a role here, too; the immigrants and their descendants who controlled the machines were anti-Negro and gerrymandered ghetto neighborhoods so that they would not have to share their power with Negroes.

The differences between the immigrant and the Negro experience should not be exaggerated, for many immigrants suffered intensely from poverty, unemployment, and discrimination. Family breakdown, desertion, alcoholism, and all the other forms of social and individual pathology rampant in the ghetto today were equally prevalent in the slums of the early twentieth century. Moreover, white Americans tend to overestimate the speed with which their ancestors escaped from poverty in comparison with Negroes. The fact is that among the various ethnic groups who came to America in the last big waves of immigration, only the Jews, who were already urbanized, have totally escaped from poverty. The Italians, Poles, Greeks, Slovenians—and even the Irish—who, like Negroes, came to America with peasant backgrounds, are only now, after three generations, in the final stages of that escape. Until the last ten years or so, the majority of the members of these ethnic groups were employed in blue-collar jobs, and only a small proportion of their children had entered the college-educated white-collar class. In short, it took these ethnic groups three and sometimes four generations to achieve the kind of middle-class income and status that means affluence in today's America.

Negroes have been in the city for only two generations, and they have come under much less favorable conditions. Indeed, their escape from poverty has been blocked in part by the very slowness of the European ethnic groups in moving up, for their exclusion from the building trades and other unions and their inability to move into better neighborhoods beyond the ghetto have been brought about by the descendants of the European immigrants who control these unions and neighborhoods, and have not yet given them up for middle-class occupations and residential areas. Negroes who first came to the cities from the South were, like the European immigrants, apathetic or resigned to their fate, and what we see now is the rebellion of the urban-born second generation against that fate.

Still, only a small proportion of the Negro second generation has joined in the rebellion. No one even knows whether further rebellions will occur, although the mere fact that they are expected may help to bring them about. The expectation itself will not cause rebellions, but if federal and local governments do not deal with the ghetto's many grievances, emphasizing riot-control measures instead, and if local police forces prepare for "trouble" physically and emotionally, it is likely that more police-ghetto incidents will take place, and that some will spark future rebellions.

NOTES

Slightly revised excerpts of the author's testimony before the National Advisory Commission on Civil Disorders, October 6, 1967. The final section also draws on a memorandum written for the commission in January 1968 entitled "Escaping from Poverty: The Negro and Immigrant Experience Compared," which subsequently formed the basis for Chapter 9 of the commission's report.

SOCIAL CHANGE IN THE "THIRD WORLD":

THE PLURAL SOCIETY, DECOLONIZATION,

AND NATION-BUILDING

No set of events has had a greater impact on the development of race relations on a world scale than the fundamental shift in power symbolized by the process of decolonization. This great movement, the break up of colonial empires during the third quarter of the twentieth century, has influenced both colonial and metropolitan societies. The papers in this section consider various aspects of colonial and postcolonial society as they relate to questions of race and ethnicity.

One type of tropical colonial society was called by J. S. Furnivall "the plural society." It consisted of a number of distinct racial or ethnic groups coexisting in a state with a minimal degree of common values. In such a situation there was a thoroughgoing division of society into several highly discrete racial, ethnic, and cultural communities whose sole contact was in the impersonal environment of the market place. Furnivall's classic description of the plural society was based on certain Southeast Asian countries like Burma and Java, and he attributed many of the special properties of its social systems to the structure of colonial domination.

Furnivall's formulation of a plural society has been developed, modified, and in some cases basically changed by later writers concerned with the dynamics of multiracial colonial and excolonial nations. Malcolm Cross raises two major objections to those later theories of the plural society and argues that the concept is both incomplete and static. On the one hand, it ignores important class, status, and power divisions that also exist in these societies, and, on the other hand, it fails to account for the dynamic interaction of the various communities within the total social system. For these reasons Cross is skeptical of the value of the concept of the plural society, as it has been generally employed, and argues in favor of a continued search for an adequate theoretical framework within which to analyze complex multiethnic relationships.

The process of decolonization brought fundamental changes to many plural societies. Few writers have captured the social and psychological forces involved in struggles for national liberation as perceptively as Frantz Fanon. It is hardly surprising, since much of Fanon's life was spent trying to make practical and theoretical sense of race relations: first in his native Martinique, then in France where he studied to be a doctor, and finally in Algeria where he participated in the strug-

gle for independence. Fanon argues that a Marxist analysis has to be modified
when considering colonial relationships and examines the role of violence both as
a foundation of settler society and as a means of overturning the social and psychological domination of colonialism.

The last paper by Walker Connor makes a critical examination of the recent
political science literature on nation-building and modernization. Connor stresses
the tendency to play down the role of ethnicity as a factor that undermines attempts at national integration and shows that the common assertion that social mobilization will cause ethnic awareness to decline has no factual basis. Connor then
exposes twelve basic fallacies to account for this surprising discrepancy between
theory and reality. The persistence, if not the growth and flowering, of ethnicity
seems to be an enduring fact of the modern world.

20   The Plural Society

J. S. Furnivall

All tropical dependencies, and indeed all tropical countries, so far as they have
been brought within the modern world, have in common certain distinctive characters in their social structure. In Dutch colonial literature they are often said to
present a dual economy, comprising two distinct economic systems, capitalist and
pre-capitalist, with a western superstructure of business and administration rising
above the native world in which the people, so far as they are left alone, lead their
own life in their own way according to a traditional scale of values in which economic values rank so low as to be negligible. It is unquestionably true that there is
a wide difference between the social standards of tropical peoples and those of the
modern West, that the natives are slow to assimilate western values, and that over
native life there is a western superstructure representing an outpost of Europe and
not rooted in the soil. Yet the Dutch picture of a native world, in which economic
values are disregarded, seems, so far as it is based on facts, to be drawn from Java,
where for some two hundred years employers secured labour through compulsion
rather than by appealing to the desire of gain. In Africa likewise, as we have just
noticed, a popular belief in the native disregard of economic values has been held to
justify compulsion as a means of securing labour. But everywhere experience has
shown that the desire of gain can easily be stimulated or, rather, liberated from
the control of custom. In British colonies under indirect rule, interpreted according
to the British tradition of the rule of law, economic forces soon permeate the native

From J. S. Furnivall, *Colonial Policy and Practice,* (Cambridge: Cambridge University Press,
1948), pp. 304–11. Reprinted by permission of Cambridge University Press.

world and, in colonies under direct rule, it is just in the economic world that all men meet, if not on equal, yet on the same terms. Even in respect of Dutch dependencies some of their own writers vehemently dispute the theory of a dual economy.[1] Yet in all tropical dependencies the western superstructure over native life is a prominent feature in the economic landscape.

But the western superstructure is only one aspect of a distinctive character, common to all tropical dependencies, that cannot fail to impress even the most casual observer; the many-coloured pattern of the population. In Burma, as in Java, probably the first thing that strikes the visitor is the medley of peoples—European, Chinese, Indian and native. It is in the strictest sense a medley, for they mix but do not combine. Each group holds by its own religion, its own culture and language, its own ideas and ways. As individuals they meet, but only in the market-place, in buying and selling. There is a plural society, with different sections of the community living side by side, but separately, within the same political unit. Even in the economic sphere there is a division of labour along racial lines. Natives, Chinese, Indians and Europeans all have different functions, and within each major group subsections have particular occupations. There is, as it were, a caste system, but without the religious basis that incorporates caste in social life in India. One finds similar conditions all over the Tropical Far East—under Spanish, Portuguese, Dutch, British, French or American rule; among Filipinos, Javanese, Malays, Burmans and Annamese; whether the objective of the colonial power has been tribute, trade or material resources; under direct rule and under indirect. The obvious and outstanding result of contact between East and West has been the evolution of a plural society; in the Federated Malay States the indigenous inhabitants number barely a quarter of the total population. The same thing has happened in the South Pacific. The Fiji chieftains invited British protection, and one result has been that half the inhabitants are immigrants from India. In African dependencies there are Indian immigrants in East Africa and Syrians in West Africa, and in some regions the 'coloured', or Eurafrican, population forms a separate caste. Sometimes a section of the native population is westernized: 'there are some territories, of which those in West Africa are perhaps most typical, in which sections of the population most closely in contact with European influences have attained a development out of all relation to the rest of the population . . . which is often still living in primitive conditions and has interests different from those of an urban or industrial society'.[2] One finds much the same thing in Java, and in all tropical dependencies 'westernized' natives are more or less cut off from the people, and form a separate group or caste. The plural society has a great variety of forms, but in some form or other it is the distinctive character of modern tropical economy.

Outside the tropics society may have plural features, notably in South Africa, Canada and the United States, and also in lands where the Jew has not been fully assimilated into social life; in other countries also there are mixed populations with particularist tendencies. But in general these mixed populations have at least a common tradition of western culture, and, despite a different racial origin, they meet on equal terms and their relations are not confined solely to the economic sphere.

There is a society with plural features, but not a plural society. It is significant that, in Canada and the United States, and also in Australia, when the influx of alien elements threatened national life and common social standards, barriers were raised against free immigration. In tropical dependencies there was no common social will to set a bar to immigration, which has been left to the play of economic forces. The plural society arises where economic forces are exempt from control by social will. It is general in the modern tropics because everywhere and always the social order seems to have had plural features. In Burma under native rule the people were not organized territorially but on quasi-feudal lines by race and occupation, and that is the normal character of tropical society, based on personal authority. But in such lands, apart from minor backward groups, there is a common cultural tradition; there is a society with plural features but not a plural society. Again, in the great fairs held annually in medieval times in ports and market towns, each company of merchants was governed by its own heads according to its own customs. But the concourse did not form a plural society, because it lasted no longer than the fair. All that happened was that, during the fair, the town was transformed into a bazaar. In the modern tropics the bazaar lasts throughout the year, and the whole country is converted into a shop or factory; from a social organism into a business concern. Despite certain plural features, tropical society was distinct from the plural society which has been created by economic forces. This is a modern invention because, only in modern times, have economic forces been set free to remould the social order. The result is a social structure quite distinct in its political and economic properties from the homogeneous unitary society of western lands and, for a solution of colonial problems, it is essential that its properties should be clearly understood. Let us examine it first in its political aspect and then in its economic aspect.

Political Features. On looking at a plural society in its political aspect one can distinguish three characteristic features: the society as a whole comprises separate racial sections; each section is an aggregate of individuals rather than a corporate or organic whole; and as individuals their social life is incomplete.

To Europeans the incompleteness of individual social life is most readily apparent in the European section. The European works in the tropics, but does not live there. His life in the tropics centres round his business, and he looks at social problems, political or economic, not as a citizen but as a capitalist or an employer of labour. Many Europeans spend twenty years or more in the tropics, and, on retiring from work to live at home, they know no more of the country than on the day they landed; nothing of the people or even of the language. Foreign orientals, likewise, are transient; they come merely to make money and their interest in the country is purely economic. The life of the ordinary native is similarly incomplete. He is a cultivator and nothing more. Under native rule the people lived within a little world, but their cultural horizon was co-extensive with its boundaries; under western rule their horizon is contracted to their life as cultivators and their social life is less comprehensive than before.

If we look above the individual to the group in which he forms a unit, we find a similar contrast between the plural society of tropical dependencies and the unitary society that western peoples take for granted. In all accounts of the modern tropics we read of the collapse of corporate tribal or village life and the atomization of society. In the foreign sections the individual stands even more alone; even among Indians caste loses its validity, and in every census in Burma it has been found impossible to compile useful returns of Indian castes. Among the Indian immigrants in South Sea Islands one may even find mixed marriages between Moslims and Hindus. Europeans often deplore the isolation of the individual in their own section. Men are continually on the move; they form business acquaintances but not friends; there are no children in the home; the club and not the home is the centre of social life, and all look more or less eagerly to going 'home' on retirement. Each section in the plural society is a crowd and not a community.

On a wider survey of the plural society as a whole comprising separate groups, we may find the nearest analogy in a confederation of allied states, united by treaty or within the limits of formal constitution merely for certain common ends, but otherwise, in matters outside the terms of union, each living its own life as a separate province. Yet this analogy fails to bring out the full complexity of a plural society. In a confederation each unit is segregated within its own territorial limits; there is contact between the states but not between their members as individuals; the union is voluntary; the terms of union are definite and limited; and any party can at will withdraw from the confederacy. In a plural society the sections are not segregated; the members of the several units are intermingled and meet as individuals; the union is not voluntary but is imposed by the colonial power and by the force of economic circumstances; and the union cannot be dissolved without the whole society relapsing into anarchy.

Like a confederation, a plural society is a business partnership rather than a family concern, and the social will linking the sections does not extend beyond their common business interests. It might seem that common interest should tie them closely, for a dissolution would involve the bankruptcy of all the partners. But the tie is strong only so far as this common interest is recognized. Perhaps the only plural society inherently stable is the Hindu society in India. Here there are separate groups or classes, partly racial, with distinct economic functions. But in India caste has a religious sanction, and in a plural society the only common deity is Mammon. In general, the plural society is built on caste without the cement of a religious sanction. In each section the sectional common social will is feeble, and in the society as a whole there is no common social will. There may be apathy even on such a vital point as defence against aggression. Few recognize that, in fact, all the members of all sections have material interests in common, but most see that on many points their material interests are opposed. The typical plural society is a business partnership in which, to many partners, bankruptcy signifies release rather than disaster.

Economic Features. The political aspect of the plural society is reflected in its economic aspect. A plural society is no ordinary business partnership. In form it is also a political society and is, or should be, organized for 'the good life', the welfare of the people, enabling them to live as well as possible. As a business partnership its function is solely economic, to produce goods as profitably as possible. But as a social institution also it has an economic aspect, and is concerned with both production and consumption, supply and demand. It is in the interest of a society that its members shall get what is best and not merely what is cheapest; by custom or law it must regulate demand. It is also in the interest of society that in the supply of goods, production for profit shall be regulated by custom or law on behalf of social welfare. In a plural society both supply and demand take on a special character.

Let us first consider the matter of demand. In buying goods it is only common sense to pay no more than necessary. But purchasers are not always guided solely by common sense. Some will pay a higher price for home products than for foreign products, or for goods untainted by sweated labour. In such cases there is a social demand for home manufactures, or for a higher standard of wages. In this matter there is a difference between the plural society and the homogeneous society. When the recent depression flooded Java with cheap cottons from Japan, European merchants tried to boycott Japanese goods; but the boycott collapsed because Chinese merchants bought them and seemed likely to capture all the trade. When Britain annexed Upper Burma the British Government contemplated retaining the Burmese prohibition of trade in opium and alcohol, but this was impossible because the demand of the Chinese and Indians had to be met. In a plural society the feebleness of social will is reflected in the weakness of social demand, which is the economic aspect of social will. Economists deal in great detail with problems of aggregate demand but, partly it may be because they take a homogeneous society for granted, they have not given social demand so much attention as it deserves. If any town or village in the western world wants better sanitation, it can spend more on conservancy. There is a collective demand which may conflict with individual demand, and at periodical elections people can choose between better conservancy and having more money in their pockets. Economists can measure this collective demand with their supply and demand curves and schedules, but collective demand is only one form of a social demand that, in general, defies measurement. The monastic schools in Burma were a response to social demand, but no one could estimate their cost, or balance it against their value. In tropical countries social demand usually takes effect through custom. Sometimes a patch of scrub jungle round a village is reserved as a public convenience and is closed to fuel cutting. People could get their fuel with less trouble, more cheaply, by cutting timber there, but social demand, taking effect through village custom, prevails over individual demand. So long as custom retains its force, no one would think of cutting down the scrub. But we have noticed that in Rangoon Indian immigrants saw a way to make easy money, and cleared the scrub to sell fuel in the market. Individual demand for private gain prevailed over the social demand for common welfare, and prevailed the more readily because society was no longer homogeneous. Even in the West social demand is most effective when it requires no stronger support than custom, because no one thinks of encroaching on it. In London rickshaws might be cheaper than taxis, but we would walk rather than use them. The individual demand for cheaper transport is overborne by the social demand for human dignity. And because we resist the temptation of cheapness we finally attain better, and probably cheaper, transport in tubes and motor-buses. During the present century Rangoon, in common with most eastern towns, has been flooded with rickshaws. In Batavia the Dutch refused to sanction them; they disliked seeing Javanese between the shafts and already had too many Chinese. Now motor transport in the towns of Java is probably better and cheaper than in any country in the tropics. Social demand can take effect only through organic social will as embodied in the social structure, and, in default of social will, individual demand prevails over social demand. A villager in Burma may wish to spend money on schooling for his children, but the maintenance of a school is conditional on the existence of social demand and, if there is no village school, he may spend his money on giving them new clothes, or on furniture that he does not use, or even on English books that he cannot read.[3] If he cannot satisfy those wants which he has as a member of society, he will satisfy his individual wants; he must take what he can get.

Here is one of the distinctions between a homogeneous society and a plural society. A plural society is broken up into groups of isolated individuals, and the disintegration of social will is reflected in a corresponding disorganization of social demand. Even in a matter so vital to the whole community as defence against aggression, the people are reluctant to pay the necessary price. In religion and the arts, in the graces and ornaments of social life, there are no standards common to all sections of the community, and standards deteriorate to such a level as all have in common. And because each section is merely an aggregate of individuals, those social wants that men can satisfy only as members of a community remain unsatisfied. Just as the life of an individual in a plural society is incomplete, so his demand tends to be frustrated. Civilization is the process of learning to live a common social life, but in a plural society men are decivilized. All wants that all men want in common are those which they share in common with the animal creation; on a comprehensive survey of mankind from China to Peru these material wants, essential to the sustenance of life, represent the highest common factor of demand. In the plural society the highest common factor is the economic factor, and the only test that all apply in common is the test of cheapness. In such a society the disorganization of social demand allows the economic process of natural selection by the survival of the cheapest to prevail.

If, again, we examine plural economy from the standpoint of production or supply, we find a similar predominance of economic forces. In selling goods it is common sense to charge as much as one can. All those engaged in production have in common, in greater or less degree, the desire for gain, to get as much as possible while giving as little as possible. But, in a plural society, that is almost all they have in common. Everywhere, in all forms of society, the working of economic forces makes for tension between groups with competing or conflicting interests; between town and country, industry and agriculture, capital and labour. In a homogeneous society the tension is alleviated by their common citizenship, but in a plural society there is a corresponding cleavage along racial lines. The foreign elements live in the towns, the natives in rural areas; commerce and industry are in foreign hands and the natives are mainly occupied in agriculture; foreign capital employs native labour or imported coolies. The various peoples meet only in the market, as competitors or as opponents, as buyers and sellers. In Burma the Indian and Chinese middlemen form combines against both the cultivator and the European miller, and Europeans form combines against both middleman and native. In Java the nationalist movement first assumed a popular character in action against the Chinese, whom Europeans at the same time were describing as worse than ten epidemics. In Indo-China Annamese and Europeans regard the Indian moneylender as a pest. It might seem that, on a long view, all sections have a common interest in the common welfare, but the foreign elements, European or oriental, mostly need not look beyond the day when they will leave the country. In any case, the end is so remote that it is out of sight; so far as the horizon of the business man extends sectional interests are opposed. It is true that big business with large capital investments in the country must take long views, and sees further than the cultivator who does not look beyond the harvest and the coolie who looks only for to-morrow's rice, but it looks on the country as a business enterprise.

Moreover, within the economic sphere there are no common standards of conduct beyond those prescribed by law. The European has his own standard of decency as to what, even in business, 'is not done'; so also have the Chinese, the Indian and the native. All have their own ideas as to what is right and proper, but on this matter they have different ideas, and the only idea common to all members of all sections is the idea of gain. In a homogeneous society the desire of profit is controlled to some extent by social will, and if anyone makes profits by sharp practice he will offend the social conscience and incur moral, and perhaps legal, penalties. If, for example, he employs sweated labour, the social conscience, if sufficiently alert and powerful, may penalize him because aware, either instinctively or by rational conviction, that such conduct cuts at the root of common social life. But in the tropics the European who, from humanitarian motives or through enlightened self-interest, treats his employees well, risks being forced out of business by Indians or Chinese with different standards. The only deterrent to unsocial conduct in production is the legal penalty to which those are liable who can be brought to trial and convicted according to the rules of evidence of infringing some positive law. In supply as in demand, in production as in consumption, the abnormal activity of economic forces, free of social restrictions, is an essential character of a plural society.

In colonial relations then, economic forces both create a plural society and, because unrestrained by social will, continue to prevail. The dictum of Dr. Boeke, that we have already noted with reference to Java, applies to tropical economy in general: 'there is materialism, rationalism, individualism, and a concentration on economic ends far more complete and absolute than in homogeneous western lands; a total absorption in the exchange and market; a capitalist structure, with the business concern as subject, far more typical of capitalism than one can imagine in the so-called "capitalist" countries, which have grown up slowly out of the past and are still bound to it by a hundred roots'.[4] In the first half of the nineteenth century economists eulogized economic man; in the last half they said he was a myth. Unfortunately they were mistaken. When cast out of Europe he found refuge in the tropics, and now we see him returning with seven devils worse than himself. These are the devils which devastated the tropics under the rule of *laissez-faire* and which it is the object of modern colonial policy to exorcise.

NOTES

1. Meijer Ranneft, J. W., *Koloniale Studiën*, 1928, p. 151
2. Hailey, Lord. *Britain and Her Dependencies*, 1943, pp. 34, 44; Teeling, L. W. B., *Gods of Tomorrow*, 1936, p. 126
3. J. S. Furnivall, *Economic Review*, 1912, pp. 380 ff.
4. J. H. Boeke, *The Structure of Netherlands Indian Economy*. New York, 1942, p. 452

21   On Conflict, Race Relations, and the Theory of the Plural Society

Malcolm Cross

To a number of recent writers the theory of the 'plural society' is a conflict theory.[1] This paper is concerned with this question and, more specifically, it asks to what degree the theory is a theory of race relations and race conflict. I shall contend that the theory of the plural society is in fact one of the few attempts to construct a theory of overall race relations (as opposed to essentially psychological theories on the origins of racial prejudice and discrimination) but that, in the form that it has come to adopt, it tends to obscure rather than elucidate problems of racial conflict. I will argue, however, that such a theory of conflict is a necessary prerequisite for comprehending the nature and significance of racial and ethnic divisions.

I. THE WORK OF J. S. FURNIVALL

The theory of the plural society has been developed from the work of J. S. Furnivall who, on the basis of his extensive research on South-East Asia and, in particular, the Dutch East Indies, held that these tropical dependencies revealed fundamentally different kinds of social organization from the West. Furnivall perceived that:

From *Race*, Vol. XII, 4, 1971, pp. 477–94. Reprinted by permission of the Institute of Race Relations.

> Each group holds by its own religion, its own culture and language, its
> own ideas and ways.. As individuals they meet, but only in the market
> place, in buying and selling. There is a plural society, with different
> sections of the community living side by side, but separately, within the
> same political unit. Even in the economic sphere there is a division of
> labour along racial lines.[2]

It is this clear characterization which forms the basis for later developments of the
theory which, as we shall see, focus attention on such cultural and institutional
variation as the major determining force of social organization and social change.
However, on the basis of statements like that above, Furnivall's work has been completely misinterpreted and it is important to understand his real position, for in
many ways the more recent developments of this theory are less useful and acceptable than the earlier forms.

Furnivall was concerned with the effects of colonialism as an economic force.
Prior to the colonial period, societies of the East were integrated by common will:

> Under native rule everywhere, even in settled agricultural communities,
> social and political relations were customary, not legal; authority was
> personal, based on Will and not on Law, and both custom and authority
> were closely bound up with religion. The social order rested not on im-
> personal law and individual rights, but on personal authority and cus-
> tomary obligations, and authority and custom derived their sanction not
> from reason but from religion.[3]

However, colonialism brought the West into contact with the East in an unequal
relationship of economic exploitation and political dominance. One result of this
involvement was the plural society. He stated this clearly in an article on the necessity of 'political education' as a means of overcoming these fissiparous tendencies:

> The dominant impulse in Western expansion over the Tropics has been
> economic advantage, and the liberation of economic forces under foreign
> rule has transformed social life into a huge business concern with nu-
> merous departments. The social order has taken the form of a plural soci-
> ety in which distinct racial groups, devoid of any common social will,
> live side by side but separately.[4]

The plural society is therefore the product of colonial expansion while the
racial divisions which most frequently characterize it, are exacerbated by the operations of colonial policy. The problem to which colonial policy has been primarily
directed 'is how best to induce dependent peoples to acquiesce in foreign rule without prejudice to the development of the colonial estate'; a problem which can best
be overcome by the traditional colonial strategy of *divide et impera.*[5] When discussing the claims of the 1947 constitution in Burma, Furnivall again asserts the
important point that racial ascription in a colonial milieu is largely a product of

political activity designed to continue a plural order which is itself the product of economic association:

> At one stroke it [the new constitution of Burma] purported to abolish racial particularism and the plural society, the systems characteristic respectively of the political and economic aspects of colonial rule.[6]

In Burma, as elsewhere in the tropical dependencies, the importation of western capitalism had disintegrative effects not only upon traditional culture and religion, but upon the whole life of indigenous peoples.

> In the first instance the local inhabitants probably obtain a share, if only a small share, in the profits and there is a rise in their material standard of living; but in the long run the result is spiritual, cultural and, as regards the people in general, material impoverishment.[7]

To Furnivall, capitalism, wherever it occurs, is inherently disruptive and divisive but, in the West, a system of law coupled with Christian moral teaching has restrained the full effects of this economic system. In the East, however, traditional religion and mores cannot control these forces as successfully. In his own words:

> In the West it has been possible to keep capital within the limits prescribed by social interests, but only by an unceasing struggle and because of the strength of a social organization based on law and informed by Christian ideals. By virtue of the moral and material forces at its disposal the West has been able to dominate the tropics. In this process economic forces, released from the social restraints of the West, have attacked the tropical economy from outside. At the same time they have emancipated economic forces in tropical society from the restraints of custom and have thereby liberated economic forces, antagonistic to social welfare from within. In the West capitalism implies a form of social organization in which economic forces are conspicuous; in the East, there is a starker form of capitalism in which economic forces are predominant.[8]

It is clear therefore that Furnivall is indeed putting forward a theory which relates specifically to colonial societies. It is a theory of conflict in that it attempts to account for discord and division between groups and, further, it seeks to incorporate racial divisions as part of an overall approach. Neither racial divisions nor cultural variability form a plural society in themselves, for this phenomenon has to be related to an economic theory and the fact of economic exploitation. In all societies conflict takes place along economic boundaries but in a plural society racial and ethnic differences coincide with these divisions (or are *made* to coincide with them), so that instability is more likely to result. It is important to realize that Furnivall was clearly opting for a conflict view of all societies and that the only difference with those that could be labelled 'plural' was that, through the operation of economic and political forces, conflict became enhanced and intensified and more likely to be racial in character. Thus:

> Everywhere, in all forms of society, the working of economic forces makes for tension between groups with competing or conflicting interests; between town and country, industry and agriculture, capital and labour. In a homogeneous society the tension is alleviated by their common citizenship, but in a plural society there is a corresponding cleavage along racial lines. The foreign elements live in the towns, the natives in rural areas; commerce and industry are in foreign hands and the natives are mainly occupied in agriculture.[9]

This extended discussion of Furnivall's original theory has been necessary because of the misinterpretation that has accompanied its later development. Many of the weaknesses which are apparent in more recent statements do not derive from Furnivall at all. In many ways his approach has much to commend it as an holistic, comparative theory of colonialism and its effects. Notwithstanding his concern for economic forces, Furnivall was not a Marxist although there are some points of similarity between Marxist approaches to colonialism and his theory.[10]

II. THE DEVELOPMENT OF PLURAL SOCIETY THEORY

It is to the Caribbean and Africa that we have to turn for the most important revisions to the theory of the plural society in recent years and, in particular, to the writings of the Jamaican social anthropologist, M. G. Smith. There is no doubt that Smith's contribution is important, if not for theoretical advancement then at least for focusing attention on vital issues and challenging the comfortable assumptions of North American functionalism which are so patently limited in their application to colonial or post-colonial societies. In fact, it is the view of the present writer that they are inapplicable anywhere, except in a very limited sense, but that is not the major point at issue although, in contradistinction to Furnivall, many adherents to the plural society thesis seem quite prepared to accept functionalist propositions concerning non-plural societies.

For Smith the question is 'whether the plural society does not represent a different type of system from that to which consensualist theses may properly apply'.[11] His answer is that they do and that the problem is to try and 'test and apply Furnivall's ideas'. Unfortunately, it is at this stage that a fundamental error of interpretation ensues. According to Smith, Furnivall 'saw clearly that . . . economic pluralism was simply an aspect of the social pluralism of these colonies'.[12] Of course, as any reading of Furnivall would show, and as has been demonstrated here already, he said quite the opposite. This in itself would not necessarily mean the construction of a theory which could not embrace ethnic and racial conflict. It does, however, mean an inability to comprehend the significance of the economic driving force of colonialism and its consequences for social organization; an error which Furnivall certainly did not commit. In order to see exactly what the development of plural society theory does now entail, I shall look critically at the most recent elaboration on this theory, paying particular attention to efforts at accounting for racial cleavage and conflict.

As in his previous essays on the subject Smith is at first at pains to point out the significance of *institutions* in a social structure.[13] It is the institutions of a society which determine what type of society it is, since institutional differentiation 'distinguishes collectivities that differ in organization, standardized procedures, norms, beliefs, ideals, and expectations'.[14] Thus, if there is but one set of institutions within the society, then we are dealing with a *homogeneous* social order. Societies not of this type, and this must include all but the very simplest structures, are either *heterogeneous* or *plural.* They are heterogeneous if they exhibit single *basic* institutions but vary at the *secondary* level. A society like the United States is heterogeneous for Smith because there is an agreement on basic institutional forms such as the family, socialization, education, law, etc. On the other hand, there is wide diversity in occupational, political, religious, and ethnic structure. If this institutional diversity is also present at the basic level, then we are dealing with a real plural situation—the plural society. A further defining characteristic which Smith appears to insist upon in his latest work is that in a plural society the political rule, or rather domination, is exercised by a culturally distinct numerical minority. This clearly would include nearly all colonial situations but, curiously, it would exclude newly-independent post-colonial nations.

It is vital to realize the central role of *institutions* in this whole concept. They underlie an important distinction which Smith makes—that is, between *social* and *cultural* pluralism. Thus 'all institutions have two analytically distinct, internally connected aspects: the cultural and the social'. If the institutional system is plural, there must be both social and cultural pluralism. The separation of these two levels is reminiscent of traditional Parsonian functionalism and, indeed, the meaning given to them is not dissimilar. Thus cultural pluralism refers to cleavages of cultural forms such as language, religion, or ideology while social pluralism refers more specifically to divisions into corporate groups. It is suggested, however, that the two may vary independently as, for example, in the Deep South where there are pockets of social pluralism but a common cultural system between black and white Americans.[15]

Smith recognizes that there are differences of incorporation or integration of groups into societies. That is to say, there is a difference between clearly-demarcated distinctions of status, and structures where parity of esteem and equal access to resources exists. He therefore puts forward the distinction between *differential incorporation* and *consociation.* Differential incorporation will involve clear divisions of status between groups and sections and usually entails the category of 'second class citizens'. It may be: 'formal and explicit, under the law and constitution, or it may prevail substantially despite them, as, for example, among the American Negroes.'[16] A consociation, on the other hand, involves segmentation but equality of opportunity and rights as, for example, in the Lebanon or Switzerland. In the third place we may have a non-pluralist type of incorporation which Smith refers to as 'universalistic' or 'uniform' and which involves the integration:

> of individuals as citizens directly into the public domain on formally identical conditions of civil and political status, thereby eliminating the requirement of individual membership in some intermediate corporation, segmental or sectional.[17]

This would be the type of incorporation found in non-pluralist societies like Britain, France, Holland, or Denmark. The first two types represent potentially pluralist situations, differential incorporation in particular being associated with the most extreme type of pluralism, a type which Smith refers to as *structural pluralism* and which necessarily incorporates both social and cultural pluralism. In the case of structural pluralism the most common type of sectional index would be racial or ethnic variation, but Smith is insistent that the concept is not confined to such divisions.

The contributions of other recent pluralist writers have not made any fundamental alterations to the pluralist position, although some have only used the concepts on a tentative basis.[18] The American anthropologist, Leo Despres, prefers to base his distinction of the plural society on the *function* of institutions. Thus he suggests that when institutions maintain cultural variation at the local level, then we are dealing with *minimal* cultural sections. Where they also differentiate at a *maximal* or national level we have a situation which is described as a plural society. He contrasts the United States, where there is no overlapping national differentiation in such things as religion and political parties, with Nigeria where maximal cultural integration occurs with respect to the corporate groups making up the total society.[19] Institutions which integrate at the parochial level would be referred to as *local* institutions while the function of integration at the national level—and thus the creation of a plural society—is accomplished by *broker* institutions.

III. A CRITIQUE OF PLURALIST THEORY

When it comes to the question of actual conflict, the theory is less clear-cut and precise. This springs mainly from the fact that the 'theory' is little more than a classificatory system; that is, by far the greatest attention is given to the features which *characterize* a plural society, rather than the precise conditions under which conflicts between segments of it may take place. And yet it is recognized that one characteristic feature of a plural society is its instability. Although the theory is said to be applicable in cases where race is not an important divisive factor and certainly where colonialism has not been present, the theory has been most frequently applied to multiracial colonial societies.

Smith suggests that conflicts in a plural society are of a fundamentally different kind from others. In a society made up of people 'who share identical institutional organization', the antagonists 'share similar means, norms, goals, procedures, and forms of organization', while in a plural society conflicts 'are generalized rapidly and with little institutional restraints to other spheres and to other members of the outgroup'.[20] Discussing the instability which adheres to consociations—that is, institutionally differentiated societies with no clear rank ordering between them— Smith suggests that:

> Lacking any continuous external threat to their joint security, each of these institutionally differentiated segments may seek to preserve or extend its internal autonomy against aggrandizement of others, while stressing its corporate unity and exclusive identity. Beyond a certain level, such intersegmental action reconstitutes the consociation as a system of external political relations between its segments, rather than a condition of social union. Recent events in Malaysia, Uganda, Guiana, Cyprus, the Congo, and Nigeria illustrate this.[21]

Quite so, but one would have thought that the important theoretical points would have concerned the *conditions* under which this polarization took place and the point at which 'a system of external political relations' was instituted. Smith is content, however, to point out that stability in a consociation will ensue when parity of status between the parts comprising it is extant, while stability in a differentially incorporated system derives from accepted patterns of ranking. Thus:

> Whereas the manifest equivalence of components—a condition that fosters intersectional association, mobility, and assimilation—is necessary for a stable consociation, the habituation of subordinate social sections to inferior status is equally essential for a stable system of differential incorporation.[22]

In other words, in a society made up of ethnic groups with parity of status, if they stay like that, it will be stable; in a society made up of ranked groups, if they accept this ranking, it too will be stable! I think this shows that, here at least, we are not very far along the road to understanding interethnic conflicts and their relationship with social change. To be fair, Smith himself has had *his* doubts about whether or not his findings were 'illusory or tautological'.[23]

In a recent paper Leo Despres discusses the nature of protest movements in plural societies and the relevance of these for political change.[24] His argument is interesting for it clearly shows, perhaps unwittingly, that in Guyana—a country which must certainly rank as a plural society—cultural diversity and ethnicity act to extend protest movements so that necessarily they become 'political' and concerned with racial and ethnic matters. Conflict itself does not appear to derive from this pluralism which only exacerbates and extends discord induced through population pressure, or land scarcity, or unemployment, or wage differentials, or whatever. Thus from the pen of a leading pluralist writer we have what amounts to an admission that the theory of the plural society is not a conflict theory as such, although he does advance the totally unproven and overly pessimistic assertion that in a plural society any social or political change will affect the relationship between ethnic or racial groups and thus lead to conflict of a racial kind. The most we have, therefore, is the conclusion that ethnicity affects conflicts within society; a proposition with which I would certainly not wish to disagree.

Since the theory of the plural society was resurrected to counter the claims of functionalism, it is not surprising that some responses have also come from this direction. Lloyd Braithwaite, for example, puts forward the suggestion that in multi-racial colonial societies the high valuation placed upon the European and his way of life serves as a common integrating value.[25] Thus a positive reference group orientation acts as a catalyst for acculturation. This type of criticism is generally taken as the only one applicable to the theory. Smith, for example, took the work of one reputedly functionalist critic and dismissed it in these terms:

> Each criticism represents an essential feature of the general thesis that societies . . . are functional unities, normatively integrated orders of functionally interdependent parts, and all alike amenable to the same mode and framework of sociological analysis.[26]

However, there are at least two fundamental points of weakness which do not derive from a functionalist view; on the contrary, many functionalists are guilty of the very same errors.[27]

First, the theory of the plural society is basically *over-simple*. It describes a society in terms of essentially one category or set of categories; that is, those related to cultural variation expressed in terms of institutional difference and ethnic difference. While in all societies that are classified as plural, ethnic divisions are of key importance, they are not the only divisions into which groups may be formed. For example, there is seldom any mention of class differences or divisions between those with political power and those without, or those who occupy positions of high esteem or rank and those who do not. It is true that Smith discusses the importance of dominance by a minority group as one of the major determining conditions of structural pluralism and thus the plural society, and that ranking is itself a part of the definition of differential incorporation, but there is no attempt at showing how these group boundaries may be of fundamental importance either because they operate independently or, and this is particularly crucial in the case of class, they underlie what appear to be purely ethnic differences.

Second, the notion of the plural society is essentially a *static* theory. This derives from two main causes, the first of which is simply that it is a *classificatory* scheme and no classificatory scheme was ever in itself dynamic. It may give labels to various states of change in a social order (i.e. *Gemeinschaft* and *Gesellschaft*) but it does not account for how one came to change for the other. In other words, to define a society as 'plural' and to propound a concept to cope with that society is not to understand how that society came to be 'plural' and neither is it to show that in reality we are justified in applying that particular concept. Even where a concept deals with change itself, which this particular one does not, we do not necessarily understand the processes of actual change thereby. The dangers inherent in the reification of concepts and the 'nominalism' which it entails have been pertinently and succinctly stated by Ernest Gellner in a discussion of the role of concepts of change and conflict in developing countries:

> If we invent rapidly changing concepts to deal with changing societies, or contradictory concepts to cope with societies in conflict, we may find ourselves with an unmanageable language, but we shall still not be able to be sure that the concepts change or internally conflict in just the way the society is changing or conflicting.[28]

How different, therefore, is this theory from Furnivall's original which, whatever faults it may have had, was certainly a theory of change grounded in the realities of western colonialism.

Second, defining a society in terms of institutionalized segments again precludes the study of how ethnic identity came to occupy the importance which it may now have. It is probably true to say that as many societies developed and came to embrace groups characterized by markedly different cultures, like the great migration of Chinese and Indian labour, they were, at this point in time, plural societies. What the plural society thesis does not tell us anything about, of course, is the process of *acculturation* or the way that ethnic identity may 'soften' (or 'harden') by contact with other ethnic groups within society. What, for example, is the process whereby caste is 'lost' among overseas Indian communities and what effect has this had upon social mobility and traditional religious observance? As one critic of Smith's earlier work put it:

> Smith applies an 'ideal-type' concept, the validity of which is based on the structure of a certain category of societies during the *'first moment' of existence,* to a number of present day societies, which vary markedly in their evolution from pluralism to homogeneity.[29]

It may, of course, be an unwarranted assumption that the movement is towards homogeneity. The emerging identity of blacks with 'Africa' within the Caribbean, for example, or the effects of Indian independence on the five million overseas Indians may well represent cases of *enculturation.* The point is that this vital question must be *asked* and answered empirically and not merely ignored or assumed to be of little consequence.

Another process, the treatment of which is conspicuous by its absence in the theory under consideration, is that of *institutionalization,* by which is meant the process whereby *some* patterns of behaviour endure over time to become accepted institutional practices while others do not. The key concept in the plural society theory is that of 'institution' for it is these that separate one plural section from another. But if all social relations are part of traditional patterns of behaviour, then one must also consider revolutions, or sudden changes, or any activity which appears to be unregulated and uncontrolled. To deny its existence is to be guilty of a static determinism which cannot have a relevance for many of the most important conflicts and changes which constantly occur in multi-ethnic societies. We are told by M. G. Smith in his latest work that societies consist of social relations and that these are either *institutionalized* or *optional;* a point which appears to belie the argument being put forward here since it suggests a chink in the armour of determinism. The point is clarified in the next few lines:

> The range and conditions that govern optional relations at both the individual and collective levels are themselves institutionally prescribed and regulated. Thus the inclusive autonomous system of social relations which constitutes a society is directly or indirectly institutionalized.[30]

If all political behaviour is 'prescribed and regulated' by political institutions, how is it that black Americans are gaining their greatest advances in political power through using techniques not sanctioned by the established political order?

One other basic process which the plural society thesis omits to discuss could be termed 'interaction'. That is the actual relations which make up any real social situation. It is one thing to argue that a society is characterized by sections with few common values between them, but it is quite another to conclude from this that interaction between, let us say, racial groups is therefore necessarily low or 'confined only to the market place'. Indeed, it may well be that it is precisely interaction (which may, of course, include conflict) that keeps the ethnic groups in the positions they occupy. Some conclusions from a recent series of empirical studies on the processes whereby ethnic boundaries are preserved are relevant. Fredrik Barth in the Introduction to this series notes that:

> categorical ethnic distinctions do not depend on an absence of mobility, contact and information, but do entail social processes of exclusion and incorporation whereby discrete categories are maintained *despite* changing participation and membership in the course of individual life histories.[31]

In other words, the existence and continuation of ethnic divisions does not preclude interaction across these divisions. Further, it follows that the plural society notion is not going to assist greatly in understanding the nature of these relationships.

A second important conclusion that Barth reaches is that 'stable, persisting, and often vitally important social relations are maintained across (ethnic) boundaries, and are frequently based precisely on the dichotomized ethnic statuses.'[32] Far from there being a situation where it is only political domination which holds a plural society together, it may well be that interaction between ethnic groups determines the boundaries of such groups and relates them to the overall system in which they are implicated. This also raises the question, related closely to the criticism of static determinism already given, that to define a society in terms of its ethnic group boundaries is to beg the important question of the maintenance of these boundaries. If it is assumed that cultural differences define these boundaries, it is also to miss the fact that one crucial part of this boundary maintenance is the definition given to the other groups within the total society; an aspect of ethnic identity which will not be apparent from a simple listing and contrasting of cultural traits and institutional patterns.

I now intend to summarize the theoretical approach implicit in this critique and, very briefly, suggest its relevance for some complex multi-ethnic situations.

IV. TOWARDS A THEORETICAL FRAMEWORK

The 'theory'[33] advanced here is based upon three premises.

1. That social interaction between individuals in groups or quasi-groups is the basis of social organization.
2. That divisions of power, conflicts of interest and the formation of competitive situations between groups are extant phenomena in all societies at all times.
3. That processes of social change may best be understood by reference to group interaction.

In the first place, there must be a division between types of group or quasi-group boundaries and I would suggest the following five:

1. *Classes.* Defined in relation to the means of production.
2. *Deference groups*[34]. Groups defined by their position on a subjectively interpreted hierarchy of prestige.
3. *Political groups.* Groups defined in relation to the distribution of political power.
4. *Ethnic groups.* Groups defined in relation to cultural features and traits.
5. *Racial groups.* Groups defined in terms of physical appearance.

The first three categories of groups, derived as they clearly are from Marx and Max Weber, are all typically *ranked* within society and thus they refer to *power* divisions of one kind or another. The last two are not necessarily ranked although often they will be, as, for example, when racial divisions are supported by reference to a biological theory of racism. It is useful, however, to distinguish the first three, which are defined in terms of power division, from the latter two, defined in terms of properties or attributes. Accordingly, I refer to classes, deference groups, and groups defined by their access to political power as *scalar* groups while those that are defined in terms of their cultural or physical properties as *eidetic* groups, simply to emphasize the importance of their clear and visible characteristics.

While in theory groups may be defined in terms of any of these criteria, they tend to coincide within any social system. Thus, typically, within British colonies a characteristic feature was the superimposition of all five divisions when it came

to the expatriate British and, perhaps, planter or settler groups. They tended to
dominate in economic terms, occupy the summit of the prestige hierarchy, and
have an effective monopoly of political power combined with an apparent mastery
of European culture and a high degree of racial exclusiveness. Once divisions in
these terms have been recognized, it becomes a crucial research question to ascertain the *degree of superimposition* that any one group of people may possess, for
this is fundamental in understanding group conflict. While ethnic and racial divisions do not necessarily imply rank ordering, they tend to have the quality of
visibility which is likely to lead to much faster group loyalty in times of conflict.
Further, a rank ordering will normally be supplied to these groups because of superimposition with other divisions which do imply such a hierarchy as, for example,
with class divisions.

Conflict situations involving racial antagonisms may therefore result not from
complete superimposition which, though it may be violent, will be relatively stable,
but from the degree of *disjunction* between groups. To take an example, M. G.
Smith characterized Jamaica as a plural society under colonial rule and yet it is
now after independence, that the conflict potential may make itself felt.[35] This is
not because of pluralism itself, but because of this disjunction between scalar
groups which superimposition with eidetic variables will serve to intensify. There
is considerable superimposition of class and racial divisions within Jamaica and the
range of this economic division is strikingly wide. However, in potential at least,
there is now a disjunction between political and economic power and it can only
be a question of time before such disjunction is realized in more concerted opposition to the economic elite. What adds to this situation is an increasing disjunction of deference groups between the elite, with its North American aims and
aspirations, and the black masses, with their growing interest in independent black
Africa. Thus, whereas the flaunting of 'white' culture once served to unify the
system, this eidetic variable—itself superimposed to a large degree upon racial divisions—now serves to exacerbate animosities.

Within any society, there will be a number of continuous but slower processes
of change in operation. As with all such processes, they may operate in two directions. They would include the following:

1. *Acculturation/Enculturation.* The process of breaking down or building up
of cultural barriers or differences.
2. *Interaction.* The actual processes of interrelation between groups or members
of groups which may develop or decay over time.
3. *Institutionalization.* The process of forming or dissolving enduring patterns
of social relationship.

Actual social life entails all, and probably more, of these major social processes
which may well be continuing in both directions at the same time. In addition,
each may involve groups defined in the previous five ways. Thus, however a group
is defined, the attitudes expressed by the members of it, and the cultural symbols
which may be used in part to define its boundaries, will change over time. If it is an

economic group, its habits of spending and saving, for example, will be influenced by many factors not least of which may be deliberate attempts by advertisers to acculturate classes to accept particular standards and economic attitudes. In a similar way, patterns of interaction between groups will vary over time and processes of institutionalization may affect classes, deference of status groups, political groups, and ethnic or racial associations.

It is clear that this is not the end of the story for all this must be set within the context of *environmental* variables which themselves may be either *symbolic,* like overall political ideology or colonial strategy, or *physical,* such as geographical or general ecological environment. In addition, *external* variables affecting the overall structure and possibly the place of groups and processes within it have to be considered. While this can be no more than a mere sketch of an approach, it may be helpful to look briefly at some typical 'plural' situations, all of which are contained in societies that are multiracial as well as being multi-ethnic and which are also former colonial possessions. This is not to suggest that the approach is only applicable in such cases but they do often represent very clear and important cases of multi-ethnic societies.

As Furnivall was so keen to point out, most colonial societies are the product of economic forces and in such cases the relationship of class divisions to the overall structure is crucial. But then too one has to assess the importance of divisions over the distribution of political power. The crisis of May 1969 in Malaysia, for example, might then be understood to some degree in terms of the disjunction between, on the one hand, the political power and emergent nationalism of the Malays and, on the other, the economic power and dominance in the urban centres of non-Malays, most notably the Chinese.[36] In other words, despite the prominence of ethnicity in the Malaysian case, there is a need to assess the importance of other group divisions and their overlap or lack of congruence with race and ethnicity. Even where ethnic feeling can be shown to operate as an independent influence, it must be seen as a *variable* and not as part of a definition of the problem; that is, it must be seen as a factor which has been subject to many, often complex, historical forces.

In Guyana the society cannot merely be understood in plural terms despite the recent attempts to do so.[37] Again, the economic divisions, with their racial overtones, which were originally induced by colonialism are crucial. Ethnic divisions between East Indians and Afro-Guyanese were exacerbated by such factors as economic competition resulting from land scarcity and narrow racialist policies of land distribution and, at a much later date, by the intervention of outside agencies, whether this was the British Government, with its unfortunate insistence on the 'Westminster model' of political development in a country with balanced and competing racial groups, or the Pentagon with its concern over the 'Marxist' utterances by the leadership of the Peoples Progressive Party. Guyana represents a complex situation indeed where ethnic divisions themselves tended to reflect and magnify divisive forces which were rather more subtle, though no less insidious, in their operation.[38]

In Trinidad the situation is again different, although historically, culturally, and demographically, it is comparable with Guyana. In Smith's terms, it would have been a plural society with full *differential incorporation* before independence and a *consociation* after. But does that reveal a distinction without a difference? To many, the change to political independence has meant less than a significant transference of economic power.

It is impossible to understand the recent historical changes within Trinidad without looking at economic forces. For one thing the presence of a comparatively large and prosperous black, coloured, and Indian middle class has established a tradition of conservatism and has, incidentally, led to a greater disjunction between racial and economic divisions. The events of 1970, though they may be termed 'Black Power', have much more in common with the riots of 1937, when also an attempt was made to unite Africans and Indians in opposition to colonialism, than they do to the drive for nationalism and political independence, with its inevitable polarization over race, which characterized the period after the granting of adult suffrage in 1945.[39] Further, there are significant disjunctions along ethnic lines within racial groups. To talk of an 'East Indian cultural section' is to ignore or minimize the role that Moslem Indians have played in the black nationalist movement. Certainly, the process of acculturation has added to this complexity, for Christian Indians have been far more successful than Hindus in professional and entrepreneurial roles.[40] It would not be entirely unreasonable to base an argument accounting for the paucity of good leadership among the Indians in Trinidad on the divisions following from this religious and economic disjunction with purely racial identity. Dr. Jagan's non-sectarian and undoubtedly effective leadership of Indians in Guyana may have reflected a greater intrinsic unity although, on the other hand, one could argue that he achieved it by using his own powers of leadership and a strong unifying political ideology. Whichever is the case, it is certainly not true that race conflict is merely a function of ethnic difference. Even if one only conceives of pluralism in terms of value difference between cultural sections, the limited evidence that we have does not support a simple division along either racial or ethnic lines.[41]

No one could deny that ethnicity is important in relation to minority groups in East and Central Africa. And yet, despite this, the notion of the plural society has not proved of great value. H. S. Morris has pointed to the importance of ethnicity with respect to the Indians of Uganda but has reserved his judgment upon the theory of the plural society.[42] Floyd and Lillian Dotson in a recently published study of Indians in Central Africa are more positive. They were led to the conclusion that:

> a pluralistic emphasis upon the culturally unique does less than adequate justice to the observable facts of social power and tends to confuse the intimate relationship between the two.[43]

In this study the authors discuss the role of the Asians within the colonial system and their interaction and competition with both Europeans and Africans. The current position of Indians, however, can only be understood in relation to colonialism itself and the racist limitations which were put on their trading activities by the

British. Thus the argument is that the role of Indians in these former British colonies and protectorates must be seen in terms of the divisions of social power inherent in the colonial system and which itself served to unify all into one economic organization dependent to a large degree upon racial demarcation. The authors are also keen to point out the divisions within the small Indian group itself in terms of religious affiliation, caste, and generation, to say nothing of the ubiquitous divisions of power within ethnic groups of the kind that are often termed 'patron–client' by anthropologists. They criticize the commitment to institutional divisions in the notion of the plural society and accurately portray it, so far as their work was concerned, as 'static and lifeless, a descriptive categorization rather than an analysis of process'.[44]

V. SUMMARY AND CONCLUSION

In this paper I have attempted to show a number of things. First, that the theory which Furnivall advanced, whatever its limitations may be, was really a theory of conflict and process involving racial divisions and intended for general application to colonial societies. Second, in the 'developments' which have been made since Furnivall, the theory has become an over-simple and static schema for categorizing all complex multi-ethnic societies. It is as well to say that there are notable exceptions to this generalization, the most important of which is the work of Pierre L. van den Berghe. To him the concept of pluralism 'is of crucial importance'. Van den Berghe is careful, however, to reject the notion of the 'plural society' and prefers to look at pluralism as a variable. As he explains:

> I prefer to regard pluralism as a variable, and to include cases of stratification based on 'race', caste, estate, or class as instances of pluralism, even though the constituent groups share the same general culture.[45]

With such an eclectic definition, which appears to be preferred by Leo Kuper as well, it is clear that the criticisms expressed here do not apply.[46] Indeed, van den Berghe's conviction that sociological theory has to incorporate racial divisions, which he sees as a special case of 'structural' or social pluralism, and ethnic divisions, which are special cases of cultural pluralism, is not disputed here.[47]

Lastly, this paper has attempted, in a very crude and preliminary way, to suggest the sort of group definitions which have to be considered before a real understanding of multi-ethnic situations can occur. I have suggested that changes within such societies take place as a result of conflicts between groups defined in these terms, and that such conflicts are especially probable when there are disjunctions of membership within these groups. It should follow, therefore, that conditions of ethnic pluralism do not by any means predispose a society to violent ethnic and racial conflict. On the other hand, the degree of superimposition which occurs may well affect the intensity of conflict. The presence of ethnic and racial superimposition is particularly likely to raise this intensity by providing readily identifiable badges of group loyalty. Apart from this structural approach, I have also stressed the importance of not losing sight of the less dramatic historical forces of acculturation, interaction, and institutionalization.

There does not seem to be any case for continuing to define particular societies as 'plural' and, indeed, the whole concept of pluralism is fraught with such imprecise definitions and confused usage that it too is best avoided. The editors of a recent book on social stratification in Africa were also in no doubt on this point:

> Socio-cultural pluralism is no special condition that requires special descriptive methods and analytic tools. The term has been used to cover so broad a range of conditions that it has served more to obscure, rather than elucidate our enquiries, and it is better to discard it in favour of the more precise and specific indicators of class and caste.[48]

Despite the veracity of this statement and my concurrence with the recommendation it contains, the theory of the plural society and pluralism in general have the inestimable virtue of incorporating racial and ethnic divisions within a conceptual framework. The fact that they may have reified such divisions to the effective exclusion of all others is no reason to discontinue the search for a more acceptable theory of race relations and race conflict.

REFERENCES

1. This appears to be the view of Leo Kuper. See Leo Kuper, 'Plural Societies: Perspectives and Problems', in Leo Kuper and M. G. Smith (eds.), *Pluralism in Africa* (Berkeley and Los Angeles, University of California Press, 1969), pp. 7–26. Also John Horton, 'Order and Conflict Theories of Social Problems as Competing Ideologies', *American Journal of Sociology* (Vol. 71, 1966), pp. 701–13.
2. J. S. Furnivall, *Colonial Policy and Practice* (London, Cambridge University Press, 1948), p. 304.
3. Ibid., p. 3.
4. J. S. Furnivall, 'Political Education in the Far East', *Political Quarterly* (Vol. XVII, 1946), pp. 123–4.
5. Ibid., p. 132.
6. J. S. Furnivall, 'Burma: Independence and After', *Asian Horizon* (Vol. 2, No. 3, 1949), p. 40
7. J. S. Furnivall, 'Nationalism in Burma', *Asian Horizon* (Vol. 1, No. 2, 1948), p. 3. See also 'Communism and Nationalism in Burma', *Far Eastern Survey* (Vol. 18, No. 17, 24 August 1949), pp. 193–7.
8. J. S. Furnivall, 'Capitalism in Indonesia', *Pacific Affairs* (Vol. XX, No. 1, 1947), p. 67.
9. *Colonial Policy and Practice*, p. 311.
10. An approach to the Far East of a reputedly similar kind is that of the Dutch economist, J. H. Boeke. He advances a theory of 'dual societies' to account for the wide disparity between economic organization within the Western sector and that within the 'pre-capitalist' remainder of Indonesia. Despite the fact that Boeke did over-emphasize the divisions between, and autonomy of, these sectors, his work does not deserve the dismissal given it by

André Gunder Frank who pontificates thus:

> There exists no dual society in the world today and all attempts to find one are attempts to justify and/or cover up imperialism and revisionism.

It is one of the major shortcomings of the 'new' Marxists that, in their attempts to see the rest of the world as simply an extension of western capitalism, they often fail to understand the internal dynamics of 'Third World' societies (to use another unacceptable expression!). See J. H. Boeke, *Economics and Economic Policy of Dual Societies as Exemplified by Indonesia* (New York, Institute of Pacific Relations, 1953) and André Gunder Frank, 'Dialectic, not Dual Society' in his *Latin America: Underdevelopment or Revolution* (New York and London, Monthly Review Press, 1969), p. 221. For a useful discussion of the notion of dualism and pluralism with reference to Black Africa, see Luis Beltrán, 'Dualisme et Pluralisme en Afrique Tropicale Indépendante', *Cahiers Internationaux de Sociologie* (Vol. 46, 1969), pp. 93–118. On Indonesia, see: W. F. Wertheim, *Indonesian Society in Transition* (The Hague, van Hoeve, 1956).

11. M. G. Smith, *The Plural Society of the British West Indies,* (Berkeley, University of California Press, 1965), p. x.
12. Ibid., p. 75.
13. M. G. Smith, 'Institutional and Political Conditions of Pluralism' and 'Some Developments in the Analytic Framework of Pluralism', in Kuper and Smith (eds.), op. cit., pp. 27–65; 415–58.
14. Ibid., p. 28.
15. Ibid., pp. 34–5.
16. Ibid., p. 430. A similar idea has been suggested by Gerald Berreman, 'Stratification, Pluralism and Interaction: A Comparative Analysis of Caste', in Anthony de Reuck and Julie Knight (eds.), *Caste and Race: Comparative Approaches* (London, J. and A. Churchill for the C.I.B.A. Foundation, 1967), p. 56
17. Ibid., p. 434
18. For example, Maurice Freedman, 'The Growth of a Plural Society in Malaya', *Pacific Affairs* (Vol. 33, 1960), pp. 158–68.
19. See Leo A. Despres, *Cultural Pluralism and Nationalist Politics in British Guiana* (Chicago, Rand McNally, 1967); 'The Implications of Nationalist Politics in British Guiana for the Development of Cultural Theory', *American Anthropologist* (Vol. 66, 1964), pp. 1051–77; 'Anthropological Theory, Cultural Pluralism and the Study of Complex Societies', *Current Anthropology* (Vol. 9, 1968), pp. 3–16.
20. Smith, 'Analytic Framework of Pluralism', op. cit., pp. 438–9.
21. Ibid., p. 443.
22. Ibid., pp. 446–7.
23. Ibid., p. 439.
24. Leo A. Despres, *Protest and Change in Plural Societies,* Occasional Papers Series, No. 2 (Montreal, McGill University, 1969). Also 'Differential Adaption and Micro-Cultural Evolution in Guyana', *Southwestern Journal of Anthropology,* (Vol. 25, No. 1, 1969), pp. 14–44.
25. Lloyd Braithwaite, 'Social Stratification and Cultural Pluralism', *Annals of the New York Academy of Sciences* (Vol. 83, Art. 5, 1960), pp. 816–36.
26. Smith, 'Analytic Framework', op. cit., p. 421.
27. The view that many points of criticism of the plural society idea do not necessarily emanate from functionalism is a major contention in a previous paper by the present writer. See Malcolm Cross, 'Cultural Pluralism and Sociological Theory: A Critique and Re-evaluation', *Social and Economic Studies* (Vol. 17, No. 4, 1968), pp. 381–97. For other critical comment, see Herman McKenzie, 'The Plural Society Debate; Some Comments on a Recent Contribution', *Social and Economic Studies* (Vol. 15, 1966), pp. 53–60; John Rex, 'The Concept of Race in Sociological Theory', in Sami Zubaida (ed.), *Race and Racialism* (Lon-

don, Tavistock Publications, 1970), pp. 35–55, and *Race Relations in Sociological Theory* (London, Weidenfeld and Nicolson, 1970). Also David Lockwood, 'Race, Conflict and Plural Society', in Zubaida, op. cit., pp. 57–72.

28. Ernest Gellner, 'Time and Theory in Social Anthropology', *Mind* (New Series, Vol. 67, 1958), p. 192.
29. Harmannus Hoetink, 'The Concept of Pluralism as Envisaged by M. G. Smith', *Caribbean Studies* (Vol. 7, No. 1, 1967), p. 40 (emphasis in original).
30. Smith, 'Institutional and Political Conditions', op. cit., p. 30.
31. Fredrik Barth, 'Introduction' in Fredrik Barth (ed.), *Ethnic Groups and Boundaries: The Social Organization of Cultural Difference* (London, George Allen & Unwin, 1970), pp. 9–10.
32. Ibid., p. 10
33. To call the overall approach and few distinctions offered here a 'theory' is undoubtedly to use the term in a very loose sense.
34. This term is preferred to that of status group simply because of the confusion which surrounds the use of the term 'status'.
35. M. G. Smith, 'The Plural Framework of Jamaican Society', in Smith, *The Plural Society in the British West Indies*, pp. 162–75.
36. See, for example, Mahathir Bin Mohamed, *The Malay Dilemma*, (Singapore, Asia Pacific Press, 1970). For recent studies of the relative position of ethnic groups, see Victor Purcell, *The Chinese in South-east Asia* (London, Oxford University Press, 1965); Kernial Singh Sandhu, *Indians in Malaya: Immigration and Settlement* (Cambridge University Press, 1969); Sinnapah Arasaratnam, *Indians in Malaysia and Singapore* (London, Oxford University Press for the I.R.R., 1970). Also cf. Freedman, op. cit.
37. See Despres, *Cultural Pluralism and Nationalist Politics.*
38. Some of the best work on Guyana has come from R. T. Smith. See his 'People and Change', *New World* (Guyana Independence Issue, 1966), pp. 49–54; 'Social Stratification, Cultural Pluralism and Integration in West Indian Societies' in Sybil Lewis and Thomas G. Matthews (eds.), *Caribbean Integration* (Rio Piedras, Puerto Rico, Institute of Caribbean Studies, 1967), pp. 236–58. Also for a discussion of acculturation, see R. T. Smith and C. Jayawardena, 'Caste and Social Status Among the Indians of Guyana' in Barton M. Schwartz (ed.), *Caste in Overseas Indian Communities* (California, Chandler Publishing Co., 1968), pp. 43–92.
39. See Selwyn Ryan, 'The Struggle for Afro-Indian Solidarity in Trinidad, *Trinidad and Tobago Index* (Vol. 4, 1966), pp. 3–28. Also Ivar Oxaal, *Black Intellectuals Come to Power* (Cambridge, Mass., Schenkman, 1968).
40. On acculturation in Trinidad, see Daniel J. Crowley, 'Plural and Differential Acculturation in Trinidad', *American Anthropologist* (Vol. 59, No. 5, 1957), pp. 189–207; 'Cultural Assimilation in a Multi-Racial Society', *Annals of the New York Academy of Sciences*, pp. 850–4. Also, see Morton Klass, *East Indians in Trinidad: A Study of Cultural Persistence* (New York, Columbia University Press, 1961); 'East and West Indian; Cultural Complexity in Trinidad', *Annals*, pp. 855–61; Colin Clarke, 'Caste Among Hindus in a Town in Trinidad: San Fernando' in Schwartz (ed.), op. cit., pp. 165–99.
41. Malcolm Cross and Allen M. Schwartzbaum, 'Socio-cultural Pluralism: Towards an Empirical Test' (forthcoming).
42. H. S. Morris, *The Indians of Uganda: A Study of Caste and Sect in a Plural Society* (Chicago, University of Chicago Press, 1968). Also, on the theory itself, see Morris, 'The Plural Society', *Man* (Vol. 57, No. 148, 1957), pp. 124–5; 'Some Aspects of the Concept, Plural Society', *Man* (New Series, Vol. 2, 1967), pp. 169–84.
43. Floyd Dotson and Lillian O. Dotson, *The Indian Minority of Zambia, Rhodesia and Malawi* (New Haven and London, Yale University Press, 1968), p. 6.
44. Ibid., p. 394.

45. Pierre L. van den Berghe, 'Pluralism and the Polity: A Theoretical Exploration', in Kuper and Smith (eds.), op. cit., p. 68.
46. See Leo Kuper, in Kuper and Smith, op. cit., pp. 152–93; 459–87. For example, Kuper suggests that pluralism 'may be constituted by class division'. Ibid., p. 459. Also cf. R. A. Schermerhorn, *Comparative Ethnic Relations* (New York, Random House, 1970), especially Chapter 4, pp. 122–63.
47. For van den Berghe's main statements on pluralism, see *Race and Racism* (New York, John Wiley, 1967); 'Towards a Sociology of Africa', *Social Forces* (Vol. 43, 1964), pp. 11–18.
48. Arthur Tuden and Leonard Plotnicov, 'Introduction' to Tuden and Plotnicov (eds.), *Social Stratification in Africa* (London and New York, Macmillan and Free Press, 1970), p. 28.

22   Violence and Decolonization

Frantz Fanon

"National liberation, national renaissance, the restoration of nationhood to the people, commonwealth: whatever may be the headings used or the new formulas introduced, decolonization is always a violent phenomenon. At whatever level we study it—relationships between individuals, new names for sports clubs, the human admixture at cocktail parties, in the police, on the directing boards of national or private banks—decolonization is quite simply the replacing of a certain "species" of men by another "species" of men. Without any period of transition, there is a total, complete, and absolute substitution. It is true that we could equally well stress the rise of a new nation, the setting up of a new state, its diplomatic relations, and its economic and political trends. But we have precisely chosen to speak of that kind of *tabula rasa* which characterizes at the outset all decolonization. Its unusual importance is that it constitutes, from the very first day, the minimum demands of the colonized. To tell the truth, the proof of success lies in a whole social structure being changed from the bottom up. The extraordinary importance of this change is that it is willed, called for, demanded. The need for this change exists in its crude state, impetuous and compelling, in the consciousness and in the lives of the men and women who are colonized. But the possibility of this change is equally experienced in the form of a terrifying future in the consciousness of another "species" of men and women: the colonizers.

Decolonization, which sets out to change the order of the world, is, obviously, a program of complete disorder. But it cannot come as a result of magical practices, nor of a natural shock, nor of a friendly understanding. Decolonization, as we know, is a historical process: that is to say that it cannot be understood, it cannot

These extracts are taken from Frantz Fanon's *The Damned* (translated by Constance Farrington), published by *Présence Africaine*, Paris, 1963, (and subsequently as *The Wretched of the Earth* by Grove Press, Inc. and other houses).

become intelligible nor clear to itself except in the exact measure that we can discern the movements which give it historical form and content. Decolonization is
the meeting of two forces, opposed to each other by their very nature, which in
fact owe their originality to that sort of substantification which results from and
is nourished by the situation in the colonies. Their first encounter was marked by
violence and their existence together—that is to say the exploitation of the native
by the settler—was carried on by dint of a great array of bayonets and cannons.
The settler and the native are old acquaintances. In fact, the settler is right when
he speaks of knowing "them" well. For it is the settler who has brought the native
into existence and who perpetuates his existence. The settler owes the fact of his
very existence, that is to say, his property, to the colonial system.

Decolonization never takes place unnoticed, for it influences individuals and
modifies them fundamentally. It transforms spectators crushed with their inessen-
tiality into privileged actors, with the grandiose glare of history's floodlights upon
them. It brings a natural rhythm into existence, introduced by new men, and with
it a new language and a new humanity. Decolonization is the veritable creation of
new men. But this creation owes nothing of its legitimacy to any supernatural
power; the "thing" which has been colonized becomes man during the same process
by which it frees itself.

In decolonization, there is therefore the need of a complete calling in question
of the colonial situation. If we wish to describe it precisely, we might find it in the
well-known words: "The last shall be first and the first last." Decolonization is
the putting into practice of this sentence. That is why, if we try to describe it, all
decolonization is successful.

The naked truth of decolonization evokes for us the searing bullets and blood-
stained knives which emanate from it. For if the last shall be first, this will only
come to pass after a murderous and decisive struggle between the two protagonists.
That affirmed intention to place the last at the head of things, and to make them
climb at a pace (too quickly, some say) the well-known steps which characterize
an organized society, can only triumph if we use all means to turn the scale, including, of course, that of violence.

You do not turn any society, however primitive it may be, upside down with
such a program if you have not decided from the very beginning, that is to say
from the actual formulation of that program, to overcome all the obstacles that
you will come across in so doing. The native who decides to put the program into
practice, and to become its moving force, is ready for violence at all times. From
birth it is clear to him that this narrow world, strewn with prohibitions, can only
be called in question by absolute violence.

The colonial world is a world divided into compartments. It is probably unnecessary to recall the existence of native quarters and European quarters, of
schools for natives and schools for Europeans; in the same way we need not recall
apartheid in South Africa. Yet, if we examine closely this system of compartments,
we will at least be able to reveal the lines of force it implies. This approach to the

colonial world, its ordering and its geographical layout will allow us to mark out the lines on which a decolonized society will be reorganized.

The colonial world is a world cut in two. The dividing line, the frontiers are shown by barracks and police stations. In the colonies it is the policeman and the soldier who are the official, instituted go-betweens, the spokesmen of the settler and his rule of oppression. In capitalist societies the educational system, whether lay or clerical, the structure of moral reflexes handed down from father to son, the exemplary honesty of workers who are given a medal after fifty years of good and loyal service, and the affection which springs from harmonious relations and good behavior—all these aesthetic expressions of respect for the established order serve to create around the exploited person an atmosphere of submission and of inhibition which lightens the task of policing considerably. In the capitalist countries a multitude of moral teachers, counselors and "bewilderers" separate the exploited from those in power. In the colonial countries, on the contrary, the policeman and the soldier, by their immediate presence and their frequent and direct action maintain contact with the native and advise him by means of rifle butts and napalm not to budge. It is obvious here that the agents of government speak the language of pure force. The intermediary does not lighten the oppression, nor seek to hide the domination; he shows them up and puts them into practice with the clear conscience of an upholder of the peace; yet he is the bringer of violence into the home and into the mind of the native.

The zone where the natives live is not complementary to the zone inhabited by the settlers. The two zones are opposed, but not in the service of a higher unity. Obedient to the rules of pure Aristotelian logic, they both follow the principle of reciprocal exclusivity. No conciliation is possible, for of the two terms, one is superfluous. The settlers' town is a strongly built town, all made of stone and steel. It is a brightly lit town; the streets are covered with asphalt, and the garbage cans swallow all the leavings, unseen, unknown and hardly thought about. The settler's feet are never visible, except perhaps in the sea; but there you're never close enough to see them. His feet are protected by strong shoes although the streets of his town are clean and even, with no holes or stones. The settler's town is a well-fed town, an easygoing town; its belly is always full of good things. The settlers' town is a town of white people, of foreigners.

The town belonging to the colonized people, or at least the native town, the Negro village, the medina, the reservation, is a place of ill fame, peopled by men of evil repute. They are born there, it matters little where or how; they die there, it matters not where, nor how. It is a world without spaciousness; men live there on top of each other, and their huts are built one on top of the other. The native town is a hungry town, starved of bread, of meat, of shoes, of coal, of light. The native town is a crouching village, a town on its knees, a town wallowing in the mire. It is a town of niggers and dirty Arabs. The look that the native turns on the settler's town is a look of lust, a look of envy; it expresses his dreams of possession—all manner of possession: to sit at the settler's table, to sleep in the settler's bed, with his wife if possible. The colonized man is an envious man. And this the settler knows very well; when their glances meet he ascertains bitterly, always on the defensive, "They want to take our place." It is true, for there is no native who does not dream at least once a day of setting himself up in the settler's place.

This world divided into compartments, this world cut in two is inhabited by two different species. The originality of the colonial context is that economic reality, inequality, and the immense difference of ways of life never come to mask the human realities. When you examine at close quarters the colonial context, it is evident that what parcels out the world is to begin with the fact of belonging to or not belonging to a given race, a given species. In the colonies the economic substructure is also a superstructure. The cause is the consequence; you are rich because you are white, you are white because you are rich. This is why Marxist analysis should always be slightly stretched every time we have to do with the colonial problem.

Everything up to and including the very nature of precapitalist society, so well explained by Marx, must here be thought out again. The serf is in essence different from the knight, but a reference to divine right is necessary to legitimize this statutory difference. In the colonies, the foreigner coming from another country imposed his rule by means of guns and machines. In defiance of his successful transplantation, in spite of his appropriation, the settler still remains a foreigner. It is neither the act of owning factories, nor estates, nor a bank balance which distinguishes the governing classes. The governing race is first and foremost those who come from elsewhere, those who are unlike the original inhabitants, "the others."

The violence which has ruled over the ordering of the colonial world, which has ceaselessly drummed the rhythm for the destruction of native social forms and broken up without reserve the systems of reference of the economy, the customs of dress and external life, that same violence will be claimed and taken over by the native at the moment when, deciding to embody history in his own person, he surges into the forbidden quarters. To wreck the colonial world is henceforward a mental picture of action which is very clear, very easy to understand and which may be assumed by each one of the individuals which constitute the colonized people. To break up the colonial world does not mean that after the frontiers have been abolished lines of communication will be set up between the two zones. The destruction of the colonial world is no more and no less than the abolition of one zone, its burial in the depths of the earth or its expulsion from the country.

The natives' challenge to the colonial world is not a rational confrontation of points of view. It is not a treatise on the universal, but the untidy affirmation of an original idea propounded as an absolute. The colonial world is a Manichean world. It is not enough for the settler to delimit physically, that is to say with the help of the army and the police force, the place of the native. As if to show the totalitarian character of colonial exploitation the settler paints the native as a sort of quintessence of evil.[1] Native society is not simply described as a society lacking in values. It is not enough for the colonist to affirm that those values have disappeared from, or still better never existed in, the colonial world. The native is declared insensible to ethics; he represents not only the absence of values, but also the negation of values. He is, let us dare to admit, the enemy of values, and in this sense he is the absolute evil. He is the corrosive element, destroying all that comes near him; he is the deforming element, disfiguring all that has to do with beauty or morality; he is the depository of maleficent powers, the unconscious and irretrievable instrument of blind forces. Monsieur Meyer could thus state seriously in the French National Assembly that the Republic must not be prostituted by allowing the Algerian people to become part of it. All values, in fact, are irrevocably poisoned and diseased as soon as they are allowed in contact with the colonized race. The customs of the colonized people, their traditions, their myths—above all, their myths—are the very sign of that poverty of spirit and of their constitutional depravity. That is why we must put the DDT which destroys parasites, the bearers of disease, on the same level as the Christian religion which wages war on embryonic heresies and instincts, and on evil as yet unborn. The recession of yellow fever and the advance of evangelization form part of the same balance sheet. But the triumphant *communiqués* from the missions are in fact a source of information concerning the implantation of foreign influences in the core of the colonized people. I speak of the Christian religion, and no one need be astonished. The Church in the colonies is the white people's Church, the foreigner's Church. She does not call the native to God's ways but to the ways of the white man, of the master, of the oppressor. And as we know, in this matter many are called but few chosen.

At times this Manicheism goes to its logical conclusion and dehumanizes the native, or to speak plainly, it turns him into an animal. In fact, the terms the settler uses when he mentions the native are zoological terms. He speaks of the yellow man's reptilian motions, of the stink of the native quarter, of breeding swarms, of foulness, of spawn, of gesticulations. When the settler seeks to describe the native fully in exact terms he constantly refers to the bestiary. The European rarely hits on a picturesque style; but the native, who knows what is in the mind of the settler, guesses at once what he is thinking of. Those hordes of vital statistics, those hysterical masses, those faces bereft of all humanity, those distended bodies which are like nothing on earth, that mob without beginning or end, those children who seem to belong to nobody, that laziness stretched out in the sun, that vegetative rhythm of life—all this forms part of the colonial vocabulary. General de Gaulle speaks of "the yellow multitudes" and François Mauriac of the black, brown, and yellow masses which soon will be unleashed. The native knows all this, and laughs to himself every time he spots an allusion to the animal world in the other's words. For he knows that he is not an animal; and it is precisely at the moment he realizes his humanity that he begins to sharpen the weapons with which he will secure its victory.

As soon as the native begins to pull on his moorings, and to cause anxiety to the settler, he is handed over to well-meaning souls who in cultural congresses point out to him the specificity and wealth of Western values. But every time Western values are mentioned they produce in the native a sort of stiffening or muscular lockjaw. During the period of decolonization, the native's reason is appealed to. He is offered definite values, he is told frequently that decolonization need not mean regression, and that he must put his trust in qualities which are well-tried, solid, and highly esteemed. But it so happens that when the native hears a speech about Western culture he pulls out his knife—or at least he makes sure it is within reach. The violence with which the supremacy of white values is affirmed and the aggressiveness which has permeated the victory of these values over the ways of life and of thought of the native mean that, in revenge, the native laughs in mockery when Western values are mentioned in front of him. In the colonial context the settler only ends his work of breaking in the native when the latter admits loudly and intelligibly the supremacy of the white man's values. In the period of decolonization, the colonized masses mock at these very values, insult them, and vomit them up.

This phenomenon is ordinarily masked because, during the period of decolonization, certain colonized intellectuals have begun a dialogue with the bourgeoisie of the colonialist country. During this phase, the indigenous population is discerned only as an indistinct mass. The few native personalities whom the colonialist bourgeois have come to know here and there have not sufficient influence on that immediate discernment to give rise to nuances. On the other hand, during the period of liberation, the colonialist bourgeoisie looks feverishly for contacts with the elite and it is with these elite that the familiar dialogue concerning values is carried on. The colonialist bourgeoisie, when it realizes that it is impossible for it to maintain its domination over the colonial countries, decides to carry out a rearguard action with regard to culture, values, techniques, and so on. Now what we must never forget is that the immense majority of colonized peoples is oblivious to these problems. For a colonized people the most essential value, because the most concrete, is first and foremost the land: the land which will bring them bread and, above all, dignity. But this dignity has nothing to do with the dignity of the human individual: for that human individual has never heard tell of it. All that the native has seen in his country is that they can freely arrest him, bear him, starve him: and no professor of ethics, no priest has ever come to be beaten in his place, nor to share their bread with him. As far as the native is concerned, morality is very concrete; it is to silence the settler's defiance, to break his flaunting violence— in a word, to put him out of the picture. The well-known principle that all men are equal will be illustrated in the colonies from the moment that the native claims that he is the equal of the settler. One step more, and he is ready to fight to be more than the settler. In fact, he has already decided to eject him and to take his place; as we see it, it is a whole material and moral universe which is breaking up. The intellectual who for his part has followed the colonialist with regard to the universal abstract will fight in order that the settler and the native may live together in peace in a new world. But the thing he does not see, precisely because he is permeated by colonialism and all its ways of thinking, is that the settler, from the moment that the colonial context disappears, has no longer any interest in remaining or in co-existing. It is not by chance that, even before any negotiation[2]

between the Algerian and French governments has taken place, the European
minority which calls itself "liberal" has already made its position clear: it demands
nothing more nor less than twofold citizenship. By setting themselves apart in an
abstract manner, the liberals try to force the settler into taking a very concrete
jump into the unknown. Let us admit it, the settler knows perfectly well that no
phraseology can be a substitute for reality.

Thus the native discovers that his life, his breath, his beating heart are the same
as those of the settler. He finds out that the settler's skin is not of any more value
than a native's skin; and it must be said that this discovery shakes the world in a
very necessary manner. All the new, revolutionary assurance of the native stems
from it. For if, in fact, my life is worth as much as the settler's, his glance no longer
shrivels me up nor freezes me, and his voice no longer turns me into stone. I am no
longer on tenterhooks in his presence; in fact, I don't give a damn for him. Not
only does his presence no longer trouble me, but I am already preparing such efficient ambushes for him that soon there will be no way out but that of flight.

We have said that the colonial context is characterized by the dichotomy which
it imposes upon the whole people. Decolonization unifies that people by the radical
decision to remove from it its heterogeneity, and by unifying it on a national, sometimes a racial, basis. We know the fierce words of the Senegalese patriots, referring
to the maneuvers of their president, Senghor: "We have demanded that the higher
posts should be given to Africans; and now Senghor is Africanizing the Europeans."
That is to say that the native can see clearly and immediately if decolonization has
come to pass or not, for his minimum demands are simply that the last shall be first.

But the native intellectual brings variants to this petition, and, in fact, he seems
to have good reasons: higher civil servants, technicians, specialists—all seem to be
needed. Now, the ordinary native interprets these unfair promotions as so many
acts of sabotage, and he is often heard to declare: "It wasn't worth while, then, our
becoming independent . . ."

In the colonial countries where a real struggle for freedom has taken place,
where the blood of the people has flowed and where the length of the period of
armed warfare has favored the backward surge of intellectuals toward bases
grounded in the people, we can observe a genuine eradication of the superstructure
built by these intellectuals from the bourgeois colonialist environment. The colonialist bourgeoisie, in its narcissistic dialogue, expounded by members of its universities, had in fact deeply implanted in the minds of the colonized intellectual that
the essential qualities remain eternal in spite of all the blunders men may make: the
essential qualities of the West, of course. The native intellectual accepted the co-
gency of these ideas, and deep down in his brain you could always find a vigilant
sentinel ready to defend the Greco-Latin pedestal. Now it so happens that during
the struggle for liberation, at the moment that the native intellectual comes into
touch again with his people, this artificial sentinel is turned into dust. All the
Mediterranean values—the triumph of the human individual, of clarity, and of
beauty—become lifeless, colorless knickknacks. All those speeches seem like collections of dead words; those values which seemed to uplift the soul are revealed as

worthless, simply because they have nothing to do with the concrete conflict in
which the people is engaged."

NOTES

1. We have demonstrated the mechanism of this Manichean world in *Black Skin, White Masks*
   (New York: Grove Press, 1967).
2. Fanon is writing in 1961.—*Trans.*

23   Nation-Building or
           Nation-Destroying?

Walker Connor

Scholars associated with theories of "nation-building" have tended either to ignore
the question of ethnic diversity or to treat the matter of ethnic identity superficially as merely one of a number of minor impediments to effective state-integration.
To the degree that ethnic identity is given recognition, it is apt to be as a somewhat
unimportant and ephemeral nuisance that will unquestionably give way to a common identity uniting all inhabitants of the state, regardless of ethnic heritage, as
modern communication and transportation networks link the state's various parts
more closely. Both tendencies are at sharp variance with the facts, and have contributed to the undue optimism that has characterized so much of the literature on
"nation-building."

    It is not difficult to substantiate the charge that the leading theoreticians of "na-
tion-building" have tended to slight, if not totally ignore, problems associated with
ethnic diversity. A consultation of the table of contents and indices of books on
"nation-building" will quickly convince the doubtful that the matter is seldom acknowledged, much less accorded serious consideration.[1] In order to be justified,
such omissions must be occasioned either by the fact that most states are ethnically
homogeneous or that ethnic diversity poses no serious problems to integration.

    The former possibility is readily eliminated by reference to the actual ethnic
composition of contemporary states. The remarkable lack of coincidence that exists
between ethnic and political borders is indicated by the following statistics. Of a
total of 132 contemporary states, only 12 (9.1 per cent) can be described as essen-

    From Walker Connor, "Nation-Building or Nation-Destroying?" *World Politics*, vol. XXIV,
no. 3 (copyright © 1972 by Princeton University Press). Reprinted by permission of Princeton
University Press.

tially homogeneous from an ethnic viewpoint. An additional 25 states (18.9 per cent of the sample) contain an ethnic group accounting for more than 90 per cent of the state's total population, and in still another 25 states the largest element accounts for between 75 and 89 per cent of the population. But in 31 states (23.5 per cent of the total), the largest ethnic element represents only 50 to 74 per cent of the population, and in 39 cases (29.5 per cent of all states) the largest group fails to account for even half of the state's population. Moreover, this portrait of ethnic diversity becomes more vivid when the number of distinct ethnic groups within states is considered. In some instances, the number of groups within a state runs into the hundreds, and in 53 states (40.2 per cent of the total), the population is divided into more than *five* significant groups.[2] Clearly, then, the problem of ethnic diversity is far too ubiquitous to be ignored by the serious scholar of "nation-building," unless he subscribes to the position that ethnic diversity is not a matter for serious concern.

The validity of this position apparently also rests upon one of two propositions. Either loyalty to the ethnic group is self-evidently compatible with loyalty to the state, or, as mentioned earlier, ethnic identification will prove to be of short duration, withering away as modernization progresses. More consideration will be later given to the matter of the two loyalties (i.e., to the ethnic group and to the state), but clearly the two are not naturally harmonious. One need only reflect on the ultimate political dissection of what was once known as the Habsburg Empire, or contemplate the single most important challenge to the political survival of Belgium, Canada, Cyprus, Guyana, Kenya, Nigeria, the Sudan, Yugoslavia, and a number of other multiethnic states. The theoretician of "nation-building" may well contemplate some proposal that he believes will reduce the matter of competing loyalties to manageable proportions (such as confederalism or cultural autonomy); but, if so, his proposal is an important element in his model and should occupy a prominent place in his writing.[3]

As to the assumption that ethnic identity will wither away as the processes collectively known as modernization occur, it is probable that those who hold this premise have been influenced, directly or indirectly, by the writings of Karl Deutsch. It is debatable, however, whether such an opinion concerning the future of ethnic identity can be properly inferred from his works. His perception of the intereffects of what he calls "social mobilization" and of assimilation (i.e., "nation-building," so far as identity is concerned) is not always clear and appears to have undergone significant fluctuations. But given the magnitude of his influence, a closer scrutiny of his works appears warranted in order to define and evaluate more clearly his conclusions concerning the significance that ethnic identity possesses for "nation-building."

Deutsch's most famous work, *Nationalism and Social Communication,*[4] illustrates the problem of defining his position with precision. On the one hand, this work contains a few passing acknowledgements that increasing contacts between culturally diverse people *might* increase antagonisms.[5] On the other hand, there are several passages that might lead the reader to conclude that Deutsch was convinced that modernization, in the form of increases in urbanization, industrialization, schooling, communication and transportation facilities, etc., would lead to assimilation. Even the development and extensive discussion of the concept of social mobilization, in a book ostensibly dedicated to the analytical study of nationalism, implied an important relationship between the two. Moreover, it was in a chapter entitled "National Assimilation or Differentiation: Some Quantitative Relationships" that Deutsch discussed the factors that determined, in his view, the rate of social mobilization. Then, after discussing the rates of mobilization and of assimilation separately, he strongly intimated a causal or reinforcing interrelationship:

> Thus far we have treated all the rates of change as completely independent from each other. . . . However, we already know empirically that the rate of assimilation among a population that has been uprooted and mobilized—such as immigrants coming to America—is usually considerably higher than the rate of assimilation among the secluded populations of villages close to the soil. . . . Probably the theoretical investigation of these quantitative aspects of the merging or splitting of nations could be carried still further. One reason to stop here might be that we know now what statistical information is worth looking for, but that there seems little point in going further until more of the relevant statistics have been collected.[6]

Later, in summarizing the same chapter, Deutsch noted:

> A decisive factor in national assimilation or differentiation was found to be the process of social mobilization which accompanies the growth of markets, industries, and towns, and eventually of literacy and mass communication. The trends in the underlying process of social mobilization could do much to decide whether existing national trends in particular countries would be continued or reversed.[7]

In the following chapter, Deutsch discussed the rate of assimilation in terms of six balances of both quantitative and qualitative factors, and then restated what he conceived to be the relationship between the rates of mobilization and assimilation.

> Assimilation among people firmly rooted in their own communities and their native setting usually proceeds far more slowly than it would among the mobilized population, but it does proceed even though it may take many generations. . . . Any more general quantitative comparison between the relatively high assimilation speeds among mobilized persons and the considerably lower assimilation speeds among the underlying population remains to be worked out. Likewise to be worked out would have to be the *mutual interaction* of the different rates of change which thus far have been discussed as if they were wholly independent of each other.[8]

Such citations would appear to justify the interpretation that Deutsch felt that modernization, by socially mobilizing large segments of the population, would increase both the likelihood and the tempo of their assimilation. Such a conclusion was lent further credence by Deutsch's optimistic view that the matter of assimilating diverse ethnic groups is subjectable to social engineering. Concluding a discussion of the role of the policy-maker, he noted: "Too often men have viewed language and nationality superficially as an accident, or accepted them submissively as fate. In fact they are neither accident nor fate, but the outcome of a discernible process; and as soon as we begin to make the process visible, we are beginning to change it."[9]

By 1961, Deutsch's view of the relationship between social mobilization and assimilation appeared to have undergone a fundamental change. Mobilization was now seen as being apt to have the opposite effect upon assimiliation.

> Other things assumed equal, the stage of rapid social mobilization may be expected, therefore, to promote the consolidation of states whose peoples already share the same language, culture, and major social institutions; while the same process may tend to strain or destroy the unity of states whose population is already divided into several groups with different languages or cultures or basic ways of life.[10]

The practical consequences of this altered view, in terms of what it portended for the survival of that preponderant number of non-industrialized states which are multiethnic, was blunted, however, by Deutsch's immediate addendum that all things, in any event, are not equal. More specifically, he contended that ethnic identity would prove no match for the power of self-interest.

> In the last analysis, however, the problem of the scale of states goes beyond the effects of language, culture, or institutions, important as all these are. In the period of rapid social mobilization, the acceptable scale of a political unit will tend to depend eventually upon its performance. ... At bottom, the popular acceptance of a government in a period of social mobilization is most of all a matter of its responsiveness to the felt needs of its population.[11]

An essay written by Professor Deutsch two years later indicated a swing back to his earlier position. In a return to his earlier optimism concerning the impact of modernization upon ethnicity, he chided unnamed authors for maintaining that ethnic divisions constituted a long-run challenge to "nation-building."

> Tribes, we know from European history, can change their language and culture; they can absorb other tribes; and large tribes come into existence through federation or mergers of smaller tribes or through their conquest and absorption by a larger one.
>   In contrast to this picture of plasticity and change, many writings on African and Asian politics still seem to treat tribes as fixed and unlikely to change in any significant way during the next decades. Yet in con-

temporary Asia and Africa, the rates of cultural and ethnic change, although still low, are likely to be faster than they were in early medieval Europe. . . . Research is needed to establish more reliable figures, but it seems likely from the experience of ethnic minorities in other parts of the world that the process of partial modernization will draw many of the most gifted and energetic individuals into the cities or the growing sectors of the economy away from their former minority or tribal groups, leaving these traditional groups weaker, more stagnant, and easier to govern.[12]

Later in the essay, Deutsch specified four stages by which he anticipated assimilation would take place:

Open or latent resistance to political amalgamation into a common national state; minimal integration to the point of passive compliance with the orders of such an amalgamated government; deeper political integration to the point of active support for such a common state but with continuing ethnic or cultural group cohesion and diversity; and, finally, the coincidence of political amalgamation and integration with the assimilation of all groups to a common language and culture—these could be the main stages on the way from tribes to nation. Since a nation is not an animal or vegetable organism, its evolution need not go through any fixed sequence of these steps. . . . Yet the most frequent sequence in modern Asia and Africa may well be the one sketched above. How long might it take for tribes or other ethnic groups in a developing country to pass through some such sequence of stages? We do not know, but European history offers at least a few suggestions.[13]

In sharp contrast to this optimistic prediction concerning the fate of the new states of Africa and Asia are the views expressed by Deutsch in his most recent work on nationalism,[14] views which more closely approximate those expressed in his 1961 article. As in that article, and unlike the position he took in the still earlier *Nationalism and Social Communication,* Deutsch now treated assimilation and mobilization as two causally isolated processes.[15] The only relationship between the two that was discussed is chronological, i.e., the question of which antedates the other:

The decisive factor in such situations is the balance between the two processes that we have been discussing. If assimilation stays ahead of mobilization or keeps abreast of it, the government is likely to remain stable, and eventually everybody will be integrated into one people. . . . On the other hand, where mobilization is fast and assimilation is slow the opposite happens.[16]

Although this position echoed that expressed by Deutsch in 1961,[17] he no longer contended that the logical consequences of this analysis could be avoided by increasing state services and benefits. The result is a note of pessimism not detected in his 1961 analysis, and one that seems to be diametrically opposed to his unequivocal optimism of 1963:

> We have seen that the more gradually the process of social mobilization moves, the more time there is for social and national assimilation to work. Conversely, the more social mobilization is postponed, the more quickly its various aspects—language, monetization, mass audience, literacy, voting, urbanization, industrialization—must eventually be achieved. But when all of these developments have to be crowded into the lifetime of one or two generations, the chances for assimilation to work are much smaller. The likelihood is much greater that people will be precipitated into politics with their old languages, their old outlook on the world and their old tribal loyalties still largely unchanged; and it becomes far more difficult to have them think of themselves as members of one new nation. It took centuries to make Englishmen and Frenchmen. How are variegated tribal groups to become Tanzanians, Zambians, or Malavians in one generation?[18]

If Deutsch's most recent analysis of the interrelationship between social mobilization and assimilation is accepted, that is, if it is granted that the connection between the two is in no way causal but purely chronological, then it is difficult to perceive what predictive value the concept of social mobilization holds for the "nation-builder." To say, "if assimilation stays ahead of mobilization or keeps abreast of it . . . eventually everybody will be integrated into one people" is in fact to say very little. If assimilation progresses, then clearly assimilation will be achieved.[19] And to add, as Deutsch does, "where mobilization is fast and assimilation is slow, the opposite happens," is not to furnish the state planner with a guide for action, but is to deny that the matter is subjectable to social engineering. If assimilation, in those cases where and when it can be achieved, is a lengthy process requiring generations, and if Professor Deutsch is not recommending that the states of the third world be immunized from modernization (and in the preceding quotation he states that such an immunization is impossible), then what is left is the conclusion that where assimilation has not yet been achieved, it is highly unlikely to be.

Professor Deutsch's most recent book therefore provides no brief for those who assume that ethnicity will wane as modernization progresses. The opposite is the case. On the other hand, some of his earlier comments, and particularly those in which he propounded four stages of assimilative growth, could indeed by cited as supporting this school of thought. Regardless of the interpretation one places upon Deutsch, however, the doctrine that modernization dissolves ethnic loyalties can be challenged on purely empirical grounds.

If the processes that comprise modernization led to a lessening of ethnic consciousness in favor of identification with the state, then the number of states troubled by ethnic disharmony would be on the decrease. To the contrary, however, a global survey illustrates that ethnic consciousness is definitely in the ascendency as a political force, and that state borders, as presently delimited, are being increasingly challenged by this trend.[20] And, what is of greater significance, multiethnic states at all levels of modernity have been afflicted. Particularly instructive in this regard is the large proportion of states within the technologically and economically advanced region of Western Europe that have recently been troubled by ethnic unrest. Examples include (1) the problems of Spain with the anti-Castilian activities of the Basques, the Catalans, and on a lesser level, the Galicians; (2) the animosity indicated by the Swiss toward foreign migrant workers, and the demands of the French-speaking peoples of Berne for political separation from the German-speaking element; (3) the South Tyroleans' dissatisfaction with Italian rule, currently muffled by recent concessions on the part of the Italian Government; (4) evidence of Breton unhappiness with continued French rule; (5) the resurgence of Scottish and Welsh nationalism, the conflict in Northern Ireland, and the wide-scale popularity of anti-immigrant sentiments epitomized in the figure of Enoch Powell—all within the United Kingdom; and (6) the bitter rivalry of the Walloon and Flemish peoples within Belgium. Outside of Europe, the challenge to the concept of a single Canada represented by the Franco-Canadian movements, and the existence of black separatist movements within the United States also bear testimony that even the combination of a lengthy history as a state and a high degree of technological and economic integration does not guarantee immunity against ethnic particularism.

That social mobilization need not lead to a transfer of primary allegiance from the ethnic group to the state is therefore clear. Can we go beyond this to posit an inverse correlation between modernization and the level of ethnic dissonance within multiethnic states? Admittedly, there is a danger of countering the assumption that the processes of modernization lead to cultural assimilation with an opposing iron law of political disintegration which contends that modernization results, of necessity, in increasing demands for ethnic separation. We still do not have sufficient data to justify such an unequivocal contention. Nonetheless, the substantial body of data which is available supports the proposition that material increases in what Deutsch termed social communication and mobilization *tend* to increase cultural awareness and to exacerbate interethnic conflict. Again, the large and growing number of ethnic separatist movements can be cited for substantiation.

There are many statesmen and scholars, however, who would protest this macroanalytical approach because the data cited for support contain a number of former colonies. The inclusion of former dependencies in a list purporting to substantiate a correlation between modernization and ethnicity is improper, they would contend, because ethnic consciousness was deliberately kept alive and encouraged by the colonial overseers as an element in a policy of divide-and-rule. The prevalence of ethnic consciousness and antagonism in these territories is therefore held to be the product of the artificial stimuli of colonial policy. Otherwise, ethnicity would not constitute a serious problem for the new states.

The validity of such a conviction can be tested by contrasting the experience of former colonies with that of industrially retarded, multiethnic states that did not undergo a significant period as a colony. No important distinctions are discernible on this basis. Consider, for example, the cases of Ethiopia and Thailand, both of which have enjoyed very lengthy histories as independent states.[21] Diverse ethnic elements were able to coexist for a lengthy period within each of these states because the states were poorly integrated, and the ethnic minorities therefore had little contact, with either their (mostly theoretic) state-governments or with each other. Until very recent times, then, the situation of the minorities was not unlike the situation of ethnic groups within colonies where the colonial power practiced that very common colonial policy of ruling through the leadership of the various ethnic groups. In all such cases, the conflict between alien rule and the ethnic group's determination to preserve its lifeways was minimized. The governments of these underdeveloped states may well have long desired to make their rule effective throughout their entire territory, but advances in communications and transportation were necessary before a governmental presence could become a pervasive reality in the remote territories of the minorities.

As a result of this new presence, resentment of foreign rule has become an important political force for the first time. In addition, quite aside from the question of who rules, there is the matter of cultural self-preservation. An unintegrated state poses no serious threat to the lifeways of the various ethnic groups. But improvements in the quality and quantity of communication and transportation media progressively curtail the cultural isolation in which an ethnic group could formerly cloak its cultural chasteness from the perverting influences of other cultures within the same state. The reaction to such curtailment is very apt to be one of xenophobic hostility.

Advances in communications and transportation tend also to increase the cultural awareness of the minorities by making their members more aware of the distinctions between themselves and others. The impact is twofold. Not only does the individual become more aware of alien ethnic groups; he also becomes more aware of those who share his identity. Thus, the transistor radio has not only made the formerly isolated, Lao-speaking villager of northeast Thailand aware of linguistic and other cultural distinctions between himself and the politically dominant Siamese-speaking element to the west; it has also made him much more aware of his cultural affinity with the Lao who live in other villages throughout northeast Thailand and across the Mekong River is western Laos.[22] Intraethnic as well as interethnic communications thus play a major role in the creating of ethnic consciousness.

As an end result of these processes, Thailand is today faced with separatist movements on the part of the hill tribes in the north, the Lao in the northeast, and the Malays in the south.[23] Similarly, as a result of growing cultural self-awareness by minorities and an increasing presence of the central government, the state of Ethiopia, despite its three-thousand-year history, is also currently faced with a number of ethnic separatist movements.[24] Other underdeveloped, multiethnic states without a history of colonialism indicate a similar pattern.[25] The colonial and noncolonial patterns are not significantly different.

Another challenge to the contention that modernization tends to exacerbate ethnic tensions may also be anticipated. As was noted earlier, the recent upsurge in ethnic conflict within the more industrialized, multiethnic states of Europe and North America seriously challenges the contention that modernization dissipates ethnic consciousness. But does not this upsurge also run counter to the assertion that modernization increases ethnic consciousness? Given the fact that the Industrial Revolution was introduced into each of these states more than a century ago, should not the high-tide mark of ethnic consciousness have appeared long ago? Part of the answer may be found in what Marxists term "The Law of the Transformation of Quantity into Quality," a paraphrase of which might read "enough of a quantitative difference makes a qualitative difference." The processes of modernization prior to World War II did not necessitate or bring about the same measure of international contact as have developments in the postwar period. With fewer and poorer roads, far fewer and less efficient private cars, local radio rather than state-wide television as the primary channel of non-written mass communications, lower levels of education and of knowledge of events beyond one's own experience, and lower general income levels that kept people close to home, ethnic complacency could be maintained: Brittany's culture appeared safe from French encroachment, Edinburgh felt remote and isolated from London, most Walloons and Flems seldom came into contact (including artificial contact through media such as television) with members of the other group. In short, the situation of ethnic groups within these states was not totally dissimilar from that which was described earlier with regard to non-industrialized societies.[26] The difference was only one of degree until that point was reached at which a qualitative change occurred. However, the point at which a significant number of people perceived that the cumulative impact of the quantitative increases in the intensity of intergroup contacts now constituted a threat to their ethnicity represented, in political terms, a qualitative transformation.

Perhaps an even more important factor in explaining the recent upsurge of militant ethnic consciousness in advanced as well as less advanced states involves not the nature or density of the communications media, but the message. Although the expression "self-determination of nations" can be traced to 1865,[27] it did not receive great attention until its endorsement by a number of world-renowned statesmen during the World War I era. Moreover, by their failure, after the war, to apply this doctrine to the multiethnic empires of Belgium, Britain, France, the Netherlands, Portugal, and Spain, the statesmen indicated that they did not consider self-determination an axiom of universal validity. Not until after World War II was the doctrine officially endorsed by an organization aspiring to global jurisdiction.[28] It is therefore of very recent vintage. But despite its short history, it has been widely publicized and elevated to the status of a self-evident truth. Today, lip service is paid to it by political leaders of the most diverse persuasions. Admittedly, the doctrine has often been misapplied, having been regularly invoked in support of all movements aimed at dissolving a political allegiance, regardless of the basis for secession. But in its pristine form, the doctrine makes ethnicity the ultimate measure of political legitimacy, by holding that any self-differentiating people, simply because it *is* a people, has the right, should it so desire, to rule itself. In recent years, with its wide acceptance as a universal truth, the doctrine has induced minorities in Europe and North America, as well as in Africa, Asia, and Latin America, to question the validity of present political borders. It has therefore been more than a justification for ethnic movements: it has been a catalyst for them. The spreading of effective communications has had an evident impact upon ethnic consciousness, but the full impact of the communications media did not precede the message of self-determination.

Still another element contributing to the upsurge in ethnic consciousness is the evident change in the global political environment, which makes it much more unlikely that a militarily weak polity will be annexed by a larger power. During the age of colonialism, the probability of that eventuality was sometimes so great as to encourage independent units to seek the status of a protectorate in order to be able to select rule by the lesser evil. By contrast, a number of relatively recent developments, including what is termed the nuclear stalemate, cause independence to appear as a more enduring prospect for even the weakest of units. Thus, a favorable environment, the generating and justifying principle of self-determination, an expanding list of successful precedents, and a growing awareness of all these factors because of increased communications, are all involved.

A summary of our findings thus far would consist of the following points. The preponderant number of states are multiethnic. Ethnic consciousness has been definitely increasing, not decreasing, in recent years. No particular classification of multiethnic states has proven immune to the fissiparous impact of ethnicity: authoritarian and democratic; federative and unitary; Asian, African, American, and European states have all been afflicted. Form of government and geography have clearly not been determinative. Nor has the level of economic development. But the accompaniments of economic development—increased social mobilization and communication—appear to have increased ethnic tensions and to be conducive to separatist demands. Despite all this, leading theoreticians of "nation-building" have tended to ignore or slight the problems associated with ethnicity.

If we turn to an analysis of the reasons for this wide gap between theory and reality, twelve overlapping and interrelated possibilities offer themselves.

(1) Confusing Interutilization of the Key Terms, Nation and State:

It may appear whimsical to begin with the often picayune matter of semantics. It is very doubtful, however, that any discipline has been more plagued by the improper utilization of its key terms than has international relations. Anthropologists often bemoan the nebulosity underlying the concept of race—an ambiguity which has been reflected in many unscientific theories, which, in turn, have required time-consuming repudiations. But, though the concept of race is a matter of great significance to anthropology, it is not the key concept, that being *man.* By contrast, the concept of the state and of man's relationship to the state are at the heart of international relations. Yet, despite their key roles, both of these concepts are shrouded in ambiguity because of careless use of terms.

Consider first the concept of the state and the manner in which it is commonly treated as synonymous with the vastly different concept of the nation. The League of Nations, the United Nations, and, indeed, the expression *international relations* are but a few of the many available illustrations of the fact that statesmen and scholars are inclined to the indiscriminate interuse of the two concepts.[29] Why this confusion in terminology has been perpetuated is difficult to explain, for authorities are certainly well aware of the distinctions between the state and the nation. Thus, a dictionary designed for the student of global politics defines the state as "a legal concept describing a social group that occupies a defined territory and is organized under common political institutions and an effective government."[30] By contrast, a nation is defined as "a social group which shares a common ideology, common institutions and customs, and a sense of homogeneity." It carefully adds: "A nation may comprise part of a state, be coterminous with a state, or extend beyond the borders of a single state." Writers of textbooks and monographs in international relations generally also detail these same distinctions between state and nation. Unfortunately, however, these same writers are then apt to revert to the indiscriminate interutilization of the two terms.[31]

It is probable that the tendency to equate the two expressions developed as alternative shorthand substitutes for the hyphenate, *nation-state*. This term is also supposed to have a precise meaning, referring to a situation in which the borders of the nation approximate those of the state. We have noted that, technically speaking, less than 10 per cent of all states would qualify as essentially homogeneous. But authorities nevertheless tend to refer to all states as nation-states.[32]

The confusion wrought by the misuse of these terms has long hampered the study of many aspects of interstate relations, but it has especially impeded the understanding of nationalism. More particularly, loyalty to the nation has often been confused with loyalty to the state. Again, this confusion has been reflected in, and largely caused by, inappropriate terminology.

The definitions of state and nation quoted above make clear that what we have thus far been calling self-differentiating ethnic groups are in fact nations. Loyalty to the ethnic group, therefore, should logically be called nationalism. But nationalism, as commonly employed, refers to loyalty to the state (or to the word *nation,* when the latter has been incorrectly substituted for state).[33] Thus, the same dictionary whose precise definitions of state and nation we have just cited defines *nationalism* as a mass emotion that "makes the *state* the ultimate focus of the individual's loyalty." (Emphasis added.) With the term *nationalism* thus preempted, scholars have felt compelled to offer a substitute to describe loyalty to the nation. Regionalism, parochialism, primordialism, communalism, ethnic complementarity, and tribalism are among those that have been advanced. Unfortunately, however, the perpetuation of the improper use of the word *nationalism* to refer to devotion to the state, while using other terms with different roots and with fundamentally different connotations to denote devotion to the nation, is hardly conducive to dissolving the confusion surrounding the two loyalties.[34] On the contrary, it is conducive to dangerously underestimating the magnetism and the staying power of ethnic identity, for those terms simply do not convey the aura of deeply felt, emotional commitment that *nationalism* does. Every schoolboy is made aware, for example, that the German and Celtic tribes of antiquity became obliterated in a higher identity; that regionalism within the United States or Germany has steadily receded in significance. By contrast with these vanquished forces, the schoolboy learns that nationalism is a vibrant force that has largely shaped the direction of global politics for the past two hundred years. But since *nationalism* is equated with loyalty to the state, the student has been preconditioned to perceive the state as the certain ultimate victor in any test of loyalties with these lower-form anachronisms that have been proven to be ephemeral.

If the nation-state were in fact the universal form of polity, the confusion would not be important. In those cases in which the nation and the state essentially coincide, the two loyalties mesh rather than compete. A common pitfall of scholarship, however, has been to equate the resulting emotional attachment to a nation-state with loyalty to the state alone. The study of nationalism in the late twentieth century has been heavily influenced by the experiences of Germany and Japan, perceived as illustrations of the extreme dedication that nationalism is able to evoke. The implication is that other states have the potential for evoking the same type of mass response, though, it is to be hoped, in a less fanatical form. Largely ignored is the fact that these two states are among the very few that are ethnically homogeneous.[35] As such, *Deutschland* and *Nippon* have been something far more profound to their populations than mere territorial-political units called states; they have been ethno-psychological inclinations called nations. To perceive German or Japanese nationalism as loyalty to the state is to miss the mark badly. It is also to distort beyond recognition the power to evoke loyalty to the state in the absence of a linking of state and nation in the popular psyche. With that linkage, the leaders can voice their appeals in terms of the state (*Deutschland*) or the nation (*volksdeutsch, Volkstum, Volksgenosse*), because the two trigger the same associations. The same is true for members of the politically dominant group in some multiethnic states. Thus, the Han Chinese are apt to view the state of China as the state of their particular nation, and are therefore susceptible to appeals either in the name of China or in the name of the Han Chinese people. But the notion of *China* evokes quite different associations, and therefore quite different responses, from Tibetans, Mongols, Uighurs, and other non-Han people. The confusing use of terminology has diverted scholars for some time from asking the key question: How many examples come to mind of a strong "state-nationalism" being manifested among a people who perceive their state and their nation as distinct entities?

The likelihood of contemporary scholars being diverted from the posing of this question would have been greatly reduced had the misnomer, "nation-building," not been adopted. Since most of the less developed states contain a number of nations, and since the transfer of primary allegiance from these nations to the state is generally considered the *sine qua non* of successful integration, the true goal is not "nation-building" but "nation-destroying." Would scholars have been less sanguine concerning the chances of success if proper terminology had been employed? Certainly they would have been less likely to ignore, or to dismiss lightly, the problem of ethnic identity, the true nationalism.[36]

(2) A Misunderstanding of the Nature of Ethnic Nationalism and a Resulting Tendency to Underrate its Emotional Power:

In its broadest implications, this reason for the failure of authorities to pay proper heed to ethnicity is the end product of all other reasons. If so understood, it is a statement of the problem rather than an explanation. However, as used here, it is intended to point to the tendency of scholars to perceive ethnic nationalism in terms of its overt manifestations rather than in terms of its essence. The essence of the nation is not tangible. It is psychological, a matter of attitude rather than of fact.

In accordance with an earlier quoted definition, we can describe the nation as a self-differentiating ethnic group. A prerequisite of nationhood is a popularly held awareness or belief that one's own group is unique in a most vital sense. In the absence of such a popularly held conviction, there is only an ethnic group. A distinct group may be very apparent to the anthropologist or even to the untrained observer, but without a realization of this fact on the part of a sizable percentage of its members, a nation does not exist.

Because the essence of the nation is a matter of attitude, the tangible manifestations of cultural distinctiveness are significant only to the degree that they contribute to the *sense* of uniqueness. Indeed, a sense of vital uniqueness can come about even in the absence of important, tangible cultural characteristics of a distinctive nature, as evidenced by the ethnopsychological experience of the American colonists, the Afrikaners, and the Taiwanese with regard to their former British, Dutch, and Han Chinese identities. Conversely, the concept of a single nation can transcend tangible cultural distinctions, such as the Catholic-Lutheran division within the German nation.[37]

Any nation can, of course, be described in terms of its particular amalgam of tangible characteristics, for example, in terms of the number of its members, their physical location, their religious and linguistic composition, and so forth. But one can so describe any human grouping, even such an unimportant categorization as the New Englander. By intuitively valuing that which they have in common with other Americans more than that which makes them unique, the New Englanders have self-relegated themselves to the status of a subnational element. By contrast, the Ibos clearly place greater importance on being Ibo than on being Nigerian. It is, therefore, the self-view of one's group, rather than the tangible characteristics, that is of essence in determining the existence or non-existence of a nation.

The abstract essence of ethnic nationalism is often not perceived by the observer. There is an understandable propensity, when investigating a case of ethnic discord, to perceive the struggle in terms of its more readily discernible features. Thus, Ukrainian unrest is popularly reported as an attempt to preserve the Ukrainian language against Russian inroads; Belgium's major problem is also viewed as essentially linguistic; the Ethiopian-Eritrean, as well as the Northern Ireland conflict, is seen as religious; the Czecho-Slovak, the West Pakistani-Bengali, and the Serbo-Croatian disputes are characterized as essentially matters of economic differentiation. Linguistic, religious, and economic distinctions between peoples are all easily discerned and, what is of at least equal moment, are easily conveyed to one's audience.

This propensity to perceive an ethnic division in terms of the more tangible differences between the groups is often supported by the statements and actions of those most involved. In their desire to assert their uniqueness, members of a group are apt to make rallying points of their more tangible and distinguishing institutions. Thus, the Ukrainians, as a method of asserting their non-Russian identity, wage their campaign for national survival largely in terms of their right to employ the Ukrainian, rather than the Russian, tongue in all oral and written matters. But would not the Ukrainian nation (that is, a popular consciousness of being Ukrainian) be likely to persist even if the language were totally replaced by Russian, just as the Irish nation has persisted after the virtual disappearance of Gaelic, despite pre-1920 slogans that described Gaelic and Irish identity as inseparable?[38] Is the language the essential element of the Ukrainian nation, or is it merely a minor element which has been elevated to *the symbol* of the nation in its struggle for continued viability? National identity may survive substantial alterations in language, religion, economic status, or any other tangible manifestation of its culture. Nevertheless, not only do those involved in an ethnic dispute tend to express their own national consciousness in terms of tangible symbols, but they also tend to express their aversion to the other nation in terms of ostensibly readily identifiable attributes. Seldom will a person acknowledge that he dislikes a member of another group simply because the latter is Chinese, Jewish, Ibo, Afro-American, Italian, or what have you. There is a very common compulsion to express what are fundamentally emotional responses to foreign stimuli (prejudices) in more "rational" terms. "They" are inclined to laziness (or aggressiveness), crime, having too many children, and, if a minority, to disloyalty. "They" are prejudiced toward us, haughty in their dealings, disparaging of our culture, determined to take unfair economic advantage, intent on forcing their culture and standards upon us, and relegating us to an inferior status.[39] Employment, crime, birth, income, emigration, life-expectancy, and bilingual statistics of varying reliability and applicability are among the data commonly advanced as tangible evidence of such allegations. Thus is the "idea" made flesh.

As a result of the tendency for both participant and reporter to describe ethno-psychological phenomena in terms of tangible considerations, the true nature and power of ethnic feelings are not probed. Indeed, in many cases analysts fail to realize they are dealing with ethnic nationalism. Northern Ireland offers a contemporary case in point.

Strife in the northern six counties of Ireland has been treated almost exclusively as a religious conflict, a quaint echo of the intranational religious wars of a bygone age that saw Frenchmen pitted against Frenchmen, German against German, and so forth. To the degree that Northern Ireland's problem has not been viewed as religious, it has been treated as a civil rights struggle for political and economic reform. In fact, it is neither in its essence; rather, it is a struggle predicated upon fundamental differences in national identity. Contrary to the typical account, the people of Northern Ireland do not uniformly consider themselves Irish.[40] Indeed, a survey, conducted in 1968 by representatives of the University of Strathclyde, indicates that a majority do not. Although 43 per cent of the respondents thought of themselves as being Irish, 29 per cent considered themselves to be British, 21 per cent Ulster, and the remaining 7 per cent considered themselves to be of mixed, other, or uncertain nationality.[41]

Unfortunately, the survey failed to correlate national identity with the religion of the respondents, but it is safe to assume, on the basis of the ethnic and religious histories of the island, that there exists a close correlation between self-identification as Irish and adherents to Catholicism.[42] The important distinction, however, lies between those who consider themselves Irish, and those who either do not so consider themselves or are not so considered by the bulk of the Irish element. That the religious issue is largely extraneous helps to account for the fact that the consistent urging of tolerance by all but a handful of religious leaders has gone unheeded.[43] Indeed, with at least as much accuracy, the conflict could be described as one of surnames rather than religions. Despite some intermarriage, the family name remains a relatively reliable index to Irish heritage, as compared to English or Scottish.[44] It is for this reason that a surname is apt to trigger either a negative or positive response. One tragic manifestation of this phenomenon has been the tendency of militant Irishmen (described as Catholics) to be particularly aggressive toward Scottish units of the British forces sent from the island of Great Britain, because of the preponderance of Scottish names among Northern Ireland's non-Irish population.[45] In popular Irish perception, their local enemies and the Scottish troops are linked in their common foreignness and Scottishness.

To the knowledge of this writer, there has been only one account of the strife in Northern Ireland that has placed it in its proper context:

> In Ulster, especially, much of the tension dates to the 17th century. After yet another round of fighting the Irish Catholics, the British encouraged Englishmen and Scotsmen to settle in Northern Ireland and tame the natives. The native Catholics have hated these invading Protestants ever since—not only as Protestants but also as outsiders with different customs and greater privileges. Then as now, the friction was as much social as religious.[46]

If one substitutes *ethnic* or *nationalistic* for *social* in the last sentence, one will perceive that the conflict in Northern Ireland is not very distinct in its primary cause from the struggle between Flem and Walloon in Belgium, between *les Anglais* and *les Canadiens* in Canada, Lao and Thai in Thailand, Ibo and Hausa in Nigeria, or "Asian" and "African" in Guyana. But how different is the image of the nature, depth, and intractibility of Northern Ireland's problem raised by this analysis from the image raised by C. L. Sulzberger's statement that "they are all Irish and therefore love a fight: formidable men and easily stirred to passion. . . . All Irish, whether they favor Green or Orange, enjoy a fight."[47]

In summary, ethnic strife is too often superficially discerned as principally predicated upon language, religion, customs, economic inequity, or some other tangible element. But what is fundamentally involved in such a conflict is that divergence of basic identity which manifests itself in the "us–them" syndrome. And the ultimate answer to the question of whether a person is one of us, or one of them, seldom hinges on adherence to overt aspects of culture. This issue has been at the core of the Israeli Government's long and still unsuccessful attempt to define a Jew. For political and legal purposes, the government may demand adherence to one of the denominations of the Judaic faith as a test of Jewishness. But, as the government is well aware, there are many self-proclaimed agnostics, atheists, and converts to other faiths who are, in the most thorough and psychologically profound sense of the word, Jewish. And there are practicing members of the Judaic faith who are not ethnically Jewish. The Judaic faith has, of course, been an important element of Jewish nationalism, as, to a lesser degree, Catholicism and Irish nationalism are related. But an individual (or an entire national group) can shed all of the overt cultural manifestations customarily attributed to his ethnic group and yet maintain his fundamental identity as a member of that nation. Cultural assimilation need not mean psychological assimilation.

(3) An Unwarranted Exaggeration of the Influence of Materialism upon Human Affairs:

A number of authorities have noted a propensity on the part of American statesmen and scholars of the post-World War II era to assume that economic considerations represent the determining force in human affairs. Programs of foreign assistance, for example, have been promoted and defended on the ground that the economic status of a state correlates directly with its form of government, political stability, and aggressiveness.[48] Policy-makers in the United States have also attempted to defuse a number of highly charged interstate (and interethnic) conflicts by making cooperation between the adversaries a condition of material recompense (for example, the Jordan, Indus, and Mekong River projects). The Marshall Plan, Point Four, the Eisenhower Doctrine, and the Alliance for Progress could all be interpreted as attempts to alter attitudes by appealing to material self-interest.

This presumption—that economic considerations constitute the primary force which shapes the basic ideas and attitudes of man—has had an evident impact upon much of the literature concerned with political integration. An ethnic minority, it is implicitly or explicitly held, will not secede from a state if its living standards are improving, both in real terms and relative to other segments of the state's population.[49] Such a prognosis again underestimates the power of ethnic feelings and ignores contrary evidence: With regard to the matter of economic inequity among groups, for example, there are a number of cases in which the ethnic consciousness of a minority and its animosity toward the dominant element became accentuated although the income gap between the group and the dominant element was being rapidly closed. The Flemish of Belgium and the Slovaks of Czechoslovakia are cases in point.[50] Indeed, there are even cases in which separatist movements exist despite the fact that the group from which they emanate is more advanced economically than is the politically dominant element. The Croatians and Slovenes of Yugoslavia and the Basques and Catalans of Spain exemplify this situation. As to the matter of real rather than comparative economic status, we have noted earlier that multiethnic states at all economic levels have been troubled by growing ethnic discord. Economic considerations may be an irritant that reinforces ethnic consciousness. And, as noted, those most involved in the conflict may present the issue in economic terms. But economic factors are likely to come in a poor second when competing with the emotionalism of ethnic nationalism. Numerous colonial ties were severed irrespective of whether or not they were economically beneficial to the colonial people. Separatists (whether Anguillan, Eritrean, Naga, or Welsh) are not apt to be dissuaded by the assertion that the nation is too small to comprise an economically viable unit. There is a simple, yet profound message of the broadest applicability in the slogan, "Better a government run like hell by Filipinos than one run like heaven by Americans."

(4) Unquestioned Acceptance of the Assumption that Greater Contacts among Groups Lead to Greater Awareness of what Groups Have in Common, rather than of what Makes Them Distinct:

A number of authorities have also noted that American foreign policy is heavily influenced by an optimistic view of human affairs in which man is seen as essentially rational and possessed of good will, and therefore preordained to find reasonable answers to problems.[51] As applied to ethnicity, this optimism is manifest in the conviction that misunderstandings among nations are due to lack of knowledge concerning each other. Greater contacts, it would follow, should lead to greater understanding and harmony. One manifestation of this belief is the person-to-person diplomacy that forms the rationale of the Peace Corps and official sanctioning of massive cultural and educational exchange programs. It is also evident in the lack of official concern that the presence of large numbers of Americans in a foreign state is apt to trigger a xenophobic response.[52] This view also probably helps to account for the slighting of ethnicity in works dealing with political integration. If greater contacts, brought about by more intensive communication and transportation networks, promote harmony, ethnic heterogeneity is not a matter worthy of serious consideration.

We have noted, however, that the contacts occasioned by modernization have in fact had the opposite tendency. The optimistic position fails to consider that, while the idea of being friends presupposes knowledge of each other, so does the idea of being rivals. Indeed, the self-awareness which is the *sine qua non* of the nation requires knowledge of non-members. The conception of being unique or different requires a referent, that is, the idea of "us" requires "them." Minimally, it may be asserted that increasing awareness of a second group is not certain to promote harmony, and is at least as likely to produce, on balance, a negative response. With an empirical eye to the evidence of growing ethnic consciousness and discord, we can add that the latter is much more likely.

(5) Improper Analogizing from the Experience of the United States:

Many works on political integration contain direct reference to the successful assimilationist history of the United States as evidence that the basic identity of people can be rather easily transferred from the ethnic group to a larger grouping coterminous with the state.[53] It is probable, moreover, that the "melting pot" idea has had an unarticulated influence upon much larger numbers. If broad-scale assimilation could occur within the United States, practically without design, why not elsewhere? If an extremely diverse ethnic hodgepodge became quite naturally a single American nation, one may well expect the same process to occur quite naturally elsewhere. The analogy is a dangerous one, however.

A denial of the pertinence of the American experience does *not* rest upon the recent surge of interest in ethnic matters within the United States. There has been a recent spate of monographs and articles clearly documenting that the melting process has not yet caught up with the myth, and that pre-American national heritage remains an important index to neighborhood, voting patterns, associations, and so forth.[54] Moreover, large numbers of people within the United States who formerly played down their pre-American heritage have recently been demonstrating a new pride in it. But these facts are not necessarily germane to the study of ethnic nationalism. Nor do they materially alter the fact that an impressively high level of assimilation has been achieved within the United States. Total melting has not yet occurred and may never occur, but it has made great strides and is progressing on a significant scale. In addition, even if the upsurge in ethnic pride should prove to be more than a vogue, it does not follow that the upsurge is a manifestation of ethnic nationalism. It was noted earlier that the concept of a single nation does not preclude internal divisions. Lesser "us—them" relationships can exist within a single nation, so long as in any test of allegiance the larger "us" of the nation proves more powerful than the divisive call of a particular region, religion, pre-American ethnic heritage, or whatever. There is nothing necessarily incompatible between stressing one's Italian or Polish cultural heritage and the American nation.

Black nationalism, by contrast, may directly challenge the larger "us" of the American nation. Although many diverse attitudes and goals are cloaked under the single rubric of black nationalism, an essential element is its insistence that what has hitherto been known as the American nation has in fact been a white nation. In refusing to identify with the American nation, and in postulating a rival black nation, black nationalism constitutes a nationalism in the most correct sense of the word.[55] This is so whether the nationalist advocates "two nations, one state" or actual political separation. Black nationalism is therefore a legitimate object of inquiry in the study of ethnicity as a global phenomenon. But, as noted, assimilation among white Americans is not an appropriate model for situations elsewhere.

The key factor that differentiates the process of assimilation in the United States is that the impetus for assimilation has come principally from the unassimilated, not from the dominant group. The typical non-African immigrant *voluntarily* left his cultural hearth and traveled a substantial distance, in both a physical and a psychological sense, to enter a different ethnopolitical environment which recognized no notable political or psychological relationship with his former homeland. Moreover, in any one generation, he and other immigrants of his particular ethnicity were few in number relative to the dominant, Anglo-Saxonized, American population. Although he may well have lived (and his descendants may still live) in an ethnic ghetto where his native language and customs lingered on, the ghetto was neither sufficiently large nor economically adequate to permit the fulfillment of his most ambitious aspirations, whether of an economic-, prestige-, or power-oriented nature. He was constantly aware of being part of a larger cultural entity that pervaded and shaped the ghetto in countless ways,[56] and he realized that cultural assimilation was necessary if the more obvious limits to his ambitions were to be pushed back. As a result of all this, ethnic problems within the United States have not been characterized primarily by the resistance of minorities to assimilation, but by the unwillingness or inability of the dominant group to permit assimilation at the rate desired by the unassimilated.

Elsewhere, the typical ethnic problem is reversed, with the pressure for assimilation popularly being viewed by the minority as originating with the dominant group. Consider the case of a French-Canadian living within the large, predominantly French Province of Quebec. He lives in an ethnic homeland, which has been continuously inhabited by Frenchmen since before the coming of *les Anglais* and which is laden with emotional overtones. English-speaking people and their culture are therefore seen as invaders, aliens in a French-Canadian land. Moreover, the French-Canadian community is sufficiently large to accommodate visionary success totally within the ethnic confines.[57] As a result, there is little to entice the individual to surrender his own culture, and much—in terms of the reinforcing quality of the forces and symbols of his environment—to cause him to resent and resist the intrusion of the outside culture. In contrast to the United States where assimilation has, on balance, been viewed by the minority as a voluntary act, anything that necessitates a degree of assimilation takes on an aura of either physical or psychological coercion.[58] The universality of this response has led to the rapid spread of the expression "cultural imperialism." And the response is self-generating, as it exacerbates ethnic sensibilities and causes what was considered innocent yesterday to be perceived as offensive today. Interethnic tensions are thereby magnified and the pale hopes of assimilation made still more dim.

In sum, then, analogies drawn from the experience of the United States are apt to be specious. A proportionately small number of people who have voluntarily left their cultural milieu to enter an alien politico-cultural environment in which cultural assimilation is perceived positively as indispensable to success is one thing; a situation characterized by two or more large groups, each ensconced in a territory it considers its traditional homeland and cultural preserve is something quite different. The second situation characterizes the overwhelming number of ethnic struggles.

(6) Improper Analogizing from the Fact that Increases in Communications and Transportation Help to Dissolve Cultural Distinctions among Regions within what Is Fundamentally a One-Culture State, to the Conclusion that the Same Process Will Occur in Situations Involving Two or More Distinct Cultures:

It is evident that increased contacts between regions of the United States have tended to weaken sectionalism. Country-wide media of communication (particularly television and motion pictures), the interregional movement of people, the geographic suffusion of industry and its products, and the increasing standardization of education have all tended to homogenize the United States. Among the more evident factors that attest to this trend are the fading of formerly clear election patterns along sectional lines (for instance, "the Solid South," or Republican northern New England) and the progressive elimination of sharp distinctions among local customs in matters such as dialect, humor, dress, and music. But if one is dealing not with variations of a single culture-group, but with distinct and self-differentiating culture groups, then increased contacts, as we have noted, tend to produce disharmony rather than harmony. Discord between the Basques and Castilians, the Czechs and Slovaks, the Russians and Ukrainians, the Walloons and Flemish, the Welsh and English, the French-speaking and English-speaking Canadians, and the Serbs and Croats has increased with increased contacts. The same development has been noted in the case of Thailand and of Ethiopia. Increased contacts tend to have one impact in a one-culture situation, and quite a different impact in a variegated culture area.[59]

(7) The Assumption that Assimilation is a One-Directional Process:

If assimilation is assumed to be irreversible, then any evidence of a move toward assimilation becomes an irrevocable gain and a basis for optimism. Thus, because the Scottish and Welsh people had undergone generations of acculturation, including almost total linguistic assimilation, and because the concept of a British national identity did indeed possess an important measure of meaning to the preponderant numbers of Scots and Welshmen, authorities were for years almost unanimous in their conviction that homogeneity of identity had once and for all been achieved.[60] The sudden upsurge in Scottish and Welsh nationalism during the 1960's illustrates, however, that assimilation may indeed by reversed so long as some glimmer of a separate ethnic identity persists.

(8) Interpretation of the Absence of Ethnic Strife as Evidence of the Presence of a Single Nation:

The existence of a single national consciousness that is shared by all segments of the population of a state *cannot* be deduced simply from the absence of overt ethnic conflict. Such a conclusion is always dangerous, for, just as the fervor with which ethnic nationalism is embraced and the form in which it is manifested can vary substantially among individuals, so too, can it fluctuate widely within a particular nation over time. Few would contend that German nationalism is dead, although it is obviously more subdued, and following different channels, than was the case in the 1930's. Periods in which nationalism takes on more passive forms may be followed by periods of militant nationalism and vice versa. In addition, the bilateral relations between ethnic groups, just as those between states, vary greatly. They may range along a continuum from a genocidal relationship to a symbiotic one. The fact that Canada and the United States have dwelt for generations alongside one another without warfare has not meant that they form a single state. So, too, the absence of hostilities between neighboring ethnic groups does not confirm a single trans-group identity. We have already noted that separate ethnic groups may coexist, at least for a time, within the same political structure. Influential factors include the degree of cultural self-awareness, the minority's perception of the nature and magnitude of the threat to the preservation of the group as a unique entity, and the reputation of the government for the relative ruthlessness with which it is apt to respond to "treasonable" acts. But coexistence—even when peaceful—should not be construed as proof of a single nation.

The error of misconstruing the absence of strife between ethnic groups as indicative of national unity has not been restricted to peaceful situations. Another common pitfall has been to impute a single national consciousness to militant movements whose ranks include members of different ethnic groups. Ethnic consciousness is not an automatic bar to cooperative, nor even to coordinated or integrated, activities against a mutually perceived enemy or in pursuit of a mutually desired goal. A number of ethnic groups can, and often do, march under the same banner and shout the same slogans. All too often, however, such a composite movement has been misidentified as a manifestation of a single, all-embracing nationalism. In the waning days of colonialism, for example, diverse segments of the population of British India were agreed upon the desirability of ridding the subcontinent of alien rule, and this movement for the eradication of British control was generally described as Indian nationalism (further subdivided into Indian and Moslem nationalism after 1930). It would have been more accurate to characterize the movement as a wartime alliance, similar in many respects to those entered into by states. Just as alliances among states tend to weaken as the threat recedes or the goal nears attainment, so too the period dating from the British announcement of intention to withdraw has been one of rather steady deterioration of the interethnic bonds within the successor states. Comparable multiethnic, anti-colonial movements exist today in a few remaining colonies, such as Angola and Mozambique. They also prevail in a number of post-colonial situations, as in Burma, northern Borneo, western New Guinea, and throughout the cordillera of Indochina. Any such multi-ethnic alliance is comprised of a number of national movements, but it is not itself coincidental with a single nation. The absence of ethnic discord between specified ethnic groups—whether manifested by passivity or by positive, cooperative action—cannot be assumed to be evidence of one national consciousness.

The tendency to see ethnic unity in the absence of overt ethnic discord has had an important impact upon theories of "nation-building." It helps to explain the very common habit of describing Western Europe as though it were composed of fully integrated states, which, as we have noted, most certainly is not the case. Western Europe is therefore held up as a model of something it is not, as proof that something can be achieved elsewhere that is in fact far from achieved there.[61] A second outgrowth of this tendency is to view outbreaks of ethnic nationalism on an *ad hoc* basis rather than as only one contemporary manifestation of a more enduring global phenomenon. An outbreak of ethnic hostilities in Malaysia, in Jamaica, in Burundi, in Spain, or in Canada is viewed as an isolated phenomenon, soon forgotten by most outside observers after a more peaceful relationship has been reinstituted. The ubiquity and significance of ethnic nationalism are therefore not fully appreciated.

(9) Improper Regard for the Factor of Chronological Time and Intervening Events When Analogizing from Assimilationist Experiences prior to "The Age of Nationalism":

In emphasizing the manner in which the nations of Western Europe and Eastern Asia were created from rather disparate ethnic materials, authorities have failed to consider that the fact that the models predate the nineteenth century may obviate their pertinence to the current scene. No examples of significant assimilation are offered which have taken place since the advent of the age of nationalism and the propagation of the principle of self-determination of nations.

By and large, those peoples who, prior to the nineteenth century, were seduced by the blandishments of another culture—those who became "them"—were not aware of belonging to a separate culture-group with its own proud traditions and myths. There was no keen competition for group allegiance. By contrast, peoples today are everywhere much more apt to be cognizant of their membership in a group with its own mythical genesis, its own customs and beliefs, and perhaps its own language, which *in toto* differentiate the group from all others and permit the typical individual to answer intuitively and unequivocally the question, "What are you?" The spontaneous response, "I am Luo" rather than Kenyan, or "Bengali" rather than Pakistani, does not bode well for the architect of a nation-state.

As we have noted, there are numerous reasons for this increase in ethnic consciousness since the early nineteenth century, among them the great increase in the frequency, scope, and type of interethnic and intraethnic group contacts. At least in terms of "assimilationist time" (the time required to produce full assimilation), the radio, telephone, train, motor vehicle, and aircraft are recent innovations, post-dating the advent of the age of nationalism and its standard of ethnicity as the basis of political legitimacy. As noted, there is little evidence of modern communications destroying ethnic consciousness, and much evidence of their augmenting it. The movement prior to the nineteenth century appears to have been toward assimilation into a number of larger nations, but since that time the movement appears to be toward the freezing of existing ethnic groups. Examples from the other side of the watershed must therefore be approached most cautiously.

(10) Improper Regard for Durative Time by Failing to Consider that Attempts to Telescope "Assimilationist Time," by Increasing the Frequency and Scope of Contacts, May Produce a Negative Response:

If the matter of chronological time could be overcome, there would remain the matter of durative time. As indicated by the resurgence of Scottish nationalism, the total assimilation of a large people predominating in a particular territory requires a period of long duration extending over several generations. To be successful, the process of assimilation must be a very gradual one, one that progresses almost without visibility and awareness.[62] Since the essence of national identity is psychological and involves self-acceptance, a greater intensity of contacts, whether by accident or design, will conceivably not only fail to speed up the process, but will prove to be counterproductive. By their very numbers, the Han Chinese furnish proof of being history's most successful assimilators; but the many people of riverine and coastal China were *sinified* only over many centuries. Programmed attempts since 1949 to speed up the process of sinifying the remaining minorities has led to increased ethnic consciousness and anti-Han resentment on the part of the minorities. So, too, the Soviet Union, despite more than a half-century of programmed assimilation, finds its "national question" not only unresolved but growing in intractability. Similarly, Franco's stepped-up attempt to eradicate Basque, Catalan, and Galician self-consciousness seems only to have magnified them. Rather than telescoping the process, more intensive contacts appear to generate a psychological rebuff. Variations in the tempo of contacts may determine whether a people moves slowly toward assimilation or rapidly toward ethnocentrism.

This relationship of assimilation to durative time casts serious doubt on whether the process of assimilation is subjectable to social engineering. Planning is more geared to action than to inaction, and more to a time span of one generation or less than to a multigenerational period. More important, however, is the fact that modernization largely dictates its own timetable. There is an inbuilt accelerator in the technological advances and other forces that causes a continuous "shrinking of the world" and the shrinking of its states as presently defined. The frequency and pervasiveness of intergroup contacts appear, therefore, to be fated to increase exponentially, regardless of the desire of the planner.

(11) Confusing Symptoms with Causes:

Most of the theoretic writings on political integration, as noted earlier, have been characterized by an unwarranted degree of optimism. But as the newly formed states proved less cohesive than had been anticipated, explanations for their political disintegration have become increasingly common. Many of these explanations, however, confuse some of the symptoms and minor contributing elements of political decay with its primary cause.

For example, a paper dealing with political decay in sub-Sahara Africa[63] lists among its causes, in addition to colonialism and neocolonialism, (a) exaggerated notions of the actual power of the centralized government, (b) the weakening of "mass parties," (c) the lessening of political mobilization, (d) the reduction of the links between the state government and segments of the population, (e) inability of the state to satisfy the perceived needs of its human components, (f) the loss of charismatic aura earlier enjoyed by the key figure, and (g) a "praetorian impulse." The question of primary loyalty and, more particularly, of ethnic identity, is not listed. And, clearly, those factors which are listed do not constitute causes, but either symptoms [(a), (b), (d), (e), (f)] or minor elements applicable to only a few specific situations [(c) and (g)]. A giant step toward identifying the primary cause would be made by asking *why* the power of the central government proved to be exaggerated, *why* the "mass" parties proved unstable, *why* the government was not able to forge solid links with all segments of the population, and *why* the father-figures could not retain their popularity.

The prime cause of political disunity is the absence of a single psychological focus shared by all segments of the population. Admittedly, ethnic homogeneity is not in itself sufficient to guarantee such a consensus. The intraethnic Vietnamese struggle illustrates this point. But in the case of the multiethnic state, we have noted that, for most of the inhabitants, primary identity will not extend beyond the ethnic group. And all but a handful of the new states are multiethnic.

To illustrate the importance of ethnic consciousness as a barrier to the political integration of the multiethnic state, let us return to the example at hand. Surely ethnic nationalism is the single most momentous political fact of sub-Sahara Africa, and the fundamental identity that it posits goes far toward answering the questions we have posed. Earlier estimates of the strength of the central governments proved exaggerated because the loyalty of the people seldom extended beyond their own ethnic group. Indeed, considering sub-Sahara's short, post-colonial history, a remarkably large number of states (more than one-third) have already experienced ethnic fragmentation in its most flagrant form of civil war along ethnic lines.[64] Similarly, in most states the mass party has been primarily a means of masking ethnic rivalry; identification of the individual with the party has been missing.[65] As to the father-figures, they have tended to retain their position in the eyes of those who see them as ethnic leaders. Kenyatta still possesses charisma for the Kikuyu; his problem is with the Luo and other non-Kikuyu who see him as one of "them."[66]

It bears repeating that ethnic homogeneity is not by itself sufficient to guarantee a bond of unity so infrangible that it can withstand any and all fissiparous forces. The impact of institutions, economic opportunities, geography, literacy, urbanization, and a host of other factors may therefore be very germane to the study of the components of an efficacious identity. But the experience of multi-ethnic states, past and present, strongly suggests that the ethnic nation may well constitute the outer limits or that identity. If there are means of transferring primary identification and allegiance from the nation to the state, or if there are ways of satisfying national aspirations within a multiethnic state, these possibilities should certainly be explored. But the potent fissiparous force of ethnic particularism should not be obscured by ascribing its role of prime mover to its symptoms.

(12) The Predispositions of the Analyst:

The last in this list of possible contributing factors to the broadscale underassessment of the ramifications of ethnic nationalism is the most difficult to document: it involves the influence that the ideals of the analyst exert upon his perception. Given the multitude of overt manifestations of ethnic nationalism throughout Africa and Asia (as well as elsewhere), it is difficult to reconcile its total absence or cursory treatment in so many studies on development. Even *in toto,* the preceding eleven considerations do not satisfactorily account for this failure to recognize the significance of the ethnic factor. Eventually it is difficult to avoid the conclusion that the predispositions of the analyst are also involved; that the "nation-builder" passionately wishes the people of his academic purview well; that he is convinced that their ultimate well-being is tied to the vehicle of the state as presently constituted; and that his compassion has colored his perception so that he perceives those trends that he deems desirable as actually occurring, regardless of the factual situation. If the fact of ethnic nationalism is not compatible with his vision, it can thus be willed away. A related factor is the fear that ethnic nationalism will feed on publicity. In either case, the treatment calls for total disregard or cavalier dismissal of the undesired facts. Such an approach can be justified for the policy-maker, but not for the scholar.

NOTES

This article is an expanded version of a paper presented at the Seventh World Congress of the International Sociological Association, held at Varna, Bulgaria, in September, 1970.
  1. A representative sampling of the literature on integration theory might well include the following titles: (1) Gabriel Almond and James S. Coleman, *The Politics of Developing Areas* (Princeton 1960); (2) Gabriel Almond and G. Bingham Powell, *Comparative Politics: A Developmental Approach* (Boston 1966); (3) Gabriel Almond and Sidney Verba, *The Civic Culture* (Boston 1963); (4) David Apter, *The Politics of Modernization* (Chicago 1965); (5) Willard A. Beling and George O. Totten, eds., *Developing Nations: Quest for a Model* (New York 1970); (6) Karl W. Deutsch and William Foltz, eds., *Nation-Building* (New York 1966); (7) Jason Finkle and Richard Gable, eds., *Political Development and Social Change* (New York 1966); (8) Philip E. Jacob and James V. Toscano, eds., *The*

Integration of Political Communities (Philadelphia 1964); (9) Lucian Pye, ed., *Communications and Political Development* (Princeton 1963); and (10) Lucian Pye, *Aspects of Political Development* (Boston 1966). The inclusion of five readers on the list, with an aggregate of well over fifty separate contributions, substantially broadens the sample.

None of these ten works dedicates a section, chapter, or major subheading to the matter of ethnic diversity. By contrast, the roles of the military, the bureaucracy, social classes, personality, industrialization, urbanization, and transaction flow and other modes of communication are common entries in tables of contents. In instances in which the tables of contents contain categories that might be expected to include a serious discourse on the ramifications of ethnicity—categories such as "Internal Legitimacy" or "National Identity" —further investigation proved unrewarding.

The slighting of ethnicity is further evidenced by the indices. Six of the ten show not a single reference to ethnic groups, ethnicity, or minorities. Two make a single passing reference to ethnicity, and still another accords to all types of minorities less than two pages, limiting the discussion to their impact upon democracy. The tenth work, a collection of papers, represents only a partial exception. Discussion of the impediments that ethnicity, *per se*, poses to state-integration is limited to general comments in an introductory essay. Moreover, in this essay the author assumes that the matter is one of relatively short duration, in line with the second tendency described in this paper's introductory sentence.

It should be acknowledged that readers dealing with "nation-building" are apt to contain a few regional or country studies whose authors are well aware of the fissiparous impact of ethnic diversity therein. (In one of the above works, for example, a contribution on sub-Sahara Africa and another on Ceylon clearly demonstrate such an awareness.) But the significant fact is that the issue of ethnic diversity is not perceived by the editors as one that transcends the particular case(s). If the format of a book, as reflected in both its table of contents and index, fails to recognize the problem of ethnicity as more than a local phenomenon, the user of the book is hardly likely to do so.

The above ten works, as noted, are believed to be representative. But two decidedly nonrepresentative titles should be noted: The concept of ethnicity pervades Rupert Emerson, *From Empire to Nation* (Boston 1960); and an important segment of Charles W. Anderson and others, *Issues of Political Development* (Englewood Cliffs 1967) is dedicated to a serious treatment of the issue.

2. The 132 units include all entities that were generally considered to be states as of January 1, 1971, with the exception of a few microunits such as Nauru and Western Samoa. However, East and West Germany, North and South Korea, and North and South Vietnam were treated as single entities in the belief that such treatment would minimize their distorting effects. It should not be assumed that the inclusion of all microunits would substantially alter the statistics in favor of homogeneity. In the case of Nauru, for example, despite a population of only 6,500, the largest ethnic element fails to constitute a majority.

3. See, for example, Arnold Rivkin, *Nation-Building in Africa* (New Brunswick 1969). After reviewing a number of problems throughout Africa, many of which he readily acknowledges are essentially ethnic (e.g., pp. 35–37, 195, 196, and 226), the author concludes (p. 238): "Although the divided populations of Africa—of different tribes, ethnic origin (as the Watusi and Bahutu in Rwanda and Burundi), religions (Christian, Islamic, animistic, etc.), and historical background—pose serious and major problems for nation-building, compared to the Latin American divisions, developed over centuries, and involving an intermixture or race, social structure, and economic status, they seem relatively manageable and over time susceptible of solution." No further details concerning a solution are offered, however, and the reader is therefore asked to accept this optimistic forecast solely on faith.

One of the most perplexing illustrations of a failure to confront a problem of ethnic diversity is offered by Lucian Pye, *Politics, Personality and Nation Building: Burma's Search for Identity* (New Haven 1962). Although the politically dominant Burmese have been involved in open ethnic warfare with that country's minorities almost uninterruptedly since that state achieved independence and although this continuing struggle unquestionably represents that state's most visible and significant barrier to integration, a passing reference to some of the minorities is limited to a single page.

4. *Nationalism and Social Communication: An Inquiry into the Foundations of Nationality* (Cambridge, Mass.). The first edition was published in 1953 and the second, which contains no substantive changes, in 1966. All references to page numbers in this paper correspond to the second edition.

5. See, for example, p. 126: "Linguistically and culturally, then, members of each group are outsiders for the other. Yet technological and economic processes are forcing them together, into acute recognition of their differences and their common, mutual experience of strangeness, and more conspicuous differentiation and conflict may result."

6. *Ibid.*, 152.

7. *Ibid.*, 188.

8. *Ibid.*, 162, 163; emphasis added.

9. *Ibid.*, 164.

10. Karl Deutsch, "Social Mobilization and Political Development," *American Political Science Review*, LV (September 1961), 501.

11. *Ibid.* It may be instructive that Deutsch offered negative examples of this phenomenon (e.g., the secession of the U.S. and Ireland from Britain), but no examples of ethnic groups submerging their identity because of effective government.

12. Karl Deutsch, "Nation-Building and National Development: Some Issues for Political Research," in Deutsch and Foltz (fn. I), 4–5.

13. *Ibid.*, 8–9. It is worth noting that in discussing these prospective stages of assimilation, Deutsch cited several of his own works, including *Nationalism and Social Communication*, thereby indicating his feeling that that work was fully compatible with this view of the ultimate eradication of ethnic divisiveness.

14. Karl Deutsch, *Nationalism and Its Alternatives* (New York 1969).

15. One indication of a change of attitude toward the problem of assimilation is that while it played a central role in *Nationalism and Social Communication*, the process of assimilation is allocated less than two pages in his most recent work and is treated in terms of its "dimensions" rather than its "components." See pp. 25–27.

16. Deutsch (fn. 14), 27.

17. See above, p. 240–41, (identified in note 10).

18. Deutsch (fn. 14), 73.

19. Another example of this tautology can be found on page 68, *ibid.* Referring to earlier cases of national integration, Deutsch concludes that "*the combined processes of social mobilization and* assimilation eventually turned them into consolidated peoples and nations." If the italicized words are omitted, the statement is an evident truism in that it defines assimilation. Indeed, to the degree that social mobilization presupposes the industrial age and relatively modern transportation and communication networks, the statement as worded is false. The Chinese nation, and nearly all others, antedate the Industrial Revolution.

20. For a treatment of this trend as a global phenomenon, see Connor, "Self-Determination: The New Phase," *World Politics*, xx (October 1967), 30–53.

21. It is assumed that Ethiopia's very short period of domination by Italy in the 1930's does not invalidate its use as an example of a state without a colonial history.

22. For a more complete discussion of the relationship of communications distance to physical distance, see Connor, "Myths of Hemispheric, Continental, Regional, and State Unity," *Political Science Quarterly*, LXXXIV (December 1969), particularly 565–67.

23. For a fascinating account of how increased contacts have strengthened Lao identity, see Charles F. Keyes, "Ethnic Identity and Loyalty of Villagers in Northeast Thailand," *Asian Survey*, VI (July 1966), 362–69.

24. See the perspicacious comment concerning Ethiopia by a newspaper reporter: "Lack of communications helped hold this empire together. Now developing communications and

the political awareness they encourage are straining its unity." (Frederick Hunter in the *Christian Science Monitor*, January 8, 1970).

Problem areas include not just the rather recently acquired Eritrea, but also Bale and Gojam Provinces. See the *New York Times*, April 1, 1969.

25. Cases in point would include Afghanistan, Iran, and Liberia. Many of the Latin American States would also qualify. For a treatment of the latter, see Anderson and others (fn. 1), 45–56. For more details on growing ethnic awareness in Thailand and South Asia, see Connor, "Ethnology and the Peace of South Asia," *World Politics*, XXII (October 1969), 51–86.

26. One piece of evidence that there are substantial distinctions in the pervasiveness of pre- and post-World War II *inter*group, *intra*state contacts is offered by American regionalism. As will be noted below, regionalism, in contradistinction to ethnicity, does tend to evaporate in direct proportion to the intensity of interregional communication and transportation networks. Yet regionalism, as manifested in concepts like "states' rights" and in voting blocs and voting patterns, was still strong following World War II. The most enduring manifestation of American regionalism, "the Solid South," has shown symptoms of dying only in recent years.

27. The expression appeared as part of the Proclamation on the Polish Question, endorsed by the London Conference of the First International. The Proclamation noted "the need for annulling Russian influence in Europe, through enforcing the right of self-determination, and through the reconstituting of Poland upon democratic and social foundations." Cited in G. Stelkloff, *History of the First International* (New York 1968), 85. For a reference to a still earlier use of the expression by Karl Marx in his *Herr Vogt* (1860), see Stefan Possony, "Nationalism and the Ethnic Factor," *Orbis*, X (Winter 1967), 1218.

28. United Nations Charter, art. I, par. 2

29. *The Worldmark Encyclopedia of the Nations [sic]*, 3d ed., I (New York 1967), 254–57, lists fifty intergovernmental organizations whose names begin with *International*. Not one of them has anything to do with nations.

30. Jack C. Plano and Roy Olton, *The International Relations Dictionary* (New York 1969).

31. See, for example, A.F.K. Organski, *World Politics* (2d rev. ed., New York 1968), 12: "The story we are about to tell is a tale of nations. Nations are the major characters, and it is with their actions, their goals and plans, their power, their possessions, and their relations with each other that we shall be concerned." See also Deutsch (fn. 14), where, despite defining the word nation to mean a people (i.e., an ethnic group) in charge of a state (p. 19), the author refers to the multiethnic populations of Spain (p. 13), and of Belgium (p. 70), as nations. See, too, the concluding paragraph of Dankwart Rustow. *A World of Nations* (Washington 1967) in which he notes that "more than 130 nations, real or so-called, will each make its contribution to the history of the late twentieth century." The author had earlier (e.g., p. 36) differentiated between state and nation. For evidence that studies dealing specifically with the problems that ethnic diversity poses for state integration are also not necessarily immune from improper interuse of terminology, see Donald Rothchild, "Ethnicity and Conflict Resolution," *World Politics*, XXII (July 1970), particularly 597–98. "First, in spite of the oft-used distinction between a fairly coercive domestic order and a fairly noncoercive international order, the jockeying for power of ethnic groups within states corresponds markedly to that of *nation* and *nation*. . . . New and more productive 'decades of development,' with their presumed attempts at re-allocation, may be as indispensable to the comity among ethnic groups within the state as they are among the *nations* of the world." (Emphasis added.) Examples abound of this tendency to use key terms improperly, so the authorities who are singled out in this and the following footnotes are *not* selected because they have been unusually uncircumspect in their terminology. On the contrary, they have been selected, in part, because they are acknowledged scholars.

32. See for example Norman J. Paddleford and George A. Lincoln, *The Dynamics of International Politics* (2d ed., New York 1967), 7: "The actors in the international political system are the independent nation-states." Or Louis J. Halle. *Civilization and Foreign Policy*

(New York 1952), 10: "A prime fact about the world is that it is largely composed of nation-states." And Elton Atwater and others, *World Tensions: Conflict and Accommodation* (New York 1967), 16: "Since there are some 120 different nation-states in the world . . ." Karl Deutsch also regularly refers to all states as nation-states. See, for example, *Nationalism and Its Alternatives* (fn. 14), 61, 125, and 176. For his description of the multi-ethnic states of Czechoslovakia, Rumania, and Yugoslavia as nation-states, see 62–63.

33. Meanwhile, expressions such as *statism* or *étatisme*, which should refer to loyalty to the state, have been assigned still other meanings that have little to do with loyalty of any sort.

34. See, for example, the section in Edward Shils, *Political Development in the New States* (The Hague 1968), entitled "Parochialism, Nationality, and Nationalism," 32–33. As used therein, parochialism refers to loyalty to the ethnic group, and nationality and nationalism refer to identity with, and loyalty to, the state.

35. One manifestation has been the grouping of the *nationalism* of Japan and Germany during the 1930's and early 1940's with that of Italy and of multiethnic Argentina and Spain under the single rubric of Fascism, a doctrine positing the superiority of the corporate state.

36. See, for example, Rothchild (fn. 31), 598. "Second, the interethnic confrontation raises questions about the unifying potential of nationalism. Although nationalism has effectively repulsed the claims of metropolitan hegemony in a number of crucial confrontations, it has still to demonstrate the ability to overcome 'primordial sentiments' and to foster a sense of common purpose." By equating nationalism with loyalty to the state, Rothchild is unwittingly criticizing nationalism for not being able to overcome itself. Nonetheless, if his pessimism persisted, his basic analysis concerning the relative strength of ethnic and state loyalty would be sound. However, he later criticizes the authors of a number of books dealing with ethnic problems for emphasizing the depth of the cleavages rather than the positive possibilities for "ethnic balancing." They represent "an all-too-general preoccupation with the nature of past cleavages and conflicts instead of with the evolving dimensions of the process of political integration" (p. 612). "They tell us more about cleavages than about links, more about conflict than about cooperation and reciprocity. Their details are sharply delineated; however, the complete picture requires somewhat greater attention to adjustment, interrelatedness, adaptation, and exchange" (p. 615). One suspects that the author might have been more likely to question whether he was not asking for answers to the unanswerable if he had been aware that nationalism was on the side of state-disintegration rather than state-integration.

37. Since the concept of the nation does not preclude significant internal divisions, it actually embodies two important levels of attitudes. Relative to *intranational* distinctions and similarities, the stress, when need be, is upon those traits that unite; relative to distinctions and similarities among nations, the ultimate stress is upon those that divide.

38. Still other examples would include the resurgence of Scottish and Welsh nationalism even among those who are linguistically assimilated to English.

39. The pioneering efforts of the late Hadley Cantril in the study of the stereotype images that one group holds of another are of great pertinence and value to the study of ethnic nationalism. The value of the work of Cantril and of those scholars most influenced by him is lessened only slightly because the objects described are the populations of countries rather than ethnic groups. When asked to select those adjectives that best describe the people of another country, it is probable that the respondent envisages the politically dominant ethnic group of that state (e.g., British is perceived as English, South African as Afrikaner, Czechoslovakian as Czech, etc.). A more important limitation lies in the fact that the responses are not tabulated according to the ethnicity of the respondents. There is still another factor: the adjectives which are usually employed in such studies cannot adequately convey the depth of irrational hatred which may be involved. Negative attributes, such as *backward, domineering, conceited,* and even *cruel,* are of a different order than are the unarticulated passions that can cause Cambodians to massacre huge numbers of unarmed

Vietnamese civilians; Balinese, Javanese, and Malays to massacre Chinese; the Bahutu to massacre the Watusi; the Hausa, the Ibo; or the Turks, the Armenians.

40. For an example of a typical account, see Linda Charlton's article in the *New York Times,* August 15, 1969, in which she describes the crisis as "Irishman against Irishman" and "Prods" (Protestants) against Catholics.

41. Richard Rose, *The United Kingdom as a Multinational State* (Glasgow 1970), 10.

42. The religious composition is 35 per cent Catholic, 29 per cent Presbyterian (Church of Scotland), 24 per cent Episcopal (Church of England), 10 per cent other Protestant, and 2 per cent other. *Ibid.,* 13.

43. See the *New York Times,* January 24, 1971, for an account of a protest demonstration by Belfast women before a Catholic Bishop's house because he had given a sermon advising Catholics not to have anything to do with the outlawed Irish Republican Army.

   Evidence that the basic driving force of Irish militancy has been not simply the desire for civil reform is offered by the fact that reforms promoted by the moderate government of Chichester-Clark were followed by greater militancy on the part of the Irish element.

44. A notable exception is Terrence O'Neill, the former, moderate Prime Minister. An awareness within Northern Ireland's political community that strong emotions are often associated with surnames caused his colleagues to presume that his name would prove a real asset in gaining the respect and trust of the Irish minority.

45. See the *New York Times,* April 30, 1970. See also the *New York Times* of two days earlier, where it was reported that order was restored in Belfast only after Scottish troops were replaced by English troops.

   As is evident from the above-mentioned survey on national identification, the term Scotch-Irish is a misleading ethnic description. It simply refers to people whose Scottish ancestors emigrated to Ireland, but it need not indicate any Irish ancestry.

46. *Wall Street Journal,* August 16, 1969. A somewhat similar analysis appeared in the letter to the editor column of the *New York Times* on July 12, 1970, signed John C. Marley. "But the religious persuasions of the opposing elements are only incidental to the underlying political question, which is whether the six counties of Northern Ireland shall be ruled by a foreign power. The overwhelming majority of the Irish people, North and South, are united in their desire that the British get out of Ireland. The only exception to this view comes from a British ethnic group which constitutes a local majority, not in the entire six occupied counties, but in a small enclave within a thirty mile radius of Belfast."

47. *New York Times,* July 10, 1970.

48. For descriptions of this tendency, see Hans Morgenthau, "The American Tradition in Foreign Policy," in Roy C. Macridis, ed., *Foreign Policy in World Politics* (3d ed., Englewood Cliffs 1967), 254, and Stanley Hoffman, *Gulliver's Troubles in the Setting of American Foreign Policy* (New York 1968), 120–21.

49. As noted earlier, Karl Deutsch explicitly held this opinion in 1961.

50. Afro-Americans within the United States may offer a comparable case.

51. Particularly significant for the present discussion is the comment of Gabriel Almond: "This overt optimism is so compulsive an element in the American culture that factors which threaten it, such as failure . . . are pressed from the focus of attention and handled in perfunctory ways." *The American People and Foreign Policy* (New York 1961), 50–51. See also Frederick Hartman, *The New Age of American Foreign Policy* (New York 1970), 58.

52. Contrast, for example, the American practice of encouraging huge numbers of American troops to furlough in Bangkok, to the Soviet practice of minimizing the Russian presence in such states as the United Arab Republic. For a discussion of the impact of a foreign presence upon a guerrilla struggle, and the sharp contrast in awareness of this impact between the United States on the one hand, and China, the Soviet Union, and North Vietnam on the other, see Connor (fn. 25), 51–86.

53. See, for example, Karl Deutsch's comment, cited above on p. 239–40.

54. Particularly recommended for their incisiveness are the works of Nathan Glazer, Milton Gordon, and Daniel Moynihan.

55. It is not implied that most Afro-Americans are black nationalists. The percentage is not known. An incisive study would have to learn also what percentage of black nationalists are separatists. It is highly probable that a substantial percentage of those who would be apt to identify themselves as black nationalists have not speculated concerning the precise goal they have in mind beyond a concept of true equality. Attitudes concerning the desirability of various forms of assimilation (schools, business, sports, marriage, etc.) would probably represent the best index as to whether or not one envisaged a separate nation. But it does not follow that attitudinal surveys can validly determine such attitudes. For a thoughtful critique of such surveys by an experienced practitioner, see Arnold Rose, *Migrants in Europe* (Minneapolis 1969), 100 ad passim.

56. Government institutions and services (particularly schools), trans-ghetto communications media, advertising, and elections are but a few of the outside forces affecting the ghetto.

57. This aspect of size helps to account for the fact that professional people are often disproportionately represented among those desiring total separation. Belgium, Canada, and Ceylon all offer cases in point. Since goals in a less sophisticated society are apt to be of lesser magnitude, a smaller community may suffice in less modern situations.

58. The need to be fluent in the dominant tongue in order to obtain a decent position in the central bureaucracy is a common example.

59. This inverse relationship causes the use of the term *regionalism* to be a particularly dangerous and inappropriate substitute for *ethnic nationalism.*

60. Richard Rose is among those authorities. In 1964 he observed that "today politics in the United Kingdom is greatly simplified by the absence of major cleavages along the lines of ethnic groups, language, or religion. . . . The solidarity of the United Kingdom today may be due to fortuitous historical circumstances; it is nonetheless real and important." *Politics in England* (Boston 1964), 10 and 11. But by 1970, the situation had changed so drastically that Professor Rose entitled a work *The United Kingdom as a Multi-National State* (fn. 41). On page 1, Rose lists L. S. Amery, Samuel Beers, Harry Eckstein, Jean Blondel, and S. E. Finer as recent writers who have failed to detect the potential significance of ethnic divisions within the United Kingdom. These men were hardly unique in their failure to anticipate the great change in attitude about to manifest itself in Scotland and Wales. See, for example, Connor (fn. 20), 39n., in which this author acknowledged but underestimated the imminent power of the Scottish nationalist idea. See, also, J. D. Mackie, *A History of Scotland* (Baltimore 1964), 367–70, in which a scholar also fails to appreciate the submerged but emerging power of Scottishness among his own people.

61. For a number of illustrations of this tendency to confuse the absence of ethnic warfare with the presence of nation-states throughout Western Europe, see Connor (fn. 20). Those who have been confused include such notables as John Stuart Mill, Lord Acton, Ernest Barker, and Alfred Cobban; their errors extended *inter alia* to the United Kingdom, Belgium, Switzerland, and Spain. Similarly, the perspicacious Frederick Engels once wrote: "The Highland Gaels (Scottish) and the Welsh are undoubtedly of different nationalities to what the British are, although *nobody* will give to these remnants of peoples *long gone by* the title of nations, any more than to the Celtic inhabitants of Brittany in France. . . ." Cited in Roman Rosdolsky, "Worker and Fatherland: A Note on a Passage in the Communist Manifesto," *Science and Society*, XXIX (Summer 1965), 333; emphasis added. In his most recent work, *Nationalism and Its Alternatives* (fn. 14), Karl Deutsch also employs Western Europe as a regional model of successfully integrated states. And in both editions of *Nationalism and Social Communication* (fn. 4), Deutsch describes the Bretons, Flemish, Franco-Canadians, Franco- and German-Swiss, Scots, and Welsh as totally assimilated.

62. This statement presupposes that the government is not prepared to take such extreme measures as coercive population transfers and forced intermarriages.

63. Christian P. Potholm, "Political Decay in Post-Independence Africa: Some Thoughts on its Causes and Cures." Paper presented at the 1970 Annual Meeting of the New York State Political Science Association.

64. Burundi, Cameroon, Chad, Congo (Kinshasa), Ethiopia, Ivory Coast, Kenya, Nigeria, Rwanda, Sudan, Tanzania (Zanzibar), Uganda and Zambia. Congo (Brazzaville) also experienced open ethnic warfare on the eve of independence and Nkrumah suppressed Ashanti and Ewe separatist movements within Ghana early in his reign. Coups that took place in Dahomey and Sierra Leone were also justified as a means of avoiding ethnic warfare. Within Liberia, Tubman's government found an official guilty of treasonably attempting to start a civil, ethnic war. Ethnicity also plays an important role within the anti-Portuguese struggle in Angola and Mozambique, and ethnic violence has occurred in the French Territory of Afars and Issas.

65. Edward Feit has orally referred to African political parties as "the continuation of tribal warfare by other means." See also his comment to this effect in "Military Coups and Political Development: Some Lessons from Ghana and Nigeria," *World Politics*, XX (January 1968), 184.

66. Although not involving an African state, the overthrow of Norodom Sihanouk offers an instructive case concerning a very popular figure who for many years purposefully played the role of—and was popularly viewed by the Khmer people of Cambodia as—the foremost national (read "ethnic") leader. Following the palace coup, it was essential for the coup's leadership that Khmer loyalty to Sihanouk be transferred rapidly to the new government. To this end, the new government publicized a number of charges against the character and record of Sihanouk, most of which were false or exaggerated. The most effective charge, however, was, in effect, that Sihanouk had been "soft on Vietnamese," permitting the Viet Cong and other Vietnamese to violate the Khmer homeland with impunity. This charge, together with the unleashing of a general hate campaign against all ethnic Vietnamese, posed a dilemma for Sihanouk: How to maintain the mantle of Khmer nationalism while simultaneously acknowledging an alliance with Hanoi and the Viet Cong—an alliance he needed if he were to counter the forces at the disposal of the new Cambodian government. The anti-Sihanouk strategy was, therefore, to turn Khmer ethnic nationalism against its former foremost figure by depicting him as a traitor who was aiding the cause of an ethnic enemy of long standing.

VALUE CONFLICTS

AND THE DYNAMICS OF

RACE RELATIONS

The part played by values and ideas in generating social change is a critical problem for sociology and one particularly associated with the writings of Karl Marx and Max Weber. Are ideas and values all-powerful forces shaping history and society; do they play an intermediary role interacting with material factors; or are they mere epiphenomena derived solely from the more fundamental influences of economic and technological change? These questions are especially significant for the study of race relations because of the distinctive role that deterministic beliefs play in the development of racial interaction.

Gunnar Myrdal's famous analysis of American race relations in terms of the conflict between the values and the actions of the white community raises just that problem. Together with critics like Robert Merton, Marxist sociologists such as Cox and Aptheker have challenged Myrdal's verdict, claiming that a literal reading of the "American Creed" was a naive misunderstanding of bourgeois ideology: the so-called "Dilemma" was little more than a smoke screen covering up a situation of class exploitation. Whatever the truth of that interpretation, Marxist social critics have had to come to terms with a related question linked to socialist societies. How can the universalistic creed of Soviet communism be reconciled with the practices of the Russian authorities towards their various national and religious minorities? Recent charges of anti-Semitism have dramatized this issue, and Goldhagen's paper, written more than a decade before the Yom Kippur and Seven Days Wars, provides the essential background for assessing the extent of a "Soviet Dilemma."

Roger Bastide continues the discussion with reference to another set of universalistic beliefs, those associated with the Christian religion. He explores the deep-rooted color symbolism that has permeated both Catholicism and Calvinism and served as an ideological reflection of, and rationalization for, racial domination. The complex manipulation of color symbolism by different religious groups, and by dominant and subordinate groups in societies with different religious traditions, provides fascinating insight into the interaction of religious values and race and ethnic relations.

270

24 The Negro Problem as a Moral Issue

Gunnar Myrdal

There is a "Negro problem" in the United States and most Americans are aware of it, although it assumes varying forms and intensity in different regions of the country and among diverse groups of the American people. Americans have to react to it, politically as citizens and, where there are Negroes present in the community, privately as neighbors.

To the great majority of white Americans the Negro problem has distinctly negative connotations. It suggests something difficult to settle and equally difficult to leave alone. It is embarrassing. It makes for moral uneasiness. The very presence of the Negro in America[1]; his fate in this country through slavery, Civil War and Reconstruction; his recent career and his present status; his accommodation; his protest and his aspiration; in fact his entire biological, historical and social existence as a participant American represent to the ordinary white man in the North as well as in the South an anomaly in the very structure of American society. To many, this takes on the proportion of a menace—biological, economic, social, cultural, and, at times, political. This anxiety may be mingled with a feeling of individual and collective guilt. A few see the problem as a challenge to statesmanship. To all it is a trouble.

These and many other mutually inconsistent attitudes are blended into none too logical a scheme which, in turn, may be quite inconsistent with the wider personal, moral, religious, and civic sentiments and ideas of the Americans. Now and then, even the least sophisticated individual becomes aware of his own confusion and the contradiction in his attitudes. Occasionally he may recognize, even if only for a moment, the incongruence of his state of mind and find it so intolerable that the whole organization of his moral precepts is shaken. But most people, most of the time, suppress such threats to their moral integrity together with all of the confusion, the ambiguity, and inconsistency which lurks in the basement of man's soul. This, however, is rarely accomplished without mental strain. Out of the strain comes a sense of uneasiness and awkwardness which always seems attached to the Negro problem.

The strain is increased in democratic America by the freedom left open—even in the South, to a considerable extent—for the advocates of the Negro, his rights and welfare. All "pro-Negro" forces in American society, whether organized or not, and irrespective of their wide differences in both strategy and tactics, sense that this is the situation. They all work on the national conscience. They all seek to fix everybody's attention on the suppressed moral conflict. No wonder that they are often regarded as public nuisances, or worse—even when they succeed in getting grudging concessions to Negro rights and welfare.

At this point it must be observed that America, relative to all the other branches of Western civilization, is moralistic and "moral-conscious." The ordinary American is the opposite of a cynic. He is on the average more of a believer and a defender of the faith in humanity than the rest of the Occidentals. It is a relatively important matter to him to be true to his own ideals and to carry them out in actual life. We recognize the American, wherever we meet him, as a practical idealist. Compared with members of other nations of Western civilization, the ordinary American is a rationalistic being, and there are close relations between his moralism and his rationalism. Even romanticism, transcendentalism, and mysticism tend to be, in the American culture, rational, pragmatic and optimistic. American civilization early acquired a flavor of enlightenment which has affected the ordinary American's whole personality and especially his conception of how ideas and ideals ought to "click" together. He has never developed that particular brand of tired mysticism and romanticism which finds delight in the inextricable confusion in the order of things and in ineffectuality of the human mind. He finds such leanings intellectually perverse.

These generalizations might seem venturesome and questionable to the reflective American himself, who, naturally enough, has his attention directed more on the dissimilarities than on the similarities within his culture. What is common is usually not obvious, and it never becomes striking. But to the stranger it is obvious and even striking. In the social sciences, for instance, the American has, more courageously than anywhere else on the globe, started to measure, not only human intelligence, aptitudes, and personality traits, but moral leanings and the "goodness" of communities. This man is a rationalist; he wants intellectual order in his moral set-up; he wants to pursue his own inclinations into their hidden haunts; and he is likely to expose himself and his kind in a most undiplomatic manner.

In hasty strokes we are now depicting the essentials of the American *ethos.* This moralism and rationalism are to many of us—among them the author of this book—the glory of the nation, its youthful strength, perhaps the salvation of mankind. The analysis of this "American Creed" and its implications have an important place in our inquiry. While on the one hand, to such a moralistic and rationalistic being as the ordinary American, the Negro problem and his own confused and contradictory attitudes toward it must be disturbing; on the other hand, the very mass of unsettled problems in his heterogeneous and changing culture, and the inherited liberalistic trust that things will ultimately take care of themselves and get settled in one way or another, enable the ordinary American to live on happily, with recognized contradictions around him and within him, in a kind of bright fatalism which is unmatched in the rest of the Western world. This fatalism also belongs to the national *ethos.*

The American Negro problem is a problem in the heart of the American. It is there that the interracial tension has its focus. It is there that the decisive struggle goes on. This is the central viewpoint of this treatise. Though our study includes economic, social, and political race relations, at bottom our problem is the moral dilemma of the American—the conflict between his moral valuations on various levels of consciousness and generality. The "American Dilemma," referred to in the title of this book, is the ever-raging conflict between, on the one hand, the valuations preserved on the general plane which we shall call the "American Creed," where the American thinks, talks, and acts under the influence of high national and Christian precepts, and, on the other hand, the valuations on specific planes of individual and group living, where personal and local interests; economic, social, and sexual jealousies; considerations of community prestige and conformity; group prejudice against particular persons or types of people; and all sorts of miscellaneous wants, impulses, and habits dominate his outlook.

NOTES

1. The word *America* will be used here as a synonym for continental United States.

25   Communism and Anti-Semitism

Erich Goldhagen

> *"Judaism kills the love for the Soviet Motherland."*
>
> > —*Sovetskaia Moldavia,* July 23, 1959.

> *"They do not like collective work, group discipline . . . They are individualists. . . . Jews are interested in everything, they want to probe into everything, they discuss everything, and end up by having profoundly different opinions."*
>
> > —Khrushchev in an interview with Serge Goussard, correspondent of *Le Figaro* (Paris), April 9, 1958.

The existence of anti-Semitism in the USSR, its employment as a tool by the Communist leadership, and its absorption into the *Weltanschauung* of the "New Class" should no longer come as a surprise to anyone familiar with the realities of Soviet life. Yet few are aware of the genealogy of this unique phenomenon—of its historical roots and ideological evolution. For it is a fact that anti-Semitism is not alien to the radical tradition—in Western Europe, and more particularly in Russia. Indeed, the ancestry of Communist anti-Semitism may be traced to the precursors of

From *Problems of Communism,* Vol. IX, 3, 1960, pp. 35–43.

Leninism and Stalinism—the revolutionary terrorists, the so-called "Populists," who dominated the revolutionary scene in Russia in the second half of the 19th century.

"Lubricant on the Wheel of Revolution"

When socialism as a current of political thought made its appearance in Western Europe, it tended to look upon the Jews with unfriendly eyes, regarding them as the embodiment of those qualities of social life which socialists denounced as evil and which they were sworn to undo. Barred from the ownership of land and excluded from the Guilds, the Jews had long ago been driven to devote themselves primarily to the pursuit of commerce; and throughout Western Europe the name Jew came to be almost synonymous with that of trader. The belief was thus born that the pursuit of money was a national vocation of the Jews, enjoined by their religion and practiced with unrivaled skill and zeal. It seemed that the spirit of commerce had found its purest embodiment and its consummate practitioners in the Jews.[1]

The Jews thus incurred the contempt and hatred that socialists harbored against the world of finance. The comprehensive condemnation of commerce and finance as useless and parasitic occupations, as unproductive activities whereby those who shun honest labor could derive undeserved riches from the toil of others was bound to embrace the Jews. This attitude was reinforced by the sinister tales which popular lore came to weave around the name of Rothschild, whose enormous wealth was believed to be a source of evil power—swaying monarchs, making and unmaking governments, and determining the destinies of nations. The vagaries of history, its irrationalities, the injustices and sufferings which it inflicted were traced not to the impersonal forces of economic and social processes but to villains of flesh and blood to whom one could assign guilt and upon whom one could discharge that hatred in which suffering and discontent often seek relief.

It was this outlook which Marx in part echoed in his famous essay *Zur Judenfrage:*

> What is the object of the Jew's worship in this world?
> Usury What is his worldly god? Money. . . .
> Money is the zealous one God of Israel, beside which no other God may stand. Money degrades all the gods of mankind and turns them into commodities. Money is the universal and self-constituted value set upon all things. It has therefore robbed the whole world, of both nature and man, of its original value. Money is the essence of man's life and work, which have become alienated from him. This alien monster rules him and he worships it.[2]

In Russia, too, disdain towards the Jews was the prevalent attitude of the early revolutionaries. The abysmal conditions of the Jews—constrained in their movement, compelled to live only in assigned regions known as the Pale of Settlement, and reduced (save for a tiny minority) to a state of poverty verging on starvation—

evoked little sympathy in the breasts of the radical intellectuals of the 1870's and 1880's, however virulent their hatred of the Tsarist autocracy. To be sure, the Jews were wretched and poor, but their wretchedness and poverty was not graced by those lofty virtues which the fertile imagination of the revolutionaries ascribed to the Russian peasantry. Unlike the peasants, who earned their meager subsistence by toil and who were regarded by the intellectuals as noble beings endowed with the qualities of selflessness and instinctive communalism, the Jews were a work-shirking lot, engaging in the "parasitic" and "exploitative" occupations. Even poverty, their only reward, could not redeem them.

But some revolutionaries did not content themselves with passive disdain; they acclaimed and encouraged active violence against the Jews.

In the spring and summer of 1881 a wave of violence swept through the southern part of the Pale of Settlement. Over one hundred Jewish communities were visited by orgies of destruction, claiming, apart from enormous material damage, scores of dead and hundreds of wounded. This outbreak of unprovoked brute force visited upon a defenseless community moved the Executive Committee of the Narodnaya Volya (People's Will)—the largest revolutionary-terroristic organization at that time—to issue a proclamation in Ukrainian on August 30, 1881, blessing the riots and exhorting the peasants to further violence against "the parasitic Jews" and the "Tsar of the Jews." "The people of the Ukraine," the proclamation stated, "suffer more than anyone else from the Jews . . . you have already begun to rise against the Jews . . . you have done well."[3]

This proclamation cannot be simply explained, of course, by the anti-Semitic spirit of the radical intelligentsia. No doubt its authors were imbued with anti-Semitic prejudices; yet it would be naive to assume, for instance, that they were in earnest in affixing the label "Tsar of the Jews" on Alexander III: his disdain for the Jews, and his oppressive and discriminatory policies against them were certainly known to the leaders of the Narodnaya Volya. Thus there is little doubt that the proclamation was first and foremost a *calculated device.* Underlying it, apart from the Bakuninist conviction that the "passion for destruction is a constructive passion," lay Machiavellian calculation, the wish and the hope that the violence against the Jews would be extended to the autocracy. By linking the Jews with the Tsar, the leaders of the Narodnaya Volya sought to telescope the pogroms into the social revolution, to fan its fire into a conflagration engulfing the authorities. They were consciously lying, but to their minds this was a "noble lie," graced by the lofty purpose it served. The blood of the Jews might have been wholly innocent, but it was nonetheless the "lubricant on the wheels of revolution."

In the society of radical émigrés in Geneva, one by the name of Zhukovsky defended the pogroms in the following terms:

> Sixty percent of the Jewish population are engaged in commerce. This is the background against which the peasant hunts down the Jew. . . . To be sure, from a humanitarian standpoint, it is a piece of barbarism when peasants fall like savages upon a frightened Jew and beat him until he bleeds. However,

take this event in the context of social dynamics. Why does he beat? Because [beating] is his political ballot. He has no other way of venting his wrath against his exploitation by the government. It is indeed a pity that the peasant beats the Jew—the most innocent of his exploiters. But he beats, and this is the beginning of his struggle for liberation. When . . . his fists will have grown strong and hard he will strike those who are above the Jews.[4]

But even those radicals who did not view the pogroms with approval could not bring themselves to call for an end to the bloodshed. Anti-Semitism was endemic to the Russian peasantry. It was its daily psychic bread designed to still the grievances and frustrations born of hunger—hunger for land and hunger for food. The Russian intelligentsia which had for two decades tried with only limited success to strike roots in the Russian peasantry, to secure its confidence and to persuade it to follow the intellectuals as the champions of its aspirations, feared that by showing concern for the Jews they would unwittingly alienate the peasants. To come out in defense of the Jews would have branded them as "Jewish stooges." Was it worth endangering, for the sake of a small national minority, the cause of socialism? These were the arguments with which radicals who had dissociated themselves from violence justified their refusal to come out publicly against the pogroms. The radical philosopher P. L. Lavrov, who was to describe anti-Semitism as the "most tragic epidemic of our era," declined to print a pamphlet against the pogroms submitted to him by the Social Democratic leader Akselrod:

> I must confess that I regard this question as a very complicated one, indeed an exceedingly difficult one for a party which seeks to come closer to the people. Theoretically, on paper, the question can be easily answered. But in view of the prevailing popular passions and the need of the Russian socialists to have the people on their side whenever possible the question is quite different.[5]

The New Spirit

The succeeding generation of Russian revolutionaries did not share the Populist view that anti-Semitic outrages have a redemptive quality. Manifestations of anti-Semitism were not tolerated in the Marxist-Socialist movement which dominated the Russian revolutionary scene during the next two decades. In his pamphlet *Our Differences* (1884), which set forth the program of the Social Democrats and the reasons for their opposition to the Narodnaya Volya, Plekhanov, the "father of Russian Marxism," condemned the proclamation of 1881 as "a base flattery of the national prejudices of the Russian people."[6] Similarly Lenin, after the notorious Kishinev pogrom in 1903, recalled with shame the "infamous proclamation" and called on all socialists to defend the Jews against the mob as a matter of honor.

Indeed, by the turn of the century both Russian and West European socialists tended to view anti-Semitism in a new light. Hitherto, socialists had regarded it as a misguided protest against existing social conditions by petty bourgeois and proletarians—"the socialism of fools," in the words of August Bebel. They had hoped that sooner or later those ensnared by it would recognize that not only capitalist Jews were the cause of their misery but Gentile and Jewish capitalists alike; and that this recognition would bring them into the fold of socialism. But when it seemed that instead of being a vestibule of socialism, anti-Semitism had become a useful tool in the hands of the ruling class, the socialist attitude changed. Anti-Semitism came to be treated unequivocally as a hostile ideology. During the two decades before 1917, there were few recorded overt expressions of anti-Jewish bias in the Russian socialist movement. In fact, there is no doubt that by and large the leaders of the Russian socialist parties did not harbor anti-Semitic sentiments. Such sentiments were certainly absent from Lenin, who was a genuine "internationalist," singularly free from national intolerance, and determinedly hostile to any manifestations of xenophobia or "Great Russian chauvinism" on the part of his comrades-in-arms.

Nevertheless, the Russian Social Democrats still shunned prominent association with specifically Jewish causes. To be sure, the central organs of their press denounced anti-Semitism in forceful terms; but they did not carry these denunciations in popular leaflets and pamphlets. For a socialist agitator, working among the grass-roots of the working-class, it was still unwise to appear in the role of an advocate of the Jews.

After the October Revolution the Bolsheviks adopted an uncompromising attitude against anti-Semitism. As the White armies converged to extinguish the infant regime with the battlecry "Beat the Jews and Save Russia," the denunciation of anti-Semitism as counter-revolutionary became not only a duty enjoined by faith but a course dictated by the imperatives of the struggle in which the Bolsheviks were engaged. The weapon had to be wrested from the hands of those seeking to restore the *ancien regime*. Anti-Semitism was outlawed and suppressed; and the Red Army was hailed by the Jews as a protector and liberator from the White troops which were bringing upon them nothing but death and destruction. There was exaggeration but no falsification in the picture of Eastern Europe drawn by the American-Yiddish poet, A. Liesin, who was not a Communist: "While in all the countries surrounding Bolshevik Russia anti-Semitism is fanned with increasingly infernal power . . . Bolshevik Russia presents an example of humaneness and justice, the like of which the history of the Jewish Diaspora has never seen before."[7] Anti-Semitism could not figure in any indictment drawn up against the Soviet dictatorship during the 1920's. But with the advent of the 1930's a new picture began to unfold itself.

Stalinist Nationalism

The revival of Great Russian nationalism under Stalin's dispensation in the early 1930's created a climate less congenial to the Jews than that which had prevailed throughout the preceding decade. With the building of "socialism in one country" proceeding apace, Bolshevik Russia began to shed many of the features which revolutionary enthusiasm and devotion had bestowed upon her. A new spirit pervaded the party, disillusioned by the dearth of revolutionary outbreaks in West Europe to which it had looked forward in the days of Lenin and Trotsky, and deeply immersed in its own "revolution from above." Under these circumstances, the Russian nationalist tradition, renounced and abused by the sweeping wave of revolutionary triumph, gradually reasserted its claims, casting the revolutionary *élan* into more traditional mold. Within these confining walls the cosmopolitan radiance of the revolution grew dimmer and dimmer. The old revolutionary leadership reared in the tradition of Marxist internationalism was replaced by a new generation of bureaucrats imbued with that peculiar mixture of Marxist militancy and Russian chauvinism which henceforth was to mark the ethos of Soviet society.

A chilly wind began to envelop the Jews, especially the Jewish intelligentsia which had been everywhere in the modern world the bearer of cosmopolitanism. In this new climate the dictatorship was less disposed to resist the envious and subdued demands that the high proportion of the Jews in administrative positions and universities be reduced and that the vacancies thus created be filled by native sons. Indeed, the dictatorship viewed such restrictive measures as salutary: they would earn the regime fresh popularity at home, and at the same time blunt the edge of anti-Communist propaganda throughout the world (emanating from the extreme right) that Mother Russia had fallen under the domination of the Judeo-Communist conspiracy. Accordingly, the Soviet government proceeded to reduce sharply the number of Jews in the leading bodies of the party and government, to introduce a *numerus clausus* into some institutions of higher learning, and virtually to exclude Jews from the diplomatic service.[8] To be a Jew again became a source of discomfort and a handicap.

These measures did not spring from anti-Semitic sentiment in the strict traditional sense of the term, but were motivated by coldly calculated *raison d'état*. They were sometimes accompanied by regrets (privately voiced) about the necessity of sacrificing principles to this greater consideration. *Lex revolutiae suprema est,* Plekhanov had proclaimed in faulty Latin at the Second Congress of the Russian Social Democratic Party (1903), scarcely aware of the horrifying deeds with which that tenet was pregnant. Would a movement which could massacre proletarians in the name of the dictatorship of the proletariat, practice terror in order to achieve social harmony, glory in autocracy in order to establish universal self-government— would such a movement shrink from the appeasement of anti-Semitism if it thought such appeasement would further the "lofty" cause of communism? The head of the Central Committee's department on national minorities met the complaints of a Yiddish writer, Katcherginski, concerning the discrimination against Jews practiced by Soviet authorities in Lithuania, with the explanation that "the Jews of Lithuania may have to be sacrificed to the general cause."[9] The rich and indiscriminate armory of means wherewith bolshevism professed to pursue Utopia acquired a fresh instrument, time-honored and of proven efficacy; and the anti-Semitic spirits, which had been outlawed by bolshevism and driven to lead a repressed existence in the subterranean dwellings of Soviet society, were now emboldened to emerge and engage in their practice in the guise of a Communist *raison d'état*.[10]

From Intolerance to Repression

In 1948 Soviet policy towards the Jews acquired a fresh and disturbing dimension. If hitherto anti-Semitism had been a tool wielded with dispassion and calculated moderation without deeply engaging the spirit of the Communist leaders, and affecting only those Jews aspiring to careers in certain fields, now it was fed by passion and conviction, and was directed against the entire Jewish community. It was not only anti-Semitism *de logique,* to paraphrase Camus' famous phrase; it was at once logical and passionate.

The affection and enthusiasm displayed by the Jews of Russia for the newly created state of Israel, to whose birth the Soviet Union itself had made a modest contribution, provoked Stalin's suspicion that the Jews were an untrustworthy element whose ties with their numerous brethren abroad made them potential traitors. He proceeded to treat them accordingly. He decided not only to render them harmless by encouraging their removal from jobs as security risks, but also to extinguish their ethnic consciousness. With characteristic totalitarian swiftness all Jewish cultural institutions were abolished and several hundred Yiddish writers were arrested: the more prominent among them were executed after a secret trial (in 1952), while others expired in the penal camps of the arctic wasteland. The entry "Jews" in the Soviet Encyclopedia appearing during that period described the Jews as if they were an extinct tribe.[11] Before World War II an elaborate network of cultural institutions had served the Jews of Russia: schools attended by over 100,000 children, a Yiddish press, a large and prolific Yiddish literary community, and a theatre rated among the best in the Soviet Union. By the autumn of 1948 almost nothing was left in existence. By a stroke of the dictator's pen all organized Jewish endeavor came to an abrupt end. Only a score or so of defunct synagogues survived. These and the withered label of Birobidzhan still incongruously attached to that region on the Amur, which had never acquired a Jewish character and in which the Jews formed a hopeless minority, were the only visible signs of a community of two and a half million.[12]

From 1948 until the death of Stalin Soviet Jews lived under a reign of terror amid rumors of their imminent mass deportation.[13]

Rehabilitation with a Difference

The death of Stalin and the acquittal of the doctors involved in the "Doctors' Plot," as well as *Pravda's* (April 6, 1953) admission that the affair of the doctors was a "fabrication" intended to "inflame nationalist hostilities among the Soviet peoples," removed the nightmare which had hovered over the Jewish community. The terror relented. But the fundamentals of Stalin's policies towards the Jews were retained. As in many other spheres of Communist endeavor the Stalinist aims were preserved, only the methods were changed. The carrot gained ascendancy over the stick, the peaceful incentive over terror, the indirect approach over the direct brutal assault.

Stalin's heirs, in the process of their cautious detachment from the most severe features of Stalin's legacy, set out to right the wrongs inflicted on some nationalities. It will be recalled that seven other ethnic groups had fallen victim to Stalin's suspicion and vindictiveness: the Ingush, the Chechens, the Volga Germans, the Crimea Tatars, the Kalmyks, the Karachai and the Balkars. All of them were uprooted at various times during World War II and banished in their entirety, including members of the party and the Komsomol, to remote places. While the expulsion of the Volga Germans was justified by the authorities as a security measure—and it was perhaps a more rational measure than the removal of the Japanese-American from the Pacific coast during World War II—the deportation of the other national groups was undertaken on the principle of collective guilt. The sins of the few were visited upon the entire community. The preamble to the official decree published in *Izvestia,* June 26, 1946, announcing, two years after the expulsion, the dissolution of the Chechen-Ingush and the Crimean Tatar autonomous republics, stated that collective punishment had been meted out for the failure of the peoples to combat those in their midst who were collaborating with the German enemy. It was this tribal notion of justice which Khrushchev included in his indictment of Stalin at the 20th Party Congress:

> Not only a Marxist-Leninist but also no man of common sense can grasp how it is possible to make whole nations responsible for inimical activity, including women, children, old people, Communists and Komsomols, to use mass repression against them, and to expose them to misery and suffering for the hostile acts of individual persons or groups of persons.[14]

The repressed nationalities have since been restored to their public identity and some have even been permitted to return to their native lands. They ceased to be Orwellian "un-peoples." Their names reappeared on maps and in reference works. Even the Volga Germans have been provided with schools and newspapers.[15]

This wholesale rehabilitation has not embraced the Jews. To be sure the Jews had not been deported—although Soviet Jews are convinced that only Stalin's death saved them from that fate.[16] But condemned to the status of an "un-people," they had been marked out for cultural extinction and their institutions had been destroyed. However, it would seem that in Khrushchev's view this particular action of Stalin did not fall into the category of "monstrous acts" and "rude violations of the basic Leninist principles of the nationality policy of the Soviet society"[17]; it was a deed of prudent statesmanship. In the course of an interview with a Canadian Communist delegation, Khrushchev, in one of the unguarded moments of candor to which he is so often given, showed himself to share Stalin's view of the Jews as inherent security risks. "Khrushchev," relates the Canadian Communist, Salsberg, "agreed with Stalin that the Crimea, which had been depopulated at the war's end, should not be turned into a Jewish colonization center, because in case of war it would be turned into a base for attacking the USSR. . . ."[18]

Surely, a people harboring such a ready propensity to treason could not be allowed to possess cultural institutions fostering and perpetuating that tendency.

Assimilation through Attrition

Stalin's heirs are determined not to revoke the edict against the cultural life of the Jews. The pleadings of a British Communist group asking that Yiddish schools and the theatre be restored were met by Suslov with a categorical refusal befitting that grim guardian of orthodoxy: "No, these things will not be reinstituted."[19]

This obduracy has been maintained by the Soviet leaders in spite of its unfavorable impression on Western opinion, which has displayed anxiety over the lot of the Jews, and in spite of the injuries inflicted on Communist parties with a substantial proportion of Jewish members. Three Communist delegations have taken up the Jewish question with the highest Soviet leaders: a Canadian delegation in August 1956; a British delegation in October of the same year; and a deputation of French Jewish Communists which journeyed to Moscow with the blessing of Thorez early in 1958 for the express purpose of dissuading the Soviet leaders from their present policy towards the Jewish minority. All returned empty-handed.

Disillusioned and embittered, Jewish Communists in Canada, the United States and Britain deserted their parties in large numbers. For many years they had nourished a vision of Soviet Russia which bore little resemblance to reality. Their imagination had seen a land in which a multi-national brotherhood informed by love was laboring towards the realization of Utopia under the guidance of dedicated leaders, all of them paragons of Leninist virtue, stern, determined, ruthless against enemies but full of solicitude for the oppressed everywhere. In the aftermath of Stalin's death the veil of illusion dissolved. J. B. Salsberg, leader of the Canadian CP and a member of the delegation to the USSR, after an interview of two hours, found the First Secretary of the Communist Party and presumed custodian of Marxism-Leninism to be a man possessed of "a backward prejudice against the Jewish group as a people . . . a prejudice which sharply contradicts the Marxist mode of thought." His "statements smack of Great Russian chauvinism. . . . His approach to the problem of Jewish nationality is an unforgivable violation of socialist democracy."[20] Soon afterwards, Salsberg resigned from the party and was followed in this action by a large number of Jews and non-Jews. The Canadian party lost some of its ablest leaders and dedicated members. In Montreal, where the Communists had once been strong enough to elect a member of Parliament, the party organization virtually ceased to exist.

In explanation of the absence of Jewish cultural institutions, Soviet spokesmen usually advance the theory of "integration." According to this theory, the Jews have become so integrated into the body of the Russian people that they have lost all will or capacity for ethnic self-expression. Eager to submerge in the Russian majority, they have abandoned Yiddish for Russian. The breath of life has departed from Jewish culture; it has died from inanition. This consummation, marking an advance on the road of history, deserves the applause of all progressive persons, including Jews. Only reactionaries could lament it. The revive Jewish institutions would, therefore, be tantamount to reviving a corpse in defiance of the will of History. According to Salsberg:

> Khrushchev repeated the view . . . that the majority of Soviet Jews have become integrated into the country's general life. He emphasized that such integration is historically progressive, whereas the maintenance of a separate group existence is reactionary.[21]

It is true, of course, that the majority of Jews have come to use Russian in their daily lives—to a large extent as a result of the assimilationist policies that have been enforced on them. Still, according to the last census, 20.8 percent of Soviet Jews have declared Yiddish to be their most intimate medium of communication. To be sure, the percentage is lower than that of any other ethnic group claiming its national language as the "mother tongue." Yet two factors must be borne in mind: (1) That it must have taken a certain amount of courage for Jews to claim Yiddish as their tongue in the face of official hostility, and that the actual figure may therefore be considerably larger; and (2) that 20.8 percent still embraces 472,000 people—in absolute figures, a far larger number than that of two dozen or so other Soviet nationalities (such as the Buriats, Avars, Ossetians, and so on) whose languages are not only tolerated, but actively encouraged by the Soviet authorities. Such, indeed, are the canons of the Soviet nationality policy that 472,000 Jews are served by a meager sheet whose circulation of 1,000 is largely confined to Birobidzhan, while, say, the 12,000 Chukchi inhabiting the northern region of the RSFSR are served by a comparable organ of 800 copies.[22]

The picture becomes fuller when we add that about 80 Yiddish writers, survivors of the decimation of the Yiddish literary intelligentsia, who are denied a public forum in their own tongue for their creative talents. A chosen few may have their works translated into Russian, if their theme is not of a specific Jewish content. The others must find contentment in manuscripts languishing in the obscurity of desk drawers. According to a highly literate French Jewish Communist, Chaim Sloves:

> The Soviet Jewish writers are more creative today than perhaps ever before. "Not a day passes that I don't write," everyone tells you. And everyone has his own work ready for the press—volumes of poetry, novels, stories, dramas. It is not merely literary impetus or prolific creativity: It is, in the highest sense, sacred dedication.[23]

Immediately after the Revolution Hebrew was declared a counterrevolutionary language. Since 1948 Yiddish literature has been treated as a force inimical to the purposes of the Soviet government. A unique application, indeed, of the official formula "socialist in content—national in form"!

Pursuing the goal of total assimilation of the Jews, the regime has for the past three years embarked on a campaign against the last fragments of communal life in Russia—the synagogues and the religious life associated with them. The purpose of this campaign, conducted through the familiar medium of the feuilleton in the press and the occasional radio broadcast, and practically reinforced by the closing of synagogues in outlying regions, is to deter the Jews from congregating in compact groups. The process of atomization is to be brought to its ultimate conclusion. By insulating the Jews from their co-religionists and co-nationals in the rest of the world, and by isolating them from each other, the regime hopes to extirpate the consciousness of kind and thus remove what it thinks is a source of disaffection from within the Soviet Union. For Judaism, Soviet propagandists insist, is not only "opium for the people," but also a creed implanting in its adherents allegiance to foreign powers and infidelity to the Soviet Union. In a recent broadcast (December 9, 1959) emanating from Kirovograd in the Ukraine (a town, incidentally, with a notorious record of pogroms in pre-revolutionary Russia, including the one which the Narodnaya Volya welcomed with such glee), the speaker inveighed in language of unusual virulence against the local synagogue and its officials:

> . . . the Jewish faith has been strongly intermixed with Jewish bourgeois nationalism and Zionism, already possessing a strong reactionary essence. . . . Sermons by Rabbi Ayzik Pektor hardly differ from the woeful theory of the uniqueness of the Aryan race and its destiny to rule over the peoples of the entire world. . . .

The broadcast was saturated with sheer medievalism:

> Among the numerous Jewish feasts, a special place belongs to Saturday, which should be inspiringly observed by every Orthodox Jew, for according to the teaching of the Talmud this is the day of absolute inactivity. And so, on a Saturday, when the divine service ends, the faithful disperse, and . . . the table is laid, vodka, wine and snacks appear, and toasts to the health of "God's servants" are raised. The drinking feast *(sic)* is led by the rabbi's wife Roza Spektor.

* * * * *

> Jewish ministers and circumcisers execute the rite of circumcision, which has a strikingly nationalistic character. Its specific significance lies in the fact that it gives proof of belonging to the "chosen" people—the Jews. At the same time it imbues Jews with repugnance and hatred of those who do not possess this special sign. . . .
>
> Judaic sermons are sermons of bourgeois Zionists. Such sermons are tools of the nationalistic, Israeli, cosmopolitan American bourgeoisie. With their tentacles, the Jewish bourgeois nationalists, with the help of Judaism, try to reach into our Soviet garden. But they will never succeed.[24]

The treatment of the Jews by the Soviet dictatorship is without a full parallel among its policies toward the other national minorities. A unique people, the Jews have drawn themselves singular treatment. As Stalinism departed from the ideals of internationalism and cosmopolitanism which had inspired the Bolshevik Revolution, it cynically resorted to anti-Semitism as a tool of its designs, harkening back to the tradition of the Narodnaya Volya, in many ways its spiritual ancestor. The xenophobia born of its totalitarian isolation—a xenophobia incongruously linked to its international aspirations and professions—exposed the Jews to grave suspicion. They were members of the worldwide fraternity, the greater part of which lived in the camp of "imperialism," and the creation of the state of Israel intensified that suspicion. Alone among all the national minorities the Jews have been condemned to total assimilation. The Jews are indeed a "chosen people" in Russia—chosen for cultural extinction.

NOTES

1. It is interesting to note, in this connection, that all utopian reformers viewed money as a pernicious force serving no purpose save that of breeding injustice and perverting authentic human values, and foresaw its disappearance in the desired society of the future. The citizens of Thomas More's *Utopia*, for instance, "hold gold and silver up to scorn in every way. . . . They hang gold rings from the ears of criminals, place gold rings on their fingers, gold collars around their necks, and gold crowns on their heads." (T. More, *Utopia*, New York, 1949, p. 44.) And Karl Marx, in his *Nationale Ekonomie und Philosophie*, had the following to say about the evil influence of money: "It turns loyalty into disloyalty, love into hate, virtue into vice, vice into virtue, slave into master, master into slave, stupidity into intelligence, intelligence into stupidity." (Quoted in Kenneth Muir's "Marx's Conversion to Communism," *The New Reasoner*, London, No. 3, Winter 1957-58, p. 63).

2. Karl Marx, *A World Without Jews*, New York 1959, p. 41. This is not to say that Marx was anti-Semitic in the accepted sense of the term. Indeed, the main theme and purport of his essay was to expose the hollowness of the civic equality granted by the bourgeois order. As for Marx's linking of Jews and capitalism, the most original and freshest explanation of it, in this author's opinion, was offered by the East German scholar L. Kofler, in his *Zur Geschichte Der Buergerlichen Gesellschaft* (On the history of the Bourgeois Society) *n.d.*, Halle/Saale, pp. 478–496—a unique exception to the otherwise dreary gibberish that passes off as "social science" in the Communist bloc. According to Kofler, capitalism found its purest manifestation in the Jewish ethos because unlike Gentile capitalists who, being linked to the native proletariat by ties of common nationhood, have endeavored to disguise and temper their avarice and exploitative ambitions, the Jews knew no such restraint. Strangers to the society in which they have lived, they pursued their vocation with uninhibited ruthlessness and without an embellishing guise. They thus have mirrored capitalism in its stark nakedness.

3. Quoted in E. Tcherikover, *geshikhte fun der yidisher arbeter bavegung in di fareynikte shtatn* (History of the Jewish Labor Movement in the USA—in Yiddish) New York, 1945, Vol. II, p. 174.

4. F. Kurski, "di zhenever grupe sotsialistn yidn un ir oyfruf" (The Geneva Group of Jewish Socialists and its proclamation—Yiddish), *Historishe Shriftn*, Vilna/Paris 1939, Vol. III, p. 561.

5. *Iz Arkhiva P. G. Akselroda* (From the P. G. Akselrod archive—in Russian) Berlin 1924, Vol. II, p. 30.

6. G. V. Plekhanov, *Izbrannye filosofskie proizvedeniia* (Collected Philosophical Works), Moscow 1956, Vol. I, p. 217.

7. A. Liesin, in *di tsukunft* (Yiddish), January 1920, p. 1.

8. Hitler revealed in the course of one of his celebrated table talks that "Stalin made no secret before Ribbentrop that he was waiting only for the moment of maturation of a sufficiently large indigenous intelligentsia to make short shrift (Schluss zu machen) of Jews as a leadership stratum which he still needs today." *Hitlers Tischgespraeche,* Bonn, 1951, p. 119.

9. Sh. Katcherginsky, *tsvishn hamer un serp* (Between hammer and sickle—Yiddish), Buenos Aires 1950, p. 96.

10. Trotsky diagnosed the first stealthy manifestations of official anti-Semitism in Soviet Russia as symptoms of the bureaucratic degeneration afflicting Soviet society. According to him, having usurped the dictatorship of the proletariat and betrayed the spirit of the Marxist-Leninist legacy, the Stalinist bureaucracy was seeking to use the Jews as a scapegoat for its misrule and betrayal. L. Trotsky, "Thermidor and Anti-Semitism," *The New International* (New York), May 1941, pp. 91–94. The article bears the date February 22, 1937. This diagnosis, however, was less applicable for the 1930's than to the period after World War II. Thus in 1956 during the ferment in the Polish Communist Party which brought Gomulka to power, the Stalinist elements, known as the Natolin faction, proposed that the popular hatred besieging the Communist rulers be placated by offering the Jewish party members as a sacrificial lamb. They advocated, in the words of a contemporary revisionist account, that the governmental and party apparatus be reconstructed by applying "the criterion of pure Aryan blood." Ryszard Turski, in *Po Prostu* (Warsaw), October 28, 1956. See also Czeslaw Milosz, "Anti-Semitism in Poland," *Problems of Communism,* May–June 1957.

11. *Bolshaia Sovetskaia Entsiklopedia,* 2nd ed., Vol. 15, Moscow 1952, pp. 377–79.

12. Birobidzhan, an area in eastern Siberia, was set up in the late 1920's as a "Jewish autonomous region," but due to its geographic location and severe climatic conditions it never attracted many Jews, whose roots were in the Ukraine and Belorussia primarily.

13. See Communist weekly *World News* (London), Jan. 12, 1957.

14. See Khrushchev's "secret speech" in *The Anti-Stalin Campaign and International Communism,* Columbia University Press, New York, 1956, pp. 57–58.

15. For an account of the rehabilitation, see Walter Kolarz, "Die Rehabilitierung de liquidierten Sowjetvolker," (The rehabilitation of Soviet nationalities), *Ost Europa* (Stuttgart), June 1957, pp. 414–20.

16. See *World News, op. cit.*

17. Khrushchev, *op. cit.,* p. 57.

18. Quoted in *The New Leader* (New York), Sept. 14, 1959, p. 9.

19. *World News, op. cit.*

20. *New Leader, op. cit.* That Khrushchev harbors anti-Semitic feelings of a rather vulgar nature has been evidenced by many of his utterances made in private. One such adverse pronouncement on the Jews, made in the course of an interview with a French correspondent of *Le Figaro* (Paris), April 9, 1958, described the Jews as averse to collective work and group discipline, and stung even the most hardened Jewish Communists in the West, whose loyalty survived the *crise de conscience* produced by revelations after Stalin's death. "It is incomprehensible how such a statement could come from the leader of the Soviet state"—quoted from *morgn frayhayt,* New York, April 13, 1958. It would be a mistake, however, to infer that the personal feelings of the dictator govern Soviet policy towards the Jews. The operative logic of the Soviet system is sufficient to account for it, although the dictator's sentiments lend a particular acerbity to some of its features.

21. *New Leader, op. cit.*

22. See census report in *Pravda,* Feb. 4, 1960. Also in *Current Digest of the Soviet Press* (New York), March 2, 1960.
23. *Yiddishe kultur* (Yiddish culture), New York, Feb. 1959.
24. Throughout 1959, a high percentage of the feuilletons appearing in the Soviet press were devoted to the pillorying and denunciation of individuals bearing unmistakable Jewish names, and of synagogues: *e.g.,* 20–25 percent of the pieces in *Vechernaia Moskva;* 20 percent in *Sovetskaia Kultura;* 10 percent in *Komsomolskaia Pravda;* 33 percent in *Sovetskaia Latvia.* For representative samples see *Prikarpatska Pravda,* September 24, 1958; *Vechernaia Moskva,* March 13, 1959; and *Sovetskaia Moldavia,* November 12, 1959. See also *The New Leader, op. cit.*

26   Color, Racism, and Christianity

Roger Bastide

Sartre has brought out quite well the part the eye plays in racial attitudes, but he does not go far enough. The eye has its substitutes. Some time ago, we discovered in talking to blind persons that they recognize immediately the race of persons whom they meet—without any mistake—by smell, by the texture of the skin, and especially by the voice. On the basis of this sensory information, they react exactly as the sighted do: with antipathy or aloofness if they are racially sensitive, or with a kind of physical attraction if they are not. This shows that any kind of perception can serve as a stimulus to racial attitude. Color is neutral; it is the mind that gives it meaning.

What is important is not so much the ability to see but the ability to see what others see. It is not so much my eye as the eyes of those who surround me. A blind person knows that he is seen. The voice—high-pitched or hoarse—of anyone who speaks to him releases instantly the reactions that society has built up in him. These reactions are the same as those of the sighted. Colors are not important in themselves as optical phenomena, but rather as bearers of a message.

The blind people whom we interrogated were Brazilians. They belonged to a country in which prejudice is based not on race but on color, where discrimination varies in direct proportion to the blackness of the skin. The ideal woman is not a blond or a fair-skinned woman but a brunette or dark-skinned woman and especially a "rosy-tinted" mulatto woman.[1] A blind Brazilian replaces the entire gamut of color tints by shades of voice, and he reacts in the same way as a person who can see. He performs immediately the transposition from one register to another and finds in the sonorities recorded by his ear the message that the sighted attach to color. This experiment led us to concentrate our attention on the symbolic perception of color and of differences in racial attitude in the various Christian faiths.

Reprinted by permission of *Daedalus,* Journal of the American Academy of Arts and Sciences, Boston, Massachusetts. Spring 1967, *Color and Race.*

To study these particular dimensions, the Christian religion must be disassociated from the churches. While religion "transcends" the world, the church itself is very much in the world. It always finds itself in a particular social situation, and its reactions are determined by its environment. The church, whose history began in the Pentecost, may deserve and try to be in Tertullian's phrase a *genus tertium,* a third race over and above the conflict between the "Greeks" and the "Barbarians." It is, nevertheless, established in a world of Babel, a world of disunity and discord.

Although the most liberal Christians of South Africa recognized, for example, the brotherhood of men before God, they were willing to accept segregation of worship if providing the same church for the white and black natives—the Afrikaners and the Bantus—were considered harmful to the cause of Christ among the Christians. René Ribeiro describes in this connection a rather curious case that occurred in Brazil[2]: A Protestant pastor from North America, serving in Recife, Brazil, showed himself to be extremely tolerant and unbiased while there. The moment he stepped on the airplane to return to the United States, however, all his southern prejudice immediately returned. He had not changed his faith; he had simply found himself in a different social situation.

Sociologists have shown that the Negro churches were, above all, instruments of self-expression for the colored community as a separate community. As is the case with the Muslim faith today, they were instruments of protest and of racial revolt. They were in essence more social than religious. But we do not wish to place ourselves in this article in the field of sociology of human—only too human—institutions, but rather in the field of religious feeling and experience (phenomenology).

I

Christianity has been accompanied by a symbolism of color. This symbolism has formed and cultivated a sensitivity to color that extends even to people who claim to be detached from religion. It has created a "backwash" of fixed impressions and attitudes difficult to efface.

Racial hatred has not evolved solely from this Christian symbolism; nor can it be fully explained by economic causes alone. Its roots extend much farther and deeper. They reach into sexual complexes[3] and into religion through the symbolism of color. In human thought every gulf or separation tends to take the form of a conflict of color. This holds not only for concrete obstacles of tribal separation—as between the Indians of the plain and the ancient Mexicans—but also for obstacles between men—as in the social structure of ancient Egypt or the castes of India. Christianity has brought no exception to this very general rule.

There is a danger of confusing in Christianity that which belongs to the scope of rationalization—that which can, as in all ideology, be explained in the final analysis by the economic infrastructure—and the symbolism of color, which falls within the scope of pure religion. When Christians tried to justify slavery, they claimed black skin was a punishment from God. They invoked the curses cast upon Cain, the murderer of his brother, and upon Ham, son of Noah, who had found his drunken father naked in his tent. Against the background of this symbolism, they invented causes for the malady, intended to justify in their own eyes a process of production based upon the exploitation of Negro labor. Later, other rationalizations and counter-rationalizations got woven around the same symbolism.

The Christian symbolism of color is very rich. Medieval painting makes full use of it. Some colors are, however, more pertinent to this discussion than others. The color yellow, or at least a dull shade of yellow, has come to signify treason. When Westerners think of Asiatics, they unconsciously transpose this significance to them, converting it into a trait of ethnic psychology. Consequently, they treat Asiatics as persons in whom they cannot have confidence. They can, of course, give excellent reasons in defense of their behavior: the closed or uncommunicative character of the Japanese, the smiling impassiveness of the Chinese, or some historic case of treason—but these are all reasons invented after the fact. If Westerners could have prevented themselves from being influenced by a symbolism centuries old, they could just as easily have found reasons to justify an impression of the yellow race as loyal and affectionate.

But the greatest Christian two-part division is that of white and black. White is used to express the pure, while black expresses the diabolical. The conflict between Christ and Satan, the spiritual and the carnal, good and evil came finally to be expressed by the conflict between white and black, which underlines and synthesizes all the others. Even the blind, who know only night, think of a swarm of angels or of devils in association with white and black—for example, "a black soul," "the blackness of an action," "a dark deed," "the innocent whiteness of the lily," "the candor of a child," "to bleach someone of a crime." These are not merely adjectives and nouns. Whiteness brings to mind the light, ascension into the bright realm, the immaculateness of virgin snow, the white dove of the Holy Spirit, and the transparency of limpid air; blackness suggests the infernal streams of the bowels of the earth, the pit of hell, the devil's color.

This dichotomy became so dominant that it dragged certain other colors along with it. Celestial blue became a simple satellite of white in painting the cloak of the Immaculate Virgin, while the red flames of hell became a fit companion for the darkest colors. Thinking is so enslaved to language that this chain of associated ideas operates automatically when a white person finds himself in contact with a colored person. Mario de Andrade has rightly exposed the evils of this Christian symbolism as being rooted in the very origins of the prejudice of color. In America, when a Negro is accepted, one often says, in order to separate him from the rest of his race, "He is a Negro, of course, but his soul is white."

II

Although Christ transcends all questions of race or ethnology, it must not be forgotten that God incarnated himself in a man of the Jewish race. The Aryans and the Gentiles—even the most anti-Semitic—worship their God in a Jewish body. But this Jewish body was not white enough for them. The entire history of Western painting bears witness to the deliberate whitening or bleaching effort that changed Christ from a Semitic to an Aryan person. The dark hair that Christ was thought to have had came to be rendered as very light-colored, and his big dark eyes as blue. It was necessary that this man, the incarnation of God, be as far removed as possible from everything that could suggest darkness or blackness, even indirectly. His hair and his beard were given the color of sunshine, the brightness of the light above, while his eyes retained the color of the sky from which he descended and to which he returned.

The progressive Aryanization of Christ is in strict accordance with the logic of the color symbolism. It did not start, however, until Christianity came into close contact with the other races—with the African race, in particular. Christian artists began to avoid the darker tints in depicting Christ in order to remove as much as possible of their evil suggestion.

The Middle Ages did have their famous Black Madonnas which were and still are the object of a devotion perhaps even deeper than that which is dedicated to many of the fair-complexioned images of the Holy Virgin. But the Black Virgin represents to her devotees not so much the Loving Mother as a sorceress, a rain maker, a worker of miracles. She has the magnetism of the strange, smacking of Gypsies and Moors; she stirs the heart as if a bit of magic—even a near-diabolical sorcery—were involved in her miracles. She is not the beloved mother who clasps the unfortunate to her white breast and comforts them with her milky white arms, drying their childish tears with the fair tresses of her bright-colored hair, but a mysterious goddess endowed with extraordinary powers. The symbolism of her dark color is not eliminated in the cult; it is only repressed—and badly repressed—because it infiltrates into the prayers that are directed toward her. Nevertheless, the Black Virgin helps one to understand the appeal used by Catholicism in its efforts to convert pagan peoples to the faith.

References must again be made to painting. The Three Kings or Three Wise Men who came to worship the newborn child were depicted as white men at first. They later came to represent the three great continents: Europe, Asia, and Africa. Balthasar was the Negro King who came to bring his tribute to the fair-haired child amidst the golden straw. He was pictured behind the other two Magi and even sometimes kneeling closest to the Babe, but never between the other two— that would have been equivalent to ignoring his color. Racism subsisted in the disguised form of a patronizing attitude in this first attempt to remove the demoniac symbolism from the black skin.

A similar effort can be seen in the creation of colored saints intended for races other than the white race. St. Mauritius, a commander of the Roman legions in Egypt who was martyred there, was originally depicted as white but then as a Moor, and finally in the thirteenth century as a Negro.[4]

Such changes were exploited for purposes of evangelism as the frontiers of the known world extended farther. The church long ignored St. Benedict of Palermo, known as St. Benedict the Moor, but finally officialized him with the development of missions in Africa and of slavery in the Western Hemisphere. This case illustrates another rationalization on the part of the church intended to break the nominal chain of symbolism. In order to escape from feminine temptations, St. Benedict prayed to God to make him ugly—so God turned his skin black.

To see only symbolism in these cases would, however, be a mistake. Because the symbolism is merely repressed, it returns from another angle. From the mystical, it is converted into the aesthetic. Evil takes the form of ugliness. Above all, the colored saints—St. Mauritius, St. Benedict the Moor, St. Iphigenia the Mulatto, and St. Balthasar the Negro King—are only intermediaries, well below the Virgin Mary and Christ, who stayed white. They express more the difference, the abyss, between people of different races than the unity. They stand for stratification in a multi-racial society.[5] The color black found only a subordinate place in the hierarchy descending from white to black.

In the desire of the church to become universal, the color black became detached from its symbolic significance only to be subsumed in an ideology. This ideology reflected the religious dimension of the paternalism white Catholic masters felt toward Indian serfs and African slaves. When color became a part of an ideology, it was obvious that colored people would react by a counter-ideology. Mulattos prayed to white saints to show that they belonged to the race of the masters. According to folk rumor, a mulatto in Brazil would put the portrait of his Negro mother in the kitchen and that of his white father in the parlor. He would shun colored saints and invoke only the aid of white saints, even though these were claimed by pure white people to belong exclusively to them. The mulattos invented the brotherhood of the Cord of St. Francis in order to enter, by the back door so to speak, the aristocratic church of the Franciscans and to mingle with the white people there.

Negroes whose skin was entirely black set out to reverse the values of the traditional Catholic iconographic system. They first invented black angels with kinky hair and flat noses. Then, prompted by a sentence in the Gospels referring to the Holy Virgin, *Niger erat sed pulchra* ("Black she was, but beautiful"), they conceived of a Black Virgin. This happened only in comparatively recent times, however. Furthermore, Christ himself was left untouched, as though to make him black would have been a sacrilege. Paternalism was still too strong for the hierarchy of color to be upset entirely.

Only in a country where segregation became the rule, as in Anglo-Saxon, Protestant North America and African colonies, did the revolt of the Negro go so far as to create a Black God and a Black Christ. In the African colonies, Messianism represented an effort on the part of the Africans to free themselves from the dominance of the white missions and to establish Black Messiahs as saviors of their own rejected, downtrodden, and exploited race.

Systems of imagery can never do more than reflect the social and economic infrastructure in a form that can never be entirely reversed. This color imagery represents only the reactions of the church to a social situation imposed upon it from without. This imagery could not, therefore, abolish the more powerful pressure of the underlying symbolism.

Catholic Latin America, with its racial interbreeding which it considers an expression of racial democracy, offers a new chain of associations between the color black, the devil, and sin. Anyone wishing to study the manifest content of these associations need only consult the work of Baudelaire, who was profoundly steeped in Catholicism in spite of—or because of—his taste for "Le Fleurs du Mal." Indeed, Baudelaire actually sought in his colored sweetheart the sensation of sin through carnal love with a woman whose color suggested the flames of Hades.

These sensations, although less clearly evident in the cult of the Black Venus in the Tropics, are there in the essence. South Americans are deeply branded by Catholicism. Sin occupies a larger place in South American literature than in European. A distinction is always made between a white woman, the object of legitimate courtship and marriage who is worshiped like the Holy Virgin, and the colored woman, the mistress who is an object of pleasure. A woman of color is considered to be a person of sheer voluptuousness. The slightest gesture she makes, such as the balanced sway of her body as she walks barefoot, is looked upon as a call of the female sex to the male. On the other hand, the white woman is desexualized, if not disincarnated or at least dematerialized.

In Latin American society, marriage limited to one's own color led to a mystic transposition of the wife before the altar of God. The symbolism of the color white played a preponderant role in this transposition. A too carnal enjoyment of the wife would have taken on the aspect of a kind of incest, degrading to both the white man and the white woman. White signified purity, innocence, and virginity. A woman whose skin was not entirely white suggested the carnal merely by her color. She became, therefore, the legitimate object of enjoyment.

The South American perhaps does not realize so fully as Baudelaire did the workings of this symbolism. It does, nevertheless, operate to the detriment of physiological reality. When, for instance, the antislavery poet Castro Alves wanted to express his reaction against the stereotyped mentality anchored in the symbolism of color, he found no other resource than to cast his colored heroine into a waterfall where thousands of brilliant drops created a white bridal veil around her dusky skin.

III

The Protestant's association of the color black with the devil and sin was as strong as the Catholic's. But the Protestant, feeling sure that his soul would go straight to hell, placed the bulwark of Puritanism between himself and the temptation of the woman with color-tinted skin.

Puritanism served to strengthen and deepen the roots of the symbolic association by arousing the idea that the contagiousness of color was associated with contagiousness of sin. The mere presence of a non-white woman was sufficient to sully the eyes and mark the flesh of the white man. Without the grace of God, man was considered to be feeble in the face of worldly temptations. Satan wielded such power over the emotions that every contact with women of the African race was to be avoided. They who bore the color of the infernal master had to be fought against by building up defense reactions of an aesthetic nature.

A white man had to convince himself that colored women were ugly and had an unbearable odor and an oily skin. By maintaining that they had none of the qualities of the ideal woman, a white man could establish a moral protection. When fear was not sufficient, barricades of an institutional nature were established: segregation by color in trains, streetcars, theaters, post offices, and other public places. The schools, where Satan could most easily work his evil influence by giving white children the habit of playing with colored children, were segregated.

Rationalizations about the practical effects of mixed marriages can, of course, camouflage the action of the symbolism: Sin was defined as a stain or pollution, the white person becoming blackened. Religious doctrine was expressed by measures of spiritual hygiene accompanied by the anguish of never having taken quite all the precautions necessary. No matter how careful a person was, he might be stricken by madness in spite of himself, as if a colored woman exuded sin by her mere presence. Over and above any historical or economic factors, the roots of segregation are to be found in the idea of contagiousness of sin through color.

Thus, in the field of religious ideas, the association of the color black with sin was expressed by different behavior patterns in the Catholics and the Protestants. The Catholic brought to the New World the heritage of medieval culture. This culture was characterized not only by the taboo of the white woman, who had been elevated when knighthood was in flower to the almost inaccessible rank of a Madonna, but also by the so-called right of the feudal lord to women of lower rank. The Protestant brought with him, on the other hand, the characteristics of the middle-class culture that was coming into being in the Western world at the time of the discovery and colonization of the New World—a culture characterized by strict family morals and a stern Puritanism. This was, in particular, the culture of the Anglo-Saxon, Dutch, and Calvinist middle classes; the Italian upper-middle class had adopted the ethics of the old medieval nobility.

An examination of Calvinism unveils other impressions in which the symbolism of color is firmly entrenched. Calvin believed that "the knowledge of God was deeply rooted in the minds of men," be they pagan or Christian. This knowledge could, however, be stifled by superstition, which blinded the intelligence, or by sin, which corrupted the senses. Contrary to any concept of racial hatred, Calvin considered reason to be proper to all men whether pagan or Christian. Concomitantly, all men were sinners. Because the pagans had not been able to trace nature back to its Creator, they had stifled the knowledge of God. They had reduced the sacred to phenomena of the senses. Even if they were moral in conduct, they deviated from the true objective of morality—the honor of God, not the glory of man.

Throughout the *Institutes,* Calvin grounds sin in human nature. Ignorance of Christ did not automatically acquit the pagans who had never heard of him. Their souls, too, were made of mud and filth. When the Calvinists came to America and found themselves in the presence of pagan Indians, it was perfectly natural that they should set about with missionary fervor to destroy the corrupt nature of these pagans. They had not come to the New World with any racial attitude, but, on the contrary, with an idea of essential equality. Indians and colonists were equal—equal in sin on the lowest level and in divine grace on the highest. This theoretical equality could be made actual. The Indian had only to give up his natural liberty, which was anarchical, troublesome, and diabolical, and bow to the superior law of the Christians as laid down in the Good Book. Unfortunately, the Indian preferred his liberty to servitude and his diabolical practices to the rules of Holy Writ. This was, in the eyes of the Puritan, an infallible sign of negative predestination, the unavoidable damning of the Indian's soul.

Although the judgment of God regarding these Indians remained a mystery, their perseverance in diabolical practices proved to the Calvinists that God had refused to shed his grace upon them.[6] What a spectacle the Indian presented to the white colonizer. The tyrannical rule of the tribal chief instead of democracy, wretched poverty happily accepted instead of economic prosperity—all evidence of a diabolical persistence in sin that doomed the Indian to eternal damnation. The association of the darker color of the skin with a parallel blackness of the soul became for the Puritans arriving in the New World a fact of experience. The symbolism of color was confirmed as an obvious truth.

As Max Weber has shown, success in life was, for the Calvinists, a sign of selection:

> The Lord God in multiplying his graces upon his servants and conferring upon them new graces every day shows thereby that the work that they have begun is agreeable to him and he finds in them the matter and the occasion to enrich and increase their benefits. . . . To him who has it shall be given. . . . I therefore confess that the faithful shall expect this benediction, that the better they have used these graces of God the more shall other new and greater benefits be added to them every day.[7]

Some curious passages in the *Institutes* take on a special significance when the problem of the religious origins of racism is considered. Man is assailed from all sides by temptations and living in a doubtful world; Calvin includes in the dangers that threaten man life among the savages and the pitfalls of country life.[8] Although he condemns racism, he maintains that the precept of salvation must be limited to those who have some alliance or affinity with Christians.[9] He adds in his *Commentary on Matthew* that God esteems more highly the small company of his own than all the rest of the world.[10]

These ideas—the danger of pagan contagion and the priceless value of the small flock—constitute the religious basis for the "frontier complex" or restricted-group sentiment. South Africa has institutionalized this attitude in the form of *apartheid.*[11] White culture becomes identified with defense of the faith. The white community feels itself to be a community elected by God to make fertile a land that the non-Europeans could not exploit. The natives have cast themselves away from divine election because they have not used properly the talents God has given them.

In some cases, the natives have even made perverse use of the gifts of God. For example, the white people strove to perfect a race of cattle that could furnish great monetary wealth to the Africans. The Bantus, however, preferred quantity. They made the number of cattle a sign of wealth and used them as the price of women in marriage, not as objects of productivity. The white people tried to teach the natives the value of saving money and the use of capital, their Calvinist standard of ethics for labor, morals, and divine vocation, but the natives worked only for the needs of immediate consumption and spent the surplus in feasts—feasts which in the eyes of the whites were always of a licentious or erotic nature.

Thus, the Calvinists reached the same conclusion about the African natives as they had about the Indians. The Calvinist missionary had given the Bantu the opportunity to enter into the economy of salvation, but he had refused. He preferred to continue living in his diabolical manner. Even when converted, the African mixed into his Christian ideas a whole series of superstitions. He interpreted the Christian dogma he was taught according to the dictates of his pagan mentality, inventing prophetesses and messiahs.

The community of the whites had no sense of loss when it came to consider itself as the small flock of the select. Its economic success was proof of divine grace, just as the situation of the blacks was the sign of their rejection. The "frontier complex" or restricted-group feeling rests, therefore, in the final analysis upon the Calvinist idea of predestination and visible signs of divine election.

In this way, dark skin came to symbolize, both in Africa and in America, the voluntary and stubborn abandonment of a race in sin. Contact with this race endangered the white person's soul and the whiteness of his spirit. The symbolism of color thus took on one of the most complicated and subtle forms, in both Protestantism and Catholicism, through the various steps through which darkness of color became associated with evil itself.

IV

The ramifications of this symbolism must now be traced through the double process of secularization in America and of de-Christianization in Europe. Western culture, even among atheists, still remains profoundly steeped in the Christian culture of the past. The symbolism of color continues, therefore, to be effective even when it goes unrecognized. Secularization and de-Christianization do involve, however, new phenomena that cannot be overlooked.

With the coming of independence to America, the philosophy of the European Enlightenment replaced to a great extent the Puritanism of the early colonists. It was first espoused by the aristocratic class of the South, of which Jefferson was the representative figure, and then by the hard-working classes of New England. American democracy is still undoubtedly colored by religion, but Americans tend more and more to retain only that part of Christianity which is based on reason, which is something quite close to what the philosophers used to call "natural religion."

Ralph Barton Perry, in his book *Puritanism and Democracy,* explains well the significance of this transition from Calvinism to an acceptance of the philosophy of the Enlightenment: Puritanism taught that men should distrust their own inclinations and their natural faculties, seeking both their origin and their salvation in a supernatural order. It was a religion of misanthropy. The philosophy of the Enlightenment, on the other hand, was human, optimistic, and eudaemonic.

Such a revolution of thought and feeling should have been marked by a revision of racial values. It was, in fact, the philosophy of the Enlightenment that precipitated the abolition of slavery. Why, then, was there no serious attack upon the symbolism of color, since it was no more founded upon reason than the social institution of slavery which got carried away by a tidal wave of thought and reason?

First of all, Calvinism still remained just under the surface, ready to be revived at the slightest opportunity. The migration toward the West, as Perry has also pointed out, was considered to be further proof corroborating the idea that the Puritans and founders of American democracy had formed of their destiny. The pioneering success was interpreted as a sign of divine grace. The Puritan felt sure that he was among the chosen few when he succeeded in standing up under adversity and triumphing over obstacles.

With the consolidation of national groups in the Western world and the triumph of the spirit of Enlightenment, nothing remained of Calvinism except the barriers forged by the "frontier complex" or restricted-group-boundary concept. The positive elements of Calvinism ceased to exercise their dynamic effect with the rise of secularization and the transition from the old Christianity to a rational religion of democracy. Nevertheless, the barriers fostered by Calvinism still stood as signs of distinction between white men and colored men.

The worst was to happen when the descendants of the slaves finally assimilated North American values and gave themselves over to a "white narcissism." They could see no other way to demonstrate their identification with America than by adopting a kind of Puritanism. The introduction of this factor into Negro Protestantism defined the religion of the colored middle class. By introducing into its religion a factor historically linked to the condemnation of the Indian and the Negro as inveterate savages, the Negro middle class introduced also its own condemnation. The Christian symbolism of color, interiorized in the Negro, gave rise to the neuropathic character, marked by a guilt complex, of the Negro middle class.

It must not be thought, however, that Catholic Latin America did not experience similar phenomena. But interracial sexuality was accepted there, and the drama found its solution in the mingling of blood. White blood acted as a tonic both physically and morally for the Negro, in a process Brazilians call "purging the blood." The progressive whitening of the African race was coupled with its progressive spiritualization.

In Europe, while capitalism had sources in Calvinism, as has been brought out by Max Weber, its development was destined to destroy the Calvinistic code of ethics. The multiplication of productive power could not maintain its pace without the parallel multiplication of needs. This gave rise to an ethic of consumption and finally to materialism. Moreover, scientific thought was undermining the supernatural foundations of the religious concept. The universe was becoming a system of laws that human reason could discern. Capable of being expressed in equations, it was consequently devoid of everything sacred.

The Africans whom the white man was to meet in the colonies had neither this materialistic concept of life nor this rational concept of the universe. Tribal life continued, even after contact with the white man, to follow the ancestral norms. It took no account of the value of time or money.[12] The school introduced by the colonizers had no other purpose than to change the mentality of the African, to prepare him to become a good worker in the service of the white man's plantations and factories and a good consumer capable of buying the white man's products. It destroyed the African's concept that everything is penetrated with something sacred and implanted a more materialistic view of life.

This change of perspective ought to have caused the Christian symbolism of color to disappear entirely. But the change in the African mentality did not come about as rapidly as was anticipated by the founders of the lay schools. Money was not used in accordance with Western standards but lavishly for the purchase of wives and the prestige of family groups. The relations of the African with his employer still followed the archaic pattern of familial or tribal relationships, and not that of the modern contractual ethic of industrialization. In short, it appeared to the white man that the native remained alien to the materialistic approach of the capitalistic economy and also to the rational spirit of science, which had become the new religion of that economy.

Thus, in the symbolic association of color which we have been discussing, some of the elements have disappeared. Associations with the devil and sin have no place in the concept of the universe introduced in the late-nineteenth century. But the "frontier complex" between two conflicting mentalities has held firm. Black and white have taken on other meanings: These meanings still follow, however, the basic antithesis founded centuries before on the white purity of the elect and the blackness of Satan. Because this symbolism became secularized, it survived the collapse of the old Christian code of ethics and the advent of another system of ideas. The Christian tree had been uprooted, but had left root fragments that continued to creep obscurely under the surface.

Mircea Eliade has taught us to discover in the present the remnants of primitive archetypes, such as the nostalgia for Paradise Lost and the Center of the World. It is not surprising, then, that a symbolism of color associations could survive the disappearance of its mystical Christian roots. A change of polarization is taking place today, however. The conflict between light and dark is not so much expressed by the two colors—white and black—as by a chain of experience of white men in their relations with races of non-European stock. A black or dark color has come to symbolize a certain social situation, class, or caste. There still remains, even in this process of secularization, something of the antithesis of darkness and light—the brightness of the sky and the darkness of anguish.

REFERENCES

1. Brazilian films are typical of this point of view. In Europe, a blond is usually the heroine, and a brunette the dangerous woman. In Brazil, the dark woman is loving and faithful, while the blond is the vamp who leads a man to ruin.
2. René Ribeiro, *Religiaõ e Relaçoẽs Raciais* (Religion and Racial Relations; Rio de Janeiro, 1956).
3. Roger Bastide, *Sociologie et Psychanalise* (Sociology and Psychoanalysis; Paris, 1951).
4. Wolfgang S. Seiferth, "St. Mauritius, African," *Phylon*, No. 4 (1941), pp. 370–76.
5. St. Benedict became the Saint of the Indians and Negroes. Most statues of him are to be found in homes, and it is there that his Saint's Day or Feast Day is celebrated. There may be, however, a special chapel for him in churches where numbers of Indians or Negroes worship. For illustrations from Venezuela, see R. Olivares Figueiroa, "San Benito en el folklore occidental de Venezuela," *Acta Venezolana*, Vol. 2, Nos. 1–4 (St. Benedict in the Western Folklore of Venezuela; 1946–47).
6. Juan A. Ortega y Medina, "Ideas de la Evangelización anglosajona entre los indígenas de los Estados Unidos de Norte-América," *América Ingigena*, Vol. 18, No. 2 (Ideas Used in the Anglo-Saxon Evangelization of the Indians in the United States; 1958).
7. Jean Calvin, *Institution de la religion Chrétienne*, ed. F. Baumgartner, Vol. 2, Part 3 (The Christian Institutes of Calvin [author's translation]; Geneva, 1888), p. 11.
8. *Ibid.*, Vol. 1, Part 17, p. 10.
9. *Ibid.*, Vol. 2, Part 8, p. 54.
10. *Ibid.*, Vol. 9, pp. 37–38.
11. Concerning this frontier complex and its various dimensions, including the cultural aspects which are generally the most stressed but which we consider as only derivatives of the first, see Kenneth L. Little, *Race and Society* (Paris, 1952). The reader may be surprised that we have quoted here two passages from Calvin which the Afrikaners do not use in their justification of *apartheid* and that we have not quoted the passages of Calvin (*Works*, Parts 36–51, pp. 400–803; Commentary on Jeremiah, Part 24, p. 2; Sermon on the Ephesians, Part 6, pp. 5–9) which the South Africans do use for that purpose. These latter passages are utilized as rationalizations of the racial situation and therefore after the fact, deforming Calvin's thought. (Cf. Benjamin J. Marais, *Colour, Unsolved Problem of the West* [Cape Town, n.d.], pp. 300ff.) The passages that we have quoted appear to have been stimuli acting upon both the conscious and the subconscious mind of the Dutch pioneers long before the advent of the *apartheid* situation.
12. Concerning this development of Calvinism in regard to science and its impact on the blacks, see Michael Banton, *West African City: A Study of Tribal Life in Freetown* (London, 1957).

GROUP BOUNDARY MAINTENANCE:

THE RIGIDITY AND FLUIDITY

OF RACIAL AND ETHNIC BARRIERS

In his brilliant analysis of the French Revolution, Alexis de Tocqueville observed that in order to discover whether the "caste" system, with its age-old conventions and social barriers, had been definitely eradicated in any country, the "acid test [is] that country's marriage customs." There can be no doubt that endogamy is an important mechanism and index of group boundary maintenance whether it is applied to social or to racial stratification. What is in dispute is the use of the term "caste" with reference to French, or any other non-Indian, society simply because of the presence of the apparently similar practice of endogamy. Louis Dumont would argue that this is an example of "socio-centrism": the tendency to interpret a society and culture in terms of another. It produces a bias that ignores the variety of functions that the "same" social institution may serve in different social systems and overlooks the vital significance of value systems and ideologies in creating such distinctions. We cannot fully understand a society divorced from other societies; so we cannot appreciate that society solely in terms derived from the outside.

Julian Pitt-River's paper focuses on the relatively fluid racial definitions and boundaries found in most Latin American societies. In these situations endogamy has never been rigidly enforced, and there is a more flexible system of stratification where color is "an ingredient, not a determinant of class." The concept of "raza" has none of the finality of the North American or Western European concept of "race"; the term *casta* has little relationship to the Hindu castes. Pitt-Rivers points to the transformations of ethnicity in Latin America and to the potentially important rise of a new sense of Indian consciousness.

In contrast to Latin America the United States has a much more rigid tradition of racial categorization in which the color bar is a central institution. E. U. Essien-Udom interprets the rise of black nationalism, and particularly the Black Muslim sect, in terms of a sociological and psychological reaction to inflexible racial discrimination. Unlike the situation in Latin America, lower class blacks who aspired to be upwardly mobile could not "change their race" by acquiring the culture, customs, or dress of the dominant group. Still less could they bridge the color barrier by inter-

298

marriage or by the accumulation of wealth. While the black bourgeoisie might build up a separate subsociety, relatively insulated from the discrimination of the white community, no such avenue of escape presented itself to the poorest members of the black ghettoes. This doubly rejected group was particularly hard pressed to find a constructive path out of its predicament.

The Muslim ideology provides a means of eradicating the inferiority complex, a legacy of slavery and continued segregation, in the most oppressed of the black masses. It achieves this end by the dual rejection of two value systems: the subculture of the ghetto and the cultural ideals of the dominant (middle-class) white society. Instead, it substitutes a set of beliefs that transposes the racism of the wider community into a doctrine of black superiority and dominance. While the direct appeal of the Muslims among blacks has been limited—as Essien-Udom, writing in the early sixties, correctly predicted—its indirect contribution to the revival of black cultural nationalism, black power, and the development of black consciousness has not been insignificant. The reason for its partial success does not rest on the logical strength of the doctrines but on the function they serve for the ghetto poor. By creating a sense of separate yet worthwhile identity the Black Muslim ideology has responded to the changing needs of the black community as a whole.

27   Caste, Racism and 'Stratification'
Reflections of a Social
Anthropologist

Louis Dumont
To E. E. Evans-Pritchard

In a recent article Professor Raymond Aron writes about sociology: 'what there exists of a critical, comparative, pluralist theory is slight'.[1] This is indeed the feeling one has when, after studying the caste system in India, one turns to comparing it with other social systems and to seeing, in particular, how it has been accommodated within the theory of 'social stratification' as developed in America. To begin with, the problem can be put in very simple terms: is it permissible, or is it not, to speak of 'castes' outside India? More particularly, may the term be applied to the

From *Homo Hierarchicus. The Caste System and its Implications.* (London: Weidenfeld and Nicolson, 1970; Chicago: The University of Chicago Press, 1970), pp. 239–58. Reprinted by permission of Weidenfeld and Nicolson and The University of Chicago Press.

division between Whites and Negroes in the southern states of the United States of America? To this question a positive answer has been given by some American sociologists[2] —in accordance with the common use of the word—while most anthropologists with Indian experience would probably answer it in the negative.[3] Ideally, this question might appear as a matter of mere terminological choice: either we accept the former alternative and adopt a very broad definition, and as a result we may have to distinguish sub-types, as some authors who have opposed the 'racial caste' (U.S.A.) to the 'cultural caste' (India); or we refuse any extension of the term and apply it exclusively to the Indian type precisely defined, and in this case other terms will be necessary to designate the other types. But in actual fact, a certain usage has been established, and perhaps it is only by criticizing its already manifest implications that a way can be opened to a better comparative view. I shall, therefore, begin by criticizing the usage which predominates in America in the hope of showing how social anthropology can assist sociology in this matter. Two aspects will particularly require attention: what idea the authors in question have formed of the Indian system, and which place they give to the concept of 'caste' in relation to neighbouring concepts such as 'class' and to the broad heading of 'social stratification' under which they often group such facts. Thereafter I shall tentatively outline the framework of a true comparison.

A. CASTE AS AN EXTREME CASE OF CLASS: KROEBER

A definition of caste given by Kroeber is rightly regarded as classical, for the whole sociological trend with which I am concerned here links up with it.

In his article on 'Caste' in the *Encyclopoedia of Social Sciences* (Vol. iii, 1930, 254b–257a), he enumerates the characteristics of caste (endogamy, heredity, relative rank) and goes on to say: *'Castes, therefore, are a special form of social classes,* which in tendency at least are present in every society. Castes differ from social classes, however, in that they have emerged into social consciousness to the point that custom and law attempt their rigid and permanent separation from one another. *Social classes are the generic soil from which caste systems have at various times and places independently grown up . . .'* (my italics).

By 'caste systems' he means in what follows, apart from India, medieval Europe and medieval Japan. He implicitly admits, however, that the last two cases are imperfect: either the caste organization extends to only a part of the society, or, as in the Japanese 'quasi-caste system', the division of labour and the integration with religion remain vague.

For us, the essential point here is that 'caste' is considered as an extreme case of 'class'. Why? Probably in the first place because of the 'universality of anthropology', as Lloyd Warner says while accepting Kroeber's definition.[4] In the second place, because 'caste' is at once rigid and relatively rare, whereas 'class' is more flexible, vaguer and relatively very widespread. But the problem is only deferred, for in such a perspective it should be necessary to define 'class', which is much more difficult than to define 'caste'. Never mind, 'class', after all, is familiar to us, while 'caste' is strange. . . . We are landed at the core of the sociocentricity within which the whole school of authors under discussion develops. Actually, if one were prepared to make light of the relative frequency with which the supposed 'class' occurs, and if one were solely concerned with conceptual clarity, the terms could just as well be reversed, and one could start from the Indian caste system, which offers in a clear and crystalline form what is elsewhere diluted and blurred in many ways. The definition quoted reduces a society's consciousness of itself to an epiphenomenon—although some importance is attached to it: 'They have emerged into social consciousness.' The case shows that to do this is to condemn oneself to obscurity.

B. DISTINCTION BETWEEN CASTE, ESTATE, AND CLASS

The oneness of the human species, however, does not demand the arbitrary reduction of diversity to unity, it only demands that it should be possible to pass from one particularity to another, and that no effort should be spared in order to elaborate a common language in which each particularity can be adequately described. The first step to that end consists in recognizing differences.

   Before Kroeber gave his definition, Max Weber had made an absolute distinction between 'class' and *Stand,* 'status-group', or 'estate' in the sense of pre-revolutionary France—as between economy on the one hand and 'honour' and 'social intercourse' on the other.[5] His definition of class as an economic group has been criticized, but it has the merit of not being too vague. Allowing that social classes as commonly referred to in our societies have these two aspects, the analytical distinction is none the less indispensable from a comparative point of view, as we shall see. In Max Weber as in Kroeber, caste represents an extreme case; but this time it is the status-group which becomes a caste when its separation is secured not only through convention and laws, but also ritually (impurity through contact). Is this transition from status-group to caste conceived as genetic or only logical? One notes in passing that, in the passage of *Wirtschaft und Gesellschaft* which I have in view here, Weber thinks that individual castes develop some measure of distinct cults and gods—a mistake of Western common sense which believes that whatever can be distinguished must be different. Into the genesis of caste, Weber introduces a second component, namely a reputedly ethnic difference. From this point of view, castes would be closed communities (*Gemeinschaften*), endogamous and believing their members to be of the same blood, which would put themselves in society (*vergesellschaftet*) one with the other. On the whole, caste would be the outcome of a conjunction between status-group and ethnic community. At this juncture a difficulty appears. For it seems that Weber maintains the difference between *Gesellschaft* and *Gemeinschaft*: on the one hand the *Vergesellschaftung* of a reputedly ethnic group, a 'Pariah people', tolerated only for the indispensable economic services it performs, like the Jews in medieval Europe, on the other the *Gemeinschaft* made up of status-groups or, in the extreme case, of castes. If I am not mistaken, the difficulty emerges in the concluding sentence, which has to reconcile the two by means of an artificial transition from the one to the other: 'Eine umgreifende *Vergesellschaftung* die ethnisch geschiedenen Gemeinschaften zu einem spezifischen, politischen *Gemeinschaftshandeln* zusammenschliesst' (my italics), or, freely translated, 'the *societalization* of ethnically distinct communities embraces them to the point of uniting them, on the level of political action, in a *community* of a new kind'. The particular group then acknowledges a hierarchy of honour and at the same time its ethnic difference becomes a difference of function (warriors, priests, etc.). However remarkable the conjunction here achieved between hierarchy, ethnic difference and division of labour may be, one may wonder whether Weber's failure is not due to the fact that to a hierarchical view he added 'ethnic' considerations through which he wanted to link up widespread ideas on the racial origin of the caste system with the exceptional situation of certain minority communities like Jews or Gypsies in Western societies.

What remains is the distinction, as analytical as one could wish, between economic group and status-group. In the latter category, one can then distinguish more clearly, as Sorokin did,[6] between 'order' or 'estate' and caste. As an instance, the clergy in prerevolutionary France did not renew itself from within, it was an open 'estate'.

C.   'CASTE' IN THE U.S.A.

At first sight there is a paradox in the works of the two most notable authors who have applied the term 'caste' to the separation between White and Negroes in the U.S.A. While their purpose is to oppose the 'colour line' to class distinctions, they both accept the idea that caste is a particular and extreme form of class, not a distinct phenomenon. We have seen that Lloyd Warner accepts Kroeber's idea of continuity; however he immediately insists, as early as his article of 1936, that whilst Whites and Negroes make up two 'castes', the two groups are stratified into classes according to a common principle, so that the Negroes of the upper class are superior from the point of view of class to the poor Whites, while at the same time being inferior to them from the point of view of 'caste'.[7] Gunnar Myrdal also states that 'caste may thus in a sense be viewed as the extreme form of absolutely rigid class', in this sense 'caste' constitutes 'a harsh deviation from the ordinary American social structure and the American Creed'.[8] The expression '*harsh* deviation' is necessary here to correct the idea of continuity posited in the preceding sentence. In other words, the supposed essential identity between class and caste appears to be rooted in the fact that, once equality is accepted as the norm, any form of inequality appears to be the same as any other because of their common deviation from the norm. We shall see presently that this is fully conscious, elaborately justified in Myrdal. But if, from the standpoint of comparative sociology, one purports to describe these forms of inequality in themselves and if, moreover, one finds that many societies have a norm of inequality, then the presumed unity between class on the one hand and the American form of discrimination on the other becomes meaningless, as our authors themselves sufficiently witness.

The use of the term 'caste' for the American situation is justified by our two authors in very different ways. For Myrdal, the choice of a term is a purely practical matter. One should take a word of common usage—and not try to escape from the value judgments implicit in such a choice. Of the three available terms, 'class' is not suitable, 'race' would give an objective appearance to subjective justifications and prejudices, so there remains only 'caste' which is already used in this sense, and which can be used, in a monographic manner, without any obligation to consider how far it means the same thing in India and in the U.S.A.[9] In point of fact, the pejorative coloration of the word by no means displeases Myrdal. While the word 'race' embodies a false justification, the word 'caste' carries a condemnation. This is in accordance with American values as defined by the author in the following pages. The American ideology is egalitarian to the extreme. The 'American Creed' demands free competition, which from the point of view of social stratification represents a combination of two basic norms, equality and liberty, but accepts inequality as a result of competition.[10] From this one deduces the 'meaning' of differences of social status in this particular country, one conceives classes as the 'results of the restriction of free competition', while 'caste', with its draconian limitations of free competition, directly negates the American Creed, creates a contradiction in the conscience of every White, survives only because of a whole system of prejudices, and should disappear altogether.

All this is fine, and the militant attitude in which Gunnar Myrdal sees the sole possibility of true objectivity could hardly be more solidly based. In particular, he has the merit of showing that it is in relation to values (a relation not expressed by Kroeber and Warner) that the assumed continuity of class and caste can be best understood. But was it really necessary in all this to use the word 'caste' without scientific guarantee?[11] Would the argument have lost in efficacy if it had been expressed only in terms of 'discrimination', 'segregation', etc.? Even if it had, ought one to risk obscuring comparison in order to promote action? Gunnar Myrdal does not care for comparison. Further, does he not eschew comparative theory, in so far as he achieves his objectivity only when he can personally share the values of the society he is studying?

Unlike Myrdal, Lloyd Warner thinks that 'caste' can be used of the Southern U.S.A. in the same sense as it is used of India. This is seen from a 'comparative study' by Warner and Allison Davis,[12] in which the results of their American study are summarized, 'caste' defined, and two or three pages devoted to the Indian side. This Indian summary, though based on good authors, is not very convincing. The variability of the system in time and space is insisted upon to the point of stating that: 'it is not correct to speak of an Indian caste system since there is a variety of systems there.'

In general, caste here is conceived as a variety of class, differing from it in that it forbids mobility either up or down. The central argument runs as follows: in the Southern States, in addition to the disabilities imposed upon the Negroes and the impossibility for them to 'pass', there is between Whites and Negroes neither marriage nor commensality; the same is true in India between different castes. It is the same kind of social phenomenon. 'Therefore, for the comparative sociologist and social anthropologist they are forms of behaviour which must have the same term applied to them' (p. 233).

This formula has the virtue of stating the problem clearly, so that if we do not agree with Warner we can easily say why. A first reason, which might receive ready acceptance, is that under the label of 'behaviour pattern' or 'social phenomena' Warner confuses two different things, namely a collection of particular features (endogamy, mobility and commensality prohibition, etc.) and a whole social system, 'caste' in the case of India obviously meaning 'the caste system'. It is not asked whether the sum of the features under consideration is enough (to the exclusion of all the features left out of consideration) to define the social system: in fact there is no question of a system but only of a certain number of features of the Indian caste system which, according to the author, would be sufficient to define the system. There is really here a *choice* which there is no necessity to follow.[13]

Let me try to indicate the reasons against the proposed choice. It is generally admitted, at any rate in social anthropology, that particular features must be seen in their relations with other particular features. There follows, to my mind, a radical consequence—that a particular feature, if taken not in itself but in its concrete position within a system (what is sometimes called its 'function'), can have a totally different meaning according to the position it occupies. That is to say, from a sociological standpoint it is *actually different*. Thus as regards the endogamy of a group: it is not sufficient to say that the group is 'closed', for this very closure is perhaps not, sociologically speaking, the same thing in all cases; in itself it is the same thing, but in itself it is simply not a sociological fact, as it is not, in the first place, a conscious fact. One is led inevitably to the ideology, overlooked in the behaviouristic sociology of Warner and others, which implicitly posits that, among the particular features to be seen in relation to each other, ideological features do not have the same status as the others. Nevertheless a great part of the effort of Durkheim (and of Max Weber as well) bore on the necessity of recognizing in them the same objectivity as in other aspects of social life. Of course this is not to claim that ideology is necessarily the ultimate reality of social facts and delivers their 'explanation', but only that it is the condition of their existence.

The case of endogamy shows very clearly how social facts are distorted through a certain approach. Warner and Davis treat it as a fact of behaviour and not as a fact of values. As such it would be the same as the factual endogamy of a tribe having no prejudice against intermarriage with another tribe, but which given circumstances alone prevent from practising it. If, on the contrary, endogamy is a fact of values, we are not justified in separating it in the analysis from other facts of values, and particularly—though not solely—from the justifications of it the people give. It is only by neglecting this that racial discrimination and the caste system can be confused. But, one might say, is it not possible that analysis may reveal a close kinship between social facts outwardly similar and ideologically different? The possibility can be readily admitted, but only to insist the more vigorously that we are as yet very far indeed from having reached that point, and that the task for the moment is to take social facts as they are given, without imposing upon them a discrimination scientifically as unwarrantable as is, in American society, the discrimination which these authors attack. The main point is that the refusal to allow their legitimate place to facts of consciousness makes true sociological comparison impossible, because it carries with it a sociocentric attitude. In order to see one's own society from without, one must become conscious of its values and their implications. Difficult as this always is, it becomes impossible if values are neglected. This is confirmed here from the fact that, in Warner's conceptual scheme, the continuity between class and caste proceeds, as we have seen, from an unsuspected relation to the egalitarian norm, whilst it is presented as a matter of behaviour.

The criticism of the 'Caste School of Race Relations' has been remarkably carried out by Oliver C. Cox.[14] From the same sources as Warner, Cox, with admirable insight, has evolved a picture of the caste system which is infinitely truer than that with which Warner was satisfied. It is true that one cannot everywhere agree with Cox, but we must remember that he was working at second and even at third hand (for instance from Bouglé). Even the limits of Cox's understanding show up precisely our most rooted Western prejudices. He is insufficient mainly in what regards the religious moorings of the system (purity and impurity); because for the Westerner society exists independently of religion and he hardly imagines that it could be otherwise. On the other hand, Cox sees that one should not speak of the individual caste but of the system (pp. 3–4), and that it is not a matter of racial ideology: '. . . Although the individual is born heir to his caste, his identification with it is assumed to be based upon some sort of psychological and moral heritage which does not go back to any fundamental somatic determinant' (p. 5).

Elsewhere he writes (p. 14): 'Social inequality is the keynote of the system . . . there is a fundamental creed or presumption (of inequality) . . . antithesis of the Stoic doctrine of human equality. . . .' We see here how Cox strikes on important and incontrovertible points whenever he wishes to emphasize the difference between India and America. I will not enlarge on his criticism of Warner and his school; we have already seen that he makes the essential point: the Indian system is a coherent social system based on the principle of inequality, while the American 'colour bar' contradicts the egalitarian system within which it occurs and of which it is a kind of disease.[15]

The use of the word 'caste' to designate American racial segregation has led some authors, in an effort to recognize at the same time the ideological difference, to make a secondary distinction. Already in 1937 John Dollard was writing: 'American caste is pinned not to cultural but to biological factors.'[16] In 1941, in an article called 'Intermarriage in Caste Society' in which he was considering, besides India, the Natchez and the society of the Southern United States, Kingsley Davis asked: how is marriage between different units possible in these societies, while stratification into castes is closely dependent on caste endogamy? His answer was, in the main, that a distinction must be made between a 'racial caste system' in which hybrids present an acute problem, and a 'non-racial caste system' where this is not so. In India, hypergamy as defined by Blunt for the north of India, i.e. marriage between a man of an upper subcaste and a woman of a lower subcaste within the same caste can be understood in particular as a factor of 'vertical solidarity' and as allowing for the exchange of prestige in return for goods (p. 386). (The last point actually marks an essential aspect of true hypergamy, in which the status or prestige of the husband as well as the sons is not affected by the relatively inferior status of the wife or mother.) Another difference between the two kinds of 'caste systems' is that the 'racial' systems rather oppose two groups only, whereas the other systems distinguish a great number of 'strata'. Finally, K. Davis remarks that the hypothesis of the racial origin of the Indian caste system is not proven and that at any rate it is not racial today (n. 22). It is strange that all this did not lead Davis to reflect upon the inappropriateness of using the same word to denote so widely different facts. For him caste, whatever its content may be, is 'an extreme form of stratification', as for others it was an extreme case of class. This brings us to the question of the nature of this category of 'stratification'.

D. 'SOCIAL STRATIFICATION'

Though the expression deserves attention in view of the proliferation of studies published under this title in the United States and the theoretical discussions to which it has given rise, it does not in effect introduce anything new on the point with which we are here concerned. We meet again the same attitude of mind we have already encountered, but here it runs up against difficulties. As Pfautz acknowledges in his critical bibliography of works published between 1945 and 1952, it is essentially a matter of 'class'.[17] However, Weber's distinction has made its way in the world: one can distinguish types of social stratification according to whether the basis of inequality is power, or prestige, or a combination of both, and classes are usually conceived of as implying a hierarchy of power (political as well as economic), castes and 'estates' a hierarchy of prestige (pp. 392-3). One notes however that the community studies of Warner and others conclude that the status hierarchy is a matter of prestige and not of power. Let us stress here the use of the word 'hierarchy', which appears to be introduced in order to allow different species to be distinguished within the genus 'stratification'. But here are two strikingly different concepts: should the quasi-geological impassibility suggested by the latter give way to the consideration of values?

A theoretical controversy in the columns of the *American Sociological Review* is very interesting for the light it throws on the preoccupations and implicit postulates of some sociologists.[18] The starting-point was an article published in 1945 by Kingsley Davis and Wilbert E. Moore. Davis had, three years earlier, given basic definitions for the study of stratification (*status, stratum,* etc.). Here the authors raised the question of the 'function' of stratification. How is it that such palpable inequalities as those referred to under the name of social classes are encountered in a society whose acknowledged norm is equality? Davis and Moore formulate the hypothesis that it is the result of a mechanism comparable to that of the market: inequality of rewards is necessary in a differentiated society in order that the more difficult or important occupations, those demanding a long training in special skills or involving heavy responsibilities, can be effectively carried out. Buckley objected that Davis and Moore had confused true stratification and pure and simple differentiation: the problem of stratification is not, or is not only, one of knowing how individuals potentially equal at the start find themselves in unequal positions ('achieved inequality'), but of discovering how inequality is maintained, since terms like stratum or stratification are generally taken as implying permanent, hereditary, 'ascribed' inequality. In a rejoinder to Buckley, Davis admitted the difference of points of view; he added that the critic's animosity seemed to him to be directed against the attempt to explain inequality functionally. In my opinion, Davis was right in raising the question of inequality; he was wrong, as Buckley seems to imply, in raising it where inequality is weakest instead of tackling it where it is strongest and most articulate. But in so doing he remained within the tradition we have observed here, which always implicitly refers itself to equality as the norm, as this controversy and the very use of the term 'inequality' show.

In a recent article Dennis H. Wrong sums up the debate. He points out the limitations of Davis's and Moore's theory and quotes from a work of the former a passage which again shows his pursuit of the functional necessity of stratification, as illustrated for instance by the fact that sweepers tend to have an inferior status in all societies (he is thinking of India).[19] In the end, Wrong asks for studies on certain relations between the egalitarian ideal and other aspects of society, such as the undesirable consequences of extreme equality or mobility (p. 780). It appears that equality and inequality are considered here as opposite tendencies to be studied on the functional level. Referring to the Utopians, Wrong recalls the difficulty of 'making the leap from history into freedom' (p. 775).

Something has happened then in this branch of American sociology. With the multiplication of studies on social classes, one has been led to introduce values and that value-charged word, 'hierarchy'; one has been led to search for the functions (and disfunctions) of what our societies valorize as well as of what they do not valorize ('in-equality') and which had been called for that reason by a neutral and even pejorative term, 'stratification'. What is in fact set against the egalitarian norm is not, as the term suggests, a kind of residue, a precipitate, a geological legacy, but actual forces, factors or functions. These are negated by the norm, but they nevertheless exist; to express them, the term 'stratification' is altogether inadequate. Nelson N. Foote wrote in a preface to a series of studies: 'The dialectical theme of American history . . . has been a counterpoint of the principles of hierarchy and equality.'[20] The 'problem' of social classes, or of 'social stratification' as it appears to our sociologists springs from the contradiction between the egalitarian ideal, accepted by all these scholars as by the society to which they belong, and an array of facts showing that difference, differentiation, tends even among us to assume a hierarchical aspect, and to become permanent or hereditary inequality, or discrimination. As Raymond Aron says: 'At the heart of the problem of classes I perceive the antinomy between the fact of differentiation and the ideal of equality.'[21] There are here realities which are made obscure to us by the fact that our values and the forms of our consciousness reject or ignore them. (This is probably still more so for Americans.) In order to understand them better, it is advantageous to turn to those societies which on the contrary approve and emphasize them. In so doing we shall move from 'stratification' to hierarchy.

E. HIERARCHY IN INDIA

It is impossible to describe the caste system in detail here. Rather, after briefly re-calling its main features, I shall isolate more or less arbitrarily the aspect which con-cerns us. Bouglé's definition can be the starting-point: the society is divided into a large number of permanent groups which are at once specialized, hierarchized and separated (in matter of marriage, food, physical contact) in relation to each other.[22] It is sufficient to add that the common basis of these three features is the opposition of pure and impure, an opposition of a hierarchical nature which implies separation and, on the professional level, specialization of the occupations relevant to the op-position; that this basic opposition can segment itself without limit; finally, if one likes, that the conceptual reality of the system lies in this opposition, and not in the groups which it opposes—this accounts for the structural character of these groups, caste and subcaste being the same thing seen from different points of view.

It has been acknowledged that hierarchy is thus rendered perfectly univocal in principle.[23] Unfortunately, there has sometimes been a tendency to obscure the issue by speaking of not only religious (or 'ritual') status, but also 'secular' (or 'so-cial') status based upon power, wealth, etc. which Indians would also take into con-sideration. Naturally Indians do not confuse a rich man with a poor man but, as specialists seem to become increasingly aware, it is necessary to distinguish between two very different things: the scale of statuses (called 'religious') which I name hierarchy and which is absolutely distinct from the fact of power: and the distribu-tion of power, economic and political, which is very important in practice but is distinct from, and subordinate to, hierarchy. It will be asked then how power and hierarchy are related to each other. Precisely, Indian society answers this question in a very explicit manner.[24] Hierarchy culminates in the Brahman, or priest; it is the Brahman who consecrates the king's power, which otherwise depends entirely on force (this results from the dichotomy). From very early times, the relationships between Brahman and king or Kshatriya are fixed. While the Brahman is spiritually or absolutely supreme, he is materially dependent; whilst the king is materially the master, he is spiritually subordinate. A similar relation distinguishes one from the other the two superior 'human ends', *dharma* (action conforming to) universal or-der and *artha* (action conforming to) selfish interest, which are also hierarchized in such a way that the latter is legitimate only within the limits set by the former. Again, the theory of the *gift* made to Brahmans, a pre-eminently meritorious action, can be regarded as establishing a means of transformation of material goods into values (*cf.* hypergamy, mentioned above, p. 306: one gets prestige from the gift of a girl to superiors).

This disjunction of power and status illustrates perfectly Weber's analytical distinction; its interest for comparison is great, for it presents an unmixed form, it realizes an 'ideal type'. Two features stand out: first, in India, any totality is expressed in the form of a hierarchical enumeration of its components (thus of the state or kingdom for example), hierarchy marks the conceptual integration of a whole, it is, so to say, its intellectual cement. Secondly, if we are to generalize, it can be supposed that hierarchy, in the sense that we are using the word here, and in accord with its etymology, never attaches itself to power as such, but always to religious functions, because religion is the form that the universally true assumes in these societies. For example, when the king has the supreme rank, as is generally the case, it is very likely not by reason of his power but by reason of the religious nature of his function. From the point of view of rank at any rate, it is the opposite to what one most often supposes, namely that power is the essential which then attracts to itself religious dignities or finds in them support and justification.

One may see in the hierarchical principle, as it appears in India in its pure state, a fundamental feature of complex societies other than our own, and a principle of their unity; not their material, but their conceptual or symbolic unity. That is the essential 'function' of hierarchy: it expresses the unity of such a society whilst connecting it to what appears to it to be universal, namely a conception of the cosmic order, whether or not it includes a God, or a king as mediator. If one likes, hierarchy integrates the society by reference to its values. Apart from the general reluctance which searching for social functions at this level is likely to encounter, it will be objected that there are societies without hierarchy, or else societies in which hierarchy does not play the part described above. It is true for example that tribes, while they are not entirely devoid of inequalities, may have neither a king nor, say, a secret society with successive grades. But that applies to relatively simple societies, with few people, and where the division of labour is little developed.

F. THE MODERN REVOLUTION

There remain the societies of the modern Western type, which go so far as to inscribe the principle of equality in their constitutions. It is indeed true that, if values and not behaviour alone are considered, a profound gap has to be acknowledged between the two kinds. What has happened? Is it possible to take a simple view of it? The societies of the past, most societies, have believed themselves to be based in the order of things, natural as well as social; they thought they were copying or designing their very conventions after the principles of life and the world. Modern society wants to be 'rational', to break away from nature in order to set up an autonomous human order. To that end, it is enough to take the true measure of man and from it deduce the human order. No gap between the ideal and the real: like an engineer's blueprint, the representation will create the actuality. At this point society, the old mediator between man in his particularity and nature, disappears. There are but human individuals, and the problem is how to make them all fit together. Man will now draw from himself an order which is sure to satisfy him. As the source of this rationality, Hobbes posits not an ideal, always open to question, but the most general passion, the common generator of human actions, the most assured human reality. The individual becomes the measure of all things, the source of all 'rationality'; the egalitarian principle is the outcome of this attitude, for it conforms to reason, being the simplest view of the matter, while it most directly negates the old hierarchies.[25]

As against the societies which believed themselves to be natural, here is the society which wants itself to be rational. Whilst the 'natural' society was hierarchized, finding its rationality in setting itself as a whole within a vaster whole, and was unaware of the 'individual', the 'rational' society on the other hand, recognizing only the individual, i.e. seeing universality, or reason, only in the particular man, places itself under the standard of equality and is unaware of itself as a hierarchized whole. In a sense, the 'leap from history into freedom' has already been made, and we live in a realized Utopia.

Between these two types which it is convenient to contrast directly, there should probably be located an intermediary type, in which nature and convention are distinguished and social conventions are susceptible of being judged by reference to an ideal model accessible to reason alone. But whatever may be the transitions which make for the evolution of the second type from the first, it is in the modern revolution which separates the two types, really the two leaves of the same diptych, that the central problem of comparative sociology most probably lies: how can we describe in the same language two 'choices' so diametrically opposed to each other, how can we take into account at once the revolution in values which has transformed modern societies as well as the 'unity of anthropology'? Certainly this cannot be done by refusing to acknowledge the change and reducing everything to 'behaviour', nor by extending the obscurity from one side to the other, as we should by talking of 'social stratification' in general. But we remark that where one of the leaves of the diptych is obscure and blurred, the other is clear and distinct; use can be made of what is conscious in one of the two types of society in order to decipher what is not conscious in the other.

G. FROM HIERARCHY TO DISCRIMINATION

One can attempt, in broad terms, to apply this comparative perspective to the American racist phenomenon. It is obvious on the one hand that society did not completely cease to be society, as a hierarchized whole, on the day it willed itself to be simply a collection of individuals. In particular, the tendency to make hierarchical distinctions continued. On the other hand, racism is more often than not understood to be a modern phenomenon. (Economic causes of its emergence have sometimes been sought, whilst much closer and more probable ideological connections were neglected.) The simplest hypothesis therefore is to assume that racism fulfils an old function under a new form. It is as if it were representing in an egalitarian society a resurgence of what was differently and more directly and naturally expressed in a hierarchical society. Make distinction illegitimate, and you get discrimination; suppress the former modes of distinction and you have a racist ideology. Can this view be made more precise and confirmed? Societies of the past knew a hierarchy of status bringing with it privileges and disabilities, amongst others the total juridical disability of slavery. Now the history of the United States tells us just this, that racial discrimination succeeded the slavery of the Negro people once the latter was abolished. (One is tempted to wonder why this all important transition has not been more systematically studied, from a sociological point of view, than it seems to have been, but perhaps one's ignorance is the answer.[26]) The distinction between master and slave was succeeded by discrimination by White against Black. To ask why racism appears is already to have in part answered the question: the essence of the distinction was juridical; by suppressing it the transformation of its racial attribute into racist substance was encouraged. For things to have been otherwise the distinction itself should have been overcome.

In general, racism certainly has more complex roots. Besides the internal difference of status, traditional societies knew an external difference, itself coloured by hierarchy, between the 'we' and the others. It was normally social and cultural. For the Greeks as for others, foreigners were barbarians, strangers to the civilization and society of the 'we'; for that reason they could be enslaved. In the modern Western world not only are citizens free and equal before the law, but a transition develops, at least in popular mentality, from the moral principle of equality to the belief in the basic identity of all men, because they are no longer taken as samples of a culture, a society or a social group, but as *individuals* existing in and for themselves.[27] In other words, the recognition of a cultural difference can no longer ethnocentrically justify inequality. But it is observed that in certain circumstances, which it would be necessary to describe, a hierarchical difference continues to be posited, which is this time attached to somatic characteristics, physiognomy, colour of the skin, 'blood'. No doubt, these were at all times marks of distinction, but they have now become the essence of it. How is this to be explained? It is perhaps apposite to recall that we are heirs to a dualistic religion and philosophy: the distinction between matter and spirit, body and soul, permeates our entire culture and especially the popular mentality. Everything looks as if the egalitarian-identitarian mentality was situated within this dualism, as if once equality and identity bear on the individual *souls,* distinction could only be effected with regard to the *bodies.* What is more, discrimination is collective, it is as if only physical characteristics were essentially collective where everything mental tends to be primarily individual. (Thus mental differences are attributed to physical types). Is this far-fetched? It is only emphasizing the Christian ancestry of modern individualism and egalitarianism: the individual has only fellow-men (even his enemies are considered, not only as objects, but also as subjects), and he believes in the fundamental equality of all men taken severally; at the same time, for him, the collective inferiority of a category of men, when it is in his interest to state it, is expressed and justified in terms of what physically differentiates them from himself and people of his group. To sum up, the proclamation of equality has burst asunder a mode of distinction centred upon the social, but in which physical, cultural and social characteristics were indiscriminately mixed. To reaffirm inequality, the underlying dualism demanded that physical characteristics be brought to the fore. While in India heredity is an attribute of status, the racist attributes status to 'race'.

All this may be regarded as an arbitrary view of the abstract intellect. Yet, the hypothesis is confirmed at least in part in Myrdal's work. Dealing with the American facts, this author discovers a close connection between egalitarianism and racism. To begin with, he notes in the philosophy of the enlightenment the tendency to minimize innate differences; then, generally everywhere and especially in America, the essentially moral doctrine of the 'natural rights' of man rests on a biological egalitarianism: all men are 'created equal'. The period 1830–1860 sees the development of an ideology for the defence of slavery: slavery being condemned in the name of natural equality, its champions argue against this the doctrine of the inequality of races; later the argument is used to justify discrimination, which becomes established from the moment when, about 1877, the North gives up enforcing assimilation. The author's conclusions are worth pondering upon: 'The dogma of racial inequality may, in a sense, be regarded as a strange fruit of the Enlightenment. . . . The race dogma is nearly the only way out for a people so moralistically egalitarian, if it is not prepared to live up to its faith. A nation less fervently committed to democracy could probably live happily in a caste system . . . race prejudice is, in a sense, a function (a perversion) of egalitarianism'.[28]

If this is so, it is permissible to doubt whether, in the fight against racism in general, the mere recall of the egalitarian ideal, however solemn it may be, and even though accompanied by a scientific criticism of racist prejudices, will be really efficient. It would be better to prevent the passage from the moral principle of equality to the notion that all men are identical. One feels sure that equality can, in our day, be combined with the recognition of differences, so long as such differences are morally neutral. People must be provided with the means for conceptualizing differences. The diffusion of the pluralistic notions of culture, society, etc., affording a counterweight and setting bounds to individualism, is the obvious thing.[29] Finally, if the tendency to hierarchize still exists, if the affirmation of the modern ideal is not sufficient to make it disappear but, on the contrary, by a complicated mechanism, can on occasion make it ferocious and morbid, the antagonisms and interests which exploit it should not be lost sight of—but this is beyond our subject.

Cutting short here the attempt to define racism comparatively, I should like to recall, albeit too briefly, a structural relation which is essential to the possible developments of comparison. Equality and hierarchy are not, in fact, opposed to each other in the mechanical way which the exclusive consideration of values might lead one to suppose: the pole of the opposition which is not valorized is none the less present, each implies the other and is supported by it. Talcott Parsons draws attention, at the very beginning of his study, to the fact that distinction of statuses carries with it and presupposes equality within each status (*op. cit.,* p. 1). Conversely, where equality is affirmed, it is within a group which is hierarchized in relation to others, as in the Greek cities or, in the modern world, in British democracy and imperialism, the latter being tinged with hierarchy (e.g., incipient racism in India in the second half of the nineteenth century).[30] It is this structural relation that the egalitarian ideal tends to destroy, the result of its action being what is most often studied under the name of 'social stratification'. In the first place the relation is inverted: equality contains inequalities instead of being contained in a hierarchy. In the second place a whole series of transformations happen which can perhaps be summarized by saying that hierarchy is repressed, made non-conscious: it is replaced by a manifold network of inequalities, matters of fact instead of right, of quantity and gradualness instead of quality and discontinuity. Hence, in part, the well-known difficulty of defining social classes.

H. CONCLUSION

To conclude in general terms, comparative sociology requires concepts which take into account the values that different societies have, so to speak, chosen for themselves. A consequence of this choice of values is that certain aspects of social reality are clearly and consciously elaborated, whilst others are left in the dark. In order to express what a given society does not express, the sociologist cannot invent concepts, for when he attempts to do so he only manages, as in the case of 'social stratification', to translate in a way at once pretentious and obscure the prejudices of his own society. He must therefore have recourse to societies which have expressed those same aspects. A general theory of 'inequality', if it is deemed necessary, must be centred upon those societies which give it a meaning and not upon those which, while presenting certain forms of it, have chosen to disavow it. It must be a theory of hierarchy in its valorized, or simple and direct forms, as well as in its non-valorized, or devalorized, or complex, hybrid, covert forms. (Let us note, following Talcott Parsons,[31] that such a theory is only one particular way of considering the total social system.) In so doing one will of course in no way impose upon one society the values of another, but only endeavour to set mutually 'in perspective'[32] the various types of societies. One will try to see each society in the light not only of itself but of the others. From the point of view of social anthropology at any rate, this appears to be not only the formula for an objective comparison, but even the condition for understanding each particular society.

NOTES

[This is an English version of a paper first published in French in *Cahiers Internationaux de Sociologie,* Paris, XXIX, 1960, pp. 91–112. The dedication and sub-title were part of the original text and have been reintroduced here.] The following reflections have sprung mainly from the preparation of an article on 'caste' for the *Vocabulary of Social Sciences* (Unesco). The question of the proximate extensions of the term 'caste', for instance to societies of South-East Asia, is left out. Only a remote extension is considered which appears to require that sociological and anthropological approaches be confronted, even if in a somewhat hasty and temporary manner.

1. Raymond Aron, 'Science et conscience de la société', *European Journal of Sociology*, I, 1, 1960, p. 29.

2. The tendency, which its only systematic opponent, O. C. Cox, has called 'the Caste School of Race Relations', seems to have won the day. Another, more moderate, tendency consists in applying the word 'caste' to U.S.A. in a monographic manner, without comparative prejudice (Myrdal, etc., see below). The dictionaries give, besides the proper sense of the word, the extended meaning, e.g., *Shorter Oxford English Dictionary*, *s.v.*: '3. *fig.* A class who keep themselves socially distinct, or inherit exclusive privileges 1807.' [The French text has here a reference to Littré instead of O.S.D.]

3. Yet, among recent authors who are familiar with the Indian system, a sociologist working in Ceylon insists on the fundamental difference between India and U.S. (Bryce Ryan, *Caste in Modern Ceylon*, New Brunswick, N.J., 1953, p. 18, note), while F. G. Bailey asserts *a priori* that this comparison must take place under the word 'caste' (*Contributions*, III, p. 90). Morris Carstairs is less categorical, but he accepts, with Kroeber's definition (below), the American usage, because of its advantages as compared with 'race' (*The Twice-Born*, London, 1957, p. 23). Much earlier an Indian author, Ketkar, insisted on a hierarchical division of American society based on race and occupation, and he enumerated ten groups (based in fact on the country of origin). He did not use the word 'caste' but he underlined with some relish the features which in his view were reminiscent of the Indian system. (Shridar V. Ketkar, *The History of Caste in India*, I, Ithaca, N.Y., 1909, pp. 100 n., 102 n., 115 n. 5.) The general question has recently been discussed in: E. R. Leach (ed.), *Aspects of Caste in South India, Ceylon and N.-W. Pakistan*, Cambridge, 1960 (Cambridge Papers in Social Anthropology, No. 2), notably p. 5.

4. W. Lloyd Warner (Dir.), *Deep South, A Social Anthropological Study of Caste and Class*, Chicago, c. 1941, ed. 1946, p. 9. B. S. Ghurye's position is close to that of Kroeber: well marked status groups are common in Indo-European cultures; comparatively, the Indian caste system represents only an extreme case (untouchability, etc.), see *Caste and Race in India*, New York, 1932, pp. 140, 142.

5. Max Weber, *Wirtschaft und Gesellschaft*, II, pp. 635–7. Discussed by Cox, *Caste, Class and Race*, p. 287, and: 'Max Weber on Social Stratification', *American Sociological Review*, II, 1950, pp. 223–7; cf. also Hans Gerth, 'Max Weber vs. Oliver C. Cox', *American Sociological Review, ibid.*, pp. 557–8 (as regards Jews and castes).

6. Pitrim A. Sorokin, *Society, Culture and Personality, Their Structure and Dynamics*, New York, c. 1947, p. 259 (the 'order' or 'estate' as a 'diluted caste', *cf.* what has been said above about class and caste). Max Weber distinguishes between open and closed status groups (*Ges. Aufs. z. Religions-soziologie*, II, ed. 1923, pp. 41–2). It is to be noted that a recent work recognizes two fundamental types of 'social stratification', the caste type which comprises 'orders' or 'estates', and the open class type, related respectively to the poles of Talcott Parsons' alternative of particularism-universalism (Bernard Barber, *Social Stratification, A Comparative Analysis of Structure and Process*, New York, 1957).

7. W. Lloyd Warner, 'American Caste and Class', *American Journal of Sociology*, XLII, 1936, pp. 234–7.

8. Gunnar Myrdal, *An American Dilemma, The Negro Problem and Modern Democracy* (with the assistance of Richard Sterner and Arnold Rose), New York and London, c. 1944, p. 675; also p. 668: 'The scientifically important difference between the terms "caste" and "class" as we are using them is, from this point of view, *a relatively large difference in freedom of movement between groups*' (his italics). Same justification for the use of the term (practical reasons, not indicating identity with the Indian facts), in Westie and Westie, *American Journal of Sociology*, LXIII, 1957–1958, p. 192, n. 5.

9. *Op. cit.*, pp. 667–8. In a footnote, Myrdal takes up an objection made in particular by Charles S. Johnson: the word 'caste' connotes an invariable and stable system in which the tensions and frictions which characterize the relations between Whites and Blacks in the United States are not found; he replies that he does not believe that a caste system having such characteristics exists anywhere (pp. 1374–35, n. 2) and says earlier (p. 668) that Hindu society today does not show that 'stable equilibrium' that American sociologists, observing from a distance, have been inclined to attribute to it. We see here some trace of the egalitarian Creed. The author has, since, had first-hand experience of India and one wonders whether he would maintain this today, whether, even, he would continue to use the word 'caste' for American phenomena.

10. *Ibid.*, pp. 670–1. There is here an interesting judgment on the Lloyd Warner school: according to Myrdal, one must take account of the extreme egalitarianism in the 'popular national theory' in order to understand both the tendency among these authors to exaggerate the rigidity of distinctions of class and caste in America, and the interest aroused by their works, which has been greater than their strictly scientific novelty.

11. It is a little surprising to find, next to the ideas here summarized, a rather narrow idea of the place of concepts in science: 'Concepts are our created instruments and have no other form of reality than in our usage. Their purpose is to help make our thinking clear and our observations accurate' (p. 667).

12. W. Lloyd Warner and Allison Davis, 'A Comparative Study of American Caste', in Edgar T. Thomson, ed., *Race Relations and the Race Problem*, Durham, North Car., 1939, pp. 219–45; for India see pp. 229–32.

13. The operation of this choice is clear in principle: the caste system of India has been characterized by only those of its traits that it is thought may be found in America, where however they do not constitute a complete system but only part of a system which is called a class-and-caste system.

14. Oliver C. Cox, 'Race and Caste, A Distinction', *American Journal of Sociology*, 1944–1945, pp. 306–8, and above all *Caste, Class and Race, A Study in Social Dynamics*, New York, 1948, to which the references in the text relate.

15. Cox's thesis appears to have had little effect. Sorokin however refers to his article and takes a similar position: the relation between Blacks and Whites has some of the elements of relations between castes but it differs fundamentally (*op. cit.*, p. 258, n. 12).

16. John Dollard, *Caste and Class in a Southern Town*, New York, *c.* 1937, ed. 1940, p. 64; Kingsley Davis, 'Intermarriage in Caste Society', *American Anthropologist*, XLIII, 1941, pp. 376–95.

17. Harold W. Pfautz, 'The Current Literature on Social Stratification, Critique and Bibliography', *American Journal of Sociology*, LVIII, 1953, pp. 391–418. The theory of stratification is approached, not starting from class, but from an absolutely general point of view, by Talcott Parsons in 'A Revised Theoretical Approach to the Theory of Social Stratification' (R. Bendix and S. M. Lipset, ed., *Class, Status and Power, A Reader in Social Stratification*, Glencoe, Ill., 1953). While it adopts the same label, the work is outside the current here criticized; the general conception (*in fine*) removes the habitual implications of the word. The argument proceeds from values and the hierarchy which necessarily results from them. The conceptual framework is that of the general theory.

18. Kingsley Davis, 'A Conceptual Analysis of Stratification', *American Sociological Review*, VII, 1942, pp. 309–21; K. Davis and Wilbert E. Moore, 'Some Principles of Stratification', *A.S.R.*, 10, 1945, pp. 242–9; W. Buckley, 'Social Stratification and Social Differentiation', *A.S.R.*, 23, 1958, pp. 369–75; K. Davis, 'A Reply to Buckley', *A.S.R.*, 24, 1959, p. 82; Dennis H. Wrong, *A.S.R.*, 24, pp. 772–82. Reference will be found in the articles of Buckley and Wrong to other articles not used here.

19. I was unfortunately unable to consult during the preparation of this article Kingsley Davis's book, *Human Society*, New York, 1949, quoted by Wrong, and which would have been of particular interest since the author was concerned with India at that time (*cf. The Population of India and Pakistan*, Princeton, 1951).

20. Nelson N. Foote, 'Destratification and Restratification', Editorial Foreword, *American Journal of Sociology*, LVIII, 1953, pp. 325-6.

21. *European Journal of Sociology*, I, 1, 1960, p. 14.

22. Célestin Bouglé, *Essais sur le régime des castes*, Paris, 1908, p. 4. The English translation of Bouglé's thesis, and a commentary on his book together with that of Hocart, which poses the problem of power, is in *Contributions*, II, 1958.

23. Talcott Parsons, *loc. cit.*

24. What follows is summarized from my chapter on the conception of Kingship in ancient India, to appear in L. Renou and J. Filliozat, *L'Inde Classique*, III.

25. On Hobbes and the artificial society, 'rational' in the sense of being devised according to the reality of man (the individual) and not inspired by an ideal order, *cf.* Léo Strauss, *Natural Right and History*, Chicago, 1953, Chapter 5; Élie Halévy, *La formation du radicalisme philosophique*, 3 vols., Paris, 1901-1904, I, pp. 3, 41, 53, 90; III, pp. 347-8, etc.

26. *Cf.* Gunnar Myrdal, *ibid.*, p. 581 ff., the 'Jim Crow Laws', etc. The reaction to the abolition of slavery was not immediate but developed slowly. Discrimination appears as simple separation under the slogan 'separate but equal'. For the period before the civil war also, Myrdal gives a succinct history, but the analysis, apparently, remains to be done. It promises to be fruitful, see for example the declarations of Jefferson and Lincoln (*cf. Times Literary Supplement*, July 22, 1960, pp. 457-8, according to J. W. Schulte-Nordholt, *The People That Walk in Darkness*, London, Burke 1960). Recent articles by P. L. Van der Berghe partly satisfy my wish. *Cf.* the last one: 'Apartheid, une interprétation sociologique de la ségrégation raciale', *Cahiers internationale de sociologie*, XXVIII, nouv. sér., 7ᵉ année, 1960, pp. 47-56. According to this author, segregation has replaced etiquette as mode of social distance. The change would correspond to the movement from slavery to racism.

27. The fact that the transition from 'equality' to 'identity' operates chiefly at the level of popular mentality makes it more difficult to seize on than if it were present in the great authors. I propose nevertheless to study elsewhere more closely this particular complementarity between egalitarianism and racism.

28. Gunnar Myrdal, *ibid.*, pp. 83 ff., the quotations are from p. 89. Myrdal also takes account of the development of the biological view of man: *Homo sapiens* as a species in the animal world; *cf.* also p. 591: 'The persistent preoccupation with sex and marriage in the rationalization . . . is, to this extent, an irrational escape on the part of the whites from voicing an open demand for difference in social status . . . for its own sake.'

29. *Cf.* Claude Lévi-Strauss, *Race et histoire*, UNESCO, *c.* 1952.

30. Machiavelli observes that a 'republic' which wishes to extend its empire and not remain small and stagnant, should like Rome confide the defence of liberty to the people and not, like Sparta and Venice, to the great. (*Discourses on the First Decade of T. Livy*, I, chapters V-VI.)

31. *Cf.* n. 17.

32. E. E. Evans-Pritchard, *Social Anthropology*, London, 1951, p. 129.

28   Race in Latin America:
The Concept of 'Raza'

Julian Pitt-Rivers

I

It is well known that the attitudes of the Latin Americans toward *race* are not the same as those of the inhabitants of Europe and the United States. This observation led scholars as distinguished as Gilberto Freire and Arnold Toynbee to put forward the view that there is no 'race prejudice' in Latin America, a view that has been criticised by more recent writers. In Latin America distinctions of 'race' are indeed made, but not on the basis of the same premises as in North America and, though *raza* and *race* are the same word, they do not bear the same connotations in Spanish-speaking as in English-speaking countries—outside scientific circles, perhaps. 'Race' is a system of classifying individuals and, as such, part of each culture, and therefore liable to vary from one to another. But what science has done with the word is another matter.

It is easy enough to smile when told that someone is of a different 'raza' to his parents or even that "he used to be a negro, but now he's white" but our smile is one of ethnocentric satisfaction and it springs from the assumption that we can allow ourselves to feel patronising toward those who use such words like a simpleton. This is a pleasure we can ill afford, for our own usage harbours a host of contradictions also.

The reason why it appears comic to suppose that a man can belong to a different race from his parents or change his race is that, for us today, the essence of the word is physical heredity, and therefore these usages are by definition nonsense: one cannot be of a different race to one's parents. Thanks to the work of modern geneticists we have some fairly firm ideas about how physical heredity is transmitted. Yet this is so only since the last half century and the word *race* had already held sway for much longer in senses which owed nothing to genetics and rested upon a notion of descent that was social rather than biological.

* * * * *

Let us now turn to Spanish America to see how the concept of *raza* is used there. It applies to two rather different categories of people who can both be opposed to the culturally hispanic and supposedly white rulers of those countries: the Negroes who are thought to be different racially on account of their phenotype and, above all, the Indians who are thought to be different in phenotype also but

Extract reprinted by permission from the *European Journal of Sociology*, XIV (1973), pp. 12-30.

who are opposed to the Hispanics essentially on account of their culture and social status as members of Indian communities. The ways in which Indians are in fact different from Hispanics are by no means constant. The notion of race therefore hinges upon the definition of the Indian and varies accordingly, making it impossible to define Indians by their overt characteristics. This creates a difficulty not only for anthropologists but for the census-takers of those countries where an attempt is made to record the racial composition of the nation. A comprehensive view of race relations depends upon these figures, yet they are scarcely comparable from one country to another. Moreover they are hard to compare from one period to another, since the criteria of the census-takers change in accordance with what each age thinks about race, as Kubler's study of the census data of nineteenth century Peru shows[1]. We do not need to go so far back in order to find the problem posed, for example, in Guatemala where the criteria have varied radically within the present century.

Its census of 1940 tried to use a physical concept of race and classified the population as either Indian, Mestizo, Negro, White or Oriental. The 1950 census-makers recognised the failure of this attempt and reverted to a simple dichotomy of *Indian* or *Ladino* (as those of Hispanic status are called in Guatemala). They placed in the latter category all those who were not Indian, including the Chinese, the Mormon missionaries, etc. The 1960 census rather logically changed the name of this category to *'non-indigena'*.

In preparation for the 1950 census, an investigation was carried out with the aim of deciding how an Indian should be defined. It discovered that the overt criteria vary from one community to another. "Thus", says the prologue to the census, "if in one municipality the principal characteristic identifying a person was dress, in another this was secondary. The same might be said of language, style of living, etc. Recognising the difficulty of formulating a definition, the instructions given to the census-takers required them to base their decisions on the social esteem in which the person was held in the place in which he was counted. In the small communities there is a certain public opinion that qualifies an individual as indian or ladino. For this reason the taking of the census was entrusted, whenever possible, to members of the local community who know quite well how people are classified there."

The census thus assumed that the ethnic distinction is a purely social one, to be isolated from the various cultural phenomena to which it is attached in any particular instance. The differing bases of this social distinction are clearly revealed, since the census also gives a wealth of statistics on the number of *Indians* in each community who speak Spanish in the home (rather than an Indian language), eat wheat bread rather than tortillas, dress as Indians, wear shoes, sandals or go barefoot, go to school till what age, etc. It is possible to see from this that there is no straightforward correlation between culture and 'race'—the census-makers are thus justified in their approach—and that the complexity of defining the Indian, especially in Guatemala, is great.

This is due to the nature of the Indians. Those who live in the jungle present no problem of definition, though they may be difficult to count. But the Indians who were baptised under the empire (and those of Guatemala almost all belong to this category) present a different problem, for they possess a recognised status in the national society, participate to some extent in the national economy, yet not in the national community. They are administered within the framework of the national state, yet they are *not part* of it, in the sense of participating fully in the national culture and possessing full citizenship. This difference of status is expressed in the idiom of *race*.

The concept of *raza* is also invoked, however, to mark distinctions of social status within the non Indian sector of the population. Thus, in Central America, a person may still be said to be Indian despite the fact that he is recognised as a Ladino. Here the distinction is a purely individual qualification which affects his class standing *within* civilised society; it does not exclude him *from* it. In the same way a Ladino may also be said to be a Negro: his colour implies that he is of African, i.e. of slave, descent. Thus there is a fundamental distinction to be made between *individual* racial identity within soi-disant civilised society and *collective* ethnic status attaching to a community. Indians are identified by the culture of their community, not their individual phenotype, even though there is a strong statistical correlation between phenotype and ethnic status. Hence a Ladino may be called 'Indian' if he looks Indian. He is not thought to be, nor treated as though he were socially an Indian. In fact many Ladinos "look Indian". Conversely, many members of Indian communities look European, but they are no less Indian on that account, either in Hispanic or in Indian eyes. *Raza* can be seen, then, to be employed in two rather different ways: it qualifies individual standing within Hispanic national life on the basis of phenotype but it is then only one of many indicators of social status: economic, educational, occupational and so forth. But it also defines people as to their ethnic status without regard to phenotype, but on account of their membership of an Indian community. Hence we reach the paradox: that *raza* only refers to phenotype when it marks a social distinction among persons who are recognised to belong to the same ('civilised') *raza*; phenotype is not the criterion for distinguishing between the Indian and Hispanic *razas*.

Descent is the central notion of the popular concept of race, but in the Hispanic half of society it is *implied* by phenotype, whereas in the case of the Indians, it is asserted by social affiliation and manifest in culture. Consequently there is only a limited difficulty for Indians, once they have learned Spanish, to change their ethnic identity and become Ladinos. If they happen to belong to a community which dresses in traditional style, they will also have to change their dress. The term *indio revestido* (redressed Indian) applies to those who have decided to change their race, but whose antecedents have not yet been forgotten.

People also change their race in the Andes, but here there is a recognised category for those who do so. They are called *cholos:* they are no longer Indians, but 'civilised Indians', Hispanics who are thought to be 'really' Indians. They constitute an ethnic status intermediary between the Indians and the Mestizos, for which there is no equivalent outside South America.

People have been changing their race in Spanish America ever since the sixteenth century. They have changed as individuals and also as communities, when a whole generation decides to do so in a given place. They have done so in ever-increasing numbers as the census figures of the last two centuries make clear. The ethnic division can therefore only be understood in *time* and one is tempted to say that the Indian, today, is simply the descendant of those who, for one reason and another, have not decided to change. The presence of the Indian is best explained then by the nature of his relationship to those who are *not*. This explanation concords with the social definition of race suggested above; the Indian is someone who is denied recognition as a full member of the human community, one who is thought to be naturally inferior. His status is a function of the total social structure which uses the cultural differences between Indian and Hispanic to maintain the social distinction. This is not the way anthropologists have usually viewed the matter, so let us glance at the more conventional approaches.

The anthropologists who first went to Middle America were concerned with the most traditional Indians they could find. In many cases their intention was to use the data of their investigations in the present to verify their hypotheses regarding the culture of the *ancient* peoples. They saw in every modern Indian a replica of his forbears and picked through the culture they surveyed in search of "pre-Columbian customs", which they labelled in terms of origins. This viewpoint concorded happily with the ideology of revolutionary Mexico which attached a similar value to the relics of the pre-conquest past. Thus anthropologists became very popular in that country and among those who, in neighbouring countries, sympathised with its revolution.

These cultural anthropologists were not in the least preoccupied by the Indians' place in the total society, nor indeed by his social relations at all, but only by his culture. Consequently race relations received scant attention from them and, insofar as the Hispanic half of the population was taken into consideration at all, it was only in that it furnished inducements to the Indians to abandon their cultural heritage.

However, it became apparent that the Indians' culture was not simply Mayan or Aztec, but contained a whole number of aspects which could only be attributed historically to the influence of the Spanish missionaries. Their religion was a case in point, since, wildly unorthodox as it was, it nevertheless centered on the catholic hagiology and, to crown it, the Indians obstinately asserted themselves to be catholics. Brave attempts were made to save the situation by distinguishing cultural form from the essence of culture. The Spaniards had imposed the superficial form but, underneath, the Indians were still pre-Columbians: the form of the *cofradías* was Spanish but this was only the superficial appearance in which the organization of earlier times lived on. The catholic saints were *really* the pre-Hispanic deities in disguise. Thus they reversed the formula of those early missionaries who had been struck by the resemblances between Indian beliefs and Christianity and maintained that the Indians were not pagans but abandoned Christians fallen into error, that

Quetzalcoatl was *really* St. Thomas the Apostle. For the anthropologists of the twentieth century St. Thomas was *really* Quetzalcoatl.

Nevertheless such considerations forced them to take account of cultural *change* and in accordance with their concept of culture (which covered all aspects of behaviour) social change was subsumed by cultural change. External pressures there were, but cultures remained wholes in the sense that, though they lost traits or borrowed them from other cultures, they were endowed with a dynamic of their own which was expressed in the theory of acculturation (whose founders, be it noted, were all Americanists: Linton, Herskovits and Redfield).

Acculturation, the process of cultural change when peoples of different culture come into contact, was to be recognised by observing the passage of traits between the initial stereotypes of pre-Columbian or Hispanic culture: this trait was lost, that one acquired, though, as Aguirre Beltrán has pointed out[2], it was not firmly decided whether loss or acquisition was the referent—whether the word 'acculturation' was compounded of *ab* or of *ad*. One finds in the *Heritage of Conquest*[3] that it is used about equally in both senses by the different contributors. The outcome of this way of thinking was the measurement of "degrees of acculturation" from the initial contact period to the present. This was accomplished according to a scale chosen by the investigator, which was arbitrary both in the choice of the traits and in the importance it attached to one aspect of culture or another. The preference of the investigator and his suppositions regarding pre-Columbian culture, therefore, determined the measurement of acculturation, so it was hardly surprising that little agreement was reached on the subject. Such arbitrariness would have mattered less if we could be sure that there was a single river of acculturation down which the Indians were travelling from their pre-Hispanic source to their integration into the ocean of the modern nation. This, however, is rather obviously not the case. One village learns Spanish but retains its traditional dress, another fails to learn Spanish but adopts Ladino clothing. A third does neither but is converted to Protestantism.

There is a further objection to the concept of acculturation: the view of history it implies is curiously unhistorical; for the vital problem in the history of culture is how the stereotypes of the cultures themselves change in time, and the stereotypes of Latin America changed very rapidly after the initial turmoil of the conquest period. Thus elements of culture which once identified the *Indians* cease to do so as soon they have been adopted by Spaniards or Ladinos, while, on the other hand, many of the cultural indices of Indian status today are in fact of sixteenth century Spanish origin and designate the Indian only because the Hispanics have dropped them. Therefore to take ancient Aztec, Mayan or Inca and ancient Spanish culture as yardsticks for the analysis of change in modern Latin America is like attempting to interpret the problems of modern British politics in the idiom of the Wars of the Roses. It commits the error of anachronism, or perhaps one should say, "reverse anachronism", for, rather than look at the past through twentieth century eyes, it attempts to view the present through the spectacles of a reconstructed and largely speculative past.

The concept of culture on which 'acculturation' is founded, because it fails to distinguish between culture and social relations and therefore attributes ethnic status uniquely to culture, is unable to cope with history. In fact, it suffers the same fate as the nineteenth century concepts of race that assumed a given number of pure races and attempted to view history in terms of their mixture: it would be alright if only the original definitions remained valid throughout time, but the whole point about history is that they do not.

It is not surprising, then, that the use of the word 'acculturation' has declined among anthropologists. But the way of thinking about Indians that was implied by it remained. Thus Whetten[4], writing about Guatemala, divided the Indians into *traditional* and *transitional*, and Adams[5], marking a finer distinction, devised three categories: *traditional, modified* and *"Ladino-ised"*. The criteria are still cultural rather than social. Their classification rests upon the hypothesis that the degrees of cultural resemblance to the Ladinos mark the path of evolution down which the Indians are moving, at greater or lesser speed. These are the stages of 'acculturation' which lead to ultimate assimilation into the Hispanic world. The Ladinos view the matter in similar terms, assuming that progress will lead to the 'civilisation' of the Indians and that to be civilised is to be like themselves, but if all the Indians saw it in that light, it is hard to see why they have not all changed before now.

Adams' scheme does not in fact fit even the whole of Guatemala, for the western plateau produces characteristics which are hardly to be interpreted in this way. Here the great majority of the population is Indian and there are even quite large towns where there are almost no Ladinos. Consequently there are Indians who occupy positions in the division of labour which elsewhere are the preserves of the Ladinos; dealers, shop-keepers, specialists of various sorts. There is an Indian upper-class. This is also an area where land is scarce and from which Indians go down to the coffee plantations of the lowlands to work. The proportion of Indians remained stable throughout the first half of the century until recently, because the only people who chose to become Ladinos were those who settled among the Ladinos of the coast. The Indian upper-class, powerful and respected in their communities, speaking Spanish and knowing enough about Hispanic culture to hold their own against the Ladinos, had no reason to change their status and become the despised members of a Ladino community they did not respect. Hence on the western plateau there is a paradox from the viewpoint of Whetten and Adams in the fact that the more competent in Spanish culture the Indian becomes (the more "Ladino-ised" in Adams' terms), the less he has to gain by becoming a Ladino. Knowledge of Spanish culture gives prestige in the Indian community. It does not in that part of Guatemala make anyone socially less Indian. Hence we find a large number of ladies who speak Spanish in the home but still wear Indian dress (24 per cent of Indian women in the department of Quetzaltenango, 46 in San Marcos, according to the census of 1950). These Indians are not anxious to change their status or they would not assert their Indian identity in this way, when there is no longer any cultural impediment to their changing it.

The acquisition of Ladino culture is a necessary condition for becoming a

Ladino, but not a sufficient one and this can be seen most clearly in the example of Quetzaltenango, the largest city in the country after the capital, where an Indian commercial class continues to speak Quiché as well as Spanish. Its women mostly wear Indian dress and the Ladino commercial class complains bitterly that the Indians are running them out of business. Here Adams' explanation of ethnic status in terms of acculturation is as firmly contradicted as if he were to try it among the Basques. His approach is based on the unconscious assumption that Indians all want to become Ladinos. Ladinos think they do or should do, but in fact in a number of places (Zapotecs of the isthmus, Tlascalans, Tarascans, etc.), they have shown that they don't. The evaluation of ethnic status in terms of the moral inferiority of Indians is a Ladino evaluation, not an Indian one, and the anthropologist can see that the difference between the two halves of the society is not a difference of evaluation within a single system which makes the Ladinos superior and the Indians inferior, but the difference between two systems of value. The model of social mobility which inspires Adams and Whetten seems quite inadequate to explain the problems of cultural change and the crossing of the ethnic barrier.

The North American cultural anthropologists are not the only ones to feel the influence of acculturation-theory. It has had a profound effect on the thinking of Mexican anthropologists. The National Indian Institute sought to reach a compromise between the conflicting demands of respect for Indian culture and the necessity for national integration and expressed this in a motto which is sometimes written large upon the walls of its premises. "To redeem the Indian is to integrate the fatherland". Like so many political mottoes this is a logical nonsense, for it maintains that Indians can become part of the national community without ceasing to be Indian, but the notion of redemption is open to fine interpretations. 'Redeem', in fact, means 'civilise' which to Hispanics means hispanicise. It thus implies the same underlying suppositions as the theory of Adams. It might seem nonetheless that this is contradictory of the indigenist ideology of the Mexican Revolution which looked to anthropology to discover the hidden treasures of the past and bring them forth to symbolise the new national neo-Aztec image, but as I have explained elsewhere, a national Indian ideology seeking a return to pre-Columbian identity does not require the existence of contemporary Indians[6]. They rather prove an embarrassment to the ideologists by their presence in a socially subordinate role. The Indian identity proclaimed by *indigenismo* does not look to the modern Indian for its ideal but to an image from the past that will validate the Indian descent of the modern Mestizo. As Bourricaud has put it, speaking of Peru: *"Indigenismo is an ideology for Mestizos"*[7].

The notion of Indian culture has thus been overexploited by the cultural anthropologists and abused by their cousins, the national indigenists, who saw in it the means of asserting a convenient untruth: i.e. that they themselves were not *really* Hispanic, that they were free at last from the burden of their colonial past. Now that the period of enthusiasm is over, the inadequacy of this theory of culture to explain (or avoid) the realities of social status has become patent. It is therefore understandable that there have been other scholars who decided that culture was not really the crucial factor in the ethnic distinction and that it should be explained rather in social terms. With this conclusion we cannot but agree, yet it remains to be seen how successful they have been.

II

I have suggested that the two uses of the word 'race', the physical and the social (assuming that we retain the word at all in scientific discourse), should be treated as quite distinct from the theoretical point of view. In practice there is frequently a close correspondence between phenotype and ethnic status, even in Latin America where the two concepts are most clearly distinguishable. Whites *tend* to look white, Mestizos *tend* to look mixed and Indians *tend* to look Indian. This helps to maintain the image of what an Indian is and provides the basis within the Hispanic half of society for those social, rather than ethnic, distinctions which are dressed up in the guise of race. Yet the ethnic distinction still needs to be explained, even if it is not simply a matter of physique. Those anthropologists who attempted to explain it by means of the theory of acculturation were mistaken because they subsumed social relations under the rubric of culture, and this led them into contradictions.

I am not the first to reject the cultural interpretation of the Indians. Already forty years ago Mariátegui proclaimed that the Indian problem was a socio-economic problem, depending above all on the land question, and various authors since him have offered sociological, as opposed to cultural, interpretations—among them anthropologists. There have also been cultural explanations offered by sociologists. So it is not a question of the discipline to which the authors belong, but whether they base their explanation on social or cultural considerations. There has even been a polemic in which an article by Colby and Van den Berghe, a sociologist, was criticised by Goldkind, an anthropologist, for attempting to give a cultural explanation of race relations in Chiapas[8] : Goldkind maintained that the Indians are simply poor peasants and their values and behaviour can be explained without any appeal to their Maya origins, by the fact that they are rustic while the Ladinos are urban—a contention that is very far from the facts, since the majority of the Ladinos of Chiapas are poor peasants also. If the cultural explanation is inadequate, I fear the sociological interpretation all too often falls into the reverse error, of thinking that the Indians' race relations can be accounted for *without* their culture, that the ethnic barrier is *really* a purely social matter to be explained like any other class distinction. In the extreme version of this approach it is suggested that culture is simply a 'bourgeois' red herring, aimed to conceal the reality of "capitalist exploitation".

The sociological theses can be grouped roughly into two versions of which a composite account must here suffice. The first equates ethnic status with class: Indians are not a race, but simply a despised rural proletariat, kept in poverty and subjection by the Whites or Ladinos or hacienda-owners, thanks to their inability to handle the language of their rulers and the discrimination to which they are subject. The facts are *commonly* thus, but this does not make the explanation valid. Indians *are* usually poor, their average standard of living is always much lower than the average of the Hispanics on the national scale of any country of Latin America. They *are* usually rural: either peons on an hacienda or providing marginal labour for it from a nearby community or emigrating to work on a seasonal basis to supplement the inadequate resources of their eroded lands. The *majority* of Indians speak no Spanish or speak it poorly. They are commonly discriminated against and the habits of fear and submission predispose them to avoid conflict with Hispanics and centre their hopes and ambitions in their local community rather than in the Hispanic world outside it.

Yet none of these facts is true everywhere. One finds individual Indians who are quite prosperous—the 1950 census of Guatemala shows that five per cent of the owners of farms of 111 acres or more are Indians. Moreover one also finds in Guatemala Ladino communities poorer than their Indian neighbours, and like them mainly subsistence farmers.

Indians are not always rural, while Hispanics frequently are. There are a number of cities with a large Indian population. In a number of countries there has been an attempt to escape from the discourtesy which the word 'Indian' implies and call the Indians *campesinos* (countrymen). This has been the government policy in Bolivia ever since the Revolution. But we are there faced with the anomaly that miners have to be referred to as 'countrymen', *campesinos,* even when they have nothing to do with the land at all, but simply because they speak only Quetchua. The solution to social problems seldom comes from attempts to reform popular vocabulary by law (though such attempts have been made even since Charles III of Spain sought to solve the gypsy problem by proscribing the word *gitano*). Outlawing the word *indio* or *indito* or *indígena* does not stop the Indian from being an Indian, for euphemisms are soon known for what they are and the final result is only to complicate the lexicon. As an informant in Colombia put it soon after denying that there were any Indians in the neighbourhood: "Los Indios, o, mejor dicho, los campesinos [...]" (The Indians, or rather, I should say, the countrymen [...]). A diminished discourtesy towards Indians is implied by the use of a euphemism, but that is all.

Indians are commonly the object of the Hispanics' contempt, but it is not by a long way always the case that they are discouraged from changing their status. Governments go to great efforts to 'civilise' which means 'hispanicise' their Indians and one may be told proudly by the mayor of some small town: "There are no Indians here any more. They are all civilised now". Nor does Indian status correspond to any particular role in the division of labour, nor to any specific relation to the modes of production. Most Indians are agricultural labourers. They may be collective subsistence farmers, peons, or independent peasant proprietors and as such sometimes employers. They may be artisans, and, in this capacity rather exceptionally, they can be employers of Hispanics—an Indian of Otavalo has a cloth factory in which he employs ten mestizos. They can be traders and dealers and

political leaders, even upon the national scene, though it becomes doubtful in such
a case whether they can still be called Indians. Just as a member of Hispanic society
can be said to be *"really* an Indian" (on account of his phenotype or antecedents),
so an Indian can be said to be *"really* a mestizo" on account of his social activities.
There was an Indian cacique of Chiapas who was said by others to be a Ladino disguised as an Indian and, when it is said that, for example, ex-president Cárdenas is an
Indian, it is hard to know quite what is meant. Ideologically perhaps, but not
culturally, nor socially, nor still less, physically.

The ethnic frontier wears thin at the fringe, but this does not detract from the
significance of the fact that there are numerous examples of Indians, morally and
socially integrated into their *Indian* community, participating in its culture and attached to their identity as Indians, who must none the less be defined as middle-
class, whatever criterion of class is chosen. Hence those who have attempted to
equate the ethnic division with a class division and explain it in economic terms
face anomalies of one sort or another, wherever they go. They have committed the
time-honoured error of mistaking a statistical probability for a cause. Whatever
ethnicity is, it is *not just class.*

Ethnic status is a *kind* of social status in the widest sense, but it differs from
class status in that it also involves the notion of *race*, and to apply a framework
borrowed from a society which has no ethnic status (or has a quite different concept of ethnic status such as the United States) is simply ethnocentrism.

A more perceptive view was taken by writers who admitted that Indians were
distinguished by a social division, which was not just class but something of a
different nature, and they called this 'caste'. The credentials of this word must also
be examined for, like 'race', it too conceals confusions[9].

In the sixteenth century it meant species of animal or plant and hence race or
lineage of men. It expressed the notion of progeny and a classification according
to descent.

It is understandable therefore that the Portuguese should have used the word
casta, given its sense of lineage or breed, to describe the castes they encountered
in India. The English and French took the word over from the Portuguese, when
they arrived in India, and thereafter gave the Hindus a privileged position in its
denotation. However, by dividing the pagan world between the Spanish and the
Portuguese, Pope Alexander also divided the destiny of the word *casta:* the Spaniards found nothing in any way resembling Hindu castes in the New World and
their own conduct there hardly conduced to implanting the ideal of purity. They
used the word, in the normal way for that period, to designate animal species and,
in the human realm, lineages or clans. Indeed it is still used in these senses in Latin
America to apply to the patri-lineages of the Andes or the matrilineal clans of the
Guajira. The term became elaborated in the Spanish empire, moreover, in a sense
yet more antithetical to that of India: it came to mean all those who were neither
purely Spanish nor Indian. In the seventeenth and eighteenth centuries it signified
above all, not the pure, but the *im*pure, the half-breeds, that is to say, the very
people who, in endogamous India, would be regarded as outside the caste system.

The *castas* were people of mixed ancestry and a pseudo-biological vocabulary was elaborated from popular zoology and the slang of the day to accord a distinct social identity to each combination of White, Indian or Negro. Inherited status was what counted, not actual colour, so that anyone who could claim one eighth or less of non-white descent was classed as white and the status of white could in any case at one period even be purchased without regard for antecedents.

Once the notion of descent had ceased, after Independence, to have any juridical value, the *castas* were no longer distinguished within the general category of *Mestizos.* Today the word *casta* is used only in its ordinary figurative senses (save in the antique local usages already mentioned). It does not refer to any social status. Yet its demise at the ethnographical level was followed by its resurrection at the hands of the social scientists who found their precedent nowhere in the Hispanic tradition, but rather in that of English sociological literature. But for the preponderance of this, it might have remained simply what it was in the vernacular. Thus it is found now, as in English, indicating a certain type of social distinction and applying, in particular, to that which divides the population of Latin America into Indian and Hispanic. This sense is quite different to that of lineage or clan or the categories of breed which were distinguished in the imperial epoch or the hierarchised endogamous occupational groups of the Hindus. It refers to no collectivity of any sort, but simply to a division of the entire population into two statuses: a superior one which is Hispanic and an inferior one which is Indian.

This usage owed its entry into Latin America to an analogy with the distinction between coloured and white people in the United States, which in turn is owed to an analogy with the castes of India. The reappearance of the term *casta* upon the Spanish scene was therefore anything but a simple revival of a usage which had fallen out of fashion there, but rather the invasion of a territory where the term once existed on the ethnographical level by the same word which, thanks to its sojourn on the far side of the world, had "made it" to analytical status.

Richard N. Adams[10] attempted to distinguish different types of social relations which the different types of Indians had with Ladinos. He suggested rather plausibly that "traditional Indians" had a race relationship with Ladinos, that "modified Indians" had a relationship which could be called "caste-like" and that "Ladino-ised Indians" were simply distinguished by class. Thus he not only destroys the unity of the notion of ethnicity, which becomes equivalent to *either* race *or* caste *or* class, but typically he makes the type of social relations a function of the Indians' culture and dependent upon their place upon the 'ladder' of acculturation. In this scheme the same 'Ladinocentric' assumptions that I outlined above are visible. It looks forward to the day when the Indians, 'Ladino-ised' and assimilated, will vanish into a flexible class system similar to that of the United States, from which it is hoped that "race prejudice" will be eliminated.

The society of the United States resolves the conflict between its egalitarian ideology and the fact of its material and moral inequalities by a doctrine which glorifies social mobility; the self-made man is regarded as the ideal. It was a doctrine which, until fairly recently, was favoured by exceptional circumstances. The country

was largely populated by immigrants who did not know English and rose in the
social scale as they became Americanised and were replaced in the most menial
ranks and the least esteem by fresh immigrants who abandoned their homeland
penniless in search of a better living in the expanding opportunities of the United
States. Thus the system offered the possibility of social mobility for all—on condition that the immigrants continued to arrive, and to arrive penniless. It would
hardly have worked had the immigrants been relatively well-to-do. It is not surprising, then, that American thinkers should be particularly attached to the ideal
of social mobility, since it is part of their national ethos. It is this attachment
which makes the Hindu caste system repugnant to them and gives to the definition
of the word 'caste', in this sociological sense, its critical term: absence of social
mobility or 'rigidity'. The other features stressed to justify the usage of the word
'caste' to describe the colour-bar in the deep south are: absence of intermarriage
between coloured and white (which they assimilate, rather rashly, to the endogamy
of the Hindu castes) and the fear of pollution through intimate contact with members of the lower caste.

The ethnic distinction in Latin America (though it is also repugnant to egalitarian sentiment) is not at all the same as in the U.S. In Latin America there is a
great deal of ethnic mobility. There is no prohibition of intermarriage and no fear
of pollution. If its social structure resembles that of India in any way, it is only in
the absence of a "colour-bar" and, in the case of the Andes, the possession of a
hierarchy of as many as four ethnic statuses: *blanco, mestizo, cholo, indio.* These
features differentiate it from the United States. It is difficult, then, to avoid the
conclusion that, if the word *caste* be extended from India to North America, the
same reasoning prohibits its usage in Latin America, and vice versa. The only
definition of caste which will apply to India, to the deep South and to Latin
America would be a residual one: any system of social differentiation offensive
to the egalitarian ideology of the modern West. It appears that the extensions rest
upon no solider basis than this.

It is not always easy to know what is intended when we encounter the word
casta in academic writings. Is it meant simply in the ethnographic sense, i.e., what
the people themselves say, or is it meant to have theoretical implications? The
problem is the same in English: is caste meant simply as a transliteration of *casta,*
as it is used in Latin America, or does it bear an analytical load? All too often it
appears that the word is introduced with no more serious intention than to utilise
an analogy that comes to hand.

In view of the facile analogies which have been used in the writings on race
relations in the New World, which disregard the distinctions between the cultures
of the conquerors (English, Spanish or Portuguese), between those of the conquered
or subordinate (Indians or Negroes), between tribal and sedentary (high-culture)
Indians, and between the nature of the colonisation *and* the period in which it
took place *and* the subsequent changes in social structure due to economic and
demographic pressures, it is not surprising that the usage of the word *caste* in the
New World should be a source of contradictions as numerous as the word *race.*

Indeed the confusions to which the word *caste* lends itself resemble those to which race gives rise in that the popular usage is ever striving to be taken seriously as a scientific term; in fact it appears very often that an author has accepted the word *casta* because it appears in the ethnography and has then gone on to assume that its technical sense was implied, i.e., that there is a rigid, endogamous caste system like the Hindus. In fact, to put the matter succinctly: in identifying the Guatemalan Indians as a caste[11], the sociologists of the twentieth century repeated the error of Columbus: arriving in Middle America they thought they had reached Asia.

* * * * *

How then shall we define the difference between Indians and Ladinos, if neither biological race, nor culture, nor class, nor caste are appropriate concepts? It is a social distinction, but one which manifests itself in culture. It is a division in the social structure, but social structures repose always on principles embedded in culture which they put to their own ends. Therefore the distinction can be understood neither in purely social nor in purely cultural terms but in the relation between these two aspects.

When the Spaniards first encountered the Indians, the word *race* applied in every sense: population isolates, languages, cultures and social groupings, but time has transformed its meaning by transforming the objects to which it applied. The criteria have become dispersed.

The physical criterion first multiplied its categories by crossbreeding and then dissolved in the chaotic miscegenation of the *castas;* race became a matter of inherited legal status and, after Independence, of social status. Under the Empire, the *República de Indios* remained outside and subordinate to colonial society within which the *castas* multiplied. After Independence the Indians, no longer a 'Republica', were summoned to join the new nation. This meant in fact joining it in the capacity of peon. The lands of the Indians were taken over by Hispanics on a far greater scale than before in order to encourage them to do so, because their labour was needed for the new markets which opened up. (The motive was stated explicitly at times.)

Debt-peonage and the hacienda system underlined the economic aspects of ethnic status, which marked, ever more clearly, the boundaries of citizenship, the new citizenship of the new nation from which the Indians were in fact excluded. From the point of view of Hispanic society the Indians formed a pool of unskilled labour to be drawn into the orbit of civilisation, as required, and to the degree necessary to fulfil their economic function.

Throughout these transformations the poles of the system remained in place, ordering the hierarchy: that which derived from Spain was above and that which was indigenous was below. Social status was justified by the attribution of descent from one *raza* or the other. But descent in anthropological terms is no more than a system whereby society accords identity to its new members. It can be physical, cultural, social or even religious in its basis, like the concept of purity of blood in sixteenth century Spain which depended on the religious orthodoxy of grandparents. In Latin America the notion of descent divides the population into those whose essential nature is thought to derive from the conquerors and those who are heirs to the natives in this regard, a connection almost as mystical as the totemic affiliation of Australian tribesmen, but none the less effective for that! The presence within the national frontiers of people who follow a different tradition in dress and speak a different language (in fact their dress is mainly European in origin and their language is stuffed with Spanish loans) is enough to keep in place the poles between which ethnic identity is divided, even though the criteria by which it is recognised vary from context to context and from place to place. Local social structures interpret the division as they will, but the existence of the two traditions, one attached to the centre of society and the function of government and the other vested in a local community opposed to it, is enough to perpetuate, in one transformation or another, the social heritage of the conquest. Hence the ethnic distinction, which appears at first sight so arbitrary, is so only to those who conceive of *races* as concrete entities, cultural or social, that is to say, defined by cultural traits or by social factors, such as economic position or occupation—rather than, as has been suggested, as relationships of a specific type which exist as a function of a total social structure, but are not reducible to either culture or class structure.

If this may be granted, then all the conflicting usages of the word *Indian* can be explained:

1) A *mestizo, ladino, racional, gente decente,* etc., in brief, Hispanic, marks the difference between himself and someone he regards as belonging to another race, i.e., of a different essential nature, by calling him an Indian; whether he dresses like one or not and whether he speaks Spanish or not, he belongs to the opposed tradition.

2) But he can also refer to someone as Indian, even though he recognises that he belongs to the same Hispanic 'race' as himself, that is, to the same tradition, if his object is to increase the social distance between the two of them, to deny their common nature. The one who is socially inferior is then said to be an Indian or "really an Indian" in spite of appearances, or "a redressed Indian". 'Cholo' has this sense too and the highly variable usage of the word can equally be explained in this way. There is nothing extraordinary in this. Long before Boulainvilliers propounded it as a doctrine, the aristocracies of Europe had claimed to be different by race to the plebeians: Gothic in Spain, Frankish in France. Upper classes do indeed habitually attempt to invoke race, i.e., nature, to validate their social superiority. The invocation of race has no other sense in Latin America.

3) Finally there is the fighting insult *indio* which is heard whenever a drunken brawl becomes serious. It is aimed at the person whom one wishes to exclude from common humanity, i.e., whom one is prepared to assassinate.

If the denotata differ, the meaning is none the less always the same: an Indian is someone excluded from full common humanity by his *raza,* one with whom there is no *community.*

It is only to be expected that Indians do not use the same terms, nor use them in the same way. When speaking Spanish they usually refer to themselves as *naturales* (persons born in the place, natives), in somewhat the same sense as in Spain where the word is used to define a person's nature by his place of birth. When speaking an Indian language, the term they use for themselves is likely to mean something like "a true man", i.e., fully human. This is so in the Tzeltal dialect of Maya which also refers to itself as the "true speech", as opposed to Spanish, the language of the *gente de razón,* the self-styled people of reason. Thus, if the Indian is excluded from common humanity by the Hispanic, at least he returns the judgement.

'Race' can be seen, then, to be a matter of social context, and the analysis of context allows us to explain the apparent contradictions between the different denotations of words such as *indio* or *cholo.* But this is not to deny that the terms used to define ethnic status have certain permanent associations attaching to one or other of the poles.

These, however, are necessarily subject to a certain ambivalence in their evaluation. First of all, Hispanic valued, Indian devalued:

I (a) Hispanic means descended, in the mystical sense, from the conquerors, of Spanish *origin,* hence associated with the Madre Patria, as Spain is still sometimes called, the source of civilisation and of Christianity. It implies 'clever', "socially superior", related to the national government, politically empowered (Spanish is the language of political power), modern in orientation: oriented to the outside world and towards the future.

I (b) Indian means descended from the conquered, 'native' in the sense of savage, uncivilised, pagan in origin, socially inferior, coming from the backwoods, stupid, backward, oriented away from the centre, towards tradition and the past.

But without changing the association these terms can be given a contrary evaluation:

II (a) Hispanic implies foreign in origin; usurpers, oppressors, destroyers of autochthonous culture, hence ambitious, calculating, heartless, and since it also implies colonial, it can be made to mean "behind the times".

II (b) Indian, valued now instead of devalued, means native to the land, and hence the rightful owners, *naturales.* Legitimate because vested with the values of antiquity—hence the role of the *quetzal* in the imagery of Guatemalan nationalism (autochthonous bird and symbol of the Quiché kings). Sincere, honest, modest, uncalculating. In the ideology of *indigenismo,* it means politically progressive, since opposed to colonial. The attempt to present measures of land-reform as a return to the *calpul* or the *ayllu* is an obvious example.

Hispanic, whether evaluated positively or negatively, relates to the centre of the nation, the capital, urban society, the function of dominance, while the concept of Indian relates to the periphery, the community, the countryside, the function of submission.

The first equation (Hispanic plus, Indian minus) goes with colonial rule, the second (Hispanic minus, Indian plus) goes with modern populism. It was the second equation which inspired the ideology of the Mexican Revolution, but the apotheosis of the Indian met with the difficulty (or perhaps it was the advantage) that there were too few Indians left and those there were, were not much interested in indigenist ideology. None of the revolutionary leaders spoke an Indian tongue and the language of power and administration continued to be Spanish. The tide was still running towards centralisation, politically, economically and culturally, at least at the national level. In fact it was precisely this development of modern popular nationalist sentiment that challenged the dominance of the ideal of things Spanish.

The tide seems to be turning today and we see everywhere a reassertion of regional sentiment, the legitimacy of the pre-eminence of the centre put in doubt. Though the movement towards economic centralisation continues in a certain sense, by the very nature of such a movement the division of labour between centre and periphery is destroyed. Just as the economic expansion of the eighteenth century led to the rebellion of the colonies and the foundation of the modern nations of Latin America, so the economic expansion of the twentieth seems to be leading to conflict between national centre and periphery, and where Indians remain, we see the new Indian middle classes emerging and yet retaining their Indian identity. The centre loses its power to command emulation and middle class Indians sometimes hang on to their regional ethnic affiliation even after they have moved to the capital—like the Isthmus Zapotecs in Mexico City. Where Indians refuse to change their ethnic status after they have acquired education in Spanish and acceded to middle class occupations, they create situations where the polarity of the social structure breaks down and a new consciousness emerges uniting Indians no longer on the basis of their community but of their region. The breach between ethnic and social status is thus consecrated. This is what appears to be happening today among the Quiché of western Guatemala, the Zapotecs of the Isthmus, the Tlascalans, the Tarascans and the lowland Maya of Yucatán. It remains to be seen how these developments will progress and whether they will be followed by a pan-Indian Quetchua movement in the Andes. But, whatever the outcome, we are clearly approaching a point of transition where Indian identity is changing its meaning once again. Ethnicity in Latin America will be transformed.

For, once *Indian* no longer implies the opposite of the ruling class, its opposition to Hispanic can only mean opposition to the centre which is every where Hispanic. Once Indian consciousness attaches to the region, not to a community, the possibility exists of claiming autonomy for it on the basis of its autochthonous culture and, where Indians are already found in middle class occupations, they are equipped to realise this possibility. So, I fear the maxim of the Mexican National Indian Institute, *Redimir al indio es integrar la patria,* is not only a piece of self-deception in the cause of indigenist ideology as I suggested, it is *wrong:* truly to redeem the Indian, that is, to redeem him *as* an Indian is to *dis*integrate the fatherland[12]

NOTES

1. George Kubler, *The Indian Caste of Peru, 1795–1940* (Washington 1950).
2. Gonzalo Aguirre Beltrán, *El Proceso de Aculturación* (Mexico 1957).
3. Sol Tax (ed.), *Heritage of Conquest* (Glencoe 1952).
4. Nathan Whetten, *Guatemala, the Land and the People* (New Haven 1961).
5. Richard N. Adams, *Cultural Surveys of Panama, Nicaragua, Guatemala, Honduras, El Salvador* (Washington 1957).
6. Julian Pitt-Rivers, Who are the Indians?, *Encounter,* XXV (1965), 41–49.
7. François Bourricaud, *Changements à Puno* (Paris 1962), p. 216.
8. Benjamin Colby *and* Pierre Van den Berghe, Ethnic Relations in Southeastern Mexico, *American Anthropologist,* LXIII (1961), 772–792; Victor Goldkind, Ethnic Relations in Southeastern Mexico: a methodological note, *American Anthropologist,* LXV (1963), 394–399; Benjamin Colby *and* Pierre Van den Berghe, Reply to Goldkind's "Critique of Ethnic Relations in Southeastern Mexico", *American Anthropologist,* LXVI (1964), 417–418. Woodrow Borah, a historian well aware of cultural anthropology, nevertheless preferred a sociological explanation: Race and Class in Mexico, *The Pacific Historical Review,* XXIII (1954), nº 4.
9. For a more detailed account of the etymology of the word, see J. Pitt-Rivers, On the word 'caste', *in* T. O. Beidelman (ed.), *The Translation of Culture. Essays in honour of Evans-Pritchard* (London, Tavistock Press, 1971).
10. Adams, *op. cit.*
11. The common usage of the term owes much to Melvin Tumin, *Caste in a Peasant Society; a case-study in the dynamics of caste* (Princeton 1952).
12. I am grateful to Professor Kenneth Kirkwood for the invitation to lecture upon this topic in St. Antony's College, Oxford, May 1969, when some of the ideas presented in this paper were first expressed.

29   The Social Significance of the Black Muslims

E. U. Essien-Udom

Broadly, the study of black nationalism is a case study of the social and psychological consequences of what Gunnar Myrdal aptly summed up as 'an American Dilemma' on the personal and group life of American Negroes. The sum total of these consequences—psychological constraints, institutional weaknesses, contradictory 'value systems' of the subculture, and the absence of an ethos—is what we described as the Negro dilemma, dramatized in the doctrines of black nationalism. These con-

From *Black Nationalism: A Search for Identity in America* (Chicago: The University of Chicago Press, 1962, abridged edition, 1966), pp. 262–275. Reprinted by permission of The University of Chicago Press.

straints are deeply rooted in the subculture although they depend on and are supported by the white society. The Negro dilemma, in a subtle and profound way, exercises a constraint, which is by no means easy to specify, on the social advancement of the masses of Negroes, especially in northern United States. Although the study points to a possible relationship between these constraints and the obstacles imposed on Negroes by the white society, it does not, however, tell us much about the relative weight to be attached to one or the other on the advancement of the masses of Negroes. Common sense suggests, however, that the attitudes and actions of the white society are more decisive. Nevertheless, both are inextricably interwoven, and analytically, they are difficult to disentangle. The uneasy coexistence between them is not adequately understood or appreciated. Black nationalism, especially the Muslim movement, is an attempt to 'break through' the vicious circle which emerges from this relationship.

Furthermore, the study underscores the Negroes' ambivalence towards assimilation, i.e. the loss of their identity, cultural traits, and history. Black nationalism, the Muslim movement in particular, raises such questions: Can the majority of Negroes be assimilated into American society? Do they really want to be assimilated? What 'price' will they have to pay for assimilation or non-assimilation? If they want to be assimilated, what are they themselves doing to facilitate this process? If not, are there discernible attitudes among Negroes which impede this process? Were there a rational choice, can the Negro subculture successfully resist the pressure for conformity exerted upon it by the dominant culture? Can they (Negroes) revitalize and regenerate the subculture?

Negroes will argue, and often glibly, that they are not concerned with assimilation but with integration (i.e. total acceptance without discrimination) and that the prospects for the former are very remote. Hence, they dismiss the question as academic. Although the probability of assimilation is remote, the question is not psychologically insignificant for the Negroes. It is significant, in part, because one's attitude towards assimilation may or may not foster the feeling of separateness and will determine the intensity of one's effort to merge into the larger culture and society. However, the question is particularly important during this period of rapid improvement in the Negro's status and the trend towards integration. These changes, in themselves, are sources of anxiety to many Negroes. Although Negroes do not express their concern publicly, the writer found that it was widely, but privately, voiced in and outside the Muslim movement. This concern and their ambivalent attitudes—be it at the level of conscious or unconscious awareness—explain, in part, why so many Negroes pay attention to black nationalism but do not actively support the Muslim movement, which is only a specific manifestation of their uncertainties. This question involves the 'destiny' of the Negro people in America. We should seek to understand it; we should not explain it away. The price for assimilation is clear; the price for nonassimilation is not obvious. If, however, the sense of separateness and ethnic consciousness, now developing, were to dominate, society at large would have to pay a price for minority exclusiveness, especially for the kind now fostered by the Muslim movement.

Ideologically and culturally, however, the assimilationist strand has been stronger among Negroes. The dominance of this strand is already discernible and much stronger among the middle- and upper-class Negroes and intellectuals. But this strand is somewhat weaker among the lower classes because the realities of their social situation do not support their assimilationist mentality. Consequently, the sense of separateness and ethnic consciousness actually dominate their lives. This feeling has always been present, but lacked positive articulation. The intensification of these feelings is one of the most important developments in the contemporary social situation of American Negroes.

Perhaps, the black nationalists' agitation is the loudest expression of a 'manifesto of identity'—the Negroes' conscious, though slow, awakening to their heritage of abuse and degradation, and, especially, to their possible destiny as human beings. It may well signal the beginning of the end of the Negroes' aimless and vain desire to hide their dark skins behind a white mask. The manifesto of identity is a subjectivity: its voice reflects the past and the present and perhaps the future as well. It requires no real objects and relationships for its expression; yet in a significant way, the manifesto brings to public attention 'voices from within the veil' and subtle and imperceptible changes which are occurring among the black masses. They are voices heralding perhaps the psychological and spiritual liberation of the black masses from the shackles of a past that still haunts the present. The manifesto announces their 'presence' in America and their impatience and disaffection with the limitations imposed upon their 'equality in opportunity'. Their impatience and disaffection cannot be disassociated from the important changes (most contributing significantly to the general improvement of the Negroes) in the United States as a whole, and in the Negro community or from the rising protest of millions in the non-white world against discrimination and exploitation based solely on racial or religious distinctions.

The 'voices from within the veil' and the manifesto of identity do not deny the Negro's Americanism. Indeed, they affirm what is commonly known: that the Negro is American in heart, loyalties, and in everything else. In its mild forms the manifesto of identity is best expressed in the 'Negro History Week' and by such organizations as the American Society of African Culture or the Afro-American Heritage Association. Its voice is a reaffirmation of the Negroes' faith in the possibilities offered by the pluralistic character of American society for their cultural, intellectual, and spiritual development. In its extreme form, the Muslim movement is the best example; it reveals how deeply the cancer of American racism has infected all its parts, making the oppressed and the oppressor mutually depraved.

The study of black nationalism illustrates the desperate character of the social situation of the lower-class Negroes in the large northern cities and the tensions which arise from this situation. We tried to show that their life is devoid of meaning and purpose. They are estranged from the larger society which they seek to enter, but which rejects them. Similarly, they are estranged from their own group which they despise. The result of this feeling of dual alienation is apathy, futility, and emptiness of purpose. In a psychological sense, many are lonesome within and outside their own group. They are rootless and restless. They are without an identity, i.e. a sense of belonging and membership in society. In this situation, there is neither hope nor optimism. In fact, most lower-class Negroes in these large cities see little or no 'future' for themselves and posterity. This is partly because they have no faith in themselves or in their potential as black men in America and especially because important decisions which shape their lives appear entirely beyond their control. We should stress, however, that the sense of social estrangement and alienation is not limited to the Negroes. In fact, it is a problem common to urban dwellers. The consequence for a meaningful life is, in varying degrees, the same for Negroes as well as others in comparable social situations. The point, however, is that the impact of contemporary urban tensions and anxieties on an already marginal and despised group is dramatic and paralyzing. It corrupts the personality of its victims, depriving them of any sense of human worth and dignity.

Three more factors in the contemporary social situation of Negroes help to explain the growing sense of separateness and ethnic consciousness among the Negro masses: the bifurcation of the Negro caste, i.e. the emergence of a real Negro middle class and the Negro's redefinition of himself not only in terms of the whites but in relation to this 'new' class; his redefinition of himself in relation to Africa; and his reactions to the traditional Negro institutions and leadership groups in terms of the new definitions.

The bifurcation of the caste, especially in the North, is an important development of which the implications are not generally recognized. Nevertheless, the emergence of a Negro middle class may have serious consequences for the Negro masses, creating an 'imbalance' within the Negro community. One obvious consequence is that lower-class Negroes are beginning to redefine themselves not only in relation to the white society but also to the Negro middle- and upper-class 'society' For this reason, they resent middle-class Negroes whose social situation is incomparably better than theirs. This situation is important for understanding the character of race relations in the North. First, the position of the middle-class Negroes tends to obscure the problems of the lower-class Negroes, in part because Negro 'progress' (with some justification) is defined largely in middle-class terms; it is measured by the conspicuous consumption of the middle- and upper-class Negroes, who, in fact, have found their identity with the white middle class. As individuals, they can escape the open contempt which Northern whites have for the less fortunate of their race. They, too, display haughtiness towards the lower-class Negroes. The 'bonds of solidarity in chains' which previously characterized the relationship between them are no longer apparent, i.e. the fact that in the past middle- and upper-class Negroes were able to identify with the struggles and aspirations of lower-class Negroes. The interests of the middle class are different and, in some measure, lower-class Negroes are estranged from them. But, like middle classes everywhere, the essentially middle-class Negro leadership takes for granted that its strivings represent unquestionably the interest of the masses. This may well be, but the estrangement between the two classes is incontestable. The important point is that precisely because lower-class Negroes are beginning to define themselves in relation to the Negro 'image' portrayed by the middle class and are attracted to it, they are also repelled by it because their actual conditions do not permit genuine identification with the middle-class Negroes. As it is in their relations with the white society, lower-class Negroes tend to withdraw and disassociate themselves from the middle- and upper-class Negroes. This estrangement suggests the beginning of class consciousness and conflict among the Negro masses, directed not against whites but against the Negro middle and upper classes. This development aggravates tensions in the Negro community and produces distrust of the middle-class leadership among the lower-class Negroes.

These Negroes feel powerless not only in relation to the white power complex but also to what appears to them as the monopoly of power by Negro middle-class leadership. Black nationalism, especially the Muslim movement, reflects this sense of dual marginality and impotence in both power centres. But an important distinction should be made here: although black nationalism is a general reaction against whites as 'possessors' of vital social, economic, and political power, the nationalists do not question, except in utopian and religious terms, the legitimacy of the white power monopoly, nor have they sought to alter it. Instead, their sense of impotence produces a need for withdrawal and racial separation (a desire for a homeland) as the means by which Negroes might become masters of their destiny. However, the Muslim movement reflects the increasing class consciousness and conflict among the lower-class Negroes and questions, specifically, the legitimacy of the Negro middle-class leadership. In other words, the movement questions the 'monopoly' of power by the middle-class leadership in defining both the 'needs' and 'destiny' of the Negro people in America. It questions the trend towards integration which its leaders see as a trend towards assimilation. Furthermore, its leaders question the 'balance' between the ideal of integration and the definition of lower-class Negro 'needs' in practical terms. The Muslim movement, in a real sense, is an attempt to alter the power relationship within the Negro community. The concerns now voiced by the black nationalists may well determine the character and style of future Negro leadership in their communities.

Another defect in the contemporary social situation of the urban Negro masses is the impotence of traditional Negro institutions in dealing with either the psychological or practical needs of their community. For a long time, these institutions and leadership groups have been the interpreters of the social scene for the masses of Negroes. Of these, the Negro church is the most important. There is evidence that the Negro church has lost its significance for the urban proletarian who seeks to define his situation in terms of the church. However, where its influence is still felt, the Negro church is particularly culpable for its general lack of concern for the moral and social problems of the community. Rather than face the problem of the degradation of its people and take positive action for moral, cultural, and economic reconstruction, it has been accommodatory. Fostering indulgence in religious sentimentality, and riveting the attention of the masses on the bounties of a hereafter, the Negro church remains a refuge, an escape from the cruel realities of the here and now. Furthermore, evidence abounds of the misuse of the pulpit for furthering personal ambitions at the expense of the already harshly exploited masses. The grim fact is that the pulpit, with exceptions spread far and wide, has become, during the present century and especially in the large cities of the North, a route to social mobility for the charlatans in the Negro community. There is some evidence, however, of a growing realization of their social responsibilities among many Negro church leaders. The most important evidence is the Southern Christian Leadership Conference, led by the Reverend Dr. Martin Luther King, Jr. The same concern was shown by Dr. Joseph H. Jackson, president of the five-million-member National Baptist Convention, who recently announced the purchase of 600 acres of farmland for resettlement of Negro tenant and sharecropper families dispossessed of any means of livelihood by whites in Fayette and Haywood Counties as reprisals for their attempt to exercise the right to vote. In large measure, however, both the Negro church and other traditional leadership groups do not seem to appreciate how debased the life of the urban lower-class Negro is, nor the magnitude of effort in thought and action required for the reconstruction of the 'Souls of Black Folk'.

Lastly, the liberation movements and the emergence of the independent African states have had a significant impact on the Negro's total redefinition of himself, in relation to both his situation in America and to Africa. These events have not only awakened an unprecedented interest in Africa but have led, in a limited way at least, to what may be called 'an African orientation'. This does not mean that their effort to redefine themselves in relation to Africa is an expression of their desire to emigrate there. The practical importance of their African orientation should not be exaggerated. It should be balanced against the strong integration and assimilationist trends. We may observe, however, that recent developments in Africa have led a great many Negroes to identify with the struggles and aspirations of the African people. This, together with the domestic development and changes, appears to create a psychological situation fostering and intensifying the sense of separateness and ethnic consciousness among the masses. This psychological situation fosters among Negroes a new self-image, pride, and an impatient and urgent desire for equality, personal dignity, and self-assertion. In some measure, the consequences of their 'new' psychology are evident in the confidence shown by southern Negro student 'sit-in' demonstrations. Similarly, the emotional appeal, though otherwise limited, of black nationalism to the Northern urban Negro masses suggests the same psychological changes. We might add, qualifiedly, that the Negro's need for an identity and his desire for equality and dignity lead him increasingly to merge his aspirations with those of millions throughout the non-white world who are protesting against discrimination and exploitation. They, too, are caught in the 'revolution of rising expectations'!

Elijah Muhammad, then, emerges against this background of tensions, change, and of neglect by the traditional Negro institutions and leaders; the failure of the white society to extend 'equality in opportunity' to the Negro people; the Negro's dual sense of alienation and marginality; and the increasing sensitivity of the masses to their lowly material fortunes and the anxieties about their 'destiny' in America. Keeping this background in mind, and disregarding but not condoning the excesses of Muhammad's ideological concoctions or racial mysticism, it is clear that his is a unique effort to reconstruct the Negro soul, by providing a 'world' (a *mystique*) in which one could be black and unashamed, and by regenerating the Negro's moral and social values. So far as the writer knows, no Negro has ever dared to tackle the bewildering problems of the 'Negro in the mud' with equal vigour and such obdurate determination as Mr. Muhammad. Seen in this light, and in the light of the limited alternatives open to these Negroes, the Nation of Islam, with its moral and economic reforms, provides a way out for these Negroes. The ideological and racialist excesses are more symptomatic and symbolic than crucial in themselves. They reflect the harsh cruelties, discontent, and the grave social malaise which afflict millions of Negroes in America. Stated simply, the message of the Nation of Islam is this: Despite important, though slow, changes which have occurred in the Negro's formal status as citizen, the lot of the masses of Negroes in the North has not changed in substance. Evidence of pauperization, cultural disorientation, and moral degradation persist in spite of, and perhaps because of, the façade of public progress. These, Muhammad asserts, exist in spite of the fact that inequalities between blacks and whites are not legislated in the North; that the subordination of the masses of Negroes in the North reveals a few stubborn facts of social life which no amount of declarations of good intentions or wishful optimism can obviate. The first, he says, is the unequal distribution of political and economic power between blacks and whites. The possibility of an equalization of this distribution of vital social power is too remote to warrant speculation; but for a long time there shall exist Negro communities, and the position of Negroes is likely to remain marginal. Thus, Negroes striving for advancement, Mr. Muhammad says, are fundamentally circumscribed by their awareness of this fact. Their formal freedom is concomitantly limited by the substantive limitations as well as by their perception of the limitations. Yet within these restrictions, Negroes can give meaning to their freedom.

Formal freedom, insists Muhammad, without a substantive basis is, in effect, meaningless. Substantive freedom, a people's style of life—material, cultural, moral, and a sense of human dignity—cannot be bestowed upon people who do not want it, and if they do, are not prepared to help themselves and make the sacrifice necessary for its attainment; they must help create the conditions for it. Thus, if the masses of Negroes are to rise in the social scale, if they are to gain respect from others, if they are to be regarded as human beings rather than social outcasts, they must become consciously aware of their predicament, their degradation which is the bond of their common identity. They must also become conscious of their opportunities, however limited, and must take advantage of them. It is pointless to indulge in the fantasy that through some biological miracle black Americans will be transformed into white Americans or that the Negro communities will disappear in the foreseeable future.

Muhammad is convinced that the chief obstacle to be overcome is the 'mentality' of the masses of Negroes. This is the true enemy of their advancement and progress. The result of centuries of oppression, it has helped to produce the moral and material conditions in which the Negro masses now find themselves. The enemy of the Negro people, he maintains, is not simply white people but also the 'value system' of the subculture.

The writer is convinced that Muhammad's ideological pronouncements, which are popularly termed 'black supremacy', are aimed at purging lower-class Negroes of their inferiority complex. The 'real' rather than the 'ostensible' enemy of the Nation of Islam or of the Negro masses in general, is not the white people *per se* but the Negro himself—his subculture, his image of himself and of his 'place' in society, his attitude towards white people, and his idealization of all that is white. From the point of view of all black nationalists, the Negro can never be really free until he has purged from his mind all notions of white superiority and Negro inferiority and thus ceases to despise himself and his group. In doing so, he may have to shed the outward appearances of white culture and, most important, the 'old-time' religion. Indeed, they insist that Negroes should proudly accept rather than deny any contrasts between them and whites. Thus, it seems, the mission of the Nation of Islam is to reverse the process towards assimilation by means of militant separatism.

The process by which whites have been able to create and sustain the Negro's image of his own inferiority is known in common parlance as 'brainwashing'. In Muhammad's teaching, this process is known as 'tricknowledgy'. It would appear to the observer that it takes another kind of 'tricknowledgy' to undo the former. This, in the writer's view, is in part the significance of the racial doctrines, especially the eschatology emphasizing the eventual 'supremacy' of the Black Nation. If, indeed, Muhammad is aware that whites used 'tricks' to 'fool' the Negro, then it is plausible that his eschatology or other doctrines of 'racial supremacy' are gimmicks meant for the consumption of his followers and for combating the 'enemy within'—the Negro's 'mentality'. If this is correct, the frequent comparison of the Muslim movement with the Ku Klux Klan or with the White Citizen Council misses the point and has only a superficial relevance. Although alike in the crudity of their racial diatribes, they differ significantly in their objectives—for instance, the Muslims do not seek to deprive their fellow citizens of their political rights.

The Nation of Islam represents an esoteric, in-group struggle to provide standards by which the social, cultural, and moral life of the Negro masses can be raised to a meaningful community fabric. It seeks an outlet for Negro striving and performance. The movement combines the attractions of religion, nationalism, and political 'pies in the sky' with a peculiar sense of belonging and achievement, and proposes the possibility of 'greater' achievement for its members. The Nation assists its members to strive for traditional American middle-class values while maintaining their identity with the Negro community.

However, these values are interpreted for the members *via* the dogma of Islam, which in a direct and uncompromising way, assists them to overcome lower-class values which are held to impede the advancement of the Negro masses. Religious and nationalistic symbols, combined with a mutilated version of Western eschatology, endow the practical and moral concerns of the members with meaning and a strong sense of purpose and destiny. However, these ideological strands seem to dominate the 'community' fabric and conceal the socially relevant aspects of Mr.

Muhammad's teachings, the primary concern of which is the 'quality' of life of the urban lower-class Negroes. Although the ideological strands give the Nation of Islam an appearance of a wholly anti-white movement, properly conceived, it is uncompromisingly anti-lower-class Negro values, anti-Negro middle-class complacency and opportunism, and anti-white paternalism and injustice. Perhaps, more than the movement has been credited, it is far more opposed to the entire 'way of life' of the lower-class Negro and the 'dependence' mentality of their leaders than it appears.

The Nation of Islam is important not because it tells whites how bitterly Negroes feel about their present conditions but for showing the Negro masses 'why' they feel the way they do, 'how' they may get out of their degradation, and 'how' they may become self-respecting citizens. The Nation sets standards of achievement and excellence for its members and interprets for them standards of morality and economic norms generally cherished by middle-class Americans. (Of course there are some deviations.) The Nation recognizes the needs of Negroes, like other human beings, for membership and identity in some community. It insists that Negroes have the capacity to redeem themselves and recover their sense of human worth; that they must take the initiative in their struggle for human dignity. The alternative to these admonitions, says Muhammad, is continued complacency, moral deterioration, cultural degradation, crime, juvenile delinquency, and social and cultural stagnation.

Negro middle-class leadership being what it is and white attitudes being essentially unchanged in the vital areas of housing, equal opportunities in employment, etc., even in the Northern cities—what logical type of leadership can one envisage emerging from the deplorable conditions of the northern ghettoes? What alternatives exist for meeting the urgent needs of the Negro communities except through an appeal to Negro initiative? It seems conceivable that if the masses of Negroes were in the mood for the Nation of Islam or for something akin to it, under the right kind of conditions and leadership, communal initiative (call it nationalism or what you will) not chauvinism, holds some promise as a way out for them. If this should happen, then it would be tragic if the white society did not understand it. The white society may even encourage it. In fact, it promises to be for the good of society. In communal oriented activities, presently woefully lacking, Negroes would discover their identity and would best reflect what is good about America through self-assertion. It might enable them to develop their potential, a greater sense of the 'public interest' and to participate more constructively in the society. The Negro is unquestionably an American, 'reluctantly' at times, even as the deviant doctrines of Mr. Muhammad show; yet he is a member of a group with four centuries of unique experiences and traditions that cannot be easily wished away. Besides, the Negro, though removed by centuries from Africa, has never been, and cannot now be expected to be, indifferent to the land of his forbears. This remote heritage, no matter how insignificant its content may be, is part and parcel of the Negro's being. This too, like his Americanism, should be understood. In these circumstances, sentimentality towards assimilation or towards chauvinistic nationalism is blatantly wishful, unrealistic, and contrary to fact, in so far as the masses of Negroes are concerned.

American Negroes have contributed to American culture not by denying their identity (or contrasts) but by asserting it through music, folklore, etc., in spite of the harsh circumstances in which they found themselves. Indeed, they stand to contribute more to the culture and welfare of their society by recognizing and appreciating their own identity, rather than by despising themselves. Until most have been assimilated, the desire for ethnic self-assertion will continue to manifest itself in their social and cultural life, in private as well as in public matters, though taking various forms.

The Muslim movement is a grand reaction to the American scene and especially, the Negro's position in it; yet the scenery (the stage-set) shackles and delimits the drama—the potential for meaningful political or social action. Herein lie the factors which limit its social usefulness. It is also handicapped by the 'style of life'—i.e. the mentality, the social and moral values and economic habits—of the group which it seeks to redeem. Its separatist ideology is irreconcilably in conflict with the dominant assimilationist thinking of the vast majority of Negroes. On the other hand, it is limited by its anti-white ideology which strikes deep at the Negroes' fears as well as those of whites—their fear of a possibility of a 'Black Revenge'. The stark reality is that there can be no substantial or disruptive political action by the Nation of Islam other than that akin to the campus gadfly—a nuisance, mildly frightening, but actually not as deadly as the tse-tse fly.

PART THREE

The Enduring Debate: Racial Harmony or Racial Conflict?

The final section of the book presents four perspectives on the development of race and ethnic relations that, while raising issues of worldwide significance, concentrate particularly on trends in the United States and South Africa. Moynihan and Glazer review the conclusions of *Beyond the Melting Pot,* their important study of group life in New York City, in the light of the resurgence of ethnicity that seemed to follow in the wake of the Black Power movement. They argue that ethnic identity has increased in salience during the decade of the sixties as a consequence of a number of factors: the downgrading of working-class occupational roles, the displacement of international events by domestic issues as a focus for ethnic identification, and the relative decline of religion as a source of primary group loyalty. Glazer and Moynihan discuss the thorny problems of using ethnicity as a basis for communal life, of whether one can distinguish between "positive" or "negative" discrimination, and of what relation those concepts have to racism. Is ethnicity simply a new rationalization for racist beliefs and discriminatory actions, or is it rather a foundation upon which all groups can maintain a legitimate sense of identity within a pluralistic society?

While the example of the Black Power movement also helped to inspire the growth of white ethnic identity, its influence has been by no means confined to the United States. Just as the position of the American blacks has been influenced by the changing status of African nations in the postcolonial era, so the internal developments of the American black community have affected race relations in other parts of the world. Heribert Adam analyzes the Black Consciousness movement in South Africa, which started out when a group of African students broke

343

away from the multiracial, but white dominated, National Union of South African Students (NUSAS) to form their own exclusively black student body, the South African Student Organization (SASO). The spokesmen for Black Consciousness reject not only the path of the white liberals but also the pragmatic collaboration of African leaders, like Chief Buthelezi, who attack apartheid while using its institutions. Black Consciousness can be seen as a reaction to the failure of liberal nonracialism in South Africa during the past half century. The SASO leaders have arrived at the conclusion that liberation can only be achieved through separation, but a separation very different from that proposed by the supporters of apartheid. The overall impact of Black Consciousness is hard to assess. Will it form a prelude, perhaps in alliance with the new industrial militancy, to profound social change; or will it serve solely as an opiate for the black intellectual?

This question also applies to the various types of black nationalist ideology in the United States. William Wilson traces the changing character of black protest from the Civil Rights strategies of the fifties and early sixties, to the more militant tactics of the Black Power movement and its successors. He explains the transition in terms of the balance between resources available to the black community and the forces of constraint operating against it and as a result of the discrepancy between the expectations raised and the successes achieved by conventional, nonviolent means. Despite the many forms that the new quest for black power has assumed, a sense of "cultural nationalism" has a wide appeal in the black community and, significantly enough, seems to transcend class lines.

In the final selection, T. F. Pettigrew explores the same basic themes of separatism, integration, and liberation against the principles and findings of social-psychological theory and research. He emphasizes the potential dangers of separatism and examines in detail five major assumptions that underlie the separatist arguments of blacks and whites. Pettigrew concludes that separatism and integration are not mutually exclusive, and that a balanced program combining integration and communal enrichment would be feasible and desirable. Thus, it is highly probable that American society will witness increased black separation in certain spheres and more integration in others, for the two are by no means incompatible. As to the long-term outcome, the previous selections should warn us against attempting premature and dogmatic predictions. What can be said, with a considerable degree of certainty, is that American, South African, and every other pattern of race and ethnic relations will develop under the limelight of international scrutiny and, increasingly, in the context of international intervention.

30   A Resurgence of Ethnicity?

Nathan Glazer & Daniel P. Moynihan

The over-all ethnic pattern of the city has not changed since 1960, though the proportions have. There are still six major, fairly well-defined groups. The most visible is the Negro, which is rapidly increasing its proportion of the city's population, and has risen from 14 per cent in 1960 to an estimated 20 per cent today. The second most visible and sharply defined group is the Puerto Rican, whose proportion within the city population has increased since 1960 from 8 to 11 per cent. Substantial numbers of Latin Americans—Cubans and others—have come into the city since 1960 and tend to be lumped in public identification with Puerto Ricans, though they resist this. The largest single ethnic group in the city is the Jewish. Our data on their numbers are very poor. We guess they are declining from the quarter of the city's population they have long formed, to more like a fifth, but they are still probably more numerous than the Negroes. The next largest white group is the Italian. The Italian-born and their children alone formed 11 per cent of the city's population in 1960, leaving out the entire third generation and beyond. Perhaps they form one-seventh of the city's population. The Irish are a steadily declining part of the city's population, owing to heavy movements to the suburbs (also true, but in lesser degree, of Jews and Italians). They form probably some 7 per cent of the city.[1]

White Anglo-Saxon Protestants form the sixth most important social segment of the city in ethnic terms. If Irish identity becomes questionable in the later generations, WASP identity is even less of a tangible and specific identity. It is a created identity, and largely forged in New York City in order to identify those who are not otherwise ethnically identified and who, while a small minority in the city, represent what is felt to be the "majority" for the rest of the country.

Even in New York they bear the prestige of representing the "majority," whatever that may be, and, more significantly, they dominate the large banks, the large insurance companies, the large corporations that make their headquarters in the city. Young people flock to the city to work in its communications industries, advertising agencies, in the corporate office buildings, and discover they have become WASPs. This odd term includes descendants of early Dutch settlers (there are still a few), of early English and Scottish settlers (there are still some of these, too), immigrants and descendants of immigrants to the city from Great Britain, and migrants to the city from parts of the country which have had substantial proportions of settlers of British, English-speaking background. Merged into this mix may be persons of German background who no longer feel ethnically identified as German-Americans. The Germans, who formed along with the Irish the dominant

Reprinted from *Beyond the Melting Pot* by Nathan Glazer and Daniel P. Moynihan by permission of The M.I.T. Press, Cambridge, Massachusetts. ©1970 by The M.I.T. Press.

ethnic group of the late nineteenth and early twentieth century in the city, have not maintained, as a group, a prominence in the city proportionate to their numbers. (And yet in the 1960's the Steuben Day parade became a major event, at which the attendance of city officeholders was obligatory.)

Beyond the six major defined segments that are crucial to politics, to self-awareness, and also to the social description of the city, there are numerous others, but they tend to have a more local significance. In any given area, one must be aware of Poles, Russians, Greeks, Armenians, Chinese, Cubans, Norwegians, Swedes, Hungarians, Czechs, and so on, and so on, but even the largest of these groups forms no more than a few per cent of the city's population.

The Chinese community has grown, owing to the revision of the immigration laws in 1965, which eliminated the last references to race and national origin. The Cuban community is the largest new addition to the city's ethnic array. The over-all pattern, however, remains the familiar one of the early 1960's, with the trends then noted continuing: the growth of the Negro and Puerto Rican populations; the decline of the older ethnic groups, Irish and German; the continued significance of the two major groups of the "new immigration" of 1880 to 1924, the Jews and the Italians. This is the statistical pattern. Politically, economically, and culturally, however, two groups have outdistanced all others in the sixties: Jews and White Anglo-Saxon Protestants. The life of the city in the late sixties reflected nothing so much as an alliance between these groups, or parts of them, and the growing Negro group, against the remaining white, largely Catholic, groups. We shall say more later concerning why this has come about and what it means for the city.

Have ethnic identity and the significance of ethnic identity declined in the city since the early 1960's? The long-expected and predicted decline of ethnicity, the fuller acculturation and the assimilation of the white ethnic groups, seems once again delayed—as it was by World War I, World War II, and the cold war—and by now one suspects, if something expected keeps on failing to happen, that there may be more reasons than accident that explain why ethnicity and ethnic identity continue to persist. In *Beyond the Melting Pot,* we suggested that ethnic groups, owing to their distinctive historical experiences, their cultures and skills, the times of their arrival and the economic situation they met, developed distinctive economic, political, and cultural patterns. As the old culture fell away—and it did rapidly enough—a new one, shaped by the distinctive experiences of life in America, was formed and a new identity was created. Italian-Americans might share precious little with Italians in Italy, but in America they were a distinctive group that maintained itself, was identifiable, and gave something to those who were identified with it, just as it also gave burdens that those in the group had to bear.

Beyond the accidents of history, one suspects, is the reality that human groups endure, that they provide some satisfaction to their members, and that the adoption of a totally new ethnic identity, by dropping whatever one is to become simply American, is inhibited by strong elements in the social structure of the United States. It is inhibited by a subtle system of identifying, which ranges from brutal discrimination and prejudice to merely naming. It is inhibited by the unavailability of a simple "American" identity. One is a New Englander, or a Southerner, or a Midwesterner, and all these things mean something too concrete for the ethnic to adopt completely, while excluding his ethnic identity.

In any case, whatever the underlying fault lines in American society that seem to maintain or permit the maintenance of ethnic identity beyond the point of cultural assimilation, the fact is ethnic identity continued in the sixties.

We have precious few studies of ethnic identity, despite the increasing prominence of its role in the mass media in recent years, and we speak consequently quite hypothetically. Yet we would like to suggest three hypotheses on the changing position of ethnic identity in recent years.

First: ethnic identities have taken over some of the task in self-definition and in definition by others that occupational identities, particularly working-class occupational identities, have generally played. The status of the worker has been downgraded; as a result, apparently, the status of being an ethnic, a member of an ethnic group, has been upgraded.

There is no question that many occupational identities have lost a good deal of their merit and virtue, not to say glamour, in the eyes of those who hold them, and in the eyes of those in positions of significance in communications and the mass media who do so much to dispense ideas of merit, virtue, and glamour. The unions, the organizations of the working class, have certainly lost much of their glamour. What young bright man coming out of college would think that the most attractive, personally satisfying, and useful job he could hold would be to work for a union, as the authors did in 1944? Indeed, the intelligentsia has been quietly departing from unions and moving into government and the universities for ten years and more. But more significant has been the downgrading of working-class occupations. In the depression, in World War II, even after the war, the worker held an honored and important position. Radicals fought over his allegiance, the Democratic party was happy in his support, one could even see workers portrayed in the movies by men such as Humphrey Bogart, John Garfield, Clark Gable, and these heroes portrayed occupations, whether as truck drivers or oilfield workers or even produce marketmen, that had some reputation and value.

Similarly, to be a homeowner after the war, and many workers became homeowners, was meritorious. It indicated rise in status, setting down roots, becoming a part of the community. Today, if one were to test associations to word "worker" and "homeowner" among television newscasters and young college graduates, one is afraid one of the chief associations would be "racist" and "Wallaceite." It is hard to recall any movie of the late sixties, aside from *Pretty Poison,* in which a factory worker was a leading character, and in *Pretty Poison* the factory spewed chemical filth into the countryside, and the worker himself was half mad.[2]

Lower-middle-class statuses have also suffered, but the clerk or teacher or salesman never did do well in the mass media. The worker did; he formed part of that long-sustained and peculiar alliance that has always seemed to link those of higher status, in particular aristocrats and intellectuals, with lower-class people, leaving the middle classes in the middle to suffer the disdain of both. What has

happened in recent years is that the lower pole of the alliance has shifted downward, leaving out the working class, and now hooking up the intellectuals and the
upper-middle-class youth with the Negro lower class.

The Wallace movement and the Procaccino campaign were in part efforts to
take political advantage of the declining sense of being valued in the working- and
lower-middle class, and to ascribe to these groups a greater measure of credit and
respect, as against both the more prosperous and better educated, who have supported measures designed to assist Negroes and the poor, and the Negroes and the
poor themselves. If these class and occupational statuses have been downgraded,
by that token alone ethnic identity seems somewhat more desirable. Today, it may
be better to be an Italian than a worker. Twenty years ago, it was the other way
around.

Thus, one reason we would suggest for the maintenance of ethnic identities is
the fact that working-class identities and perhaps some other occupational identities
have lost status and respect.

Let us suggest a second hypothesis as to changes in ethnic identity in this decade: international events have declined as a source of feelings of ethnic identity,
except for Jews; domestic events have become more important. The rise of Hitler
and World War II led to an enormous rise in feelings of ethnic identification. Nor
was there much decline after the war, as the descendants of East European immigrants who had been aroused by Hitler's conquests now saw their homelands
become Russian satellites, and as other nations were threatened. But aside from
Jews, no group now sees its homeland in danger. (Israel barely qualifies as a "homeland," but the emotional identification is the same.) Even the resurgence of conflict
between Catholics and Protestants in Northern Ireland has evoked only a sluggish
response among American Irish. By this very token, as involvement with and concern for the homelands decline, the sources of ethnic identification more and more
are to be found in American experiences, on American soil. This is not to say that
identification with homelands in danger or in conflict cannot rise again. But for the
first time a wave of ethnic feeling in this country has been evoked not primarily by
foreign affairs but by domestic developments. This is a striking and important development—it attests to the long-lived character of ethnic identification and raises
the curtain somewhat on the future history of ethnic identity in this country.

A third hypothesis: along with occupation and homeland, religion has declined
as a focus of ethnic identification. Just as ethnicity and occupation overlap, so do
ethnicity and religion. For some time, it seemed as if new identities bases on religion
were taking over from ethnic identities. This was the hypothesis of Will Herberg.[3]
The Jews remained Jews, with a subtle shift from an ethnic identification in the
first and second generation to more of a religious identification in the third; the
Irish became ever more Catholic in their self-image, and so did the Italians. Even
the P in WASP stands for Protestant, as part of the identity. Only for Negroes did
racial identity seem clearly far more significant than religion. In *Beyond the
Melting Pot,* we argued that religion and race seemed to be taking over from ethnicity. Yet in the last few years, the role of religion as a primary identity for

Americans has weakened. Particularly in the case of Catholics, confusion and uncertainty have entered what was only a few years ago a very firm and clear identity. Thus, for Irish and Italians alike, Catholicism once confirmed a basic conservatism; it was not only anti-Communist, obviously, but, more significantly, it took conservative positions on issues of family, sex, culture, education. Catholics formed the core of the Democratic party in New York, which, alongside its pronounced and decisive liberalism in social policy, remained conservative on issues of family and culture. The revolution in the Catholic Church has shaken this monolithic institution, and the identity of Catholic is no longer self-evident, to those holding it or to those outside the Church. The change is symbolized by the radical changes in ritual, in this most conservative of institutions, and in the possibility of changes in such ancient patterns as the celibacy of the clergy.

For the purposes of race relations, the most striking development is the divergence between clergy and laity (some clergy and some laity) on the issue of Negro militancy. When priests marched with Martin Luther King in Chicago, it was reported that Catholic workers who opposed the move of Negroes into their neighborhoods said, "Now even they are with them, and we are alone." Nothing as striking as this has happened in New York, where the laity are not as conservative as in Chicago (with its strong Polish and Lithuanian representation), and where the priests have not come up with a prominent radical leader. But if there is no equivalent of Father Groppi in New York, there are many smaller versions of Father Groppi. Catholicism no longer confirms as fully as it did some years ago the conservative tendencies of Italians and Irish.

We have suggested three aspects of the current prominence of ethnicity: that it is related to the declining merit of certain occupational identifications, that it increasingly finds its sources in domestic rather than foreign crises, and that the revolution in the Catholic Church means that, for the first time, it does not complement the conservative tendencies of Catholic ethnic groups. Now we come to a fourth aspect. In a word, is the resurgence of ethnicity simply a matter of the resurgence of racism, as is now often asserted? Is the reaction of whites, of ethnic groups and the working and middle class, to the increasingly militant demands of Negroes a matter of defense of ethnic and occupational turfs and privileges or is it a matter of racial antipathy, and more of racism, that large and ill-used term, which means, if it means anything, that those afflicted with it see the world primarily in racial categories, in black and white, and insist that black should be down and white up?

In the fifties, Herberg argued that religion was rising, not because of any interest really in its doctrines, but because religion was a more respectable way of maintaining ethnic primary groups than ethnicity itself. To be Italian or Jewish (ethnic rather than religious) was somehow not reputable and raised the issue of conflict with the demands of American citizenship, a potential conflict that became particularly sharp in World War II and that has remained alive for American Jews since the establishment of the State of Israel. Now, it is argued, religion, owing to the liberalism of the clergy, cannot serve to keep the Negroes out—of neighborhoods, schools, jobs. But ethnicity can still serve that function. So, by emphasizing ethnicity and ethnic attachment, the argument goes, one can cover one's racism and yet be racist.

Thus, it may be argued, just as religion in the 1950's covered for ethnicity, ethnicity in the 1960's covers for racism. The issue remains simply one of white against black, and to speak of Jews, Italians, Irish, is merely to obfuscate it. We disagree with this point of view and argue that ethnicity is a real and felt basis of political and social action.

To begin with, we have always been forced to recognize the validity of some degree of discrimination—difficult to call simply racist—if it was for the purpose of defending something positive rather than simply excluding someone because of his race. For example, while city, state, and federal laws prohibit discrimination on account of race, creed, color, or national origin, they do accept the fact that certain institutions will want to discriminate positively, for purposes of the kind of mission in which they are engaged. The headquarters of the Armenian Church will want to hire Armenians, a Polish cultural foundation will hire Poles, and so on. Similarly, when Jewish organizations fought discrimination in vacation resorts in New York State in the 1940's and 1950's, they had the difficult issue of deciding whether the note in resort advertisements, "churches nearby," indicated discrimination. The argument was made that Jewish resorts could freely advertise, "dietary laws observed." In both cases, one could argue, something *positive* was being accented, rather than something defined as negative excluded. To emphasize the virtues of maintaining an ethnic neighborhood is different from emphasizing the exclusion of Negroes, in sense and logic, though the acts that serve one aim are hard to distinguish from the acts that serve the other.

Legally, the problem of permitting this kind of positive discrimination is enormously difficult. Morally and socially, it appears to have some value. Just as blacks now want to gather together in distinctive institutions where they can strengthen specifically black social, cultural, and political tendencies, so do other groups; in both cases, the pervasiveness of antidiscrimination statutes and regulations introduces difficulties.

It may be granted that there is some legitimacy to what we call positive discrimination, which can be defined simply as the effort to bring together people of distinctive backgrounds or interests or potential interests for some socially valued end. "Religion" is such an end. "Ethnicity" can be considered such an end. But what about "race"? "Race," we all agree, has been rejected as such an end. Thus, we do not want to see "white" institutions maintained or established in this country. For the purpose of "white," as most of us see it, is not to defend or maintain a "white" culture or religion but to exclude blacks. By the same token, is not the maintenance and creation of black institutions illegitimate? We do not think so, because whatever some black militants may think, "black" defines not a race but a cultural group, in our terms, an ethnicity. Thus, it is hardly likely that Moslem, Swahili-speaking blacks of Zanzibar would find much in common with the black institutions and culture that are now being built up in this country. They would

not have any predilection for soul music or soul food, would find the styles of
dress, hair, walk, and talk that are now popular as defining blackness distinctly
foreign. "Blackness" in this country is not really and simply *blackness,* it is an
American Negro cultural style. Blackness would be as unacceptable in this country
as whiteness, if it were really only blackness. We can accept it because we recognize in blackness not simply the negative exclusion of white but the positive discrimination designed to strengthen and develop a distinctive group, with a distinctive
history, defined interests, and identifiable styles in social life, culture, and politics.

But the matter is not so simple. This is one way of seeing blackness, of course,
and a way that makes it conformable to the main trends in American society,
where ethnic distinctiveness is to some degree accepted and accommodated. But
it is not necessarily the way blacks see it today or will see it. Certainly, many blacks
do insist on the racial formulation. They base it on the common oppression of all
"colored" races by all "whites," and even more by "capitalistic' and "imperialistic"
whites, something that is a rough summary of history, but very rough indeed,
when one considers that Japan built up a great empire over other yellow and brown
people, that Arabs for centuries dominated and enslaved black Africans, that
Russia maintains dominion over white groups, and so on. To our minds, whether
blacks in the end see themselves as ethnic within the American context, or as only
black—a distinct race defined only by color, bearing a unique burden through
American history—will determine whether race relations in this country is an un-
ending tragedy or in some measure—to the limited measure that anything human
can be—moderately successful.

Indeed, much of the answer to the question we have posed—ethnicity or
racism?—is a matter of definition and self-definition, and much of the future of
race relations in the city and the country depends on what designations and definitions we use. For just as a "nigger" can be made by treating him like a "nigger"
and calling him a "nigger," just as a black can be made by educating him to a new,
proud, black image—and this education is carried on in words and images, as well
as in deeds—so can racists be made, by calling them racists and treating them like
racists. And we have to ask ourselves, as we react to the myriad cases of group
conflict in the city, what words shall we use, what images shall we present, with
what effect? If a group of housewives insists that it does not want its children
bussed to black schools because it fears for the safety of its children, or it does
not want blacks bussed in because it fears for the academic quality of the schools,
do we denounce this as "racism" or do we recognize that these fears have a base
in reality and deal seriously with the issues? When a union insists that it has nothing
against blacks but it must protect its jobs for its members and their children, do
we deal with those fears directly, or do we denounce them as racists? When a neighborhood insists that it wants to maintain its character and its institutions, do we
take this seriously or do we cry racism again?

We believe the conflicts we deal with in the city involve a mixture of *interests:*
the defense of specific occupations, jobs, income, property; of *ethnicity:* the
attachment to a specific group and its patterns; and of *racism:* the American

(though not only American) dislike and fear of the racial other, in America's case in particular compounded by the heritage of slavery and the forcible placing of Negroes into a less than human position. We believe we must deal with all these sources of conflict, but to ignore the ethnic source, or the interest source, in an exclusive fixation on the racist source, will undoubtedly encourage the final tearing apart of the community and the country between groups that see each other as different species rather than as valued variants of a common humanity.

Politically, we think it is wise to recognize these varied sources of conflict. Empirically, we think that to insist that ethnic concerns are only a cover for racism is wrong. Recent research throws some light on the persistence of ethnic cohesion, and it lasts longer than many people believe. The sociologist Nathan Kantrowitz, studying the patterns of residence of racial and ethnic groups in the New York City metropolitan area, points out that the degree of separation between white groups that we often consider similar is quite high. No group, except the Puerto Rican, is as segregated from others as the Negro. When we contrast the residence of Negroes as compared with the residence of foreign-born whites and their children, we find a "segregation index" averaging 80; that is, 80 per cent of Negroes would have to move to be distributed throughout the metropolitan area the way specific groups of foreign-born whites and their children are. We find the same figure when we compare the residences of Puerto Ricans and foreign-born whites and their children; by this measure, then, Puerto Ricans are as segregated as Negroes. But when we compare different *white* groups, we also find a high degree of separation. Thus, for example,

> The segregation index between Norwegians and Swedes, 45.4, indicates a separation between two Protestant Scandinavian populations which have partially intermarried and even have at least one community in common (the Bay Ridge neighborhood in Brooklyn). But the high [segregation index] does represent ethnic separation, for each national group still maintains its own newspaper, and each lives in neighborhoods separate from those of the other. If Swedes and Norwegians are not highly integrated with each other, . . . they are even less integrated with other ethnic populations.[4]

And if this is the case for these groups, we would expect Italians and their children, immigrants from Russia and their children to have even *higher* segregation indices— and indeed they do.

Thus, the data show, on at least this point of residential segregation, that the pattern of distinctive residence characterizes almost all ethnic groups. This is not to say that they all face discrimination: they do not. Negroes do face discrimination in housing, and as we know, severe discrimination. But if groups that do *not* face discrimination *also* show a high degree of segregation, we must resort to two additional explanations of the Negro pattern of residence: one is the economic— they can't afford to move into many houses and many areas (as is true of Puerto Ricans, and, in lesser degree, of other groups); and the second is simply that there is also a positive element in the association of Negroes in given areas, something which is very often totally ignored. Formal and informal social life, churches and other institutions, distinctive businesses, all serve to make neighborhoods that are desirable and attractive for a given group, and to think that this pattern, which operates for all groups, is suspended for Negroes, is to be racist indeed.

NOTES

1. The estimates of Negroes and Puerto Ricans in the city have some official standing; they are from the City Planning Commission. The others are based on sample surveys conducted for the 1969 election. These are rather contradictory, and we have simply made some educated guesses.
2. See William Simon, John H. Gagnon, and Donald Carns, "Working-Class Youth: Alienation Without An Image," *New Generation*, Vol. 51, No. 2, Spring 1969, pp. 15–21.
3. Will Herberg, *Protestant, Catholic, Jew*, New York: Doubleday, 1955.
4. Nathan Kantrowitz, "Ethnic and Racial Segregation in the New York Metropolis, 1960," *American Journal of Sociology*, Vol. 74, No. 6, May, 1969, 685–695.

31　　The Rise of Black Consciousness in South Africa

Heribert Adam

While outside attention focuses on guerrilla incursions, industrial strikes, UN missions or similar events of a spectacular nature, subtle changes are taking place almost unnoticed inside South Africa. Divergent trends emerge in less publicized events whose accumulated impact could nevertheless account for potential changes. Focus on the static nature of entrenched White rule and Black subordination easily overlooks the latent dynamics of the contradictions of apartheid. White domination is not monolithic nor has the seemingly total subjugation of Black people rendered all opposition powerless. Racial supremacy, at the very least, has to legitimize itself at the end of the colonial era and cannot afford to rely on the brute and cynical use of force alone. This interplay between legitimizing ideology and contradictory reality opens one avenue of challenge to the existing power. Its necessary interconnection with outside forces and its reliance on external economic and political support, constitutes a lever of influence absent in an isolated fortress. Finally, the internal economic scene with its own dictates would seem to lead to an alternative setting in

From *Race*, Vol. XV, 2, 1973, pp. 149–165. Reprinted by permission of the Institute of Race Relations.

favour of the subordinates. Not that economic expansion will automatically or necessarily lead to different race relations, as the old liberal illusion asserts; but the inclusion of better skilled Blacks into a diversified economy will change the constellation of power whereby the powerless are able to act with more likely success in a strike situation. An economy which has to invest in individual African productivity through various schemes also becomes more dependent on its workers if they decide to challenge their conditions

In these crucial moments—far from hypothetical since widespread strikes started in January 1973 in Durban and have continued ever since on an almost daily basis in different parts of the country, mainly Natal[1]—the political consciousness of the participants and differing policy goals of various leaders become of decisive importance in dampening, channelling, or directing popular grievances. In this sense, the so-called 'Black Consciousness Movement' of African, Indian, and Coloured students, though not directly related to the spontaneous strikes, gains political significance beyond the esoteric student circles. It signals potentials and sparks which could perhaps overflow to those whose real power counts more than student dreams. So far, to my knowledge, no comprehensive, detached critical assessment of the Black Consciousness ideas has been attempted, apart from propagandistic descriptions or, more frequently, sweeping condemnation.

The new movement started when African students in 1968 split away from the always White-dominated liberal, though, in the South African context, often radical, 'National Union of South African Students' (NUSAS), forming their own exclusively Black group under the name of 'South African Student Organisation' (SASO).[2] Apart from the ideological justification given, this departure from organizational multiracialism by the African opponents of apartheid had several objective reasons. It reflected the different problems and perceptions of Africans, studying since the beginning of the sixties in isolated, separate ethnic universities, which in their disciplinary code as well as exposure to outside issues differed considerable from the cosmopolitan English-language institutions with a long tradition of academic freedom.[3] But above all, the Black students unconsciously realized an insight which sociologists have labelled 'interracial interaction disability'.[4] This notion expresses the results of empirical research which showed that initial differences in social status in the larger society produce a similar power and prestige order in new small groups where competence at the task has no rational relationship to the state of the status characteristics. In such situations White dominance inevitably results when races interact or Blacks compare themselves to 'significant others' of the two races.[5] Where objective status differences and belief systems are so powerful and overwhelming that they infect interracial organizations against the conscious intentions of their participants, separation might indeed be the appropriate answer to overcome the structural disabilities.

Several years later the SASO philosophy encouraged the creation of a new political body, the 'Black Peoples Convention', formed in 1971, among whose goals is 'the principle and philosophy of Black communalism—the philosophy of sharing.' SASO has become the student wing of this body, while other branches attempted to organise all-Black trade unions (Black Allied Worker's Council, initiated by Drake

Koka), or concerned themselves with theological (African Independent Church's Association, AICA), or educational projects (ASSECA).

The ideas of Black Consciousness are not new in South Africa and were similarly expressed by earlier organizations, particularly the Pan African Congress. However, the new movement differs in: (1) the exclusion of all Whites from its ranks; (2) the emphasis of organizational unity of all three non-white groups under the label 'Black'; and (3) the rejection of Black sympathizers who co-operate with Whites in apartheid institutions in order to fight the system on its own terms. Historically, the emergence of Black Consciousness must be seen as a counterview to the institutionalized apartheid opposition which encouraged and paved the way for the cautious airing of more uncompromising African perspectives. It would seem decisive that for the first time since the suppression of organized legal Black resistance a decade earlier, African organizations and leaders have publicly reemerged on a platform of outspoken opposition to White domination. During the sixties, individual attempts to air Black frustrations were quickly silenced through banning orders and other intricate provisions of the 'Suppression of Communism Act', although Black underground activity continued in a limited way, as evidenced in various court cases. Verbal attacks on the White system by Black spokesmen were now tolerated to a greater degree, compared with the earlier South African tradition and the practice in other authoritarian states both of a right-wing and 'socialist' doctrine. Indeed, the reasons for this surprising shift can hardly be viewed as a newly adopted tolerance of the South African government which, on the whole, has responded with more intransigence than concessions to demands for change of its institutionalized racialism. It would seem that both the content of the Black Consciousness creed in relation to the official apartheid doctrine as well as its limited impact thus far, were mostly responsible for its initial legal survival. When this impact became a more realistic possibility during the Durban strikes in February 1973, eight of the leading SASO organizers were quickly silenced by banning orders, together with an equal number of White NUSAS officials or sympathizers. It remains to be seen how far the intimidating effect of such measures alone will cripple the organization as has been the case in similar circumstances a decade earlier. From a manipulative White point of view, Black outspokenness is also useful for the White minority system in so far as it signals explosive frustrations and aspirations and allows for easier surveillance of its most dangerous leaders. The question is, how far can this 'repressive tolerance' backfire? Is the new opposition—which can be crushed by an ever more powerful state machinery whenever it may be deemed expedient— likely to develop its own dynamic in the meantime? Can a dialectic of oppression be discovered, contributing to the downfall of a racial oligarchy by the very methods which it adopted for its security?

SOURCES AND CONTENTS

The advocates of Black Consciousness in South Africa owe much of their philosophy to the inspiration gained from its famous predecessors, the ideas of negritude

and Black identity elsewhere. Although Leopold Senghor, Aimé Cesaire or Frantz
Fanon are seldom acknowledged, Black Consciousness in South Africa marks their
success in universalizing the experience of the colonized in different geographical
settings. The accusation of plagiarizing and importing a foreign philosophy, not fit-
ting the unique South African circumstances, therefore overlooks the common insights of a colonial existence. Many observers have wondered why the Black awareness
in its present form has appeared so late on the South African scene. One reason
would seem to be that opposition to White rule had been absorbed in other forms
of African nationalism which in coalition with a few White supporters always
aimed at a non-racial, common, western-type society whose values supposedly
everyone would share. This old alternative of separation or integration is no longer
relevant to the politically conscious new Black. His goal has changed into 'liberation' and this includes a rejection of many Western values to which the earlier Black
nationalists claimed the same adherence as their White monopolizers.[6]

In the absence of real liberation and the means to achieve it, Black Consciousness essentially represents verbal resistance. However, even in the realm of
rhetoric it has to select its weapons carefully, considering the overwhelming White
power structure. But more fundamental factors distinguish the South African movement from Black Power of the American version. First of all, the idea of Black Consciousness in South Africa differs from Black Power ideologies in the United States
by addressing itself to a different structural and historical setting. Blacks in South
Africa have no power—not the power of a gun, nor the power of a vote, or pressure
groups to influence decisions affecting their lives at their urban homes or work
places. The law aims at their separation in South Africa and does not support
attempts for equality as in the United States. South African subordinates are at the
mercy of their rulers without even the hope for an individual escape in a race-caste
system which ascribes status without exception for the rich or educated. However,
83 per cent of the population in South Africa are classified African, Indian, or
Coloured, and this numerical majority allows for the realistic expectation of an
eventual Black political and cultural system, which the 11 per cent Black people in
the United States can never hope to achieve on a national level. This factor, together with the severity of disprivilege, backed by racist laws in addition to racist
social practice as in the U.S., would seem to account for a much more political outlook of the movement in South Africa. There is less concern with a life-style and
the cultural assertion of a different personality.

Moreover, the two situations of current racial discrimination result from different historical backgrounds of settler colonialism. The American sociologist Robert
Blauner has suggested 'that cultural penetration is less effective and extreme when a
people are colonized within their original territory.'[7] Africans in South Africa were
defeated militarily, their land was taken over by the settlers, and they were pushed
back into overcrowded so-called 'tribal areas', but for the most part they were
never enslaved in the sense that their American counterparts were. The historical
situation of American Blacks resembles much more that of South African Coloureds. Africans, on the other hand, could fall back on cultural traditions which

survived conquest and remained essentially intact. A Black Consciousness spokesman confirms this with the statement 'that the basic tenets of our culture have succeeded to a great extent to withstand the process of bastardisation.'[8] In South Africa there is less need to reconstruct a lost history but only to correct white distorted history books which dwell on the civilizing mission of the culturally superior Europeans. For many Black South African intellectuals, a sense of their own past is much more present than it is for their counterparts in America, although in the latter instance the specific slave culture and history have long been neglected or denied. An important difference in the two historical accounts is the not always unsuccessful resistance to white conquest, particularly by the Zulus. The unbroken memory of this dimension relates frequently to interpretations of current events.[9] Although the migratory labour system, urbanization and industrialization would seem to have destroyed cultural tradition and its economic base in the subsistence economy for many of the urban proletariat, there exists at the same time an awareness of the alternative which is in South Africa not artificial decoration but living reality. It would seem that the Indian community in South Africa in particular has preserved facets of a traditional culture and customs which served as an immunizing shield against discrimination. In another context Amilcar Cabral stressed the 'cultural resistance of the people, who when they are subjected to political domination and economic exploitation find that their own culture acts as a bulwark in preserving their identity'.[10] There can be little doubt that the specific Black identity in South Africa ameliorated the harshness of individual suffering and thus far has prevented extreme forms of outrage against the real source of frustration. Within the protective group membership the consequences of racial discrimination are obviously not attributed to individual failures but to the collective stigma. This decreases frustrations and the resulting aggression. In a perceptive analysis of inhibiting factors of earlier forms of African nationalism, Fatima Meer has pointed to a remarkable 'absence of violence in the face of the most dire provocation'. Contrary to racist beliefs, she suggests, 'that far from being wild and violent, Africans are singularly unaggressive'.[11] The relatively unbroken cultural tradition of South African Blacks appears to have contributed to this situation, where individual frustrations are channelled into group comfort.

Black Consciousness aims above all at strengthening this group cohesion in the face of threatening anomie and white imposed fragmentation. Its slogans are solidarity and brotherhood, 'drawing strength from our common plight'.[12] Central in all the statements, and almost identical with similar pronouncements in the United States, is the call for psychological liberation. Since the colonized have frequently internalized the norms and orders of their oppressors, they first of all must rid themselves of their 'slave mentality'. Inferiority feelings, distrust of themselves, and self-hate are seen as the cardinal sins and obstacles of liberation. There is almost a pathological self-assertion, rejecting what is essentially obvious and not worth-while to be negated: 'We are not genetic errors, nor are we God's mistakes'.[13] An American Black writer has stated a similar reservation: 'It is important to be aware of one's cultural origin, but a waste of energy to feel it necessary to disprove all white lies and to present a black counter for everything the white world holds in esteem. My father could give a damn if someone painted a Black Madonna. The goal of Black people should not be to attain the same level of mediocrity as White people.'[14]

The adopted ridicule and deprecation of the conquereds' traditional way of life is seen as the root of continued subjugation, for which the victims are sometimes blamed more than the aggressor. 'We Black people contribute to our own oppression more than our oppressor enslaves us.'[15] Reminiscent of nineteenth century idealistic philosophers, not real liberation from material and political bondage alone, but spiritual freedom, is viewed as being able to achieve the desired state, in spite of continuing subjugation. 'If one is free at heart, no human-made chains can bind one to servitude', writes the first president of SASO.[16] The dehumanization of racism is countered and the violated dignity and degraded personality restored by an assertion of the 'intrinsic worth' of the Black man, a call for pride and self-reliance and a rejection of White guardianship, patronization, and paternalism in any form.

The new Blacks apply a much more realistic perspective to racism than earlier Black leaders, who basically tried to impress the White with their 'civilized' standards, appeals for justice and moral arguments. Contrary to this tactic of persuasion, the new Black generation expects that a ruling group does not give up its privileges voluntarily, unless pressured into doing so by the strength of its opponent. Racial prejudice is not to be changed by enlightenment, since racial attitudes reflect and rationalize group interests and privileges.

If this generalization is basically correct, then the Black Consciousness proponents must equally face the fact that 'self-love', 'identity', and 'cultural assertion' are not sufficient to effect real change. The crucial question remains how this cultural revolution in the minds of the subordinates can be translated into political action. It might be the first phase and necessary prerequisite for a successful mobilization—but there is also the danger that it may become an end in itself, in much the same way as cultural nationalism, the obsession with soul, and a unique life-style have frequently become a substitute for political activity among Black people in the U.S. As Cabral has pointed out elsewhere: 'But the "return to the source" is not and cannot in itself be an act of struggle against foreign domination (colonialist and racist) and it no longer necessarily means a return to tradition.'[17]

The strength of the apartheid ideology lies precisely in the official encouragement of an apolitical ethnic orientation as an end in itself. It is hoped that cultural revitalization, culminating in stronger ethnic ties, will weaken national unity, as it did elsewhere in Africa, given the cultural diversity of a multi-ethnic society. Unlike the notion of the 'melting pot', which so obviously has failed in the United States, the Afrikaner policy of multinationalism uses ethnicity maintenance as its basis.[18]

Apartheid gambles with the strength of traditional definitions, while Black Consciousness on the other hand relies on the shared experience of oppression. The Black Consciousness proponents also want to utilize cultural revitalization, but eventually to redirect it into political mobilization. A prediction about failure or success of both strategies appears not as easy as political theorists would make us believe and earlier Panafricanists have come to learn. Increasingly, more Anglo-American social scientists, who earlier unanimously predicated continuing assimilation and acculturation, are now beginning to grapple with the very opposite of their predictions. As Blauner has observed, ethnic groups in many plural societies readily seem to seize upon their supposedly lost identity, because it provides a bulwark of identification in the face of increasing anxieties. The continued appeal of independent African churches and sects, now believed to number about 3,000 and comprising 25 per cent of all Africans, may be similarly explained.

Symbolic liberation then substitutes easily for a political programme. The rhetoric reconfirms faith and purges doubts about the ultimate success, and the meetings tend to become a cult, regenerating the spirit by confirming the pride and worth. For example, being now called Black, instead of Non-white,[19] is regarded as progress in much the same way as the liberal White feels his outlook proven by being kind to his servants, or the Nationalist feels on the left because he shifted to 'the pat on the head instead of the sjambok on the back' as Nadine Gordimer[20] illustrates the South African way of tokenism. Among the patted, too, there are already signs of delusions and confusion over priorities. For instance, one reads: 'We sincerely believe that we the Black people of this world hold the key to the future well-being and peace that is so urgently required on this planet.'[21] It is doubtful whether that author holds the key to the immediate needs of his community, let alone a realistic assessment of the existing power structure in South Africa. As a sympathetic White political scientist has commented: 'If black leaders believe that they have an intuitive understanding of the needs of the black people, and no need to motivate them to act politically, then they are not likely to be very effective leaders'.[22]

THE POLITICAL GOAL: INTEGRATION OR SEPARATION

Before any adequate evaluation can be made of the potential for change by Black Consciousness, a closer evaluation of its political goals has to proceed an analysis of its tactics in light of the specific South African social structure and history of resistance. Three related issues seem to recur in all discussions about Black Consciousness: (1) the question of integration; (2) the role of the White liberal and Whites in general; and (3) the notion of a reverse racism as a reaction to White discrimination.

For the more sophisticated spokesmen of Black Consciousness, the question of integration or separation is irrelevant, because the alternative does not exist. If it were to exist, it would depend on the answer to the question: integration into what? There is a deeply felt conviction that white society is essentially corrupt and that it is, therefore, not worth being part of such a tradition. White technical and economic superiority is seen as having developed and being maintained on the basis of exploitation at home and abroad. Integration into this system on White terms would only compromise Blacks. 'It is an integration in which Black will compete with Black, using each other as stepping stones up a steep ladder leading them to White values. It is an integration in which the Black man will have to prove himself in terms of these values before meriting acceptance and ultimate assimilation.'[23] Behind inarticulated outbursts against a 'stinking capitalism'[24] in the statements of some spokesmen lies a remarkably clear understanding by others that, contrary to the policies of the United and Progressive Party, only economic equality can ultimately solve the racial problem: 'Racial integration requires economic integration, and this in turn, requires a recognition that the race problem cannot be solved without profound structural modification in the country, without real changes in the tax structure and the relations between the private and public sectors; without a redefinition of all values and a redistribution of income and power.'[25]

The role of the White liberals in South Africa is seen as directing their efforts 'merely at relaxing certain oppressive legislations' in order to 'allow Blacks into a White-type society.'[26] This argument, though correct as far as the official policy of the few remaining liberal institutions is concerned, overlooks, however, a small group of Whites (Radicals, Socialists, and Communists) who share the criticism of a profit-oriented colonial system and always were and could be allies in the struggle for an alternative society. The reaction against all Whites by the New Blacks may be interpreted, above all, as retaliation against a deeply despised paternalism. Adam Small summarizes his experience: 'White antagonists of apartheid love to cast themselves in the role of guardians for us, love to approach us as little children are approached, love to tell us "you too have beautiful values, can't you see"?'[27] This patronizing attitude, together with the close but unsuccessful involvement of White opponents of apartheid with the Black resistance in the past, has paradoxically made the helpless White liberal now a more frequent target for verbal attacks than Afrikaners ever have been. In the words of an African student, those who kick us are almost less hated than those who tell us how to respond to the kick. Liberal activists, such as Alan Paton, resent this unjustified condemnation, while the government press rejoices at the unexpected African support. Both blame each other for the rise of Black exclusivism and anti-White feelings. But more than the irrelevancy of liberals for Black needs and their parallel failure to dent the status quo with more than rhetoric, it is the very goal of the two philosophies which are diametrically opposed. The aims of the South African Institute of Race Relations, the most significant and almost sole institutional representative of traditional liberalism in South Africa, can best illustrate this predicament. The Institute is careful to define itself as a non-militant body, 'committed to long-term strategies of peaceful change' and 'not cataclysmic overthrow', its 'main appeal has been to the moderates of all racial groups.'[28] The liberal aims of 'inter-racial peace, harmony and co-operation'[29] clash with a situation where, in the views of progressive Blacks, only conflict, confrontation, and non-cooperation can achieve a change of the White power structure. In this sense the new Black aggressiveness poses indeed 'an inherent threat to much that the Institute has striven for.'[30] And yet it is only because White liberals have a sensitive relationship to Blacks, that the two most outspoken opponents of the Government are interlocked in bitter arguments with each other. As van Wyk rather aptly observes about the White liberals, only 'theirs is an exposed nerve system'.

The militant rhetoric of Black Consciousness has naturally led to accusations of a Black racism. Some officials have charged that Black Consciousness 'is a well-known old snake again raising its head ... the Pan-African Congress and Poqo in a new guise.'[31] Although the undifferentiated attacks against *all* Whites and frank statements of hate suggest some infection, for the oppressed, colour has a different meaning. Above all, they are not in a position to harm anyone nor do they expose pseudo-justification of privilege. Black Consciousness simply reflects the fact that the supposedly colour-blind ethos of liberalism has become an anachronism as long as an all pervasive racial structure continues to differentiate between people solely on the basis of their skin colour. The victims did not make this situation and some are well aware of the ambiguity of their organizing principle: 'History has charged us with the cruel responsibility of going to the very gate of racism in order to destroy racism—to the gate not further.'[32] The dangerous illusion such statements would seem to foster lie in the naive expectation that once a Black counter-racism has been unleashed it could be stopped after being successful. There is indeed the strong possibility that Black racial antagonism, like its White counterpart, soon develops its own dynamic over which its manipulators lose control. Those who believe in a human consciousness, instead of a Black or a White one, can only hope that this synthesis will finally emerge out of a conflict in which both groups suffer in different ways. If one can generalize Blauner's observation in the context of the United States that 'the groups and the individuals with the strongest sense of ethnic culture seem to have the least need for anti-White feelings',[33] then there is much more hope for an eventual peaceful co-existence in South Africa where both Africans and Afrikaners do not lack a sense of their own identity. Before this stage is reached, however, it would seem that the African's 'feeling of non-solidarity with men who stand in the way of solidarity'[34] becomes an inevitable phase.

TACTICS AND STRATEGIES

The weakest point of the Black Consciousness movement would appear to be the methods it utilizes to realize its ideals. So far, these consist of hardly more than calls for unity and more organizations: 'Black-based youth camps, centres, colleges, welfare organizations etc.'[35] Others talk in the fashion of U.S. Black capitalism, but without its resources and opportunities, about examining 'the possibilities of establishing business co-operatives, whose interests shall be ploughed back into community development programmes. We should think along such lines as the 'buy black' campaign once suggested in Johannesburg and to establish our own banks for the benefit of the community.'[36]

While Black Consciousness certainly has left its mark on the political debate in South Africa, its significance so far lies in its potential, not in its actual, strength and response. There are severe obstacles in the path of the proclaimed solidarity of the three subordinate groups. The objective condition of shared stigmatization is nevertheless experienced differently, partly because there are distinctive degrees of exploitation among Africans, Coloureds, and Indians. This decisive hierarchy among the subordinate castes is perhaps best illustrated in the pay gap among Black workers in South Africa's public sector. The 251,000 Whites in this category earned an average of R 330 a month ($462) in 1972, the 67,900 Coloureds earned R 122 ($161), the 14,580 Asians R 162 ($227), and the 314,200 Africans made only R 50 ($70).[37] Indians in particular have not fully identified with the Black label and even revived the Natal Indian Congress (N.I.C.) in opposition to the Black Consciousness advocates as well as the government sponsored South African Indian Council. The overwhelming majority of Indians fear more than White rule a 'genuine danger of Black Consciousness leading to Black racism' and, therefore, stand for mobilization 'towards the goal of a common society'.[38] The Natal Indian Congress, originally established by Gandhi, now represents to a large extent the expanded Indian professional class with a certain stake in the status quo. Their career interests and middle-class background still colour the perspective of most Indian students in an anti-confrontation fashion. The widespread support for a SASO inspired strike at two Indian institutions in summer 1972 does not disprove this assessment. Although the strike started as a solidarity protest against the expulsion of African students in Turfloop, the Indian students were much more motivated by similar grievances at home. A similar mechanism operated among the White students who joined the walkout. As a visiting American observed: 'Sympathy for the oppressed "others" acted as a catalyst in bringing about a reaction in defence of one's own rights . . . quickly the sympathy issue was submerged by the "defence of our rights" aspect of the protest.'[39]

In a little publicized vote at the only Black medical school at the University of Natal, the majority decided against a lecture boycott and the division was mostly along ethnic lines—Indians against and Africans in favour.[40] On the other hand, the SASO philosophy seemed to have gained much more support at the Coloured university, partly because of the stand by some influential Coloured intellectuals but partly because of the different social background of Coloured students who generally have weaker family and community ties than Indians. In a situation of cultural diversity such as in South Africa, Black Power, defined as comprising all three subordinate groups, faces many more obstacles than in a relatively culturally homogeneous situation such as in the U.S. In a different context, Donald L. Horowitz has pointed out that 'cultural differences may shield groups from conflict by focusing their attention on quite different objects of gratification.'[41] If an alliance between Africans, Coloureds, and Indians is ever to receive mass support, as compared with the mutual flirtations of esoteric intellectual elites, it can only be on the basis of a common *political* cause and not *cultural* unity. The rejection of the label 'Black' by the overwhelming majority of the Indian and Coloured population signals the desire to retain a specific cultural status rather than a dismissal of a political alliance. Despite the shared resentment towards Afrikaner dominance there is, nevertheless, a reluctance to express itself as a common Black cultural front, at least as far as Coloureds and Indians are concerned. By emphasizing the common *non-political* bonds of all 'Non-Whites', Black Consciousness spokesmen advocate fictitious links with little bases in reality. The denouncement of Indian or Coloured parents, for example, who frown upon inter-Black marriages and favour group traditions, only alienates large sections from the common goal and obscures the political issues. The same holds true for the rejection of non-African cultural symbols, such as the wearing of saris in favour of the adoption of African life-styles and habits, which must remain artificial and alien in an Indian subcultural setting. Petty as these issues may seem compared with the overall struggle, they are relevant at the level of mass perception by unintentionally discrediting the desired Black political unity. Due to geographical and occupational fragmentation as well as considerable cultural differences, various subordinate groups perceive of their supposedly 'common plight' quite differently, and the racist treatment of ethnic group members in Uganda has certainly not made the Black alliance in South Africa more attractive.

While unity envisaged by Black Consciousness seems at present a remote utopia, the government policy of tribalization through differential rewards and fragmentation appears to be also unsuccessful in a much more significant realm. The three most important Bantustan leaders, Chiefs Buthelezi, Mantanzima, and Mangope, have in 1972 for the first time publicly stressed the need for Black unity, transcending the imposed ethnic fragmentation. These traditional African leaders, frequently denounced as government stooges, have reiterated their willingness to serve under each other in a projected united African federation. While the White government had been embarrassed by this rejection of Nationalist blueprints and the vivid demands for more land, it cannot silence this potential threat without jettisoning its entire ideological base.

Zulu Chief Gatsha Buthelezi, above all, has increasingly emerged as a widely respected leader who fearlessly exposes the gap between the promise and reality of apartheid and thereby strikes a deep accord with ordinary Africans, both in the townships and the hinterland. The semi-official *Transvaler* warned that 'if he continues along the road he is on today he will undoubtedly be heading for a confrontation of such a dimension that he could only do damage and harm.'[42] His appeal seemed to be due to his realism and the recognition of African powerlessness. Unlike earlier African leaders he does not beg for the deliverance of Black demands, thereby subjecting himself to the contempt of the donor. More than any other African, Buthelezi symbolizes the new pride and self-respect, in spite of or because of his role as underdog. In an analysis of earlier expressions of African nationalism, Fatima Meer observed that 'the more militant African leaders appeared never to project themselves beyond the role of revolutionaries into that of governmental dignitaries manipulating state power.'[43] Though without power to manipulate, Buthelezi plays this role symbolically, preparing the ground for the future crunch. In reminding the Afrikaners of their own historical struggle against British imperialism, he claims the same justification for the cause of his own people.

It is indicative of the uncompromising attitude of Black Consciousness advocates that they do not wish to find common ground with such pragmatism. With a remarkable insensitivity for the politically possible, they insist on moral purity. Elitism as well as non-political aloofness must not be spoilt by pragmatic involvement with collaborators of 'white racist institutions.' When former SASO president

Temba Sono suggested such a possibility in a speech, he was immediately expelled from the organisation and asked to leave the hall. Sono had argued for a policy 'to accommodate even contradictions in our struggle', and to 'avoid stagnating in the certitude of ideology', which 'must not restrict the scope of human action'.[44] The rejection of such pragmatism by SASO has had the paradoxical effect of making the pragmatic opponents of apartheid from within its own institutions more respectable and perhaps protected them, as newly defined 'moderates', from otherwise more severe attacks. In this sense a Buthelezi can only welcome his critics on the left, given the certainty of his mass support even among many African students.

For if there is any realistic hope of gradual change inside South Africa in the absence of external intervention, it would seem to result from the combined pressures, operating from within the system. Above all, what would appear decisive, is the only weapon which Blacks share, their withdrawal of labour and its potential effects. A mobilization or pacification by nationally recognized leaders could make the difference in the degree of success of spontaneous strikes. In the absence of African union negotiators, official African spokesmen are likely to be called upon to play a mediating role. The potential mobilizing strength of Black Consciousness in affecting real change of the fossilized South African structure would seem to lie foremost in such eventualities. The test of the most appropriate Black tactics and strategies is yet to come.

REFERENCES

1. By the end of April 1973, it was officially estimated that 61,000 Black workers had participated in strike actions over the recent months in spite of this constituting a criminal offence.
2. On South African students politics see, H. W. van der Merwe and David Welsh (eds.), *Student Perspectives on South Africa* (Cape Town, Philip, 1972); and for the history of NUSAS, also M. Legassick and J. Shingler, 'South Africa', in D. Emmerson (ed.), *Students and Politics in Developing Nations* (London, Pall Mall, 1968), pp. 103–45. For the official attitude see also the recent report of the 'Schlebusch Commission' and its controversial reception.
3. See Kogila Adam, 'Dialectic of Higher Education for the Colonized: The Case of Non-White Universities in South Africa', in Heribert Adam (ed.), *South Africa: Sociological Perspectives* (London, Oxford University Press, 1971), pp. 197–213.
4. E. G. Cohen, 'Interracial Interaction Disability', *Human Relations* (Vol. 25, February 1972), pp. 9–24.
5. See J. Berger, M. Zelditch, Jr., and B. Anderson (eds.), *Sociological Theories in Progress* (Boston, Houghton Mifflin, 1966), pp. 29–46. Also E. G. Cohen and Susan S. Roper, 'Modification of Interracial Interaction Disability', *American Sociological Review* (Vol. 37, December 1972), pp. 643–57.
6. On liberation as a goal of Black Consciousness, see particularly Bennie A. Khoapa, 'Black Consciousness', *South African Outlook* (June/July 1972), pp. 100–2.
7. Robert Blauner, *Racial Oppression in America* (New York, Harper & Row, 1972), p. 119.
8. Steve Biko, 'Black Consciousness and the Quest for a True Humanity', in Mokgethi Motlhabi (ed.) *Essays on Black Theology* (Johannesburg, University Christian Movement, 1972), p. 25. This publication was soon banned in South Africa but has been published in Britain by C. Hurst.

9. A good example is Chief Gatsha Buthelezi addressing an American University audience on 'The Past and Future of the Zulu People' and elaborating with obvious ease and satisfaction on the successful battles of heroes in his lineage. See Munger Africana Library No. 4., California Institute of Technology, Pasadena.

10. Amilcar Cabral, 'Identity and Dignity in Struggle', speech at Lincoln University, in *Southern Africa* (Vol. V, November 1972), pp. 4–8.

11. Fatima Meer, 'African Nationalism—some Inhibiting Factors', in Heribert Adam (ed.) *South Africa: Sociological Perspectives* (London, Oxford University Press, 1971), p. 145.

12. Biko, op. cit., p. 27.

13. SASO leaflet, 'Towards Realising Ourselves', undated and without author attribution.

14. Donald Reeves, *Newsweek* (9 April 1973), p. 28.

15. Strini Moodley, 'Black Consciousness, the black artist and the emerging black culture', SASO *Newsletter* (May/June 1972), pp. 18–20.

16. Biko, op. cit., p. 21.

17. Cabral, op. cit., p. 5.

18. For an insightful analysis of this topic see George Devos, 'Social Stratification and Ethnic Pluralism: an Overview from the Perspective of Psychological Anthropology', *Race* (Vol. XIII, No. 4, April 1972), pp. 435–60.

19. It is symptomatic for the South African domestic debate how both Whites and Blacks are preoccupied with labels at the expense of the real issues. Thus the South African Institute of Race Relations asked the public to search for a more appropriate name for the country's subordinate castes before deciding to use the term Black, as did the *Rand Daily Mail* in 1972, while the 'Progressive Party' resolved after an elaborate debate to use only the group names: African, Coloured, Indian. SASO delegates continued in the same vein by evicting journalists whose papers continued to use the term non-white. A glance at the fate of 'Negroes' in America would have been useful.

20. Nadine Gordimer, 'White Proctorship and Black Disinvolvement', *Reality* (November 1971), pp. 14–6.

21. 'Towards Realising Ourselves'.

22. Richard Turner, 'Black Consciousness and White Liberals', *Reality* (July 1972), p. 20. Turner, too, has been banned.

23. Biko, op. cit., p. 21.

24. Jerry Modisane, SASO *Newsletter* (May/June 1972), p. 17.

25. Khoapa, op. cit., p. 102.

26. SASO Manifesto, Point 5.

27. Adam Small, 'Blackness versus Nihilism', in *Essays on Black Theology*, p. 15.

28. F. J. van Wyk, 'Black Consciousness—The Institute's Position as I see it', RR 120/72, (mimeographed) Johannesburg (15 December 1972), p. 3.

29. See the statement on 'The Nature and Aims of the S.A. Institute of Race Relations', Annual *Survey of Race Relations in South Africa 1972*, last page.

30. Black Consciousness, A Report on a seminar held by the Cape Western Region of the South African Institute of Race Relations, RR 64/72 (mimeographed).

31. J. H. T. Mills, a retired civil servant in the Transksei, as reported in *Rand Daily Mail* (31 August 1972).

32. Khoapa, op. cit., p. 101.

33. Blauner, op. cit., p. 118.

34. Khoapa, op. cit.

35. Ibid.

36. Biko, op. cit., p. 26.

37. Department of Statistics, as quoted in *The Star*, Air Mail Edition (23 December 1972), p. 6. Excluded are figures from Railways, Harbours, and Post Office employees.

38. Fatima Meer, 'The Natal Indian Congress', *Reality* (July 1972), pp. 5–6.

39. Edward K. Steinhart, 'White Student Protests in South Africa: The Privileged Fight for their Rights', *Africa Today* (Vol. 19, No. 3, Summer 1972), p. 50.

40. *Natal Mercury* (29 May 1972).
41. Donald L. Horowitz, 'Multiracial Politics in the New States: Toward a Theory of Conflict',
    in Robert J. Jackson and Michael B. Stein, *Issues in Comparative Politics* (New York, St.
    Martin's Press, 1971), p. 166.
42. *Die Transvaler* (4 September 1972).
43. Meer, op. cit., p. 145.
44. *Sunday Times* (2 July 1972); *Star* (3 July 1972).

32   Power and the Changing Character
of Black Protest

William J. Wilson

Throughout the discussion of black social thought and protest in the United States,
one pattern of behavior seems to emerge: *the changing goals of black advancement*
tend to be associated with the changing definition of black despair, and both the
defined problem and the conceived goal are ultimately associated with the choice of
possible pressure or constraint resources that blacks can mobilize in pressing for the
desired solution. However, it should be noted that despite the definition of the
problem and the conception of the goal, the choice of pressure resources is influenced or determined by the extent to which blacks find themselves in competitive
relations with whites. The now more conservative black protest movements, such
as the NAACP and the National Urban League, developed and gained momentum
when racial accommodations were undergoing change but when the dominant-
group controls were so strong that the pressure tactics of the mid-twentieth century
activist movements would not have been tolerated.[1]

Before the emergence of the activist black protest movements, the drive for
civil rights was therefore in the hands of a few professionals competent to work
through controlling legal and educational channels.[2] The NAACP achieved great
success through these agencies, and its definition of the problem facing black
people signified its planned strategy. Specifically, prior to 1960 the NAACP tended
to define the racial problem as legal segregation in the South, and its major goal,
popularized by the slogan "free by 1963," was the elimination of all state-enforced
segregation. Although the officials of the NAACP have lacked a power orientation,
the mobilization of their legal machinery has represented a display of power—the
power of litigation—in this instance, a power resource of high liquidity. Working
through prevailing institutional channels, the NAACP was able to win an overwhelming number of cases in the Supreme Court and thus helped to produce laws

designed to improve racial conditions in America, although white Southerners ingeniously circumvented the new laws and thus usually prevented their implementation. Lewis M. Killian has discussed this matter:

> It is ironic that the white South was extremely successful in minimizing the impact of the desegregation decision of the federal court without arousing the indignation of the rest of the nation. As much as the White Citizens Council and the Ku Klux Klan are invoked as symbols of the southern resistance, they and their extra-legal tactics did not make this possible. Far more effective were the legal strategems, evasions, and delays that led Negroes to realize that although they had won a new statement of principle they had not won the power to cause this principle to be implemented.[3]

White procrastination made it apparent to many black leaders that both the goal and the problem had been too narrowly defined. A new definition of the problem thus emerged—token compliance to the newly created laws—and a corresponding new goal—the elimination of both de facto and de jure segregation. Litigation, no longer an effective pressure resource in the face of white procrastination, was replaced by passive or nonviolent resistance. The fact that the power balance between blacks and whites had undergone some alteration also helped bring about the shift to nonviolent direct-action protest. As blacks increased their political and economic resources, as the Supreme Court rendered decisions in favor of desegregation, and as the United States government became increasingly sensitive to world opinion of its racial situation, black expectations were heightened, continued white resistance became more frustrating, and consequently support for direct-action (albeit nonviolent) protests quickly mushroomed. Although some writers have identified the successful Montgomery bus boycott of 1955–1956 as the beginning of the black revolt,[4] Meier and Rudwick have maintained that "the really decisive break with the pre-eminence of legalistic techniques came with the college student sit-ins that swept the South in the Spring of 1960."[5] These demonstrations set a chain of nonviolent resistance movements to desegregation into motion that subsequently swept the country from 1960 to 1965. Even though the initial emphasis was on persuasion resources rather than constraint resources, the technique of nonviolence was in reality an aggressive manifestation of pressure. Its twofold goal was to create and to implement civil rights laws. Even though many of the nonviolent protests were not specifically directed at the federal government, they were in many cases intended to apply indirect pressure on it. Black leaders recognized that because of their political and pressure resources and because of the United States' concern for world opinion, the government was not in a position to ignore their stepped-up drive for civil rights.

For a brief period of time, the nonviolent resistance strategy proved to be highly effective. In addition to forcing local governments and private agencies to integrate facilities in numerous Southern cities and towns, the nonviolent demonstrations pressed the federal government into passage of civil rights legislation in 1964 and voting rights legislation in 1965—acts that satisfied many of the black demands of the early 1960s. There are several reasons why the federal government responded favorably to many of the demands emanating from the nonviolent protest movement: (1) the demands that accompanied the protests tended to be fairly specific, e.g., "end discrimination in voting," and hence the government was able to provide "remedies" that clearly approximated the specifications in the demands; (2) the attempt to satisfy these demands did not call for major sacrifices on the part of whites, and hence there was little likelihood that a significant political backlash against the government would occur in sections of the country other than the South; (3) the demands were consistent with prevailing ideals of democracy and freedom of choice, and hence they could not be easily labeled "extreme" either by the white citizens or by governmental authorities; (4) the more blacks pressed their demands and carried out their protests, the more violent was the Southern response, and because these developments were receiving international attention, the government became increasingly concerned; (5) the government was sensitive to the political resources blacks had developed and became cognizant of the growing army of Northern whites sympathetic to the black cause; (6) blacks' political strength seemed to be magnified by the united front they presented, as groups ranging from the relatively conservative NAACP to the radical Student Nonviolent Coordinating Committee all joined in nonviolent protests to effect change.

To understand why many blacks shifted away from nonviolence both as a philosophy of life and as a technique to achieve racial equality, it is necessary to understand the dynamics of minority protest: if an extended period of increased expectations and gratification is followed by a brief period in which the gap between expectations and gratifications suddenly widens and becomes intolerable, the possibility of violent protests is greatly increased. Davies applies this analysis to the black rebellion of the 1960s:

> In short—starting in the mid-1950's and increasing more or less steadily into the early 1960's—white violence grew against the now lawful and protected efforts of Negroes to gain integration. And so did direct action and later violence undertaken by blacks, in a reciprocal process that moved into the substantial violence of 1965–67. That 3 year period may be considered a peak, possibly the peak of the violence that constituted the black rebellion. It merits reemphasis that during this era of increased hostility progress intensified both the white reaction to it and the black counteraction to the reaction, because everytime a reaction impeded the progress, the apparent gap widened between expectations and gratification.[6]

Even though there was no sudden or sharp increase in black unemployment and no sudden reversal in the material gains blacks had accumulated during the prosperous 1960s, "there was, starting notably in 1963, not the first instance of violence against blacks but a sudden increase in it. This resurgence of violence came after, and interrupted, the slow but steady progress since 1940. It quickly frustrated rising expectations."[7] For the first time, there was a real sense of apprehension among blacks that, not only would conditions stop improving, but gains already achieved could very well be lost unless steps were taken to counteract mounting white violence.

Birmingham, Alabama, in 1963 was the scene of this initial wave of white violence and black counterreaction. In April, Birmingham police used high-pressure water hoses and dogs to attack civil rights marchers, and blacks retaliated by throwing rocks and bottles at the police; in May, segregationists bombed the homes of black leaders, and blacks retaliated by rioting, setting two white-owned stores on fire and stoning police and firemen; on September 15, whites enraged by school desegregation bombed a black church, killing four small girls and injuring twenty-three other adults and children, and blacks angrily responded by stoning police.[8]

However, racial violence was not restricted to Birmingham, Alabama, in 1963. Medger Evers, an NAACP official in Jackson, Mississippi, was shot to death in front of his home on May 28, 1963. Whites and blacks in Cambridge, Maryland, engaged in a gun battle after blacks had stormed a restaurant to rescue sit-in demonstrators beaten by whites; the black quarter in Lexington, North Carolina, was attacked by a white mob after blacks had attempted to obtain service at white restaurants, and in the ensuing gun battle a white man was killed; mounted police at Plaquemine, Louisiana, galloped into a group of civil rights demonstrators and dispersed them with electric cattle prods—fifteen demonstrators were injured; police used tear gas, shotguns, and high-pressure water hoses in Savannah, Georgia, to break up a protest demonstration that turned into a riot—at least ten whites and thirteen blacks were injured; and mass arrests of civil rights activists took place in Athens, Georgia; Selma, Alabama; Greensboro, North Carolina; Orangeburg, South Carolina and several other Southern towns.[9]

The gap between expectations and emotional gratifications[10] increased black support for violent protest and was reflected, not only in the way blacks responded to white attacks beginning with the Birmingham incident in 1963, but also in the changing philosophy of younger civil rights activists. In the early months of 1964, members of the Student Nonviolent Coordinating Committee (SNCC) and the Congress of Racial Equality (CORE) openly challenged the philosophy of non-violence and called for more belligerent forms of protest.[11] It was during this same period that Malcolm X, shortly after he resigned from the Nation of Islam, called for blacks to arm themselves and abandon nonviolence and that the Brooklyn chapter of CORE attempted to tie up New York traffic (on April 22, the opening of the World's Fair) by emptying the fuel tanks of 2000 automobiles and abandoning them on the freeways leading to the fairgrounds (lacking support, the strategy failed).[12] Continued white violent acts such as the murder of civil rights workers by white terrorists in Mississippi in 1964, Ku Klux Klan terrorism in Mississippi and Alabama in 1965, attacks against CORE organizers in Bogalusa, Louisiana, in 1965, the beating and murder of civil rights activists in Selma, Alabama, in 1965, and police brutality that precipitated rioting in Northern ghettoes in 1964 deepened the militant mood in the black community and widened the gap between expectations and emotional gratification.

In the face of these developments, the call by some black leaders for greater militancy was based on the optimistic belief that the larger society was more likely to respond properly to black demands backed by belligerent and violent protests than to those reinforced by nonviolent resistance. Theoretical analysis suggests either that blacks believed they possessed sufficient resources not only to disrupt the larger society but also to prevent an all-out repressive reaction by whites, or that they felt that by the mid-1960s the system had developed a high tolerance for minority protests.[13] However, it was lower-class urban blacks who dramatically demonstrated that a more belligerent mood had gripped the black community when they rocked the nation with a proliferation of ghetto revolts from 1964 to 1968. In the early 1960s, nonviolent protests were heavily populated by middle-class or higher-educated blacks, who were far more likely at this period to participate in a drive for social justice that was disciplined and sustained.[14] Ghetto blacks for the most part were not directly involved in the nonviolent resistance movement of the early 1960s, and many of the gains achieved did not materially benefit them (the civil rights movement up to 1965 produced laws primarily relevant to privileged blacks with competitive resources such as special talents or steady income);[15] nevertheless, the victories of the nonviolent movement increased expectations among all segments of the black population.[16] In the age of mass communication, Northern ghetto blacks, like blacks throughout the country, were very much aware of and identified with the efforts of Martin Luther King, Jr., and other civil rights activists. By the same token, they were also cognizant of the white violence that threatened to halt the gradual but steady progress toward racial equality.

Accordingly, ghetto rebellions cannot be fully explained in isolation or independently of the increasingly militant mood of the black community. However, what made the situation of ghetto blacks unique was the fact that the gap between expectations and emotional gratification was combined with concrete grievances over police brutality, inferior education, unemployment, underemployment, and inadequate housing. It is true that these conditions have always existed in ghetto life and did not suddenly emerge during the 1960s, but the important point is that increased expectations and greater awareness of racial oppression made these conditions all the more intolerable.[17] Charles Silberman was essentially correct when he stated that "it is only when men sense the possibility of improvement, in fact, that they become dissatisfied with their situation and rebel against it. And 'with rebelling' as Albert Camus put it 'awareness is born,' and with awareness, an impatience 'which can extend to everything that [men] had previously accepted, and which is almost always retroactive.' "[18] Likewise, as the number and intensity of ghetto revolts increased, black complaints about human suffering became more explicit and focused.

The Harlem revolt in 1964 actually marked the beginning of ghetto uprisings of the 1960s (where groups of blacks looted stores, burned buildings, and attacked firemen and police in the black community), but the most serious revolts occurred in 1965 in Watts (resulting in 34 deaths, 900 injuries, 4000 arrests, and an estimated property damage of $100,000,000), in 1967 in Detroit (43 deaths, 1500 injuries,

5000 arrests, and $200,000,000 in property damage), and Newark (26 deaths, 1200 injuries, 1600 arrests, and $47,000,000 in property damage). The assassination of Dr. Martin Luther King, Jr., precipitated the final series of ghetto rebellions in the spring of 1968. During that four-year period (1964–1968) of intense racial violence, thousands of persons, mostly black, were killed or injured, and the property damage was estimated in the billions of dollars.

In addition to these manifestations of greater black militancy, the emergence of the Black Power Movement in 1966, with its shift in emphasis to racial solidarity and its explicit repudiation of nonviolence as a strategy of protest and way of life, can also be associated with the sudden gap between rising expectations and emotional gratification. In a fundamental sense, however, the Black Power Movement represented a return to the self-help philosophy and emphasis on black solidarity that usually occurs "when the Negroes' status has declined or when they experienced intense disillusionment following a period of heightened but unfulfilled expectations."[19]

Unlike the self-help nationalistic philosophies that developed in the 1850s following increased repression in the free states, in the Booker T. Washington era as a response to the growth of biological racism and resurgence of white supremacy, and in the post World War I period as a reaction to white violence perpetrated against black urban immigrants in the North, the Black Power Movement developed during a period when blacks had achieved a real sense of power.

Killian has commented on this new feeling of power:

> The nonviolent demonstrations of SCLC, CORE, and SNCC . . . had not solved the bitter problems of the Negro masses, but they had shown that the Negro minority could strike terror into the hearts of the white majority. They had produced concessions from white people, even though the triumph of winning these concessions had soon turned to despair because they were never enough. Watts and other riots reflected no clearly formulated demand for new concessions. They did reflect the basic truth that Negroes, mobilized in ghettoes to an extent never before experienced and made confident by earlier victories, were no longer afraid of white power. Within a few months after Watts, they would begin to proclaim their faith in Black Power.[20]

This new sense of power was reflected not so much in the programs actually introduced under the banner of Black Power as in the revolutionary rhetoric used to articulate Black Power philosophy. That certain black radicals dared, through national media, to call openly for the use of violence to overthrow racial oppression was a clear indication that blacks felt secure enough to threaten the very stability of the larger society. In actual fact, however, although Black Power advocates often disagreed about the aims and purposes of the movement, their various demands and programs were more reformist in nature than revolutionary[21] (e.g., programs emphasizing black capitalism, the running of black candidates for political office, self-help in the area of jobs and housing, black studies in high schools and colleges, and black culture and identity). Some of the programs introduced by

Black Power spokesmen were an extension of the conservative separatism advocated by the Nation of Islam (Black Muslims) under the leadership of Elijah Muhammad. From the 1950s to the first half of the 1960s, when black social thought continued to be overwhelmingly supportive of integration,[22] the Nation of Islam served as the major medium for a black nationalist philosophy.[23] Commenting on Muslim philosophy, Cruse wrote that the

> Nation of Islam was nothing but a form of Booker T. Washington economic self-help, black unity, bourgeois hard work, law abiding, vocational training, stay-out-of-the-civil-rights-struggle agitation, separate-from-the-white-man, etc., etc. morality. The only difference was that Elijah Muhammad added the potent factor of the Muslim religion to race, economic, and social philosophy of which the first prophet was none other than Booker T. Washington. Elijah Muhammad also added an element of "hate Whitey" ideology which Washington, of course, would never have accepted.[24]

The most significant influence on the radical flank of the Black Power Movement was ex-Muslim minister Malcolm X. Because of differences with Elijah Muhammad, Malcolm X resigned from the Muslim organization and moved beyond its program of territorial separation and bourgeois economic nationalism. Shortly before he was assassinated in 1965, he had begun to formulate a philosophy of revolutionary nationalism (that "views the overthrow of existing political and economic institutions as a prerequisite for the liberation of black Americans, and does not exclude the use of violence[25]) subsequently adopted by militant Black Power leaders such as Stokely Carmichael and H. Rap Brown and incorporated into the philosophy of the newly emerging Black Panther Party in the late 1960s.

Yet, of all the philosophies of nationalism or racial solidarity that emerged under the banner of Black Power, none has received as much support from black citizens as has cultural nationalism.[26] Cultural nationalism is concerned mainly with positive race identity, including the development and/or elaboration of black culture and history. One of the most illustrative statements of this theme has come from Blauner:

> In their communities across the nation, Afro-Americans are discussing "black culture." The mystique of "soul" is only the most focused example of this trend in consciousness. What is and what should be the black man's attitude toward American society and American culture has become a central division in the Negro protest movement. The spokesmen for black power celebrate black culture and Negro distinctiveness; the integrationists base their strategy and their appeal on the fundamental "American-ness" of the black man. There are nationalist leaders who see culture building today as equal or more important than political organization. From Harlem to Watts there has been a proliferation of black theater, art, and literary groups; the recent ghetto riots (or revolts, as they are viewed from the nationalistic perspective) are the favored materials of these cultural endeavors.[27]

But certainly we must not lose sight of the fact that cultural nationalism, like other forms of nationalism has become popular during certain periods in history — periods when black disillusionment follows a brief interval of black optimism and commitment to integration. It is not so important that structural assimilation,[28] especially for middle-class blacks, is occurring at a greater rate than ever before; what is important is the black perception of the racial changes that are occurring. Black awareness has been heightened by the efforts of both the civil rights and the Black Power activists, and impatience and frustration with the pace of racial equality have become more intense. Whereas the cultural nationalism of the 1850s and of the Harlem Renaissance period was largely confined to segments of the black intelligentsia,[29] the cultural nationalism of the late 1960s and early 1970s has transcended class lines. Awareness of the evils of racial oppression and of white resistance to racial equality is characteristic of all segments of the black population; support for racial solidarity with emphasis on black culture and racial identity has reached unprecedented heights.

NOTES

1. See Clarence E. Glick, "Collective Behavior in Race Relations," *American Sociological Review*, 13:287–293 (June 1947).
2. James H. Laue, "The Changing Character of Negro Protest," *Annals of the American Academy of Political and Social Science*, 357:120 (Jan. 1965).
3. Lewis M. Killian, *The Impossible Revolution?: Black Power and the American Dream* (New York: Random House, 1968), p. 70.
4. See, for example, Louis Lomax, *The Negro Revolt* (New York: Signet, 1962).
5. August Meier and Elliot Rudwick, *From Plantation to Ghetto: The Interpretative History of American Negroes*, rev. ed. (New York: Hill and Wang, 1970), p. 227.
6. James C. Davies, "The J-Curve of Rising and Declining Satisfactions as a Cause of Some Great Revolutions and a Contained Rebellion," in *Violence in America: Historical and Comparative Perspectives*, ed. Hugh Davis Graham and Ted Robert Gurr (New York: Bantam Books, 1969), p. 721.
7. Davies, op. cit., p. 723.
8. Keesing's Research Report, *Race Relations in the USA, 1954–68* (New York: Scribner's, 1970), pp. 152–153.
9. Ibid., pp. 154–155.
10. A number of writers have not made full use of Davies' "J-curve" theory because they have restricted the notion of "gratification" to material gains or physical gratification and have ignored the factor of "emotional gratification." See, for example, James A. Geschwender, "Social Structure and the Negro Revolt: An Examination of Some Hypotheses," *Social Forces*, 43:248–256 (Dec. 1964), and Thomas F. Pettigrew, *Racially Separate or Together?* (New York: McGraw-Hill, 1971), chap. 7.
11. Keesing's Research Report, op. cit., pp. 164–165.
12. Ibid., p. 164.
13. For a discussion of this latter point, see L. H. Massotti and D. R. Bowen, eds., *Riots and Rebellion: Racial Violence in the Urban Community* (Beverly Hills, Calif.: Sage, 1968), and Pettigrew, op. cit., chap. 7.
14. As M. Elaine Burgess observed in 1965, "Neither the lower class nor the upper class could

have mounted the resistance movement we are now witnessing throughout the South. The former does not possess the resources, either internal or external, essential for such a movement, and the latter is much too small and, very frequently, too far removed from the masses to do so. Such activity had to wait the development of an ample middle class that was motivated to push for validation of hard-won position, thus far denied by the white power structure. The question of unequal distribution of status and power between Negroes and whites would consequently appear as a special case of the more basic problems of order and change. By no means are we saying that all challenges to established social structures or power distributions are class oriented, or directly concerned with relative social position. Nevertheless, it is true that one of the major sources of tension and therefore of change and potential change in the South, as in the broader society, stems from the new middle-class Negro's disbelief in past rationales for inequality and the desire for substitution of new rationales." M. Elaine Burgess, "Race Relations and Social Change," in *The South in Continuity and Change*, ed. by John C. McKinney and Edgar T. Thompson (Durham, N.C.: Duke U.P., 1965), p. 352.

15. As Martin Luther King, Jr., once observed, "What good is it to be allowed to eat in a restaurant if you can't afford a hamburger?"

16. See, for example, William Brink and Louis Harris, *Black and White: A Study of U.S. Racial Attitudes Today* (New York: Simon & Schuster, 1966), p. 42; H. Cantrell, *The Pattern of Human Concerns* (New Brunswick, N.J.: Rutgers U.P., 1965), p. 43; and Pettigrew, op. cit., chap. 7.

17. See *Report of the National Advisory Commission on Civil Disorders* (New York: Bantam, 1968), and Nathan S. Caplan and Jeffrey Paige, "A Study of Ghetto Rioters," *Scientific American*, 219:15–21 (Aug. 1968).

18. Charles Silberman, *Crisis in the Classroom* (New York: Random House, 1970), pp. 19–20.

19. John H. Bracey, August Meier, and Elliot Rudwick, eds., *Black Nationalism in America* (Indianapolis: Bobbs-Merrill, 1970), p. xxvi. It is true, as John Bracey has argued, that black nationalist philosophy has always existed among some segments of the black population (see "John Bracey Sketches His Interpretation of Black Nationalism," Ibid., pp. lvi–lix), but what available research there is clearly establishes the fact that support for this philosophy increases and declines during certain periods in history.

20. Killian, op. cit., pp. 105–106.

21. Harold Cruse, *Rebellion or Revolution* (New York: Apollo, 1968), chap. 13, and *The Crisis of the Negro Intellectual* (New York: Morrow, 1967), pp. 554–565.

22. According to Bracey et al., "The proliferation of nationalist ideologies and organizations that reached a climax during the 1920's was followed by a thirty year period in which nationalism as a significant theme in black thought was virtually nonexistent. From the thirties until the sixties, with few exceptions, leading Negro organizations stressed interracial cooperation, civil rights, and racial integration. Among the chief reasons for the temporary demise of nationalism were the effects of the Depression and the consequent necessity of relying on the New Deal for survival, and the influx of trade Unionists and Communists into the black community preaching and practicing racial equality and brotherhood. The principal ideological concerns of articulate blacks during the Depression decade focused on very practical aspects of the Negro's relationship to New Deal agencies and the Roosevelt Administration, on the role of industrial unions in the advancement of the race, and on the relevance of Marxist doctrines of the Negro's problem." Bracey et al., op. cit., p. xiv.

23. Founded in the early 1930s, the Nation of Islam became a viable institution around 1950. It achieved its greatest popularity after the late Malcom X became a convert to the Muslim sect and one of its most influential ministers until he resigned in 1964.

24. Cruse, *Rebellion or Revolution*, op. cit., p. 211.

25. Bracey et al., op. cit., p. xxviii. Also see *The Autobiography of Malcolm X* (New York: Grove, 1964).

26. For example, the Opinion Research Corporation survey in 1968 revealed that 86 per cent of the blacks in their sample felt that black people should be taught subjects in school that added to their feeling of pride in being black. In their study of black attitudes in fifteen American cities, Angus Campbell and Howard Schuman have found that "There is a strong trend in the data that is related to, but different from and much stronger than 'separation.' It concerns the positive cultural identity and achievements of Negroes, rather than their political separation from whites. The finding appears most strikingly in the endorsement by 42 percent of the Negro sample of the statement 'Negro school children should study an African Language.' Two out of five Negroes thus subscribe to an emphasis on 'black consciousness' that was almost unthought of a few years ago." Angus Campbell and Howard Schuman, "Racial Attitudes in Fifteen American Cities," in *The National Advisory Commission on Civil Disorders, Supplemental Studies* (Washington, D.C.: G.P.O., 1968), p. 6.

    Despite the strong sentiment for cultural nationalism in the black community, institutional nationalism—i.e., the efforts of black citizens to gain control of the political, economic, and social institutions in their community and/or to establish separate institutions free of control by the dominant white society—although increasing in popularity, still receive support from only a minority of blacks. See, for example, Brink and Harris, op. cit.; *Report of the National Advisory Commission on Civil Disorders*, op. cit.; Campbell and Schuman, op. cit.; Caplan and Paige, op. cit.; and Gary T. Marx, *Protest and Prejudice: A Study of Belief in the Black Community*, rev. ed. (New York: Harper, 1970).

27. Robert Blauner, "Black Culture: Myth or Reality?" in *Americans from Africa: Old Memories, New Moods*, ed. by Peter I. Rose (New York: Atherton, 1970), pp. 417–418.

28. Following Milton M. Gordon, "structural assimilation" is defined as "large scale entrance into cliques, clubs, and institutions of host society on primary group level." Milton M. Gordon, *Assimilation in American Life* (New York: Oxford U.P., 1964), p. 71.

29. As Robert A. Bone has noted, "Even at the peak of Renaissance nationalism the middle-class writers could never muster more than token enthusiasm for a distinctive Negro culture." Robert A. Bone, "The Negro Novel in America" in *Americas' Black Past*, ed. by Eric Foner (New York: Harper, 1970), p. 385.

33   Racially Separate or Together?

Thomas F. Pettigrew

The United States has had an almost perpetual racial crisis for a generation. But the last third of the twentieth century has begun on a new note, a change of rhetoric and a confusion over goals. Widespread rioting is just one expression of this. The nation hesitates: it seems to have lost its confidence that the problem can be solved; it seems unsure as to even the direction in which a solution lies. In too simple terms, yet in the style of the fashionable rhetoric, the question has become: Shall Americans of the future live racially separate or together?

This new mood is best understood when viewed as part of the eventful sweep of recent years. Ever since World War I, when war orders combined with the curtailment of immigration to encourage massive migration to industrial centers, Negro Americans have been undergoing rapid change as a people. The latest products of this dramatic transformation from Southern peasant to Northern urbanite are the second and third generations of young people born in the North. The most significant fact about this "newest new Negro" is that he is relatively released from the principal social controls recognized by his parents and grandparents, from the restraints of an extended kinship system, a conservative religion, and an acceptance of the inevitability of white supremacy.

Consider the experience of the 20-year-old Negro in 1971. He was born in 1951; he was only 3 years old when the Supreme Court ruled against *de jure* public school segregation; he was only 6 years old at the time of the disorders over desegregation in Little Rock, Arkansas; he was 9 years old when the student-organized sit-ins began at segregated lunch counters throughout the South; he was 12 when the dramatic march on Washington took place and 15 when the climactic Selma march occurred. He has witnessed during his short life the initial dismantling of the formal structure of white supremacy. Conventional wisdom holds that such an experience should lead to a highly satisfied generation of young black Americans; but newspaper headlines and social-psychological theory tell us that precisely the opposite is closer to the truth.

The young black surveys the current scene and observes correctly that the benefits of recent racial advances have disproportionately accrued to the expanding middle class, leaving the urban lower class ever further behind. While the middle-class segment of Negro America has expanded from roughly 5 to 25 percent of the Negroes since 1940,[1] the vast majority of blacks remain poor. The young Negro has been raised on the proposition that racial integration is the basic solution to racial injustice, but his doubts grow as opportunities open for the skilled while the daily lives of the unskilled go largely unaffected. Accustomed to a rapid pace of events, many Negro young people wonder if integration will ever be possible in an America where the depth of white resistance to racial change becomes painfully more evident: in 1964, the equivocation of the Democratic Party Convention when faced with the challenge of the Mississippi Freedom Democratic Party; in 1965, the brutality at the bridge in Selma; in 1966, the summary rejection by Congress of anti-discrimination legislation for housing; in 1968, the wanton assassinations within ten weeks of two leading symbols of the integration movement; and, finally, the retrogression in Federal action for civil rights under the Nixon administration. These events create understandable doubts as to whether Dr. Martin Luther King's dream of equality can ever be achieved.

It is tempting to project this process further, as many analyses in the mass media unhesitantly have done, and suggest that all of black America has undergone this vast disillusionment, that blacks now overwhelmingly reject racial integration and are instead turning to separatist goals. As we shall note shortly when reviewing evidence from surveys, this is not the case. Strictly separatist solutions for the black ghettos of urban America have been most elaborately and enthusiastically advanced not by Negro writers but by such popular white writers as the newspaper columnist Joseph Alsop and William H. Ferry, formerly of the Center for the Study of Democratic Institutions.[2] These white analysts, like many white spokesmen for three centuries before them, are prepared to abandon the American dream of equality as it should apply to blacks, in the name of "hard realities" and under a conveniently mistaken notion that separatism is what blacks want anyway.

Yet the militant stance and rhetoric have shifted in recent years. In a real sense, integration has not failed in America, for it still remains to be tried as a national policy. Many Negroes of all ages sense this; they feel that the nation has failed integration rather than that integration has failed the nation. Influential black opinion turned in the late 1960s from integration as the primary goal to other goals—group power, culture, identity, integrity, and pride. Only a relatively small segment of blacks see these new goals as conflicting with integration; but this segment and their assumptions are one focus of this paper, for they play a disproportionately critical role in racial integration and white racism. The principal contention here is *that integration is a necessary condition for the eradication of white racism at both the individual and institutional levels.* No treatment of this thesis in America of the 1970s could be complete unless it included a brief discussion of this new black mood and its apparently separatist fringe.

Even much of this fringe of young ideological blacks should be described as "apparently" separatist, for the labels that make sense for white Americans necessarily must shift meaning when applied to black Americans. Given the national events that have occurred in their short lives, it is not surprising that this fringe regard racial integration less as an evil than as irrelevant to their preoccupations. They often call for *selective* separatism of one or more aspects of their lives while also demanding their rights of entry into the society's principal institutions. It is no accident that the most outspoken members of this faction are college students in prestigious and predominantly white universities.

Through the eyes of some whites, this behavior seems highly inconsistent; it looks as though they talk separation and act integration. But actually the inconsistency is often, though not always, more apparent than real. Consistent with the new emphasis upon power and pride, these young blacks are attempting to define their situation for themselves with particular attention to group autonomy. They are generally as opposed to forced separatism as were Negroes of past generations, and they reject other imposed doctrines as well. And for many of them, integration appears to be imposed by white liberals. "Why is it that you white liberals only insist on *racial* integration," they often ask, "when separation by class and ethnicity is a widespread fact of American life? Why is it no one gets upset by Italian separatism or Jewish separatism, only black separatism?" That the imposed separation of Negroes in America is qualitatively different and more vast than that practiced against or by any other sizable American minority, that integration as a doctrine was a creation not of white liberals but of their own fathers and grandfathers—these answers to the young blacks' insistent question are intellectually sound. But such responses do not relate to the feelings underlying the question, for they ignore the positive functions of the new emphasis which excite many young black Americans today.

The positive functions of the new militancy and ideology are exciting precisely because they go to the heart of many young blacks' personal feelings. If the new ideology's analysis of power at the societal level is incomplete, its analysis of racial self-hate at the individual level is right on the mark. Its attention to positive identity and "black is beautiful" is needed and important. Indeed, the abrupt shift from "Negro" to "black" is an integral part of this movement. Many members of older generations would have taken offense at being called "black"; it was considered a slur. But in facing the issue squarely, young blacks want to be called by the previously forbidden term in order to externalize the matter and convert it into a positive label. The fact that the historical justification sometimes cited for the shift is thin at best is not the point.[3] The important consideration is psychological, and on this ground there is every reason to believe that the change is healthy.

But the point often overlooked about this new movement is that its cultural and psychological aspects do not require racial separatism. We shall review evidence indicating that this fact is clearly perceived by the great majority of black Americans, who want racial pride and integrity together with integration. Not only is there no necessary contradiction between these two goals, but, once established, group pride is developed best in heterogeneous settings which allow for both individual and group autonomy.

Racial integration has shifted, then, in much black thought from the status of a principal goal to that of one among other mechanisms for achieving "liberation." "Liberation," in its broadest meaning for American race relations, means the total elimination of racial oppression. Similar to the older usage of "freedom," "liberation" means the eradication of the burden of racism that black Americans have borne individually and collectively since 1621. From this particular black perspective, "racially separate or together" is not the issue so much as what mix of strategies and efforts can actually achieve liberation. This view predominated in the August, 1970, issue of *Ebony,* which was completely devoted to the topic: "Which Way Black America? Separation? Integration? Liberation?" *Ebony's* Senior Editor, Lerone Bennett, Jr., puts it forth bluntly:

> . . . The fundamental issue is not separation or integration but liberation. The either/or question of integration or separation does not speak to that proposition; for if our goal is liberation it may be necessary to do both or neither.[4]

We shall return to this point shortly; and we will note that when the much-abused term "integration" is adequately defined, our position resembles Bennett's in all but rhetoric.

There are, then, positive functions internal to black communities and individuals which this new stance and line of thought appear to have. Much of the present writing in race relations is devoted to these positive functions. But what do these trends spell for the possibility of effectively combating white racism? While accepting the conclusion of the Kerner Commission that this is the basic problem, some recent black thought takes the position that wholly *black* concerns must take such precedence that the fight against white racism is, if not irrelevant, at least of secondary importance. Worse, some elements of the separatist fringe actively contribute to the growth and legitimacy of white racism. Hence, when Roy Innis, the national chairman of the Congress of Racial Equality (CORE), goes on a publicized tour to meet governors of the Deep South in order to advocate his program of separate-but-equal public schools, it hardly helps the effort to eliminate white racism.

This truly separatist fringe, then, is neither necessary to nor typical of the new black thrust. It gains its importance from, and becomes potentially dangerous because of, the way it nourishes white racism at both the individual and institutional levels. And it is for this reason that we need to compare it with white segregationist thought. Obviously, the two groups of separatists have sharply different sources of motivation: the blacks to withdraw, the whites to maintain racial supremacy. Nor are their assumptions on a par for destructive potential. But the danger is that black and white separatism could congeal as movements in the 1970s and help perpetuate a racially separate and racist nation. Because of this danger, it is well to examine the basic assumptions of both groups.

SEPARATIST ASSUMPTIONS

White segregationists, both in the North and in the South, base their position upon three bedrock assumptions. *Assumption 1* is that separation benefits both races because each feels awkward and uncomfortable with the other: *Whites and Negroes are happiest and most relaxed when in the company of "their own kind."*[5]

Assumption 2 is blatantly racist: *Negroes are inherently inferior to whites, and this is the underlying reality of all racial problems.* The findings of both social and biological science place in serious jeopardy every argument put forward for this assumption, and a decreasing minority of white Americans subscribe to it.[6] Yet it remains the essential substratum of the thinking of white segregationists; racial contact must be avoided, according to this reasoning, if standards of whites are not to be lowered. Thus, attendance at a desegregated school may benefit black children, but it is deemed by segregationists to be inevitably harmful to white children.[7]

Assumption 3 is derived from this assumption of white superiority: *Since contact can never be mutually beneficial, it will inevitably lead to racial conflict.* The White Citizens' Councils in the Deep South, for example, insist that they are opposed to violence and favor racial separation as the primary means of maintaining racial harmony. As long as Negroes "know their place," as long as white supremacy remains unchallenged, strife will be at a minimum.

Black separatists base their position upon three somewhat parallel assumptions. They agree with Assumption 1, that both whites and Negroes are more at ease when separated from each other. It is a harsh fact that blacks have borne the heavier burden of desegregation and have entered previously all-white institutions where open hostility is sometimes practiced by segregationist whites in order to discourage the process, and this is a partial explanation of agreement among blacks with Assumption 1. Yet some of this agreement stems from more subtle situations: the demands by some black student organizations on interracial campuses for all-black facilities have been predicated on this same assumption.

A second assumption of black separatists focuses directly upon white racism. Supported by the chief conclusion of the National Advisory Commission on Civil Disorders, black separatists consider that white racism is the central problem, and that "white liberals" should confine their energies to eradicating it.[8] Let us call this *Assumption 4: White liberals must eradicate white racism.* This assumption underlies two further contentions: namely, that "white liberals" should stay out of the ghetto except as their money and expertise are explicitly requested, and that it is no longer the job of black militants to confront and absorb the abuse of white racists.

The third assumption of black separatists is the most basic of all, and is in tacit agreement with the segregationist notion that interracial contact as it now occurs makes only for conflict. Interaction between black and white Americans, it is held, can never be truly equal and mutually beneficial until blacks first gain personal and group autonomy, self-respect, and power. This makes *Assumption 5: Autonomy is necessary before contact.* It often underlies a two-step theory of how to achieve meaningful integration: the first step requires separation so that Negroes can regroup, unify, and gain a positive self-image and identity; only when this is achieved can the second step, real integration, take place. Ron Karenga, a black leader in Los Angeles, states the idea forcefully: "We're not for isolation, but interdependence. But we can't become interdependent unless we have something to offer. We can live with whites interdependently once we have black power."[9]

Each of these ideological assumptions deserves examination in the light of social-psychological theory and findings.

SOCIAL-PSYCHOLOGICAL CONSIDERATIONS OF SEPARATIST ASSUMPTIONS

Assumption 1: Whites and Negroes Are More Comfortable Apart than Together

There can be no denying that many black and white Americans initially feel uncomfortable and ill at ease when they encounter each other in new situations. This reality is so vivid and so generally recognized that both black and white separatists use it widely in their thinking, though they do not analyze the nature and origins of the situation.

The literature of social science is replete with examples of the phenomenon.

Irwin Katz has described the initial awkwardness in biracial task groups in the laboratory: white partners usually assumed an aggressive, imperious role, black partners a passive role. Similarly, Yarrow found initial tension and keen sensitivity among many Negro children in an interracial summer camp, much of which centered on fears that they would be rejected by white campers.[10] But, more important, such tension does not continue to pervade a truly integrated situation. Katz noted that once blacks were cast in assertive roles, behavior in his small groups became more equalitarian and this improvement generalized to new situations. Yarrow, too, observed a sharp decline in anxiety and sensitivity among the black children after two weeks of successful integration at the summer camp. As was discussed previously, similar increments in cross-racial acceptance and reductions in tension have been noted in new interracial situations in department stores,[11] the Merchant Marine,[12] the armed forces,[13] and public housing,[14] and even among the Philadelphia police.[15]

This is not to say that new interracial situations invariably lead to acceptance. As we have seen, the *conditions* of the interracial contact are crucial; and even under optimal conditions, the cross-racial acceptance generated by contact is typically limited to the particular situation which created it. A segregated society restricts the generalization effects of even truly integrated situations; and at times like the present, when race assumes such overwhelming salience, the racial tension of the larger society may even poison previously successful interracial settings.

Acquaintance and similarity theory helps to clarify the underlying process. Newcomb states the fundamental tenet as follows:

> Insofar as persons have similar attitudes toward things of importance to both or all of them, and discover that this is so, they have shared attitudes; under most conditions the experience of sharing such attitudes is rewarding, and thus provides a basis for mutual attraction.[16]

Rokeach has applied these notions to race relations in the United States with some surprising results. He maintains that rejection of black Americans by white Americans is motivated less by racism than by assumed differences in beliefs and values. In other words, whites generally perceive Negroes as holding beliefs contrasting with their own, and it is this perception—not race *per se*—that leads to rejection. Indeed, a variety of subjects have supported Rokeach's ideas by typically accepting in a social situation a Negro with beliefs similar to their own over a white with different beliefs.[17]

Additional work has specified the phenomenon more precisely. Triandis and Davis have shown that the relative importance of belief and race in attraction is a joint function of personality and the interpersonal realm in question. Similarity of beliefs is most critical in more formal matters of general personal evaluation and social acceptance, where racial norms are ambiguously defined. Race is most critical in intimate matters of marriage and neighborhood, where racial norms are explicitly defined. For interpersonal realms of an intermediate degree of intimacy, such as friendship, both beliefs and race appear important. There are wide individual differences in the application of these concerns, however, especially in areas where the degree of intimacy is intermediate.[18]

Seen in the light of this work, racial isolation has two negative effects, both of which operate to make optimal interracial contact difficult to achieve and initially tense. First, isolation prevents each group from learning of the beliefs and values they do in fact share. Consequently, Negroes and whites kept apart come to view each other as very different; this belief, combined with racial considerations, causes each race to reject contact with the other. Second, isolation leads in time to the evolution of genuine differences in beliefs and values, making interracial contact in the future even less likely.[19]

A number of findings of social-psychological research support this extrapolation of interpersonal-attraction theory. Stein et al. noted that relatively racially isolated white ninth-graders in California assumed an undescribed Negro teen-ager to be similar to a Negro teen-ager who was described as being quite different from themselves.[20] Smith et al. found similarity of beliefs was more critical than racial similarity in desegregated settings, less critical in segregated settings.[21] And the U.S. Commission on Civil Rights, in its study of *Racial Isolation in the Public Schools,* found that both black and white adults who as children had attended interracial schools were more likely as adults to live in an interracial neighborhood and hold more positive racial attitudes than comparable adults who had known only segregated schools.[22] Or, to put it negatively, Americans of both races who experienced only segregated education are more likely to reflect separatist behavior and attitudes as adults.

Racial separatism, then, is a cumulative process. It feeds upon itself and leads its victims to prefer continued separation. In an open-choice situation in Louisville, Kentucky, black children were far more likely to select predominantly white high schools if they were currently attending predominantly white junior high schools.[23] From these data, the U.S. Commission on Civil Rights concluded: "The inference is strong that Negro high school students prefer biracial education only if they have experienced it before. If a Negro student has not received his formative education in biracial schools, the chances are he will not choose to enter one in his more mature school years."[24] Similarly, Negroes who attended segregated schools, the Civil Rights Commission finds, are more likely to believe as adults that interracial schools "create hardships for Negro children" and are less likely to send their children to desegregated schools than are Negroes who attended biracial schools.[25] Note that those who most fear discomfort in biracial settings are precisely those who have experienced such situations *least.* If desegregation actually resulted in perpetual and debilitating tension, as separatists are so quick to assume, it seems unlikely that children already in the situation would willingly opt for more, or that adults who have had considerable interracial contact as children would willingly submit themselves to biracial neighborhoods and their children to biracial schools.

Moreover, in dealing with the fact that some tension does exist, a social-cost analysis is needed. The question becomes: What price comfort? Racially homogeneous settings are often more comfortable for members of both races, though, as we have just noted, this seems to be most true at the start of the contact and does not seem to be so debilitating that those in the situation typically wish to return to segregated living. But those who remain in racial isolation, both black and white, find themselves increasingly less equipped to compete in an interracial world. Lobotomized patients are more comfortable, too, but they are impaired for life.

Moreover, there is nothing inevitable about the tension that characterizes many initial interracial encounters in the United States. Rather, tension is the direct result of the racial separation that has traditionally characterized our society. In short, separation is the cause of awkwardness in interracial contacts, not the remedy for it.

Assumption 2: Negroes Are Inferior; and Assumption 4:
White Liberals Must Eradicate White Racism.

These two assumptions, though of vastly different significance, raise related issues; and both also are classic cases of self-fulfilling prophecies. Treat a people as inferior, force them to play subservient roles,[26] keep them essentially separate, and eventually the people produced by this must come to support the initial racist notions. Likewise, assume that whites are unalterably racist, curtail efforts by Negroes to confront racism directly, separate Negroes from whites even further, and the result will surely be a continuation, if not a heightening, of racism.

The core of racist attitudes, the assumption of innate racial inferiority, has been under sharp attack from social science for over three decades.[27] Partly because of this work, attitudes of white Americans have undergone massive change over these years. Yet a sizable minority of white Americans, perhaps still as large as a fifth of the adult population, persist in harboring racist attitudes in their most vulgar and naive form. This is an important fact in a time of polarization, such as the present, for this minority becomes the vocal right anchor in the nation's process of social judgment. Racist assumptions not only are nourished by separatism but in turn rationalize separatism. Equal-status contact is avoided because of the racist stigma placed on black Americans by three centuries of slavery and segregation. But changes are evident both here and in social-distance attitudes. Between 1942 and 1963 the percentage of white Americans who favored racially desegregated schools rose from 30 to 63; the percentage of those with no objections to a Negro neighbor rose from 35 to 63.[28] And recall, too, that this trend did not abate during the mid-1960s of increasing white polarization mistakenly labeled "white backlash." This trend slowed, however, at the very close of the 1960s and in the early 1970s—possibly as a result of less insistence for integration.

The slow but steady erosion of racist and separatist attitudes among white Americans occurred during years of confrontation and change, although the process has been too slow to keep pace with the Negro's rising aspirations for full justice and complete eradication of racism. In a period of confrontation, dramatic events can stimulate surprisingly sharp changes in a short period of time.[29] Consider the attitudes of white Texans before and after the assassination of Martin Luther King, Jr., the riots that followed his murder, and the issuance of the forthright Report of the National Advisory Commission on Civil Disorders.[30] Table 1 shows the data collected before the assassination (in November, 1967, and February, 1968) and after the assassination (in May, 1968, and August, 1968). Observe that there were especially large changes in the four areas of relatively formal contact—desegregation in buses, jobs, restaurants and hotels. In areas of relatively informal contact—desegregation of schools and churches—there was moderate change. And in areas of intimate contact—desegregation of social gatherings, housing, swimming pools, house parties, and college dormitories—there was no significant change. Despite the ceiling effect,[31] approval increased most for those items already most approved. One is reminded of Triandis and Davis's breakdown of racial realms by degree of intimacy.[32] The changes in attitudes also varied among different types of white Texans; the young and the middle class shifted positively the most, again despite ceiling effects.[33] The tentative generalization growing out of these data is that in times of confrontation, dramatic events can achieve positive attitude changes among those whites and in those areas least subject to separatist norms.

The most solid social-psychological evidence about changes in racial attitudes comes from the studies of contact. Repeated research in a variety of newly desegregated situations showed that the attitudes of whites and blacks toward each other markedly improved: in department stores, public housing,[34] the armed services,[35] and the Merchant Marine,[36] and among government workers,[37] the police,[38] students,[39] and general small-town populations.[40] Some of these findings can be interpreted not as results of contact, but as an indication that more tolerant white Americans seek contact with Negro Americans. A number of the investigations, however,

TABLE 1

Percent of White Texans Who Approve*

Area of Desegregation	Nov. 1967	Feb. 1968	May 1968	Aug. 1968	$\frac{May + Aug.}{2} - \frac{Nov. + Feb.}{2}$ Raw change
Formal contact					
Same buses	62.9	64.5	74.3	69.7	+8.3
Same jobs	66.8	69.1	76.1	76.4	+8.2
Same restaurants	57.9	59.9	66.8	66.4	+7.7
Same hotels	53.0	53.8	60.2	59.6	+6.5
Informal contact					
Same schools	53.7	57.6	61.4	61.7	+5.8
Same churches	57.4	60.0	62.5	65.4	+5.2
Teach your child	49.4	51.2	54.3	55.6	+4.7
Intimate contact					
Same social gatherings	39.3	38.9	41.8	44.2	+3.9
Live next door	29.5	32.1	32.0	36.6	+3.5
Same swimming pools	30.9	27.1	29.5	34.6	+3.1
Same house party	26.2	26.2	26.5	29.0	+1.5
College roommate of your child	17.4	17.8	17.1	18.0	0.0

*These results are taken from R. T. Riley and T. F. Pettigrew, "Dramatic Events and Racial Attitude Change" (unpublished paper, Harvard University, August, 1970). The data are from probability samples of white Texans drawn and interviewed by Belden Associates of Dallas, Texas.

restrict this self-selection factor, making the effects of the new contact itself the only explanation of the significant alterations in attitudes and behavior.

Surveys bear out these findings on a national scale. Hyman and Sheatsley found that among whites the most extensive changes in racial attitudes have occurred where extensive desegregation of public facilities had already taken place.[41] Recall, too, that data from the Coleman Report indicate that white students who attend public schools with blacks are the least likely to prefer all-white classrooms and all-white "close friends"; and this effect is strongest among those who began their interracial schooling in the early grades.[42] This fits neatly with the findings of the U.S. Commission on Civil Rights for both black and white adults who had attended biracial schools as children.[43]

Not all intergroup contact, of course, leads to increased acceptance; sometimes it only makes matters worse. Keep in mind Allport's criteria: prejudice is lessened when the two groups (1) possess equal status in the situation, (2) seek common goals, (3) are cooperatively dependent upon each other, and (4) interact with the positive support of authorities, laws, or customs.[44] These criteria are actually an application of the broader theory of interpersonal attraction. All four conditions maximize the likelihood that shared values and beliefs will be evinced and mutually perceived. Rokeach's belief-similarity factor is, then, apparently important in the effects of optimal contact. Following Triandis and Davis's findings,[45] we would anticipate that alterations in attitudes achieved by intergroup contact, at least initially, will be greatest in formal areas and least in intimate areas—as was true of the changes in attitudes of white Texans, brought about by dramatic events in the early spring of 1968.

From this social-psychological perspective, the assumption of black separatists that "white liberals" should eliminate white racism seems to be an impossible and quixotic hope. One can readily appreciate the militants' desire to avoid further abuse from white racists; but their model for change is woefully inadequate. White liberals can attack racist attitudes publicly, conduct research on racist assertions, set the stage for confrontation. But with all the will in the world they cannot accomplish by themselves the needed push, the dramatic events, the actual interracial contact which have gnawed away at racist beliefs for a generation. A century ago the fiery and perceptive Frederick Douglass phrased the issue pointedly:

> I have found in my experience that the way to break down an unreasonable custom is to contradict it in practice. To be sure in pursuing this course I have had to contend not merely with the white race but with the black. The one has condemned me for my presumption in daring to associate with it and the other for pushing myself where it takes it for granted I am not wanted.[46]

Assumption 3: Contact Must Lead to Conflict; and
Assumption 5: Autonomy is Needed before Contact

History reveals that white separatists are correct when they contend that racial change creates conflict, that if only the traditions of white supremacy were to go unchallenged racial harmony might be restored. One of the quietest periods in American racial history, 1895-1915, witnessed the construction of the massive system of institutional racism as it is known today—the "nadir of Negro American history," as Rayford Logan calls it.[47] The price of those two decades of relative peace is still being paid by the nation. Even if it were possible now to gain racial calm by inaction, the United States could not afford the enormous cost.

But if inaction is clearly impossible, the types of action necessary are not so clear. Black separatists believe that efforts to further interracial contact should be abandoned or at least delayed until greater personal and group autonomy is achieved by Negroes. This view and the attitudes of white separatists just mentioned are two sides of the same coin. Both leave the struggle against racism in attitudes completely in the hands of "white liberals." And the two assumptions run a similar danger. Racism is reflected not only in attitudes but, more importantly, in institutionalized arrangements that operate to restrict the choices open to blacks. Both forms of racism are fostered by segregation, and both have to be confronted directly by Negroes. To withdraw into the ghetto, psychologically tempting as this may be for many, is essentially to give up the fight to alter the racially discriminatory operations of the nation's chief institutions. The Rev. Jesse L. Jackson, the Chicago black leader of Operation Breadbasket, makes the same point in forceful terms:

> Let's use this analogy. Assuming that racism is a hot fire. If we're gonna take over things and run them and destroy racism; we got to get to the core of the fire. You can't destroy it by running away from it. The fact is, at this point in American history, racism is in trouble in terms of the government, economy, political order and even the psychological order.[48]

The issues involved are shown schematically in Figure 1. By varying contact—separation and an ideologically vague concept of "autonomy," four cells may be set up that represent the various possibilities under discussion. Cell A, true integration, refers to institutionalized biracial situations where there is cross-racial friendship, racial interdependence, and a strong measure of personal and group autonomy. Such situations do exist in America today, but they are rare islands in a sea of conflict. Cell B represents the autonomous ghetto postulated by advocates of black separatism, relatively independent of the larger society and far more viable than is commonly the case now. This is an ideologically derived hypothetical situation, for no such urban ghettos exist today. Cell C stands for merely desegregated situations. These are often mistakenly called "integrated." They are institutionalized biracial settings which involve little cross-racial acceptance and, often, patronizing legacies of white supremacy. Cell D represents today's typical highly separate urban ghetto with little or no personal or group autonomy.

Definitional confusions may obscure the meaning of Figure 1, especially the definition of "integration." This term became almost a hallowed symbol of the civil rights movement of previous decades, and its present disparagement in newer black

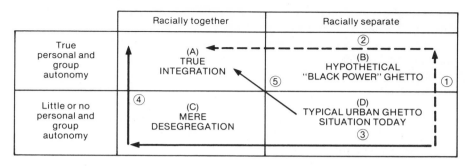

Figure 1.   Schematic diagram of autonomy and contact-separation. Dotted lines denote hypothetical paths; solid lines, actual paths. The author is indebted to Professor Karl Deutsch of Harvard University for several stimulating conversations out of which came this diagram.

thought may be traced in part to this fact. But most disparagement of "integration" is due to definitional confusion between it and "assimilation" and between it and desegregation as diagramed in Figure 1. As Lerone Bennett rightly points out, these confusions among both whites and blacks stem from employing exclusively a white standard of reference:

> . . . One of the greatest enemies of integration in America today is the word integration. Contrary to the hopes of some and the fears of others, integration does not mean black elimination. Integration may or may not lead to assimilation, but assimilation does not necessarily mean the disappearance of a minority. . . . /D/ifferences can be eliminated in favor of a creative minority. Both "integrationists" and "separatists" forget that there is a blackening process as well as a whitening process. Liberationists, who recognize this dialectic, say blacks must assimilate and not be assimilated. . . . Integration is not disappearance; nor is it simple contiguity . . . since men have given the word integration a bad name, we shall use the word *transformation* to refer to the real thing.[49]

Cell A refers to "the real thing," to the integration of *whites* as well as blacks, to the end product of Lerone Bennett's "transformation."

Except for white separatists, observers of diverse persuasions agree that the achievement of true integration (cell A) should be the ultimate goal. But there are, crudely speaking, three contrasting ways of getting there from the typical current situation (cell D). The black separatist assumes that only one route is possible: from the depressed ghetto of today to the hypothetical ghetto of tomorrow and then, perhaps, on to true integration (lines 1 and 2 in Figure 1). The desegregationist assumes precisely the opposite route: from the present-day ghetto to mere desegregation and then, hopefully, on to true integration (lines 3 and 4 in Figure 1). But there is a third, more direct route, right across from the current ghetto to true integration (line 5 in Figure 1). Experience to date combines with a number of social-psychological considerations to favor the last of these possibilities with some important qualifications.

The route favored by black separatists has a surprising appeal for an untested theory; besides those whites who welcome any alternative to integration, it seems to appeal to militant black leaders searching for a new direction into which to channel the ghetto's rage, and to blacks who just wish to withdraw as far away from whites as possible. Yet, on reflection, it can be seen that the argument involves the perverse notion that the way to bring two groups together is to separate them further. One is reminded of the detrimental consequences of isolation in economics, through "closed markets," and in genetics, through "genetic drift." In social psychology, isolation between two contiguous groups generally leads to: (1) the development of diverse values, (2) reduced intergroup communication, (3) uncorrected perceptual distortions of each other, and (4) the growth of vested interests within both groups for continued separation. Race relations in the United States already suffer from each of these conditions; and the proposal for further separation, even if a gilded ghetto were possible, can only exacerbate them.

In fairness, it should be emphasized again that the criticisms here are directed against the concept of the insulated ghetto, not the shrewder and more subtle notions of power and regrouping combined with challenges to the restriction of choice imposed by the nation's leading institutions. As was mentioned at the beginning of this paper, a much larger segment of militant blacks, judging from their actions, adheres to the latter program. The fascinations of the more romantic notions of a totally self-sufficient black community and even occasional expressions of black chauvinism are apparently diminished by many of the unromantic facts of the situation.

We will not pursue the many economic and political difficulties inherent in the concept of the insulated ghetto, but it should be mentioned that the resources immediately available in the ghetto for the task are meager. Recognizing this limitation, black separatists call for massive Federal aid with no strings attached. But this requires a national consensus. Some separatists consider that the direct path to integration (line 5 in Figure 1) is idealistic dreaming, then turn and assume that the same racist society that resists integration will unhesitatingly pour a significant portion of its treasure into the ghetto. "Local control" without access to the necessary tax base is not control. This raises the question of the political limitations of this route. Irish-Americans entered the mainstream through the political system, and this method is often cited as appropriate to black separatism—but is it really? Faster than any other immigrant group except Jewish Americans, the Irish have assimilated on the direct route of Figure 1. Forced to remain in ghettos at first, the Irish did not settle for "local control" but strove to win city hall itself. Boston's legendary James Michael Curley won "Irish power" not by becoming mayor of the South Boston ghetto, but by becoming mayor of the entire city. Analogies between immigrants and blacks contain serious inaccuracies, however, since immigrants never suffered from slavery and legalized segregation. But to the extent an analogy is appropriate, Mayor Carl Stokes of Cleveland, Mayor Richard Hatcher of Gary, and Mayor Kenneth Gibson of Newark are far closer to the Irish-American model than are black separatists.

A critical part of the thinking of black separatists centers on the psychological concept of "fate control"—more familiar to psychologists as Rotter's internal control of reinforcement variable.[50] "Until we control our own destinies, our own schools and areas," goes the argument, "blacks cannot possibly achieve the vital sense of fate control." Data from the Coleman Report are cited to show that fate control is a critical correlate of achievement in school for black children.[51] But no mention is made of the additional fact that levels of fate control among black children were found by Coleman to be significantly higher in interracial schools than in all-Negro schools. Black separatists brush this important finding aside because all-Negro schools today are not what they envision for the future. Yet the fact remains that interracial schools appear to be facilitating the growth of fate control among Negro students now; the ideological contention that fate control can be developed as well or better in uniracial schools remains an untested and hypothetical assertion.

Despite the problems, black separatists feel that their route (lines 1 and 2 in Figure 1) is the only way to true integration, in part because they regard the indirect route of desegregation (lines 3 and 4) as an affront to their dignity. Anyone familiar with the blatantly hostile and subtly rejecting acts that typify some interracial situations will understand this repudiation of nonautonomous desegregation (cell C).[52] The U.S. Commission on Civil Rights, in reanalyzing Coleman's data, found that this provided the tool for distinguishing empirically between effective and ineffective biracial schools where whites form the majority. Achievement, college aspirations, and the sense of fate control by Negro students proved to be highest in truly integrated schools when these schools are independently defined as biracial institutions characterized by no racial tension and widespread cross-racial friendship. Merely desegregated schools, defined as biracial institutions typified by racial tension and little cross-racial friendship, have scant benefits over segregated schools.[53]

This finding reflects Allport's conditions for optimal contact. Truly integrated institutions afford the type of contact that maximizes cross-racial acceptance and the similarity of beliefs described by Rokeach.[54] They apparently also maximize the positive and minimize the negative factors which Katz has isolated as important for performance of Negroes in biracial task groups.[55] And they also seem to increase the opportunity for beneficial cross-racial evaluations, which may well be critical mediators of the effects of biracial schools.[56] Experimental research following up these leads is now called for to detail the precise social-psychological processes operating in the truly integrated situation.[57]

The desegregation route (lines 3 and 4 in Figure 1) has been successfully navigated, though the contention of black separatists that Negroes bear the principal burden for this effort is undoubtedly true. Southern institutions that have attained integration, for example, have typically traveled this indirect path. This route, then, is not as hypothetical as the route advocated by black separatists, but it is hardly to be preferred over the route of direct integration (line 5).

Why not the direct route, then? The standard answer is that it is impossible, that demographic trends and resistance from whites make it out of the question in our time. One is reminded of the defenders of slavery in the 1850s, who attacked the Abolitionists as unrealistic dreamers and insisted that slavery was so deeply entrenched that efforts should be limited to making it into a benign institution. If the nation acts on such speculations, of course, they will probably be proven correct. What better way is there to prevent racial change than to act on the assumption that it is impossible?

The belief that integration is impossible, however, is based on some harsh facts of urban racial demography. Between 1950 and 1960, the average annual increment of Negro population in the central cities of the United States was 320,000; from 1960 to 1966 the estimated annual growth climbed to 400,000, though reduced in-migration from the rural South has lowered this annual growth rate considerably since 1966.[58] In the suburbs, however, the average annual growth of the Negro population declined from 60,000 between 1950 and 1960 to an estimated 33,000 between 1960 and 1966, though it has sharply increased since 1966.[59] In other words, it would require several times the present trend in growth of Negro populations in the suburbs just to maintain the sprawling central-city ghettos at their present size. In the nation's largest metropolitan areas, then, the trend is still pushing in the direction of ever increasing separatism.

But these bleak data are not the whole picture. In the first place, they refer especially to the very largest of the metropolitan areas—to New York City, Chicago, Los Angeles, Philadelphia, Detroit, Washington, D.C., and Baltimore. Most Negro Americans do not live in these places, but rather in areas where racial integration is in fact possible in the short run if attempts in good faith are made. There are more Berkeleys—small enough for school integration to be effectively achieved—than there are New York Cities. In the second place, the presumed impossibility of reversing racial trends in the central city is based on anti-metropolitan assumptions. Without metropolital cooperation central cities—and many suburbs, too—will find their racial and other basic problems continuing. Do we need to assume such cooperation impossible? We previously proposed effective state and Federal incentives to further this cooperation. Moreover, some large black ghettos are already extending into the suburbs (e.g., east of Pittsburgh and west of Chicago); the first tentative metropolitan schemes to aid racial integration are emerging in a variety of cities (e.g., Boston, Hartford, Rochester, and Portland, Oregon); and several major metropolitan areas have even consolidated (e.g., Miami-Dade County and Nashville-Davidson County). Once the issue is looked at in metropolitan terms, its dimensions become more manageable. Black Americans are found in America's metropolitan areas in almost the same ratio as white Americans: about two-thirds of each group reside in these 212 regions. On a metropolitan basis, therefore, Negroes are not disproportionately metropolitan.

Yet it must be admitted that many young blacks, separatist and otherwise, are simply not convinced by such arguments. Such large-scale proposals as metropolitan educational parks strike them as faraway pipe dreams of no significance to their immediate problems. Contact theory holds little appeal. They rightfully argue that Allport's four conditions do not typify the American national scene. How often, they ask, do blacks actually possess equal status in situations with whites? And in struggles for racial power, as they view it, can there be a cooperative seeking of common goals? And as for the possibility that true integration of cell A will be sanctioned by those in authority, they say ruefully, consider the public images on racial matters of Nixon, Mitchell, Agnew, Carswell. Maybe the demographic arguments against the possibility of integration are overdrawn, they concede, but can one realistically expect Allport's conditions of positive contact to become the rule in the foreseeable future of the United States?

Underlying this criticism is less a theoretical and ideological difference than a sharply contrasting assessment of the probabilities and possibilities of America's race relations. These black spokesmen may well be right. The United States may indeed be so racist both as to individuals and structure that the type of institutional changes we have advocated will never be achieved. No footnoting of references or social-psychological theory can refute this possibility, but I hope it is wrong. Our entire analysis is predicated on the more optimistic view that somehow American society will muddle through. To assume otherwise, once again, is to risk contributing to the problem by engaging in a self-fulfilling prophecy.

Moreover, the attack on contact theory is based in part on a misreading of it. *Situations* meeting Allport's four conditions do exist in the United States, and we have seen that they are becoming more numerous in such realms as employment. True, as noted, these truly integrated situations are still isolated islands and together do not constitute a critical mass nationally. Yet the status of Negroes is rising in the United States. Indeed, the personal lives of the black critics themselves typically attest to this social mobility, for roughly 90 percent of middle-class blacks today derive from families which were lower class in 1940. But we noted how these very gains create rapidly rising expectations and a keen sense of relative deprivation, some of which gets channeled among some blacks into the separatist ideology under discussion.

Nor are power struggles as completely racial and competitive as critics claim. For one thing, power conflicts almost invariably involve class as well as racial interests, and to the extent that class is involved there are at least potential white allies. White Americans, after all, are an even more diverse assortment than black Americans. Thus, Mayor Carl Stokes received 22 percent of the white vote in Cleveland in November of 1969, Thomas Bradley 40 percent in the Los Angeles mayoralty runoff in June of 1969, Mayor Kenneth Gibson 16 percent in Newark in June of 1970. The percentages are low because of racism, but they do occur and rise over time (Stokes received in general elections only 11 percent in 1965, and 19 percent in 1967). But actually the theory requires only that blacks and some whites share common goals to the point where coalitions become important to both; one of these coalitions is called the Democratic Party, which since Franklin Roosevelt has consisted of a precarious combination of minorities which together total a registration far larger than that of the rival party.

Finally, concerning Allport's fourth condition on the sanction of laws and authorities, there is solid evidence in civil rights legislation and other institutional changes that moving toward the sanctioning of true integration. By and large, of course, America's institutions still do not play this role; they are racist, in the Kerner Commission's plain language, in that their normal operations still act typically to restrict choice for blacks. But positive change is evident from the appearance of Negroes on television to their participation in former bastions of white privilege. True, as far as race is concerned the Nixon Administration is a throwback to the naivete of early twentieth-century administrations; it offers no "authority sanction," nor does it promise to in its remaining years. Yet there are other political alternatives which would willingly offer the racial leadership the nation so desperately needs. To opt out of the opposition, to assume that the Mitchells and Agnews are inevitable and typical products of the American political system, is to ensure that such men will in fact remain in power.

To argue for route 5 in Figure 1 is not to assume that it will be easy to achieve, or that Allport's optimal conditions for intergroup contact apply generally throughout America at present. The direct path does stress that *simultaneous* attention must be given to both integration and individual and collective autonomy, for today's cell D has neither and tomorrow's cell A must have both. And neither the desegregation (paths 3 and 4 of Figure 1) nor the separatist (paths 1 and 2) route gives this simultaneous attention. Once again, Bennett phrases the argument cogently:

> It is impossible, Simon de Beauvoir said, to draw a straight line in a curved space. Both "integrationists" and "separatists" are trying to create right angles in a situation which only permits curves. The only option is Transformation of a situation which does not permit a clear-cut choice in either direction. This means that we must face the fact that it is impossible to move 30 million African-Americans anywhere.[60]

IMPLICATIONS FOR POLICY

Much of the confusion over policy seems to derive from the assumption that since *complete* integration in the biggest cities will not be possible in the near future, present effort toward opening opportunities for integration for both Negro and white Americans are premature. This thinking obscures two fundamental issues. First, the democratic objective is not total racial integration and the elimination of black neighborhoods; the idea is simply to provide an honest choice between separation and integration. Today only separation is available; integration is closed to blacks who would choose it. The long-term goal is not a complete obliteration of cultural pluralism, of distinctive Negro areas, but rather the transformation of these ghettos from racial prisons to ethnic areas freely chosen or not chosen. Life within ghettos can never be fully satisfactory as long as there are Negroes who reside within them only because discrimination requires them to.

Second, the integrationist alternative will not become a reality as long as we disparage it or abandon it to future generations. *Exclusive* attention to programs for enriching life in the ghetto is almost certain, to use Kenneth Clark's pointed word, to "embalm" the ghetto, to seal it in even further from the rest of the nation (making line 2 in Figure 1 even less likely). This danger explains the recent interest of conservative whites in enrichment programs for the ghetto. The bribe is straightforward: "Stop rioting and stop demanding integration, and we'll minimally support separatist programs within the ghetto." Even black separatists are understandably ambivalent about such offers, as they come from sources long identified with opposition to all racial change. Should the bargain be struck, however, race relations in the United States will be dealt still another serious blow.

Yet a policy concentrating *exclusively* on integration, like one concentrating exclusively on enrichment, runs its own danger of worsening the situation. As many black spokesmen correctly point out, a single-minded pursuit of integration is likely to blind us to the urgent requirements of today's black ghettos. Either policy followed mechanically and exclusively, then, has serious limitations which the rival strategy is designed to correct. This fact strongly suggests that a national transformation from a racist society to an open society will require a judicious mix of both the strategies.

The outlines of the situation, then, are these: (1) Widespread integration is possible everywhere in the United States except in the largest central cities. (2) It will not come unless present trends are reversed and considerable resources are provided for the process. (3) Big central cities will continue to have significant concentrations of Negroes even with successful metropolitan dispersal. (4) Large Negro ghettos are presently in need of intensive enrichment. (5) Some enrichment programs for the ghetto run the clear and present danger of embalming the ghetto further.

Given this situation and the social-psychological considerations we have been discussing, the overall strategy needed must contain the following elements:

1. A major effort toward racial integration must be mounted in order to provide genuine choice to all Negro Americans in all realms of life. This effort should envisage complete attainment of the goal in smaller communities and cities by the late 1970s and a halting of separatist trends in major central cities, with a movement toward metropolitan cooperation.

2. A simultaneous effort is required to enrich the vast central-city ghettos of the nation, to change them structurally, and to improve life in them. In order to avoid

"embalming" them, however, strict criteria must be applied to proposed enrichment programs to insure that they will not hinder later dispersal and integration. Restructuring the economics of the ghetto, especially by developing urban cooperatives, is a classic example of productive enrichment. Effective job training programs offer another example of productive enrichment. The building of enormous public housing developments within the ghetto presents a good illustration of counterproductive enrichment. Some programs, such as the decentralization of huge public school systems or the encouragement of business ownership by Negroes, can be either productive or counterproductive depending upon how they are focused. A decentralization plan of many small homogeneous school districts for New York City is clearly counterproductive for later integration; a plan involving a relatively small number of heterogeneous school districts for New York City could well be productive. Likewise, black entrepreneurs who are encouraged to open small shops and are expected to prosper with an all-black clientele are not only part of a counterproductive plan, but are probably commiting economic suicide. Negro businessmen who are encouraged to pool their resources to establish somewhat larger operations and to appeal to white as well as black customers on major traffic arteries in and out of the ghetto could be an important part of a productive plan.

In short, a mixed strategy is called for—both integration and enrichment—and it must contain safeguards that the two aspects will not impede each other. Results of recent surveys strongly suggest that such a mixed strategy would meet with widespread approval among black Americans. On the basis of their extensive survey of black residents in fifteen major cities in 1968, Campbell and Schuman conclude:

> Separatism appeals to from five to eighteen per cent of the Negro sample, depending on the question, with the largest appeal involving black ownership of stores and black administration of schools in Negro neighborhoods, and the smallest appeal the rejection of whites as friends or in other informal contacts. Even on questions having the largest appeal, however, more than three-quarters of the Negro sample indicate a clear preference for integration. Moreover, the reasons given by respondents for their choices suggest that the desire for integration is not simply a practical wish for better material facilities, but represents a commitment to principles of nondiscrimination and racial harmony.[61]

Young men prove to be the most forthright separatists, but even here the percentages of men aged 16 to 19 who were separatists ranged only from 11 to 28. An interesting interaction between type of separatism and educational level of the respondent appears in Campbell and Schuman's data. Among the 20- to 39-year-olds, college graduates tended to be more separatist in those realms where their training gives them a vested interest in positions free of competition—black-owned stores for black neighborhoods, black teachers in mostly black schools. The poorly educated were most likely to believe that whites should be discouraged from taking part in civil rights organizations and to agree that "Negroes should have nothing to do with whites if they can help it" and that "there should be a separate black nation here."[62]

But if separatism draws little favorable response even in the most politicized ghettos, positive aspects of cultural pluralism attract wide interest. For example, 42 percent endorse the statement that "Negro schoolchildren should study an African language." And this interest seems rather general across age, sex, and education categories. Campbell and Schuman regard this as evidence of a broadly supported attempt ". . . to emphasize black consciousness *without* rejection of whites. . . . A substantial number of Negroes want *both* integration and black identity."[63] Or, in the terms of this chapter, they prefer cell A in Figure 1—"true integration."

When viewed historically, this preferred combination of black consciousness without separation is not a new position for black Americans. It was, for example, their dominant response to the large-scale movement of Marcus Garvey in the 1920s. Garvey, a West Indian, stressed pride in Africa and black beauty and successfully mounted a mass movement throughout the urban ghettos of the day, but his famous "back to Africa" separatist appeals were largely ignored as irrelevant.

Campbell and Schuman's data indicate little if any change from the prointegration results of earlier surveys.[64] And they are consistent with the results of surveys in Detroit, Miami, New York City, and other cities.[65] Data from Bedford-Stuyvesant in Brooklyn are especially significant, for here separatist ideology and a full-scale enrichment program are in full view. Yet when asked if they would prefer to live on a block with people only of the same race or people of every race, 80 percent of the Negro respondents chose an interracial block. Interestingly, the largest Negro segment choosing integration—88 percent—consisted of residents of public housing where a modest amount of interracial tenancy still prevails.[66]

A final study from Watts links these surveys to the analysis here. Ransford found that willingness of Negroes to use violence was closely and positively related to a sense of powerlessness, feelings of racial dissatisfaction, and limited contact with whites. Respondents who indicated that they had no social contact with white people, "like going to the movies together or visiting each other's homes," were significantly more likely to feel powerless and express racial dissatisfaction as well as to report greater willingness to use violence.[67] The personal, group, and national costs of racial separatism are clearly great.

A FINAL WORD

Racially separate or together? Our social-psychological examination of separatist assumptions leads to the assertion of one imperative: the attainment of a viable, democratic nation, free from personal and institutional racism, requires extensive racial integration in all realms of life as well as vast programs of ghetto enrichment. To prescribe more separation because of discomfort, racism, conflict, or the need for autonomy is like getting drunk again to cure a hangover. The nation's binge of *apartheid* must not be exacerbated but alleviated.

NOTES

An earlier draft of this paper was the author's presidential address to the Society for the Psychological Study of Social Issues, delivered at the annual convention of the American Psychological Association in San Francisco, California, on September 1, 1968.

1. These figures derive from three gross estimates of "middle class" status: annual family income of $6,000 or more, high school graduation, or white-collar occupation. Thus, in 1961 roughly one-fifth of Negro families received in excess of $6,000 (a percentage that now must approach one-fourth, even in constant dollars); in 1960, 22 percent of Negroes over 24 years of age had completed high school; and in 1966, 21 percent of employed Negroes held white-collar occupations.

2. J. Alsop, "No More Nonsense About Ghetto Education!" *New Republic,* July 22, 1967, Vol. 157, pp. 18–23; and "Ghetto Schools," *New Republic,* Nov. 18, 1967, Vol. 157, pp. 18–23. (For answers to these articles, see: R. Schwartz, T. Pettigrew, and M. Smith, "Fake Panaceas for Ghetto Education," *New Republic,* Sept. 23, 1967, Vol. 157, pp. 16–19; and "Is Desegregation Impractical?" *New Republic,* Jan. 6, 1968, Vol. 157, pp. 27–29.) W. H. Ferry, "Black Colonies: A Modest Proposal," *The Center Magazine,* January 1968, Vol. 1, pp. 74–76. Ferry even proposes that "black colonies" be formally established in American central cities, complete with treaties enacted with the Federal government. The position of black militants is in sharp contrast to this; they complain of having a colonial status now and do not consider it a desirable state of affairs.

3. It is sometimes held that "Negro" was the term for slaves; but actually both "Negro" and "black" were frequently used in documents concerning slaves. Some critics argue that the true skin color of Negro Americans is basically brown, not black, and that the term "black" is therefore inappropriate. But of course "white" Americans are seldom white either; besides, "Negro" is simply the Spanish word for "black." The importance of the term "black" is in fact basically psychological. I have used both terms interchangeably because surveys indicate each is preferred by different segments of the Negro community.

4. Lerone Bennett, Jr., "Liberation," *Ebony,* August 1970, Vol. 25, pp. 36–43.

5. C. P. Armstrong and A. J. Gregor, "Integrated Schools and Negro Character Development: Some Considerations of the Possible Effects," *Psychiatry,* 1964, Vol. 27, pp. 69–72.

6. T. F. Pettigrew, *A Profile of the Negro American* (Princeton, N.J.: Van Nostrand, 1964).

7. Analysis specifically directed on this point shows that this contention is not true for predominantly white classrooms as contrasted with comparable all-white classrooms. [United States Commission on Civil Rights, *Racial Isolation in the Public Schools* (Washington, D.C.: U.S. Government Printing Office, 1967), Vol. 1, p. 160.]

8. National Advisory Commission on Civil Disorders, *U.S. Riot Commission Report* (Washington, D.C.: Government Printing Office, 1968).

9. B. E. Calame, "A West Coast Militant Talks Tough But Helps Avert Racial Trouble," *The Wall Street Journal,* July 26, 1968, Vol. 172, No. 1, p. 15. Karenga's contention that blacks presently have nothing "to offer" a racially interdependent America strangely echoes similar contentions of white racists.

10. I. Katz, "Review of Evidence Relating to Effects of Desegregation on the Performance of Negroes," *American Psychologist,* 1964, Vol. 19, pp. 381–399; and M. R. Yarrow (ed.), "Interpersonal Dynamics in a Desegregation Process," *Journal of Social Issues,* 1958, Vol. 14, No. 1, pp. 3–63.

11. J. Harding and R. Hogrefe, "Attitudes of White Department Store Employees Toward Ne-

gro Co-workers," *Journal of Social Issues*, 1952, Vol. 8, pp. 18-28; and G. Saenger and E. Gilbert, "Customer Reactions to the Integration of Negro Sales Personnel," *International Journal of Opinion and Attitude Research*, 1950, Vol. 4, pp. 57-76.

12. I. N. Brophy, "The Luxury of Anti-Negro Prejudice," *Public Opinion Quarterly*, 1946, Vol. 9, pp. 456-466.

13. S. A. Stouffer, E. A. Suchman, L. C. DeVinney, S. A. Star, and R. M. Williams, Jr., *Studies in Social Psychology in World War II*, Vol. 1, *The American Soldier: Adjustment During Army Life* (Princeton: Princeton University Press, 1949).

14. M. Deutsch and M. Collins, *Interracial Housing: A Psychological Evaluation of a Social Experiment* (Minneapolis: University of Minnesota Press, 1951); M. Jahoda and P. West, "Race Relations in Public Housing," *Journal of Social Issues*, 1951, Vol. 7, pp. 132-139; D. M. Wilner, R. Walkley, and S. W. Cook, *Human Relations in Interracial Housing: A Study of the Contact Hypothesis* (Minneapolis: University of Minnesota Press, 1955); and E. Works, "The Prejudice-Interaction Hypothesis from the Point of View of the Negro Minority Group," *American Journal of Sociology*, 1961, Vol. 67, pp. 47-52.

15. W. M. Kephart, *Racial Factors and Urban Law Enforcement* (Philadelphia: University of Pennsylvania Press, 1957).

16. T. M. Newcomb, R. H. Turner, and P. E. Converse, *Social Psychology: The Study of Human Interaction* (New York: Holt, Rinehart and Winston, 1965).

17. M. Rokeach, P. Smith and R. Evans, "Two Kinds of Prejudice or One?" in M. Rokeach (ed.), *The Open and Closed Mind* (New York: Basic Books, 1960); M. Rokeach and L. Mezei, "Race and Shared Belief as Factors in Social Choice," *Science*, 1966, Vol. 151, pp. 167-172; C. R. Smith, L. Williams, and R. H. Willis, "Race, Sex and Belief as Determinants of Friendship Acceptance," *Journal of Personality and Social Psychology*, 1967, Vol. 5, pp. 127-137; D. D. Stein, "The Influence of Belief Systems on Interpersonal Preference," *Psychological Monographs*, 1966, Vol. 80, No. 616; and D. D. Stein, J. A. Hardyck, and M. B. Smith, "Race and Belief: An Open and Shut Case," *Journal of Personality and Social Psychology*, 1965, Vol. 1, pp. 281-290.

18. H. C. Triandis and E. E. Davis, "Race and Belief as Determinants of Behavioral Intentions," *Journal of Personality and Social Psychology*, 1965, Vol. 2, pp. 715-725. This resolution of the earlier controversy between Triandis and Rokeach takes on added weight when the data from studies favorable to Rokeach's position are examined carefully. (H. C. Triandis, "A Note on Rokeach's Theory of Prejudice," *Journal of Abnormal and Social Psychology*, 1961, Vol. 62, pp. 184-186; and M. Rokeach, "Belief versus Race as Determinants of Social Distance: Comment on Triandis' Paper," *Journal of Abnormal and Social Psychology*, 1961, Vol. 62, pp. 187-188). That interpersonal realms lead to varying belief-race weightings is borne out by Table 4 in Stein *et al., op. cit.;* that intensely prejudiced subjects, particularly in environments where racist norms even extend into less intimate realms, will act on race primarily is shown by one sample of whites in the Deep South in Smith *et al., op. cit.*

19. Both black and white observers tend to exaggerate racial differences in basic values. Rokeach and Parker note from data from national surveys that, while there appear to be real value differences between the rich and the poor, once socioeconomic factors are controlled there are no sharp value differences between black and white Americans. M. Rokeach and S. Parker, "Values as Social Indicators of Poverty and Race Relations in America," *Annals of the American Academy of Political and Social Science*, 1970, Vol. 388, pp. 97-111.

20. Stein *et al., op. cit.*

21. Smith *et al., op. cit.*

22. United States Commission on Civil Rights, *op. cit.*

23. For twelve junior highs, the Spearman-Brown rank-order correlation between the white junior high percentage and the percentage of Negroes choosing predominantly white high schools is +.82 (corrected for ties)—significant at better than the 1 percent level of confidence.

24. United States Commission on Civil Rights, *Civil Rights USA: Public Schools, Southern States, 1962* (Washington, D.C.: U.S. Government Printing Office, 1963).

25. United States Commission on Civil Rights, *Racial Isolation in the Public Schools, op. cit.*

26. For a role-analysis interpretation of racial interactions in the United States, see Pettigrew, *A Profile of the Negro American, op. cit.*

27. One of the first significant efforts in this direction was the classic intelligence study by O. Klineberg, *Negro Intelligence and Selective Migration* (New York: Columbia University Press, 1935). For a summary of current scientific work relevant to racist claims regarding health, intelligence and crime, see Pettigrew, *A Profile of the Negro American, op. cit.*

28. H. H. Hyman and P. B. Sheatsley, "Attitudes Toward Desegregation," *Scientific American*, July, 1964, Vol. 211, pp. 16–23; and P. B. Sheatsley, "White Attitudes Toward the Negro," in T. Parsons and K. B. Clark (eds.), *The Negro American* (Boston: Houghton Mifflin, 1966).

29. R. T. Riley and T. F. Pettigrew, "Dramatic Events and Racial Attitude Change" (unpublished paper, Harvard University, August, 1970).

30. National Advisory Commission on Civil Disorders, *op. cit.*

31. "The ceiling effect" occurs when initial approval is already so high, so near its "ceiling" of 100 percent, that further gains in approval would not generally be as large as when there is less initial approval.

32. Triandis and Davis, *op. cit.*

33. Similar to these results was an overall shift of approximately 5 percent toward favoring the racial desegregation of public schools noted among white Texans between two surveys taken immediately before and after the 1957 school crisis in Little Rock. And once again, the most positive shifts were noted among the young and the middle class. (R. T. Riley and T. F. Pettigrew, *op. cit.*)

34. Deutsch and Collins, *op. cit.;* Jahoda and West, *op. cit.;* Wilner *et al., op. cit.;* and Works, *op. cit.*

35. Stouffer *et al., op. cit.;* and B. MacKenzie, "The Importance of Contact in Determining Attitudes Toward Negroes," *Journal of Abnormal and Social Psychology*, 1948, Vol. 43, pp. 417–441.

36. Brophy, *op. cit.*

37. MacKenzie, *op. cit.*

38. Kephart, *op. cit.*

39. MacKenzie, *op. cit.*

40. R. M. Williams, Jr., *Strangers Next Door: Ethnic Relations in American Communities* (Englewood Cliffs, N.J.: Prentice-Hall, 1964).

41. Hyman and Sheatsley, *op. cit.* This is, of course, a two-way causal relationship. Not only does desegregation erode racist attitudes, but desegregation tends to come first to areas where white attitudes are least racist to begin with. Hyman and Sheatsley's finding, however, specifically highlights the former phenomenon: "In those parts of the South where some measure of school integration has taken place official action has *preceded* public sentiment, and public sentiment has then attempted to accommodate itself to the new situation."

42. J. S. Coleman, E. Q. Campbell, C. J. Hobson, M. McPartland, A. M. Mood, F. D. Weinfield, and R. L. York, *Equality of Educational Opportunity* (Washington, D.C.: U.S. Government Printing Office, 1966).

43. U.S. Commission on Civil Rights, *Racial Isolation in the Public Schools, op. cit.*

44. G. W. Allport, *The Nature of Prejudice* (Cambridge, Mass.: Addison-Wesley, 1954).

45. Triandis and Davis, *op. cit.*

46. F. Douglass, *Life and Times of Frederick Douglass: The Complete Autobiography* (New York: Collier Books, 1962), pp. 366–367 (original edition in 1892).

47. R. W. Logan, *The Negro in the United States: A Brief History* (Princeton, N.J.: Van Nostrand, 1957).

48. J. L. Jackson and A. F. Poussaint, "A Dialogue on Separatism," *Ebony*, August, 1970, Vol. 25, pp. 62–68.

49. Bennett, *op. cit.*, pp. 37–38.

50. J. B. Rotter, "Internal versus External Control of Reinforcement," *Psychological Monographs*, 1966, Vol. 80, No. 609.

51. Coleman *et al., op. cit.*

52. For extreme examples of this phenomenon in public schools in the Deep South, see: M. Chessler, *In Their Own Words* (Atlanta: Southern Regional Council, 1967).

53. U.S. Commission on Civil Rights, *Racial Isolation in the Public Schools, op. cit.* More recent evidence for this distinction is provided in: S. Koslin, B. Koslin, R. Pargament, and H. Waxman, "Classroom Racial Balance and Students' Interracial Attitudes," (unpublished paper, Riverside Research Institute, New York City, 1970).

54. Another white observer enthusiastic about black separatism even denies that the conclusions of the contact studies are applicable to the classroom and other institutions which do not produce "continual and extensive equal-status contact under more or less enforced conditions of intimacy." Stember selectively cites the investigations of contact in public housing and the armed forces to support his point (C. H. Stember, "Evaluating Effects of the Integrated Classroom," *The Urban Review*, June, 1968, Vol. 2 [3–4], pp. 30–31); but he has to omit the many studies from less intimate realms which reached the same conclusions—such as those conducted in schools (T. F. Pettigrew, "Race and Equal Educational Opportunity," *Harvard Educational Review*, 1968, Vol. 38, pp. 66–76) and employment situations (Harding and Hogrefe, *op. cit.*; Kephart, *op. cit.*; MacKenzie, *op. cit.*; and Williams, *op. cit.*), and even one involving brief contact between clerks and customers (G. Saenger and E. Gilbert, "Customer Reactions to the Integration of Negro Sales Personnel," *International Journal of Opinion and Attitude Research*, 1950, Vol. 4, pp. 57–76).

55. I. Katz, *op. cit.*; and I. Katz, "The Socialization of Competence Motivation in Minority Group Children," in D. Levine (ed.), *Nebraska Symposium on Motivation, 1967* (Lincoln: University of Nebraska Press, 1967).

56. T. F. Pettigrew, "Social Evaluation Theory: Convergences and Applications," in D. Levine, *op. cit.*

57. Pettigrew, "Race and Equal Educational Opportunity," *op. cit.*

58. U.S. Depts. of Labor and Commerce, *The Social and Economic Status of Negroes in the United States, 1969* (Washington, D.C.: U.S. Government Printing Office, 1970), pp. 5–7.

59. *Ibid.*

60. Bennett, *op. cit.*, p. 38.

61. A. Campbell and H. Schuman, "Racial Attitudes in Fifteen American Cities," in The National Advisory Commission on Civil Disorders, *Supplemental Studies* (Washington, D.C.: U.S. Government Printing Office, 1968), p. 5.

62. *Ibid.*, p. 19.

63. *Ibid.*, p. 6.

64. W. Brink and L. Harris, *The Negro Revolution in America* (New York: Simon and Schuster, 1964); and W. Brink and L. Harris, *Black and White: A Study of U.S. Racial Attitudes Today* (New York: Simon and Schuster, 1967).

65. P. Meyer, *A Survey of Attitudes of Detroit Negroes after the Riot of 1967* (Detroit, Mich.: Detroit Urban League, 1968); P. Meyer, "Miami Negroes: A Study in Depth," *The Miami Herald*, 1968; and Center for Urban Education, "Survey of the Residents of Bedford-Stuyvesant." Unpublished paper, 1968.

66. *Ibid.*

67. H. E. Ransford, "Isolation, Powerlessness, and Violence: A Study of Attitudes and Participation in the Watts Riot," *American Journal of Sociology*, 1968, Vol. 73, pp. 581–591.